Encyclopedia of
Women Social Reformers

Encyclopedia of
Women Social Reformers

Helen Rappaport

A B C ⬤ C L I O

Santa Barbara, California   Denver, Colorado   Oxford, England

Library of Congress Cataloging-in-Publication Data

Rappaport, Helen.
    Encyclopedia of women social reformers / Helen Rappaport.
        p. cm.
    Includes bibliographical references and index.
    ISBN 1-57607-101-4 (hardcover : alk. paper) ; 1-57607-581-8 (e-book)
    1. Women social reformers—Encyclopedias. 2. Women political
activists—Encyclopedias. 3. Women's rights—Encyclopedias. I. Title.
    HQ1236 .R29 2001
    303.48'4'03—dc21

                                        2001005601

06 05 04 03 02 01   10 9 8 7 6 5 4 3 2 1

This book is also available on the World Wide Web as an e-book.
Visit abc-clio.com for details.

ABC-CLIO, Inc.
130 Cremona Drive, P.O. Box 1911
Santa Barbara, California 93116–1911

This book is printed on acid-free paper ∞.

Manufactured in the United States of America

For my good friend Ruth Marris Macaulay

But the effect of her being on those around her was incalculably diffusive: for the growing good of the world is partly dependent on unhistoric acts; and that things are not so ill with you and me as they might have been, is half owing to the number who lived faithfully a hidden life, and rest in unvisited tombs.

—George Eliot, *Middlemarch* (1871–1872)

Contents

Foreword, Marian Wright Edelman, xv
Preface, xvii
Acknowledgments, xxi
Women Social Reformers by Country, xxiii
Women Social Reformers by Cause, xxix

Encyclopedia of Women Social Reformers

Contents

Contents

Volume 2: M–Z

Contents

Contents

Foreword

This encyclopedia celebrates women's role as social reformers, because in private and public ways women have always been at the forefront of every important social movement. The quest for a better world has been and is the daily work of thousands and thousands of women around the world. What we know from the past and what we know from contemporary experience is that women have always stepped forward to accept the challenge a moral moment presents. Women have been catalysts and implementers of change. They have not been afraid to change things.

An American slave woman, Harriet Tubman, ushered slaves to freedom on an Underground Railroad. Another slave woman, Sojourner Truth, consistently spoke out against slavery and unjust treatment of women and told her detractors that even if they didn't care any more for her than they would for a flea, with God's help she would keep them "scratching." Dorothy Day, cofounder of the Catholic Worker Movement, dedicated her work and her life to the poor and homeless, speaking boldly about the duty one owed to one's neighbor—"anyone in need." Jane Addams and other prominent women "settlers" started settlement houses and worked for the poor and for peace. Poor women in India struggling to feed their children and families walked with empty plates and spoons to protest rising food prices. Rachel Carson's groundbreaking book *Silent Spring* launched the modern environmental movement in the United States.

Courageous environmental pioneer Amrita Devi gave her life three hundred years ago to protect the trees in her village because she believed them sacred. Her sacrifice inspired others who bravely repeated it—and saved the trees and sparked the Chipko movement in India. Thousands of Chilean women faced death and demonstrated in the streets to demand the resignation of a military junta leader. Black women were the backbone of the American Civil Rights Movement: Jessie Daniel Ames, Ella Baker, Fanny Lou Hamer, Mary McCleod Bethune, Rosa Parks, Mary Church Terrell, Ida Wells-Barnett, and on and on. South African women fought and helped win an end to murderous apartheid policies. And there are more stories to tell and more history being made each day.

Many of these women's stories are told in this book. The *Encyclopedia of Women Social Reformers* features women from the United States to New Zealand, from Argentina to Japan, from Hungary to South Africa, from Iran to India—women from around the world who have been willing to stand up and make a difference. Women *and* men—and girls *and* boys—all need to hear the stories of what these women have done to make the world a better place not just for women but for everyone in it. Their example should inspire all of us to continue doing everything we can to fight for change in our own communities, nation, and world. But they can also be a special encouragement to those of us who are women and girls, because they remind us that even in places and times where women have been marginalized by those in power, we have always still managed to be mighty instruments for transforming change.

American anthropologist Margaret Mead said, "Never doubt that a small group of thoughtful, committed people can change the world. Indeed, it is the only thing that ever has." This book profiles some of the thoughtful, committed women who have changed their worlds. I hope many of its readers will go on to do the same.

Marian Wright Edelman
President
Children's Defense Fund

Preface

The epigraph to this book, written by George Eliot in 1871–1872, still attests 130 years later to the fact that "the growing good of the world is partly dependent on unhistoric acts." In the course of researching the hundreds of women's stories included here, the sorry fact remains: the self-sacrifice, courage, and endurance of many pioneering women in so many spheres of activism, welfare, and philanthropy are yet to be uncovered or accorded the credit they deserve. The list of entries, as it now stands, differs quite dramatically from the original I drew up three years ago—the further I progressed with my research, the more and more totally unsung or undervalued women I found. Even in the final days of writing, I was still encountering new and wonderful stories. But in the process of resdicovering the lives of numerous fascinating and inspiring women whose stories had been seldom told, some of the "usual suspects" had to be sacrificed to make way for them. I therefore make no apologies for the fact that there are sure to be some women reformers whom readers expect to find here but who are not included; but, in compensation, I hope they find many new women about whose work they previously knew nothing or very little.

It would have been an easy option to allow the white, middle-class, well-heeled majority from the United Kingdom and United States, about whom much has already been said, to dominate this text. There are enough extremely worthy women from these two countries alone—particularly in the nineteenth century—to have filled these two volumes almost to the exclusion of all others. From the outset, therefore, I had to make some ruthless decisions about whom to include and whom to leave out. These choices were primarily dictated by the nationality and cause in which each woman was engaged; for this reason

a number of British and American suffragettes had to be cut to make way for women who have worked in other much more specialized and little-known areas such as antivivisectionism, conservation, prison reform, religious reform, Third World human rights, and so on.

In order to strike a balance between ethnic background and nationality, I have been liberal in my application of the term *social reformer* so as to be able to include women from some countries who might not otherwise have been considered appropriate within a stricter definition of social reform. These choices were influenced by the cultural environments and historical periods in which some women lived. In some countries, women's activism was so constrained by religious and political controls or social conventions that the only way in which the subject of reform could be broached by them was through writing or through modest charitable work, rather than on the soapbox. Thus, for example I have included some women writers, such as Fredrika Bremer in Sweden, who were not necessarily activists but whose intellectual or moral influence made a considerable impact on the movement for social reform. Similarly, some women active in philanthropic or charitable work, who mainly gave of their money and whose activism was often constrained by a very narrow religious or moral outlook, have been included either to balance the nationalities or because their contribution—patronizing, imperialist, or discriminating though it might be perceived now—was significant. I am referring here to women such as Angela Burdett-Coutts, without whose money much philanthropic and welfare work in Britain could not have been undertaken.

It had been my original intention to include women throughout history, from as far back as

Theodora in sixth-century Byzantium, through early feminists such as Christine de Pisan and Sor Juana Inés de la Cruz, to some fascinating early medical pioneers in the seventeenth century. But with a text that, like Topsy, "just growed," the project threatened to become impossibly unwieldy, and a decision was made to restrict the current two volumes to the period from the French Revolution to the second wave of feminism in the 1970s, with a few important contemporary figures. Again, this criterion necessitated the exclusion of some women from the modern movement in order to retain the balance.

In terms of political activism, with one or two exceptions (based on a value judgment of whether the woman in question made other important contributions to social change), only women involved in peaceful lobbying and protest have been selected. (Although, of course, I must here concede the window smashing and letterbox burning of the militant suffragettes.) Those women who took part in armed insurrection, assassination, and bomb throwing have been omitted. For this reason, some Russian and Latin American revolutionaries have been left out, but influential leaders such as Qiu Jin of China and Louise Michel of France—both of whom were leaders of important civil liberties movements that became revolutions—have been included.

The most difficult aspect of researching and writing a book of this kind, single-handedly, proved to be the frustrating lack of sources and the inevitable inconsistencies and contradictions that constantly arose between those sources that do exist, particularly regarding names and founding dates of organizations. Many of the lives of women in the Third World, despite huge advances in feminist scholarship over the last thirty years, are still only described in the thinnest of sources. Many will never be properly told because no documentary record exists. The stories of other women, sad to say, have only come down to us through the records of their better-known husbands and sons. A particular case in point is the Australian suffragist and writer Louisa Lawson, whose 1978 biography was entitled *Louisa Lawson: Henry Lawson's Crusading Mother,* presumably deemed necessary in order to persuade readers that she was worth reading about (Henry Lawson was a notable poet). Similarly, virtually the only English-language source available at the time of writing on

the Filipina suffragist Agnes de Silva is a biography of her politician husband George. This has meant that many of the Third World and even some First World entries have had to be pieced together from sparse facts found in a wide range of disparate sources, as well as on the Internet; this involved much random searching, but occasionally bore wonderful fruit. Despite my best efforts, I regret that some of the life dates of women included in this book could not be traced; I would be grateful to hear from any reader able to fill in such gaps from more specific knowledge.

With regard to foreign-language bibliographical sources, in the case of Latin American women in particular, there is now a considerable body of academic study available in Spanish, with monographs in print on several women included in this book. Unfortunately, it was beyond my ability to research foreign-language sources for so many nationalities in anything but superficial detail; a decision was made from the outset to write the encyclopedia for the general reader who may not necessarily possess specific foreign-language skills. This restriction led to another difficult decision, made for reasons of space and for the purpose of avoiding confusion: the many published works and names of foreign organizations and women's societies in entries are cited in English only (a few foreign titles are given in cases where ambiguity might occur). For the interested reader or student who wishes to pursue an individual woman further, an appendix can be found at the end of this book, giving the most-cited organizations with the title in the original language. Consultation of books in the further reading section of each entry will also provide the user with foreign-language attributions and titles. The changing demands of the new world of electronic publishing have meant that the traditional presentation of the end-of-entry further reading system, which in reference works of this kind has tended in the past to employ a system of title abbreviation referring to a full bibliography in the back matter of the book, has been replaced with full citations at the end of each entry.

The number of historical and critical sources now available on women's history is vast and rapidly growing, but there is still a great need for more comprehensive biographical reference sources. An extensive select Bibliography of the books I found most useful in the preparation of this text (although it is by no means exhaustive), divided into lists of dictionaries and encyclopedias and primary and secondary sources, can be found at the end of the book. The book also includes indexes of the entries by cause (for example, birth control, education, human rights, medicine, prison reform, suffrage, temperance, etc.) as well as by nationality and primary country of activism, along with a chronology of significant events since the French Revolution.

The British political diarist and socialite Henry "Chips" Channon remarked in his diary of 7 July 1936, "Reformers are always finally neglected, while the memoirs of the frivolous will always eagerly be read." It has been my sincere hope in the writing of this book that I might be able to restore some of the many neglected and forgotten lives of women activists—of all colors, creeds, and political persuasions—to history and to disprove Channon's remark by illustrating that accounts of the lives of women reformers need never be dull. It has been, at its low point, an exhausting, frustrating, and even dispiriting experience trying to uncover the facts of many of the lives described in this book, but an experience that has never ceased to be enlightening, fascinating, stimulating, and frequently humbling. It is an honor to have this opportunity of restoring a little bit of women's lost and underrated history. But there are still many more stories out there waiting to be told.

Helen Rappaport
Oxfordshire, England

Acknowledgments

This book could not have been written without the pioneering work on women's history by other scholars around the world, many of whose works are listed in the bibliography. Those who have done so much to disseminate the history of the women's suffrage movement, in particular, are now too many to single out. But with regard to the less accessible stories of women outside the United Kingdom, United States, and western Europe, I would like, in particular, to commend the work of the following, whose groundwork greatly assisted me in my research: Asunción Lavrin, K. Lynn Stoner, Judith Hahner, and Shirlene Soto (Latin America); Sharon Sievers (Japan); Elizabeth Croll and Christina Kelly Gilmartin (China); Margot Badran, Valentine Moghadam, and Nawal el-Saadawi (Egypt and the Middle East); Haleh Afshar (Islamic women, particularly in Iran); Kumari Jayawardena (India and the Far East); Antoinette Burton and Geraldine Forbes (India); Richard Stites, Linda Edmondson, and Barbara Alpern Engel (Russia). Richard Evans was one of the first to explore European feminism, and, nearer home, Maria Luddy deserves a special mention for her outstanding work on Irish women.

I spent many happy hours in the Bodleian Library in Oxford doing the research for this book, and I am grateful to the staff—particularly in my regular haunt, the Lower Library—for their help and cheerfulness, as I am to the staff at the Indian Institute, Rhodes House, Queen Elizabeth House, and the Radcliffe Science Library. Joan Countryman and her library staff at Lincoln School, Providence, allowed me the free run of their excellent collection during a visit to the United States in 2000. The financial assistance of the Society of Authors, through whose Authors' Foundation I was awarded a bursary to "buy time" for writing some of this book, provided a welcome respite.

I would like to express my gratitude to friends and scholars who shared information and offered help, advice, and moral support: Elizabeth Crawford, Orlando Figes, Ann Hardy, Barbara Harlow, Ann Heilmann, Jane Jordan, Graham Law, Ruth Marris Macaulay, Christina Malkowska Zaba, Sybil Oldfield, Liz Pride, Seunghee Han, Nayereh Todi, and Lori Williamson. My thanks to Tony Sloggett at ABC-CLIO in Oxford for his continuing support and Melanie Stafford in the Denver office for her good humor and professionalism. A special commendation is due to my long-suffering, painstaking, and ever-vigilant copy editor, Beth Partin; proofer, Lori Kranz; and indexer, Ingrid Becher. I am also grateful to photo researchers Julie Mason and Liz Kincaid for turning up some rare pictures of women we thought we would never find.

Women Social Reformers by Country

Afghanistan
(mostly anonymous)

Albania
Mother Teresa

Algeria
Auclert, Hubertine
M'rabet, Fadela

Argentina
Chertkoff de Repetto, Fenia
Grierson, Cecilia
Lanteri-Renshaw, Julieta
Laperrière de Coni, Gabriela
Moreau de Justo, Alicia
Muzzilli, Carolina
Perón, Eva
Rawson de Dellepiane, Elvira

Australia
Bates, Daisy
Caldicott, Helen
Chisholm, Caroline
Dugdale, Henrietta
Goldstein, Vida
Greer, Germaine
Lawson, Louisa
Montefiore, Dora
Noonuccal, Oodgeroo Moongalba
Scott, Rose
Spence, Catherine
Street, Jessie

Austria
Mayreder, Rosa
Pappenheim, Bertha
Popp, Adelheid
Schreiber, Adele
Suttner, Bertha Félice Sophie von

Belgium
Bol Poel, Martha
Popelin, Marie

Bolivia
Barrios de Chungara, Domitla

Brazil
Lutz, Bertha

Canada
Cary, Mary Ann Shadd
Casgrain, Thérèse
MacPhail, Agnes
McClung, Nellie
Murphy, Emily Gowan
Rutnam, Mary
Stowe, Emily Jennings

Chile
Labarca Hubertson, Amanda

China
Cai Chang
Deng Yingchao
Deng Yuzhi
Ding Ling
He Xiangning
Liu-Wang Liming
Qiu Jin
Song Qingling
Tang Qunying
Wang Huiwu
Xiang Jingyu

Cuba
Collado, María
Domínguez Navarro, Ofelia
Gómez de Avellaneda y Arteaga,
    Gertrudis

Rodríguez Acosta, Ofelia
Sabas Alomá, Mariblanca

Czechoslovakia
Masarykova, Alice
Plamínková, Františka

Denmark
Bajer, Mathilde

Egypt
Barakat, Hidiya Hanim
al-Ghazali, Zeinab
Musa, Nabawiyya
Nabarawi, Saiza
Nasif, Malak Hifni
el-Saadawi, Nawal
al-Said, Aminah
Shafiq, Durriyah
Sha'rawi, Huda

Finland
Furujhelm, Annie
van Gripenberg, Alexandra

France
Armand, Inessa
Auclert, Hubertine
Beauvoir, Simone de
Deraismes, Marie
Deroin, Jeanne
Durand, Marguerite
Gouges, Olympe de
Michel, Louise
Mink, Paule
Niboyet, Eugénie
Pelletier, Madeleine
Potonié-Pierre, Eugènie
Richard, Marthe
Roland, Pauline
Roussel, Nelly
Sand, George
Séverine
Tristan, Flora
Vérone, Maria
Vincent, Eliska
Weiss, Louise

Germany
Anneke, Mathilde Franziska
Augspurg, Anita
Bäumer, Gertrud

Braun, Lily
Cauer, Minna
Dohm, Hedwig
Heymann, Lida Gustava
Juhacz, Marie
Lange, Helene
Otto-Peters, Luise
Salomon, Alice
Stöcker, Helene
Stritt, Marie
Tiburtius, Franziska
Zakrzewska, Marie
Zetkin, Clara

Ghana
Dorkenoo, Efua

Greece
Parren, Callirhoé Siganou

Guatemala
Menchú Tum, Rigoberta

Hong Kong
Benson, Stella

Hungary
Glücklich, Vilma
Schwimmer, Rosika

India
Besant, Annie
Bhatt, Ela
Carpenter, Mary
Chattopadhyaya, Kamaladevi
Chaudharani, Saraladevi
Dutt, Saroj Nalini
Hossain, Begum Rokeya Sakhawat
Joshi, Anandibai
Kaur, Rajkumari Amrit
Mother Teresa
Naidu, Sarojini
Pandit, Vijaya Lakshmi
Patkar, Medha
Pechey-Phipson, Edith
Ramabai, Pandita Saraswati
Ranade, Ramabai
Rau, Dhanvanthi Rama
Reddi, Muthulakshmi
Rukhmabai
Saghal, Manmohini Zutshi
Sister Nivedita

Sister Subbalakshmi
Sorabji, Cornelia
Sorabji, Susie
Tata, Lady Mehrbai Dorab

Indonesia
Kartini, Raden Adjeng
Santoso, Maria Ullfah
Soewondo-Soerasno, Nani

Iran
Azmudeh, Tuba
Behruzi, Mariam
Daulatabadi, Sadiqa
Kar, Mehrangiz
Manuchehrian, Mehrangiz
Qurratul-Ayn
Rahnavard, Zahra
Taleqani, Azam

Ireland
Bates, Daisy
Bennett, Louie
Blackburn, Helen
Carmichael, Amy Wilson
Cobbe, Frances Power
Cousins, Margaret
Despard, Charlotte
Edgeworth, Maria
Gonne, Maud
Gore-Booth, Eva
Haslam, Anna
Jameson, Anna Brownell
Jellicoe, Anne
Markievicz, Constance de
McAuley, Catherine
Noble, Christina
O'Brien, Charlotte Grace
Parnell, Anna
Sheehy-Skeffington, Hannah
Sister Nivedita
Tod, Isabella
Wheeler, Anna Doyle
Wollstonecraft, Mary

Israel
Szold, Henrietta

Italy
Alma Dolens
Beccari, Alaide Gualberta
Gwis-Adami, Rosalia

Kuliscioff, Anna
Montessori, Maria
Mozzoni, Anna Maria

Jamaica
Marson, Una
Seacole, Mary

Japan
Fukuda Hideko
Hani Motoko
Hiratsuka Raicho
Ichikawa Fusae
Ishimoto Shizue
Ito Noe
Kanno Suga
Kishida Toshiko
Yajima Kajiko
Yamada Waka
Yosano Akiko

Kenya
Maathai, Wangari Muta

Korea
Lee Tai-Young

Lebanon
Ziyadah, Mai

Lithuania
Goldman, Emma

Mexico
Caballero de Castillo Ledón, Amalia
   Gonzalez
Carrillo Puerto, Elvia
García, Maria del Refugio
Gutiérrez de Mendoza, Juana Belén
Jiménez y Muro, Dolores
Torres, Elena

Mozambique
Machel, Graça Simbine

Myanmar (Burma)
Aung San Suu Kyi

Netherlands
Jacobs, Aletta
Manus, Rosa

New Zealand
Sheppard, Kate
Stout, Lady Anna
Te Puea

Nigeria
Ransome-Kuti, Fumilayo

Norway
Collett, Camilla
Krog, Gina

Pakistan
Bukhari, Shahnaz
Jilani, Hina, and Asma Jahangir
Jinnah, Fatima
Khan, Raana Liaquat Ali
Nawaz, Begum Jahanarah Shah

Palestinian National Authority
Ashrawi, Hanan

Peru
Alvarado Rivera, María Jesus

Philippines
Felix, Concepción

Poland
Malkowska, Olga
Orzeszkowa, Eliza
Rose, Ernestine
Schneiderman, Rose

Portugal
Osório, Ana da Castro

Russia/Soviet Union
Armand, Inessa
Bonner, Yelena
Filosova, Anna
Kollontai, Alexandra
Kovalevskaya, Sofya
Krupskaya, Nadezhda
Kuliscioff, Anna
Mirovich, Zinaida
Pokrovskaya, Mariya
Shabanova, Anna
Shishkina-Yavein, Poliksena
Starovoitova, Galina
Stasova, Nadezhda
Suslova, Nadezhda
Trubnikova, Mariya

Scotland
Wright, Frances

Sierra Leone
Casely Hayford, Adelaide Smith

Somalia
Dirie, Waris

South Africa
Blackburn, Molly
Cornelius, Johanna
First, Ruth
Hobhouse, Emily
Joseph, Helen Beatrice
Kuzwayo, Ellen
Maxeke, Charlotte Manye
Ngoyi, Lilian
Ramphele, Mamphela
Schreiner, Olive
Sisulu, Nonsikelelo Albertina
Suzman, Helen

Spain
Arenal, Concepción
Campoamor, Clara
Gómez de Avellaneda y Arteaga, Gertrudis
Nelken i Mausberger, Margarita
Pardo Bazán, Emilia

Sri Lanka
de Silva, Agnes
Rutnam, Mary
Wickremasinghe, Doreen

Sweden
Bremer, Fredrika
Key, Ellen
Lind-af-Hageby, Louise
Myrdal, Alva
Nelken i Mausberger, Margarita

Switzerland
Goegg, Marie Pouchoulin

Trinidad and Tobago
Jeffers, Audrey Lane

Turkey
Edip, Halide

United Kingdom
Anderson, Elizabeth Garrett

Ashby, Margery Corbett
Astor, Nancy
Bamber, Helen
Beale, Dorothea
Becker, Lydia
Benson, Stella
Besant, Annie
Billington-Greig, Teresa
Black, Clementina
Blackburn, Helen
Blackwell, Elizabeth
Bodichon, Barbara
Bondfield, Margaret
Booth, Catherine
Boucherett, Jessie
Brittain, Vera
Burdett-Coutts, Angela
Buss, Frances
Butler, Josephine
Byrne, Lavinia
Caird, Mona
Carpenter, Mary
Castle, Barbara
Chew, Ada Nield
Chisholm, Caroline
Clough, Anne Jemima
Cobbe, Frances Power
Cooper, Selina
Courtney, Kathleen D'Olier
Cunard, Nancy
Davies, (Sarah) Emily
Davison, Emily Wilding
Despard, Charlotte
Diana, Princess of Wales
Dilke, Emilia
Fawcett, Millicent Garrett
Ford, Isabella
Fry, Elizabeth
Gaskell, Elizabeth
Grand, Sarah
Greer, Germaine
Heyrick, Elizabeth
Hill, Octavia
Hobhouse, Emily
Holtby, Winifred
Hopkins, (Alice) Ellice
How-Martyn, Edith
Inglis, Elsie
Jebb, Eglantyne
Jex-Blake, Sophia
Kenney, Annie
Kingsford, Anna
Lind-af-Hageby, Louise

Linton, Eliza Lynn
Lytton, Lady Constance
MacMillan, Chrystal
Marshall, Catherine
Martineau, Harriet
McMillan, Margaret
Mitchell, Hannah
Montagu, Lily
Montefiore, Dora
More, Hannah
Neilans, Alison
Nightingale, Florence
Norton, Caroline
Pankhurst, Christabel
Pankhurst, Emmeline
Pankhurst, (Estelle) Sylvia
Paterson, Emma
Pechey-Phipson, Edith
Peckover, Priscilla
Pethick-Lawrence, Emmeline
Pizzey, Erin
Rathbone, Eleanor
Robins, Elizabeth
Royden, Maude
Rye, Maria
Sheppard, Kate
Shirreff, Emily Anne
Somerset, Lady Isabella
Spence, Catherine
Stopes, Marie
Swanwick, Helena
Taylor, Harriet
Twining, Louisa
Ward, Mary
Webb, Beatrice
Wickremasinghe, Doreen
Wollstonecraft, Mary
Wolstoneholme-Elmy, Elizabeth

United States
Abbott, Edith
Abbott, Grace
Addams, Jane
Ames, Jessie Daniel
Anneke, Mathilde Franziska
Anthony, Susan B.
Astor, Nancy
Baker, Ella
Baker, (Sara) Josephine
Balch, Emily Greene
Barton, Clara
Bates, Daisy
Beard, Mary Ritter

Beecher, Catharine Esther
Belmont, Alva
Bethune, Mary McCleod
Blackwell, Alice Stone
Blackwell, Antoinette Brown
Blackwell, Elizabeth
Blatch, Harriot Stanton
Bloomer, Amelia Jenks
Bloor, Ella Reeve
Bonnin, Gertrude
Brown, Charlotte Hawkins
Brown, Olympia
Caldicott, Helen
Carson, Rachel
Cary, Mary Ann Shadd
Catt, Carrie Chapman
Child, Lydia Maria
Chisholm, Shirley
Day, Dorothy
Dennett, Mary Ware
Dix, Dorothea Lynde
Dodge, Grace
Dreier, Mary Elisabeth
Dworkin, Andrea
Eastman, Crystal
Edelman, Marian Wright
Farnham, Eliza Wood
Flynn, Elizabeth Gurley
Foster, Abby (Abigail) Kelley
Friedan, Betty
Fuller, (Sarah) Margaret
Gage, Matilda Joslyn
Gibbons, Abigail Hopper
Gilman, Charlotte Perkins
Goldman, Emma
Grimké, Angelina Emily and Sarah Moore
Hale, Clara
Hamer, Fanny Lou
Hamilton, Alice
Howe, Julia Ward
Huerta, Dolores
Jackson, Helen Hunt
Jacobi, Mary Putnam
Jones, Mary
Kehew, Mary Morton
Keller, Helen
Kelley, Florence
La Flesche, Susette
Lathrop, Julia

Livermore, Mary
Lockwood, Belva Ann
Lowell, Josephine Shaw
McDowell, Mary
Mott, Lucretia Coffin
Nation, Carry
O'Brien, Charlotte Grace
Ovington, Mary White
Parks, Rosa
Paul, Alice
Peabody, Elizabeth
Perkins, Frances Coralie
Prejean, Sister Helen
Rankin, Jeanette
Robins, Elizabeth
Robins, Margaret Dreier
Roosevelt, (Anna) Eleanor
Rose, Ernestine
Salomon, Alice
Sanger, Margaret
Schlafly, Phyllis
Schneiderman, Rose
Schwimmer, Rosika
Scudder, Vida
Shaw, Anna Howard
Stanton, Elizabeth Cady
Steinem, Gloria
Stone, Lucy
Stowe, Harriet Beecher
Szold, Henrietta
Tarbell, Ida
Terrell, Mary Church
Thomas, Martha Carey
Truth, Sojourner
Tubman, Harriet Ross
Wald, Lillian D.
Wells-Barnett, Ida B.
Willard, Emma Hart
Willard, Frances
Woodhull, Victoria Claflin
Wright, Frances
Zakrzewska, Marie

Uruguay
Abella de Ramírez, María
Luisi, Paulina

Vietnam
Noble, Christina

Women Social Reformers by Cause

Abolition of Slavery
Anneke, Mathilde Franziska
Anthony, Susan B.
Cary, Mary Ann Shadd
Child, Lydia Maria
Foster, Abby (Abigail) Kelley
Gibbons, Abigail Hopper
Gómez de Avellaneda y Arteaga, Gertrudis
Grimké, Angelina Emily and Sarah Moore
Haslam, Anna
Heyrick, Elizabeth
Howe, Julia Ward
Lowell, Josephine Shaw
Mott, Lucretia Coffin
Stone, Lucy
Stowe, Harriet Beecher
Truth, Sojourner
Tubman, Harriet Ross
Wright, Frances

Abolition of State-Regulated Prostitution
Beccari, Alaide Gualberta
Benson, Stella
Blackwell, Elizabeth
Butler, Josephine
Carmichael, Amy Wilson
Deraismes, Marie
Goegg, Marie Pouchoulin
Haslam, Anna
Hopkins, (Alice) Ellice
Jacobs, Aletta
Luisi, Paulina
Martineau, Harriet
Mozzoni, Anna Maria
Neilans, Alison
Pappenheim, Bertha
Reddi, Muthulakshmi
Richard, Marthe
Shishkina-Yavein, Poliksena
Stritt, Marie
Yajima Kajiko

Anti-Suffrage/Anti-Equal Rights
Beecher, Catharine Esther
al-Ghazali, Zeinab
Linton, Eliza Lynn
More, Hannah
Perkins, Frances Coralie
Schlafly, Phyllis
Tarbell, Ida
Ward, Mary
Yamada Waka

Anti-Vivisection/Animal Rights
Blackwell, Alice Stone
Blackwell, Elizabeth
Caird, Mona
Carson, Rachel
Cobbe, Frances Power
Deraismes, Marie
Durand, Marguerite
Heymann, Lida Gustava
Heyrick, Elizabeth
Kingsford, Anna
Lind-af-Hageby, Louise

Children's Rights
Abbott, Grace
Baker, (Sara) Josephine
Campoamor, Clara
Carmichael, Amy Wilson
Carpenter, Mary
Carrillo Puerto, Elvia
Domínguez Navarro, Ofelia
Edelman, Marian Wright
Jebb, Eglantyne
Jones, Mary
Kelley, Florence
Lathrop, Julia
Machel, Graça Simbine
Malkowska, Olga
Manuchehrian, Mehrangiz
McAuley, Catherine

McMillan, Margaret
Montessori, Maria
Noble, Christina
Ramabai, Pandita Saraswati
Ranade, Ramabai
Rathbone, Eleanor
Reddi, Muthulakshmi
Robins, Margaret Dreier
Rukhmabai
Sabas Alomá, Mariblanca

Civil Rights

Ames, Jessie Daniel
Aung San Suu Kyi
Baker, Ella
Bates, Daisy (Aus.)
Bates, Daisy (U.S.)
Bethune, Mary McCleod
Blackburn, Molly
Brown, Charlotte Hawkins
Chisholm, Shirley
Cunard, Nancy
Domínguez Navarro, Ofelia
Edelman, Marian Wright
First, Ruth
García, Maria del Refugio
Hamer, Fanny Lou
Holtby, Winifred
Joseph, Helen Beatrice
Keller, Helen
Kuzwayo, Ellen
Lockwood, Belva Ann
Marson, Una
Maxeke, Charlotte Manye
Menchú Tum, Rigoberta
Ngoyi, Lilian
Noonuccal, Oodgeroo Moongalba
Ovington, Mary White
Parks, Rosa
Prejean, Sister Helen
Rahnavard, Zahra
Ramphele, Mamphela
Roosevelt, (Anna) Eleanor
Schreiner, Olive
Sisulu, Nonsikelelo Albertina
Steinem, Gloria
Suzman, Helen
Taleqani, Azam
Te Puea
Terrell, Mary Church
Wells-Barnett, Ida B.

Education

Alvarado Rivera, María Jes?s
Armand, Inessa
Azmudeh, Tuba
Beale, Dorothea
Beard, Mary Ritter
Beecher, Catharine Esther
Bethune, Mary McCleod
Blackwell, Elizabeth
Brown, Charlotte Hawkins
Buss, Frances
Carpenter, Mary
Casely Hayford, Adelaide Smith
Cauer, Minna
Chisholm, Caroline
Chisholm, Shirley
Clough, Anne Jemima
Daulatabadi, Sadiqa
Davies, (Sarah) Emily
Dutt, Saroj Nalini
Edgeworth, Maria
Edip, Halide
Filosova, Anna
Glücklich, Vilma
Hani Motoko
Hossain, Begum Rokeya Sakhawat
Jameson, Anna Brownell
Jeffers, Audrey Lane
Jex-Blake, Sophia
Jiménez y Muro, Dolores
Kartini, Raden Adjeng
Kehew, Mary Morton
Kovalevskaya, Sofya
Krupskaya, Nadezhda
Labarca Hubertson, Amanda
Lange, Helene
Lutz, Bertha
Machel, Graça Simbine
McMillan, Margaret
Montessori, Maria
More, Hannah
Musa, Nabawiyya
Nasif, Malak Hifni
Osório, Ana da Castro
Parren, Callirhoé Siganou
Peabody, Elizabeth
Ramabai, Pandita Saraswati
Ranade, Ramabai
Ransome-Kuti, Fumilayo
Shabanova, Anna
Shirreff, Emily Anne
Sister Nivedita
Sister Subbalakshmi

Sorabji, Cornelia
Sorabji, Susie
Stasova, Nadezhda
Stowe, Emily Jennings
Suslova, Nadezhda
Taylor, Harriet
Terrell, Mary Church
Thomas, Martha Carey
Tiburtius, Franziska
Tod, Isabella
Torres, Elena
Trubnikova, Mariya
Wickremasinghe, Doreen
Willard, Emma Hart
Yosano Akiko
Zakrzewska, Marie

Emancipation of Women
Abella de Ramírez, María
Afghan Women Social Reformers
Astor, Nancy
Beauvoir, Simone de
Bloomer, Amelia Jenks
Bodichon, Barbara
Bremer, Fredrika
Brittain, Vera
Buss, Frances
Caballero de Castillo Ledón, Amalia Gonzalez
Caird, Mona
Chaudharani, Saraladevi
Collett, Camilla
Daulatabadi, Sadiqa
Deng Yingchao
Deraismes, Marie
Ding Ling
Dohm, Hedwig
Dugdale, Henrietta
Edip, Halide
Felix, Concepción
Friedan, Betty
Fukuda Hideko
Fuller, (Sarah) Margaret
García, Maria del Refugio
Gilman, Charlotte Perkins
Goegg, Marie Pouchoulin
Gómez de Avellaneda y Arteaga, Gertrudis
Gouges, Olympe de
Grand, Sarah
Greer, Germaine
Grimké, Angelina Emily and Sarah Moore
Hani Motoko
He Xiangning
Hossain, Begum Rokeya Sakhawat

Ishimoto Shizue
Ito Noe
Jameson, Anna Brownell
Kartini, Raden Adjeng
Kishida Toshiko
Krupskaya, Nadezhda
Lee Tai-Young
Liu-Wang Liming
Marson, Una
Martineau, Harriet
Mayreder, Rosa
McClung, Nellie
Michel, Louise
Moreau de Justo, Alicia
Mozzoni, Anna Maria
M'rabet, Fadela
Musa, Nabawiyya
Nabarawi, Saiza
Naidu, Sarojini
Nasif, Malak Hifni
Nawaz, Begum Jahanarah Shah
Osório, Ana da Castro
Otto-Peters, Luise
Pardo Bazán, Emilia
Potonié-Pierre, Eugénie
Qiu Jin
Qurratul-Ayn
Rahnavard, Zahra
Robins, Elizabeth
Rodríguez Acosta, Ofelia
Roland, Pauline
Rose, Ernestine
Sabas Alomá, Mariblanca
al-Said, Aminah
Sand, George
Schreiner, Olive
Sha'rawi, Huda
Stanton, Elizabeth Cady
Steinem, Gloria
Suttner, Bertha Félice Sophie von
Tata, Lady Mehrbai Dorab
Taylor, Harriet
van Gripenberg, Alexandra
Wang Huiwu
Wheeler, Anna Doyle
Wollstonecraft, Mary
Wright, Frances
Yosano Akiko
Ziyadah, Mai

Environmental Issues
Caldicott, Helen
Carson, Rachel

Hill, Octavia
Maathai, Wangari Muta
Patkar, Medha

Health Care
Anderson, Elizabeth Garrett
Baker, (Sara) Josephine
Bamber, Helen
Barton, Clara
Dirie, Waris
Dix, Dorothea Lynde
Dorkenoo, Efua
Gibbons, Abigail Hopper
Grierson, Cecilia
Hamilton, Alice
Inglis, Elsie
Jacobi, Mary Putnam
Jex-Blake, Sophia
Joshi, Anandibai
Kaur, Rajkumari Amrit
Kingsford, Anna
Kuliscioff, Anna
Lanteri-Renshaw, Julieta
Laperrière de Coni, Gabriela
Lathrop, Julia
Livermore, Mary
Luisi, Paulina
Martineau, Harriet
Nightingale, Florence
Pechey-Phipson, Edith
Pokrovskaya, Mariya
Rawson de Dellepiane, Elvira
Rutnam, Mary
Sanger, Margaret
Seacole, Mary
Shabanova, Anna
Suslova, Nadezhda
Tiburtius, Franziska
Twining, Louisa
Wald, Lillian D.
Zakrzewska, Marie

Human Rights
Ames, Jessie Daniel
Ashrawi, Hanan
Bamber, Helen
Barrios de Chungara, Domitla
Barton, Clara
Blackburn, Molly
Bonner, Yelena
Bonnin, Gertrude
Butler, Josephine
Cunard, Nancy

Diana, Princess of Wales
Hobhouse, Emily
Huerta, Dolores
Jackson, Helen Hunt
Jilani, Hina, and Asma Jahangir
Joseph, Helen Beatrice
Kar, Mehrangiz
Kuzwayo, Ellen
La Flesche, Susette
Menchú Tum, Rigoberta
Mother Teresa
Myrdal, Alva
Ngoyi, Lilian
Niboyet, Eugénie
Prejean, Sister Helen
Roosevelt, (Anna) Eleanor
Sisulu, Nonsikelelo Albertina
Starovoitova, Galina
Street, Jessie
Suzman, Helen
Szold, Henrietta
Wells-Barnett, Ida B.

Immigrant Rights
Abbott, Edith
Abbott, Grace
Addams, Jane
Balch, Emily Greene
Chisholm, Caroline
Masarykova, Alice
McDowell, Mary
Montagu, Lily
O'Brien, Charlotte Grace
Scudder, Vida
Szold, Henrietta

Labor Rights/Trade Unionism
Barrios de Chungara, Domitla
Bennett, Louie
Besant, Annie
Bhatt, Ela
Black, Clementina
Blackburn, Helen
Bloor, Ella Reeve
Bondfield, Margaret
Cauer, Minna
Chertkoff de Repetto, Fenia
Chew, Ada Nield
Collado, María
Cooper, Selina
Cornelius, Johanna
Deng Yuzhi
Deroin, Jeanne

Dilke, Emilia
Dreier, Mary Elisabeth
First, Ruth
Flynn, Elizabeth Gurley
Ford, Isabella
Gilman, Charlotte Perkins
Goldman, Emma
Gore-Booth, Eva
Hamilton, Alice
Huerta, Dolores
Ichikawa Fusae
Jellicoe, Anne
Jones, Mary
Kehew, Mary Morton
Kelley, Florence
Kenney, Annie
Laperrière de Coni, Gabriela
Markievicz, Constance de
Maxeke, Charlotte Manye
McDowell, Mary
Mink, Paule
Mitchell, Hannah
Muzzilli, Carolina
Otto-Peters, Luise
Parnell, Anna
Parren, Callirhoé Siganou
Paterson, Emma
Perkins, Frances Coralie
Pethick-Lawrence, Emmeline
Popp, Adelheid
Robins, Margaret Dreier
Rye, Maria
Saghal, Manmohini Zutshi
Schneiderman, Rose
Tristan, Flora
Vincent, Eliska
Webb, Beatrice
Wickremasinghe, Doreen
Xiang Jingyu
Zetkin, Clara

Marriage/Divorce/Custody Rights
Abella de Ramírez, María
Behruzi, Mariam
Lawson, Louisa
Norton, Caroline
Rau, Dhanvanthi Rama
Rawson de Dellepiane, Elvira
Santoso, Maria Ullfah
Soewondo-Soerasno, Nani

Peace/Anti-militarism
Addams, Jane

Alma Dolens
Ashby, Margery Corbett
Ashrawi, Hanan
Auclert, Hubertine
Augspurg, Anita
Bajer, Mathilde
Balch, Emily Greene
Beccari, Alaide Gualberta
Bennett, Louie
Bondfield, Margaret
Braun, Lily
Bremer, Fredrika
Brittain, Vera
Brown, Olympia
Catt, Carrie Chapman
Courtney, Kathleen D'Olier
Day, Dorothy
Dennett, Mary Ware
Despard, Charlotte
Dohm, Hedwig
Dreier, Mary Elisabeth
Eastman, Crystal
Gilman, Charlotte Perkins
Glücklich, Vilma
Goegg, Marie Pouchoulin
Goldstein, Vida
Gwis-Adami, Rosalia
Heymann, Lida Gustava
Hiratsuka Raicho
Hobhouse, Emily
Holtby, Winifred
Jacobs, Aletta
Jebb, Eglantyne
Keller, Helen
Kelley, Florence
Key, Ellen
Lind-af-Hageby, Louise
Lockwood, Belva Ann
MacMillan, Chrystal
MacPhail, Agnes
Manus, Rosa
Marshall, Catherine
Mayreder, Rosa
Nabarawi, Saiza
Niboyet, Eugénie
Pankhurst, (Estelle) Sylvia
Peckover, Priscilla
Plamínková, Frantisˇka
Popelin, Marie
Potonié-Pierre, Eugénie
Rankin, Jeanette
Robins, Elizabeth
Royden, Maude

Salomon, Alice
Schreiner, Olive
Schwimmer, Rosika
Scott, Rose
Séverine
Suttner, Bertha Félice Sophie von
Swanwick, Helena
Tarbell, Ida
Weiss, Louise

Philanthropy/Charity Work
Barakat, Hidiya Hanim
Belmont, Alva
Bol Poel, Martha
Boucherett, Jessie
Burdett-Coutts, Angela
Chattopadhyaya, Kamaladevi
Diana, Princess of Wales
Dodge, Grace
Filosova, Anna
Jellicoe, Anne
Noble, Christina
Pandit, Vijaya Lakshmi
Peabody, Elizabeth
Perón, Eva
Roosevelt, (Anna) Eleanor
Scudder, Vida
Sha'rawi, Huda
Séverine
Somerset, Lady Isabella
Song Qingling
Sorabji, Cornelia
Sorabji, Susie
Stasova, Nadezhda
Stout, Lady Anna
Tata, Lady Mehrbai Dorab
Trubnikova, Mariya
Ward, Mary

Political and Legal Reform
Astor, Nancy
Aung San Suu Kyi
Beauvoir, Simone de
Behruzi, Mariam
Billington-Greig, Teresa
Blatch, Harriot Stanton
Bloor, Ella Reeve
Bonner, Yelena
Braun, Lily
Cai Chang
Caldicott, Helen
Casgrain, Thérèse
Castle, Barbara

Chattopadhyaya, Kamaladevi
Chaudharani, Saraladevi
Chertkoff de Repetto, Fenia
Chisholm, Shirley
Deng Yingchao
Deng Yuzhi
Deroin, Jeanne
Ding Ling
Dworkin, Andrea
Flynn, Elizabeth Gurley
Friedan, Betty
Fukuda Hideko
Fuller, (Sarah) Margaret
Furujhelm, Annie
Gonne, Maud
Gouges, Olympe de
Gutiérrez de Mendoza, Juana Belén
He Xiangning
Hiratsuka Raicho
Ito Noe
Jackson, Helen Hunt
Jiménez y Muro, Dolores
Jinnah, Fatima
Kanno Suga
Kar, Mehrangiz
Kaur, Rajkumari Amrit
Khan, Raana Liaquat Ali
Kishida Toshiko
Kollontai, Alexandra
Kuliscioff, Anna
Laperrière de Coni, Gabriela
Lee Tai-Young
Liu-Wang Liming
Lockwood, Belva Ann
Lutz, Bertha
Masarykova, Alice
Michel, Louise
Mirovich, Zinaida
Montefiore, Dora
Murphy, Emily Gowan
Muzzilli, Carolina
Naidu, Sarojini
Nelken i Mausberger, Margarita
Pandit, Vijaya Lakshmi
Pankhurst, Christabel
Parnell, Anna
Paul, Alice
Perkins, Frances Coralie
Perón, Eva
Plamínková, Frantis'ka
Popp, Adelheid
Qiu Jin
Ransome-Kuti, Fumilayo

Rawson de Dellepiane, Elvira
al-Said, Aminah
Santoso, Maria Ullfah
Shafiq, Durriyah
Sheehy-Skeffington, Hannah
Song Qingling
Spence, Catherine
Stanton, Elizabeth Cady
Starovoitova, Galina
Steinem, Gloria
Street, Jessie
Taleqani, Azam
Tang Qunying
Torres, Elena
Vérone, Maria
Wang Huiwu
Webb, Beatrice
Xiang Jingyu
Zetkin, Clara

Prison Reform

Arenal, Concepción
Farnham, Eliza Wood
Fry, Elizabeth
Gibbons, Abigail Hopper
Gonne, Maud
Heyrick, Elizabeth
Howe, Julia Ward
Lowell, Josephine Shaw
Lytton, Lady Constance
MacPhail, Agnes

Property Rights

Becker, Lydia
Lanteri-Renshaw, Julieta
Norton, Caroline
Rose, Ernestine
Wheeler, Anna Doyle

Religious Reform

Blackwell, Antoinette Brown
Bukhari, Shahnaz
Byrne, Lavinia
Cobbe, Frances Power
Cousins, Margaret
Deraismes, Marie
Dirie, Waris
Foster, Abby (Abigail) Kelley
Gage, Matilda Joslyn
Jinnah, Fatima
Montagu, Lily
M'rabet, Fadela
Nawaz, Begum Jahanarah Shah

Qurratul-Ayn
Royden, Maude
Rukhmabai
el-Saadawi, Nawal
Stanton, Elizabeth Cady

Reproductive Rights

Besant, Annie
Carrillo Puerto, Elvia
Dennett, Mary Ware
Goldman, Emma
How-Martyn, Edith
Ishimoto Shizue
Jacobs, Aletta
Kollontai, Alexandra
Luisi, Paulina
Pelletier, Madeleine
Rau, Dhanvanthi Rama
Roussel, Nelly
Rutnam, Mary
Sanger, Margaret
Stöcker, Helene
Stopes, Marie
Stritt, Marie
Wright, Frances

Sexual Freedom

Goldman, Emma
Grand, Sarah
Greer, Germaine
Kanno Suga
Key, Ellen
Kollontai, Alexandra
Pelletier, Madeleine
Rodríguez Acosta, Ofelia
Roland, Pauline
el-Saadawi, Nawal
Sand, George
Schreiber, Adele
Stöcker, Helene
Stopes, Marie
Stritt, Marie
Wollstonecraft, Mary
Wolstenholme-Elmy, Elizabeth
Woodhull, Victoria Claflin

Social Welfare/Poverty

Abbott, Edith
Arenal, Concepción
Armand, Inessa
Barakat, Hidiya Hanim
Bates, Daisy (Aus.)
Bäumer, Gertrud

Bhatt, Ela
Booth, Catherine
Burdett-Coutts, Angela
Castle, Barbara
Cobbe, Frances Power
Day, Dorothy
Dodge, Grace
Fry, Elizabeth
Gaskell, Elizabeth
al-Ghazali, Zeinab
Gonne, Maud
Grierson, Cecilia
Hamer, Fanny Lou
Hill, Octavia
Hopkins, (Alice) Ellice
Inglis, Elsie
Jacobi, Mary Putnam
Jeffers, Audrey Lane
Juhacz, Marie
Khan, Raana Liaquat Ali
Lowell, Josephine Shaw
Manuchehrian, Mehrangiz
McAuley, Catherine
Mother Teresa
Myrdal, Alva
Orzeszkowa, Eliza
Ovington, Mary White
Pappenheim, Bertha
Pizzey, Erin
Ramphele, Mamphela
Rankin, Jeanette
Rathbone, Eleanor
Roussel, Nelly
Rye, Maria
Saghal, Manmohini Zutshi
Salomon, Alice
Spence, Catherine
Stout, Lady Anna
Tristan, Flora
Twining, Louisa
Wald, Lillian D.

Suffrage
Alma Dolens
Alvarado Rivera, María Jes?s
Anderson, Elizabeth Garrett
Anneke, Mathilde Franziska
Anthony, Susan B.
Ashby, Margery Corbett
Auclert, Hubertine
Augspurg, Anita
Bajer, Mathilde
Becker, Lydia

Belmont, Alva
Bennett, Louie
Benson, Stella
Billington-Greig, Teresa
Black, Clementina
Blackburn, Helen
Blackwell, Alice Stone
Blackwell, Antoinette Brown
Blatch, Harriot Stanton
Bloomer, Amelia Jenks
Bodichon, Barbara
Bondfield, Margaret
Bonnin, Gertrude
Boucherett, Jessie
Brown, Olympia
Caballero de Castillo Ledón, Amalia Gonzalez
Campoamor, Clara
Cary, Mary Ann Shadd
Casgrain, Thérèse
Catt, Carrie Chapman
Cauer, Minna
Chew, Ada Nield
Child, Lydia Maria
Collado, María
Cooper, Selina
Courtney, Kathleen D'Olier
Cousins, Margaret
Davies, (Sarah) Emily
Davison, Emily Wilding
de Silva, Agnes
Despard, Charlotte
Dohm, Hedwig
Domínguez Navarro, Ofelia
Dreier, Mary Elisabeth
Dugdale, Henrietta
Durand, Marguerite
Eastman, Crystal
Fawcett, Millicent Garrett
Felix, Concepción
Ford, Isabella
Foster, Abby (Abigail) Kelley
Furujhelm, Annie
Gage, Matilda Joslyn
Gilman, Charlotte Perkins
Goldstein, Vida
Gore-Booth, Eva
Gutiérrez de Mendoza, Juana Belén
Hamilton, Alice
Haslam, Anna
Heymann, Lida Gustava
Howe, Julia Ward
How-Martyn, Edith
Ichikawa Fusae

Jacobs, Aletta
Kenney, Annie
Key, Ellen
Krog, Gina
Labarca Hubertson, Amanda
Lanteri-Renshaw, Julieta
Lawson, Louisa
Livermore, Mary
Lockwood, Belva Ann
Lutz, Bertha
Lytton, Lady Constance
MacMillan, Chrystal
Manus, Rosa
Markievicz, Constance de
Marshall, Catherine
McClung, Nellie
Mink, Paule
Mirovich, Zinaida
Mitchell, Hannah
Montefiore, Dora
Moreau de Justo, Alicia
Mott, Lucretia Coffin
Murphy, Emily Gowan
Neilans, Alison
Niboyet, Eugénie
Noonuccal, Oodgeroo Moongalba
Pankhurst, Christabel
Pankhurst, Emmeline
Pankhurst, (Estelle) Sylvia
Paterson, Emma
Paul, Alice
Pelletier, Madeleine
Pethick-Lawrence, Emmeline
Plamínková, Frantisˇka
Pokrovskaya, Mariya
Popelin, Marie
Popp, Adelheid
Rankin, Jeanette
Rathbone, Eleanor
Rawson de Dellepiane, Elvira
Robins, Elizabeth
Rose, Ernestine
Royden, Maude
Schneiderman, Rose
Schreiber, Adele
Schwimmer, Rosika
Scott, Rose
Shafiq, Durriyah
Shaw, Anna Howard

Sheehy-Skeffington, Hannah
Sheppard, Kate
Shishkina-Yavein, Poliksena
Soewondo-Soerasno, Nani
Stanton, Elizabeth Cady
Stone, Lucy
Stout, Lady Anna
Stowe, Emily Jennings
Stowe, Harriet Beecher
Stritt, Marie
Swanwick, Helena
Tang Qunying
Thomas, Martha Carey
Tod, Isabella
Truth, Sojourner
Tubman, Harriet Ross
van Gripenberg, Alexandra
Vérone, Maria
Vincent, Eliska
Weiss, Louise
Willard, Frances
Wolstenholme-Elmy, Elizabeth

Temperance/Drug and Alcohol Abuse
Blackwell, Alice Stone
Bloomer, Amelia Jenks
Booth, Catherine
Brown, Olympia
Hale, Clara
Haslam, Anna
Livermore, Mary
Nation, Carry
Shaw, Anna Howard
Sheppard, Kate
Somerset, Lady Isabella
Willard, Frances
Yajima Kajiko

Violence against Women
Afghan Women Social Reformers
Bukhari, Shahnaz
Dirie, Waris
Dorkenoo, Efua
Dugdale, Henrietta
Dworkin, Andrea
Jilani, Hina, and Asma Jahangir
Kar, Mehrangiz
Pizzey, Erin

A

Abbott, Edith
(1876–1957)
United States

With her sister Grace, the reformer and social theorist Edith Abbott was a pioneer of women's social work in the United States and became renowned for establishing a highly professional, scientific basis for social administration as its "passionate statistician." Both sisters were the products of a compassionate, reformist Quaker mother who encouraged their concern for social welfare.

Abbott was born in Grand Island, Nebraska, and, after attending Brownell Hall boarding school in Omaha, taught school in Nebraska while studying for her degree at the University of Nebraska by correspondence course. Awarded her degree in 1901, she took up postgraduate studies at the University of Chicago. After receiving a doctorate in economics in 1905 for a thesis on unskilled labor in the United States from 1850, Abbott won a Carnegie Fellowship, which enabled her to travel to England in 1906 to study at University College and the London School of Economics. During the course of her research into women in industry, she became an admirer of the reformer Charles Booth, met the socialist leaders Sidney and Beatrice Webb, and observed for herself the workings of the English Poor Laws in London's East End. In 1910 Abbott published the results of her research as *Women in Industry: A Study in American Economic History.*

On her return to the United States in 1907, Abbott taught economics at Wellesley College for a year and then, having heard so much about the pioneer work of Jane Addams from her sister Grace, joined her at Hull House in Chicago. She took a post as assistant to Sophonisba Breckinridge at the Chicago School of Civics and Philanthropy and developed a program in social work, which, when the school ran into financial difficulties, was successfully transferred to the University of Chicago in 1920. Together, Abbott and Breckinridge also worked for women's, immigrants', and trade union rights and were active in the suffrage campaign. In 1927 they cofounded the *Social Science Review,* which Abbott edited until 1953.

In 1924 Abbott became dean of the graduate School of Social Service Administration (as the former School of Civics and Philanthropy was now known), remaining there until 1942. During this period she further expanded fieldwork and the training of social workers in the community, as well as applying her considerable skills as a statistician to studies of truancy, juvenile delinquency, and the penal system.

In 1935, having advised on federal aid programs during the Great Depression, Abbott was disappointed in the provisions of the new Social Security Act, which she had helped draft. In 1937 she began campaigning for the abolition of the means test applied to old age pensioners, offering the Fabian and socialist alternatives of social insurance and a public welfare system that she had encountered during her time in England. In 1940 she advocated the nationalization of medical care and welfare and provisions for the retraining of the unemployed—all to be financed out of taxes.

During her career, Abbott produced a considerable body of statistical and analytical work, including *Historical Aspects of the Immigration Problem* (1926), *Report on Crime and the Foreign Born* (1931), and *Social Welfare and Professional Education* (1931). She also served as an adviser to the International Office of the League of Nations and was president of both the National Conference of Social Work and the American Association of Schools of Social Work.

See also Abbott, Grace; Addams, Jane; Webb, Beatrice.

References and Further Reading
Costin, Lela B. 1983. *Two Sisters for Social Justice: A Biography of Grace and Edith Abbott*. Urbana: University of Illinois Press.
Current Biography. 1941. New York: H. W. Wilson.
Davidson, Cathy N., and Linda Wagner Martin, eds. 1995. *Oxford Companion to Women's Writing in the United States*. New York: Oxford University Press.
Dictionary of American Biography 1946–1958, and indexes to Supplements 1–10, 1981–1996. New York: Scribner's.
Encyclopedia of Social Work. 1995. New York: NASW Press.
Fitzpatrick, Ellen. 1991. *Endless Crusade: Women Social Scientists and Progressive Reform*. New York: Oxford University Press.
Kendall, Katherine A. 1989. "Women at the Helm: Three Extraordinary Leaders." *Affilia* 4(1): 23–32.
Sicherman, Barbara, and Carol Hurd Green, eds. 1980. *Notable American Women 1607–1950: A Biographical Dictionary*, vol. 4, *The Modern Period*. Cambridge, MA: Belknap Press of Harvard University.

Abbott, Grace
(1878–1939)
United States

As with her older sister Edith, the impetus for Grace Abbott's humanitarian and civic work came from her Quaker background and the example of her reformist mother and her administrator father, who was the first lieutenant governor of Nebraska. She became an influential public figure, serving during five U.S. presidencies as head of the Children's Bureau, where she promoted the protection of the child worker, continuing the work begun by Florence Kelley against inhumane child labor. Abbott also made it her particular lifelong concern to defend the rights of immigrants to the United States.

Born in Grand Island, Nebraska, Abbott attended Brownell Hall boarding school and studied for a degree at Grand Island College. Like her sister Edith, she initially worked as a teacher (1899–1907) and encouraged Edith to join her in working at Jane Addams's Hull House in Chicago, where she supported the labor rights of immigrant women in Chicago's garment industry and provided moral and practical support during their strike of 1911–1912. After completing her M.A. in political science at the University of Chicago (1909), she began writing a series of weekly articles entitled "Within the City's Gates" (1909–1910) for the *Chicago Evening Post*, in which she highlighted the problems of poverty in the immigrant community.

Abbott was appointed head of the Immigrants' Protective League (IPL), which she had initiated along with a committee of the Women's Trade Union League in Chicago in 1908. She worked with the immigration authorities both in Chicago and at Ellis Island in New York, organizing teams of volunteer workers and translators to meet, greet, and set up assistance for newly arrived immigrants in finding accommodations and work, thus avoiding their exploitation by unscrupulous travel ticket brokers, employers, and landlords. A particular concern of the IPL was the protection of vulnerable single immigrant women, who all too frequently were being entrapped into prostitution and vice. Under Abbott the IPL sought to defuse public hostility toward immigrants by emphasizing their value to the community and the need for respect to be shown to their cultures. The IPL supported immigrants' rights to citizenship and provided them with legal assistance in the courts; it also lobbied for the eventual passage (in 1913) of a bill to introduce official immigration and naturalization inspectors at all points of entry into the United States. Abbott herself made a particular point of defending immigrants from eastern Europe against the introduction of literacy tests aimed at dramatically reducing their numbers and made many practical suggestions, based on her own careful research, for legislation to protect the rights of immigrants.

In 1917, the year she published a detailed account of her years of research in *The Immigrant and the Community*, Abbott accepted a post in Washington in the child labor division of the U.S. Children's Bureau, where she worked on limiting the employment of juveniles under the child labor clause of the 1916 Keating-Owen Act. Her careful work of two years in setting up the enforcement of the new law was brought to a halt in 1918 when the act was declared unconstitutional. In 1919 she returned to immigrant work in Chicago as director of the short-lived Illinois State Immigrants' Commission. Here she made further studies of literacy levels among immigrants leading to the introduction of adult education programs before once more working for the Immigrants' Protective League. Abbott returned to Washington to serve as director of the Children's Bureau from 1921 until 1934.

During her thirteen years as head of the bureau, Abbott continued to set standards for maternal and child welfare under the provisions of the Sheppard-Towner Maternity and Infancy Protection Act of 1921, overseeing the establishment of 3,000 health clinics for children and mothers across the United States and resisting government moves to bring the work of the bureau under the control of the Public Health Service. In 1922 she was invited to become a U.S. delegate to the League of Nations Advisory Committee on Traffic in Women and Children.

In 1934 Abbott returned to Chicago to join her sister Edith at the School of Social Service Administration as professor of public welfare, a post she held until her death in 1939. During her remaining years, she edited the *Social Service Review* (1934–1939) and in 1935 and 1937 was a delegate to the International Labour Organization. In 1938 she published her two-volume study, *The Child and the State*. A year before her death, she saw some of her work on child labor realized in the passing of the 1938 Fair Labor Standards Act.

Abbott was a lifelong pacifist and in 1915 attended the landmark women's peace congress in the Hague that attempted to set up peace mediation during World War I. When she died, she was given a Quaker funeral.

See also Abbott, Edith; Addams, Jane.

References and Further Reading

Costin, Lela B. 1983. *Two Sisters for Social Justice: A Biography of Grace and Edith Abbott.* Urbana: University of Illinois Press.

Dictionary of American Biography 1946–1958, and indexes to Supplements 1–10, 1981–1996. New York: Scribner's.

Encyclopedia of Social Work. 1995. New York: NASW Press.

Fitzpatrick, Ellen. 1991. *Endless Crusade: Women Social Scientists and Progressive Reform.* New York: Oxford University Press.

Howard, Angela, and Frances M. Kavenik, eds. 2000. *Handbook of American Women's History.* 2d ed. Thousand Oaks, CA: Sage.

Lindenmeyer, Kriste. 1997. *"A Right to Childhood": The U.S. Children's Bureau and Child Welfare, 1912–1946.* Urbana: University of Illinois Press.

Abella de Ramírez, María
(1866–1926)
Uruguay

In the history of Uruguayan feminism, the liberal reformer and humanitarian María Abella de Ramírez had a significant influence on the establishment of women's groups in Uruguay in the twentieth century, although she lived for most of her life in Argentina. She sought a reevaluation of the roles of women as wives and mothers and an affirmation of their right to have equal status with men and to be treated as free, autonomous beings. She also called for the legal protection of their children.

Abella's influence was most apparent through her work as contributor to and editor of her journal *We Women* (*Nosotras*), which she founded in 1902 and ran until 1904, and *The New Woman* (1910–1912, the journal of the National Feminist League). She was an early member of the freethinker movement in Argentina and in 1903 supported the establishment of a feminist center as a meeting place for like-minded women. In 1906 she laid out what she described as her "minimum plan of female vindications" at the Freethinker Congress, elaborating on women's need for equal access to education, work opportunities, and rates of pay. In 1909 she founded the National League of Women Freethinkers with Julieta Lanteri-Renshaw, which brought together women from several Latin American countries.

In 1910 Abella attended the First International Women's Congress. Its title, however, was somewhat misleading; held in Buenos Aires, the congress was composed mainly of women from Argentina, Chile, Paraguay, Peru, and Uruguay as well as a few foreign observers, but despite having only 200 or so delegates it provided a valuable forum in which Latin American feminists could exchange ideas and mutual support. That same year, inspired by the congress, Abella founded the National Women's League in La Plata and in its four-point plan affirmed her objectives on women's civil and political rights, divorce, and the protection of children. The league also made clear its support for women's suffrage and affiliated itself with the International Woman Suffrage Alliance and its support for reform of the Argentine civil code. In 1946, twenty years after Abella's death, a major reform of the code was enacted.

Abella's program of reform upheld the equal responsibility of men and women for their children, the rights of illegitimate children under the law, and the same access to absolute divorce (rather than simply legal separation) for women as men. Divorce legislation, a particularly hard case to argue in the face of a wall of opposition from the Roman Catholic Church, was of particular importance to Abella. Without access to legal divorce, women in unhappy marriages would be condemned to go on suffering physical and psychological abuse with no hope of escape. Abella's campaigning on divorce bore fruit in 1907, with the passage of new divorce laws in Uruguay that became a model for the rest of Latin America.

Abella had no desire to see traditional roles overturned. As the mother of four daughters, she upheld the importance of motherhood, which she felt was grossly undervalued, and fought hard against the entrenched view that women, once married, were assumed to have no desire for any autonomy. It was the value placed on motherhood by society that was in need of reappraisal. Like many of her Latin American feminist contemporaries, Abella believed motherhood to be fundamentally empowering rather than disabling. Women who opted for this role should be protected by the state and should not have to forfeit their economic and civil rights as a result.

Equally, Abella argued in support of women who eschewed conventional roles. She took an egalitarian view of women in all levels of society. For her, there were no moral or social borders dividing members of her own sex but rather a sense of oppression by and unequal opportunity with men that united them. She argued against the popular misconception of feminists as having no comprehension of or respect for social traditions: "she [the feminist] is accused of being useless for love and a ridiculous being from whom man should keep away. The contrary is the truth. The feminist woman is an intelligent woman who wishes to disengage her economic and social standing from that of the male of the family" (Lavrin 1995, 34). And if women chose to enter the workplace, Abella believed that they should be able to do so on an equal footing with men and not be hedged round with separate rules and regulations that ghettoized them.

See also Lanteri-Renshaw, Julieta.

References and Further Reading
Carlson, Narifran. 1988. *Feminismo! The Woman's Movement in Argentina from Its Beginnings to Eva Perón.* Chicago: Academy Chicago Publications.
Lavrin, Asuncion. 1995. *Women, Feminism, and Social Change in Argentina, Chile, and Uruguay 1890–1940.* Lincoln: University of Nebraska Press.

Addams, Jane
(1860–1935)
United States

The social reformer, pacifist, and temperance campaigner Jane Addams had, as a young woman, enjoyed an enviable social position as the daughter of a wealthy state senator in Illinois. Highly intelligent and attractive, she could have led a comfortable, conventional, and relatively unchallenged life but chose instead to reject marriage and domesticity to seek personal fulfillment in helping the impoverished and mainly immigrant communities of Chicago's industrial heartland, becoming founder of the Hull House settlement there. The Hull House, inspired in turn by pioneering work in England, would serve as a prototype for many similar ventures that grew up elsewhere in the United States and around the world and would change the face of social work among the underprivileged.

Born in Cedarville, Illinois, and educated at a select establishment, the Rockford Female Seminary, Addams was the eighth of nine children. She was well provided for by her widowed banker father. As a Quaker abolitionist, senator, and supporter of women's emancipation, John Addams endorsed his daughter's desire to train as a doctor after she rejected missionary work, but he died in 1881, the year Addams joined the Woman's Medical College in Philadelphia. Her depression at his loss, coupled with illness and a lack of conviction that she had found the right vocation, caused her to abandon her studies. Having the means to be a free agent, she undertook a rest cure, traveling in Europe first with her stepmother, then with college friend Ellen Gates Starr from 1883 to 1885 and 1887 to 1888.

Addams visited England in 1887–1888, where she observed the work of social reformers, drawing inspiration from the Toynbee Hall project in Whitechapel, a slum district in London's East End. Named after the English social reformer Arnold Toynbee, this institution served as a

Jane Addams (The Nobel Foundation)

study center where students and reformers from Oxford and Cambridge Universities lived among the poor and studied social conditions, establishing a precedent for social work *within* the community. It also ran a center to offer legal aid, welfare, cheap meals, and literacy classes to the poor and largely immigrant community.

On her return to the United States in 1889, much to her family's disapproval, Addams made clear her intentions to be independent when she turned down attempts to marry her off to her stepbrother. She had already come to the conclusion that private acts of charity would have no impact on the great levels of deprivation and suffering that were now proliferating in Chicago and other cities, and over the next forty-six years, she set out to mitigate the suffering of America's "huddled masses." With Starr, she settled in the immigrant, multiracial area of South Halsted Street in Chicago, where in September 1889 she rented the derelict Charles Hull mansion, built by a real estate developer in 1856, and renovated it to serve as a welfare center run by volunteers. With time, a complex of thirteen buildings would be added to what would become known as the Hull House settlement.

Addams attracted to her work at Hull House a core of dedicated middle-class women volunteers who lived together in cooperative apartments and assisted in what would effectively become the first institution to train social workers. Hull House pioneers would include Grace and Edith Abbott, Julia Lathrop, Alice Hamilton, and Florence Kelley; the settlement also frequently invited women from Europe to visit and observe their work, such as Alice Salomon, who would establish the first school of social work in Germany, and Alice Masarykova, who would do the same in Czechoslovakia. Under Addams's leadership, Hull House began by setting up a playground and gymnasium for physical fitness activities; a day nursery; a dispensary that issued free medicines; and instruction in arts and crafts (including bookbinding), sewing, and cookery. It also staged concerts, art exhibitions, and other entertainments. More important, the settlement also offered immigrants help and advice on matters relating to their working hours and safety, child labor, and delinquency. Overnight accommodation was offered for working girls, and eventually educational courses to prepare girls for college were established, as was a summer camp at Lake Geneva in Wisconsin. In 1891 Addams initiated the Jane Club to offer cooperative housing to female factory workers. A network of forty subsidiary branches of the settlement would, by 1893, be helping 2,000 women a week. Such was the popularity of the venture that Addams and her colleagues relied on the financial support of many rich patrons in Chicago to keep it going.

Addams and her colleagues at Hull House also initiated social research projects, adopting investigative methods to study the causes of crime and poverty along the lines introduced by Charles Booth in England, by interviewing immigrant families in Chicago's eighteen national communities and observing the conditions in which they lived and worked. Detailed statistical analysis and recommendations for reform were published in *Hull House Maps and Papers* (1895). These resulted in the Illinois Factory Inspection Act of 1893 and the establishment of a juvenile court in 1899. Other innovations prompted by Addams were the "Mother" Pension Act, the eight-hour working day for women, a compensation system for workers injured on the job, and the regulation of tenement housing. In 1903 Addams cofounded and served as vice president of the Women's Trade Union League, which fought for the rights of many immigrant working women, with their specific needs in mind. In 1908 Addams and others in the league set up an Immigrants' Protective League to provide advice and help to newly arrived immigrants.

As a believer in women's natural compassion and nurturing qualities, Addams joined the suffrage campaign in Chicago in 1907, in the hope that the improved political status of enfranchised women would sooner effect social reform. She also supported racial equality and was a prime mover behind the establishment in 1909 of the National Association for the Advancement of Colored People. A succession of important roles were taken up by Addams over the next few years: in 1910 she scored two firsts for women, becoming president of both the National Conference of Social Work and of the National Conference of Charities and Corrections. In later years she founded and was appointed head of the National Federation of Settlements (1911–1935) and became the first vice president of the National American Woman Suffrage Association (1911–1914). In 1912 Addams worked in the election campaign for the Progressive Party's nomination of Theodore Roosevelt, being the first woman to publicly nominate a candidate at an election rally. The party made use of the research compiled at Hull House as a basis for its social reform program.

Addams was appalled by the outbreak of World War I in 1914 and led a women's peace parade in New York. Her unswerving support for humanitarian activities and pacifism over the next four years was incomparable, as she sought to open up channels of peace mediation by neutral nations. In January 1915 she joined other pacifists, including Carrie Chapman Catt, at a meeting in Washington, D.C., to call for the abolition of war. At the end of the conference, Addams and Catt founded the Woman's Peace Party and produced an eleven-point program for peace mediation. Later that year, a women's peace conference was held in The Hague, which established the International Committee of Women for Permanent Peace, soon known as the Women's International League and after 1919, known as the Women's International League for Peace and Freedom (WILPF). Addams served as its presi-

dent until 1929. On her return to the United States, she joined other American pacifists in trying to get President Woodrow Wilson to mediate in the war, but after the United States entered the fighting in 1917, her opposition to the draft and women's participation in war work earned her much vilification, as did her defense of the civil liberties of German immigrants to the United States who had been subjected to considerable persecution. The effects were felt at Hull House, support for which dwindled during the war.

When the war was over, in 1919 Addams presided over the second women's peace congress that was held by WILPF in Zurich, which set about fund-raising to help the victims of war. Addams, Alice Hamilton, and Carolina Wood traveled to Germany on behalf of the American Friends Service Committee, a Quaker organization, to investigate the terrible depredations of war, taking with them $30,000 worth of aid and 25 tons of clothing to distribute among the needy. One of Addams's final significant contributions to human rights came in 1920, when she was one of the founders of the American Civil Liberties Union after she had become disillusioned with the lack of support given the League of Nations by the U.S. government.

In 1931, by which time her health was failing, Addams was nominated for the Nobel Peace Prize as "the right spokesman for all the peace-loving women of the world." She shared it with Nicholas Murray Butler, becoming the second woman so honored. She immediately donated half of her prize money to the WILPF.

Addams published accounts of her work in *Twenty Years at Hull-House* (1910) and *The Second Twenty Years at Hull-House* (1930). She was also the author of many groundbreaking social studies, including *Democracy and Social Ethics* (1902), *Newer Ideals of Peace* (1907), and *The Spirit of Youth and the City Streets* (1909). A complex and often difficult personality, Addams, who retained close links with the Quakers throughout her life, was a woman of great emotional depths who nevertheless maintained a carefully constructed aura of personal detachment both from her work and her associates. She was referred to mockingly as "Saint Jane" by male sociologists of the time, who disparagingly viewed social welfare as women's work and as a subsidiary to what they perceived as their own superior domain—that of the still male-dominated discipline of social science. Addams herself remained modest about her life's work, which she considered to have been nothing but "a drop in the bucket" of human suffering (Bolt 1993, 267). Although her contribution to social science was undervalued in her lifetime, the wider dissemination of women's history since the 1970s has elevated Addams to her rightful position in the forefront of America's pantheon of distinguished pioneers, as a woman who recognized the importance of respect for the dignity of the individual in all fields of social welfare.

In 1963 development of the new university campus at Chicago necessitated the relocation of the Hull House settlement to Chicago's north side, with new community centers established in Lakeview and Uptown Center, where Addams's work continues under the auspices of the Hull House Association. For information, contact http://www.hullhouse.org/. The original Charles Hull mansion, now protected as a National and Chicago Historic Landmark, remains on Halsted Street as a memorial to and museum of Jane Addams's work. For visiting times, contact http://www.uic.edu/jaddams/hull/hull_house. html.

See also Abbott, Edith; Abbott, Grace; Catt, Carrie Chapman; Hamilton, Alice; Kelley, Florence; Lathrop, Julia; Masarykova, Alice; Salomon, Alice; Suttner, Bertha Félice Sophie von.

References and Further Reading

Bolt, Christine. 1993. *The Women's Movements in the United States and Britain from the 1790s to the 1920s.* London: Harvester Wheatsheaf.

Chambers, Clarke A. 1963. *Seedtime of Reform: American Social Service and Social Action, 1918–1933.* Minneapolis: University of Minnesota Press.

———. 1967. *Spearheads for Reform: The Social Settlements and the Progressive Movement 1890–1914.* New York: Oxford University Press.

Davis, Allen F. 1967. *Spearheads for Reform: The Social Settlements and the Progressive Movement 1890–1914.* New York: Oxford University Press.

———. 1973. *American Heroine: Life and Legend of Jane Addams.* New York: Oxford University Press.

Ferrell, John. 1967. *Beloved Lady: A History of Jane Addams's Ideas on Reform and Peace.* Baltimore: Johns Hopkins University Press.

Josephson, Harold, Sandi Cooper, and Steven C. Hause et al., eds. 1985. *Biographical Dictionary of Modern Peace Leaders.* Westport, CT: Greenwood Press.

Lasch, Christopher. 1965. *The New Radicalism, America 1889–1963: The Intellectual as Social Type.* New York: W. W. Norton.

———. 1982 [1965]. *The Social Thought of Jane Addams.* Reprint, New York: Irvington.

Linn, James Weber. 1999 [1935]. *Jane Addams: A Biography.* Reprint, New York: Appleton-Century.

Marchand, C. Roland. 1972. *The American Peace Movement and Social Reform, 1898–1918.* Princeton: Princeton University Press.

Schott, Linda K. 1997. *Reconstructing Women's Thoughts: The Women's International League for Peace and Freedom before World War II.* Stanford: Stanford University Press.

Sklar, Kathryn Kish. 1998. *Social Justice Feminists in the United States and Germany: A Dialogue in Documents 1885–1933.* Ithaca: Cornell University Press.

Solomon, Barbara Miller. 1985. *In the Company of Educated Women: A History of Women and Higher Education in America.* New Haven: Yale University Press.

Tims, Margaret. 1961. *Jane Addams of Hull House, 1860–1935: A Centenary Study.* London: Allen and Unwin.

Afghan Women Social Reformers

The case of women in Afghanistan requires a special entry in honor of the collective efforts of the by necessity largely anonymous women campaigners whose message on the abuse of human rights in that country is now attracting widespread media attention and the concern of humanitarian groups around the world.

The focus for the defense of women's and human rights in general in Afghanistan has, since 1977, been the Revolutionary Association of the Women of Afghanistan (RAWA), which is based in Pakistan. It was founded in Kabul by a group of academics and intellectuals, led by a feminist poet named Meena (1957–1987), initially to campaign for democratic reform by the old regime, which had long placed women in a subordinate position, and to call for the establishment of education and health projects. But with the Soviet invasion of 1979 the Afghan women's movement turned to resistance against the occupation—a bitter struggle during which 2 million Afghans are thought to have died.

In 1981 Meena established a journal, *Women's Message,* as a focus for women's protest in Afghanistan, but in 1987 she was assassinated in Pakistan (where she had gone to work among the thousands of Afghan refugees from the war) by agents of the Afghanistan branch of the KGB, the Soviet secret police. Since her death it has been too dangerous for any one woman to assume open leadership of RAWA. During the prolonged and still continuing refugee crisis that spilled over into Pakistan and also Iran, RAWA was instrumental in creating much needed schools and hospitals for women and children in Quetta, as well as training additional nurses and teachers; but it is faced with an overwhelming task in dealing with such a major humanitarian problem, as it does not receive support from international NGOs, and is in desperate need of financial support for its crucial relief work. There are now 4 million Afghan refugees in Pakistan.

The long war of attrition in Afghanistan that lasted until the Soviets finally withdrew in 1989 resulted in the final overthrow of the communist-backed puppet government in 1992. Several more years of fighting between fundamentalist factions, during which the country's already damaged infrastructure was totally devastated, led to the establishment of the new and draconian Islamic Emirate of Afghanistan, dominated by the Taliban—the Islamic religious militia. RAWA, continuing in its long tradition of promoting a secularist, democratic society in Afghanistan, has since been drawing world attention, with ever greater urgency, to the abuse of human rights in a country where the death rate per 1,000 population is now running at 17.4, as opposed to a world average of 8.9, and where life expectancy for women has now fallen to 46.3 years. RAWA's 2,000 members, both inside and outside Afghanistan, report on the abuse of women's rights in Afghanistan through its website (see below) and *Women's Message,* which now appears in Urdu, English, and Persian editions.

A harrowing catalogue of atrocities committed by the fundamentalist regime against the civilian population of Afghanistan, and most particularly its women, is now being widely disseminated, thanks to the many nameless women of RAWA who have taken and continue to take enormous personal risks to expose the true nature of a regime that has systematically set about sending its women back into the dark ages. In twenty-first-century Afghanistan, women have become the silent sex, consigned to the role of nameless, faceless chattels. Swathed (and stifled in the heat of summer) in their *burqahs,* which allow them only a mesh slit through which to view the increasingly narrow world they inhabit, they are confined to the home and condemned to joyless lives, denied the lifeblood of education

and intellectual stimulus, denied medical care in pregnancy and childbirth, and faced constantly with the threat of the most barbaric punishments for the slightest misdemeanors deemed by the Taliban to contravene the *shari'ah*—Islamic law.

At the time of writing, all schools for girls over twelve and training establishments for women in Afghanistan have been closed down. They are also excluded from the universities, the civil service, and all professional work. A few extremely brave women continue to teach young girls clandestinely in their own homes. A 2001 Channel Four *Dispatches* documentary on women in Afghanistan, filmed secretly by Saira Shah with the assistance of women in RAWA's underground opposition network in Kabul, showed one such woman, unveiled and in Western dress, teaching a group of girls. Asked if she was worried about being recognized she shrugged her shoulders— how would they know, she asked—I am not allowed out on the streets without being totally covered. And indeed, women in Afghanistan cannot leave their homes without a male escort who is a close family member, or mix socially with other men. They are forbidden from consulting male doctors when sick or in labor, and there are virtually no women doctors still working in the country.

The Taliban have now banned the entire population from listening to taped music, playing video games, and watching films and videos. Women are forbidden all forms of recreation such as sport, dancing, cycling—nor are they even allowed the natural expression of pleasure in singing or laughing out loud. The sound of their footsteps must not be heard (thus all fashionable shoes are banned) nor must they show any part of their anatomy outside in the open— women have been attacked and even killed for inadvertently showing as much as an ankle. Makeup is strictly forbidden—although some Afghan women, as a last act of defiance, enjoy private makeup sessions with their friends behind the locked doors of their homes. And even within the confinement of their homes they are further cut off from the outside world, because all windows have been painted over so that the women inside cannot be seen from the outside.

It is not surprising therefore that such barbarity has driven many Afghan women to suicide. Now unable to work and provide for their starving children, impoverished women have been forced out onto the streets to beg. One in four Afghan children now dies before reaching his or her fifth birthday and more Afghan women die in childbirth than anywhere else in the world. Other desperate women have been driven to prostitution—a crime that carries the death penalty. One last and horrifying form of public entertainment and edification remains in Afghanistan—public executions. Women have been publicly stoned to death for extramarital sex and adultery. Homosexuals too face the death penalty. Thieves suffer the amputation of hands. Many so condemned have to face the horror of being paraded around in the back of an open truck before being publicly executed in the sports ground at Kandahar (with sickening irony, men are now hanged from the crossbar of the goalpost) or the former football stadium in Kabul. The latter was built in the 1990s as a goodwill gesture, with funding by the international community, to the "heroic" Afghan rebels who had ousted the Soviets. The Taliban are unrepentant at the misuse of a place of recreation as a place of judicial murder. Their spokesman, interviewed in the Channel Four documentary, blandly observed that if the international community would fund the building of a special, new venue designated for public executions, then football could once more be resumed at the stadium.

Taliban vigilantes of the Ministry for the Prevention of Vice and the Promotion of Virtue now patrol the streets and staff checkpoints throughout Afghanistan on the lookout for infringements of Islamic law. The ministry's name and the ominous building in Kabul from which it operates have become synonymous with terror; a place that inspires dread in the same way that the Lubyanka headquarters of the KGB in Moscow did during the worst excesses of the Stalinist purges of the 1930s. The list of proscribed activities for the civilian population is endless—it can be consulted in detail on RAWA's website at www.rawa.hackmare.com/rawa/. Readers are also recommended to consult Amnesty International's website, http://www.amnesty.org, for regular updates on the situation.

In what makes for particularly chilling reading, a recent ruling by the Taliban now states that all non-Muslims in Afghanistan must wear a distinguishing badge on their clothes to signify that they are not of the faith. Meanwhile, the Taliban

have issued a *fatwah* on the members of RAWA for their courageous resistance.

Alma Dolens (Teresita dei Bonfatti/Teresita Pasini)
(1876–?)
Italy

The forgotten Italian pacifist campaigner, suffragist, and journalist Teresita dei Bonfatti (later Signora Pasini) was known by her pseudonym, Alma Dolens, which is Latin for "a sorrowful soul" or "heavy heart," the name no doubt intended as a reflection of her emotional response to war and militarism against which she campaigned so fervently. Between 1908 and 1913, she became a prominent pacifist campaigner, but little is known of her activities after the end of World War I or of the date of her death.

Dolens was from a wealthy Umbrian family, prominent in the Italian *Risorgimento* of the nineteenth century, that had supported Giuseppe Garibaldi's unification of Italy. She married a Milanese lawyer, who supported her in her pacifist work and her interest in women's suffrage as president of the Lombardy Committee for Woman Suffrage and Workers' Rights. Dolens took a central role within the male-dominated Italian peace movement after speaking at national peace congresses in 1909 and 1910. She was driven by the conviction that the lack of women, both in the movement and in politics in general, was a major inhibiting factor to social progress. She called for closer links between the pacifist organizations and trade unions and urged that women's separate peace societies be established, arguing that too many women were reticent about joining because they equated pacifism with an absence of patriotic spirit. She was convinced that women would be a significant force for international peace arbitration, and she believed that children should be educated into a better understanding of the true nature of patriotic support for national wars and should be taught, rather, to value peace above national concerns.

For two years, Dolens toured central Italy, establishing a network of regional committees of her Women's Society for Peace, and with the help of officials from the metalworkers' union, she founded the Workers' Society for Arbitration and Disarmament in Milan, which by 1910–1911 had about 700 members. But in 1911 the Italian women's peace movement ended abruptly with Italy's declaration of war on Turkey and the Italian invasion of Libya-Cyrenaica. The pacifist movement was quickly riven between those such as Rosalia Gwis-Adami, who felt that Italian women must support the national war effort, and others like Dolens, who opposed the war. Dolens bravely took on a public campaign against the war, appealing to the Carnegie Foundation in the United States and the peace movement headquarters in Berne, Switzerland, for funds to enable Italian pacifists to regroup. Throughout 1911–1912, she persisted in leafletting, putting up posters, and organizing marches in Milan against the war, but the pacifist movement rapidly disintegrated, and Dolens was banned from public speaking. Frustrated, she turned to other social issues, writing about the living conditions of the poor in the slums of Rome, Milan, and Naples. She lent her energies to numerous women's organizations, becoming friends with the international peace campaigner Rosika Schwimmer after attending a women's conference in Budapest in 1913.

After failing in 1912 to effect the efficient regrouping of the Italian pacifist movement, by 1914 Dolens was preoccupied by the greater threat of war in Europe. In July she attended an emergency meeting called by the International Bureau of Peace and traveled to The Hague in April 1915 for a similar congress by women pacifists that attempted to conciliate in the war. She remained in the left wing of the international pacifist movement until the end of World War I, throwing her energies into relief work for Italian families forced out of their homes in the Austro-Hungarian Empire during the fighting and raising funds to buy clothes, milk, and medicines for these refugees.

After the war, Dolens toured Belgium, where she saw for herself the terrible depredations of war and became even more convinced that militarism and arms stockpiling were the enemies of the poor and underprivileged. She argued that governments had a social responsibility to eradicate such suffering: the cure for the diseases of "poverty, tuberculosis, unemployment," she averred, "is the end of formidable and costly weaponry" (Cooper 1991, 211), and countries should be obliged by international law to arbitrate in times of war.

See also Gwis-Adami, Rosalia; Schwimmer, Rosika.
References and Further Reading
Cooper, Sandi E. 1991. *Patriotic Pacifism: Waging War on War in Europe, 1815–1914.* New York: Oxford University Press.
Pierson, Ruth Roach, ed. 1987. *Woman and Peace: Theoretical, Historical and Practical Perspectives.* London: Croom Helm.
Robertson, Priscilla. 1982. *An Experience of Women: Pattern and Change in Nineteenth-Century Europe.* Philadelphia: Temple University Press.

Alvarado Rivera, María Jesus
(c. 1880s–1971)
Peru

A lone voice calling for women's rights in Peru between 1911 and 1925, Alvarado was unique for her time in opening up this debate. Although she supported women's access to education and work, she did not believe that equality of the sexes was desirable or achievable across the board, for she believed that women's maternal role was unique. Her refusal to be silenced and her stubborn campaigning for women's suffrage eventually led to imprisonment and exile to Argentina in 1926. In 1969 Alvarado was acknowledged by the National Council of Women of Peru as having been the "first modern champion of women's rights in Peru" (Chaney 1979, 69).

After attending primary school and a private high school for girls run by leading feminist Elvira García y García, Alvarado became a schoolteacher. Appalled by the antiquated system in which she worked, she began studying education methods, becoming a self-taught sociologist and eventually developing advanced ideas on vocational education, euthanasia, the health and nutritional care of schoolchildren, and the control of sexually transmitted diseases. Her interest in promoting better morals in schools spilled over into improving the welfare of and providing social activities for women, agitating for the land rights of indigenous Indians, and monitoring conditions among workers. With the help of a small inheritance, Alvarado opened a free school for the daughters of workers, where she introduced her own reformist teaching methods and also used the school printing press to publish her many pamphlets and tracts.

In 1910 Alvarado attended the First International Women's Congress in Argentina, held in

Buenos Aires, and spoke about the new term *feminism,* relating its concerns to education and the law. A year later, in October 1911, Alvarado gave a public lecture on the subject at the Geographic Society of Lima, which marked the first public exposition of feminism in Peru. She argued that social changes were needed to free women from their situation of inferiority. Better education and suitable employment would give them economic independence, but first they needed the vote to gain equal civil and political rights with men. Alvarado appealed to the government to end discrimination against women but also encouraged women to organize in their own defense. After four years of lobbying and campaigning, inspired by her experience of the 1910 congress, her efforts led to the establishment of the first feminist group in Peru, Women's Evolution (Evolución Femenina) in 1914.

The establishment of such a women's organization in a country where there was a much narrower socially aware elite, concentrated in the capital, Lima, and where society in general was far more class-bound inevitably made the political struggle for women's rights harder in Peru than it was in nearby Argentina, Brazil, and Chile. In addition, the Peruvian women's movement did not enjoy the collaboration between middle- and working-class races and castes that had occurred in the movement in Mexico. Women's Evolution was therefore greeted with a great deal of hostility, not only from the Roman Catholic Church, which saw such divisive action by women as fuelling confrontation between the sexes and unsettling traditional patriarchy, but also from more moderate upper-class, convent-educated philanthropists.

Women's Evolution's program of activities, such as the setting up of a "Labor and Moral School Workshop," initially designed to help women who had drifted into prostitution, offended respectable society. Alvarado argued that the problem of prostitution in particular should be attacked at the grass roots—by improving the economic situation of women driven to it and by providing them with a better education and training in some kind of skill. But although some more enlightened female philanthropists and liberal politicians lent their support, particularly in terms of the suffrage campaign, the vast majority were horrified, so much so that a rival organization, the Catholic Women's League, soon sprang up and went out of its way to oppose feminist activities in Peru.

During her time with Women's Evolution, Alvarado also initiated a drive to reform the civil code and to allow women to hold government posts. For nine years she campaigned to get women accepted as directors of (male-run) public welfare societies, which played an important social role in selling or renting out land in order to raise money to fund hospitals, orphanages, and welfare programs. Her campaign became increasingly political, carried on in the media and in the Chamber of Representatives. In 1915 the chamber approved legislation allowing women to be committee members of public welfare societies, but it did not become law until 1922.

In 1923 Alvarado was invited by Carrie Chapman Catt, who was visiting Lima as president of the International Woman Suffrage Alliance, to become secretary of an affiliated organization in Peru. This led to the establishment in 1924 of a National Council of Women, but one that was soon rent with divisions between more radical women who sought reform of the civil code and women's equality with men in all things before the law and those campaigning merely for suffrage. Catholics both within the council and in society at large took issue with what they saw as the more seditious elements of Alvarado's advanced social objectives. Alvarado, who had long been ostracized for her more militant views, was arrested, along with other dissidents, and spent Christmas 1924 in Santo Tomás jail. After three months of solitary confinement, she was deported by President Augusto B. Leguia's regime and spent the next twelve years in exile in Argentina. With Alvarado's departure the embryonic feminist movement in Peru was stillborn; it was not until 1955 that women there achieved the vote.

See also Catt, Carrie Chapman.

References and Further Reading

Chaney, Elsa M. 1979. *Supermadre: Women in Politics in Latin America.* Austin: Institute of Latin American Studies, University of Texas Press.

Miller, Francesca. 1992. *Latin American Women and the Search for Social Justice.* Hanover, NH: University Press of New England.

Tenenbaum, Barbara A., ed. 1996. *Encyclopedia of Latin American History and Culture.* Vol. 2. New York: Charles Scribner's Sons.

Ames, Jessie Daniel
(1883–1972)
United States

Although the black activist Ida B. Wells-Barnett undoubtedly holds center stage in the long anti-lynching campaign in the United States, less attention has been paid to the work of the Texan Jessie Daniel Ames, who during the 1930s was in the forefront of a movement of southern white women to combat racial violence. As founder of the Association of Southern Women for the Prevention of Lynching (ASWPL), Ames led a significant movement that worked toward reconciling bitter racial differences during a period of economic hardship in the South.

Ames was born in Palestine, in eastern Texas, and grew up near Austin, where her father was a railroad station master. She studied at Southwestern University, graduating in 1902. Her marriage in 1905 to an army medical officer resulted in long separations and his untimely death from fever in 1914. Despite the strains of bringing up her three children alone, she set up a telephone company with her mother and became proud of her hard-won independence. She joined the latter stages of the women's suffrage movement as treasurer of the Texas Equal Suffrage Association in 1918 and in 1919 was a founder and president of the Texas League of Women Voters.

After women won the vote in the United States in 1920, Ames acted as a Democratic Party delegate to national conventions in 1920, 1924, and 1928 and sought to galvanize support for progressive reform in the South. She began to broaden her social and feminist activities, as a member of the Texas branch of the American Association of University Women and of the Federation of Women's Clubs. Prison reform also became a concern through her involvement in the Committee on Prisons and Prison Labor. In all her work she became increasingly frustrated by the exclusion of black women from social activism in the South and by the failure of white women to address the pressing issue of racial inequality and persecution. Seeking to lead white southern women into greater public involvement in such issues, she took an important role in the Texas branch of the Commission on Interracial Cooperation in 1924. In 1929, as regional director of its Women's Committee and by then living in Atlanta, Georgia, Ames began

to build a major support base for women's activism against lynching.

In 1930 she founded the ASWPL, which eventually built up a core membership of 43,000 members who had signed its antilynching pledge and gained a great deal of support from the Methodist Woman's Missionary Council. The ASWPL enlisted its members in attempts to forestall mob violence and lynchings by gathering petitions, making speeches, distributing pamphlets and resolutions, and conducting poster campaigns. It urged members to reject their traditional role as helpless white women. In the rabidly pro-white, antiblack environment of the 1930s South, Ames came up against considerable intimidation from the Ku Klux Klan and also the reactionary ultra-right-wing Women's National Association for the Preservation of the White Race.

In her campaigning, Ames was one of the first white women to join the ranks of the many black women who since the nineteenth century had sought to confront southern racism head-on. She sought to demolish the widely held view among white males that their womenfolk in the South were especially vulnerable to rape by black men; she did so by attempting to deconstruct the demeaning myth of extreme racial stereotypes: the chaste white lady at the mercy of the rapacious black man. She felt that the time was long overdue for white southern women to throw off "the crown of chivalry which has been pressed like a crown of thorns on our head" (Berkin and Norton 1979, 366). Ames also understood, as had Wells-Barnett (who had begun fighting against lynching in the 1880s), that racial violence and lynching had little to do with the supposed "rape" of white women but were deeply rooted in economic factors. Much of it sprang from white southern hostility to black business enterprise that might in some way set up a challenge to its own economic security, particularly with white poverty on the increase in southern rural communities during the Great Depression. Ames also exposed the hypocrisy of the double sexual standard whereby white men would have no qualms about preying sexually upon black women.

In the atmosphere of racial hysteria that followed in the wake of the notorious 1931 Scottsboro case, in which nine black youths were convicted of the sexual assault of two white women, Ames set up a study of lynching statistics between

1889 and 1929 that demonstrated of those lynched, only 6.9 percent had actually been guilty of rape. She lobbied with other members of the ASWPL for the Scottsboro death sentences to be commuted to life and considered the case a serious blow to the antilynching cause because of the huge publicity attached to it. It prompted her to further question the injustices of the U.S. legal system, where far more draconian punishments were meted out to black men, often on flimsy evidence, than to white lynchers, who all too often were allowed to evade prosecution. She concluded that this disparity resulted from the black defendants' poor standards of education and their inability to afford proper legal representation; it is a situation still being confronted by penal and prison reformers today in the contentious debate over the continuing use of the death penalty in certain U.S. states. In the end, Ames also came to question the sexual reputation and behavior of white women involved in cases of supposed rape (such as the later discredited white women in the Scottsboro case). Her conclusion that many white women voluntarily entered into sexual relationships with black men prompted her to schedule discussion of the double standard of ethical and moral conduct at ASWPL meetings and urge members to work toward greater respect for the chastity of black women.

In 1937 Ames took over running the Commission on Interracial Cooperation (CIC) and set up a monthly publication entitled the *Southern Frontier*. During 1937 she led a concerted drive to expose sheriffs who acquiesced in the abduction and lynching of black prisoners by white mobs, and also that year published *Southern Women Look at Lynching*. After a federal antilynching law was introduced in 1939, no lynchings occurred during the period May 1939 to May 1940, and their incidence declined thereafter. In 1942, optimistic that her work was now over, Ames published *The Changing Character of Lynching*, in which she welcomed the dramatic decline in lynchings. She did urge against complacency, however, warning that when the war was over and men returned to the labor force, they must be offered productive work that would not rekindle racial rivalries or the specter of lynching. The future of the South, she argued, rested on the ability not just of whites to recognize the civil and economic rights of blacks but also of blacks to join in a renewed sense of postwar purpose.

In 1943 the ASWPL and the CIC both became part of the Southern Regional Council. Ames gave up activism and settled in the Blue Ridge Mountains, where she supported the Democrats and took up philanthropic work for her local Methodist church. She was honored at the age of eighty-eight for her civil rights activism and her brave repudiation of white supremacy in the South. She died in Austin.

See also Prejean, Sister Helen; Wells-Barnett, Ida B.

References and Further Reading

Berkin, Carol Ruth, and Mary Beth Norton. 1979. *Women of America: A History.* Boston: Houghton Mifflin.

Cimbala, Paul A. 1997. *Against the Tide: Women Reformers in American Society.* Westport, CT: Praeger.

Hall, Jacqueline Dowd. 1993 [1979]. *Jessie Daniel Ames and the Women's Campaign against Lynching.* Reprint, New York: Columbia University Press.

Olson, Lynn. 2001. *Freedom's Daughters: The Unsung Heroines of the Civil Rights Movement from 1830 to 1970.* New York: Scribner.

Scott, Anne Firor. 1970. *The Southern Lady: From Pedestal to Politics, 1830–1930.* Chicago: University of Chicago Press.

Anderson, Elizabeth Garrett
(1836–1917)
United Kingdom

The first woman to qualify as a doctor in England, Elizabeth Garrett Anderson had to endure the usual pattern of male hostility and the obduracy of the British medical establishment in her objective of establishing women's medical training there. Having become a seasoned and persistent campaigner for the opening up of medical training to women at her London hospital, she also lent her energies to the women's suffrage movement and endorsed her friend Emily Davies's crusade to open up higher education for women. Anderson scored other notable landmarks for women in England, becoming, with Davies, one of the first women to be elected to the London School Board and the first woman in England to be elected to the office of mayor.

Anderson was one of ten children born in Whitechapel, in London's East End. Her family moved to the Suffolk coast when she was a child, where her father, Newson Garrett, was a prosperous grain malter, brewer, and ship owner. Anderson returned to London to attend Miss Browning's school in Blackheath until the age of fifteen and afterward made a European tour. She was bolstered in her desire to enter medical training after reading articles endorsing women's entry into the professions in the *Englishwoman's Journal,* which was established by a group of London feminists who met at the home of Barbara Bodichon in Langham Place, London. In 1859, when the Langham Place Circle, as it became known, advertised a series of lectures by the British-born doctor Elizabeth Blackwell, who had trained in the United States, on "Medicine as a Profession for the Ladies," Anderson was one of several eager young women who attended the first lecture, afterward meeting Blackwell and becoming a member of the circle.

In her quest to enter medicine, Anderson had to overcome her father's initial violent opposition, eventually winning his staunch support—both moral and financial—although she was never able to entirely persuade her mother of the acceptability of her vocation. Through Newson Garrett's friendship with one of the male governors of Middlesex Hospital, a post was obtained for Anderson as a nurse trainee in 1859. There she was allowed to observe operations and dissections but was forbidden from active participation.

Anderson did exceptionally well in her first exams in surgical nursing, coming out first in an all-male class, whose members responded by having her banned from the lecture hall. With the way to further study blocked to her because women were refused admittance to medical school at that time, Anderson continued with her own private study, obtaining some private tuition from Dr. Joshua Plaskitt in Greek, Latin, and *materia medica.* In May 1861 she was allowed to sit in on chemistry lectures at the Middlesex Hospital Medical School, but the administrators refused her permission to enter medical studies there, despite a petition in support of her application from sympathetic male students. A familiar trail of application and rejection ensued, as Anderson, supported by loyal friends such as Emily Davies, applied to one medical school after another. She was rejected by London University (where there was, in fact, only one vote cast against her) and then Oxford, Cambridge, Glasgow, and Edinburgh Universities. Even the support of leading politicians such as William Gladstone and the reformer Richard Cobden could not overcome the prejudice against women's entry into the medical profession.

As a last resort, Anderson approached the Society of Apothecaries after finding a loophole in its charter that failed to specify that women could *not* be admitted to its courses. After checking the legality of this nondiscriminatory policy, the society reluctantly allowed Anderson to study for their license as an apothecary. She undertook her own studies privately, first as an apprentice with Plaskitt and then traveling to Scotland, where she studied with Professor George Day at St. Andrews and gained valuable experience in midwifery with Alexander Keiller at the Edinburgh Maternity Hospital.

In August 1865 Anderson applied to take the Society of Apothecaries examination. By this time, the society had become deeply perturbed about adverse criticism it might receive for granting Anderson a license. It was only her father's threat of legal action if it reneged on its charter that ensured that Anderson did take the exam in September 1865. After receiving her Final Certificate, Anderson was entitled to be placed on the medical register as a licentiate of the Society of Apothecaries, which basically allowed her to dispense medicines, and soon after, with financial support from her father, she set herself up in practice in London. Meanwhile, the Society of Apothecaries ensured that Anderson's license would be the exception rather than the rule by passing a resolution categorically excluding women from its license. Anderson's contemporary Sophia Jex-Blake would thus have to find a different route to medical training in her own battle to become a doctor soon after.

In 1866 Anderson opened the St. Mary's Dispensary for Women and Children in Seymour Place, London, which was very quickly administering to sixty to ninety women a day. It would become known as the New Hospital for Women and Children in 1872, the first teaching hospital in the United Kingdom staffed by women and offering medical courses for female students. Anderson would later give moral support to the campaign for female students to be allowed to study for medical degrees at the University of Edinburgh, led by Jex-Blake and Edith Pechey-Phipson during the 1870s.

During the 1860s, despite her feminist sympathies, Anderson did not join with other members of the Langham Place Circle or even with other reformers in her own family in protesting the passage of the Contagious Diseases Acts and the institution of state-regulated prostitution. As a doctor who all too often witnessed the ravages of venereal disease on innocent wives and children, she supported the legislation on the grounds of public health, believing that regular inspection of prostitutes was the only way of controlling the spread of the disease and would provide an opportunity for prostitutes to be rescued from their profession and rehabilitated. Anderson's failure to endorse the campaign led by Josephine Butler would cost her the support and friendship of some of her old associates at Langham Place over the years, who viewed the laws as discriminatory and a breach of basic civil liberties.

Anderson finally gained her own medical degree in January 1870. Through the good offices of influential friends who helped her circumvent the residency requirements, she learned enough French to earn a medical degree in France, awarded by the medical faculty of the Sorbonne in Paris (women had been accepted for medical degrees there in 1868). Two months later, she secured her first official medical appointment (and indeed the first secured by a woman in Britain) as visiting medical officer to the East London Hospital for Children. That year she and Davies became the first women to take advantage of new legislation allowing women to stand for election to the London School Board, one of several set up across Britain to implement William Forster's new Education Act of 1870, which established state elementary education for children five to thirteen years old. Indeed, Anderson secured the highest numbers of votes (47,000) in the election, which provided women with a rare opportunity to enter public service. She undertook important work, encouraging working-class people to send their children to school. In 1872 she and Davies both tried and failed to persuade the London County Council to introduce equal rates of pay for men and women serving as school visitors.

In 1871 Anderson finally married at the age of thirty-five to a steamship merchant named James Skelton Anderson. She managed to successfully combine a happy married life and the rearing of two children (a third died in infancy) with her medical career, although she resisted her husband's attempts to take control of her earnings.

Responding to an article by Dr. Edward Clarke of Harvard University in 1873, Anderson was drawn into a widespread debate in the medical press on whether further education was inappropriate for women. Many male doctors like Clarke were arguing that the "overwork" involved in academic study affected women's reproductive capabilities and that menstruation was too debilitating for them to undertake such rigorous academic pursuits. Like other medical women, Anderson was appalled by this argument and published a rebuttal in the *Fortnightly Review*, outlining the feminist argument against male perceptions of women's inherent "invalidism" and their inability to perform certain tasks when menstruating. For too long, she believed, the medical establishment had overstated this case; after all, working women had for centuries carried on working despite the sometimes debilitating effects of menstruation. (Anderson's argument would be endorsed in 1877 by the American doctor Mary Putnam Jacobi in her book *Question of Rest for Women during Menstruation*.) In 1874, Anderson responded to a similar article, "Sex in Mind and in Education," by Dr. Henry Maudsley in the *Fortnightly Review*, arguing against the adoption of games and gymnastics in progressive women's schools. Endorsing the work of her friend Emily Davies at Cambridge, where gentle exercise was part of the curriculum, Anderson argued that it was precisely a lack of exercise that harmed women's physical well-being rather than the reverse. The introduction of physical education in women's schools in Britain was an important issue pioneered by other women educators such as Dorothea Beale and Frances Buss.

In 1873 the British Medical Association finally acknowledged Anderson by electing her to its hallowed portals; she would remain its sole female member until 1892. In 1874 she accepted an appointment as a lecturer in midwifery (until 1897) at the newly opened London School of Medicine for Women, established with only fourteen students by the equally determined medical pioneer, Sophia Jex-Blake. Despite her personal and professional differences with Jex-Blake, Anderson served the school as dean for twenty years, from 1883 to 1903, while working as the senior physician at the New Hospital for Women until 1892. The following year, Anderson contributed a substantial endowment to a new medical school at Johns Hopkins University in Baltimore, Maryland, on the understanding that it would admit women students.

Outside of medicine, throughout her life Anderson took an interest in the women's suffrage movement. In 1865 she was a founder of the Kensington Society, a group of about fifty people (including Anderson's educationist friends Beale and Buss) who met four times a year to discuss topics such as parental authority and women's entry into the professions, and whose support for women's suffrage, Elizabeth Crawford argues, was "a catalyst for the birth of the suffrage movement" in England (1999, 322). A Women's Suffrage Committee established by the group in 1866 obtained more than 1,500 signatures on a petition calling for women householders to be given the vote, which Anderson and Davies presented in person, at Parliament, to women's rights advocate John Stuart Mill. But for many years thereafter, Anderson's support for the suffrage campaign was passive rather than active, for she was reluctant to take on the fight for an additional cause that, like women's medical training, faced intense public hostility. In 1889 Anderson finally joined her sister Millicent Garrett Fawcett on the Central Committee of the National Society for Women's Suffrage, but it was not until after her husband's death in 1907 and her election as mayor of Aldeburgh in 1908 that she began taking part in committees and deputations to Parliament. For a short while she joined in activism for the Women's Social and Political Union (WSPU) and went on a short lecture tour in 1909 with Annie Kenney, but the increasing violence of the militants eventually alienated Anderson, and she retired from public activism by 1912. Her daughter Louisa, however, who also entered medicine and ran the first women's field hospital during World War I, was imprisoned for her militant suffrage campaigning in 1912.

In 1907 under the new Qualification of Women Act, which made women eligible for service on county and borough councils and for holding office in them, Anderson stood for and was elected as mayor in her hometown of Aldeburgh, Suffolk. She served two terms (until 1909), during which she took an interest in local issues relating to public health and sanitation.

After Anderson died, the New Hospital was renamed the Elizabeth Garrett Anderson Hospital (1918). It was later incorporated into the University of London and is still in operation today, having fought off attempts to close it down in the 1970s.

See also Beale, Dorothea; Blackwell, Elizabeth; Bodichon, Barbara; Buss, Frances; Butler, Josephine; Davies, (Sarah) Emily; Fawcett, Millicent Garrett; Jacobi, Mary Putnam; Jex-Blake, Sophia; Kenney, Annie; Pechey-Phipson, Edith.

References and Further Reading
Anderson, Louisa G. 1939. *Elizabeth Garrett Anderson.* London: Faber.
Banks, Olive, ed. 1985, 1990. *The Biographical Dictionary of British Feminists,* vol. 1, *1800–1930;* vol. 2, *1900–1945.* Brighton: Harvester Wheatsheaf.
Baylen, J. O., and N. J. Gossman, eds. 1979–1984. *Biographical Dictionary of Modern British Radicals.* 3 vols. Hassocks, Sussex: Harvester Press.
Bell, Enid Moberley. 1953. *Storming the Citadel: The Rise of the Woman Doctor.* London: Constable.
Blake, Catriona. 1990. *The Charge of the Parasols: Women's Entry to the Medical Profession.* London: Women's Press.
Bonner, Thomas Neville. 1992. *To the Ends of the Earth: Women's Search for Education in Medicine.* Cambridge, MA: Harvard University Press.
Cole, Margaret. 1938. *Women of To-Day.* London: Thomas Nelson and Sons.
Crawford, Elizabeth. 1999. *The Women's Suffrage Movement, 1866–1928: A Reference Guide.* London: University College of London Press.
Fancourt, Mary St. John. 1965. *They Dared to Be Doctors: Elizabeth Blackwell and Elizabeth Garrett Anderson.* London: Longman's Green.
Hollis, P. 1987. *Ladies Elect: Women in English Local Government, 1865–1914.* Oxford: Clarendon Press.
Manton, Jo. 1965. *Elizabeth Garrett Anderson.* London: Methuen.
Walsh, Mary Roth. 1977. *"Doctors Wanted: No Women Need Apply": Sexual Barriers in the Medical Profession, 1835–1975.* New Haven: Yale University Press.

Anneke, Mathilde Franziska
(1817–1884)
Germany/United States

The feminist Mathilde Anneke was one of the first women in Germany to write as a professional. Forced to flee after taking part in the revolutionary upheavals there in 1848, she was called one of the "three Amazons of the German Revolution" by Clara Zetkin. Although Anneke never really settled into her adopted home of Milwaukee, remaining one of a tight-knit community of German exiles, she played an important role in the U.S. antislavery and suffrage campaigns.

Born in Westphalia, Anneke came from a middle-class, Roman Catholic family of twelve children. She was married off at seventeen to a French wine merchant much older than herself but left her husband soon after and in 1846 fought a custody battle to bring up her small daughter, struggling to support them both by her writing. For a while, Anneke lived a quiet and pious life as a devout Catholic, writing religious poetry, publishing a book of prayers, and translating the work of others. In 1844 she published the play *Oithono,* which was staged in Münster. In 1846–1847, to express sympathy for Louise Aston, another woman married young who had fought a battle for divorce, Anneke wrote the pamphlet "Woman in Conflict with Social Conditions." Her second marriage to Prussian officer, radical, and freethinker Fritz Anneke in 1847 brought her into a whole new world of revolutionary ideas through his work as editor of the workers' daily *The New Cologne Newspaper* and their activities in Rhenish political circles. When her husband was imprisoned for his links with communist agitators, Anneke, who had renounced her religion and become a freethinker, took over editing the paper from September 1848. After it was suppressed in December 1848, she launched her own *Women's Newspaper,* which in its sole issue discussed the separation of German schools from the control of the church.

During 1848–1849 the Annekes took part in the resistance to the Prussians in the Rhenish Palatinate, with Mathilde riding alongside her husband and serving as his orderly and messenger. Her account was later published in German in Newark in 1853 (*Memoirs of a Woman from the Campaigns in Baden and the Palatinate*). But Prussian successes and the fall of Rastatt in July 1849 forced the couple to flee to the United States via Switzerland as part of a group of "forty-eighters" (as the German exiles were known).

They settled in Milwaukee, Wisconsin, where Anneke became an active supporter of the abolitionist cause. In 1846–1847 she had written on the subjection of women in her pamphlet

"Woman in Conflict with Social Conditions," and in 1852 she established the *German Woman's Newspaper,* which advocated women's emancipation, the first German-language journal in the United States to be run by a woman. Despite the hostile reception it received, Anneke kept the paper going for another two and a half years by giving lectures. In 1853 she met and became good friends with Susan B. Anthony and Elizabeth Cady Stanton, the leaders of the U.S. women's movement, and with their encouragement founded a suffrage association in Wisconsin. From 1869 Anneke regularly attended conventions of the National Woman Suffrage Association, where she was admired as an eloquent speaker. In 1858 tragedy struck the family when three of the Annekes' six children died in a smallpox epidemic.

In 1860 Anneke joined her husband in Europe, where he had gone to work as a newspaper correspondent. When he returned to the United States in support of the Unionists in the Civil War, Anneke, by then used to living an independent life, remained in German-speaking Switzerland with their children, supporting them through her journalism. She wrote in support of the Union cause, producing antislavery stories such as "The Slave Auction" (1862) and underlining the particularly cruel double enslavement of black women. She returned to the United States at the end of the Civil War in 1865 and turned her attention to women's education and training, believing them to be essential if women were to achieve equality with men both in society and in the professions. She opened the Milwaukee Tochter Institut, a German-language girls' school (also known as Madam Anneke's German-French-English Academy), acted as its administrator, and also taught there while raising funds to keep the school going by giving lectures and selling articles to the *Illinois State Times.*

See also Anthony, Susan B., Stanton, Elizabeth Cady; Zetkin, Clara.

References and Further Reading
Cocalis, Susan L., and Kay Goodman, eds. 1982. *Beyond the Eternal Feminine: Critical Essays on Women and German Literature.* Stuttgart: Akademischer Verlag Dans-Dieter Heinz.
McFadden, Margaret. 1999. *Golden Cables of Sympathy: The Transatlantic Sources of Nineteenth-Century Feminism.* Lexington: University of Kentucky Press.

Stanton, Elizabeth Cady, Susan B. Anthony, and
Matilda Joslyn Gage. 1881–1886. *History of
Woman Suffrage.* Vol. 1. New York: Fowler and
Wells, pp. 571–573.
——. 1881–1886. *History of Woman Suffrage,* vol. 2.
New York: Fowler and Wells, pp. 392–399.

Anthony, Susan B.
(1820–1906)
United States

It is difficult to separate the life of American
women's rights pioneer Susan B. Anthony from
that of her close friend and colleague, Elizabeth
Cady Stanton, with whom she journeyed
through fifty years of highs and lows on the road
toward women's suffrage. Neither was to see
women win the vote in her own lifetime. In her
photographs, all the stresses and strains and disappointments of that long, hard battle seem to
be inscribed on Anthony's gaunt and austere
face. Eschewing marriage and personal relationships, she was a woman who dedicated everything to the cause of women's equality and gave
her limitless energies to the efficient organization of a political women's movement, traveling
widely in the United States and to Europe at a
time when such journeys were far from easy.
Starting out as a shrewd and combative militant,
with time Anthony mellowed into the figurehead
of the U.S. suffrage campaign after becoming, in
1892, the president of the National American
Woman Suffrage Association.

Some of the stern demeanor of Susan B. Anthony was the product of her strict Quaker upbringing. She was educated at district school and
later at a Quaker boarding school. Her father, a
Quaker abolitionist who owned a cotton mill in
Battenville, New York, lost his business in the financial crash of 1837. In 1846 after a split in her
local Quaker meeting, Anthony joined the Unitarian church but retained her links with the
Quaker community in Rochester throughout her
life and encouraged the city's particularly energetic suffrage movement.

From the outset, Anthony made a conscious
decision to reject domesticity and marriage; indeed, her campaigning years up to 1890 kept her
so constantly on the move that she never had a
place to call home. Having made the choice to be
neither "drudge" nor "doll" (the two polarized

Susan B. Anthony (Library of Congress)

roles of married women, as she perceived them),
she chose the only path then open to her—teaching (the need to earn her own living having become a necessity after her father's financial ruin).
During 1846–1849 Anthony taught at a female
academy in New York state, after which, with the
family fortunes on the mend, she went to manage the family farm in Rochester, New York. In
1848 she also took up work for the Daughters of
Temperance.

Anthony's activism had begun in 1837 when
she had attended the first antislavery convention
held by women in the United States, in New
York. Thanks to the support given the U.S. anti-
slavery campaign by many enlightened women,
who drew the obvious analogy between slavery
and the domestic drudgery of the wife (Anthony
among them), the abolitionist movement became closely allied with the campaign for
women's rights. Anthony did not, however, attend the first women's rights convention at
Seneca Falls in 1848, her primary interest at that
time being temperance, but in 1851 she was in-

troduced to Elizabeth Cady Stanton by Amelia Jenks Bloomer and struck up a lifelong friendship with her.

Although the cause of suffrage would later become all-consuming for Anthony, the first campaigns waged by her were for dress reform, temperance, and women's economic emancipation. During 1851–1852 she joined with Stanton and Bloomer in attempting to overturn conventions of female dress, calling for an end to tight corseting and bulky crinoline skirts and supporting the new "bloomer" costume, which she herself wore during 1853–1854, as did Stanton. Meanwhile, Anthony continued to concentrate her attention on temperance. But in 1852 when she found herself prohibited from speaking at a male-dominated Albany temperance rally, she joined with Stanton to found the Woman's State Temperance Society. For Anthony, temperance was an important way to control the physical violence of men against their wives and children, and she believed that women should have the right to divorce drunken or violent husbands. When Anthony was again prevented, as a woman, from speaking at the World's Temperance Convention in 1853, she went one better and organized a Whole World's Temperance Convention. Such would be the tenor of all her indomitable campaigning: a dogged refusal to be restrained, as a woman, from pursuing the causes in which she believed. She turned to campaigning for improvements to women's economic position, with Stanton working toward reform of the law regarding women's right to own property. In 1854 Anthony got up a petition with 6,000 signatures, demanding that New York state pass a Married Women's Property Act that would allow them to keep some of their own earnings, to retain some of their possessions if they divorced, and to be given custody of their children. Anthony also tagged on a demand for suffrage to this petition, which was ignored. But in 1860 the act was passed acceding to most of the other demands.

Anthony and Stanton had by now become close collaborators. They were a good mix: Anthony the born organizer and business manager, self-effacing, hardworking, restrained, and possessed of considerable political acumen; Stanton the ideologist and thinker, the passionate public speaker, emotional, compassionate, a mother-earth figure with small children of her own. As Stanton would later observe of their partnership:

"she is slow and analytical in composition, I am rapid and synthetic. I am the better writer, she the better critic. She supplied the facts and statistics, I the philosophy and rhetoric" (Stanton, Anthony, and Gage 1881, 459). In addition, of all the early feminist pioneers in the United States, Anthony was probably the most traveled. As Margaret Hope Bacon asserts, Anthony was the proactive one willing to "do the legwork to make the dream a reality" (Bacon 1986, 116). Indeed it was a necessity, with Stanton tied to her domestic duties and eventually eight children. Over the years, Anthony would endure endless journeys by carriage, cart, and, failing that, wagon across bumpy roads to remote towns, only to be rewarded for her pains by often encountering hostile audiences.

Anthony proved a passionate abolitionist, helping escaped slaves on the Underground Railroad and in 1856 taking over the work of Lucy Stone as New York agent of the American Anti-Slavery Society. In 1863 she and Stanton founded the Woman's National Loyal League to petition against slavery and in 1866 Anthony agreed to take on another role as corresponding secretary of the American Equal Rights Association. During the Civil War, Anthony and other women's rights campaigners supported the Union in hopes that they would thereby win women's suffrage from the victorious Republican Party for their loyalty. But Anthony was appalled when the Fourteenth Amendment to the Constitution was introduced in 1866, defining the voter as *male*, and thus granting the vote only to freed, male slaves when it was ratified in 1868. Anthony violently objected to the fact that black men, many of whom were illiterate, should be emancipated ahead of better-educated white women, seeing this as a betrayal of their work against slavery. After the slave leader Frederick Douglass upheld the amendment (despite his avowed support for women's emancipation), Anthony became convinced that women could no longer rely on male-led movements for the achievement of their political rights. The ratification of the Fifteenth Amendment in 1870 was for her the last straw: it legislated against political disenfranchisement solely on the grounds of *race* and not of sex, thus upholding the continued exclusion of women from suffrage. As a result, Anthony and Stanton would withdraw their support from the American Anti-Slavery Society.

In January 1868, with financing from an eccentric Irish entrepreneur, George Francis Train, Anthony set herself up as a publisher in New York City to produce a weekly national journal on women's rights, *The Revolution,* which featured the slogan "Men, their rights and nothing more; women, their rights and nothing less." Aside from denouncing the Fourteenth and Fifteenth Amendments, this very forward-looking journal was not afraid to tackle controversial and distasteful issues such as prostitution, abortion, rape and wife beating, and infanticide. (On its pages, Anthony famously supported Hester Vaughan, who was accused of infanticide, organizing a petition and campaigning to win her a pardon.) But in early 1870, *The Revolution* folded with debts of $10,000, and Anthony was faced with having to pay them. She did so by embarking on regular lecture tours in the Midwest and the West Coast and finally paid off the debts in 1876.

Also in 1868, Anthony, long a supporter of the rights of working women, helped to organize the New York Working Women's Association in support of a campaign for an eight-hour workday and equal pay for women. But by that time, there was a pressing need for women to have their own organization dedicated to the fight for suffrage. In January Anthony organized a woman suffrage convention in Washington, D.C., and in May 1869 Anthony and Stanton founded the National Woman Suffrage Association, with the objective of taking their case right up to the federal level. In so doing, they caused a split in the suffrage movement. The more conservative wing, led by Lucy Stone and her husband Henry Blackwell, who disliked Anthony's denigration of suffrage for black males, founded the American Woman Suffrage Association.

In 1872 Anthony decided to test the precise wording of the Fourteenth Amendment. She felt that its first section specifying that states shall not abridge the rights of "citizens" could be interpreted as referring to women. She also challenged the Fifteenth Amendment, which forbade the withholding of suffrage to citizens "on account of race, color, or previous condition of servitude," asserting that it thus upheld the rights of married women to vote because they too were technically enslaved. She joined with fourteen other women to cast votes in elections in Rochester, New York. As the ringleader, Anthony was made the sacrificial lamb for a government test case: after being arrested and then eventually freed on bail, she went on a lecture tour of Monroe County, New York (in which Rochester is located), publicizing her stand on women's rights. She was fined $100 at her trial in early 1873, at the end of which she launched a sharp attack on the judge for the abuse of her civil and political rights and for having "trampled underfoot every vital principle of our government" (Bacon 1986, 131). Anthony refused to pay her fine, hoping to contest her case in a higher court. The authorities defused this attempt at publicity by not pursuing the fine.

During the 1870s and 1880s, Anthony narrowed her activism to the fight for suffrage by relentlessly lobbying politicians for changes to the Constitution. She eventually won the introduction of a new federal amendment in Congress in 1878, which stated that a person's sex should not exclude her from the right to vote. It became known as the Susan B. Anthony Amendment and was annually and endlessly debated and rejected, while Anthony continued campaigning for its support across the United States. In 1881 she and Stanton published a "Message to Future Generations," in which they vowed women would not give up the fight until they enjoyed the same rights as men. At this time, Anthony also began setting down a record of the women's suffrage movement with Stanton and Matilda Joslyn Gage. They produced the first three volumes of the *History of Woman Suffrage* during 1881–1886; in 1902 Anthony would eventually finish editing volume 4 with the help of Ida Husted Harper, and the remaining two volumes would finally appear in 1922. Harper would also write a two-volume hagiography, *The Life of Susan B. Anthony,* in 1898 (a third volume appeared in 1908), but this book has since been shown to be unreliable for its deliberate alterations to and censorship of some of Anthony's letters.

From the early 1880s, Anthony began advocating the establishment of an international women's suffrage association, and in 1888 her goal was realized when she founded the International Council of Women in Washington. In 1890, after many years of trying to bring together the moderates and militants of the American suffrage movement and heal the rift between them, Anthony was the impetus behind the amalgamation of the two main suffrage organizations under the title of the National American Woman Suffrage Association. Anthony served as its president from 1892 to 1900 and nominated Carrie Chapman Catt as her successor. In 1904, two years before her death, Anthony was one of a group of women involved in the foundation of the International Woman Suffrage Alliance after a meeting of the ICW in Berlin. Anthony was made its honorary president.

Undoubtedly one of the most forceful pioneers of women's suffrage in the United States, Anthony never gave up hope of winning. Shortly before her death, she attended a national suffrage convention in Baltimore, where she famously remarked that "failure is impossible" (Bacon 1986, 187). It was her eloquent collaborator Elizabeth Cady Stanton who summed up the secret of their successful teamwork: "I forged the thunderbolts, and she fired them" (Stanton, Anthony, and Gage 1881, 458).

Susan B. Anthony's home in Rochester, New York, is now a National Historic Landmark and is maintained through private support. For information, contact http://www.susanbanthonyhouse.org/. The Women's Rights National Park at Seneca Falls, which commemorates the women's rights convention held there in 1848, has ongoing events, news, and exhibitions relating to the work of Anthony and her contemporaries. Contact http://www.nps.gov/wori/.

See also Bloomer, Amelia Jenks; Catt, Carrie Chapman; Gage, Matilda Joslyn; Stanton, Elizabeth Cady; Stone, Lucy.

References and Further Reading

Anthony, Katharine Susan. 1954. *Susan B. Anthony: Her Personal History and Her Era.* Garden City, NY: Doubleday.

Bacon, Margaret Hope. 1986. *Mothers of Feminism: The Story of Quaker Women in America.* San Francisco: Harper and Row.

Barry, Kathleen. 1988. *Susan B. Anthony: A Biography of a Singular Feminist.* New York: New York University Press.

Buhle, Mari Jo, and Paul Buhle, eds. 1978. *The Concise History of Woman Suffrage: Selections from the Classic Work of Stanton, Anthony, Gage, and Harper.* Urbana: University of Illinois Press.

DuBois, Ellen Carol. 1981. *The Elizabeth Cady Stanton–Susan B. Anthony Reader: Correspondence, Writings, Speeches.* Rev. ed. Boston: Northeastern University Press.

Helsinger, Elizabeth K., Robin Lauterbach Sheets, and William Veeder. 1983. *The Woman Question: So-cial Issues, 1837–1883,* vol. 2, *Society and Literature in Britain and America, 1837–1883.* Manchester: Manchester University Press.

Kerber, Linda K., and Jane DeHart-Mathews. 2000. *Women's America: Refocusing the Past.* New York: Oxford University Press.

Lutz, Alma. 1959. *Susan B. Anthony: Rebel, Crusader, Humanitarian.* Reprint, Boston: Beacon Press.

Sherr, Lynn. 1995. *Failure Is Impossible: Susan B. Anthony in Her Own Words.* New York: Times Books.

Stanton, Elizabeth Cady, Susan B. Anthony, and Matilda Joslyn Gage. 1881–1886. *History of Woman Suffrage,* vol. 1. New York: Fowler and Wells.

Arenal, Concepción
(1820–1893)
Spain

The prison reformer, humanist, and protosociologist Concepción Arenal was a unique voice in nineteenth-century Spain. Alongside Emilia Pardo Bazán and Gertrudis Gómez de Avellaneda, she was one of the first to write in Spanish about the position of women and the underprivileged at a time when the women's movement in that country had yet to develop. Arenal's writings on penal science and international law became the model to which many later Spanish women writers and reformers aspired.

Arenal was born in Galicia and brought up in Santander. In 1835 her family settled in Madrid, where during the 1840s, she defied her family's sense of propriety and dressed as a man in order to be admitted to lectures at the Central University. After marrying in 1848, she began publishing articles in the progressive newspaper *Iberia.* Left a widow with three children in 1857, she turned to journalism as a major means of financial support. In 1860 she published her first, groundbreaking essay: "Beneficence, Philanthropy and Charity." Madrid's Academy of Moral and Political Science was so impressed that it awarded the essay a major prize, but it had been published by Arenal under a male name—her son's. Shortly afterward, Arenal published what would become a prototype for charitable and philanthropic work, a manual known as *The Visitor of the Poor* (1860), the first of its kind to attempt to explain the condition of poverty and the nature of the sorrow of the underprivileged. In it, she urged philanthropists to examine their own inner selves: "In order to enter the homes of the poor with humility of heart and of mind, we must decide whether in their place we would conduct ourselves better. In viewing their faults, vices, and crimes, we must ask ourselves this question: would the poor be what they are, if we were what we ought to be?" (Smith 1989, 215).

In 1863 Arenal initiated a lifetime's work on penal reform when she was appointed a visitor of the Women's Prison at Corunna, publishing her findings as *Letters to Delinquents* in 1865 and offering up suggestions for reform of the penal code of 1850. In a brief reformist period in Spanish history that followed the 1868 revolution and the dethronement of Queen Isabella, Arenal became inspector of the correctionals for women, a post she held until 1873. During this period, Arenal joined the organizing committee of the Ladies Athenaeum (1869) and founded a newspaper, the *Voice of Charity,* which ran until 1884.

Meanwhile, Arenal had turned to exploring the wider issues of women's civil and professional position in her writings. In 1868 she published *The Woman of the Future,* a collection of twelve studies on the social position of Spanish women. In it, she pointed out, among other absurdities, that a woman could be "the Mother of God" but was not allowed to be a priest and that a woman was classified with children in civil law yet could suffer the same punishment as an adult male under criminal law. In "Women's Work," published in 1871 in the *Bulletin of the Free Institute of Education,* she argued for equal pay and child care facilities for working women. She supported the rights of workers, advocating collective ownership after the International Workers Association was founded in Madrid in 1868, and in 1872 donated money toward the construction of workers' homes. Her pacifism grew during the Carlist Wars that followed the proclamation of a Spanish republic in 1873, when she worked for the Red Cross and ran a hospital for the wounded. She published her account of this period as *War Notebooks* (1874). Arenal became increasingly radical after the restoration of the monarchy in 1875 and in 1876 moved to Asturia. She once more returned to an exposition of the problems of the middle-class woman, in 1881 attacking the sterility of married life in *The Woman in Her House.*

Middle-class women in Spain were constrained by a narrow existence, Arenal argued, which both denied them a sense of purpose and consigned them to silence and immobility. If they dared aspire to any form of work, they found it doubly difficult to do so if they were married because work for middle-class women in an intensely Catholic Spain, as Catherine Davies explains in her excellent study (1998), was not only disapproved of as unseemly by church and society but also considered to be a dishonor to their husbands. Acutely aware of the lack of professional opportunity open to women, in an 1892 essay Arenal famously pronounced that the only options open to women were to be "a schoolmistress in a girls' school, telegraphist, telephonist, tobacconist and Queen" (Davies 1998, 24). After her death, the association Arenal had founded, the Women of Charity, went into decline, and with it the first flowering of middle-class feminism in Spain. Arenal's vivid and compelling arguments on women's rights still await a wider audience outside the Spanish-speaking world.

See also Gómez de Avellaneda y Arteaga, Gertrudis; Pardo Bazán, Emilia.

References and Further Reading

Davies, Catherine. 1998. *Spanish Women's Writing 1849–1996.* London: Athlone Press.

Smith, Bonnie G. 1989. *Changing Lives: Women in European History since 1700.* Lexington, MA: D. C. Heath.

Armand, Inessa (Elizabeth d'Herbenville/ Elizabeth Inès Stéphane)
(1874–1920)
France/Soviet Union

Much has been made in recent biographies of the Bolshevik leader Vladimir Ilich Lenin of the role of the socialist feminist Inessa Armand in his life. In a rare revelation of the more human side to Lenin, biographers have indicated that he and Armand had a very close relationship from about 1911 to Armand's death in 1920. Had she not died young, Comrade Inessa (as the Soviets referred to her), a highly articulate figure in the Women's Department of the Communist Party (known as the Zhenotdel), might have come to exert a greater influence over the Soviet leader in her work for women's issues.

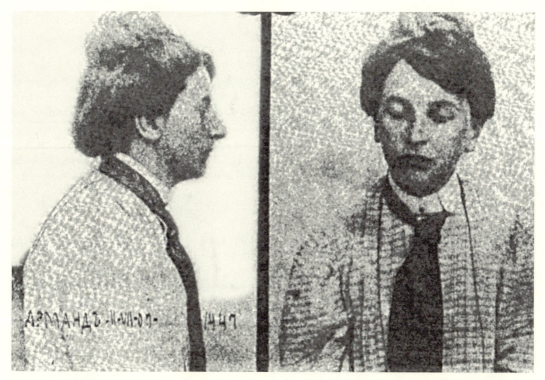

Inessa Armand (Susan Lang)

Armand was born in Paris as Elizabeth d'Herbenville, the daughter of a French father and a Scottish mother who were traveling music hall performers. After the death of her father, Armand and her sister were sent to Russia by their mother to join their aunt and grandmother, who were tutors there to the children of a rich Russian industrialist, Evgeny Armand. When she was nineteen, Inessa married Evgeny's son Alexander and subsequently had four children by him. An intelligent woman, Armand read widely and embraced the emergent women's movement. She ran a school for peasants on the family estate, and in Moscow in 1899 she joined with a group of women reformers to found the Moscow Society for Improving the Lot of Women, which became affiliated with the Women's International Progressive Union in England and shared similar objectives with the Russian Women's Mutual Philanthropic Society. The Moscow society worked on various philanthropic projects, including temperance and the campaign against state-regulated prostitution and for the rehabilitation of prostitutes. It also set up hostels and vocational workshops for poor women. Armand became chair of its Educational Commission

and served as president of the society from 1900 to 1903.

At this time, Armand also attended the Sunday gatherings of M. K. Gorbunova-Kablukova, an ardent supporter of women's education and their entry into the professions. Armand herself tried to open a Sunday school for poor and illiterate working women in 1900, but this school and an attempt to set up a women's newspaper in 1902 were quashed by the authorities. She was allowed to establish a "shelter for downtrodden women" in 1901, however, which aided women in their social rehabilitation by teaching them sewing, cooking, and other simple domestic skills. But by 1903, after four years of charitable work conducted in the face of a barrage of official objections and with very limited results, Armand had become convinced by her reading of the literature of Marxism and contacts with socialist political groups that only radical social and political change would ever combat such deep-seated social ills.

During 1903 Armand had an affair with her brother-in-law Vladimir and gave birth to a fifth child that October. She joined the Russian Social Democratic Workers' Party and over the next five years worked for it, mainly in Moscow and Pushkino (a town northeast of the city), disseminating revolutionary propaganda and stealing back and forth from Russia to Europe between arrests and periods of imprisonment. After her fourth arrest, she was sent to Archangel in 1907 to serve out her sentence in exile. Her health was poor, and the conditions in the frozen north of Russia were arduous. In October 1908 Armand absconded, returned to Moscow, and from there escaped to Europe, eventually arriving in France in January 1909. Seeking to prepare herself better for party work in exile and reunited with three of her children, she went to the New University of Brussels to study economic science. After completing her studies, in September 1910 she took up work in Paris with French socialists and Russian émigrés and adopted the name Inessa Armand.

As far back as the 1890s, Armand had read the writings of Lenin and had exchanged letters with him. Between that time and the October Revolution in 1917, they crossed paths constantly in Europe, with Armand becoming a close collaborator and friend of Lenin's wife, Nadezhda Krupskaya. In Paris Armand was a very energetic worker for the Bolsheviks, disseminating literature, indoctrinating and training new members, and helping to fund a Socialist Party summer school at Longjumeau in 1911. She also translated Bolshevik literature into French, including some of Lenin's writings. In July 1912 Armand returned to St. Petersburg to do undercover work for the party. She was arrested in September and spent another six months in solitary confinement. In August 1913 she left Russia again, worked with Lenin for a while in Cracow, Poland, and eventually returned to Paris. There, with Krupskaya and Alexandra Kollontai she started a Bolshevik journal for women, the *Woman Worker*, in which they urged Russia's female proletariat to rebel against their exploitation by the capitalist system. The journal was short-lived, but during her six months of work for it, Armand initiated discussions within the party on the status of women.

During World War I, much of Armand's time was taken up working for Lenin and the party in Paris. She also organized pacifist conferences against the war and represented the Bolsheviks at international socialist conferences held at Zimmerwald and Kienthal in Switzerland. In 1915 she sent Lenin a résumé of a pamphlet she wanted to write drawn from her own experiences, setting out her views on love, marriage, and the family and emphasizing freedom of choice, personal commitment, and sexual equality. A detailed correspondence between Armand and Lenin on the subject followed. Lenin's bureaucratic and highly pedantic responses concentrated on Armand's interpretation of the concept of "free love" (that bothersome topic—as far as the Bolshevik leadership were concerned—that so preoccupied other Bolshevik women like Kollontai). Lenin's conclusion was simple: free love was a "bourgeois demand" and a class issue. What Armand saw as a basic human need, Lenin viewed as a license to promiscuity, as "leftist deviation"; what is more, in his view, such emotional aspirations were disruptive to the work for socialism. Nothing ever shifted the puritanical streak in Lenin's attitude toward sexuality and the relationships of male and female revolutionaries. He was still locked into the view perpetuated in the revolutionary bible of the 1860s—Nikolay Chernyshevsky's novel *What Is to Be Done?*—a paean to the aesthetic ideal of men and women working in celibate harmony within the revolutionary collective.

After the February Revolution broke in 1917, Armand was one of a select group who accompanied Lenin back to Russia in a sealed train, arriving at St. Petersburg's Finland Station in April. In Moscow she became a familiar figure on the podium at political meetings as a member of the Bolshevik Party's Central Committee. She set up the journal *Working Woman's Life* in June 1917, publishing articles accentuating the work of the female proletariat and encouraging women to join the party. After the October Revolution it was rumored that Lenin had wanted to live openly with Armand but that the Bolshevik leadership had refused to condone this. Instead, in 1918, Armand was discreetly installed in an apartment in the Kremlin, along with Lenin's wife and his sister Maria. In 1918 Armand became chair of the Moscow branch of the Economic Council, involved herself in the establishment of new schools, and occasionally gave lectures in schools on the "woman question" and other issues. She also organized the First All-Russian Congress of Women Workers and Peasants with Kollontai and Konkordiya Samoilova.

Armand's major contribution to the restructuring of Soviet society came with her party work for women from August 1919 as founder and first director of the Zhenotdel, the new women's department of the Communist Party, a concept that had been advocated as far back as 1908 by Kollontai. The Zhenotdel would promote the education, emancipation, and integration into the workplace of women under Soviet rule—or that, in theory, was its aim. It ambitiously set out to unite women across a great diversity of ethnic, social, and religious communities in the economic reconstruction of the country by improving standards of productivity in the factories and extending political education to illiterate workers. But in reality, the Zhenotdel's role was soon commandeered by the male Bolshevik leadership to impose uniformity of political thought and mobilize even more women (particularly those in remote rural areas) for even more work.

For her part, Armand worked hard to ensure that nurseries, clinics, communal laundries, kitchens, and canteens were set up to help factory women all over the Soviet Union. Having access to such services would not only enable them to perform better at their jobs but also free up time for them to become active in workers' committees, attend literacy classes and trade union meetings, and thus be politicized. She also set up a Zhenotdel newspaper called the *Communist Woman,* on which she collaborated with Nadezhda Krupskaya, and supervised the publication of much other literature, including a sixteen-page pamphlet titled "Why I Have Become a Defender of Soviet Rule." But in the course of its work the Zhenotdel ran up against many difficulties. Russian peasant women in remote areas had long been resistant to strangers who came to their villages to proselytize, particularly communist organizers who rode roughshod over traditional social customs and religious practice. This problem became particularly acute among Muslim women in the Soviet republics who were forced to unveil. In any event, the party itself would become increasingly wary of any separate sphere of women's activity that could not be kept under its tight control.

There is no doubt that Armand wore herself out in service of the Zhenotdel and the Communist Party, often working sixteen hours a day. Together with Alexandra Kollontai and Samoilova, she organized the First Conference of Interna-

tional Women Communists in Moscow in July 1920, but by then she was on the point of physical collapse. Lenin begged her to take a rest in the Caucasus, but shortly after her arrival there, Armand contracted cholera and died. Lenin was distraught at Armand's death and ensured that she was accorded the honor of being buried alongside other revolutionary heroes by the Kremlin Wall in Red Square.

The flame of Armand's work was kept alive until Lenin's own death in 1924, but before the decade was out, Joseph Stalin had set about destroying her legacy, and by the 1930s her work had been forgotten. The Zhenotdel to which she had dedicated her health and energies was abolished by Stalin in 1930. Its abolition symbolized the death of Bolshevik feminism in the Soviet Union.

See also Filosova, Anna; Kollontai, Alexandra; Krupskaya, Nadezhda.

References and Further Reading

Clements, Barbara Evans. 1997. *Bolshevik Women.* Cambridge: Cambridge University Press.

Elwood, Carter. 1992. *Inessa Armand: Revolutionary and Feminist.* Cambridge: Cambridge University Press.

Service, Robert. 2000. *Lenin: A Biography.* London: Macmillan.

Stites, Richard. 1991 [1978]. *The Women's Liberation Movement in Russia: Feminism, Nihilism, and Bolshevism, 1860–1930.* Reprint, Princeton: Princeton University Press.

Volkogonov, Dmitri. 1994. *Lenin: Life and Legacy.* London: HarperCollins.

Ashby, Margery Corbett
(1882–1981)
United Kingdom

Margery Corbett Ashby had a long and distinguished career in public service that was dominated by her promotion of women's rights and her beliefs in individual liberty. As a respected figure in liberal politics and the international women's movement, she also took a particular interest in the enfranchisement of women in developing countries through her long presidency (1923–1946) of the International Woman Suffrage Alliance (IWSA).

Born in Sussex, Ashby was educated at home by her parents and by French and German governesses. As the daughter of a Liberal Party member of Parliament and a socially active mother (who had campaigned for dress reform in her day), she grew up in a family that advocated progressive reform and from her teens helped her mother campaign for the women's suffrage movement. At the age of only sixteen, she made her first political speech, and at eighteen with her younger sister and some friends, she founded a group known as the Young Suffragists.

After studying classics from 1900 to 1903 at Newnham College, Cambridge University, where she was active in the Cambridge branch of the National Union of Women's Suffrage Societies (NUWSS), Ashby spent a year at a teacher-training college. But after accompanying her mother to the inaugural congress of the IWSA, held in Berlin in 1904, she decided against a career as a teacher.

In 1907 Ashby briefly took a job as organizing secretary of the NUWSS and was subsequently elected to its executive committee. With her mother, she founded the Liberal Suffrage Group, and in 1909 she joined the executive committee of the Cambridge Women's Suffrage Association. After her marriage in 1910 to barrister Arthur Ashby, she restricted herself to local affairs for a while, serving as a poor law guardian in Putney in 1913. She resigned from the NUWSS executive in 1914 and took up voluntary relief work during World War I. She was invited by the British War Office to advise on the problems that developed during Germany's postwar occupation by Allied troops and assisted in the establishment of a women's police force in Cologne to help control the growing problem of prostitution in the city during its occupation.

After women in Britain gained the vote in 1918, Ashby's primary objective was to enter Parliament, where she could better promote women's rights and the greater involvement of women in British political life. In 1918 she was one of seventeen women who stood for the first time for election to the House of Commons, but, unfortunately, it was the first of seven unsuccessful attempts in seven different constituencies that she would make between then and 1944.

Ashby was a delegate of the IWSA to the Versailles Peace Conference (1919–1920) and attended the first of the IWSA's postwar congresses in 1920, at which she was elected secretary. Three years later, at the alliance's Rome conference, she was elected to succeed Carrie Chapman Catt as president. During her twenty-three years as president she toured the world, much encouraged in her work and financially assisted by her parents, especially during the 1920s. She visited all the member countries of the IWSA in Europe between 1924 and 1928 and also the United States. She spoke on women's issues, notably her own hobbyhorses of women's equal rights with men in the workplace and the adoption by men of the same moral standards as women, in thirty-seven different countries, putting to good use her ability to converse in French, German, Italian, and Turkish. In 1926, with suffrage having been awarded to women in many countries, the IWSA was renamed the International Alliance of Women for Suffrage and Equal Citizenship (IAWSEC), and it concentrated on extending its activities to wider issues of women's rights in employment, education, and their encouragement to hold public office. Ashby continued to emphasize women's peace campaigning and worked hard to overcome differences with feminists in countries seeking independence from British rule, collaborating with Egyptian feminist leader and nationalist Huda Sha'rawi to further women's suffrage in Egypt. Several years after her tenure as president ended in 1946, Ashby edited the IWSA journal *International Woman Suffrage News* from 1952 to 1961.

When the vote in Britain was extended from women over thirty to all women over twenty-one in 1928, Ashby joined with Eva Hubback to work under the auspices of the National Union of Societies for Equal Citizenship, again encouraging women to play their part in British political and cultural life and calling upon government to introduce family allowances. She cofounded the Townswomen's Guilds during the late 1920s, organizations intended to further promote women's public service throughout the counties of the United Kingdom in no matter how limited a capacity.

Throughout the 1930s, Ashby also became increasingly preoccupied with the peace movement. During 1932–1934 she was British alternate delegate to the League of Nations Disarmament Conference and supported the work of the league in peace mediation, although she was dismayed that it did not accord women greater involvement in its administration. But her faith in the efficacy of the league in averting war evaporated, as did her ambition of galvanizing a broad base of support for the peace movement among members of the International Alliance of Woman. Ashby resigned as a delegate in 1935, deeply discouraged that so little had been achieved by the British government in forwarding the cause of collective security.

In 1942 Ashby went to Sweden to conduct anti-Nazi propaganda during World War II. Although she gave up her work for the IWSA in 1946, she continued to attend its conferences and lectured on pacifism and women's rights, traveling in India, Sri Lanka, and Iran. A lifelong liberal, Ashby was also active in the Association for Moral and Social Hygiene, the British Commonwealth League, and the Women's Freedom League. She was made a Dame of the British Empire in 1967 and remained an important figure in the international women's movement until her death at the age of ninety-nine.

See also Catt, Carrie Chapman; Sha'rawi, Huda.

References and Further Reading
Alberti, Johanna. 1989. *Beyond Suffrage: Feminists in War and Peace, 1914–1928*. London: Macmillan.
Ashby, Dame Margery Corbett. 1996. *Memoirs*. Privately printed.
Bosch, Mineke. 1990. *Politics and Friendship: Letters from the International Woman Suffrage Alliance, 1902–1942*. Columbus: Ohio State University Press.
Brookes, Pamela. 1967. *Women at Westminster: An Account of Women in the British Parliament 1918–1966*. London: Peter Davies.
Harrison, Brian. 1987. *Prudent Revolutionaries: Portraits of British Feminists between the Wars*. Oxford: Clarendon Press.
Rupp, Leila J. 1997. *Worlds of Women: The Making of an International Women's Movement*. Princeton: Princeton University Press.
Schreiber, Adele, and Margaret Mathieson. 1955. *Journey towards Freedom: Written for the Golden Jubilee of the International Alliance of Women*. Copenhagen: International Alliance of Women.
Stott, Mary. 1978. *Organization Woman: The Story of the National Union of Townswomen's Guilds*. London: Heinemann.
Whittick, A. with Frederick Muller. 1979. *Woman into Citizen*. London: Atheneum.

Ashrawi, Hanan
(1946–)
Palestinian National Authority

Since taking a leading role in peace talks to try to end the Arab-Israeli conflict in Israel in the early 1990s, the Palestinian human rights activist and peace negotiator Hanan Ashrawi has remained at the forefront of consciousness-raising on humanitarian issues and the achievement of a just and permanent peace in Israel. As an informed and articulate defender of the *intifada,* Ashrawi became the acceptable face of the Palestine Liberation Organization (PLO) for the media and the public at large, with sympathetic Israelis on the left seeing her as epitomizing the "good Arab." A woman of considerable intellect and commanding presence, she has done much to maintain the high profile of the legitimacy of the Palestinian cause during the often extremely fraught Israeli-Palestinian negotiations.

Ashrawi was born into a Palestinian Christian family at Nablus, in what was then part of the British mandate of Palestine and is now the Israeli-occupied West Bank. Her father, a prosperous medical practitioner, Daoud Mikhail, had been active in the Palestinian nationalist movement and was a founder of the PLO. She grew up in comfortable middle-class surroundings in Ramallah and entered the American University of Beirut, in Lebanon, where she earned a degree in English literature. While studying in Beirut, Ashrawi joined the General Union of Palestinian Students, which had undertaken welfare work among Palestinian refugees in Lebanon. When the Arab-Israeli Six-Day War broke out in 1967, she was trapped in Beirut, unable, as an "absentee" under a new law introduced by the Israelis, to return home.

After graduating in 1969, she decided to go to the United States to do postgraduate studies in medieval and comparative literature at the University of Virginia. There she joined in left-wing student activism and the women's movement and was finally allowed to return to Ramallah in 1973. She was offered the chair of Medieval and Comparative Literature at the Anglican Teachers' College at Bir Zeit on the West Bank, which was then being upgraded to Bir Zeit University. In 1986 she was appointed dean of the Faculty of Arts. She resigned as dean in 1990, although she continued her association with the faculty until 1995.

After the raids on Palestinian refugee camps by Lebanese Christians in 1982, Ashrawi became an important spokesperson for the rights of Palestinians and an open advocate of an independent Palestinian state. In the late 1980s, she became heavily involved in the Palestinian cause and the activism of the PLO as a member of the Intifada Political Committee. In interviews on American news programs—notably a three-hour, live Arab-Israeli debate in a 1988 edition of ABC's *Nightline*—she lent a newfound weight and seriousness to the legitimacy of Palestinian claims with her intelligent, reasoned responses and drew attention to the unraveling humanitarian crisis among Israel's dispossessed Palestinian population.

In 1991, when Norwegian negotiators initiated Middle East peace talks, Ashrawi was appointed by Yasser Arafat to join the Palestinian delegation in Madrid; she led a protest when the Israelis called for all delegates linked to the PLO to be excluded, and although the ruling stood, such was the respect for Ashrawi that she was allowed to take on the role of official spokesperson of the Palestinian delegation during what became the Middle East peace process.

Under the Oslo Accords of 1993, self-rule was established for Palestinians in parts of the Israeli-occupied West Bank and the Gaza Strip. Ashrawi again played a crucial role, but with some Muslims reluctant to have her, as a Christian and feminist, as their representative, she resigned as official spokesperson at the end of the year in order to concentrate on human rights issues in the Israeli-occupied territories. She founded and became commissioner general (1993–1996) of the Palestinian Independent Commission for Citizens' Rights in Jerusalem, a human rights group within the newly established Palestinian National Authority (PNA). After the first free elections were staged in the Palestinian West Bank and Gaza in 1996, she was elected to the Palestinian Legislative Council as an independent member for Jerusalem and served for two years (1996–1998) as minister of higher education and research under Yasser Arafat. However, in 1998, dissatisfied with Arafat's leadership of the PNA and concerned about the erosion of its democratic principles and the rise of political corruption, Ashrawi resigned. She founded a new body, the Palestinian Initiative for the Promotion of Global Dialogue and Democracy, dedicated to democratic and candid dialogue in the resolution of conflict and the free exchange of ideas based on humanitarian rather than ideological considerations.

Revered by her admirers as the "First Lady of the Palestinians," Ashrawi has consistently promoted the politics of peace rather than confrontation; she has denounced Israel's failure to comply with the terms of the Oslo Accords but has also condemned extremism and the abuse of human rights by the PNA. She has extended her work for human rights beyond the confines of the Middle East as a member of the Independent International Commission on Kosovo. She continues to speak out with characteristic compassion against the victimization of ordinary Palestinians in what she perceives as a punitive peace process that is perpetuating rather than resolving conflict, but she is determined that a democratic resolution will be achieved. Her work continues in the international arena as a member of advisory bodies such as the Council on Foreign Relations and the United Nations Research Institute for Social Development. She is now holder of the Weissberg chair in international studies at Beloit College.

Ashrawi is the author of numerous academic works on literature, including *Contemporary Palestinian Literature under Occupation* (1976) and *From Intifada to Independence* (1989); and in 1995 published her autobiography, *This Side of Peace: A Personal Account,* about the Palestinian fight for autonomy.

References and Further Reading

Ashrawi, Hanan. 1995. *This Side of Peace: A Personal Account.* London: Simon and Schuster.

Encyclopedia Britannica: Book of the Year 1993. Chicago: University of Chicago Press and Encyclopedia Britannica.

Golden, Kristen, and Barbara Findlen. 1998. *Remarkable Women of the Twentieth Century: 100 Portraits of Achievement.* New York: Friedman/Fairfax Publishers, in association with Corbis.

Penguin Biographical Dictionary of Women. 1998. Harmondsworth: Penguin.

Victor, Barbara. 1994. *A Voice of Reason: Hanan Ashrawi and Peace in the Middle East.* New York: Harcourt Brace and Co.

Astor, Nancy
(1879–1964)
United States/United Kingdom

The noted American-born feminist and politician Lady Nancy Astor, famous for her repartee and the coterie of privileged friends who frequented her opulent mansion at Cliveden, used her position as the first woman member of Parliament (MP) in Britain to campaign with moralistic fervor on many social issues during her twenty-six-year career. From the day she entered Parliament in 1919, Astor became a thorn in the side of the male political establishment with her idiosyncratic brand of "moral reform feminism" (Pugh 2000, 244). Refusing to accede to the role of party yes-woman or be patronized as the token woman in Parliament, she remained her own person in the firm belief that women were not the weaker but the stronger sex and could play an influential part in British political life as well as in reconciling class antagonisms. Such was her outspokenness throughout her political career that Astor was convinced that it had kept her from being given a cabinet post. She remained one of British politics' great individualists, a woman of tremendous vitality and determination who proudly asserted, "I am an agitator, not an administrator."

Born Nancy Witcher Langhorne in Danville, Virginia, Astor was one of five exceptionally beautiful and gifted daughters of a Virginia tobacco auctioneer who had worked his way up from poverty to a fortune. She made a socially advantageous marriage to Bostonian Robert Gould Shaw in 1897, but the couple proved sexually incompatible, a situation exacerbated by Gould's drinking. Mindful of the social stigma attached to divorce, Nancy only reluctantly agreed to one in 1903.

In England in 1906 Nancy met and married Waldorf Astor, the son of an American family, who was in line for both his father's title and his millions (his father had been made a British peer). In 1910 Waldorf Astor stood as a Liberal candidate for Parliament and was elected to a seat in Plymouth. The couple moved to the West Country, where Astor became active in her husband's constituency in between having five children. In 1919 the first Lord Astor died, and upon inheriting his father's title, Waldorf Astor was promoted to the House of Lords. With women in the United Kingdom having been awarded suffrage in 1918, Nancy decided to stand in the by-election to her husband's seat and became Unionist MP for the Sutton division of Plymouth in 1919. This made her the first woman in Britain to enter Parliament, which she did in a blaze of publicity and much public curiosity (the

Irish Sinn Fein member, Constance de Markievicz, had been elected in 1918 but had declined to take her seat in protest at British rule in Ireland). Not all feminists, however, delighted in Astor's moment of triumph. As an American and a member of the wealthy aristocracy, not only was she seen by many women as a less than ideal candidate for the honor of first woman MP, but her campaign had been a comfortable one, winning as she had her husband's safe seat. As Mary Stocks relates in her memoirs (1970), Astor's detractors were soon surprised by both the energy and commitment that she invested in her work. She proved to be no political dilettante but a woman who was genuinely interested in and passionate about every social cause she adopted.

As the only woman among 600 men, Astor was paralyzed by fear on her first day in the house, but made an impressive maiden speech on temperance, a subject close to her own heart, along with other issues relating to moral reform. Thereafter, she became renowned for her short, fiery speeches, her idiosyncratic brand of charm combined with bullishness, and the persistence with which she rudely and constantly challenged male politicians during their own speeches. For the next three years, Astor occupied a unique place in British politics as the only woman MP. She would be supported throughout her long career by her husband, who was devoted to her, and by the admiration of many women's organizations. She was assisted in her work by the feminist Ray Strachey, who offered her services free as parliamentary secretary and political adviser and once remarked that Astor became a "symbol of hope" to whom many wives and mothers appealed in the hundreds of letters she would receive daily, being "identified in the public mind with all the socials reforms which are dear to ordinary women" (Strachey 1978, 378). And Astor certainly made good use of her position in promoting a wide range of social causes that absorbed her: temperance, law and order (as a member of the Criminal Law Commission in 1922 and an advocate of women police officers), progressive education, and an increase in the age at which students might legally leave school. On a broader level, her campaigning addressed in particular the preservation of family life, and the rights and welfare of women and children. As an initiator of the Trade Boards Act, she also worked for improved standards in the distributive and catering trades and was supportive of the work of Margaret McMillan in the establishment of nursery schools.

Olive Banks (1990, 220) argues that for all her support of temperance, Astor's successful campaigning for the introduction of a private member's bill, the Intoxicating Liquors Act of 1923 (which prohibited the sale of alcohol to people under the age of eighteen), was prompted as much by her concern for equal rights and justice for the many wives abused by alcoholic husbands as it was on strictly moral terms. A devout Christian Scientist from 1914 and an admirer of Mary Baker Eddy's *Science and Health* (1875), she employed an evangelizing earnestness in her persistent attacks on prevailing double standards in sexual behavior. Many of Astor's views of moral reform reached back to the reformist traditions of the Victorian era laid down by women such as Josephine Butler, whom she greatly admired. With her emphasis on the good, solid, middle-class values of sobriety, sexual restraint, and the defense of marriage (she wanted to make divorce more difficult), Astor won approval for many of her reform campaigns from that bastion of middle England, the Women's Institutes, in the words of Brian Harrison, "the real, old-fashioned, courageous, sensible, solid cup-of-tea women" (1987, 80). It was her ability to relate to such women at large that gave Astor what Martin Pugh (2000) sees as the "common touch" akin to that of some royalty, a gift that increased support for Astor's positions on gambling, prostitution, temperance, and the protection of women and children. In 1925 Astor introduced a bill to end the controls on prostitution and replace them with legislation that would have made not just the prostitutes who solicited on the streets but also their male clients subject to prosecution. Following in the steps of Butler, Astor attached similar importance to the eradication of venereal disease through the reform of male sexual behavior. In addition, she was involved in passing legislation making child molestation a serious crime (and she was supported in this by Britain's second woman MP, the now forgotten Margaret Wintringham).

There was, however, a negative side to Astor's work: she was violently intolerant of many things, most overtly socialism and communism. No apologies can be made for her undisguised racial prejudice, although one might argue that it typified the ingrained social attitudes prevalent among the aristocracy in Britain at that time. However, there was a perverse courage, if not recklessness, to the way in which she gave short shrift to those with whose political ideas she disagreed. Thus, when she visited the Soviet Union with her husband and George Bernard Shaw in 1931, she exercised no restraint in "going on" at Joseph Stalin "like a steamroller" (Fox 2000, 430) over his repressive policies. Equally, in later years she would be just as uncompromising in her criticism of Nazism and McCarthyism.

During her years as an MP, Astor's home, Cliveden, became a notable political salon (its habitués were known as the "Cliveden set"), where some of the most eminent minds of her day met and from where they exerted considerable influence over British foreign policy in particular. Her equally grand townhouse in London's St. James's Square also became a venue for informal meetings between politicians and women voters. Although she was a Unionist MP, Astor nevertheless supported the principles of welfare legislation mooted by the British labor movement and in 1932 set up a lobby group to fight the exclusion of married women from statutory rights under the National Health Insurance and Contributory Pensions Act.

During World War II, Astor gave much moral support to her constituents, who came under fierce bombing raids by the Germans (because of the naval installations at Plymouth). Her own home there suffered bomb damage. But by the end of the war, the political climate in Britain had changed dramatically, and Astor allowed herself to be persuaded to retire from Parliament in 1945, a fact that she later regretted. With her political powers by then markedly fading, however, she may well have spared herself ignominious defeat in the subsequent Labour landslide.

In the years since her death in 1964, Astor has been remembered primarily for her gift for mimicry (as an impersonator of numerous fellow politicians) and her eccentric witticisms, ensuring her inclusion in many collections of quotations, if nothing else. As former British prime minister Clement Attlee remarked at her death, "She could exchange compliments or insults on equal terms with dukes or dockers" (*Observer* 3 May 1964). In 1923 Astor published her lively memoirs *My Two Countries,* which contain much of her thinking on women's moral superiority to men and her belief that men's derisiveness toward women by men had originated, in her view, from the day that Adam laid the blame on woman for eating the apple in the Garden of Eden. But to emphasize her wit at the expense of her genuine social concerns is to do her a disservice: Nancy Astor's humanitarian concerns, her courage, and her social activism more than demonstrated the generous undercurrents of her irreverent public persona.

See also Butler, Josephine; Markievicz, Constance de; McMillan, Margaret.

References and Further Reading

Astor, Michael. 1963. *Tribal Feeling.* London: John Murray.

Astor, Nancy. 1923. *My Two Countries.* London: W. Heinemann.

Banks, Olive. 1990. [1981.] *Faces of Feminism: A Study of Feminism as a Social Movement.* Reprint, Oxford: Blackwell.

Collis, Maurice. 1960. *Nancy Astor: An Informal Biography.* London: Faber and Faber.

Fox, James. 2000. *Five Sisters: The Langhorne Sisters of Virginia.* New York: Simon and Schuster.

Harrison, Brian. 1987. *Prudent Revolutionaries: Portraits of British Feminists between the Wars.* Oxford: Clarendon Press.

Masters, A. 1981. *Nancy Astor: A Biography.* New York: McGraw Hill.

Pugh, Martin. 2000. *Women and the Women's Movement in Britain 1914–1999.* 2d ed. Basingstoke: Macmillan.

Stocks, Mary. 1970. *My Commonplace Book.* London: Peter Davies.

Strachey, Ray. 1978 [1928]. *The Cause: A Brief History of the Women's Movement.* Reprint, London: Virago.

Sykes, Christopher. 1972. *Nancy: The Life of Lady Astor.* London: Collins.

Auclert, Hubertine
(1848–1914)
France/Algeria

It was the belief of the radical feminist and pacifist Hubertine Auclert, who revived and led the French suffrage movement in the formative phase of the French Third Republic from 1871, that women were a natural force for good in society. Their emancipation, which would make them equal partners with men in the civil, political, and economic spheres, combined with the proper support of mothers and children by the state would, in her view, provide the impetus to peaceful social change. For forty years she dedicated herself to the cause of women's suffrage.

Auclert was rebellious from an early age. Born in Allier as one of seven children, she turned her back on her conventional convent education and overcame her natural shyness to move to Paris in 1872 to work for women's rights. She later recalled: "I became a crusader, not by choice, but from duty . . . and went to war like a medieval knight" (Moses 1984, 213). She took a job as secretary on the newspaper *The Future of Women* (founded as *Women's Rights* by Léon Richer in 1869 and run by Marie Deraismes), which provided a forum for campaigns for women's education and admittance to the professions, revision of the civil code, and improved wages and property rights for women. She also produced her own pamphlets, *The Political Rights of Women* (1878) and *Social and Political Equality* (1879), arguing for women's property rights, their right to retain their maiden names, and other issues.

For a while, Auclert was active in Richer and Deraismes's group, the Association for the Rights of Women, but in 1876 she split with them because they would not commit to working specifically for women's suffrage, but supported a gradualist approach to the achievement of women's political rights. As a militant, Auclert could not agree with republican feminists such as Deraismes that women's suffrage must wait until women were more politically enlightened and less inclined to support a return of the monarchy.

Refused permission by Deraismes and Richer to make a speech on women's suffrage at the first international congress on women's rights organized by them in France in 1878, Auclert gave it the following year as a delegate to the founding congress of the French Workers Party, held in Marseilles. On this occasion, she obtained support from male activists in framing resolutions on women's political and civil equality. But although she founded the Paris branch of the Federation of the Socialist Workers' Party of France, her involvement with socialism was brief.

It is thought that Auclert was one of the first women to use the term *féministe*. Her new feminist group Women's Rights, established in 1876, had as its motto "No duties without rights; no rights without duties," and its objective was absolute equality for women with men in all spheres. The group issued an "Appeal to the Women of France" (1876), in which it challenged

Hubertine Auclert (Historical Library of the City of Paris)

the double legal standard that treated women as an incompetent subspecies of humanity, yet punished them just as severely as men. The group also questioned why women were obliged to pay the same taxes as men when they had no say in the country's financial affairs.

In 1880 Auclert tried to register to vote. When she was denied this right, she refused to pay her taxes, only to have her furniture seized. Throughout the decade she repeatedly petitioned the French government on women's rights. In 1881 she cofounded one of the most influential French feminist journals, the *Female Citizen (La Citoyenne),* which featured her polemical articles and was the rallying cry of French suffragists until it was closed down in 1891. She then wrote for the *Woman's Journal* from 1891 to 1916 and also became a regular contributor to Marguerite Durand's feminist newspaper the *Sling (La Fronde),* as well as the *Radical* and *Free Speech.*

Meanwhile, a divide had opened up between militants such as Auclert, who demanded political rights with suffrage paramount among them, and liberal, republican feminists such as Marie Deraismes, who called for a broader base of civil and political rights. In 1883, having become dissatisfied with Deraismes's lack of clear support for women's suffrage, Auclert renamed her Women's Rights group Women's Suffrage. It was the first women's organization in France specifically dedicated to this cause, as well as to reform of the divorce laws, equal pay for women, and women's entry into the professions. At this time Auclert also met in Liverpool with U.S. suffragists Elizabeth Cady Stanton and Susan B. Anthony, establishing the beginning of an international movement for the vote.

In 1885, although they were legally excluded from doing so, Auclert tested the water by joining with fourteen other women to put themselves forward as parliamentary candidates in elections. She proposed that a nurturing "mother's state" be established, in opposition to what she saw as the "Minotaur state" (a monster that devoured people), and although the attempt failed, she stood for election again in 1910.

In 1888 Auclert married Anton Levrier and

went to live in Algeria, where she studied the lives of women and in particular the imposition of French culture on Islamic Algerian women, publishing the results of her research as *Arab Women in Algeria* in 1900. When her husband died in 1892, Auclert returned to Paris only to find that after so many years away she had lost her position in the suffrage movement. Her following had been greatly reduced to a closely knit core of twenty women, and her paper, the *Female Citizen,* had been closed down.

With the French feminist movement now disintegrating as a result of increasing discord between middle-class, conservative feminists—who placed nationalism and religion ahead of women's rights—and radical socialist women, a disillusioned Auclert withdrew to concentrate on writing, contributing to the journal the *Radical* from 1896. But her built-in defiance of the French patriarchy led once again to a rebellion against taxation. She protested that if both men and women should have to pay taxes, why then was it that only men could vote? She tried to hold out against the treasury but was taken to court and forced to capitulate. In 1899 she suggested that maternity allowances should be funded by making men pay a paternal tax. In 1904 Auclert was still campaigning: now influenced by suffragette militancy in England, she ritually burned a copy of the civil code in a public act of defiance and in 1908 smashed a ballot box as a symbolic act of protest during municipal elections in Paris.

In 1903 Auclert revived the idea of state maternity allowances again, arguing that mothers should be recognized as fulfilling a valuable social function and should therefore be reimbursed for their labor by the state. She shared the belief of many feminists around the world that women were a power for good, were men's moral superiors, and were better equipped to rebuild society. As war approached, she became increasingly alarmed at escalating European militarism, which she looked upon as a peculiarly male folly. Such aggressive behavior, she felt, began with men's domination over women in the home, and children carried this behavior into public life. She became a major French peace campaigner, linking her fight for women's suffrage to a fundamental belief that enduring, international peace would only be achieved after women had won their political rights. She expanded on her pacifism in her history of suffrage, *Women's Vote* (1908), and a collection of her essays on suffrage, *Women at the Helm* (published posthumously in 1923).

See also Deraismes, Maria.
References and Further Reading
Bidelman, Patrick Kay. 1982. *Pariahs Stand Up! The Founding of the Liberal Feminist Movement in France 1858–1889.* Westport, CT: Greenwood Press.

Hause, Steven C. 1987. *Hubertine Auclert: The French Suffragette.* New Haven: Yale University Press.

Josephson, Harold, Sandi Cooper, and Steven C. Hause, eds. 1985. *Biographical Dictionary of Modern Peace Leaders.* Westport, CT: Greenwood Press.

Moses, C. 1984. *French Feminism in the Nineteenth Century.* Albany: State University of New York Press.

Offen, Karen. 2000. *European Feminisms 1700–1950: A Political History.* Palo Alto: Stanford University Press.

Sowerwine, Charles. 1982. *Sisters or Citizens? Women and Socialism in France since 1876.* Cambridge: Cambridge University Press.

Augspurg, Anita
(1857–1943)
Germany

A radical feminist and founder in 1902 of the first overtly political women's organization, the German Association for Women's Suffrage, Augspurg mounted an important campaign against the civil code in 1895–1896 and became a respected figure in the International Woman Suffrage Alliance and pacifist movement.

Born in Verden an der Aller, Augspurg came from a literary family and trained as a teacher. She pursued brief careers as an actress and as a photographer, running the Atelier Elvira photography studio in Munich before finally, as a result of her growing interest in women's rights, studying law in Zurich (1893–1897). She would later become the first woman judge in Germany. In Zurich she associated with many women forced to seek further education outside their home countries, where women's entrance to university was proscribed, and took part in the European feminist campaign against state-regulated prostitution.

In 1895 after becoming leader, with Marie Stritt and Minna Cauer, of the Federation of German Women's Associations, which had been set up in Berlin in 1894, she helped coordinate a campaign calling for changes to the German civil code. Becoming increasingly radical in her objectives, Augspurg split with moderates in the federation in 1898 and a year later, with Minna Cauer, founded the Union of Progressive Women's Associations, which had launched a campaign for women's suffrage. But it was not until 1902 that a formal women's suffrage organization was established, when Augspurg joined Cauer, Stritt, and Lida Gustava Heymann in founding the German Union for Women's Suffrage in Hamburg, the only city where the ban on women's political activities did not apply. Augspurg was elected president and, with her training as an actress, became an accomplished public speaker. She laid out three objectives for the movement: those women who already had a limited form of the vote elsewhere in Germany should be encouraged to use it; male political candidates who favored women's suffrage should be supported in elections; and women must be educated politically in the proper use of the vote.

In 1899, as a delegate to the International Council of Women's conference in London, Augspurg and her long-standing associate Heymann (with whom she worked for forty years and with whom she lived, for the most part, on a farm in Bavaria outside Munich) had mooted the idea of an international suffrage organization. In 1903 the union joined the Federation of German Women's Associations, and the following year Augspurg represented it at a seven-nation meeting held in Washington, D.C., that established the International Woman Suffrage Alliance. In the Reichstag elections in 1904 she advocated that the union canvass on behalf of the Liberal People's Party in return for its formal support for suffrage, but when its candidate was not elected, the party failed to incorporate women's suffrage into its program. Augspurg was bitterly disillusioned during 1907 to 1908, when left-wing liberals who had promised support for suffrage joined with the conservatives and national liberals. Determined never again to work with "men's parties," she turned to more militant activities led by women for women, but it was an uphill battle, for by now the suffrage movement was becoming increasingly polarized between socialist radicals and the right wing. Augspurg decided to focus instead on the international suffrage movement. In 1908 she extended her contacts with European suffragists, leading a delegation of thirty German

women at a huge suffrage demonstration in Hyde Park, London. Inspired by Emmeline Pankhurst's militant Women's Social and Political Union (WSPU), Augspurg and Heymann adopted the WSPU's colors—green, purple, and white—and moved to Munich, where they spearheaded the German militant suffrage movement.

Augspurg split from the German Union for Women's Suffrage in 1911, when she refused to take her seat in the general assembly under its new president Marie Stritt because Stritt opposed Augspurg's support of universal (rather than just women's) suffrage. Augspurg joined Heymann and Cauer in decamping to set up in 1913 the more radical German Women's Suffrage Association, with Augspurg as president, which advocated universal suffrage and aspects of moral reform. By the outbreak of war in 1914, the suffrage movement in Germany had been reduced to factional infighting, and with the conservative mainstream now supporting German militarism, Augspurg turned her energies to pacifism. She had attended a conference on disarmament initiated by Tsar Nicholas II, held in The Hague in 1899, after which she returned home to organize German women pacifists. At the inaugural peace congress held by women pacifists in The Hague in April 1915, which had been planned by Augspurg and Aletta Jacobs of the Netherlands, Augspurg led a German delegation that on its return to Germany founded the German Women's Committee for Permanent Peace. The organization, although loosely structured and run on donations, was harassed by the military police and repressed. The committee was linked to the international organization of the same name, which soon after became known as the Women's International League (and in 1919 changed its name to the Women's International League for Peace and Freedom). Augspurg remained active until its German branch was dissolved by Adolf Hitler in 1933.

After women's suffrage was achieved in 1918, Augspurg continued to work for civil rights. She stood unsuccessfully for the National Assembly in 1919 and wrote regularly for the leading pacifist women's journal, *Woman in the State* (1919–1932), in it voicing her concerns at the heavy war reparations levied against Germany under the terms of the Versailles Treaty of 1919. Later, in 1923, she supported passive resistance against French reparations in the mining district of the Ruhr and urged reconciliation between the two countries. Augspurg was on holiday in Italy when the Nazis seized power in 1933. She went into exile in Switzerland, where she lived with Heymann and other German political exiles in Geneva, who cowrote with her their memoirs, *Erlebtes-Erschautes* (which can be approximately translated as "Experienced and Seen"), published posthumously in Germany in 1972.

See also Cauer, Minna; Heymann, Lida Gustava; Jacobs, Aletta; Pankhurst, Emmeline; Stritt, Marie.

References and Further Reading

Braker, Regina. 1995. "Bertha von Suttner's Spiritual Daughters: The Feminist Pacifism of Anita Augspurg, Lida Gustava Heymann, and Helene Stöcker at the International Congress of Women at the Hague, 1915." *Women's Studies International Forum* 18(2): 103–111.

Evans, Richard. 1973. *The Feminist Movement in Germany 1894–1933*. London: Sage.

Josephson, Harold, Sandi Cooper, and Steven C. Hause et al., eds. 1985. *Biographical Dictionary of Modern Peace Leaders*. Westport, CT: Greenwood Press.

Sklar, Kathryn Kish. 1998. *Social Justice Feminists in the United States and Germany: A Dialogue in Documents 1885–1933*. Ithaca: Cornell University Press.

Aung San Suu Kyi
(1945–)
Burma (official name, Myanmar)

For long an exile from her home country, in 1988 Aung San Suu Kyi, who had married and settled in England, returned to Burma to find herself drawn into the growing pro-democracy movement that was sweeping the country. As the daughter of Aung San, leader of the Burmese independence movement of the 1940s who was assassinated in 1947, Aung San Suu Kyi decided to stay and join the struggle against the twenty-six-year dictatorship of General Ne Win. Her long fight to uphold civil rights and see democracy established in Burma seemed only natural for someone of her upbringing: at a rally on 26 August 1988 she averred that as her father's daughter she could not remain indifferent. The pacifist policy of civil disobedience that she adopted, guided by patience and an emphasis on dialogue, was inspired by the campaigns of Mahatma Gandhi and Martin Luther King, Jr.

Aung was born and educated in Rangoon. In 1960, when her mother was appointed Burmese ambassador to India, she accompanied her there and studied politics at Delhi University. She took a B.A. in philosophy, politics, and economics at St. Hugh's College, Oxford, and thereafter (1969–1971) worked as assistant secretary to the Advisory Committee on Administrative and Budgetary Questions at the United Nations Secretariat in New York. While working as a research officer in Bhutan, in 1972 she met and married British Tibetan scholar Michael Aris, who had been appointed private tutor to the royal family there. After the birth of her two sons, Aung spent time in Japan as a visiting scholar at the Center for Southeast Asian Studies at Kyoto University and in Simla, India, in 1986 as a researcher for the Indian Institute of Advanced Study.

Upon her return to Burma in 1988, Aung gave a speech calling for democratic government to 500,000 people at a rally at the Shwedagon Pagoda in Rangoon. In September 1988 Ne Win resigned the chairmanship of the Burma Socialist Program Party and allowed a military junta to take over the government (the State Law and Order Restoration Council), which in the wake of a national uprising immediately clamped down on civil rights and instituted martial law; thousands of people were killed. The junta did, however, announce free elections for the following spring. In anticipation, Aung and several other activists founded the National League for Democracy (NLD) on 27 September 1988 and during the next few months addressed numerous public rallies throughout Burma. But democratic activists were soon subjected to brutal police harassment, and on 20 July 1989 Aung was put under house arrest. Soon after her case was taken up by Amnesty International, which designated her a prisoner of conscience.

Despite the huge success of the NLD in the subsequent elections in May 1990, in which it won 82 percent of the seats, the junta refused to recognize this victory and imprisoned many members of parliament. For six years, Aung remained under house arrest, separated from her husband and sons. By the time of her release on 11 July 1995, she had become a heroic symbol of the right to democratic freedom, a defender of political integrity, and an upholder of human rights.

Aung became the focus of her country's pro-democracy movement, and her home was vener-

Aung San Suu Kyi (center; Reuters/Jonathan Karp/Archive Photos)

ated as a shrine. She was accorded many prestigious awards and honorary doctorates, including in 1990 the Thorolf Rafto Prize for Human Rights and the Sakharov Prize for Freedom of Thought. In 1991 changes to the law allowed the military junta to hold her for up to five years without charge or trial. In response, Aung was given the highest accolade—the 1991 Nobel Peace Prize—to "show the Nobel Committee's support for the many people throughout the world who are striving to attain democracy, human rights and ethnic conciliation by peaceful means." Aung used the prize money to set up a health and education trust for Burmese people. Other subsequent honors included the Victor Jara International Human Rights Award in 1993; the Jawaharlal Nehru Award for International Understanding in 1995; the W. Averell Harriman Democracy Award; and the highest honors from Cambridge, Oxford, and other universities. In 1994 her period of detention was extended to six years. After meeting with members of the junta, Aung was finally released from house arrest on 11 July 1995.

Tight controls were maintained on Aung's movements once she was freed: she was still subjected to round-the-clock surveillance, her movements were strictly limited, her mail was censored and much of it destroyed before it reached her, and her visitors were closely scrutinized. Throughout the dark years of her incarceration in her crumbling colonial villa, Aung's writings, such as *Freedom from Fear* (1999), which introduced her pacifist and Buddhist approach to resolving conflict to Western readers, were published abroad. Human rights campaigners and other Nobel laureates regularly supported her call for democratic reform. From England, her husband and sons lent unfailing moral support; but the Burmese authorities refused to grant Aris a visa to visit his wife after 1995. Sadly, he died of cancer in 1999 with Aung 5,000 miles away. She had been offered the chance to leave Burma to visit her family on several occasions but had refused this offer even when her husband was dying, knowing she would never be allowed to return to Burma. The National League for Democracy, although legally recognized by the regime, is still harassed by the authorities, who refuse to acknowledge Aung's political power, knowing full well that her free exercise of it would bring a landslide victory to the NLD.

Known simply as "the Lady" among Burmese, Aung's spirits have been kept going by her passionate sense of justice coupled with a deep spirituality and compassion. Through her work for the NLD, she has advocated wide-reaching economic and social reforms, improvements to health care and education, and the care of children of political prisoners. She has drawn attention to corruption in the government, which is selling off Burma's natural resources to foreign investors, laundering money and appropriating humanitarian aid, as well as turning a blind eye toward the escalating drug trade. Through Amnesty International, she has also alerted the world to the government's treatment of political prisoners and abuses of human rights, such as the 1998 persecution of people with human immunodeficiency virus (HIV) by the military junta. But in everything Aung's overriding commitment has been to nonviolence, buoyed up by her Buddhist beliefs that emphasize a "revolution of the spirit." As she says: "It is not power that corrupts but fear. Fear of losing power corrupts those who wield it and fear of the scourge of power corrupts those who are subject to it. . . . Truth, justice, and compassion cannot be dismissed as trite when these are often the only bulwarks against ruthless power" (1991, 180, 185). A website about Aung San Suu Kyi can be found at http://www.dassk.com.

References and Further Reading

Aung San Suu Ki. 1991. *Freedom from Fear and Other Writings.* London: Penguin.
———. 1997. *The Voice of Hope: Conversations with Alan Clements.* London: Penguin.
Ling, Bettina. 1999. *Aung San Suu Kyi: Standing Up for Democracy in Burma.* New York: Feminist Press.
Victor, Barbara. 1998. *The Lady: Aung San Suu Kyi, Nobel Laureate and Burma's Prisoner.* Boston: Faber and Faber.

Azmudeh, Tuba
(1878–1936)
Iran

A pioneer educator, Azmudeh was married at the age of fourteen to an army officer who was much older than she was. Fortunately, her husband allowed her to improve herself through private study and hired tutors to help her with Persian, Arabic, and French. As a result of her reading at home, Azmudeh developed a thirst for learning that impelled her to make it more accessible to other young women.

In 1907 a meeting held by women in Tehran had initiated lobbying for more girls' schools, and had called for the dowry system to be abolished, in order that the money might be better spent on educating young women. In the face of much local prejudice and hostility, Azmudeh set up a school for twenty girls, known as the Namus school, in her own home in Tehran. She was accused of immorality in doing so, and her pupils were criticized for breaching conventional social practice and for seeking education outside the seclusion of their own homes. Therefore it is a considerable achievement that Azmudeh's school continued to grow and even to expand its curriculum. She was able to enlist the teaching help of scholarly friends of her husband. Such was the eventual prestige of her school that it attracted the daughters of other progressive Iranians who believed, as did Azmudeh, that women's education was an integral part of Islamic faith, and not contradictory to its teachings.

Azmudeh inspired many other female educators to follow her example in Iran, and several of her pupils went on to train as much-needed female secondary school teachers. She also extended her activities to offer adult literacy classes for women, but the texts used for these courses were generally limited to the Qu'ran and other religious writings.

References and Further Reading

Very little has been written in English, and only in passing, about Azmudeh's work or the details of her life.

B

Bajer, Mathilde
(1840–1934)
Denmark

With her husband, the Danish reformer and Nobel Peace Prize winner Fredrik, the feminist and
suffragist Mathilde Bajer founded the Danish
Women's Association (DWA) in 1871, inspired in
part by publication in Danish of John Stuart
Mill's classic treatise, *The Subjection of Women*
(1869). Although Fredrik Bajer won a considerable reputation for himself, the work of his wife
has barely been recorded—or at least in English.
Like so many other loyal female supporters of
more eminent male partners, it is likely that
Mathilde's activism nurtured much of Fredrik's
own feminist sympathies. It is also said that she
did much of the work in typing up the writings
on pacifism that earned Bajer the Nobel Peace
Prize in 1908.

A brief mention of Bajer in the standard Danish national biography tells us that she was born
in Herlufmagle parish, in the Praesto district
southwest of Copenhagen, the daughter of an estate owner and that she married Bajer in 1867.
Sharing an interest in women's equality, they began contacting Swedish campaigners for
women's rights in the late 1860s. Before the Bajers took up the cause of women, the sole discussion of women's rights in Denmark had appeared in *Clara Raphael: Twelve Letters,* an 1850
work published anonymously by Mathilde
Fibiger, which in its plaintive call for women to
be allowed an intellectual life outside the narrow
confines of the family prompted considerable
debate in Denmark.

In April 1871 the Bajers founded a Danish
branch of the International Association of
Women that had been founded in Geneva in
1868 to work for peace; for women's moral and
intellectual advancement; and for their civil, economic, social, and political rights, and which was
now led by Marie Goegg. Mathilde Bajer was
elected chair of the Danish wing, but this attempt at establishing wider links in the European
women's movement appears to have failed, and
in December 1871 the International Association
of Women disintegrated in the wake of the
Franco-Prussian War and the Paris Commune.
The Bajers therefore founded a Danish Women's
Association (DWA) to replace the defunct IAW.
Fredrik was a committed pacifist, who believed
that if women were politically and educationally
emancipated they could be a greater force for
peace and a more moral society. He therefore
also established a feminist library and the
Women's Reading Society that same year, although it was made use of only by a small number of unmarried middle-class women.

Moderate in its objectives, the DWA campaigned initially on mainly economic issues, calling for married women's financial independence
and the expansion of women's employment opportunities; from 1885 it published its own magazine, *Women and Society* (edited by Elisabeth
Grundtvig). In 1872 the Bajers opened a
women's trade school in Copenhagen under the
auspices of the DWA. During the 1880s, with a
change of government bringing in a socialist-lib-
eral alliance better disposed to reform, they
worked together in the social purity movement
and the campaign against state-regulated prostitution through the Copenhagen branch of the
International Abolitionist Federation.

Within four years of the establishment of the
DWA, Mathilde Bajer had become leader of a minority who felt that women's suffrage was not
being given a high enough profile and that other

reforms affecting women's lives would not be achieved unless women first obtained the vote. Things came to a head in the DWA in the mid-1880s when internal debate on women's sexual freedom and the sexual double standard, in Bajer's view, seemed to be diverting attention away from the suffrage issue. In 1886 she broke away to found the Danish Women's Progress Association (DWPA), which included in its program pacifist and labor issues. Between 1888 and 1894 Bajer edited and occasionally contributed to the DWPA's journal, *What We Want.* Meanwhile, another breakaway group from the DWA founded the Danish Women's Suffrage Society in 1888.

In 1887 Fredrik Bajer, by then a member of Parliament, introduced a motion to grant women the vote in local elections. Its rejection galvanized women into radicalizing their campaign, during which time the moderate Danish Women's Association assumed center stage and eventually, in 1897, absorbed the Danish Women's Suffrage Society. At around the same date, Bajer's DWPA disintegrated through internal differences and was reabsorbed into the DWA, with Bajer heading its Copenhagen branch. Meanwhile, the radical element in the DWA left in 1898 to set up a Danish Women's Association's Suffrage Federation (DWASF) that collaborated with the Danish Liberal Party and concentrated on the fight for women's suffrage at the municipal level. In 1900 radical suffragists, discontented with all existing parties, founded the National League for Women's Suffrage (NLWS). Thus by 1910 three major suffrage organizations were vying for support: the NLWS, the DWASF, and the original moderate society, the DWA, which had the smallest number of members. Bajer remained in the left wing of the Danish women's movement to see women win full suffrage in 1915. She was elected an honorary member of the DWA and continued to address women's issues into her old age, becoming involved in international feminist organizations and in furthering the pacifist work of her husband.

References and Further Reading

Evans, Richard J. 1977. *The Feminists: Women's Emancipation Movements in Europe, America, and Australasia 1840–1920.* London: Croom Helm.

Baker, Ella
(1903–1986)
United States

The black civil rights leader and community organizer Ella Baker favored decentralization of the civil rights movement and its expansion among the young at the grassroots level. Having been a founder of the Southern Christian Leadership Conference, she supported the development of a separate, autonomous, student-led civil rights movement, the Student Nonviolent Coordinating Committee (SNCC).

Baker was born in Norfolk, Virginia, and grew up in North Carolina in a close, supportive family, receiving much inspiration from her grandparents who had been slaves. In 1918 she went as a boarder to a high school in Raleigh and graduated from Shaw University there in 1927. Soon after, she settled in New York, where she worked in community relations in Harlem while completing additional studies in sociology at the New School for Social Research. In 1932 she co-founded the Young Negroes Cooperative League with writer George Schuyler to help buy and distribute food to poor black families, and in 1931 became its national director. During the Depression in the 1930s, Baker took up journalism, writing for the *Negro National News* and the *American West Indian News* and in 1935 publishing an exposé in the National Association for the Advancement of Colored People (NAACP) journal *Crisis* on the exploitation of black domestic workers. She also worked on literacy projects and lectured on consumer affairs for the Workers Education Project of the Works Progress Administration and associated with women's groups such as the Harlem Housewives Co-operative, the Harlem Young Women's Christian Association (YWCA), and the Women's Day Workers. From her association with radical trade unionists, Baker became increasingly politicized, but from the outset she was determined that women's work for racial equality and civil rights should be fully integrated into national movements, and this was a principle to which she would closely adhere throughout her career as an activist.

In 1940 Baker was appointed a field secretary of the NAACP, traveling widely in the South to establish a network of branches there, train new leaders, and recruit wider support. By 1943 she had been promoted to the position of national

Ella Baker (Library of Congress)

the increasing activism of black students that was springing up throughout the South, Baker called a conference at her old university in Raleigh, North Carolina, at which she and student leaders set up SNCC. Its prime objective was to encourage an autonomous and egalitarian protest movement that would link student civil rights groups and extend their activities beyond lunch counter sit-ins. Baker was nominated as executive secretary of SNCC, which launched a wide range of sit-ins and boycotts across the South. In 1960, she left the SCLC to work for the YWCA at a regional office in Atlanta.

Baker also continued to encourage blacks in the South to utilize their vote. After having successfully led a campaign to get as many blacks as possible to register to vote—the Crusade for Citizenship of 1958—she was a founder of the Mississippi Freedom Democratic Party in 1964, which attempted to break the exclusively white control of the Democratic Party in the South and in particular challenged the segregationist policies of the Mississippi delegation to the Democratic National Convention.

During the remainder of her career, Baker served in many civil rights, women's, and youth organizations as an adviser and continued to draw attention to the considerable and often underrated contribution of women to the movement. She also continued her support for the desegregation of education through her work for the Southern Conference Educational Fund. After returning to New York in 1964, she endorsed the independence movements in South Africa and Zimbabwe. A self-effacing figure, in her lifetime Baker deliberately chose not to attract attention to her own personal contribution, and as a result her organizing skills and her dedication have not always been adequately credited.

director. As president of the NAACP's New York branch, she also led the fight against the unofficial segregation operating in the city's public schools, in 1957 establishing Parents in Action for Quality Education.

In 1956 Baker cofounded In Friendship, a society dedicated to helping the growing civil rights movement and desegregation of the schools in the South. After In Friendship's help in sponsoring the bus boycott in Montgomery, Alabama, had proved the effectiveness of nonviolent protest against segregation in the South, Baker realized that this area was where her work could be most effective. She was a prime mover in the organization of the Southern Christian Leadership Conference (SCLC) in 1957, soon after moving to Atlanta to serve as executive secretary under the leadership of Martin Luther King, Jr.

But by 1960 Baker had come into open disagreement with SCLC leaders over their emphasis on a centralized leadership that relied heavily on King's charisma and did not sufficiently involve the young or give proper accreditation to women activists. In April 1960, keen to promote

References and Further Reading

The Annual Obituary. 1986. New York: St. Martin's Press.

Cantarow, Ellen, et al. 1980. *Moving the Mountain: Women Working for Social Change.* Old Westbury, NY: Feminist Press.

Carson, Clayborn. 1981. *In Struggle: SNCC and the Black Awakening of the 1960s.* Cambridge, MA: Harvard University Press.

Crawford, Vicki L., Jacqueline Anne Rouse, and Barbara Woods, eds. 1990. *Women in the Civil Rights Movement: Trailblazers and Torchbearers.* Brooklyn: Carlson Publishing.

Dallard, Shyrlee. 1990. *Ella Baker: A Leader behind the Scenes*. Englewood Cliffs, NJ: Silver Burdett Press.

Grant, Joanne. 1998. *Freedom Bound*. New York: Wiley.

Hine, Darlene Clarke, et al., eds. 1993. *Black Women in America: An Historical Encyclopedia*. 2 vols. Bloomington: Indiana University Press.

McGuire, William, and Leslie Wheeler, eds. 1993. *American Social Leaders: From Colonial Times to the Present*. Santa Barbara: ABC-CLIO.

Morris, Aldon D. 1984. *The Origins of the Civil Rights Movement*. New York: Free Press.

Payne, Charles. 1989. "Ella Baker and Models of Social Change." *Signs* 14(4): 885–889.

Smith, Jessie Carney, ed. 1992. *Notable Black American Women*. Detroit: Gale.

Baker, (Sara) Josephine
(1873–1945)
United States

The American doctor and public-health administrator initiated groundbreaking work in child care among the immigrant communities of New York that led to a marked drop in infant mortality rates. Baker also set up agencies for fostering abandoned children and was active in the women's suffrage movement.

Born in Poughkeepsie, New York, Baker had hoped to study at Vassar College, but after the death of her father had brought financial difficulties upon the family, she trained as a doctor at the Women's Medical College of the New York Infirmary in 1894–1898. Having established herself in private practice in New York City, Baker quickly found this work did not pay, and in 1901 she took a post as a medical inspector and later (1907) as assistant to the commissioner of the Department of Public Health of New York City. In this capacity, she monitored public health among the immigrant communities of Lower East Side's "Hell's Kitchen." Alarmed at the high rates of infant mortality, particularly among Italian families, that she and a team of nurses found in 1908, Baker founded the first American health agency of its kind to be funded by taxation, the Division (later Bureau) of Child Hygiene within the U.S. Health Department. Baker was gratified to see that her guidelines on child care rapidly led to a fall in the death rate among infants on the East Side. Indeed, so significant would be her successes at combating infant deaths that by

1923 the rate for New York had become not only the lowest in the United States but also lower than that in many European cities.

In their work for the Bureau of Child Hygiene, Baker and her team of nurses set standards of infant health care by introducing registered midwives and well-baby clinics that offered advice on hygiene and medical care and offered free baby milk. They encouraged mothers to breastfeed rather than to give their babies unsafe cow's milk (which in those days was not pasteurized) and taught them the use of silver nitrate as a medication to prevent blindness in new babies. Monitoring of babies and children for infectious diseases such as diphtheria was introduced, and a widening of public awareness on the issues of baby care was promoted through Baker's organization of the Little Mothers' Leagues and, in 1911, the Children's Welfare Federation (for which she worked until 1917). By 1913 Baker had given up her own medical practice as the demands upon her expertise increased. From 1916 to 1931, she gave annual lectures on child hygiene to students at the Bellevue Hospital Medical School in New York and was closely involved in the American Child Hygiene Association from 1909 to 1918. She backed up her work in public health with numerous pamphlets and articles on child care, including *The Growing Child* in 1923 and *Child Hygiene* in 1925.

Baker retired from her directorship of the Bureau of Child Hygiene in 1923 but remained active on many medical committees. In 1935–1936 she was president of the American Medical Women's Association. She had also been active in the women's suffrage movement as a founding member of the College Women's Equal Suffrage League from 1908. The league, led by Baker, lobbied for New York University to admit women to postgraduate studies, and she had made a personal stand on this issue by declining the offer of a lectureship at the university, prompting it to later revise its policy.

References and Further Reading
Adickes, Sandra. 1997. *To Be Young Was Very Heaven: Women in New York before the Great War*. Basingstoke: Macmillan.

Baker, Sara Josephine. 1939. *Fighting for Life*. New York: Macmillan.

Dictionary of American Biography 1946–1958, and indexes to Supplements 1–10, 1981–1996. New York: Scribner's.

Penguin Biographical Dictionary of Women. 1998.
    Harmondsworth: Penguin.
Sicherman, Barbara, and Carol Hurd Green, eds.
    1980. *Notable American Women 1607–1950: A Bio-
    graphical Dictionary,* vol. 4, *The Modern Period.*
    Cambridge, MA: Belknap Press of Harvard Uni-
    versity.
Whitman, Alden, ed. 1988. *American Reformers: An
    H. W. Wilson Biographical Dictionary.* New York:
    H. W. Wilson.

Balch, Emily Greene
(1867–1961)
United States

The Quaker pacifist, economist, and educator
Emily Greene Balch was a disciple of Jane Addams. Fifteen years after Addams received the
Nobel Peace Prize, Balch herself became a recipient in 1946, in recognition not just of her work
as one of the pacifist movement's outstanding
intellectual leaders, but also for the great compassion and understanding she demonstrated for
Slavic immigrants to the United States.

Born in Jamaica Plain, Massachusetts, the
daughter of a Unitarian lawyer, Balch was in the
first group of women students to be educated at
Bryn Mawr College, graduating in 1889. She
spent two years in Paris on a European Fellowship (1890–1891), studying social science and
economics at the Sorbonne. Her study of official
French measures to combat poverty was published as *Public Assistance of the Poor in France*
(1893).

Wishing to commit herself to social work on
her return to the United States, Balch worked for
the Boston Children's Aid Society. Influenced by
the work of Jane Addams at Hull House in
Chicago, she joined with others in establishing a
similar venture, Denison House, in Boston in
1892–1893. She also joined the Federal Labor
Union in 1893 and supported working women in
Boston as a cofounder of its branch of the
Women's Trade Union League in 1903. During
1908–1909 Balch was a member of the Massachusetts Commission on Industrial Relations
and played an important role in drafting a minimum wage bill as chair of the Massachusetts
Minimum Wage Commission in 1913.

Meanwhile, Balch had become quickly dissatisfied with the limitations of her reformist work
and decided that social causes could better be
promoted through education. She pursued further studies in economics at the Harvard Annex,
the University of Chicago, and the University of
Berlin. Completing these degrees in 1896, Balch
became a lecturer in economics and political science at Wellesley College, and in 1913 she was
promoted to head of the departments of economics and sociology. Here her lectures on
Marxism, immigration, and the contribution of
women to the economy inspired lively discussion
and a new generation of women social activists.

The other primary arena of social concern for
Balch was immigration. In 1904–1906 she made
an extensive study of Slavic immigrant communities in the United States and their countries of
origin and published a compassionate account in
Our Slavic Fellow-Citizens in 1910 that sought to
erode traditional prejudices toward immigrant
groups. In 1913–1914 she served on the Massachusetts Commission on Immigration.

Balch established a close relationship with the
pacifist leader Jane Addams during World War I,
when together they helped to set up the international conference of women held in The Hague
in 1915, at which they were both founding members of the International Committee of Women
for Permanent Peace. With Alice Hamilton and
Jane Addams, Balch published a report on the
conference, entitled *Women at The Hague,* also in
1915. In the summer, on their return to the
United States, Balch and Addams founded the
Woman's Peace Party and lobbied President
Woodrow Wilson to join in attempts at mediation in the war. When he declined, they approached Henry Ford for support. When Ford
subsequently chartered a "peace ship," Balch was
one of several U.S. pacifists who sailed on it to a
conference of neutral nations held in Stockholm,
Sweden, and from there she went on a peace mission to Russia and other parts of Scandinavia.
Balch's support for conscientious objectors, her
pacifist writings in the *Nation,* and her opposition to U.S. entry into the war attracted much
suspicion and vilification for her perceived lack
of patriotism and her left-wing sympathies. At
the end of the war in 1918, the loss of her job at
Wellesley College (a direct result of her pacifism)
propelled Balch into wider activities for the
peace movement and support for organizations
such as the Fellowship of Reconciliation, the War
Resisters' International, and the League of Nations. In 1919 she attended the first postwar con-

ference of the International Committee of Women for Permanent Peace in Zurich, at which she was elected secretary-treasurer of the newly named Women's International League for Peace and Freedom (WILPF), a post that took her to Geneva for several years.

In 1925, with the backing of President Herbert Hoover, Balch took part in a WILPF fact-finding mission in Haiti. Since 1915 the country had been occupied by U.S. Marines, mainly in order to protect U.S. investments there. During a two-week fact-finding mission, Balch gathered information on the social, political, and economic state of the island, which she published with others in 1927 under the title *Occupied Haiti*. By drawing attention to the twelve-year occupation of the island, Balch is thought to have contributed to the withdrawal of troops in 1934, although the United States retained financial control there until 1947.

In 1921 Balch converted to Quakerism and continued to work closely with Jane Addams, another Quaker deeply committed to world peace. In 1927 they collaborated on a pamphlet analyzing war, entitled "What Concern Has America with World Peace? The Hopes We Inherit," which had at its moral root their Quaker beliefs.

Throughout the 1930s Balch defended the rights of Europe's Jews, who were coming under increasing racial persecution with the rise of the Nazis. She helped Jewish immigrants to settle in the United States, and in publications such as *Refugees as Assets* (1939) argued for a positive attitude toward their potential contribution to American society, citing the case of the Jews of New York's East Side, who had established a thriving garment industry. When war broke out in Europe in 1939, Balch felt compelled to contradict a lifetime's pacifism and her Quaker beliefs by supporting the Allies in what she saw as a necessary war against fascism.

After the war, Balch worked for postwar reconstruction, provided aid to refugees, and helped in the reintegration of Japanese Americans who had been interned. As a supporter of a gradualist approach to maintaining world peace and the breakdown of national boundaries, she advocated the establishment of nonpartisan international bodies, such as an international maritime body to control the world's waterways and the strengthening of the United Nations. In 1946 at the age of seventy-nine, Balch shared the No-

bel Peace Prize with Young Men's Christian Association leader John R. Mott and donated the money to the WILPF. In her many published works, she explored not only pacifism but racialism and anti-Semitism. Her Nobel speech, "Toward Human Unity or beyond Nationalism," was published as a book in 1952.

See also Addams, Jane; Hamilton, Alice.

References and Further Reading
Dictionary of American Biography 1946–1958, and indexes to Supplements 1–10, 1981–1996. New York: Scribner's.
Josephson, Harold, Sandi Cooper, and Steven C. Hause et al., eds. 1985. *Biographical Dictionary of Modern Peace Leaders.* Westport, CT: Greenwood Press.
McGuire, William, and Leslie Wheeler, eds. 1993. *American Social Leaders: From Colonial Times to the Present.* Santa Barbara: ABC-CLIO.
Palmieri, Patricia. 1995. *In Adamless Eden: The Community of Women Faculty at Wellesley.* New Haven, CT: Yale University Press.
Randall, Mercedes M. 1964. *Improper Bostonian: Emily Greene Balch.* New York: Twayne.
———, ed. 1972. *Beyond Nationalism: The Social Thought of Emily Greene Balch.* New York: Twayne.
Sicherman, Barbara, and Carol Hurd Green, eds. 1980. *Notable American Women 1607–1950: A Biographical Dictionary,* vol. 4, *The Modern Period.* Cambridge, MA: Belknap Press of Harvard University.
Whitman, Alden, ed. 1988. *American Reformers: An H. W. Wilson Biographical Dictionary.* New York: H. W. Wilson.

Bamber, Helen
(1925–)
United Kingdom

In her work, first with survivors of the Nazi concentration camps and later with the victims of extreme cruelty and torture, the British campaigner Helen Bamber has had many encounters with the unconscionable face of modern-day political repression around the world as director of the Medical Foundation for the Care of Victims of Torture. Born Helen Balmuth, the daughter of Polish-Jewish exiles and the granddaughter of a man who had espoused the anarchist ideas of Peter Kropotkin, Bamber grew up in a radical household in northeastern London dominated by her father's passionate commitment to human rights. During the 1930s, her father closely monitored the rise to power of Adolf Hitler and became increasingly obsessed with the inevitability of war, welcoming activists of all persuasions into his home. Bamber's own political activities began during the late 1930s, when she joined a group of teenage antifascists protesting the activities of Sir Oswald Mosley's British Union of Fascists.

During World War II, Bamber was evacuated to Suffolk and, after her return to London, volunteered for firewatch duty during bombing raids at the age of sixteen. Toward the end of the war, she took a job as secretary to a Harley Street doctor, where she responded to an advertisement calling for volunteers to help Jewish survivors of the Nazi concentration camps. In 1944 Bamber made her way across Europe to join the Jewish Relief Unit that was working in the British-occupied zone of Germany.

It proved the most sobering of undertakings for a young woman of only twenty when Bamber entered Belsen concentration camp in 1945 in one of the first relief teams. Having received a rudimentary training from her relief unit and from the National Association of Mental Health in England, she remained there for a year and a half, working with many of the camp's 20,000 survivors as assistant to the field director of the Jewish Relief Unit. Much of her work involved documenting the survivors and placing them on the list of displaced persons, distributing clothing and food, and struggling to overcome bureaucratic difficulties in order to get the many children there suffering from tuberculosis out of Belsen to sanatoriums in Switzerland. Even more important, however, was the role Bamber played in listening to survivors' accounts of their experiences, thus helping them grieve and come to terms with their traumatic experiences.

In 1947 Helen married Rudi Bamberger, a Jewish refugee from Nuremberg whose father had been murdered during an orgy of fascist violence against Jews known as *Kristallnacht* (9–10 November 1938); he later changed his name to Bamber. Upon her return to London, she worked for the Jewish Refugee Committee, helping Jewish survivors of the Holocaust trace families who had emigrated to the United States and join them there. She was asked to become a caseworker for the Committee for the Care of Children from Concentration Camps, which sup-ported young survivors from Auschwitz through their painful adjustment to a new life in Britain and helped place them in jobs among its Jewish community. She worked for the organization until 1954.

While working as a social worker in St. George's Hospital in London's East End in 1956, Bamber met Dr. Maurice Pappworth, who introduced her to the issue of cruelty in medicine, manifested in the incidence of unnecessary surgery; the overprescription of drugs, particularly for the mentally ill; and the exploitation of patients in often painful forms of medical research. He had begun compiling a dossier on unethical experimentation, particularly on the elderly and the very young, and asked Bamber to help him develop an archive. Thereafter, Bamber became engaged in typing his lectures on the subject, which were published in Pappworth's groundbreaking study, *Human Guinea Pigs* (1967), through which she gained a valuable grounding in medical ethics.

Bamber was working in a Middlesex hospital when she first heard of the launch of Amnesty International in May 1961, an organization dedicated to alerting society to the plight of prisoners of conscience. At this time, she also began working for the psychoanalyst Dr. Hermann Hardenberg, who had taken a strong position against the use of lobotomies in controlling psychotic patients. As a result of her experiences working in hospitals during the 1960s, Bamber began campaigning for a relaxation of visiting hours for children in hospitals. She also wanted their mothers to be allowed to stay with them so that the children could avoid suffering unnecessary trauma caused by separation from them. Through an organization called Mother Care for Children in Hospital, she lobbied nursing and medical schools and hospitals. Her campaign mushroomed, eventually leading to the foundation in 1963 of the National Association for the Welfare of Children in Hospital.

Bamber also continued in her volunteer work for Amnesty International, gathering the testimony of witnesses, documenting the stories of torture victims, and cataloguing their injuries. She developed a concern for protection of the individual from what she termed "the ethics of emergency" (Belton 1998, 207), the wartime need to introduce extreme methods of torture. Her first cases involved cataloguing the appalling physical and mental aftereffects of torture on victims taken to the notorious Villa Grimaldi torture center near Santiago, Chile, during the military regime of Augusto Pinochet (1973–1990). Bamber subsequently worked to uncover the truth about Chile's many "disappeared." In 1974 she was elected to the executive council of the British section of Amnesty International and with Dick Barbor-Might began compiling a dossier on torture in Chile that would be published as the 1974 Amnesty International *Report on Torture.*

In later years, Bamber turned her attention to the abuse of political prisoners in the Soviet Union under President Leonid Brezhnev, lending support to the campaign against psychiatric abuse there during the 1980s and in particular the use of so-called punitive medicine, which involved administering massive overdoses of tranquillizers to supposedly "mentally ill" political prisoners. Her attention also turned to Northern Ireland, to South Africa, and to the growing catalogue of medical abuse worldwide, which impelled her to set up an organization specifically to catalogue the erosion of medical ethics. Bamber resigned from the UK executive council of Amnesty International in 1980, together with other members working in the medical group, and left the organization in 1985 to undertake a more proactive role in the treatment and rehabilitation of those who had been subjected to torture, based on a program of counseling offered in a supportive environment.

Over the 1985–1986 Christmas and New Year's holidays, Bamber founded an independent charity, the Medical Foundation for the Care of Victims of Torture, setting up in rooms at the National Temperance Hospital in London and two years later relocating to premises in Kentish Town. As director of a team of interpreters and caseworkers—some paid staff and others volunteers—Bamber oversees the rehabilitation of approximately 3,000 people a year from as many as 90 different countries. The foundation begins by giving victims a careful clinical examination and recording details of their stories before referring them for treatment, which involves counseling and eventually practical help in returning to the community. The foundation also works to improve the legal status of asylum seekers and refugees. People are referred to it by Amnesty International, the UN High Commission for Refugees, various hospitals and clinics, and individual doctors and psychiatrists. It relies on charitable trusts and donations to raise the £3 million a year needed to keep up its rehabilitation programs and its campaign against the practice of torture in 117 countries worldwide. For further information on its work, contact http://www.torturecare.org.uk.

In 1993 Helen Bamber was nominated as a European Woman of Achievement in recognition of her work and in 1997 was awarded the Order of the British Empire. She holds numerous honorary doctorates and is a patron of the Belfast-based group Women Against Violence and the London-based human rights group Latin American Mothers. Her organization is now considered one of the outstanding humanitarian organizations of the postwar era, alongside Oxfam and Amnesty International. A small, soft-spoken, and entirely unpretentious woman, renowned for her relentless hard work and good humor, Bamber is an unsung modern-day heroine who has devoted more than fifty years to the welfare of others in performing what she considers the indispensable task of "bearing witness to the vulnerability of humanity" (Hattenstone 2000, 6).

References and Further Reading

Belton, Neil. 1998. *The Good Listener. Helen Bamber: A Life against Cruelty.* London: Weidenfeld and Nicolson.

Hattenstone, Simon. 2000. "Small Wonder." [*Guardian* profile.] *Guardian* (11 March): 6–7.

Oldfield, Sybil, ed. 2001. *Women Humanitarians: A Biographical Dictionary of British Women Active between 1900 and 1950.* London: Continuum.

Barakat, Hidiya Hanim
(1898–1969)
Egypt

A philanthropist and social worker, Barakat was one of many enlightened and committed upper-class women of her generation who made a major contribution to the welfare of ordinary Egyptian people. With her name almost unmentioned outside books such as Lois Beck and Nicki Keddie's *Women in the Muslim World* (1978), she remains, at present, one of the unsung pioneers of welfare in Egypt in the early twentieth century. Barakat was the galvanizing force behind many social and medical projects in Egypt from the 1920s onward, bringing together a team of women coworkers to set up a network of clinics and hospitals, schools, and orphanages in most of the major towns. Her organization also provided essential relief work during epidemics.

Barakat was born into a life of privilege as the daughter of a former magistrate and palace official. She was educated at the French convent Nôtre Dame de la Mère de Dieu until she was thirteen years old. At the age of twenty, she married the lawyer Bahieddine Barakat, a member of a leading political family (who would later serve as a minister in several Egyptian governments). She was soon drawn into political activities by her new family, who saw that her welfare activities could be used as a cover for the dissemination of Wafdist (nationalist) literature, a task she undertook covertly and with panache, protected by her genteel upper-class persona.

Through her connections at court, Barakat helped one of the princesses organize a group of women philanthropists, and in 1908 the group set up a medical clinic in a poor quarter of Cairo. Barakat brought several other women along to join in the work, including Huda Sha'rawi, and their organization in 1909 assumed the name Mabarrat Muhammad Ali (Muhammad Ali the Great Philanthropic Association), popularly known later as the Mabarrat. The association set up a clinic in Abdin, which later expanded into a hospital and outpatient clinic. But the association was determined to make health care and medicines available to people everywhere, especially in rural areas, in particular to counter the appallingly high infant mortality rates in Egypt. Barakat, as treasurer of the association, was a natural organizer and helped mastermind a network of clinics as well as coordinating epidemic relief and mobile vaccination programs. Despite their comfortable backgrounds, she and her fellow upper-class women workers often had to live in less than salubrious surroundings during the process. The association meanwhile continued to gain a wide patronage, later including that of King Farouk's sister.

In 1919 Barakat cofounded another organization, the Society of the New Woman, which extended the definition of social welfare to include education and the teaching of trades as well as child care and the establishment of orphanages, all of these activities supported thanks to Barakat's vigorous fund-raising, mainly among her own class. And indeed she and her female supporters raised huge sums of money to support their many welfare schemes, haranguing friends and relatives for donations and calling on local landlords to provide sites for the construction of clinics and dispensaries.

By the 1950s the Mabarrat had become the biggest, most wide-reaching organization in Egypt. In 1952, after the revolution that had brought in Gamal Abdel Nasser's government, Barakat was elected president of the Mabarrat. Her daughters, too, had followed in her footsteps by working as nurses during the troubles of 1948, when Egyptian forces invaded Palestine and the Suez crisis ensued in 1956; her youngest daughter eventually succeeded her as president of the association.

By 1961 the Mabarrat had set up twelve hospitals across Egypt. In 1964 these hospitals were nationalized, and the Mabarrat's various other institutions—orphanages, clinics, and child care centers—became government-run facilities. Many of the unnamed, uncredited women who threw their energies into the work initiated by Barakat gained great organizing and administrative experience as a result of their activities.

Shortly before her death, Barakat was awarded Egypt's highest honor. When she died, President Anwar Sadat, acknowledging her contribution, inaugurated a social project in her honor, stating: "We are all pupils of Hidiya Barakat" (quoted in Marsot 1978, 275). Several Egyptian institutions were also named after her.

See also Sha'rawi, Huda
References and Further Reading
Marsot, Afaf Lutfi al-Sayyid. 1978. "The Revolutionary Gentlewoman in Egypt." In L. Beck and N. Keddie, eds., *Women in the Muslim World*. Cambridge, MA: Harvard University Press.

Barrios de Chungara, Domitla
(1937–)
Bolivia

A true working-class heroine who has fought and suffered for the economic and political rights of Bolivian tin miners and their families, since the early 1960s Barrios was a leader of the Housewives' Committee of Siglo XX, once one of Bolivia's largest and richest mining complexes.

Domitla Barrios de Chungara (center; Library of Congress)

Barrios was born on 7 May 1937 into extreme poverty in Siglo XX. She then lived at Pulacayo, a remote mining settlement, until age twenty. After receiving only the most rudimentary education, she had to leave school to look after her younger siblings. She was politically active from her teens: her father was a union leader who refused to give up his militant activism despite his dying wife's wish. Not long after leaving school, Domitla joined her father in the Bolivian revolution of 9 April 1952 in the hope that the new government under Dr. Victor Paz Estenssoro would give control of the mines to the people and return ownership of agricultural land to the peasants.

In 1957 Barrios gave up her job in a mining company grocery store at Pulacayo. She married a miner and returned to Siglo XX, where she continued to educate herself by studying the Bible. She struggled to bring up her seven children during a period of political unrest and economic instability as Bolivia staggered from one military coup to another. Like many other women, Barrios had to find ways of bringing in more money: she sold *salteñas* (meat pies) on the street in order to earn enough to feed her children. But to do

so meant getting up at 4 A.M. to prepare this food before attending to her own domestic chores and standing in line for water and supplies.

Day after day, Barrios witnessed the brutally hard lives of the mining community: the lack of decent housing for miners' families, poor sanitation, no running water, and the exhausting and debilitating shift work, which required miners to spend eight hours a day underground. Many would chew on coca leaves for their narcotic effects in order to get through the working day. She saw how working conditions and the proliferation of dust particles destroyed miners' lungs, leaving them with silicosis. Yet for all the mine's riches, four-fifths of its profits went to outside capitalist tin barons, and nothing was done by government to improve the lives of the 10,000 underpaid workers who created that wealth.

Such abuse of the workers at Siglo XX inevitably led to a drive to form unions and strike for higher wages; in retaliation, many protesters were arrested. When this happened, a group of about seventy women began organizing to help those arrested and imprisoned. The Housewives' Committee of Siglo XX was founded in 1961 at a time when miners were owed three months' wages and had run out of food and medical supplies. The Housewives' Committee soon began to take part in the activities of the Bolivian Federation of Mine Workers and to join in protesting against the political oppression of workers in other countries such as Chile, Vietnam, Laos, and Cambodia. In 1961 the first of a series of major clashes with the Bolivian Mineral Corporation (COMIBOL) took place over the nonpayment of wages, and a 335-kilometer march to La Paz was organized. The leaders were arrested and jailed, and the wives of the imprisoned men staged a hunger strike in sympathy at the Federation of Factory Workers. Throughout this protest campaign, the Housewives' Committee lobbied for support on local radio, in letters to the president, and in schools and hospitals. Further clashes with COMIBOL occurred in 1963, the year that Barrios first became active in the organization, when the company refused to send the mining families medical supplies to combat an influenza epidemic.

In 1964 General René Barrientos came to power in Bolivia and was rattled by the political threat from women's groups such as the Housewives' Committee. Barrios and her colleagues did not trust him or his policies and were soon proved right when he called for a yearlong reduction in wages of mineworkers to help COMIBOL recover from bankruptcy. Violent clashes and protests ensued, and the leaders of demonstrations were deported to Argentina. In 1965 Barrios took over as secretary-general of the Housewives' Committee in the wake of reprisals against protesting miners from Siglo XX. The miners were fired on by troops, many were killed, and Siglo XX was put under curfew. In 1967 Barrios, who was then pregnant, denounced a massacre of hundreds of protesting miners in San Juan. She was arrested and thrown into a filthy prison cell, where she gave birth alone.

After her release, Barrios helped to build a village school and went to live in Oruro for two years. There she sold cooked food on the streets. After she returned to Siglo XX, her husband forbade her from taking part in any more acts of protest, insisting that her place was in the home with her children. But Barrios refused to turn her back on her political commitments and defied her husband to serve as a delegate to a Congress of Mineworkers held at Siglo XX in 1970. At the congress, the women delegates demanded that widows of miners receive indemnification and that their orphans be given grants for schooling. That same year Barrios helped organize a Committee of Unemployed to help widows and other women in Siglo XX without work. The mining company responded to this request by making these desperate women laboriously sort through rock piles for good ore. When they organized to demand proper employment, they were laid off. Throughout all these struggles, Barrios set about familiarizing herself with labor law to help people fight against unfair dismissal; she also went in a delegation to COMIBOL to ask for a women's sewing cooperative to be set up in La Paz.

In 1971 after yet another political coup and a peso devaluation, the Housewives' Committee demanded an increase in living allowances at the Siglo XX grocery store. The committee organized a demonstration of 4,000 women and achieved some improvement. By 1973 Barrios had begun trying to extend her concerns to the indigenous peasant community by setting up worker-peasant links and working with the National Peasants' Confederation. That same year she was one of three female delegates to a 500-person workers' congress in Huamini. During the 1970s the living standards of Barrios's family improved when her husband was offered a better job with higher wages and guaranteed education for the children, but Barrios turned these inducements down because she wanted to stay close to her own working-class roots and people. She remained at Siglo XX, continuing to defend the rights of the destitute families of striking miners and maintaining that their innocent wives and children should not suffer as a result.

In 1975 Barrios was invited to take part in a women's congress in Mexico as part of the International Year of the Woman being promoted by the United Nations. It was the first time she had traveled beyond her immediate locality, and she enjoyed the opportunity of discussing common concerns with other Latin American women. In 1977 she published her memoirs of the turbulent years of strikes, demonstrations, marches, and periods in prison that marked her involvement in the Housewives' Committee. *Let Me Speak* is a passionate testimony written in an uncompromising, idiomatic style that underlines the gulf of difference between the activities of the emancipated and often comfortably off reformers of the Western world and the gritty and determined women in the Third World who have risked the little they have to make the lives of their families better.

Barrios remains unrepentant in her belief that Bolivia's economic problems will never be solved under the capitalist system. Indeed, when she was once asked by moderate U.S. feminists to modify her anticapitalist militancy, she made clear that for women like her in Brazil, these really were life-and-death issues: if their husbands died or were sick or were fired from their jobs, the families would lose their homes. It has been her mission continually to remind the privileged of just how different her own deprived world is. Despite a bout of poor health and a period spent recuperating in Mexico, Barrios is still fighting for her own people, calling for wage increases for mineworkers in proportion to the cost of living. At her suggestion, a network of Housewives' Committees has now organized itself across Bolivia into a National Housewives' Federation. In 1980 she was exiled by the military junta. In 1986 Siglo XX was closed down, eliminating 23,000 miners' jobs. Barrios returned to Bolivia, running a school for itinerants in Cochabamba.

References and Further Reading
Barrios de Chungara, Domitla. 1978. *Let Me Speak.* London: Stage 1.
Miller, Francesca. 1992. *Latin American Women and the Search for Social Justice.* Hanover, NH: University Press of New England.

Barton, Clara
(1821–1912)
United States

Clara Barton, the "Angel of the Battlefield," was to the American Civil War what Florence Nightingale, the "Lady with the Lamp," was to the Crimean War. As humanitarians and nurses, both of them improved standards of care among the sick and wounded and contributed to the establishment of women's nursing. Like Nightingale, Barton never married and developed her own brand of ruthless and energetic efficiency that would not suffer fools gladly. Her determination would result in the founding of the American Red Cross in 1881; her insistence on her own unchallenged control would, however, lead to her ouster from the organization in 1904.

Born in Oxford, Massachusetts, the last of five children, Barton had grown up hearing stories from her father about his days fighting in the Indian wars and his love of the army. She would later overcome the natural timidity of her childhood to become an indomitable figure in dealing with the military authorities during the Civil War. After nursing her sick brother for two years, Barton took up teaching, first in local schools and then, in 1850, at the Liberal Institute in Clinton, New York. In 1852 she founded one of the first American public (free) schools in Bordentown, New Jersey. After commending Barton on her success, the authorities promptly appointed a man above her to take charge. Barton resigned in protest in 1854. She had for years suffered intermittently from bouts of depression, during which she would lose her voice, and she decided to move south to a warmer climate in the hope that this would help. Settling in Washington, D.C., in a bold move she entered the male preserve of the civil service. Barton was probably the first officially appointed woman to take up a clerical job there, copying documents in the Patent Office. She interrupted her appointment to return to Oxford in 1857–1860.

When the Civil War broke out in April 1861, Barton, as an independently minded supporter of the Unionist cause, wanted to play her part. She befriended casualties from the Sixth Massachusetts Regiment quartered in Washington and called for donations and supplies from their families back in her home state. The response was huge, and Barton took a mule train and wagon to distribute these supplies, which included brandy, tobacco, and sewing kits. But Barton quickly realized that small acts of charity such as hers would not be enough to alleviate the large-scale suffering of Union troops and that she had to take her work to the front lines. Her experience of the aftermath of the Second Battle of Bull Run in August 1862—in which 3,000 men were wounded and during which she helped hold down the operating table under artillery fire—galvanized her to bypass the bureaucracy and dilatoriness of official military channels and organize her own medical supplies and food for the wounded, who, at Bull Run, she had described as covering "acres."

What particularly appalled Barton was the unnecessary loss of life among wounded men who were not receiving medical attention quickly enough. With groups of volunteers, she traveled to the scenes of fighting by mule train to nurse the wounded and provide much-needed succor, such as hot soup and coffee. At Antietam in September 1862, her clothes drenched in blood, Barton attended the wounded in the thick of fire, at one point nearly being killed herself when a wounded man she was tending was hit by a bullet. It was not just on the battlefield that men suffered, however, as Barton witnessed when she saw the inadequacy of army hospitals. In 1864 Barton was given an official appointment as head nurse of the Army of the James, running corps hospitals in Virginia. Meanwhile, the official Union appointee, Dorothea Dix, had been acting as overall superintendent of women nurses for the Sanitary Commission since 1861, but Barton resisted any suggestion that she should join her nursing team, determined to act independently.

After the war, Barton would expose the sufferings of those who had died or nearly starved to death in prison camps, such as the Andersonville Prison in Georgia. This Confederate camp housed 33,000 Union prisoners by war's end, and 13,000 died there, to be buried in mass graves. Beginning in 1865, with the sanction of President Abraham Lincoln, Barton had begun working to trace and identify killed, wounded, and missing Union troops, funding her own office for the purpose in Annapolis, Maryland, and supporting it on the lecture circuit for two years. She received letters from many thousands of families anxious to trace their missing men, in return writing something like 22,000 letters herself and supervising the laying out of a proper cemetery for those who had died at Andersonville. Barton would continue her attempts to trace missing soldiers until 1869, by which time she had spent $1,750 of her own income in responding to a flood of over 63,000 letters inquiring about missing soldiers.

By the time she had come to the end of a two-year tour in which she gave 300 public lectures on her experiences of the war, Barton was exhausted. She went to Europe on a rest cure in 1869 but soon was drawn into new activities when she discovered the work of the International Committee of the Red Cross, founded in 1864. She volunteered her services and helped organize relief and military hospitals in Strasbourg, Metz, and Paris during the Franco-Prussian War of 1870–1871, distributing supplies raised by donation in the United States.

Barton returned to the United States in 1873, spent the next five years campaigning for a national organization of medical aid, and again toured with lectures on medical issues. In 1877 she was asked to establish the American Association of the Red Cross, which after its incorporation in 1881 elected Barton president. Subsequently, Barton crusaded for the United States to support the Geneva Convention on the humane treatment of prisoners of war, which it signed in 1882. Believing in the "wise benevolence" of preparing in peacetime not only for the exigencies of war but also for natural disasters, she urged the American Red Cross to set up relief programs for such emergencies as floods in Ohio and Mississippi in 1884, a hurricane on the Sea Islands off South Carolina in 1893, and a tidal wave in Galveston, Texas, in 1900. At the age of seventy-seven, still unwilling to delegate her humanitarian work to others, Barton traveled to Cuba in 1898 to work as a nurse during the Spanish-American War and organized Red Cross medical supplies and relief to Cuban civilians, traveling by her now familiar mode of mule train.

By the end of the century, Barton was struggling to keep the American Red Cross afloat as funds ran low. But by 1904 it had come perilously near to closing down, due to a continuing lack of public support and objections to Barton's dictatorial mode of leadership. The U.S. Congress insisted on less centralized control by Barton after objections raised by board member Mabel Boardman had led to an investigation of the organization's business management. Barton resigned in 1904 and returned to her home in Glen Echo, Maryland, where she lived a life of semireclusion and wrote *A Story of the Red Cross* (1904) and *Story of My Childhood* (1907). Having always endorsed the women's rights movement in the United States, Barton had become an important figure, making personal appearances at landmark events such as the first convention of the National Woman Suffrage Association, held in Washington, D.C., in January 1869. In 1902 she attended the first international woman suffrage conference. Like her contemporary Florence Nightingale, she received many honors and lived a long life—into her nineties—despite the rigors of her long years of campaigning.

A Clara Barton National Historic Site was established by the National Park Service in 1975 at Barton's home at Glen Echo, Maryland, the original headquarters of the American Red Cross, from where she had distributed relief supplies. For visiting hours, see http://www.nps.gov/clba/index.htm.

See also Dix, Dorothea Lynde.

References and Further Reading

Barton, William E. 1922. *The Life of Clara Barton, Founder of the American Red Cross.* Boston: Houghton Mifflin.

Burton, David A. 1995. *Clara Barton: In the Service of Humanity.* Westport, CT: Greenwood Press.

Dictionary of American Biography 1946–1958, and indexes to Supplements 1–10, 1981–1996. New York: Scribner's.

Massey, Mary E. 1966. *Bonnet Brigades: American Women and the Civil War.* New York: Alfred A. Knopf.

Pryor, E. B. 1987. *Clara Barton: A Professional Angel.* Philadelphia: University of Pennsylvania Press.

Reynolds, Moira Davison. 1988. *Nine American Women of the Nineteenth Century: Leaders into the Twentieth.* Jefferson, NC: McFarland.

Ross, Ishbel. 1956. *Angel of the Battlefield: The Life of Clara Barton.* New York: Harper.

Sicherman, Barbara, and Carol Hurd Green, eds. 1980. *Notable American Women 1607–1950: A Biographical Dictionary,* vol. 4, *The Modern Period.* Cambridge, MA: Belknap Press of Harvard University.

Bates, Daisy
(1861–1951)
Ireland/Australia

The Australian anthropologist Daisy Bates, who spent the best part of thirty-five years living among Aboriginal tribes in the outback, dedicated herself to their welfare and the documentary preservation of their cultural tradition. Born Daisy O'Dwyer in Tipperary, Ireland, in later, somewhat unreliable memoirs Bates would claim descent from the ancient Gaelic clan of that name. Her family was reasonably well off, providing her with a private income later in life, but her mother died when she was small. She was sent to live with a family in England when she was eight. Suspected of having tuberculosis, she emigrated to the better climate of Australia in 1884, where she stayed with family friends in Queensland and then briefly worked as a governess in New South Wales. A brief marriage to Harry Morant quickly foundered (he later became infamous as "Breaker" Morant during the Boer War in South Africa, when he was court-martialed and shot in 1902 for murdering Boer prisoners). A year later Daisy remarried—bigamously—to cattle rancher Jack Bates. But she abandoned him and their son to travel alone around Australia, and after the couple lost much of their money in financial crashes in 1894, she returned to England. There she worked as a journalist in London on the *Review of Reviews*. Commissioned by *The Times* to investigate allegations of the persecution of Aboriginals in northwestern Australia by white settlers, she went back to gather documentary evidence, staying at a Catholic mission station at Beagle Bay, near Broome.

Thus began a lifelong investigation of Aboriginal life and customs in the area of the Great Australian Bight. Espousing their welfare with a sense of maternal mission, Bates soon began living among Aboriginals in remote areas, where she enjoyed the privileges of being allowed to observe ancient religious rituals and touch sacred objects from which even Aboriginal women were excluded.

In 1902, after briefly reuniting with her husband and son for a profit-making droving trip in which they took 800 head of cattle 1,000 miles south to Perth, she left them again to take up an appointment from the government of Western Australia to conduct research into Aboriginal life and customs on the Maaba reserve at Cannington. She began documenting dozens of Aboriginal dialects and practices, in 1905 producing a study of tribal marriage laws. In 1910–1911 she was invited to join the Radcliffe-Brown anthropological expedition to Aboriginals in the northwest, during the course of which she investigated their employment on sheep stations and the life of native women working in mining towns. She became increasingly preoccupied with the welfare of sick and elderly Aboriginals, particularly those exiled from their traditional homelands. The Aboriginals responded to her dispensations of benevolent concern by revering her, calling her "Kabbarli" (grandmother).

In 1912 Bates was made Honorary Protector of Aborigines at Eucla in South Australia. From her remote camp in the bush, she worked on the first official ethnographic study of Aboriginals, among the Mirning tribe. She left the bush only briefly in 1914 to attend sessions of the Congress of the British Association for the Advancement of Science and in 1915 went to Adelaide to raise government funding for welfare projects. In 1919 Bates once more returned to the outback, to a camp at Ooldea in South Australia, where for the next sixteen years she devoted herself to welfare among transient Aboriginal tribes, using much of her own money to buy supplies, help feed them, and nurse those who were sick. She also fiercely guarded them from the encroachments of civilization, in particular the railways, which were increasingly cutting across their ancient lands, and from the dilution of their bloodlines by miscegenation and intermarriage.

By this time something of a celebrity (because of sensationalist articles about her work in the press that talked of cannibalism among Aboriginals), Bates had became an unrivalled authority on Aboriginal dialects and oral culture. In 1933 she gave evidence to a government committee in Canberra on the state of the Aboriginal peoples, recommending, as she had for many years, that a central region of Australia be made over to them as a homeland under Crown protection. In 1934 her services to anthropology were rewarded when she was made a Commander of the Order of the British Empire (CBE). She made another brief return to Adelaide in 1935, during which she serialized accounts of her life in the bush in the papers, which were later collected as *The Passing of the Aborigines,* published in the United Kingdom in 1938 and in Australia in 1946. By the 1930s entirely converted to the nomadic life, Bates took herself off again to an Aboriginal camp at Pyap on the Murray River, where she occupied herself in cataloguing and writing up her many years of anthropological notes. In 1945 her failing health finally forced Bates to give up the bush and retire to Adelaide on a government pension.

Bates's posthumous reputation has been eroded by criticism of both her character (patronizing and imperious), her old-school colonial style (she always wore corsets and Western dress, even in the outback), and the negativism of her work for Aboriginals, whom she saw as a living remnant of ancient Paleolithic humans doomed to extinction. But within her limitations, as a believer in the benevolence of British colonial rule and a defender of Aboriginal autonomy, she was a genuine friend whose invaluable work in cataloguing Aboriginal life, culture, and legend dating back to the mythical Dreamtime has yet to be properly evaluated and published. These extensive observations, contained in eighty boxes, were donated by her to the National Library of Australia in Canberra.

References and Further Reading

Blackburn, Julia. 1994. *Daisy Bates in the Desert.* New York: Pantheon.

Hill, Ernestine. 1973. *Kabbarli: A Personal Memoir of Daisy Bates.* Sydney: Angus and Robertson.

Marcus, Julie, et al., eds. 1993. *First in Their Field: Women and Australian Anthropology.* Melbourne: Melbourne University Press.

Ó Céirín, Kit, and Cyril Ó Céirín, eds. 1996. *Women of Ireland: A Biographic Dictionary.* Kinvara, County Galway: Tír Eolas.

Pike, Douglas Henry, ed. 1966– . *Australian Dictionary of Biography.* Melbourne: Melbourne University Press.

Roberts, Frank C. 1951–1960. *Obituaries from* The Times. Vol. 1. Reading: Newspaper Archive Developments.

Salter, Elizabeth. 1971. *Daisy Bates: "The Great White Queen of the Never Never."* Sydney: Angus and Robertson.

Bates, Daisy
(1914?–1999)
United States

The fight to desegregate the schools of the American South could have had no more potent historical watershed than the enrollment of nine black students at Central High School in Little Rock, Arkansas, in 1957. Much of the success of the desegregation campaign in Arkansas is due to the work of Daisy Bates, a now legendary figure in the history of the civil rights movement in the United States.

Born in a poor sawmill and lumbering town (sources conflict about whether her birth year was 1914 or 1920), Huttig, Arkansas, Bates never knew her father and was put up for adoption after her mother's rape and murder by three white men. After graduating from a local segregated high school in Huttig, she went to Memphis for two years to study psychology at Meymoyne College.

Bates married Lucious ("L. C.") Bates and settled in Little Rock in 1941. Together they leased the editorship of the *Arkansas State Press,* a highly influential newspaper that under their editorship would rise to a circulation of 20,000 and give a voice to the state's blacks. During World War II, the newspaper exposed the racism of the Arkansas police and the bias of the state's criminal justice system, when black soldiers sent to training camps in the area ran into trouble with the authorities.

In 1952 Bates was elected president of the state chapter of the National Association for the Advancement of Colored People (NAACP) and served until 1961. In this capacity, she was drawn into its desegregation campaign after the famous Supreme Court ruling of 1954, *Brown v. Board of Education of Topeka, Kansas,* upheld the right of the Reverend Oliver Brown to send his daughter to the school of his choice. With this official declaration that segregation was unconstitutional, the NAACP intensified its campaign in Little Rock. In 1955, with the city's high schools still defying this ruling, Bates and her colleagues in the NAACP decided to try to break segregation at the all-white Central High School. They began planning their strategy, first by exerting pressure on the school board to abide by the ruling. As protests, meetings, and lawsuits proliferated in an attempt to enroll black students in Arkansas's schools, an official date was finally set for integration—September 1957. Meanwhile, Bates organized a group of nine black teenagers to make this important stand for black civil rights.

After Governor Orval Faubus called in the National Guard to bar the way to these students when they arrived to enroll on 2 September 1957, President Dwight D. Eisenhower federalized the National Guard to ensure that the students were allowed to enter, which they eventually did on 25 September. Over the following year, Bates gave great moral support to the students as they ran the daily gauntlet of racial hatred at the school. She herself came constantly under verbal attack, racial abuse, and threats of violence. Incendiary bombs were thrown at her home, and Ku Klux Klan crosses burned on the lawn in 1959. That same year, Bates and her husband were forced to close their newspaper due to a drop in advertising revenue.

After leaving Little Rock, Bates continued to work as a community organizer for underprivileged blacks in Mitchellville, Desha County, after giving up her NAACP post in 1961. Active in the Community Revitalization Project, she oversaw improvements to sanitation and health care in the town. Her successful encouragement of black voters in Mitchellville also eventually led to the election of a black mayor and city council. In the early 1960s, she was appointed to the Democratic National Committee by President John F. Kennedy and toured the United States promoting voter registration. In 1972 she attacked funding cuts to the Office of Economic Opportunity in Desher County by the Nixon administration. Bates published an account of her experiences, *The Long Shadow of Little Rock,* in 1962.

References and Further Reading

Bates, Daisy. 1962. *The Long Shadow of Little Rock: A Memoir by Daisy Bates.* New York: David McKay.

Crawford, Vicki L., Jacqueline Anne Rouse, and Barbara Woods, eds. 1990. *Women in the Civil Rights Movement: Trailblazers and Torchbearers.* Brooklyn: Carlson Publishing.

Encyclopaedia Britannica: Book of the Year 2000. Chicago: University of Chicago Press and Encyclopaedia Britannica.

Hine, Darlene Clarke, et al., eds. 1993. *Black Women in America: An Historical Encyclopedia.* 2 vols. Bloomington: Indiana University Press.

Huckaby, Elizabeth. 1980. *Crisis at Central High School: Little Rock 1957–1958.* Baton Rouge: Louisiana State University Press.

Smith, Jessie Carney, ed. 1992. *Notable Black American Women.* Detroit: Gale.

Bäumer, Gertrud
(1873–1954)
Germany

Feminist, patriot, and Christian moderate in the German women's movement to 1933, Gertrud Bäumer opposed the "new morality" movement advocating sexual liberation and emphasized the separate spheres in which women could contribute their unique gifts to social welfare as wives and mothers. An eloquent speaker, under her leadership the Federation of German Women's Associations moved increasingly to the right during 1901–1914.

Born in Hohenlimburg in Westphalia, the daughter of a theologian, Bäumer's evangelical Christian background would color her activities. She became a teacher, held posts at Camnen and Magdeburg from 1892 to 1898, and studied literature and philosophy in Berlin for a year. She was an active member of the General German Women Teachers' Association led by president Helene Lange, with whom she had founded the journal *The Woman* in 1893. Bäumer became Lange's secretary in 1899, and for the next thirty years, she worked closely with Lange on women's issues.

Bäumer wrote many pamphlets and books, most notably the ambitious five-volume *Handbook of the Women's Movement* (1901–1906) edited with Helene Lange, influenced by the Christian social theorist Friedrich Naumann, whose ideas on a German brand of democratic and social reform spiced with military strength were symbolized by the sword and a kernel of wheat. In 1900, elected to the committee of the Federation of German Women's Associations, Bäumer made clear her commitment to welfare and nationalist interests. She sought to defuse class tensions through the organization of social welfare programs that emphasized the role of women as wives and mothers. Her "new ideal" of women's sacrosanct nurturing role thus viewed abortion as criminal. Under Bäumer the federation was increasingly attacked by the left wing for being traditionalist, particularly after 1910 when it merged with the German Evangelical Women's League and withdrew support for radical feminists such as Helene Stöcker, Adela Schreiber, and Marie Stritt, who sought women's sexual emancipation and the legalization of abortion. Bäumer replaced Stritt as president of the federation in 1910, together with Lange editing its journal *The Woman* (until 1929; editor-in-chief 1929–1944), and by the outbreak of World War I in 1914 the last vestiges of radicalism within the women's movement in Germany had been marginalized. Between 1912 and 1944, Bäumer also coedited the journal *Help* with Naumann.

During World War I Bäumer worked for the National Women's Service. She saw the war as a good opportunity for women to prove their worth to the fatherland and adapted her perception of the federation's objectives to patriotic rather than solely reformist goals, based on her own "ideology of republican motherhood" (Smith 1989, 398). Bäumer galvanized women to set up soup kitchens and hospital wards, to provide welfare to the families of men in the military, and to work in industry and keep the food supply going. However, she was critical of government incentives to women to produce more children, or "an arms race by mothers," as she dubbed it (Thébaud 1994, 421).

After the war and the introduction of women's suffrage in 1919, Bäumer was elected to the National Assembly and was one of the first forty-one women to take their seats in the Reichstag in 1920, remaining there until 1933 and in 1920 serving as minister of the interior. At first she supported Adolf Hitler, but in 1933 when he became chancellor, she was dismissed from her post in the ministry of the interior with only a small pension, despite her long service. All independent women's groups were ordered to disband and join a single organization, the Nazi Women's Group, which was controlled by the state. On moral grounds, Bäumer refused to allow the Federation of German Women's Associations to comply because to do so would have meant going against its constitution by expelling its Jewish members. Her links with Christian opposition to the Nazis during the war led to investigations of her by the Gestapo on several occasions, and she also suffered at the hands of the Allies at war's end for her support of German militarism. Bäumer nevertheless took up political activity again in 1949 and was instrumental in the establishment of the Christian Social Union. In the interwar years she also was a member of the first German delegation to the League of Nations and served on the Commission for the Protection of Children.

See also Lange, Helene; Schreiber, Adela; Stöcker, Helene; Stritt, Marie.

References and Further Reading

Evans, Richard. 1973. *The Feminist Movement in Germany 1894–1933.* London: Sage.

Offen, Karen. 2000. *European Feminisms 1700–1950: A Political History.* Stanford: Stanford University Press.

Sklar, Kathryn Kish. 1998. *Social Justice Feminists in the United States and Germany: A Dialogue in Documents 1885–1933.* Ithaca: Cornell University Press.

Smith, Bonnie G. 1989. *Changing Lives: Women in European History since 1700.* Lexington, MA: D. C. Heath.

Thébaud, Francoise, ed. 1994. *A History of Women: Toward a Cultural Identity in the Twentieth Century.* Cambridge, MA: Belknap Press at Harvard University.

Beale, Dorothea
(1831–1906)
United Kingdom

The educationist Dorothea Beale lived the life of the archetypal Victorian spinster, rejecting suitors and eschewing a personal life for one of duty lived for and through her pupils. She devoted herself to pioneering girls' secondary school education at Cheltenham Ladies' College. With her close friend and associate Frances Buss, who did likewise at the North London Collegiate School for Ladies, Beale shared a belief in women being better suited than men to the teaching of young girls. During her years at Cheltenham, Beale injected new life into the staid and narrow curriculum then available and promoted the health and all-around welfare of her students through the adoption of physical fitness regimes.

Born in London, one of eleven children, Beale would comment in later life that she had spent much of her youth engaged in "the inevitable sock-darning which falls to a girl's position in a family of so many boys" (Perkin 1993, 17). While receiving some education at home in Essex and at a local school, she managed to teach herself Latin and study the works of Euclid. Her father sent her to finishing school in Paris with her sister in 1847, but the 1848 revolution there forced them to return, after which Beale was fortunate in being one of the first young women to enter Queen's College for Ladies in London's Harley Street. This secondary school for girls, which provided the level of academic curriculum that would enable women to become teachers, had recently been set up by the Governesses' Benevolent Institution. Here Beale met and became friends with other future social reformers, including Frances Buss and Adelaide Procter. She became a teacher of mathematics at the school in 1849 and a senior teacher from 1854 to 1856 but resigned in protest at the lack of teacher involvement in the running of the school.

In 1857 Beale accepted an appointment as head of the Clergy Daughters' School in Casterton, Westmorland, a rigorous establishment set in a lonely environment that the Brontë sisters had attended and that Charlotte Brontë had used as the basis for Lowood School in her 1847 novel *Jane Eyre*. Although the regime had improved somewhat since Brontë's time there, Beale found its narrow curriculum stale and tedious and her duties teaching a wide range of subjects onerous. She left after a year, wrote a *Textbook of General History,* and competed with forty-nine other candidates for the post of principal at the first private girls' school established in England (1854), Cheltenham Ladies' College. At that time the school had only sixty-nine pupils and was in a state of serious financial decline.

For Beale, Cheltenham became her consuming passion, which she embraced with total dedication to the belief that a good education based on religious principles was essential in molding good character and social responsibility: "Girls must be prepared for life, taught to know the truth, feel nobly, and hence act rightly" (Perkin 1993, 37). During her forty-eight years there until her death in 1906, Beale ruled over Cheltenham with grim determination, reforming the school's financial affairs and establishing efficient management. Most important, after carefully biding her time and not alienating the parents of potential students, Beale began revising the curriculum, adding science, mathematics, and classics during the late 1860s as well as other academic subjects—innovations considered extremely radical for their time. Beale was also an advocate of fresh air and exercise; all her students were expected to spend some time out of doors engaged in gentle recreation such as walking or croquet. Lawn tennis and cycling were also introduced later at Cheltenham, as was calisthenics, considered by Beale to be a suitable antidote to the supposed mental rigors of academic study. In 1876, daily musical drills and rhythmic gymnastics were introduced. By 1905 the college would boast six trained teachers in physical education. However, Beale insisted that sporting activities at Cheltenham should not be competitive; pupils were allowed to engage in friendly cricket and hockey matches with each other but not with other schools. This was very much part and parcel of Beale's insistence that while women sought academic excellence, they should not appear manly or competitive but rather be reared up as paragons of "dutiful womanhood" (McCrone 1988, 81).

In 1864 Beale further increased the school's intake with the introduction of boarders. A nursery school followed, and in 1877 a teacher-training college, St. Hilda's (named after St. Hilda of Whitby), was established as an adjunct to the school. In 1892 St. Hilda's was transferred to a house purchased by Beale in Oxford, where it was called St. Hilda's Hall of Residence and offered a one-year teacher-training course at the university. In 1893 St. Hilda's became one of Oxford University's first female colleges.

With Emily Davies, with whom she was active in the women's discussion group the Kensington Society, Beale also promoted women's higher education and suffrage in Britain and was involved in the drawing up of the first petition on women's suffrage that was presented to Parliament by John Stuart Mill in 1866. In 1864 she gave evidence to the Royal Commission on Endowed Schools (which lasted until 1867), arguing that girls' schools should be included in the endowments that had previously only been awarded to boys' secondary schools. In 1869 Beale published the commissioners' *Report on the Education of Girls,* in her preface highlighting the low standards of teaching still prevailing in girls' secondary schools. The Endowed Schools Act provided for the establishment of new high schools for girls offering high academic standards. In all her campaigning for women's education, however, Beale made it clear that she did not seek to take women out of their conventional roles; she believed that they should be educated in order to "best perform that subordinate part in the world to which, I believe, they have been called" (Strachey 1978, 135). Nor did she approve of girls competing academically with boys and opposed women's education at the university level.

In 1884 Beale, a woman of devout Christian beliefs, extended her interests to philanthropic work in the community, when she established

the Guild of the Cheltenham Ladies' College, which set up a settlement house in Bethnal Green in London's East End. She joined the growing movement led by evangelicals in the 1880s of rescuing prostitutes through the National Vigilance Association for the Repression of Criminal Vice and Immorality (an organization to which she bequeathed money on her death). She was active in numerous educational societies, including the Froebel Society and the Child Study Association, and in 1895 succeeded Buss as president of the Association of Headmistresses; she was also active in the Teachers' Guild. Her 1898 work, written in collaboration with two other educators, *Work and Play in Girls' Schools,* endorsed the arguments of medical women such as Elizabeth Garrett Anderson that, far from being harmful, physical exercise for schoolgirls was an essential component of the school curriculum.

Beale lived a life of pious frugality and intense privacy, at the end of which she was awarded an honorary law degree by Edinburgh University in 1899. She left the then considerable sum of £55,000 to Cheltenham Ladies' College. She developed a close friendship with the Indian reformer and Christian convert Pandita Ramabai, who studied and taught for a while at Cheltenham, and was a supporter of the English suffrage movement as vice president of the Central Society for Women's Suffrage (later the London Society for Women's Suffrage), although she remained forever wary of advocating male-female rivalry, particularly in politics. Her views on women's emancipation were at all times restricted by her overriding sense of woman's ultimately dutiful and subordinate role.

See also Anderson, Elizabeth Garrett; Buss, Frances; Davies, (Sarah) Emily; Ramabai, Pandita Saraswati.

References and Further Reading

Kamm, Josephine. 1958. *How Different from Us: A Biography of Miss Buss and Miss Beale.* London: Bodley Head.
McCrone, Kathleen E. 1988. *Sport and the Physical Emancipation of English Women 1870–1914.* London: Routledge.
Perkin, Joan. 1993. *Victorian Women.* London: John Murray.
Raikes, Elizabeth. 1909. *Dorothea Beale of Cheltenham.* London: Archibald Constable.
Shillito, Elizabeth. 1920. *Dorothea Beale: Principal of the Cheltenham Ladies' College 1858–1906.* London: Society for the Promotion of Christian Knowledge.
Steadman, F. C. 1931. *In the Days of Miss Beale: A Study of Her Work and Influence.* London: E. J. Burrow.
Strachey, Ray. 1978 [1928]. *The Cause: A Brief History of the Women's Movement.* Reprint, London: Virago.

Beard, Mary Ritter
(1876–1958)
United States

Forty years before the proliferation of women's studies courses and the wider dissemination of source material on women's history began in the 1970s, the American writer and educator Mary Ritter Beard advocated the addition of women's studies to the academic curriculum and encouraged women to reject the mindset of generations that they had no value as members of society or any power to change history.

Beard was born in Indianapolis, the daughter of a lawyer who was a staunch Republican and temperance campaigner. After graduating from DePauw University in 1897, she taught German in high school before marrying Charles Austin Beard in 1900. Charles's studies took the couple to England in 1900; they spent the next two years in Oxford, where Charles was a cofounder of the trade unionist Ruskin College. They then moved to Manchester, where they both became friends with the Pankhurst family and, through them, took an active interest in class politics and the work of the Independent Labour Party. Mary also associated with women in the National Union of Women's Suffrage Societies.

After their return to the United States in 1902, Beard undertook postgraduate studies in sociology in 1904 at Columbia University. But after two years, she gave up to commit her time to working for the rights and working conditions of women through the Women's Trade Union League. She joined the league in 1907 and became involved in organizing the 1909–1910 strike by women shirtwaist makers in New York. In 1912 she left to join the more working-class-based Wage Earners' League.

At the same time, Beard also became involved in the suffrage movement, joining the National American Woman Suffrage Association in 1910,

Mary Ritter Beard (Library of Congress)

then led by Carrie Chapman Catt, and editing its journal, the *Woman Voter,* during 1910–1912. But again, she left this organization in 1913 to cofound a more militant group, the Congressional Union for Woman Suffrage, led by Alice Paul. The union, which would later become the National Woman's Party, adopted the strategies of the Pankhursts' militant Women's Social and Political Union, founded in 1903. Beard remained active with the union until 1917.

Although Beard continued to work for protective legislation for women after she left the union, she increasingly turned away from activism to the development of her own theories, becoming a notable lecturer. Her book *Woman's Work in Municipalities* (1915) established the arguments she would develop throughout her subsequent works in calling for greater recognition of the achievements of women. Noralee Frankel and Nancy S. Dye (1991) assert that this work is in itself a record of the uncredited reformist work of many American women of that time. And indeed, in its cataloguing of women's work in the inner cities, it testifies to a considerable range of activity that helped create "the first kindergartens, public libraries, adult education

programs for immigrants, industrial training schools, the first programs for public health, municipal recreation, housing reform and the new field of social work" (Spender 1983, 342).

In 1916 Beard worked with Florence Kelley on the research paper "Why Women Demand a Federal Suffrage Amendment: Difficulties in Amending State Constitution," published by the Congressional Union. After women's suffrage was granted in 1920, she opposed the Equal Rights Amendment campaign, sticking to her conviction that separate provisions should be made to protect the rights of women.

During the 1920s, Beard collaborated with her husband on the adoption of a school of writing known as the "New History," which avoided the traditional overemphasis on man-made wars. Instead, it considered social and economic factors as well as the role of women in molding historical events. Together they published other books on American history and citizenship, including a two-volume history of the United States, *The Rise of American Civilization* (1927).

In 1934 Beard's fifty-page educational pamphlet, "A Changing Political Economy as It Affects Women," offered a prototype syllabus for a course in women's studies—but one that no college was forward-thinking enough to adopt. A year later, with the Hungarian women's rights activist Rosika Schwimmer, Beard founded the World Center for Women's Archives, no doubt out of her painful awareness, as Ann J. Lane points out, that women's history was all too easily lost. But the center ran out of money by 1940, and despite a huge commitment on Beard's part and much hard work, it folded. Beard and three other women then turned in 1941 to making a detailed study of the coverage and treatment of women in the *Encyclopedia Britannica,* recommending rewrites where they thought entries were deficient. The suggestions, which had taken eighteen months of careful research and preparation, were never implemented.

But her most important works were those in which she underlined the crucial role of women in molding history. Beard's publications were many, including *A Short History of the American Labor Movement* (1920); *Force of Women in Japanese History* (1953); and a memoir of her husband, *The Making of Charles A. Beard* (1955). *On Understanding Women* (1931) illustrated how women had developed the domestic arts and crafts and highlighted their tendency to underplay their talents instead of taking credit for their achievements. Her most famous book and a work innovative for its time, *Woman as Force in History: A Study of Tradition and Realities* (1946), argued for greater weight to be given to women's contribution to history. It is a sad testament to how little attention was paid to this important study that it was quickly forgotten. Not until the 1970s would feminist interest in *Woman as Force in History* be revived, when the book was finally reprinted. In it, Beard argued that women had colluded in the perpetuation of their own oppression and invisibility by being content to accept a passive role. Until they were able to liberate their minds from preconceived notions of their own subservience and conceptualize their own collective force, they would remain impotent. And the key to power for women was, in Beard's view, independence from the kind of male-dominated official institutions—in politics, science, and education—that would seek only to subordinate them.

See also Catt, Carrie Chapman; Kelley, Florence; Pankhurst, Christabel; Pankhurst, Emmeline; Paul, Alice; Schwimmer, Rosika.

References and Further Reading

Cott, Nancy F., ed. 1991. *A Woman Making History: Mary Ritter Beard through Her Letters.* New Haven, CT: Yale University Press.

Frankel, Noralee, and Nancy S. Dye. 1991. *Gender, Class, Race, and Reform in the Progressive Era.* Lexington: University of Kentucky Press.

Lane, Ann J., ed. 1977. *Mary Ritter Beard: A Source Book.* New York: Schocken Books.

———. 1983. "Mary Ritter Beard: Woman as Force." In Dale Spender, ed. *Feminist Theorists: Three Centuries of Women's Intellectual Traditions.* London: Women's Press.

Turoff, Barbara K. 1979. *Mary Beard as Force in History.* Dayton, OH: Wright State University Press.

Simone de Beauvoir (Archive Photos)

Beauvoir, Simone de
(1908–1986)
France

As the woman who overturned thinking on women's sexuality and social position after World War II with her seminal work *The Second Sex* (1949—all dates given are of first publication in French), the radical writer and existentialist

Simone de Beauvoir inspired the new "second wave" of feminist thinking and activism that developed into the highly vocal women's rights movement of the 1970s. Born in Paris, the daughter of an upper-middle-class lawyer, de Beauvoir was educated privately at convents. She rejected her conventional upbringing after studying philosophy at the Sorbonne (graduating in 1929), where she met the French existentialist writer Jean-Paul Sartre. They collaborated closely on the development of French existentialist theory until his death in 1980, although the couple never lived together. In 1945 they cofounded the monthly magazine *Modern Times*.

Having obtained a teaching diploma, de Beauvoir worked at lycées in Marseilles and Rouen (1931–1936) and returned to teach in Paris (1937–1943), remaining there throughout the German occupation during World War II. She gave up teaching when she published her first novel, *She Came to Stay* (in French, *L'Invitée*, 1943), followed by *The Blood of Others* (1944) and *All Men Are Mortal* (1946).

De Beauvoir's theories on individual choice, freedom, and the responsibility of the individual for his or her actions through the creation of a personal moral law in a world without God are central to existentialist thinking. They also colored her extensive social study *The Second Sex,* originally published in two volumes in 1949. In it, alluding to a pantheon of literary, mythical, and historical sources, she expounded on what she defined as traditional patriarchy's perpetuation of the "eternal feminine." Because of the continued bias toward the male as being superior in all things and the placement of social constraints on women that forever subordinated them as the physically weak "other," women had failed to attain their freedom and independence. De Beauvoir attacked conventional male images that depicted women as inferior, arguing that this state of being was not the result of women's natural biology or psychology but of their passive acceptance of conditioning by men through marriage and motherhood. As she famously argued, "One is not born a woman; one becomes a woman" (1972, 295).

De Beauvoir's book sold 22,000 copies within weeks of publication, arousing both praise and outrage with its bold and outright rejection of marriage and motherhood. It urged women to exercise their free will and fight back against male domination and their own dependency in marriage and provided an intellectual framework for feminist thinking that would gather momentum in the 1970s. It was only then that de Beauvoir took a public stand on issues such as abortion, signing a 1973 manifesto by leading Frenchwomen who had themselves undergone abortions for reform of the law and organizing demonstrations through the Movement for the Liberation of Women. She also denounced the physical abuse of women by men as president of the League for the Rights of Women from 1974. During the 1960s, de Beauvoir visited communist Cuba and the Soviet Union and denounced the Algerian and Vietnam Wars. She also founded the feminist publications *New Feminism* (1974) and *Feminist Questions* (1977).

Simone de Beauvoir also produced a body of essays, four books on philosophy (including *Ethics of Ambiguity* in 1947), a play, and several other novels, including *The Mandarins,* which won the Prix Goncourt in 1954. Her four-volume autobiography provided a wide-ranging view of life in French intellectual circles from the 1930s to 1970s: *Memoirs of a Dutiful Daughter* (1958), *The Prime of Life* (1960), *Force of Circumstance* (1963), and *All Said and Done* (1970). De Beauvoir also explored the social problems of the neglect of the elderly in *Old Age* (1970) and dealt with the death of her mother from cancer in *A Very Easy Death* (1964).

References and Further Reading
Bair, Deirdre. 1990. *Simone de Beauvoir: A Life.* London: Jonathan Cape.
Beauvoir, Simone de. 1972. [1953.] *The Second Sex.* Reprint, Harmondsworth: Penguin.
Francis, Claude, and Fernand Goutier, trans. 1989. *Simone de Beauvoir.* London: Mandarin.
Heath, Jane. 1989. *Simone de Beauvoir.* Hemel Hempstead, UK: Harvester Wheatsheaf.
Whitmarsh, A. 1981. *Simone de Beauvoir and the Limits of Commitment.* Cambridge: Cambridge University Press.

Beccari, Alaide Gualberta
(1842–1906)
Italy

The focal point of the slow-to-develop women's movement in Italy was for many years a single journal—*Woman*—published by Alaide Beccari, a republican, pacifist, and pioneering writer on social issues. The journal lent its voice in the 1870s and 1880s to the campaign for the reform of the 1865 civil code and for the abolition of state-regulated prostitution in 1888 that had been introduced in the Cavour Regulation of 1860.

Beccari's father, a civil servant in Padua (then part of the Austro-Hungarian Empire), was active in the Italian *Risorgimento.* Having taken part in the 1848 revolution, during which he lost his fortune and his job, he was forced to leave Padua and took refuge with Cavour's forces in Turin. The only survivor of his twelve children, Beccari worked for a while as her father's secretary. She returned to Padua after it was liberated by forces from the state of Lombardy-Venetia and took up journalism, although she was plagued with very poor health all her life.

At the age of only sixteen, in 1868, she founded the journal the *Woman* in Venice. Published fortnightly, the journal raised the issue of women's rights in Italy—but not until after the country had been unified by Giuseppe Garibaldi in 1861. On its pages, the journal drew women's attention to the growing activism for social, moral, and political reform being embraced by women in France, the United States, and Britain. For twenty years under Beccari's editorship, *Woman* continued to consistently promote equal rights for women, emphasizing cooperation between women of all classes and acting as an important stimulus to the developing Italian women's movement. It published the feminist writings of pioneer women such as Anna Maria Mozzoni and supported her in her campaign (in tandem with Josephine Butler's similar campaign in England) from 1878 against state-regulated prostitution. The journal was also widely read by male legislators and teachers, and its pioneering articles were translated and printed in the *Englishwoman's Review*.

In 1877 Beccari was gratified to see a series of proreform articles in the *Woman* encourage 3,000 women to sign a petition on women's suffrage, no mean feat at a time when the majority of Italian women were illiterate. In the 1870s, under Beccari's pacifist impetus and her vision of woman as the "citizen mother" whose natural dignity was an antidote to male militarism, the *Woman* drew attention to the growing international peace movement. It publicized the 1870 establishment of the International Association of Women (IAW) in Geneva by Marie Goegg and printed announcements of peace conferences and new societies as they sprang up. Although Beccari fought against a tide of indifference to the cause, she continued to argue for women's right to a decent education if they were adequately to fulfill their roles as mothers; equally, she felt acknowledgement of their economic role as workers was long overdue.

In the meantime, persistent ill health had blighted Beccari's own life, so much so that she was forced to edit her journal from her bed. In December 1880 she launched a drive on its pages for women's suffrage. She moved to Bologna in 1887, but ill health finally forced her to give up editing the *Woman* a year later, and she was replaced by Emilia Mariani. Beccari continued to help other women embark on writing careers, wrote children's plays, and founded a children's magazine titled *Mamma*.

In 1892 Beccari moved to Turin. In her final years, discouraged by the lack of popular support for a women's movement in Italy, she turned in-

creasingly to socialist concerns, in so doing losing the support of moderates in the movement. She died of German measles, which she contracted after nursing a poor child.

See also Butler, Josephine; Goegg, Marie Pouchoulin; Mozzoni, Anna Maria.
References and Further Reading
Berkin, Carol R., and Clara M. Lovett. 1980. *Women: War and Revolution.* New York: Holmes and Meier.
Howard, Judith Jeffrey. 1977. "The Civil Code of 1865 and the Origins of the Feminist Movement in Italy." In B. B. Caroli, R. F. Harney, and L. F. Tomasi, eds., *The Italian Immigrant Woman in North America.* Toronto: The Multicultural History Society of Ontario.
Josephson, Harold, Sandi Cooper, and Steven C. Hause et al., eds. 1985. *Biographical Dictionary of Modern Peace Leaders.* Westport, CT: Greenwood Press.

Becker, Lydia
(1827–1890)
United Kingdom

For thirty years, the suffragist moderate Lydia Becker rallied support for women's franchise as a basic constitutional right both at the national level and in her own city of Manchester. Her outstanding *Women's Suffrage Journal* became both an important mouthpiece for the movement and an essential source for later historians of British feminism. Becker made a particular point in her campaigning of supporting the rights of middle-class women to have control over their property and earnings and of identifying the particular difficulties of their social position. Lacking the greater independence of both working women, particularly in the manufacturing industries, and those in the aristocracy, middle-class women were, in her view, more commonly the victims of social ostracization if they acted independently in defense of their rights.

Becker was the eldest of fifteen children born in Manchester to a family that had originated in Thuringia, Germany. Her father ran a calico bleaching factory and provided a relatively comfortable home environment in which Becker was educated and displayed intellectual talents and a love of reading from a young age. She took a particular interest in science, studying astronomy and botany and in 1864 publishing *Botany for Novices.* Two years later she produced a companion volume, *Elementary Astronomy,* but it was never published. She corresponded with Charles Darwin, with whom she discussed botanical research.

By the time she reached the age of forty, unmarried and without children, Becker was one of those many middle-class Victorian women desperately seeking a vocation. Her first steps toward liberation came with the establishment of the short-lived Manchester Ladies Literary Society. In its modest way, the society offered women a much-needed opportunity for intellectual advancement, emphasizing the importance of their study of philosophy and science. But it was in October 1866 at a meeting of the National Association for the Promotion of Social Science, held in Manchester, that Becker was galvanized by a paper by feminist Barbara Bodichon entitled "Reasons for the Enfranchisement of Women." In February of the following year, Becker was elected honorary secretary of the Manchester Women's Suffrage Committee—the first suffrage body, albeit provisional, to be founded in England. In March, Becker published her own article, "Female Suffrage," in the *Contemporary Review.* In the autumn of 1867, the committee became the Manchester National Society for Women's Suffrage (MNSWS), and Becker would be its guiding force until her death, both as a first-class administrator and as a tireless lobbyist for private members' bills on women's suffrage, in the preparation of which she made a study of constitutional law and parliamentary procedures.

In 1867, as the result of either clerical error or a simple oversight, the name of a woman shopkeeper, Lily Maxwell, found its way into the electoral roll for a by-election in Manchester. Becker took full advantage of the opportunity to gain publicity for the suffrage cause from this unprecedented event and persuaded the timid Maxwell duly to cast her vote. After she had done so, Becker attempted to get other women householders included on the electoral roll as their statutory right, but appeals to the courts soon quashed these claims, most notably in a test case, *Chorlton v. Lings,* mounted by Dr. Richard Pankhurst (husband of Emmeline Pankhurst) with Becker's assistance in Manchester. In this case, barristers representing 5,346 women in Manchester argued their right to the franchise under ancient English law.

In 1868 Becker chaired the MNSWS's first public women's suffrage meeting, held at the Free Trade Hall in Manchester. As a liberal and a moderate, Becker collaborated with the Liberal Party in Lancashire in supporting free trade. But in her suffrage campaigning, she fought to retain the MNSWS's political neutrality, and resisted attempts to include Liberal women's groups in the society, a fact that prompted several members to decamp to form the Central National Society for Women's Suffrage. In 1869 Becker became engaged in lecture tours for suffrage in and around the north of England. In her 1869 article for the *Contemporary Review,* "On the Study of Science by Women," she added her voice to the growing debate over women's learning capacities, and in 1870, with the passing of William Forster's Education Act, like other feminists Becker recognized an opportunity for women to take up public work by standing for election to the newly instituted school boards. She was elected in Manchester, where she criticized the excessive emphasis on domestic skills in its girls' schools. She was continuously reelected to this post until her death in 1890.

In March 1870 Becker founded the *Women's Suffrage Journal,* which she would edit and also frequently subsidize financially until 1890 (when it folded after her death), and through which she almost single-handedly "kept the question of women's suffrage alive in England for the next twenty years" (Chafetz and Dworkin 1986, 114). Thereafter the suffrage movement temporarily stalled until the Women's Franchise League established by the Pankhursts in 1889 began to gain ground. The journal, which contained many contributions from Becker, would provide later historians with a mass of invaluable material on social attitudes and the position of women in Victorian England.

Back in 1867, Becker had collaborated with Josephine Butler (whom she greatly admired and supported) in the campaign to repeal the Contagious Diseases Acts; she also worked with Elizabeth Wolstenholme-Elmy in preparing an address to the council of the National Association for the Promotion of Social Science, asking for its support in reforming the laws governing married women's right to their own property and earnings. In 1868 she became treasurer of the Married Women's Property Committee but would be forced to resign in 1874 when, after the election of a Conservative government, she endorsed the exclusion of married women from the vote in William Woodall's parliamentary bill on suffrage. This bill proposed that the franchise be awarded only to those single women and widows holding the same property qualification as men. It had been primarily a tactical decision on Becker's part, made in hopes of improving the chances of at least limited legislation on women's suffrage being passed, but it lost her friends and left her isolated in later years, during which she also increasingly became the butt of uncharitable comments about her plain, "bluestocking" appearance.

In 1880 Becker returned to suffrage campaigning as parliamentary secretary of the Central Committee of the National Society for Women's Suffrage, which was based in London. During the 1880s she spoke at several public meetings in support of women's suffrage, but her health began to fail, and she traveled to France for a rest cure, where she contracted diphtheria, dying soon after in Geneva. In her day Becker was admired for her statecraft by Christabel Pankhurst, but her somewhat forbidding personality, as Dale Spender (1982) points out, all too often made her the butt of parody by those who viewed her as an austere and embittered spinster.

See also Bodichon, Barbara; Butler, Josephine; Pankhurst, Christabel; Pankhurst, Emmeline; Wolstenholme-Elmy, Elizabeth.

References and Further Reading
Blackburn, Helen. 1971 [1902]. *Women's Suffrage: A Record of the Women's Suffrage Movement in the British Isles with Biographical Sketches of Miss Becker*. Reprint, New York: Kraus Reprint Company.
Chafetz, Janet, and Gary Dworkin. 1986. *Female Revolt: Women's Movements in World and Historical Perspective*. Totowa, NJ: Rowman and Allanheld.
Crawford, Elizabeth. 1999. *The Women's Suffrage Movement, 1866–1928: A Reference Guide*. London: University College of London Press.
Holcombe, Lee. 1983. *Wives and Property: Reform of the Married Women's Property Law in Nineteenth-Century England*. Toronto: University of Toronto Press.
Holton, Sandra Stanley. 1996. *Suffrage Days: Stories from the Women's Suffrage Movement*. London: Routledge.
Kelly, Audrey. 1992. *Lydia Becker and the Cause*. Lancaster: Centre for North-West Regional Studies.
Levine, Phillipa. 1990. *Feminist Lives in Victorian England: Private Roles and Public Commitment*. Oxford: Blackwell.
Lewis, Jane. 1987. *Before the Vote Was Won: Arguments for and against Women's Suffrage*. London: Routledge and Kegan Paul.
McHugh, Paul. 1980. *Prostitution and Victorian Social Reform*. London: Croom Helm.
Shanley, Mary Lyndon. 1989. *Feminism, Marriage, and the Law in Victorian England, 1850–1895*. Princeton: Princeton University Press.
Spender, Dale. 1982. *Women of Ideas, and What Men Have Done to Them*. London: Routledge and Kegan Paul.

Beecher, Catharine Esther
(1800–1878)
United States

The American educational and domestic reformer Catharine Beecher came from a family of campaigning evangelicals and was the elder sister of abolitionist and writer Harriet Beecher Stowe. A staunch advocate of women's separate sphere of work, which she emphasized as at all times being in the service of God, she was an opponent of the women's suffrage movement. Beecher believed that to invest political power in women would cause them to turn their backs on their duties within the home, where she saw their role as teacher-missionaries engaged in the moral regeneration of society.

Born in East Hampton, New York, Beecher was the eldest of thirteen children of congregational preacher Lyman Beecher. She was educated at home in her mother Roxana's private school and subsequently at a private school in Litchfield, Connecticut. But at the age of sixteen, Beecher became a surrogate mother to her siblings when their own mother died. In 1821 she took up a teaching post at a girls' school in New London. She was briefly engaged to a Yale mathematics professor, Alexander Fisher, and went into a deep depression when he was lost at sea in 1823. She never married, instead accepting this loss as a sign from God that she should devote her life to the cause of women's education. In 1824 she founded a school for young ladies with her sister May, which later became the Hartford Female Seminary, a few years after another educational pioneer, Emma Willard, opened her own similar establishment, the Troy Seminary.

Catharine Esther Beecher (Bettmann/Corbis)

Beecher also began writing the first of numerous essays on women's education as well as textbooks for schools, such as "Female Education" in 1827 and the 1829 pamphlet, "Suggestions Respecting Improvements in Education." In it, she advocated not only the intellectual advancement of women but also the moral training that would guide them in their leadership of the regeneration of society through the professions of nursing and teaching. Her strong support for temperance and women's role in the movement was colored by her belief, as with teaching, that women occupied a higher moral ground than men.

In 1832 Beecher moved to Cincinnati with her father when he took up a post as president of the Lane Theological Seminary there. She opened another school, the Western Female Institute, which she ran until 1837, when financial difficulties and her ill health forced her to give up her position. Believing that a whole new generation of women teachers were urgently needed in the new frontier towns of the West, Beecher preempted the later exhortation of Horace Greeley (1850) by urging not young men but young women to "go west." In her 1835 *Essay on the Education of Female Teachers,* Beecher estimated

that 30,000 teachers were needed and that women were the ideal candidates because they would accept lower wages. Throughout the 1840s, Beecher worked energetically to encourage more women to go into the teaching profession, selecting and appointing likely candidates through her membership in the Ladies' Society for Improving Education in the West and the Board of National Popular Education, which enlisted 500 women from New England to take up the teaching challenge in the West. Her founding in 1852 of the American Woman's Educational Association was instrumental in the establishment of colleges to train women teachers in Wisconsin, Iowa, and Illinois. Sadly, these ventures were short-lived.

In 1837 Beecher returned to the East Coast. In 1841 she did for American homemakers what the celebrated Mrs. Beeton would do in England by writing a housewife's "Bible," in which she lauded the vocational domestic skills of women. The *Treatise on Domestic Economy for the Use of Young Ladies at Home and at School* would be the first American manual to approach the subject of household management from a scientific as well as a domestic point of view. It proved so popular that it was regularly reprinted over the next fifteen years and provided Beecher with a welcome income. Another later revision of this work, undertaken with her sister Harriet Beecher Stowe, was published as *The American Woman's Home or Principles of Domestic Science* (1869) and laid down further ground rules for the running of an efficient and hygienic home.

Beecher's writings were considerable, including "An Essay on Slavery and Abolitionism with Reference to the Duty of American Women to Their Country" (1837), which emphasized women's pacifism and decried their involvement in combative campaigning. In her 1846 pamphlet, "The Evils Suffered by American Women and American Children," and the 1851 work, *True Remedies for the Wrongs of Women,* Beecher further argued against the lack of fresh air and exercise afforded to women and the subjection to tight corseting that caused them physical and mental damage. As an early advocate of calisthenics—a gentle form of gymnastics that had originated in Germany—she encouraged the adoption of healthy and regular exercise in her 1857 work, *Physiology and Calisthenics for Schools and Families.*

By 1871 Beecher had been obliged to compromise on her opposition to equal pay for women (she had originally justified lower pay for women as a necessity if they were to gain more work), but in *Woman Suffrage and Woman's Profession* (1871) she continued to argue for women's primary dedication to domestic roles as wives and mothers. Although Beecher's insistence on this limiting role alienated her from many feminists and suffragists, notably illustrated in her 1837 debate with Angelina Grimké over women's entry into public life (Grimké had made public speeches against slavery), she did, as Olive Banks has argued, at least prompt women to enter the less controversial movement for moral reform, which in turn "led feminism into the attempt to use the vote to transform society itself" (Banks 1990, 88).

In 1874 Beecher published her autobiography, *Educational Reminiscences*. She also tackled religious and moral issues in an opus of over thirty published works, including *Elements of Mental and Moral Philosophy* (1831), *Letters on the Difficulties of Religion* (1836), and *Common Sense Applied to Religion* (1857). Despite her frail health and recurring mental and physical crises, Beecher thrived on hard work to live to the age of seventy-eight.

See also Grimké, Angelina Emily and Sarah Moore; Stowe, Harriet Beecher; Willard, Emma Hart.

References and Further Reading

Banks, Olive. 1990 [1981]. *Faces of Feminism: A Study of Feminism as a Social Movement.* Reprint, Oxford: Blackwell.

Boydston, J., et al., eds. 1988. *The Limits of Sisterhood: The Beecher Sisters on Women's Rights and Women's Sphere.* Chapel Hill: University of North Carolina Press.

Kerber, Linda K., and Jane DeHart-Mathews. 2000. *Women's America: Refocusing the Past.* New York: Oxford University Press.

Melder, Keith E. 1977. *The Beginnings of Sisterhood: The American Woman's Rights Movement, 1800–1850.* New York: Schocken.

Rugoff, Milton. 1982. *The Beechers: An American Family in the Nineteenth Century.* New York: Harper & Row.

Sklar, Katharine. 1976. *Catherine Beecher: A Study in American Domesticity.* New Haven: Yale University Press.

Behruzi, Mariam
(1945–)
Iran

A leading female parliamentarian and lawyer since the Iranian Revolution in 1979, Behruzi began speaking out in defense of women's rights at a time when the government was calling for a return to traditional Islamic values and the exclusion of women from many areas of public life, including her own profession, the law.

Behruzi was alarmed at the way in which women were being deprived of a public role by being encouraged to go back into the home and return to their traditional roles as wives and mothers. She argued that women entering politics was not antithetical to Islamic law and that they should be allowed a role in the *majlis* (the Iranian parliament), citing the example of the Prophet Muhammad's daughter, Fatimah, who made insightful pronouncements and public speeches on political and social issues.

Born in Tehran, the daughter of a well-known cleric, Behruzi completed high school and, although she was married at age fifteen, continued her studies at the university level. She began giving lectures to women on religious practice and the Qu'ran and took an active part in anti-Shah demonstrations in the 1970s. In 1975 she was prohibited from continuing her political activities and went underground, only to be arrested and imprisoned in 1978–1979.

Behruzi was elected as one of the first female members of the new Iranian parliament in 1980. As a member of the Committee on the Family, which was set up in 1984, she called for fuller discussion of family rights, particularly with regard to the decisionmaking processes of divorce courts. In her opinion, these courts did not place sufficient emphasis on the rights of wives and children, particularly in cases of child custody, which always favored the husbands. Behruzi also lent her support to the idea of awarding compensation to divorced women for the time they had given up to their domestic roles in the home and drew attention to the need to provide welfare in the form of shelter and jobs to "unprotected" single women so that they could support themselves. However, at a congress in Beijing in 1981 she had condemned abortion and also defended the precepts of the Islamic criminal code.

In 1986 Behruzi became head of the Zeinab's

Association, a group committed to promoting women's education and raising their social and political consciousness. By 1995 the association had enrolled 150 students in its course on Islamic knowledge and had encouraged several thousand to take up the study of Arabic and English. But successes here were countered by Behruzi's failure in the *majlis* to carry an addendum to Article 42 of the Organization Bill, which would have sanctioned the establishment of a special committee to explore women's issues.

In 1991 Behruzi stood for election to the fourth *majlis* and was one of nine women to be elected. She immediately directed her energies toward issues affecting the family and women's fuller participation in national affairs and achieved ratification of a bill allowing women in the civil service to retire after twenty years and resume a role at home. She also fought to have women admitted to all the various committees of the fourth *majlis,* arguing that women had an inherent sensitivity to social needs.

Behruzi returned to campaigning in preparation for elections to the fifth *majlis* as one of only five female candidates. By now she had achieved a high public profile as a leading female politician and commentator on women's issues and had the confidence to be more sweeping in her criticism of traditional patriarchal attitudes that undervalued the contribution of women. During the campaign, she was emphatic that "women's participation in the public domain had been condoned by the Koran" and that their involvement in the foundation of Islam was "a fundamental matter of creed" (Afshar 1998, 50). Although Behruzi was not reelected, her efforts were validated when, as a result of her campaigning, the *majlis* rubber-stamped the creation of a women's committee.

After losing her parliamentary seat, Behruzi turned her attention to promoting the work of women lawyers and accentuating their unique skills and insights. This was part of a campaign to have more women appointed to the courts as legal advisers to judges, although the difficulties of avoiding contravention of religious practice by having women working in close proximity to men have made this a difficult issue. In justification of her case, Behruzi has repeatedly raised instances of women's unique contribution to the Islamic revolution and has repeated Ayatollah Khomeini's own endorsement of women taking an active part in "all domains" (Afshar 1998, 123). Again, Behruzi's campaigning led to women being allowed to once again study at the faculties of law, which had been banned under Khomeini when women had been excluded from working in the Iranian legal system. Behruzi's intelligent arguments placed within a feminist interpretation of Islamic law contributed to a change in attitude toward the role of women in the legal system. They have since been allowed to assist in the custody of minors as well as work as advisers in administrative justice and family courts.

Behruzi has served as an organizer of the Iranian Women's Islamic Association and is chair of Islamic studies at the University of Shaheed Beheshti. She advocates the wearing of the *hijab* as a symbol of chastity and has criticized the Turkish government for forbidding women from wearing the veil and traditional Islamic dress. Her son was killed during the Iran-Iraq War of 1980–1988.

References and Further Reading

Afshar, Haleh. 1998. *Islam and Feminisms.* Basingstoke: Macmillan.

Mogadam, Valentine M. 1993. *Modernizing Women: Gender and Social Change in the Middle East.* Boulder, CO: Lynne Rienner.

Belmont, Alva
(1853–1933)
United States

Of all the least likely candidates for the title "social reformer," none could have been further removed from the everyday realities of women's struggle to survive than the fantastically wealthy American socialite Alva Belmont. Married into the Vanderbilt family, she spent millions of her husband's money building and furnishing a grotesque baroque marble folly at Newport, Rhode Island. But having espoused the cause of women's suffrage with tremendous gusto, she would in later life donate much of her fortune to running the women's suffrage campaign and become one of its most efficient managers.

The daughter of a cotton planter, Alva Erskine Smith was born in Mobile, Alabama, in the deep South. After the Civil War, the family lived for a time in France, where she was educated in genteel private schools. In 1875, much to his family's alarm, she married one of the most eligible bachelors in the United States—William K. Vanderbilt, grandson of the famous shipping and railroad magnate Cornelius. With New York society of the time notoriously snobbish about who it would admit to its inner sanctums, the Vanderbilts (as relatively new social interlopers) had to buy their way into the elite of the city's "Four Hundred" top families (mainly old money), controlled by Mrs. William Astor. They did so through an orgy of expensive entertaining and the construction of their Fifth Avenue and Rhode Island mansions, the former personally supervised by Belmont, who worked closely with its architect. These two houses eventually cost the Vanderbilts about $3 million and $9 million, respectively, by the time they were completed. In 1895, having climbed her way up the greasy pole of social ambition, Belmont invited opprobrium by daring to divorce her husband for his adultery. A few months later, she regained lost social ground by pulling off a major coup, marrying their daughter Consuelo to the duke of Marlborough and into the cream of the British aristocracy. Alva herself quickly remarried, to a younger man, the banker Oliver Hazard Perry Belmont. It was not until after his death in 1908, however, that she abandoned the social whirl of New York high society to fight for women's suffrage. Like many late converts to causes from which their social status had distanced them, Belmont espoused the women's movement with the same kind of enthusiasm and energy with which she had conducted her assault on New York society, becoming closely involved with the militant suffrage wing led by Alice Paul.

From 1909, when she founded the Political Equality League (a New York suffrage group of which she served as president), Belmont's money would fund the campaign; she also paid for the National American Woman Suffrage Association to relocate its headquarters from Ohio to New York, providing it with elegant Fifth Avenue offices (at an annual rent, paid by her, of $5,000). Her various homes would also host the suffrage campaign's high-profile fund-raising events, such as the 1914 Conference of Great Women held at her Newport mansion, and provide for the comforts of visiting luminaries such as Christabel Pankhurst, whose 1914 lecture tour to the United States Belmont organized.

Aside from her many public speeches and her

Alva Belmont (Library of Congress)

articles on women's rights in journals such as *Harper's Bazaar, Collier's, Forum, North American Review,* and *Ladies' Home Journal,* Belmont took up radical activism in support of striking women garment workers, such as the famous shirtwaist makers' strike in New York, in which around 20,000 women participated during 1909– 1910. She joined them on picket lines, donated funds, hired the use of the New York Hippodrome and Carnegie Hall for major rallies, and worked for the New York Women's Trade Union League in keeping the strike alive for thirteen weeks, although it ultimately failed to achieve all its objectives. Over the next few years, Belmont embraced numerous welfare projects with enthusiasm: she organized low-cost canteens for workers; established housing projects for poor women; and donated money to hospitals, children's homes, and churches. She took to picketing and lecturing with aplomb, and poured her money into mounting eye-catching suffrage motorcades. In 1912 she headed a great suffrage parade down Fifth Avenue.

In 1913 Belmont joined the newly formed Congressional Union and was voted onto its executive board. She was also on the executive of the National Woman's Party (NWP), which succeeded the Congressional Union in 1917. Its headquarters were based at a Washington, D.C., residence bought specifically for the purpose by Belmont. Elected president in 1921, she paid for and oversaw the party's central office near the Capitol, and also funded its national press bureau, managed by Ida Husted Harper, until her death. In 1916 Belmont ventured into the world of music, with Elsa Maxwell cowriting a suffragist operetta, *Melinda and Her Sisters*. She traveled abroad on numerous occasions as a delegate of the NWP, attending conferences in Europe, such as the 1925 conference of the International Woman Suffrage Alliance in Paris and the 1930 Conference on the Codification of International Law in The Hague, and advocated an end to discrimination against women in international law.

One of the American suffrage movement's most flamboyant and wealthy figures, Belmont is said to have offered the sage advice, "Pray to God. She will help you." After the vote was awarded to American women in 1920, Belmont returned to a former interest in architectural design. She died in Paris at one of her several French residences where she had been carrying out restoration projects. Having been one of the first women admitted to the American Institute of Architects, she was brought home to be buried alongside the great and good in New York's Woodlawn Cemetery.

See also Pankhurst, Christabel; Paul, Alice.
References and Further Reading
Adickes, Sandra. 1997. *To Be Young Was Very Heaven: Women in New York before the Great War.* Basingstoke: Macmillan.
Balsan, Consuelo Vanderbilt. 1952. *The Glitter and the Gold.* New York: Harper.
Buell, Janet W. 1990. "Alva Belmont: From Socialite to Feminist." *The Historian* 52(2): 219–241.
Foner, Philip. 1979. *Women and the American Labor Movement,* vol. 1, *From Colonial Times to the Eve of World War I.* New York: Free Press.
Rector, Margaret Hayden. *Alva, That Vanderbilt-Belmont Woman.* Wickford, RI: Dutch Island Press.

Bennett, Louie
(1870–1956)
Ireland

A pacifist, suffragist, and lifelong trade unionist, Louie Bennett committed herself to nonmilitant methods in all the many areas of activism to which she devoted her life. She was particularly vigorous in promoting the interests of Irish working women right up until her death at the age of eighty-six.

Bennett was born in Dublin into a prosperous Protestant family. She was educated in England and at Alexandra College in Dublin and, as a young woman, studied singing on the Continent. She turned her hand to writing novels such as *The Proving of Priscilla* (1902) and *A Prisoner of His Word* (1908) before taking up the suffragist cause.

As cofounder, with her friend Helen Chevenix, of the Irish Women's Suffrage Federation in 1911, she took an interest not just in obtaining the franchise for women but in drawing attention to the exploitation of women in the workplace and in particular the plight of those employed in sweatshops. As a pacifist, she opposed the more militant activities of the Irish Women's Franchise League but would not condemn them. Instead, she channeled her energies into coordinating the suffrage movement with the women's labor movement. In her quest to gain basic economic justice for women workers, she cofounded the Irish Women's Reform League in 1913 and affiliated it with the federation. She was particularly incensed by the exploitation of female juveniles, who were paid even less than adult women. Because child labor in turn created high levels of unemployment among those older women, Bennett campaigned to make employment of children under the age of fifteen illegal.

During a major lockout of workers during the 1913 Dublin strike, Bennett was inspired by the relief work of Constance de Markievicz and Hannah Sheehy-Skeffington and served meals in soup kitchens and provided assistance to strikers' families. During World War I, she managed to overcome the mistrust of the trade union movement's leader, James Connolly, although she found him dictatorial to work with and resisted his interference in her trade union activities. Her firm leadership as secretary of the Irish Women Workers Union (IWWU) from 1916 to 1955 ensured that it remained separate and autonomous from male trade unions. It was a union organized by women for women, a fact that opened up its appeal to a wider membership, which reached 2,000 by 1918. Some in the trade union movement criticized this ghettoization of women within their own separate union and called for mixed-sex unions, but for Bennett having single-sex unions was the only way of guarding against the male temptation to subordinate women's trade unions to their own. In any event, Bennett's attitude toward women working was always a somewhat ambivalent one, for she looked upon their employment as being an "unfortunate necessity" and a "menace to family life" that could cause hardships for women with children (Ward 1983, 242).

Despite her private reservations, As general secretary of the IWWU, Bennett campaigned vigorously against limits being placed on women's right to work and first helped working women to exert their political muscle in 1917, when, despite hating strikes because of the misery that they caused, she was galvanized into leading a women laundry workers' strike. The women were campaigning for an extra week's holiday a year, better ventilation and sanitary conditions, and the provision of canteen facilities, as well as a reduction in the working week to fifty hours. Having seen the appalling conditions in which these women worked, in dilapidated buildings and outhouses with little or no heat and light, leaking roofs, and plagues of rats, Bennett joined them on the picket lines in the pouring rain. An employer seeing her thus engaged admonished her that this was inappropriate for someone of her class, to which Bennett responded: "It is far more important that your girls should get enough to live on than I should keep out of the wet" (Fox 1958, 73).

In 1918 Bennett declined nomination as a Labour Party candidate in the general election. During the Irish Civil War of 1922–1923, she tried to avert the fighting by acting as a conciliator and led a peace campaign by the IWWU. Although she was a passionate supporter of the Irish cause and wanted to see Ireland reunified as an independent country on a federal system, as a pacifist she did not engage in nationalist activities but instead lent her support to the wider concerns of world peace. Bennett had been one of a group of vociferous Irish women pacifists during World War I and subsequently spent much time writing and speaking in support of disarmament, endorsing the work of the League of Nations, and attending its conference in Geneva in 1928. She also represented Ireland on the International Executive of the Women's International League for Peace and Freedom, becoming president of its Fifth Congress, held in Dublin in 1926.

In 1932 Bennett became the first woman president of the Irish Trade Union Conference. Speaking on the maintenance of basic wages for skilled workers, she argued that women should be paid the same rates as men and suggested that this could be achieved through an international system of labor agreements. In 1935 she opposed changes to women's working rights proposed by Eamon de Valera's Conditions of Employment Bill. The onset of another war in 1939 did not slow Bennett down: until 1943 she served as a member of the Commission on Vocational Organization, and throughout the war she helped mobilize food and fuel supplies and organized hot meals for schoolchildren. In the 1944 general election, Bennett stood as a Labour Party candidate for Dublin County but failed to win a seat; to compensate, she threw her energies into local work for the health service and housing. At war's end in 1945, she found herself in charge of a fourteen-week strike by 1,500 female laundry workers, the resolution of which brought the workers a statutory two weeks' paid annual holiday, and a forty-five-hour working week.

During her final years, Bennett campaigned against the development of the atom bomb, the war in Korea, and high levels of military spending by governments and was called upon to speak out on behalf of exploited workers in the British colonies. As a humanitarian and moderate, she loathed the aggression of industrial confrontation and the economic suffering brought upon the families of those on strike. In all her trade union negotiating, she tried always to take a moderate stand and earned the respect of employers for her willingness to try every possible means of achieving settlement via peaceful negotiation.

See also Markievicz, Constance de; Sheehy-Skeffington, Hannah.

References and Further Reading

Fox, Richard M. 1958. *Louie Bennett: Her Life and Times.* Dublin: Talbot Press.

Ó Céirín, Kit, and Cyril Ó Céirín, eds. 1996. *Women of Ireland: A Biographic Dictionary.* Kinvara, County Galway: Tír Eolas.

Ward, Margaret. 1983. *Unmanageable Revolutionaries: Women and Irish Nationalism.* London: Pluto Press.

Benson, Stella
(1892–1933)
United Kingdom/Hong Kong

The feminist novelist and suffragist Stella Benson spent the last years of her short life leading an important campaign against the brothel system in Hong Kong and voicing her concerns for the care of women suffering from venereal disease. Educated at home because of her poor health, Benson nevertheless became active in the women's suffrage movement in England and during World War I worked in London's East End for the Charity Organisation Society, campaigning for the welfare of prostitutes. She also ran her own business in Hoxton making paper bags. She published her first novel, *I Pose,* in 1915 and her second, *This Is the End,* in 1917 before ill health forced her to seek the warmth of California in 1918. After a succession of make-do jobs, she eventually obtained a post tutoring at the University of California. Her experiences in the United States were worked into a satirical novel, *The Poor Man* (1922).

In 1920 Benson returned home via China, teaching for a while at the Diocesan Boys School in Hong Kong and working at the American hospital in Beijing. Back in London in 1921, she married James Anderson, an official in the Chinese Customs Service. The couple's honeymoon, spent traveling the United States in a Ford, formed the basis of her novel *The Little World* (1925). After the couple returned to live in China, Benson published several more novels and collections of short stories, including her most successful book, *Tobit Transplanted* (1931; published in New York as *The Run-Away Bride* in 1930), about the upheavals experienced by White Russians exiled in Manchuria after the Russian Revolution. In 1931 she set aside her writing to become involved in a League of Nations subcommittee assigned to conduct a survey of li-censed prostitution in Hong Kong as part of a wider League of Nations–backed traveling commission inquiring into the international traffic in women.

Working in conjunction with Gladys Forster and despite their different attitudes toward the causes and cures of prostitution (with Forster taking the traditional, moral, and Christian feminist view), Benson worked diligently to expose the high numbers of underage girls engaged in prostitution and the terrible toll of disease they suffered. Benson's approach to the problem, based on the need for legal changes, was in fundamental contrast to the previous work of Christian missionaries, who had offered relief and sometimes refuge but never any real solution.

During the course of their investigation, Benson and Forster interviewed many young prostitutes, and Benson took detailed and dispassionate notes that testify to the sale and enticement of young girls into prostitution, their enslavement by pimps, and the horrific disfigurement of prostitutes suffering from incurable venereal disease. Many were able to keep working only through the constant payment of bribes to inspectors, police, and other corrupt officials on top of high fees to their brothel mistresses. Benson recorded their misery, loneliness, and homesickness; but she made no moral judgments, averring that "it is the coercion of a living creature to unnatural courses that hurts me" (Hoe 1996, 207). In many cases, girls had been mortgaged by their own families; their sale to brothels raised money often used to educate and train sons of the family. Benson was appalled by the meek acquiescence of the girls themselves, who were brought up to accept traditional Asian attitudes of female subordination and filial duty.

The governor of Hong Kong attempted to curtail the work of Benson and Forster after the League of Nations report had been completed. He looked upon the women on the subcommittee as uninformed amateurs who had been interfering in a system that until then the British government had tolerated as a necessary evil (supposedly to control the spread of venereal disease among British and Chinese servicemen). But the women prevailed in their campaigning. In December 1931, and also under pressure from the British parliament, the governor was forced to agree to the phased abolition of state-regulated brothels in Hong Kong, followed by a shut-down of those run by Chinese and Europeans over the next couple of years. Two years later, at the age of forty, Benson, who had settled in Hongay in the province of Tonkin (then part of northern Indochina), took ill with pneumonia and died.

At the time of the publication of her bestseller *Tobit Transplanted* in 1931, Benson returned to England to receive the A. C. Benson Silver Medal of the Royal Society of Literature. Weak and constantly coughing (her tuberculosis was by then well advanced), she dined with Virginia Woolf, relating stories about the Hong Kong slave trade to her. A year later she was dead. As her friend, the writer Naomi Mitchison, relates: "Her books are in the chilling basement of the London Library, along with a few other good novelists and countless more bad or indifferent ones, much read in their time, now forgotten" (Mitchison 1979, 137). Also mostly forgotten is Benson's humanitarian work in China.

See also Brittain, Vera; Holtby, Winifred.

References and Further Reading

Bedell, R. Meredith. 1983. *Stella Benson*. Boston: Twayne.

Brittain, Vera. 1979 [1957]. *Testament of Experience: An Autobiographical Story of the Years 1925–1950.* Reprint, London: Virago.

Grant, Joy. 1988. *Stella Benson: A Biography.* London: Macmillan.

Hoe, Susanna. 1991. *The Private Life of Old Hong Kong.* Hong Kong: Oxford University Press.

———. 1996. *Chinese Footprints: Exploring Women's History in China, Hong Kong and Macau.* Hong Kong: Roundhouse Publications.

Mitchison, Naomi. 1979. *You May Well Ask: A Memoir 1920–1940.* London: Flamingo.

Besant, Annie
(1847–1933)
United Kingdom/India

A small woman of enormous energy, one of the first to take a stand in support of birth control in Britain, Annie Besant was an indefatigable propagandist for the causes that she so fervently adopted during an extremely active life. These ranged from freethinking, socialism, trade unionism, and the rights of working and married women to the care of the homeless and deprived. In her later years, she espoused Theoso-

phy and the nationalist cause in India, although her work on the subcontinent would eventually languish in the shadow of Mahatma Gandhi. Besant insisted that her primary objective in all things had been to follow the truth, and she proved a fine orator, admired by Elizabeth Cady Stanton, who considered her without peer among women public speakers in Britain. So too did fellow social reformer Beatrice Webb, who in 1887 described Besant as "the only woman I have ever known who . . . had the gift of public persuasion" (Taylor 1992, 35). Her life falls into two clear phases, the first one of socialist activism in England to 1885, and the second her involvement in Theosophy, which took her to India, where she would remain until her death.

Besant's family were of Irish ancestry, and she grew up with an intensely devout religious faith. The family was forced to live in straitened circumstances after her father's death when she was five. Denied the kind of education her brothers received, she was sent away to Dorset to be educated at the school of the progressive educator and friend of the family Ellen Marryatt until she was sixteen. After spending time abroad, Besant found herself cornered into accepting an offer of marriage from the uninspiring and conventional Frank Besant, a schoolmaster at Cheltenham. She did so "out of sheer weakness and fear of inflicting pain," as she later observed (Harrison 1977, 51), when she was only twenty, and lived to regret it. Two children were born in quick succession in 1869 and 1870, and Besant felt increasingly isolated and enslaved by her situation at a time when she was also rapidly losing her religious faith. When her husband took up a curacy in Lincolnshire, she tried to find an outlet in nursing local villagers during a typhoid epidemic. With her spiritual life in crisis, she wrote a pamphlet entitled "The Deity of Jesus of Nazareth by the Wife of a Beneficed Clergyman" in 1873 and refused to attend communion. Her husband asked her to leave.

After briefly trying to run her own school, Besant was drawn to the ideas of the radical atheist and freethinker Charles Bradlaugh. She also discovered a talent for public speaking (the timbre of her voice was noted by many in later years), and after Bradlaugh heard Besant speak in 1874, he offered her a job writing for and coediting a freethinker journal, the *National Reformer*. Now militant in her atheism, Besant began touring

Annie Besant (Library of Congress)

and lecturing at meetings of freethinkers in her desire to do away with religious bigotry and superstition in the fight for truth and a just society. Besant's atheism placed her always outside the suffrage movement, whose conservative mainstream could never accept this attitude nor her status as a separated wife (she would never be able to get a divorce and marry Bradlaugh). Besant's response to the hostility she constantly encountered in her defense of women's rights was pragmatic: "If the Bible and Religion stand in the way of women's rights then the Bible and Religion must go" (Longford 1981, 146).

In 1874 Besant became vice president of the National Secular Society and became fanatical in her very public advocacy of secularism to such a degree, indeed, that she alienated some would-be supporters—particularly in works such as her 1877 book, *The Gospel of Atheism*. In the late 1870s, she embraced a new cause, determined both to aid poor working-class women forced to endure endless unwanted pregnancies and to counter the high infant mortality rates and the unhealthy, overcrowded conditions in which so many poor families lived. In 1877 she and Bradlaugh organized the republication of a sixpenny

pamphlet advocating birth control, *The Fruits of Philosophy,* originally written by U.S. doctor Charles Knowlton in 1832 in support of the social, medical, and economic needs for population control. The book explained the functioning of the reproductive system and some methods of contraception with accompanying diagrams (later deemed obscene), and was brought out by Besant and Bradlaugh with additional medical notes by Dr. George Drysdale, who supported Bradlaugh and the Malthusian League as a result of his own concern over population control. The pamphlet was produced without any support from English feminists, who were fearful that any endorsement they might give to Besant's cause might damage their own.

After publication of the pamphlet, Besant and Bradlaugh were charged with obscenity and the promotion of sex outside marriage. In court, Besant distinguished herself with an eloquent and impassioned account of the suffering of the poor, describing her own firsthand observations made in the slums of the East End. The core of her argument challenged Victorian hypocrisy, with Besant asserting that "it is more moral to prevent the birth of children than it is after they are born to murder them . . . by want of food, and air, and clothing, and sustenance" (Manvell 1976, 91).

She and Bradlaugh were found guilty, fined £200 for selling an indecent book, and sentenced to six months in prison. On appeal the sentence was quashed over a legal technicality, but Besant paid a high price for her legal triumph. As a result of the scandal attached to the case and the subsequent publication by Besant of yet another controversial pamphlet, "Atheism and Malthusianism," Besant's estranged husband succeeded, after a long legal battle throughout 1878 and 1879, in gaining custody of her daughter Mabel, who had until then lived with Annie; her son Digby had remained with his father. Her access to her children was so restricted thereafter that Besant made the painful decision that it would be better for them if she cut herself off for the time being (she was reunited with them in the late 1880s, when they left their father to go and live with her).

Meanwhile, in the wake of the trial, sales of *The Fruits of Philosophy* rocketed from a few thousand to 185,000 sold between 1878 and 1881 by the Freethought Publishing Company. Besant published another pamphlet in 1879, "The Law of Population: Its Consequences, and Its Bearing upon Human Conduct and Morals," in which she updated the limited medical information provided in Knowlton's 1832 work. Dedicating this work specifically to the poor, she discussed the increasing social problems brought about by the population explosion and overcrowding in urban slums. The first birth control tract written by a woman for women, the pamphlet was targeted specifically at working-class women, describing methods of contraception such as the "safe period," coitus interruptus, and the use of douches and sponges. By 1887, when it appeared in its 110th printing (it sold 175,000 copies by 1891), Besant was also advocating the use of a kind of pessary, the new cervical cap, but it would be more than forty years before the first birth control clinic would eventually be opened by Marie Stopes in 1921. Meanwhile, in Britain, Besant's efforts to disseminate birth control literature contributed to a drop in the birth rate from the 1870s to the end of the century.

During this difficult period, Besant consoled herself by taking advantage of new university rules on the admission of women and studied for a degree in science at Birkbeck College in London, passing the preliminary exams in botany with first-class honors. The powers that be at Birkbeck chose not to publish her name in the list of results, however. The stigma of the *Fruits of Philosophy* case would dog her for the rest of her time in England.

Undaunted, in 1878 Besant produced a pamphlet in which, writing from all-too-painful personal experience, she argued against legal marriage so that unhappy marriages might be avoided and proposed that if women were accorded greater equality with men in relationships, they would not need to marry.

During 1881–1884, Besant had an intense affair with the socialist Edward Aveling, but he subsequently left her for Eleanor Marx. In 1884 after meeting George Bernard Shaw, Besant subsumed her need for passion in her life into socialism. (Shaw would later base the character of Raina in his play *Arms and the Man* on her.) She had already been active in the Social Democratic Federation and had joined the Fabians in 1885. She and journalist William Thomas Stead founded a socialist journal, *The Link,* to champion the rights of the oppressed and she also contributed to an important collection of articles edited by Shaw, the *Fabian Essays in Socialism* (1889). Along with many other women activists, Besant made use of a rare opportunity for women to enter public service by standing for election to the boards that controlled state schools. During 1887–1890 she served as a member of the London School Board for Tower Hamlets, introducing free school meals for poor children and lobbying for free medical care to be provided.

In 1888 Besant found herself at the center of another cause célèbre—this time the first strike in support of unskilled women factory workers in London's East End. In June of that year, she had published an article entitled "White Slavery in London" in *The Link,* denouncing the long hours worked by women who did piecework in their homes and in the sweatshops and singling out the plight of those employed at the Bryant and May match factory, whose lives, she argued, were sacrificed for a paltry four shillings a week in the cause of giving shareholders their 23 percent. Like Alice Hamilton in the United States, Besant catalogued the appalling physical effects of factory employment on women workers, such as hair loss and the condition known as "phossy jaw"—a degenerative disease of the teeth, gums, and jawbones caused by ingesting phosphorus fumes during the manufacturing process. She was asked with Clementina Black to organize and publicize a strike by 1,400 of these women. It became a landmark in the history of English women's trade unionism, equaling the famous shirtwaist makers strike of 1909–1910 in the United States. After a three-week strike, the management of Bryant and May's caved in and agreed to introduce a radical overhaul of working conditions. Besant herself went back into the slums and factories after the strike and wrote and lectured on the miserable lives of other workers, from those who made matchboxes in their own homes to workers in the gas and printing industries.

At the end of the 1880s, becoming dissatisfied that socialism alone could not offer her all the answers she sought to the ills in society, Besant rediscovered her spiritual self in a new esoteric religious cult, which would unfortunately invite further derision and once again set her apart from many of her former colleagues and friends, including Shaw and even her closest ally, Charles Bradlaugh. She became a member of the circle surrounding Madame Helena Petrovna Blavatsky, a Russian émigré who founded Theosophy, a religious movement that combined philosophy, mysticism, and Hindu and Buddhist teachings. Having been captivated by Blavatsky's *The Secret Doctrine* (1888), an overview of her basic Theosophical teachings, Besant visited her and by 1889 had become a dedicated handmaiden, turning to vegetarianism and spiritualism and wholeheartedly adopting Blavatsky's beliefs in reincarnation. Before long, Blavatsky's inner sanctum had decamped to Besant's home in St. John's Wood, which became the society's official headquarters. Besant took over the editorship of the Theosophist magazine *Lucifer* and, after Blavatsky's death in 1891, became head of the movement in Europe and India.

It was this newfound religion that took Besant to India, a country that, because of Theosophy, represented for her the source of all ancient wisdom and that she began to look upon as her true spiritual home. But, having arrived there in 1893, true to character she was soon expending her energies on a myriad of new causes in education and social reform—in particular campaigning against child marriage, the caste system, and the plight of the untouchables—and enlisting the support of Indian members of the Theosophical Society. She learned Sanskrit and oversaw the publication of works on Hinduism, in 1895 translating the classic Indian work *The Bhagavad Gita*. In 1898 she founded Central Hindu College at Benares, the first of several educational institutions (including the Central Hindu Girls' School in Benares) that she would establish in India, founded on Indian ideals and culture rather than Western models. In addition to all this activity, she still retained her links with English reformers and gave her continued support, from a distance, to the English suffrage movement.

From her first days in India, Besant was critical of British rule and the imposition of English mores on its ancient culture. After she was elected president of the Theosophical Society in 1907, she settled in Madras. By this time, she had adopted an Indian lifestyle and wore a sari. She encouraged the dissemination of Indian literature and philosophy and promoted indigenous Indian arts and crafts and the Swadeshi boycott of British textiles. She bought the Indian newspaper the *Madras Standard* and relaunched it

under the title *New India* as a vehicle for Indian self-government. As an associate of Mahatma Gandhi, Besant supported Indian home rule, founding the India Home Rule League in 1916. Although she rejected Gandhi's policies on civil disobedience as being too militant, she campaigned in earnest for Indian nationalism from 1913, publishing a collection of her lectures, *Wake Up India: A Plea for Social Reform,* and taking on much speech making and pamphlet writing. Her high public and political profile also attracted many Indian women into the campaign for women's suffrage in India, with Besant adamant that real reform there could only be achieved when women had the vote.

In 1917 Besant was arrested and interned on a hill station for her vociferous condemnation of British rule, but the resulting public protest in India was so unprecedented that the authorities had to release her. That year she was also elected as the first woman president of the Indian National Congress (a post she held until 1923), although she was by no means the only woman associated with it. But Besant, the ersatz Indian for all her sari, found that her appeal as a spiritual and political leader was rapidly being eclipsed by that of a native leader—Gandhi—and her influence further waned with her disapproval of his policies of noncooperation with British officials from 1919. Besant left the Indian National Congress in 1923 after disagreeing over its campaigning methods. She remained a confirmed advocate of constitutional reform in India (in 1924 founding the National Constitutional Convention) and retained the respect she had earned as a social reformer by turning to other activities, such as founding the Indian Boy Scout movement in 1917 and serving as president of the Women's Indian Association in 1917.

In her final years, Besant adopted a protégé, Jidda Krishnamurti, whom she proclaimed to be Theosophy's new spiritual leader. She toured and lectured on his behalf, until in 1929 he seceded from the movement. In 1933 Annie Besant died at the Theosophical Society's headquarters in Adyar, near Madras, still searching for the answer to life's riddles. She was given a traditional Indian cremation. In its obituary, the *Hindu Patriot* summed up her unique contribution: "An extraordinary woman, Irish by birth, English by manner, Indian by adoption" (Bennett 1988, 54). She was the author of over 100 books and pamphlets, including *On the Nature and Existence of God* (1875), *Reincarnation* (1892), *Esoteric Christianity* (1901), *Theosophy and the New Psychology* (1904), *Lectures on Political Science* (1919), and *Shall India Live or Die?* (1925).

See also Black, Clementina; Hamilton, Alice; Stanton, Elizabeth Cady; Stopes, Marie; Webb, Beatrice.

References and Further Reading
Bennett, Olivia. 1988. *Annie Besant*. London: Hamish Hamilton.
Besant, Annie. 1903. *An Autobiography*. 2d ed. London: T. Fisher Unwin.
Burton, Antoinette. 1994. *Burdens of History: British Feminists, Indian Women and Imperial Culture 1865–1915*. Baltimore: Johns Hopkins University Press.
Chaudhuri, Nupur, and Margaret Strobel, eds. 1992. *Western Women and Imperialism: Complicity and Resistance*. Bloomington: Indiana University Press.
Dinnage, Rosemary. 1987. *Annie Besant*. Harmondsworth: Penguin.
Harrison, Fraser. 1977. *The Dark Angel: Aspects of Victorian Sexuality*. London: Sheldon Press.
Jayawardena, Kumari. 1995. *The White Woman's Other Burden: Western Women and South Asia during British Rule*. London: Routledge.
Longford, Elizabeth. 1981. *Eminent Victorian Women*. London: Weidenfeld and Nicolson.
Manvell, Roger. 1976. *The Trial of Annie Besant and Charles Bradlaugh*. London: Elek/Pemberton.
Nethercot, Arthur. 1960. *The First Five Lives of Annie Besant*. London: Rupert Hart-Davis.
———. 1963. *The Last Four Lives of Annie Besant*. London: Rupert Hart-Davis.
Parker, Julia. 1988. *Women and Welfare: Ten Victorian Women in Public Social Service*. Basingstoke: Macmillan.
Reynolds, Moira Davidson. 1994. *Women Advocates of Reproductive Rights: 11 Who Led the Struggle in the United States and Great Britain*. Jefferson, NC: McFarland.
Taylor, Anne. 1992. *Annie Besant: A Biography*. Oxford: Oxford University Press.
Tuson, Penelope, ed. 1997. *The Queen's Daughters: An Anthology of Victorian Feminist Writings on India 1857–1900*. Reading, Berkshire, UK: Ithaca Press.

Bethune, Mary McCleod
(1875–1955)
United States

One of the first black women to serve as a presidential adviser on black and minority groups—to Presidents Herbert Hoover, Franklin Delano Roosevelt, and Harry S. Truman—Mary McCleod Bethune was a highly influential figure in the U.S. government. She also set out to invest a sense of pride in young black men and women by opening up further education to them and advancing their employment in the professions. But above all, she dedicated herself to obtaining for black Americans the basic civil rights enjoyed by whites as laid down in the U.S. Constitution.

Bethune's parents had been slaves in South Carolina, and during her deprived childhood at Mayesville as one of seventeen children, she struggled to educate herself while working on the family's cotton and corn fields. She won a scholarship to the Scotia Seminary, a Presbyterian school in North Carolina, in 1888 and in 1894 studied at the Moody Bible Institute in Chicago, graduating in 1895 with the intention of becoming a Presbyterian missionary in Africa. But when her application to do so was turned down, Bethune taught at mission schools in Georgia and South Carolina until 1903.

After her marriage failed, Bethune founded a small school in 1904, the Daytona Normal and Industrial Institute for Girls in Daytona Beach, Florida. Bethune's school had extremely modest beginnings in a four-room frame house with five girl pupils and her own son. She raised money by soliciting funds from local clubs, churches, and businesses, and even resorted to selling potato cakes and ice cream to workers on a nearby construction site, but such was her shortage of funds that she used "charred splinters for pencils, mashed elderberries for ink, and a packing case for a desk" (Trager 1994, 369). A year later, the number of pupils had risen to 100. Further funding given to Bethune by the industrial magnate and philanthropist James Gamble in 1912 helped the school expand its site and erect more buildings. In 1923, with the support of the Board of Education for Negroes of the Methodist Episcopal Church, the 300 pupils of Bethune's school merged with a men's college, Cookman Institute, to become Bethune-Cookman College. With its motto, "Enter to Learn, Depart to Serve," the college would eventually have 1,000 students. Bethune served as its president and was a major fund-raiser until the end of 1942.

Meanwhile, Bethune also worked tirelessly for the black community by bringing black women into the movement for civil rights, first through the National Association of Colored Women (as president, 1924–1928). In 1935 she founded the influential National Council of Negro Women (NCNW), an amalgamation of several smaller associations of black women. As its president from 1935 to 1949, working from its headquarters in Washington, Bethune liaised with other groups, such as the National Association for the Advancement of Colored People (NAACP, of which she served as vice president in 1940–1945), the Young Women's Christian Association (YWCA), and the League of Women Voters, to combat segregation and racial discrimination at the national level.

Bethune secured a first for American black women in 1936, when she became an adviser to President Roosevelt after he appointed her head of the Office of Minority Affairs (later changed to director of the Division of Negro Affairs) of the National Youth Administration (NYA). During her tenure until 1944, Bethune became a close friend of Eleanor Roosevelt. It was thanks to Bethune's tutelage that Eleanor Roosevelt would become a leading advocate of black civil rights. Bethune's work on numerous youth projects for the NYA went a considerable way toward achieving higher employment levels for blacks in the state administration and the enrollment of more black men and women in colleges and graduate programs through her administration of the Special Negro Fund, which provided grants to black college students. Bethune herself became an important voice in Roosevelt's "black cabinet," the unofficial name given to the Federal Council on Negro Affairs, which she established in 1936 to encourage greater participation by blacks in New Deal economic projects and to educate governmental officials about black civil rights.

During World War II, Bethune assisted the secretary of war in the appointment of black women to train as officers in the Women's Army Corps, and at war's end she was a delegate of the State Department at the foundation of the United Nations in San Francisco in 1945. She published numerous articles in *Ebony,* the *Journal of Negro History,* the *Pittsburgh Courier,* and the *Chicago Defender,* one of her most notable being "Certain Unalienable Rights" in the 1944 collection *What the Negro Wants.* A devout Christian who worked for the constitutional rights of all American blacks, Bethune wrote of her unshakeable commitment in a June 1941 ar-

ticle in *Who, the Magazine about People* ("Faith Can Move a Dump Heap"): "For I am my mother's daughter, and the drums of Africa still beat in my heart. They will not let me rest while there is a single Negro boy or girl without a chance to prove his worth." It was this self-sacrifice and dedication that brought her many honors during her lifetime, including the NAACP's Spingarn Medal (1935), the Francis A. Drexel Award (1936), and the Thomas Jefferson Award (1942). She also received the Italian Medal of Honor and Merit in 1949.

See also Roosevelt, (Anna) Eleanor.
References and Further Reading

Bethune, Mary McCleod. 1999. *Mary Mcleod Bethune: Building a Better World: Essays and Selected Documents.* Edited by Audrey Thomas McCluskey and Elaine M. Smith. Bloomington: Indiana University Press.

Holt, Rackham. 1964. *Mary McCleod Bethune: A Biography.* New York: Doubleday.

Lerner, Gerda, ed. 1972. *Black Women in White America: A Documentary History.* New York: Pantheon Books.

McKissack, Patricia C. 1991. *Mary McCleod Bethune: A Great Teacher.* Hillside, NJ: Enslow.

Peare, Catherine Owen. 1951. *Mary McCleod Bethune.* New York: Vanguard.

Sterne, Emma Gelders. 1957. *Mary McCleod Bethune.* New York: Alfred A. Knopf.

Trager, James. 1994. *The Women's Chronology: A Year-by-Year Record, from Prehistory to the Present.* London: Aurum Press.

Bhatt, Ela
(1933–)
India

Ela Bhatt's work as founder and general secretary of the Self-Employed Women's Association (SEWA) has made a huge difference in the working lives of poor women in India. By offering moral and legal support about issues of low pay and exploitation and by teaching self-reliance through the innovative provision of a union-run cooperative bank that provides share capital, her organization has helped many impoverished Indian women start up and maintain their own small businesses.

Following family tradition, Bhatt trained as a lawyer and, as an admirer of the work of Mahatma Gandhi, committed herself to taking up social concerns. Between 1955 and 1958, she worked on labor law proposals for the Textile Labour Association, and after the birth of her children, from the late 1960s she specialized in labor issues for the association's newly established women's section, based in Ahmadabad in west-central India, the country's sixth most populous industrial center.

Until the 1960s, the women's section had confined itself to training women in conventional skills such as sewing, embroidery, and typing, but Bhatt realized that there was a whole army of unskilled, destitute women who could benefit from access to training and welfare. She had been observing with growing concern, particularly in the light of the decline of the city's cotton industry, the struggle to make a living of poor women market sellers from Ahmadabad's slums. These women, often accompanied by their children, would sit for long hours by their stalls trying to make a few rupees; many of them were migrant workers and had only the barest kind of makeshift shelters. Bhatt recognized the desperate need for some kind of association or union to protect these women from exploitation, police and official harassment (mainly involving peremptory fines for "illegal" trading), and financial difficulty frequently brought on by recourse to unscrupulous moneylenders. Initially, she helped organize a small group of twenty-four women who worked in the cloth market carrying loads on their heads after they discovered that no proper records were being kept of the number of loads they carried and thus they were being cheated out of their full earnings.

But there were many other women in cottage industries needing Bhatt's help: women who made incense sticks and rolled cigarettes or made brooms, and women who sold a wide variety of goods from used clothes to fruit and vegetables, textiles, weaving, and basketwork. Bhatt was also approached for help by other women workers in agriculture, female carpenters and metalworkers, and even women who picked the city's rubbish heaps for waste paper.

Because 89 percent of the Indian workforce was self-employed, Bhatt was convinced that the key to economic prosperity lay with these hardworking people, in particular poor women in rural regions. The union's fundamental role would be to draw public attention to their indispensability to the economy. In addition, their accep-

Ela Bhatt (Archive Photos)

tance of hard work would be encouraged through the provision of bank loans so that they could develop their businesses and avoid being exploited by middlemen.

Bhatt set up the Self-Employed Women's Association (SEWA) on 3 December 1971, and it was recognized by the government as a legitimate trade union in April 1972. In its first years, its membership was only a few thousand, but by the end of 1995 it had grown to become the biggest trade union in India, with 218,700 members from all castes. The growth of union membership gave the union much more bargaining power and enabled it to negotiate numerous health care and maternity benefits for its members, as well as offering them help with housing and child care, life insurance, and legal aid. Bhatt also introduced literacy training. By affiliating itself with other large unions such as the International Union of Food and Tobacco Workers and the International Federation of Plantation, Agricultural and Allied Workers, SEWA increased international exposure of the abuses suffered by low-paid, self-employed workers throughout the world.

Equally important, members of SEWA were encouraged by Bhatt to set themselves up in cooperative groups according to their trade. In this way tools and expertise could be shared, production quotas could be organized, and the members could collectively buy materials in larger, cheaper quantities and subsequently even market their own goods. There are now more than seventy co-operatives, each with at least 1,000 members. The establishment in 1974 of SEWA's own bank made it possible for low-income women workers to acquire modest financial investment for improving their businesses without falling prey to money-lenders and pawnbrokers. Such was her unique experience in opening up banking to Third World women, exemplified in her 1975 book *Profiles of Self-Employed Women,* that Bhatt became founder of the Women's World Banking Association in 1980; she has been its chairperson since 1985. And the SEWA bank itself has confounded its critics with a recovery rate on loans made to poor women of 98 percent.

Bhatt's distinguished career as a trade unionist eventually led to public life as an Indian member of parliament between 1986 and 1989 and as the first woman member of the Indian Planning Commission (1989–1991). She has traveled to many countries to observe the varying levels of women's economic status and to see how different societies encourage self-sufficiency in their members. In the course of encouraging women to organize their working lives, she has also taught them awareness of other social concerns and emphasized the need for literacy.

A woman of great organizational gifts who since 1971 has inspired the belief in many people that they *can* grow and develop their own small businesses, Bhatt has received many prestigious humanitarian awards for her years of service at SEWA. These include the Susan B. Anthony Award for National Integration (1982), the Right Livelihood Award for "Changing the Human Environment" (Stockholm, 1984), the Women in Creation Award, the Alliance des Femmes (Paris, 1990), and the Ramón Magsaysay Award for Community Leadership (Manila, 1997), with this latter award given for "making a reality of the Gandhian principle of self-help among the depressed workforce of self-employed women" (Rose 1992, 28). For further information on SEWA, contact http://www.sewa.org.

References and Further Reading
Calman, Leslie. 1992. *Toward Empowerment: Women and Movement in India.* Boulder, CO: Westview Press.
Rose, Kalima. 1992. *Where Women Are Leaders.* London: Zed Books.

Sreenivasan, Jyotsna. 2000. *Ela Bhatt: Uniting Women in India.* New York: Feminist Press.

Billington-Greig, Teresa
(1877–1964)
United Kingdom

An important figure in the women's suffrage movement in Scotland, Teresa Billington-Greig was also a founder of the Women's Freedom League, after finding it impossible to countenance the Pankhursts' dictatorial leadership of the Women's Social and Political Union (WSPU). She remained discontented, however, with all the women's groups in which she became involved. As an individualist, she was unable ever to quite square her own passionately held beliefs with organized methods of protest.

Born the daughter of a shipping clerk in Preston, Lancashire, Billington-Greig was brought up a strict Roman Catholic and educated at a convent in Blackburn. After being apprenticed to a milliner, which she hated, she decamped to attend extension classes at Manchester University and train as a teacher for the Municipal Education School Service there. By the time she took up a teaching post in 1901, she had become an outspoken agnostic and was threatened with the loss of her teaching post for refusing to teach religious subjects. She appealed to Emmeline Pankhurst, who served on the education committee, for help. Pankhurst responded by securing Billington-Greig a new post in a Jewish school. At around this time, Billington-Greig also joined the Ancoats University Settlement in Manchester (1902–1905).

Having become a close friend of the Pankhursts, Billington-Greig was one of the first to join the newly founded WSPU at the end of 1903, where she worked with Annie Kenney, speaking at churches, trade unions, and debating groups. Kenney was impressed with Billington-Greig's skill at debate and her gifts of oratory, in which she wielded her "sledge-hammer of logic and cold reason" (Mackenzie 1975, 23). Through this organization, Billington-Greig also promoted equality for women teachers, from 1904 calling for equal pay for them as the founder and secretary of the Manchester Teachers' Equal Pay League.

In 1905 at the request of Emmeline Pankhurst and socialist leader Kier Hardie, Billington-Greig became the first woman organizer of the Independent Labour Party, giving up teaching and all her other commitments to take this on as a full-time job. In 1906 she was also offered work as a paid organizer for the WSPU in London, in which capacity she helped set up a major demonstration in Trafalgar Square in May 1906 in support of women's suffrage. Soon after, having been involved in scuffles outside the home of Chancellor of the Exchequer Herbert Asquith, she was sent to Holloway Prison until her fine was paid by a sympathizer.

In the summer of 1906, Billington-Greig was sent to Scotland to recruit for the WSPU and found local branches, scoring considerable success in the major cities; that year she also published *Towards Women's Liberty.* Through the semiautonomous WSPU branches in Scotland, Billington-Greig became a popular figure in the union, rivaling even Emmeline and Christabel Pankhurst. When in October 1907, Emmeline announced the inception of a virtual dictatorship of the WSPU in order to concentrate the campaign for suffrage under tightly centralized control, Billington-Greig left in protest. As a supporter of the Labour Party, she was also disenchanted with the Pankhursts' decision to forbid their members from collaborating with it, thus distancing themselves from the socialist tradition from which the WSPU had sprung. The Pankhursts too had found her presence disruptive, viewing her as a troublemaker who should be called to heel.

Billington-Greig responded by cofounding a new, democratically structured organization, the Women's Freedom League (WFL), with Charlotte Despard and Edith How-Martyn. For a short while, it operated as a splinter group within the WSPU, but by the beginning of 1908 she was setting up branches across Britain. Although it remained the smallest of the three leading suffrage organizations, according to Andro Linklater, it "defied expectations by outliving, outworking and outfeminizing every other suffrage society" (1980, 120), with Billington-Greig proving to be its outstanding strategist and theoretician and publishing numerous essays in the ensuing years. By 1914 the WFL had 4,000 members, and it did not disband until 1961.

Although Billington-Greig was elected chair and organizing secretary of the WFL, she concentrated her efforts on organizing propaganda campaigns in Scotland, where she had become a leading figure in the Scottish suffrage movement. The WFL was joined by many members of the WSPU in Scotland, and together with Despard and How-Martyn, Billington-Greig made her own political statements through acts of civil disobedience such as organizing tax resistance and a boycott of the census in 1911. But once again, Billington-Greig's volatile personality made it difficult for her to accept compromises. In her insistence on total democratic participation in the league, she became rattled by Despard's dominating personality, and the WFL leadership was often rife with dissent. Billington-Greig was depressed by this disunity and disappointed that the reality of campaigning life never matched up to her own high ideals.

Billington-Greig gave up her work for suffrage in 1911 and resigned from the WFL. She was disappointed that the British movement had opted for a narrow concentration on women's suffrage to the exclusion of other, equally pressing issues of women's rights. She gave time over to writing a scathing attack on the WSPU in her 1911 book, *The Militant Suffrage Movement,* which Brian Harrison applauds for its "rare mix of intelligent analysis and participant observation" (1987, 45), and in which she criticized the WSPU's abandonment of its labor roots and the poor by currying support among the conservative and middle-class elite. She drifted away from activism thereafter, deeply disillusioned and sidelined by financial and domestic problems. In 1914 she reemerged to give a pioneering lecture on birth control, published in 1915 as "Commonsense on the Population Question," and took a strong pacifist position during World War I, when she took in Belgian refugees. She briefly returned to activism for the WFL in 1937–1938. During World War II, she was involved in the evacuation of children from London by the London County Council. From 1946 to 1949, she served as honorary director of the WFL's Women for Westminster campaign, advocating women's greater involvement in the political life of the country through the support of women candidates in elections. But in all her activities, Billington-Greig remained on the periphery, unable to sublimate herself in the collective spirit of organized groups, and asserting, "I shall be a militant rebel to the end of my days" (Harrison 1987, 71).

See also Despard, Charlotte; How-Martyn, Edith; Kenney, Annie; Pankhurst, Christabel; Pankhurst, Emmeline.

References and Further Reading

Crawford, Elizabeth. 1999. *The Women's Suffrage Movement, 1866–1928: A Reference Guide.* London: University College of London Press.

Harrison, Brian. 1987. *Prudent Revolutionaries: Portraits of British Feminists between the Wars.* Oxford: Clarendon Press.

Leneman, Leah. 1991. *A Guid Cause: The Women's Suffrage Movement in Scotland.* Aberdeen: Aberdeen University Press.

Liddington, Jill, and Jill Norris. 2000 [1978]. *One Hand Tied behind Us.* Rev. ed., London: Virago.

Linklater, Andre. 1980. *An Unhusbanded Life: Charlotte Despard, Suffragette, Socialist, and Sinn Feiner.* London: Hutchinson.

Mackenzie, Midge. 1975. *Shoulder to Shoulder.* London: Penguin.

McPhee, C., and A. Fitzgerald, eds. 1987. *The Non-Violent Militant: Selected Writings of Teresa Billington-Greig.* London: Routledge and Kegan Paul.

Black, Clementina
(1853–1922)
United Kingdom

The English trade unionist and industrial reformer Clementina Black was one of the first British women to support the rights of unskilled women employed in sweatshops. Her output as a novelist was overshadowed by her important studies of working conditions and her defense of a legal minimum wage for women. She was also a suffragist, encouraging working women to support the cause through the Women's Industrial Council, and an advocate of cooperative housing.

Black was born in Brighton, East Sussex, where her father was town clerk. She was educated at home with her sister Constance (who later became the noted Russian translator Constance Garnett). But when Black was twenty-two, her mother died, and Black had to take over the nursing of her invalid father as well as the care of seven younger siblings. She began writing and, after the death of her father in 1877, moved to London. There she published her first novel, *A Sussex Idyll,* and continued to research several more at the library of the British Museum as well as lecturing on eighteenth-century literature.

In addition to her literary aspirations, Black developed an interest in the rights of working women and wage parity. She became friends with Eleanor Marx and through her in 1886 was introduced to the work of Lady Emilia Dilke and Emma Paterson's Women's Protective and Provident League (WPPL), one of the first organizations to attempt to provide medical care and help in old age for workers. She became secretary of the league (later known as the Women's Trade Union League) and began lecturing on behalf of women's trade unions in an attempt to establish links between middle-class feminists and the male trade union movement. Eventually, finding the WPPL insufficiently radical in its activities, she joined the Women's Trade Union Association (WTUA) in 1889 to continue her work for better conditions in Britain's sweatshops.

Blackburn began exploring new ways of lobbying manufacturers to improve the low wages paid to women workers through a new pressure group, the Consumers' League. In 1888 she and Annie Besant helped organize the strike by 1,400 East End matchgirls at the Bryant and May's factory, through the efforts of the WPPL and the London Trades Council achieving a settlement that broke new ground in women's trade unionism in Britain. In 1890 she initiated the idea that employees should work only within comfortable limits and not have to endure long hours that precluded all rest and relaxation. She lobbied the London County Council to extend its concern for welfare in the workplace by ensuring that its fair wages rules covered women sweatshop workers and that any work the council gave out went to companies that paid a "living wage" to seamstresses—suggesting four-pence an hour as the minimum.

In 1894 the WTUA merged with the Women's Industrial Council, with Blackburn chosen as president, a post she retained for twenty years. During this time, she edited its publication, *Women's Industrial News,* and published important propagandist studies of women in industry, including *Sweated Industry and the Minimum Wage* (1907); *Makers of Our Clothes: A Case for Trade Boards* (1909); and her most important contribution, *Married Women's Work* (1915), in which she advocated that women learn independence and the self-respect of undertaking work of some kind, whether or not their economic needs dictated it. She also included forceful arguments for the emancipation of those who already worked long hours in industry from the additional burden of household tasks through the introduction of cooperative housing, including nursery, cooking, and laundry facilities, and the institution of a minimum wage for unskilled workers monitored by wage boards. She advocated these and other issues relating to women's work as vice president of the National Anti-Sweating League and at a 1906 conference she organized in London on the minimum wage.

Black was also a member of the Fabian Society and was active in the suffrage movement as a member of the London branch of the National Union of Women's Suffrage Societies. She edited the suffrage journal *Common Cause* during 1912–1913, only one of her many journalistic activities. Her fiction, including the three-volume novel *Orlando* (1879) and a novel with a socialist message, *An Agitator* (1894), is now sadly forgotten.

See also Besant, Annie; Dilke, Emilia; Paterson, Emma.

References and Further Reading

Crawford, Elizabeth. 1999. *The Women's Suffrage Movement, 1866–1928: A Reference Guide.* London: University College of London Press.

Glage, Liselotte. 1981. *Clementina Black: A Study in Social History and Literature.* Heidelberg: C. Winter Universitätsverlag.

Mappen, E. 1985. *Helping Women at Work: The Women's Industrial Council, 1889–1914.* London: Hutchinson.

Nicholls, C. S., ed. 1993. *Dictionary of National Biography: Missing Persons.* Oxford: Oxford University Press.

Blackburn, Helen
(1842–1903)
Ireland/United Kingdom

The Irish suffragist Helen Blackburn, who settled in England when she was seventeen, was one of the first to recognize the important contribution women made to the industrial wealth of the nation. She became an early campaigner for the rights of women workers and argued against separate protective legislation for women. With Jessie Boucherett, Blackburn founded the Freedom of Labour Defence League, which promoted self-employment in preference to wage labor.

Born in Knightstown in County Kerry, Ireland, Blackburn was the daughter of an inventor and civil engineer who managed a quarry. The

family moved to London in 1859, and in 1874 at the age of thirty-two, Blackburn became secretary of the London Central Committee of the National Society for Women's Suffrage, remaining in that post until 1895. From 1880 to 1895, she also acted as secretary of the Bristol and West of England Suffrage Society, organizing local demonstrations in support of the cause. She published various pamphlets on women's suffrage: "Some of the Facts of the Women's Suffrage Question" and "Comments on the Opposition to Women's Suffrage" (both in 1878) and "Because: Being Reasons from Fifty Women Workers Why It Is of National Importance That the Parliamentary Franchise Be No Longer Denied to Women as Women" (1888).

In 1881 Blackburn began a long collaboration and friendship with Jessie Boucherett, former editor of the *Englishwoman's Review,* which Blackburn edited from 1889 to 1902. With Boucherett, Blackburn wrote *A Handbook for Women Engaged in Social and Political Work* (1881). For her, the issue of the self-determination of women workers as men's equals was paramount, and she opposed extension of the Factory Acts, which provided protection to female workers different from that given to male workers. In 1885 she organized an exhibition of women's industries in Bristol that emphasized women's pride in their work and its professionalism and that was later seen at the 1893 World's Columbian Exhibition in Chicago.

For two years from 1895 to 1897, Blackburn was forced to give up her activism to care for her invalid father. During that time, she worked with Boucherett on *The Condition of Working Women and the Factory,* which they published in 1896. In 1899 the two women, already active in the Liberty and Property Defence League, founded the Freedom of Labour Defence League to voice their opposition to the introduction of protective legislation for women, in the belief that limitations placed upon women's choice of professional career would erode their earning power.

In 1902 Blackburn produced a classic history, written from the moderate perspective and thus largely ignoring the contributions of radical women: *Women's Suffrage: A Record of the Movement in the British Isles.* She also contributed the chapter on the suffrage movement in Great Britain published in volume 6 of the classic American work, *The History of Woman Suffrage,* edited by Susan B. Anthony and Ida Husted Harper. In 1903 Blackburn and Norma Vynne cowrote *Women under the Factory Acts.*

See also Boucherett, Jessie.

References and Further Reading
Banks, Olive, ed. 1985, 1990. *The Biographical Dictionary of British Feminists,* vol. 1, *1800–1930;* vol. 2, *1900–1945.* Brighton: Harvester Wheatsheaf.
Crawford, Elizabeth. 1999. *The Women's Suffrage Movement, 1866–1928: A Reference Guide.* London: University College of London Press.
Lewis, Jane. 1987. *Before the Vote Was Won: Arguments for and against Women's Suffrage.* London: Routledge and Kegan Paul.

Blackburn, Molly
(1930–1985)
South Africa

A prominent white civil rights campaigner and member of the organization Black Sash, Blackburn earned a unique position of trust among the black community in the townships of the eastern Cape, with whom she worked closely in defense of their civil liberties. Blackburn's valuable work was cut short by a fatal car crash at the age of fifty-five.

Blackburn was the daughter of Edgar Bellhouse, a liberal, Progressive Party politician. She studied at the Collegiate School for Girls in Port Elizabeth and at Rhodes University in Grahamstown. Her first marriage took her to Europe (1954–1963), and on her return to South Africa in 1967 she married a doctor named Gavin Blackburn.

In 1981 she was elected as a Progressive Party candidate to the Cape Provincial Council, which provided a platform from which she tirelessly worked for civil rights and racial justice for the remaining three years of her life. In 1982, increasingly concerned with the problems of poverty and prejudice endured by the populations of the black townships, she rejoined Black Sash, an organization to which she had belonged in the 1960s. This action group of predominantly white, middle-class women had been formed in 1955 to protest the withdrawal of voting rights from Cape coloureds by the South African government and was so named because the women protesters wore black mourning sashes at civil rights demonstrations. Concentrating her efforts

in the Cradock township in the eastern Cape, Blackburn took up the defense of its inhabitants and gave them advice on forming their own civic association. She also criticized the heavy-handedness of the official administration in its treatment of blacks and the police abuse of black civil rights prisoners under arrest. She compiled a dossier on such abuses and gave the press and sympathetic South African members of parliament access to it, warning also that the populations of the black townships were becoming alienated to the point of violent protest.

Blackburn regularly courted reprisals in the form of criminal charges, abusive phone calls, and death threats for her outspokenness against apartheid at the funerals of black activists and for her confrontational attitude toward the government of the National Party. In July 1985 she was arrested after speaking at a commemorative service for black leaders held at Zwide. That same year she and another Black Sash activist, Di Bishop, led the lobbying for a commission of inquiry by six members of parliament (including Helen Suzman) into the shootings of twenty black demonstrators at Langa township at Uilenhage in March.

In December 1985 Blackburn was killed in a head-on car collision on her way back from visiting the township of Oudshoor, where the black residents had been intimidated with threats of eviction. Blackburn's funeral in Port Elizabeth was attended by 20,000 mourners, many of them black people who came to pay their respects to a woman they had come to know as "Mama Molly."

See also First, Ruth; Suzman, Helen.

References and Further Reading
Spink, Kathryn. 1991. *Black Sash: The Beginning of a Bridge in South Africa.* London: Methuen.
Uerwey, E. J., ed. 1995. *New Dictionary of South African Biography.* Pretoria: HSRC Publishers.

Blackwell, Alice Stone
(1857–1950)
United States

The only daughter of Lucy Stone and Henry Blackwell became her mother's loyal helpmate early in life. Born into a family of leading abolitionists, she was weaned on women's rights and social justice, devoting her life not just to women's suffrage but also to racial equality, the antivivisection movement, temperance, and trade union rights. Blackwell was influential in persuading her mother to agree to the reunion of the divided women's suffrage movement in the United States in 1890, when the National American Woman Suffrage Association was formed.

Born in East Orange, New Jersey, Blackwell was educated at the Harris Grammar School in Dorchester and the Chauncy Hall School in Boston. She graduated from an otherwise all-male class at Boston University in 1881 and took up writing for and later editing her parents' women's rights publication, the *Woman's Journal,* the official organ of Stone's American Woman Suffrage Association.

In 1890, Blackwell and her mother Lucy Stone concurred on the advantages the women's movement would gain if Stone's American Woman Suffrage Association merged with Susan B. Anthony's National Woman Suffrage Association. Blackwell was appointed as the new organization's recording secretary, and from the late 1890s she was also coeditor of its journal, *Progress.* For most of her life as an activist, she stayed out of the limelight; she never married but gave her time and energy to many good causes as a member of the Woman's Christian Temperance Union, the Anti-Vivisection Society, and, in support of the admission of black students to Boston University, the National Association for the Advancement of Colored People.

Blackwell's wide-ranging interests and liberal sensitivities extended increasingly to socialist causes as she grew older, particularly after her more conservative mother's death in 1893, when she spoke out against the persecution of Armenians by the Ottoman Empire and of political dissidents in czarist Russia. She set up the Friends of Russian Freedom and developed a friendship with the grande dame of Russian women revolutionaries, Ekaterina Breshko-Breshkovskaya, in 1917 editing autobiographical material in Yiddish about her as *The Little Grandmother of the Russian Revolution: Reminiscences and Letters of Catherine Breshkovsky* [sic]. In 1927 Blackwell joined with many other humanitarians in protesting the trial of Nicola Sacco and Bartolomeo Vanzetti, entering into a long correspondence with the latter. As a supporter of free speech, she also opposed the arbitrary deportation of radical "undesirables" under the terms of the 1917 U.S. Espionage Act.

In 1917 Blackwell gave up editing the *Woman's Journal* but remained active in women's politics after suffrage was won in 1920 as a member of the Massachusetts League of Women Voters. She continued her literary endeavors, publishing versions of poetry from literal translations made for her of Armenian, Russian, Yiddish, Spanish, Hungarian, French, Italian, and Spanish originals. In addition, she wrote a romanticized biography of her mother, *Lucy Stone: Pioneer of Woman's Rights,* in 1930. A lifelong Unitarian, Blackwell was also active in the pacifist movement as a member of the American Peace Society. Despite the onset of blindness, she lived until she was ninety-two.

See also Anthony, Susan B.; Stone, Lucy.

References and Further Reading

Flexner, Eleanor. 1975 [1959]. *A Century of Struggle: The Woman's Rights Movement in the United States.* Rev. ed. Cambridge, MA: Belknap Press of Harvard University.

Hays, Elinor Rice. 1967. *Those Extraordinary Blackwells: The Story of a Journey to a Better World.* New York: Harcourt and Brace.

Kraditor, Aileen. 1981 [1965]. *The Ideas of the Woman Suffrage Movement 1890–1920.* Reprint, New York: W. W. Norton.

Merrill, Marlene Deahl. 1990. *Growing Up in Boston's Gilded Age: The Journal of Alice Stone Blackwell, 1872–1874.* New Haven: Yale University Press.

Blackwell, Antoinette Brown
(1825–1921)
United States

The first woman in the United States to be ordained, in 1853, and an advocate of liberal religion, Antoinette Brown Blackwell wrote extensively on philosophy, science, religion, and women's rights. She was the sister-in-law of her friend Lucy Stone (who married Henry Brown Blackwell a year before Antoinette married his brother Samuel Blackwell) and of Elizabeth Blackwell, as well as the aunt of Alice Stone Blackwell.

Blackwell grew up in a reformist and revivalist family in Henrietta, New York, and as a young woman took up speaking in her local Congregational church. Educated at Monroe County Academy and Oberlin College, she graduated from the latter in 1847. Having discovered her

Antoinette Brown Blackwell (Library of Congress)

terest in women's rights and lectured on the subject, as well as on temperance and abolition, in Ohio and New York state after she left college in 1850. In 1853 she attended the World's Temperance Convention in New York, and in 1860 she took part in the tenth National Women's Rights Convention there, at which marriage was debated and on which occasion she opposed Elizabeth Cady Stanton's resolution on reform of divorce laws. Blackwell was a great believer in marriage as a union of equals. The first obligation of a woman in marriage, she felt, was to "maintain her own independence and her own integrity of character; to assert herself, earnestly and firmly, as the equal of man, who is only her peer" (Helsinger, Sheets, and Veeder 1983, 34). She nevertheless also endorsed women's right to find "womanly methods of working" (Leach 1981, 200) that would enable them to have fulfilling work outside the family. Women should marry later, at age twenty-five or thirty, when, she believed, they would be better equipped to choose the right partner. And after having their children, women could pursue outside activities that suited their particular natures. In particular, Blackwell endorsed the ideal of the married female doctor as a prime example of how women could successfully combine their two spheres of activity.

Blackwell herself did not marry until she was thirty-one, when she became the wife of Samuel C. Blackwell in 1856 after a long courtship. They settled in New Jersey, where she spent the next eighteen years raising their five daughters. There she carried on with her writing, in 1869 publishing the first of ten books, a discussion of her own religious theories and her interest in the new science of Charles Darwin and Herbert Spencer. Reading their theories had led her to challenge traditional Christian doctrine, upon which she elaborated in *Studies in General Science;* a novel, *The Island Neighbors,* followed in 1871. As a member of the American Association for the Advancement of Science, Blackwell would also publish articles in *Popular Science.*

In 1869, when Congress passed the Fifteenth Amendment, granting suffrage to black men while still denying women the vote, Blackwell felt that she could not, on moral grounds, join with other suffragists in opposing this recognition of black civil rights, even if it did preempt the emancipation of women. She continued the fight for women's suffrage in a theoretical rather than

vocation and wishing to be a preacher, Blackwell studied for a further three years at the Theological Seminary at Oberlin College, but because she was a woman, was not allowed to receive a degree. After 1850 she spent two years traveling around, lecturing and trying to find a congregation that would accept her, eventually becoming a pastor at the First Congregational Church in South Butler, New York, and obtaining her ordination on 15 September 1853, the first woman in the United States to do so. Soon after, however, Blackwell found that her personal philosophical beliefs and liberal attitudes placed her at odds with the church's teaching on issues such as original sin and predestination, and she left to become a Unitarian.

At about this time, Blackwell went on a lecture tour in New England with Ernestine Rose. With the encouragement of newspaper proprietor Horace Greeley, Blackwell spent time among the poor Irish and German immigrants of New York's slums and visited delinquent asylums and prisons with Abigail Gibbons. These travels would be the basis of a series of articles entitled "Shadows of Our Social System" that she wrote for Greeley's *New York Tribune* in 1855.

From her student days, Blackwell took an in-organizational capacity through her articles in the *Woman's Journal,* the publication of her sister-in-law Lucy Stone's American Woman Suffrage Association. She also took her message into the pulpit, giving sermons covering a wide range of social issues, including abolition, temperance, and women's rights. The advancement of women in science also earned her support through her vice presidency of the Association for the Advancement of Women.

In 1875 Blackwell entered the controversy prompted by publication of Charles Darwin's *Descent of Man,* seeing his theory of evolution as supporting the emancipation of women and publishing her own response in *The Sexes throughout Nature.* This book challenged the misogynistic assertion that women were not physiologically equipped for the exertions of excessive academic study and was an attempt by Blackwell to provide a scientific basis for women being different from but equal with men. However, in her arguments she succeeded only in emphasizing women's location in a separate sphere from men by highlighting their special, compassionate qualities as nurturers.

In 1878 Blackwell was finally awarded an honorary M.A. by Oberlin College, and in 1908 she became a doctor of divinity when she was appointed to the new All Souls Unitarian Church in Elizabeth, New Jersey, after donating the land on which it was built. Later appointed pastor emeritus, Blackwell continued to preach at All Souls on a monthly basis until her death, when the church went into decline. In 1902 Blackwell published a book of religious poetry (*Sea Drift: Or Tribute to the Ocean*). That same year, she preached the funeral oration at the obsequies for the suffrage leader Elizabeth Cady Stanton.

Like her niece, Alice Stone Blackwell, Antoinette Blackwell survived into her nineties, living for periods with one or another daughter after the death of her husband in 1901. But of the eminent pioneering Blackwell women, Antoinette was the only one to live to see the long fight for women's suffrage achieve its goal in 1920.

See also Blackwell, Alice Stone; Blackwell, Elizabeth; Gibbons, Abigail Hopper; Rose, Ernestine; Stanton, Elizabeth Cady; Stone, Lucy.

References and Further Reading

Cazden, Elizabeth. 1983. *Antoinette Brown Blackwell: A Biography.* New York: Feminist Press.

Hays, Elinor Rice. 1967. *Those Extraordinary Blackwells: The Story of a Journey to a Better World.* New York: Harcourt Brace.

Helsinger, Elizabeth K., Robin Lauterbach Sheets, and William Veeder. 1983. *The Woman Question: Social Issues, 1837–1883,* vol. 2, *Society and Literature in Britain and America, 1837–1883.* Manchester: Manchester University Press.

Kerr, Laura. 1951. *Lady in the Pulpit.* New York: Woman's Press.

Lasser, Carol, and Marlene Deal, eds. 1987. *Letters between Lucy Stone and Antoinette Brown Blackwell, 1846–1893.* Urbana: University of Illinois Press.

Leach, William. 1981. *True Love and Perfect Union: The Feminist Reform of Sex and Society.* London: Routledge and Kegan Paul.

Blackwell, Elizabeth
(1821–1910)
United Kingdom/United States

Elizabeth Blackwell provided herself with many mountains to climb in her determined pursuit of a medical career, not the least of which was to be rejected by twenty-nine medical schools in succession. She carried her determination to become a doctor over into her mission to establish the first medical training school for women in the United States. She also promoted the cause of women's medical education in Britain, wrote on the importance of sex education, and gave her support to most of the social causes of her day, campaigning in particular against vivisection and the Contagious Diseases Acts, the latter passed in the United Kingdom in the 1860s. She believed that woman, with her maternal instincts of self-sacrifice, was uniquely equipped for an important role in welfare as the natural opponent of cruelty and injustice.

Blackwell was born in Bristol, England, one of nine children (five of them daughters), whose father, Samuel, a well-known local dissenter and lay preacher, was in sugar refining. After the family business was destroyed by fire in 1832, the Blackwells emigrated to New York, where they became involved in the abolitionist cause, helping runaway slaves on the Underground Railroad. In 1837 the family suffered further financial losses during an economic depression. They moved to Cincinnati in 1838, but Samuel Blackwell died soon after, and Elizabeth was faced with the doleful inevitability of teaching or working as a governess in order to help support the family. She taught music for a while and then, with her sisters Anna and Marian, opened a school for girls. When three of her brothers set themselves up in a milling business, things improved for the family. Blackwell also continued to work in the abolitionist movement, at various times being active in the Abolitionist Vigilance Committee, the Anti-Slavery Working Society, the Ladies Anti-Slavery Society, and the New York Anti-Slavery Society. When her private school closed after four years, Elizabeth fell back on teaching, but she had no vocation for the work and gave up her job, seeking greater challenges.

Everything changed for Blackwell in 1845, when she visited Mary Donaldson, a sick friend suffering from uterine cancer. Donaldson admitted to her that she would certainly have turned to medical help sooner if women doctors had been available to her. Realizing how reticent women were about consulting male doctors on gynecological problems, Blackwell set her sights on training as a doctor. But the study of medicine was at that time impossible for women, and only Blackwell's exceptional resilience and determination during the course of three years of constant lobbying finally gained her admission to study. She would later recall that "the idea of winning a doctor's degree gradually assumed the aspect of a great moral struggle" (Forster 1984, 65), which once taken up she would not relinquish. She began writing a stream of letters to medical academies in the United States while teaching music at an academy in North Carolina. There she boarded with a doctor's family, and her landlord, John Dickson, allowed her to begin self-study using his books. But when the school where she was working closed, Blackwell had to move on— to Philadelphia this time. She took private anatomy lessons while applying to more than a dozen medical schools. By a stroke of luck, she was finally allowed to enter Geneva Medical School in New York state in 1847, after the question of her admittance was put to a vote by the male students. They condescendingly agreed to give her admittance their "entire approval," convinced she would never stay the course. But Blackwell completed her studies, handicapped by subjection to a constant barrage of hostility, belittlement, and isolation. Considered immoral for pursuing medical studies, she had great difficulty in finding a boardinghouse to take her and, during the two years she spent at Geneva, was os-

tracized by the female population, who resolutely refused to pay her visits or even speak to her. Undaunted, Blackwell set her sights on a career in women's surgery, having gained valuable clinical experience working in the women's syphilis ward at the Blockley almshouses in Philadelphia during the summer of 1848.

A gathering of 20,000 people witnessed Blackwell's graduation in January 1849, for which she wrote a thesis on ship fever that was published in the *Buffalo Medical Journal*. Although she became an American citizen in April, it still proved impossible for her to obtain hospital experience in the United States, and she was forced to go to Paris. There, however, she was only allowed practical training as a student midwife at the La Maternité lying-in hospital, where she had to endure a spartan life in communal dormitories with other trainees and work fourteen-hour days. It was here, too, that Blackwell first encountered the abuse of women patients in the charity wards for the poor by doctors who subjected them to painful and degrading examinations and medical procedures. She viewed the forced removal of women's ovaries in the treatment of menstrual problems as particularly inhumane. Like Anna Kingsford, who also studied at La Charité and was appalled at practices she saw there, Blackwell linked the abuse of women by medical science with that of the vivisectionists on helpless animals (see, for example, Blackwell's "Scientific Method in Biology," published in her *Essays in Medical Sociology* in 1902).

While she was in Paris, a tragedy overtook Blackwell's ambitions to be a surgeon: while treating a baby with purulent ophthalmia, she accidentally infected her own eyes. After weeks of pain and suffering, she discovered she had lost the sight in one eye (which was later removed, leaving her permanently disfigured); the vision in her other eye was also severely impaired. A long convalescence and a period of fruitless travel around Europe in search of every conceivable kind of cure ensued. Finally accepting that she would never be able to undertake surgery, Blackwell decided instead to go into general practice. She traveled to England and undertook further training in the autumn of 1850, this time under the eminent surgeon Dr. James Paget at St. Bartholomew's Hospital in London. Perversely, the hospital ruled that she was not allowed to treat female diseases. During her time in England, Blackwell made lifelong friends of feminist activists Barbara Leigh Smith (later Barbara Bodichon) and other radical women in the Langham Place Circle.

Blackwell returned to New York in August 1851, but despite her excellent credentials, no one would employ her as a doctor. Therefore, she decided to set up a private practice in March 1852, but again public antipathy toward a woman doctor meant she had so few patients that she was soon in financial difficulties. She undertook a series of public lectures, published in 1852 as *The Laws of Life, with Special Reference to the Physical Education of Girls*—effectively, the first medical book by a woman. The book attracted the attention of some Quaker women, who became her patients, and the income enabled Blackwell to open a small clinic in 1853 and to buy a house in a decent district, where she took in several of her brothers and sisters, and a medical partner, German immigrant Marie Zakrzewska. Although Blackwell had long since decided never to marry, by 1856 she began to feel she had missed out on the experience of having children, and she adopted a seven-year-old orphan named Kitty Barry.

The demand for Blackwell's clinic was such that she moved to bigger premises in a poor area on the East River. By this time, she had amassed a great deal of specialist knowledge on women's gynecological problems, and she initiated fundraising to open a hospital. Blackwell's New York Infirmary for Women and Children opened on Bleecker Street in Greenwich Village on 12 May 1857, with Blackwell and Zakrzewska joined by Elizabeth's younger sister, Emily (1826–1910). After suffering the same rejections and setbacks of her older sister, Emily had finally qualified as a doctor at Western Reserve University in 1854. The hospital became an important venue where women doctors could gain essential experience in clinical medicine, even offering home visits to the poor, and was soon extremely busy. More staff were needed, and more money had to be raised.

Blackwell decided to return to England to encourage Englishwomen to enter medical training. She met Florence Nightingale in the summer of 1858 and again in January 1859, but disagreeing with Nightingale's view that women should confine themselves to nursing, Blackwell refused to be prevailed upon to take overall charge of a training school for nurses that Nightingale was

establishing at St. Thomas's Hospital. While in England, Blackwell gave lectures on "Medicine as a Profession for the Ladies" in London, Manchester, Birmingham, and Liverpool. She was also formally enrolled on the British medical register, having already practiced in Britain before the passing of the 1858 Medical Act.

A year later, Blackwell returned to the United States, determined to establish her own medical school for women. In 1860 she and her sister Emily cowrote one of the first important books to promote her case, *Medicine as a Profession for Women*. Again, Elizabeth undertook vigorous fund-raising and bought a property on Second Avenue. But in April 1861, the outbreak of the Civil War put her plans on hold. Blackwell immediately called a meeting in New York to organize women nurses to go to the front, but the hostility of the medical profession was such that her plans were thwarted. She founded the Women's Central Association for Relief, which later became the U.S. Sanitary Commission, the official body that would train and send out nurses to the Union troops under the leadership of Dorothea Dix.

Blackwell's New York Infirmary finally opened its own Women's Medical College in 1868, which offered the most rigorous medical training yet available to women. Elizabeth was professor of hygiene for thirty years (until the school closed in 1899), and her sister Emily served as the college's dean and professor of obstetrics and diseases of women. Emily proved an efficient administrator and devoted the next forty years of her life to the infirmary's efficient management, overseeing the training of 350 women doctors during the medical college's lifetime and becoming one of the first women in the United States to undertake complex surgical procedures.

Blackwell was now able to devote time to giving lectures and spreading her message on hygiene as well as setting up a program of public sanitary inspection. In 1869 she returned to England with her adopted daughter Kitty and set up a private practice in London. There, in 1874, she cofounded the London School of Medicine for Women with Sophia Jex-Blake and was appointed chair of gynecology there and at Elizabeth Garrett Blackwell's New Hospital for Women and Children. Blackwell was also active in numerous organizations, such as the National Anti-Vivisection Society, and cofounded the National Health Society of London in 1871. In 1879, she settled on the south coast, in Hastings.

At this time, Blackwell became increasingly drawn into issues of moral reform, believing as she did in the moral superiority of women and their natural loyalty to what is right. She became a member of the Social Purity Alliance, the National Vigilance Association, and the Council of National Vigilance, and worked with Josephine Butler for repeal of the Contagious Diseases Acts to combat state-regulated prostitution. In *Counsel to Parents on the Moral Education of Their Children* (1879), she supported sex education and called for an end to double standards in sexual morality, which demanded that women remain pure, although setting no such standard of sexual behavior for men. However, in the 1880s she would oppose the use of contraceptives, seeing them as encouragement for men to increase the sexual demands they made on their wives.

Blackwell also offered her tireless energy to the campaign for women to become Poor Law Guardians; she was active in antivaccination and antivivisection campaigns and took an interest in spiritualism, rabies treatment, and psychology. In between all this, she participated in local politics in Hastings and cooperative farming in the nearby Kent countryside. After meeting Charles Kingsley, the English clergyman and novelist, she converted to Christian socialism, a movement closely allied to the Workers' Education Association, and supported the concept of workers' cooperatives and the welfare state. Many of Blackwell's ideas on these themes were outlined in her 1902 book, *Essays in Medical Sociology*.

Blackwell finally retired in 1894 and wrote her autobiography, *Pioneer Work in Opening the Medical Profession to Women*. She traveled on the Continent, but in 1907 a bad fall severely confined her, and she died of a stroke in 1910. She was buried in Kilmun, Scotland, a beautiful spot that was one of her favorite places. In all her years of vigorous work for women's medicine, she had never doubted the ability of women to take up new challenges, provided that they could overcome their own often inbred inertia, as she wrote in a letter to Matilda Joslyn Gage in 1852: "I believe that the chief source of the false position of women is *the inefficiency of women themselves*—the deplorable fact that they are so often careless mothers, weak wives, poor housekeepers, ignorant nurses and frivolous human beings.

If they would perform with strength and wisdom the duties which lie immediately around them every sphere of life would soon be open to them" (Forster 1984, 55).

See also Butler, Josephine; Dix, Dorothea Lynde; Gage, Matilda Joslyn; Jex-Blake, Sophia; Kingsford, Anna; Nightingale, Florence; Zakrzewska, Marie.

References and Further Reading

Bell, Enid Moberley. 1953. *Storming the Citadel: The Rise of the Woman Doctor*. London: Constable.

Blackwell, Elizabeth. 1914. *Work for Women*. Everyman's Library series. London: J. M. Dent. Reprinted as *Pioneer Work in Opening the Medical Profession to Women: Autobiographical Sketches* [original title]. New York: Schocken, 1977.

Blake, Catriona. 1990. *The Charge of the Parasols: Women's Entry to the Medical Profession*. London: Women's Press.

Bonner, Thomas Neville. 1992. *To the Ends of the Earth: Women's Search for Education in Medicine*. Cambridge, MA: Harvard University Press.

Fancourt, Mary St. John. 1965. *They Dared to Be Doctors: Elizabeth Blackwell and Elizabeth Garrett Anderson*. London: Longman's Green.

Forster, M. 1984. *Significant Sisters: The Grassroots of Active Feminism, 1839–1939*. London: Secker and Warburg.

Hays, Elinor Rice. 1967. *Those Extraordinary Blackwells: The Story of a Journey to a Better World*. New York: Harcourt and Brace.

Walsh, Mary Roth. 1977. "*Doctors Wanted: No Women Need Apply*": *Sexual Barriers in the Medical Profession, 1835–1975*. New Haven: Yale University Press.

Wilson, Dorothy C. 1870. *Lone Woman: The Story of Elizabeth Blackwell, the First Woman Doctor*. Boston: Little, Brown.

Blatch, Harriot Stanton
(1856–1940)
United States

As the daughter of Elizabeth Cady Stanton, one of the founding mothers of American suffragism, it was inevitable that Harriot Stanton Blatch would continue in her mother's campaigning tradition. She did so in a more assertive and proactive manner than Stanton had, leading from the front and advocating the development of a grassroots political movement supported by working women that was inspired by her experiences working for women's suffrage in England. With Alice Stone Blackwell she also facilitated the eventual reunion of the two branches of the American women's suffrage movement.

Born in Seneca Falls, New York, the sixth of seven children, Blatch was educated at private schools; she studied mathematics at Vassar College until 1878, followed by a year at the Boston School of Oratory. She then set off to Europe in 1880 as tutor cum companion to an American family. Returning home in 1881, she contributed a chapter on Lucy Stone's American Woman Suffrage Association, which she felt was underrepresented, to her mother and Susan B. Anthony's monumental *History of Woman Suffrage*. Returning to England, she married businessman William Henry Blatch in 1882, thereby losing her American citizenship under a U.S. law that designated women who were U.S. citizens as aliens if they married foreigners, a fact that she would always greatly regret (the law was not revoked until the 1922 Cable Act). She lived there contentedly, bringing up two daughters (although one died young) and returning to the United States in 1902 when her mother was dying. During her time in England, Blatch wrote an M.A. thesis for Vassar College on village life in England. She took an interest in English political life and became a member of the Fabian Society, mixing with socialists such as G. B. Shaw and Sidney and Beatrice Webb. She eventually joined the newly formed Women's Liberal Federation in 1887 and supported the election of women to local government as a member of the Society for Promoting the Return of Women as County Councillors. Drawn into suffrage activities and public speaking, Blatch became close friends with Emmeline Pankhurst. She joined the Women's Franchise League in 1890 and took part in debates on women's issues at the Pioneer Club in London.

On her resettlement in the United States in 1902 and despite her status as an alien, Blatch resolved to bring the American suffrage movement out of the doldrums of conservatism into which she felt it had descended. She injected new blood (particularly after the death of Susan B. Anthony in 1906) and new energy into a movement that, in the words of Aileen Kraditor, was stuck "in a rut of tea parties and innocuous ladylikeness" (1981, 269). Blatch inspired the staging of open-air rallies and large parades in New York from 1910 and Washington, D.C., from 1912, based on those of the suffrage movement in England. These parades became annual events; a famous

Harriot Stanton Blatch (Library of Congress)

1912 parade in New York had 10,000 marchers, underlining the heightened pace of activities in New York state under Blatch's energetic leadership and with support and money from women such as Alva Belmont, which had come in the wake of partial women's suffrage being awarded in some midwestern states. That year, suffragists also undertook a thirteen-day march from New York City to Albany and another from New York City to Washington; the marching tradition would do much to heighten public and press awareness of the suffrage campaign during the concerted two-year campaign that won women in New York state the vote in 1917.

As an advocate of the economic independence of women and the unionization of women workers, in 1907 Blatch founded the Equality League of Self-Supporting Women, which in 1910, echoing the radicalism of the Pankhursts' Women's Social and Political Union, became the Women's Political Union (WPU). This group pioneered the enlistment of working women into the women's rights movement, who were seen by Blatch as the cornerstone of large-scale activism, as they had proved to be in the suffrage movement in England. Under Blatch, the WPU began lobbying for a referendum on women's suffrage to be held in New York state, and she succeeded in further galvanizing support among women in the professions and business, with membership of the organization growing to reach 20,000. But in 1915 she rejected the opportunity to amalgamate the WPU and Carrie Chapman Catt's more moderate Empire State Campaign Committee in the drive for the vote for women in New York state; instead, in 1916 she allied the WPU with Alice Paul's more militant Congressional Union. Soon after, this organization became the National Woman's Party and worked toward winning a federal equal rights amendment that would, among other things, give the vote to women.

Blatch's energies were diverted into war work during World War I after she had witnessed that done in Europe by women in industry and agriculture. She headed the U.S. Food Administration's Speaker's Bureau and took the leadership of the Woman's Land Army, describing her work for it in her 1918 book, *Mobilizing Woman Power*. Once the war was over, she took a clear pacifist position supporting the establishment of the League of Nations, sharing the view of many women activists that the sooner their sex won the vote, the sooner it would have a greater influence over maintaining world peace. After the war and the winning of the vote, Blatch joined the Socialist Party and supported the political campaign of its presidential candidate, Robert La Follette.

Many of Blatch's later years were spent in writing works such as *A Woman's Point of View: Some Roads to Peace* (1920), editing her mother's diaries and letters with her brother Theodore (*Eighty Years and More: Reminiscences of Elizabeth Cady Stanton*, 1898), and completing her memoirs, which she wrote with Alma Lutz and published as *Challenging Years* in 1940.

Blatch maintained her friendship with the Pankhurst family and her close links with the English suffrage movement after her return to the United States. In 1907, 1909, and 1913 she organized visits to New York by Emmeline Pankhurst, and in 1912 her daughter Sylvia came to the United States for a highly successful lecture tour. Blatch's daughter Nora followed in the pioneering tradition of her mother and grandmother by becoming the first woman to be admitted to an American university to study civil engineering—at Cornell University in 1901.

See also Anthony, Susan B.; Blackwell, Alice Stone; Catt, Carrie Chapman; Pankhurst, Emmeline; Paul, Alice; Stanton, Elizabeth Cady; Webb, Beatrice.

References and Further Reading
Blatch, Harriot Stanton, and Alma Lutz. 1940. *Challenging Years: The Memoirs of Harriot Stanton Blatch*. New York: G. Putnam's Sons.
Crawford, Elizabeth. 1999. *The Women's Suffrage Movement, 1866–1928: A Reference Guide*. London: University College of London Press.
DuBois, Ellen. 1997. *Harriet Stanton Blatch and the Winning of Woman Suffrage*. New Haven, CT: Yale University Press.
———. 1998. *Woman Suffrage and Women's Rights*. New York: New York University Press.
Frankel, Noralee, and Nancy S. Dye. 1991. *Gender, Class, Race, and Reform in the Progressive Era*. Lexington: University of Kentucky Press.
Kraditor, Aileen. 1981 [1965]. *The Ideas of the Woman Suffrage Movement 1890–1920*. Reprint, New York: W. W. Norton.
O'Neill, William L. 1989. *Feminism in America: A History*. 2d ed. New Brunswick, NJ: Transaction.

Bloomer, Amelia Jenks
(1818–1894)
United States

The woman whose name was given to a mode of dress that became synonymous with the early advocates of women's emancipation did not, in fact, invent the Turkish-style trousers that were named after her. Such was the derision with which the newfangled women's dress known as "bloomers" was greeted that Amelia Bloomer and the women who wore them (including Susan B. Anthony and Elizabeth Cady Stanton) were eventually forced to concede that to persist in doing so detracted from the seriousness of the campaign for women's rights.

Born in Homer, New York, Bloomer lived a quiet backwater life, receiving a limited education followed by several years working as a teacher and then governess. Her sharp intellect found an outlet after she married the Quaker abolitionist lawyer and newspaper man Dexter Chamberlain Bloomer in 1840. Having made a feminist point in her marriage vows by deliberately excluding the word *obey*, Bloomer afterward took an interest in social reform. Over the following years, she worked as an editor of and contributor to her husband's journal, the *Seneca County Courier,* and in 1848 joined the local Ladies' Temperance Society. That same year she attended the famous Seneca Falls women's rights convention as a reporter for the *Seneca County Courier,* although she did not join in the debates. In January 1849 Bloomer established her own monthly temperance journal, the *Lily,* in Seneca Falls, the first of its kind in the United States to be owned and run by a woman. With an initial circulation of 200–300, it featured articles by Bloomer and her close associates in the women's movement, such as Stanton and Anthony, quickly moving from coverage of temperance issues to arguments for dress and marriage reform, including women's right to divorce drunken husbands, and women's suffrage. By the time it closed six years later, the magazine would have a readership of 6,000 and would have served as a valuable outlet for the first writings on women's rights in the United States.

As early as 1847, in a letter to her friend Charlotte A. Joy, Bloomer had been an advocate of the simplification of women's dress, averring that "the costume of woman should be suited to her wants and necessities. It should conduce at once to her health, comfort and usefulness" (3 June 1847). In 1851 she openly practiced what she preached when Seneca Falls again became the venue for another pioneering venture—the wearing of Turkish-style pantaloons under a shortened skirt. Like many other women, Bloomer rejected the uncomfortable, constricting corsets, tight lacing, and unwieldy skirts of her time and eagerly adopted the pantaloons, which had been introduced by Elizabeth Smith Miller on a visit to her friend Elizabeth Cady Stanton. Smith had designed these with a view to making it easier for women to take up physical exercise such as gardening, and the design had in turn been based on a style of "pantalets" worn by the English actress Fanny Kemble (the wearing of which Bloomer had defended in the *Lily* in 1849). When the garment had first appeared in London, it had been known as the "Camilla costume." But after Bloomer adopted the pantaloons as a symbol of her own emancipation and advocated their use in the *Lily,* saying "we have been and are slaves, while man in dress and all things else is free" (Rendall 1985, 258), they were nicknamed "bloomers."

Amelia Jenks Bloomer (Library of Congress)

Over the next few years Bloomer, Cady Stanton, and Anthony doggedly courted ridicule and constant accusations of sartorial immodesty by persisting in wearing their bloomers in small-town America. Anthony and Cady Stanton soon gave in to public pressure and abandoned them, but Bloomer determinedly wore her pantaloons during a speaking tour of New York state in 1853 (with more people turning up to laugh at her bloomers than listen to what she had to say) and continued to do so until she was forced to capitulate by the late 1850s. In the end, the association of bloomers with emancipated, "loose" women was having too negative an effect on the suffrage movement. Bloomer was baffled at why women themselves were generally so set against the idea of bloomers when, as she so rightly pointed out, they were prepared to tolerate Scotsmen wearing kilts.

In 1853 Bloomer and her husband moved to Mount Vernon, Ohio, from where Amelia continued to publish the *Lily,* using female typesetters. But after the couple moved farther west, to Iowa, she was no longer able to get the paper properly distributed, and she sold the *Lily* in 1855. After being published for another year by new owner Mary Birdsall, it closed down in December 1856. Nevertheless, Bloomer continued to lecture and write about temperance and women's suffrage, contributing to her husband's paper, the *Western Home Visitor*. During the Civil War, she undertook relief work for the Soldiers' Aid Society of her hometown, Council Bluffs. In 1871 she became president of the Iowa Suffrage Society, which successfully lobbied for the Iowa equal property rights code, passed in 1873.

In the late 1880s, when it was no longer considered inappropriate for polite young women to be seen riding the new, modified ladies' bicycle, bloomers were reintroduced for the purpose by women dress reformers such as Lady Florence Harberton, leader of the Rational Dress Society in the United Kingdom, a fact that no doubt led Bloomer to feel vindicated.

See also Anthony, Susan B.; Stanton, Elizabeth Cady.
References and Further Reading

Bloomer, Dexter C. 1895. *Life and Writings of Amelia Bloomer.* Boston: Arena.

Cooᴌ, Anne C., ed. 1994. *Hear Me Patiently: The Reform Speeches of Amelia Jenks Bloomer.* Westport, CT: Greenwood Press.

Gattey, Charles Neilson. 1967. *The Bloomer Girls.* London: Femina Books.

Noun, Louise. 1985. "Amelia Bloomer, a Biography: Part I, the Lily of Seneca Falls." *The Annals of Iowa* 47(7): 575–617.

———. "Amelia Bloomer: Part II, the Suffragist of Council Bluffs." *The Annals of Iowa* 47(8): 575–621.

Rendall, Jane. 1985. *The Origins of Modern Feminism: Women in Britain, France, and the United States 1780–1860.* Chicago: University of Chicago Press.

Bloor, Ella Reeve ("Mother Bloor")
(1862–1951)
United States

Ella Bloor, the indomitable labor organizer, socialist, and orator, made great sacrifices in her personal life to work for trade union rights. She frequently faced criticism and considerable logistical problems in ensuring the welfare of her six children as she traveled around the United States in her trade union work. As a socialist, she also came under fire for her communist sympathies, enduring persistent harassment to become an icon of the American labor movement.

Born on Staten Island, New York, Bloor was left in charge of her nine siblings after their mother's death in 1879. As a young woman eager to take up social reform, she was active in the Woman's Christian Temperance Union and came under the intellectual influence of her great-uncle Dan Ware, a Unitarian. But her marriage to his son Lucien foundered due to her increasing activism in the temperance and suffrage movements in Philadelphia, and in 1896 they divorced, leaving Bloor the single parent of four children (two had died in infancy). By this time, she had already become caught up in the organization of trade unions and had espoused the socialist concepts of worker control of industry and agriculture. She settled for a while in a socialist community in Delaware and remarried in 1897. But this marriage, to the socialist Louis Cohen, also ended in separation in 1902 and ultimate divorce, leaving Bloor with two more children to support.

Having joined the Social Democratic Party of America in 1897, Bloor embarked on a marked phase of activism as a labor organizer and supporter of women's rights. In 1901–1902, her increasing radicalism prompted her to join the Socialist Party of America. In 1906 she moved to Chicago to collaborate with the socialist writer Upton Sinclair in a government commission to investigate the exploitation of workers in the meatpacking industry, prompted by the huge success of Sinclair's 1906 novel, *The Jungle*. Cataloguing the widespread abuse by management of underpaid and overworked immigrants in the Chicago stockyards, as well as exposing the willful adulteration of meat products, the novel had a social impact equal to that of Harriet Beecher Stowe's 1852 work, *Uncle Tom's Cabin*. For the sake of propriety, during the course of her research Bloor adopted the name of her coresearcher Richard Bloor, and the affectionate epithet given her at the time, "Mother Bloor," would become set in stone during her itinerant activities on behalf of the poor and unemployed across the United States during the Depression years.

Bloor spent the years 1906 to 1918 organizing trade union activities for the Socialist Party in Connecticut, West Virginia, and Illinois. She also played a role in labor disputes among coal miners in Pennsylvania and among strikers in Michigan in 1913 and in Colorado in 1914, in all of her campaigning encouraging the active involvement of women.

A pacifist during World War I, Bloor opposed conscription and fund-raised for the legal defense of conscientious objectors through the Workers' Defense Union. After the war, she was a founding member in 1919 of the American Communist Party, the radical left-wing faction that had broken away from the Socialist Party of America, and she eventually served on its Central Committee from 1932 to 1948. She traveled to the Soviet Union in 1921 as a delegate to the Red International of Labor Unions to see for herself how the new Soviet experiment was working. She was not disappointed and visited again in 1937, by then deeply impressed with the state provisions made for women and children, which she outlined in her 1938 pamphlet, "Women in the Soviet Union."

Like many socialists in the United States during the 1920s and 1930s, Bloor suffered as a result of her communist sympathies but nevertheless in 1927 she campaigned for the acquittal of the Italian anarchist trade unionists Nicola Sacco and Bartolomeo Vanzetti. Throughout the Great Depression, Bloor took to the road, traveling the United States as a labor organizer in the steel and mining industries, joining hunger marches, and helping impoverished farmers in the Midwest through her work for the Farmers National Committee for Action.

In the 1930s Bloor married for the third time, to Andrew Omholt, a North Dakota farmer and member of the Communist Party. Before and during World War II, Bloor lectured regularly against fascism. She was active in the American League against War and Fascism (1934–1940), in 1934 enlisting U.S. delegates to the International Workers' Conference Against War and Fascism in Paris. Her espousal of socialist principles and activism for the Communist Party (she was head of its Philadelphia branch from 1941 to 1947) resulted in regular arrest and constant surveillance throughout her life, and she spent a month in prison when she was seventy-two. Bloor's frequent attempts to run for political office, including secretary of state for Connecticut and lieutenant governor of New York, all failed because of her uncompromising political beliefs. She recounted her experiences in her 1940 autobiography, *We Are Many,* and remained until her death a passionate defender of the working classes and the rights of women and children, both in her many speeches on the public platform and in her interviews on the radio.

See also Stowe, Harriet Beecher.
References and Further Reading
Barton, Anna. 1937. *Mother Bloor: The Spirit of '76.* New York: Workers Library.
Buhle, Mari Jo, Paul Buhle, and Dan Georgakas, eds. 1998. *Encyclopedia of the American Left.* 2d ed. New York: Oxford University Press.
Dictionary of American Biography 1946–1958, and indexes to Supplements 1–10, 1981–1996. New York: Scribner's.
Flynn, Elizabeth Gurley. 1942. *Daughters of America: Ella Reeve Bloor and Anita Whitney.* New York: Workers Library.
Sicherman, Barbara, and Carol Hurd Green, eds. 1980. *Notable American Women 1607–1950: A Biographical Dictionary,* vol. 4, *The Modern Period.* Cambridge, MA: Belknap Press of Harvard University.
Whitman, Alden, ed. 1988. *American Reformers: An H. W. Wilson Biographical Dictionary.* New York: H. W. Wilson.

Bodichon, Barbara (Barbara Leigh Smith)
(1827–1891)
United Kingdom

Born into the Unitarian tradition of social campaigning, the feminist and educator Barbara Bodichon played a central role in the development of the women's movement in nineteenth-century Britain. Yet, by the time of her death she had been larely forgotten and was susequently relegated to the footnotes of history, accorded only the most anodyne of entries in the original edition of the *Dictionary of National Biography,* which alluded only to her reputation as an artist (the entry has now been completely revised in a major overhaul of the DNB's coverage). Back in the early 1980s, when writing her book *Women of Ideas and What Men Have Done to Them,* Dale Spender complained bitterly about the difficulty she had had in finding useful biographical information on Bodichon—a situation that applied to many of Bodichon's feminist contemporaries. It was not until biographers Sheila Herstein (1985) and Pam Hirsch (1998) provided detailed accounts that Bodichon's crucial role could be properly assessed.

Bodichon and her four brothers and sisters were the products of a common-law union between Benjamin Lee Smith, a Unitarian preacher and Liberal member of Parliament (for Norwich from 1838 to 1847), and a young milliner, Anne Longden, whom he refused to marry because of her lower social status. Bodichon grew up with the stigma of illegitimacy, kept apart from her upwardly mobile and legitimate relatives, such as her cousin Florence Nightingale. She remained stubbornly unconventional in her own adult life and a sympathetic friend of the writer George Eliot, who was also a social outcast because of her long common-law relationship with George Lewes. But there were compensations: Bodichon's upbringing was progressive and unconventional, and the family home was frequented by radicals of all persuasions: abolitionists, anti–Corn Law campaigners, and supporters of the Chartist movement. Bodichon was allowed to develop her talents as a fine draughtsman and painter and might have pursued a career in art had she not become drawn into the 1850s debate, fostered by Harriet Taylor and John Stuart Mill, on women's rights. With her lifelong friend Bessie Rayner Parkes, Bodichon subsequently became a dominant force in the group of intellectual women who became known as the Langham Place Circle and who spearheaded the British campaign for women's legal rights and suffrage beginning in the 1850s.

When Bodichon was seven, her mother died of tuberculosis. Barbara and her siblings, who had been educated at home until then, were sent by their father to the progressive Westminster Infant School, one of the pioneering "ragged schools" in London. In 1848 Bodichon's father settled an income of £300 a year in stocks and shares on her, which allowed her the scope to pursue her literary and artistic interests. She studied painting and drawing at the Ladies' College in London's Bedford Square during 1849 and took lessons with the pre-Raphaelite painter William Holman Hunt. With her close friend Parkes, Bodichon spent time traveling and sketching on the Continent in 1850, the two women arousing curiosity wherever they went because they were unaccompanied and favored rational dress (no corsets and loose clothes). Bodichon would exhibit her work regularly through the Society of Female Artists (of which she was a cofounder in 1856), as well as in various galleries and at the Crystal Palace at its new site in Sydenham (from 1852), where she was awarded numerous Crystal Palace medals.

In 1854, after spending time absorbing the new theories on education then current and observing teaching methods in various primary schools, Bodichon used a large proportion of her private income to open an experimental primary school in Paddington. The Portman Hall School, inspired by the work of radical Unitarian educationists, was run on egalitarian principles. It made no distinctions regarding sex, class, or religion and rejected religious instruction, educating Jews and Roman Catholics alongside Unitarians and the children of freethinkers. This progressive school, a pioneer in coeducation, numbered among its teachers the reformer Octavia Hill. It also rejected learning by rote and corporal punishment and encouraged extracurricular activities such as physical exercise, Saturday outings, and visits to museums. Bodichon would be involved in running the school until it closed in 1862.

Bodichon first addressed the rights of married women and the need for changes to the unjust laws regarding their rights to divorce and to control their property in an 1854 pamphlet entitled "A Brief Summary in Plain Language of the Most Important Laws Concerning Women." An influential work that sold widely, it was inspired by "The Enfranchisement of Women," a pamphlet cowritten by John Stuart Mill and Harriet Taylor. Bodichon's pamphlet came out the same year that Caroline Norton argued a similar case in "English Laws for Women in the Nineteenth Century." In her pamphlet, Bodichon discussed the vulnerable economic status of married women and argued against the discriminatory laws that prevented their equality with men and deprived them of legal rights to custody of their children. The pamphlet was duly submitted to the Law Amendment Society, and Bodichon, Parkes, and other women organized a petition in 1855 in support of Bodichon's proposed reforms of marriage and divorce laws under a Married Women's Property Bill. This petition was presented to Parliament in March 1856, but its demands were not met in the 1857 Divorce Act. Although the act allowed wives to divorce their husbands (but not on the grounds of adultery alone) and retain some of their property as divorcees, it made no provisions for married women. The campaign for married women's property rights would continue until the Married Women's Property Acts of 1870, 1878, and

1882 gave wives full control over the property they brought into a marriage and their own earnings during the marriage.

In 1857, just before she married a French doctor, Eugène Bodichon, whom she had met in Algiers, Barbara published her radical tract *Women and Work*. In it, she argued that women, far from abandoning their aspirations for economic autonomy upon marriage, should seek admittance to all professions in order to secure an "honorable" independence from their husbands. She placed no qualifications on women's ability to work, seeing neither financial security nor marriage as precluding them from working if they so chose. She felt that women's paid work would have a beneficial effect on married life and would go some way toward alleviating the unremitting boredom of many middle-class women's lives. Bodichon adhered to this belief in her own life, having married a man sympathetic to her feminist views who respected her need for autonomy.

During 1857–1858, Bodichon and her husband traveled in the United States, visiting the southern states where, during the course of visits to plantations and slave auctions, they observed with horror the injustices of slavery. Bodichon took time while in the United States to meet with activists in the women's movement, including Lucretia Mott and Lucy Stone. Her vivid account of this visit was published as *An American Diary 1857–1858* in 1972. In it Bodichon drew clear comparisons between the institution of slavery and the domestic subjugation of women, averring that "slavery is a greater injustice, but it is allied to the injustice to women so closely that I cannot see one without thinking of the other and feeling how soon slavery would be destroyed if right opinions were entertained upon the other question" (Bodichon 1972, 63).

After her marriage, Bodichon would spend half of each year in England and the other half in Algeria with her husband, where she became a specialist in painting watercolor landscapes; he devoted himself to homeopathic cures at his clinic, a eucalyptus-planting project in the desert, and good works among the poor. In the wake of the 1856 petition to Parliament, Bodichon was encouraged by Anna Jameson to set up the *English Woman's Journal* (later known as the *Englishwoman's Review*) with Parkes and others; the journal would also be printed by a woman, Emily Faithfull. It became the mouthpiece for the women's movement in England for many years, providing new topics of discussion for women beyond the mundane and domestic and seeking to promote legal reform favoring them as well as lobbying for women to be admitted into higher education and the medical profession. Some of Bodichon's conclusions on the inadequate education then available for girls were outlined in her 1860 article in the *English Woman's Journal*, entitled "Middle Class Schools for Girls." The journal's editorial group also placed a particular emphasis on assisting the many respectable but so-called superfluous middle-class women in financial difficulty in obtaining employment other than as governesses—a market that Jameson declared was already "glutted." The Langham Place Circle did so by setting up their own Society for Promoting the Employment of Women in 1859 to act as an employment bureau. A library, the Victoria Press (Faithfull's imprint, which published books by women and trained women to be typesetters), and an emigration society run by Maria Rye would all eventually be based at Langham Place.

Bodichon was one of the first women in Britain to publish articles on women's suffrage. In 1866, encouraged by the election to Parliament of the feminist sympathizer John Stuart Mill (for whose electoral campaign she had worked), she produced two seminal tracts: her "Reasons for the Enfranchisement of Women" and "Objections to the Enfranchisement of Women Considered." These were subsequently read out at various venues, including the Kensington Society and the congress of the National Association for the Promotion of Social Science in Manchester. She became a member of the Enfranchisement of Women Committee in 1866, which she served as secretary until June 1867. She helped to organize committees in Manchester and Edinburgh, which gathered 1,499 signatures on a petition that was presented to Mill in June 1866. The proposed legislation contained in the petition was finally discussed in Parliament in May 1867, at the time the Reform Bill was being debated, but was defeated.

During the 1870s Bodichon turned her attention to her friend Emily Davies's campaign to establish university education for women at Cambridge University. In 1862 she had joined a committee set up by Davies to lobby for women to be allowed to take local university examinations, and in 1869 Bodichon's donation of £1,000 enabled Davies to set up a women's college at nearby Hitchin, which in 1873 moved to new premises in Cambridge and became Girton College. Bodichon would develop close and affectionate ties with many of the college's first students and teachers, visiting the college regularly and frequently mending rifts between students and staff caused by Davies's dictatorial regime as college principal. Bodichon financed scholarships and made a bequest of £10,000 on her death; her library of 395 volumes was also acquired by the college in 1954. Girton College's website has useful background on Bodichon's contributions at http://www.girton.cam.ac.uk/html.

Barbara Bodichon suffered a debilitating stroke in 1877 at the age of fifty and only partially recovered. She was able to publish her autobiography, *Perverse and Foolish: A Memoir of Childhood and Youth,* shortly before her death at Scalands, her country home at Robertsbridge on the Sussex coast. A woman of considerable beauty and charisma, Bodichon remained an individualist who was generous with her friendship and her money. In the light of her posthumous feminist reputation, her landscape watercolors and sketches—well reviewed in her day and then neglected for many decades—now command considerable prices in the auction rooms. Her friend George Eliot modeled the eponymous heroine of her novel *Romola* (1863) on Bodichon.

See also Davies, (Sarah) Emily; Hill, Octavia; Jameson, Anna Brownell; Mott, Lucretia Coffin; Nightingale, Florence; Norton, Caroline; Rye, Maria; Stone, Lucy; Taylor, Harriet.

References and Further Reading
Bodichon, Barbara. 1972. *An American Diary 1857–1858.* London: Routledge and KeganPaul.
Bradbrook, M. C. 1975. *Barbara Bodichon, George Eliot and the Limits of Feminism.* Oxford: Blackwell.
Burton, Hester. 1949. *Barbara Bodichon.* London: John Murray.
Crawford, Elizabeth. 1999. *The Women's Suffrage Movement, 1866–1928: A Reference Guide.* London: University College of London Press.
Herstein, Sheila. 1985. *A Mid-Victorian Feminist: Barbara Leigh Smith Bodichon.* New Haven: Yale University Press.
Hirsch, Pam. 1998. *Barbara Leigh Smith Bodichon 1827–1891: Feminist, Artist, and Rebel.* London: Chatto & Windus.
Holcombe, Lee. 1983. *Wives and Property: Reform of the Married Women's Property Law in Nineteenth-Century England.* Toronto: University of Toronto Press.
Hughes, Kathryn. 1998. *George Eliot: The Last Victorian.* London: Fourth Estate.
Lacey, Candida A., ed. 1987. *Barbara Leigh Smith Bodichon and the Langham Place Group.* London: Routledge and Kegan Paul.
Matthews, Jacquie. 1983. "Barbara Bodichon: Integrity in Diversity." In Dale Spender, ed., *Feminist Theorists: Three Centuries of Women's Intellectual Traditions.* London: Women's Press.
Spender, Dale. 1982. *Women of Ideas, and What Men Have Done to Them.* London: Routledge and Kegan Paul.

Bol Poel, Martha
(1877–1956)
Belgium

The Belgian social reformer and fifth president of the International Council of Women (ICW) from 1936 to 1947 was also a noted wartime heroine of the Belgian resistance. Born Marthe de Kerchove de Denterghem into an aristocratic family in Ghent that had a reputation for philanthropy, Bol Poel's middle school education was completed at the Kerchove Institute founded by her grandfather. In 1895 she studied for her Brévet Supérieur in Paris and entered the Académie Julien to study painting and drawing. In 1898 she became a baroness on her marriage to the rich industrialist and politician Bol Poel, who had a metalworks at La Louvière. Following in the family tradition for good works, Martha set up a maternity center at the works. As her husband's political career burgeoned and he rose to become a deputy and then a senator, the Bol Poels' home became a center of Belgian cultural and political life.

When the Germans occupied Belgium at the outbreak of World War I in 1914, Bol Poel ran an underground postal service for soldiers and their families. Arrested in 1916, she was imprisoned for two years. Because she was ill with heart disease, Bol Poel was exchanged for a German prisoner in 1917 and went into exile in Switzerland until war's end. Upon her return to Belgium, she founded a Friendly Association for ex-prisoners, to which she devoted herself for the remainder of her life. During the 1920s, she also became a leading figure in the women's movement as founder and president of the National Federation of Liberal Women, which initiated the founding of the Belgian Girl Guides and Young Women's Christian Association (YWCA), both of which involved young women in various social and cultural projects.

In 1934 Bol Poel was elected president of the Belgian National Council of Women. Such were her organizational skills that she was invited by the ICW to succeed Lady Isabella Aberdeen as its president, a post she held from 1936 to 1947 (her deputy took over during the war years).

In 1940 Belgium was once again invaded by the Germans, and Bol Poel was forced to take her political and social activities underground, holding National Council of Women meetings in secret at her home. After the war, she resumed her work for the ICW, attending the first postwar council meeting, held in Philadelphia in 1947, on which occasion she retired, opting to continue as honorary president. She was also a member of the Belgian Committee for Cooperation in the United Nations.

Bondfield, Margaret
(1873–1953)
United Kingdom

The distinguished trade union leader, pacifist, and advocate of adult suffrage Margaret Bondfield was the first woman in Great Britain appointed to a cabinet post, as minister of labor. As a member of the Independent Labour Party, she had a particular concern for the working conditions and pay of shop girls, becoming an authority on the subject through her organization of the Shop Assistants' Union and a forceful champion of work for women that was more than mere drudgery.

Born in Chard, Somerset, Bondfield was one of eleven children of a foreman in a lace workshop who had strong radical beliefs. She had very little education but nevertheless took up teaching when she was only thirteen and a year later went to work as a draper's assistant in a shop in Brighton. She continued as a shop girl after moving to London and would remain in this work for eleven years. Made miserable by the poor work-

ing conditions and long hours she had to endure—seventy-six hours a week for an annual salary of £25—as well as the rudimentary dormitory accommodations she was given, Bondfield became a socialist, joining the Social Democratic Federation in 1890 and later the Independent Labour Party. She began lobbying for regulation of her industry as a member of the National Union of Shop Assistants and wrote articles on women's work for the union's journal, the *Shop Assistant,* under the name of Grace Dare. In 1892 the Shop Act limited the working week for shop assistants under eighteen to seventy-four hours, although Bondfield would continue to assert that many girls worked an eighty-hour week.

In 1896 Bondfield was asked to conduct an investigation into the working conditions of shop assistants for the Women's Industrial Council, which prompted her to join the Women's Trade Union League, where she met and associated with Lady Emilia Dilke. In 1898, the year her report was published, Bondfield was appointed assistant secretary and paid organizer of the National Union of Shop Assistants on a salary of £2 per week, a post she held until 1908. In 1899 and on several subsequent occasions, she was the only woman delegate to the annual Trade Union Congress (TUC). Concurrent with these activities, Bondfield was an official (1898–1938) of the National Federation of Women Workers (founded in 1906) and in 1902 was called to give evidence on working conditions to a Select Committee on Shops.

In all her work, Bondfield was driven primarily by her commitment to labor politics, with her feminist concerns taking second place. Therefore, she did not devote time to campaigning in the women's suffrage movement for a limited franchise for women based on property qualifications, which she felt would inevitably penalize working-class women, but rather supported suffrage for all by chairing the Adult Suffrage Society. In 1907 she took part in a public debate in support of adult suffrage, challenging Teresa Billington-Greig, who supported limited suffrage for women.

In 1908 Bondfield gave up her work for the National Union of Shop Assistants to become a freelance lecturer for the Independent Labour Party and secretary of the Women's Trade Union League. In 1913 she was elected to the party's executive (remaining until 1921). With Margaret

Davies of the Women's Cooperative Guild, Bondfield supported a minimum wage, child welfare, and health insurance for women workers and submitted a report on the possible introduction of maternity benefits, which were incorporated in the Liberal government's 1911 Health Insurance Bill.

During World War I, Bondfield took a pacifist, conciliatory stance and refused to support the suffrage movement's endorsement of the war effort, although she monitored the pay and conditions of women munitions workers through the National Federation of Women Workers and was active in the Central Committee on Women's Employment. In 1915 she was one of 100 British women pacifists who signed an "open Christmas letter" to women in Germany and Austria, appealing to them to call for an end to the war. Bondfield also called for British women to set an example for their menfolk and support a women's peace congress to be held in The Hague that year. In April 1915 she attended a national conference of women held in London to discuss peace initiatives after the British government banned women from attending the conference in The Hague. At a subsequent meeting in May, again at London's Central Hall, she proposed a new organization, the British Committee of the Women's International Congress, which issued a manifesto entitled "Towards Permanent Peace." Later that year, this committee became the Women's International League, with Bondfield serving as an executive member. In December she spoke at a public meeting against conscription, which she considered debased the value of human life.

In the years after World War I, Bondfield continued to work for the TUC, acting as a labor delegate to numerous international labor conferences and as a TUC delegate to the Soviet Union in 1920. In 1923 she assumed the chair of the General Workers Union, which had merged with the National Federation of Women Workers in 1920, and earned the accolade of being the first woman to be made chair of the TUC, in 1923.

By this time, Bondfield had decided to enter politics, but her 1923 election as a Labour member of Parliament for Northampton lasted only a year, during which time she served as parliamentary secretary to the minister of labor. In 1926 she entered Parliament again, representing Wallsend, and was appointed minister of labor under Ramsay MacDonald in 1929, during a severe economic recession. It could not have been a more difficult time to become the first woman appointed to a government post. During her term, which ended in 1931 when the Labour government lost the general election, she presided over the Unemployment Insurance Fund, which rapidly became insolvent due to the increase in payouts during the continuing depression, forcing Bondfield to reluctantly support the government's reduction of unemployment benefits to women with the 1931 Anomalies Act. This effected the exclusion of 180,000 married women from eligibility for benefits, even though they had paid contributions while working, and the decision lost her valuable support within the trade union movement.

After being defeated in the 1931 election, Bondfield carried on with trade union work until 1938, when she spent time lecturing in Canada, the United States, and Mexico. She was preparing to stand for reelection to Parliament when war broke out in 1939, and with the general election deferred, she accepted the post of vice president of the National Council of Social Service, an organization responsible for public welfare. She maintained her interest in social reform as chair of the Women's Group on Public Welfare from 1939 to 1949.

In 1948 Bondfield was made a Companion of Honour, and in 1949 she published her autobiography, *A Life's Work.* Her views moderated in later life as she came to place greater emphasis on women's nurturing role within the family, but she would be remembered by fellow reformer Mary Stocks as "a woman of white-hot integrity, capable of selfless devotion, and withal most loveable" (Stocks 1970, 167).

See also Billington-Greig, Teresa; Dilke, Emilia.

References and Further Reading

Banks, Olive, ed. 1985, 1990. *The Biographical Dictionary of British Feminists,* vol. 1, *1800–1930,* vol. 2, *1900–1945.* Brighton: Harvester Wheatsheaf.

Baylen, J. O., and N. J. Gossman, eds. 1979–1984. *Biographical Dictionary of Modern British Radicals.* 3 vols. Hassocks, Sussex: Harvester Press.

Bellamy, Joyce M., and John Saville. 1982. *Dictionary of Labour Biography.* London: Macmillan.

Bondfield, Margaret. 1949. *A Life's Work.* London: Hutchinson.

Hamilton, Mary A. 1924. *Margaret Bondfield.* London: Leonard Parsons.

Josephson, Harold, Sandi Cooper, and Steven C. Hause et al., eds. 1985. *Biographical Dictionary of Modern Peace Leaders*. Westport, CT: Greenwood Press.

Liddington, Jill. 1989. *The Long Road to Greenham: Feminism and Anti-Militarism in Britain since 1820*. London: Virago.

Stocks, Mary. 1970. *My Commonplace Book*. London: Peter Davies.

Bonner, Yelena
(1923–)
Soviet Union/Russia

The distinguished human rights activist Yelena Bonner was a leader, with her husband Andrey Sakharov, of the Soviet dissident movement of the 1970s and 1980s, during which time they both endured considerable political harassment. Today Bonner continues to speak out on civil rights abuses in postcommunist Russia.

Bonner's parents were victims of the Stalinist purges of the Soviet intellectual and political elite during the 1930s. Her father, an Armenian communist, was executed in 1937, and her mother spent sixteen years in the Gulag before being released in 1954. Left alone, Bonner lived with relatives in Leningrad until they, too, were arrested. She served as a nurse at the Russian front during World War II, suffering a serious injury that would permanently affect her eyesight. Nevertheless, after the war she was able to study medicine, qualifying to be a doctor in 1953 and remaining in medical practice until 1983. During this time, she undertook medical aid work in Iraq. Like all Soviets who wanted to protect their careers, she joined the Communist Party, but she did not do so until 1965, during the brief years of the political "thaw" when Joseph Stalin had been formally denounced. When the Soviets invaded Czechoslovakia in 1968, she again became highly critical of the regime, and with the government turning the screws on internal political dissidents in the early 1970s, Bonner resigned her membership in the Communist Party.

Bonner had first married in 1947. In 1971 she married her second husband, the eminent nuclear physicist and academician Andrey Sakharov, a pioneer of the Soviet Union's first hydrogen bomb who had been one of the leading campaigners against its further development since 1961. In 1975, when the Helsinki Final Act had just been endorsed by the Soviets, dissidents such as Bonner and her husband nurtured hopes that the Soviet government would adhere to the act's clauses on human rights. Branches of the Helsinki Human Rights Group were set up across the Soviet Union to monitor the application of the agreement in that country, with Bonner becoming a leader of the Moscow group in 1976.

From the day she married Sakharov, Bonner had shared the mantle of leading spokesperson on the abuses of human rights in the Soviet Union. She and Sakharov paid a high price for their outspokenness. Their tiny apartment became a focus for dissent, and the Sakharovs were the subject of relentless harassment, KGB surveillance, and frequent arrest—so much so that it permanently impaired their health. When Sakharov denounced the Soviet invasion of Afghanistan in December 1979, the full weight of official disapproval was launched at him. He was stripped of his Soviet scientific honors and exiled to the then closed city of Gorky (now Nizhniy Novgorod). Bonner joined him there in 1984, when she too was exiled after being arrested and prosecuted for anti-Soviet activities. Here, again, their every movement was watched, with Bonner remarking that the minders followed her even when she went to buy bread.

Meanwhile, Bonner had been suffering from failing eyesight, and in 1975 she had been allowed to go to the West for an eye operation, during which time she also collected the 1975 Nobel Peace Prize awarded to her husband. She made several return visits, but not without having to go on a hunger strike (and be force-fed) to be permitted to travel to Italy in 1981 to see a specialist. She traveled abroad for further treatment in 1984, and in 1985, when she went to the United States to see doctors about her heart trouble and glaucoma, she spoke out publicly on the persecution of Soviet dissidents. In 1986 the rigors of life in exile came to an end with—as it seemed at the time—the sweeping political rebirth of the Soviet Union under Mikhail Gorbachev's policies of glasnost and perestroika. Bonner and Sakharov were allowed to return to Moscow. In April 1989 Sakharov was elected to the Congress of People's Deputies, but by that time mortally ill, he barely had time to enjoy his new intellectual freedom before dying in December.

Since the collapse of the Soviet Union in 1991, with Bonner comparing the destruction of the

Berlin Wall with the fall of the Bastille during the French Revolution, she has helped sustain the struggle for the democratization of a country that for centuries under the czars and then the Soviets had never enjoyed real political and civil freedoms. She has not let up on her hawkish criticism of the post-Soviet governments of Gorbachev, Boris Yeltsin, and Vladimir Putin, warning that postcommunist Russia was once more turning back to totalitarianism, restoring a strictly centralized rather than a multinational government, and one that was hijacking control of the media and clamping down on freedom of the press. In March 2000, in the *Moscow Times,* she urged the West to support Russian dissidents critical of the continuing conflict in Chechnya, the oppression of ethnic minorities, the uncontrolled spread of the Mafia, and the tightening of press controls under Putin, whose government she described as being little more than "modernised Stalinism." The increasing constraints upon journalists in Russia and the assassination of some leading figures in television and newspaper reporting have since highlighted the steady erosion of freedom of speech in Russia. In March 2001 Bonner appealed via Radio Free Europe to the Parliamentary Assembly of the Council of Europe, asking it to take up the issue of the ethnic cleansing of the Chechen people by Russian troops. She reminded public opinion in the West that this conflict has now claimed the lives of more than 100,000 civilians. For updates on human rights appeals in the former eastern Europe, contact Radio Free Europe at http://www.rferl.org/welcome/english/.

References and Further Reading
Bonner, Yelena. 1986. *Alone Together.* New York: Alfred A. Knopf.
———. 1992. *Mothers and Daughters.* New York: Alfred A. Knopf.
Klose, Kevin. 1984. *Russia and the Russians: Inside the Closed Society.* New York: W. W. Norton.
McCauley, Martin. 1997. *Who's Who in Russia since 1900.* London: Routledge.
Sakharov, Andrey. 1990. *Memoirs.* London: Hutchinson.

Bonnin, Gertrude (Zitkala-Ša/Red Bird)
(1876–1938)
United States

The Native American writer and progressive reformer Gertrude Bonnin, who regularly alerted government to the abuse of her people's rights and to the corrupt practices of the Bureau of Indian Affairs, was also known under her Lakota tribal name of Red Bird.

Born in South Dakota on the Yankton Sioux Reservation, she was the daughter of a Nakota mother and white father. She left her home at the age of eight to study at a Quaker mission school—White's Manual Labor Institute—in Wabash, Indiana. After leaving when she was eleven she spent the following years back on the reservation, returning to higher education in 1895, when she obtained a scholarship to Earlham College, Richmond, Indiana. But she was forced to give up her studies after two years due to ill health. During 1897–1899, Bonnin took up the violin at the New England Conservatory of Music in Boston, and left around 1899 to teach music at the Carlisle Indian School in Pennsylvania, during which time she played at the Paris Exposition of 1900 with the school's Carlisle Indian Band.

By around 1900, Bonnin had begun publishing articles on Indian life under the pen name of Zitkala-Ša (Red Bird) in the *Atlantic Monthly* and *Harper's Monthly.* She was by now becoming increasingly averse to the teaching methods instituted at Carlisle by its diehard founder, Colonel Richard Henry Pratt, who ran the school like an army camp and exploited the unpaid labor of students in local agriculture. Bonnin objected to Pratt's emphasis on assimilation and the conversion of his Native American students to Christianity in preference to nurturing their traditional Indian cultural values. Nor did the school ever encourage its students to aspire to anything more than menial vocational training. Bonnin was eventually dismissed, probably as a result of her article "The Soft-Hearted Sioux," which had appeared in *Harper's Monthly* in 1901 and in which she had illustrated the loss of cultural identity experienced by a young Indian boy after being given a Christian education.

Back in her reservation at Yankton, North Dakota, Bonnin began collecting stories of traditional Lakota Indian life for her 1901 anthology,

Old Indian Legends, which had been commissioned by the Boston publisher Ginn and Co. She took a job as a clerk at the Bureau of Indian Affairs at Standing Rock Indian Reservation in New Mexico, where she met and married a mixed-blood Nakota, Raymond Bonnin, in 1902. The couple moved soon after to Utah, living for fourteen years on the Unitah-Ouray reservation. During this time Bonnin remained active in local Indian cultural and self-help activities as a member of the Society of American Indians (SAI, founded in 1911), with which she corresponded on local native affairs. This organization, which Bonnin served as secretary from 1916 and whose journal *American Indian Magazine* she edited in 1918–1919, had dedicated itself to preserving the Indian way of life and culture. It lobbied vigorously for Indian civil and political rights; the arguments were, however, essentially assimilationist. Bonnin's critics have since argued that she and the SAI were misguided in their campaigning on citizenship and employment rights for Native Americans, for such legal changes were precisely those that contributed to the erosion of their traditional way of life, and diluted the Native Americans' sense of heritage.

One of Bonnin's responsibilities as secretary of the SAI was to conduct correspondence with the Bureau of Indian Affairs, but her increasing criticism of the BIA's corrupt practices eventually lost her husband his job. In 1916 the couple moved to Washington from where Bonnin lectured around the USA on behalf of the SAI to promote the cultural and tribal identity of Native Americans. During the 1920s Bonnin invested much time and effort in promoting the idea of a Pan-Indian movement that would unify America's many different tribes in a common cause. In 1926, with the help of her husband, she organized the National Council of American Indians (NCAI), which she served as president and major fund-raiser and speaker from 1926 until her death in 1938. But as such, the NCAI's unifying efforts remained ineffectual and it went into limbo after Bonnin's death, to be revived in 1944 under a male leadership who failed to acknowledge the long years during which Bonnin had run the organization practically single-handedly.

Bonnin also worked tirelessly for the General Federation of Women's Clubs (GFWC) from 1921, in the course of which she was involved in studies of the federal treatment of Native Americans and their right to suffrage and in which she defended tribal religion and rights to ancient homelands. In 1924, under the auspices of the GFWC, an Indian Welfare Committee was set up to launch a government investigation, led by Bonnin, of the exploitation of Native Americans in Oklahoma and, in particular, attempts to defraud them of drilling rights to their oil-rich lands there. She wrote a report on this, published by the Indian Rights Association as *Oklahoma's Poor Rich Indians: An Orgy of Graft and Exploitation of the Five Civilized Tribes—Legalized Robbery.* Its publication prompted the establishment by Herbert Hoover's government of the Merriam Commission in 1928, which reported on Native American life and eventually resulted in the passing of the Indian Reorganization Act (1934) under Roosevelt's New Deal, although ultimately Bonnin clashed with the U.S. government's Indian commissioner, John Collier, who was responsible for the wording of the act.

In her work for the NCAI, Bonnin also ran a voter-registration drive among Native Americans in 1924 in order to raise their support for the Curtis Bill, passed by Congress that year. This gave Native Americans U.S. citizenship but failed to grant them voting rights (these would not be granted in many states until as late as the 1960s). Bonnin continued to call for civil and political rights for her people and for improvements to education and health care provisions on reservations, some of which were implemented under the New Deal. Dressed in her traditional costume, she appeared regularly on the lecture circuit speaking on issues relating to the rights and culture of her people. She published *American Indian Stories* in 1921 and with William F. Hanson in 1913 collaborated on an opera, *Sun Dance,* based on Native American culture that was premiered in New York. Throughout her life Bonnin remained true to her pagan beliefs, publishing "Why I Am a Pagan" in *Atlantic Monthly* in 1902. Ironically, when she died Bonnin was buried, not according to traditional Indian rites in the homeland she loved, but in that most elitist of American resting places—Arlington National Cemetery (her husband, as a former U.S. Army captain, had had the right to be buried there). Since her death, the University of Nebraska has reissued many of Bonnin's writings on Native American culture.

References and Further Reading

Bataille, Gretchen M., and Kathleen Mullen Sands. 1984. *American Indian Women: Telling Their Lives.* Lincoln: University of Nebraska Press.

Fisher, Dexter. 1979. "Zitkala-Sa: The Evolution of a Writer." *American Indian Quarterly* 5: 229–238.

Hoefel, Roseanne. 1997. "Writing, Performance, Activism: Zitkala-Sa and Pauline Johnson." In Susan Castillo and Victor M. P. Da Rosa Porto, eds., *Native American Women in Literature and Culture.* Portugal: Fernando Pessoa University Press.

Krupat, Arnold, ed. 1994. *Native American Autobiography: An Anthology.* Madison: University of Wisconsin Press.

Spack, Ruth. 1997. "Re-visioning Sioux Women: Zitkala-Sa's Revolutionary American Indian Stories." *Legacy* 14(1): 25–42.

Zitkala-Sa. 1985 [1921]. *American Indian Stories.* Reprint, Lincoln: University of Nebraska Press.

Booth, Catherine
(1829–1890)
United Kingdom

Catherine Booth was cofounder with her husband of the Salvation Army; together they initiated a brand of fire-and-brimstone social activism, challenging armchair Victorian reformers to take their campaigning to the streets where it was really needed. A devout and rigorous Christian, Booth's evangelism was devoted to the moral and social redemption of the destitute. Unlike other reformers, she did not confine herself to conveying her message to do-gooders in the middle classes but took it to the proletariat, preaching in the pubs, open spaces, and back streets of the East End of London. In her very public campaign for moral purity and temperance, she courted hostility and derision as well as acts of violence by brothel keepers, pub landlords, and the public alike.

Born in Ashbourne Derbyshire, Booth was the daughter of a Wesleyan lay preacher and carriage builder. She grew up in Lincolnshire and spent much of her adolescence as an invalid, suffering from spine, heart, and lung trouble. She was therefore educated at home and spent much time in self-study of the Bible and theology. Her life-long abhorrence of drink took root when her own father broke his pledge and became a drunkard.

After the family moved to London in 1844, Catherine began attending the Brixton Wesleyan Methodist Church, where she met William Booth at a prayer meeting. As a woman of strong opinions and forceful personality, Catherine was ejected from the congregation for being too extreme and joined a group of Wesleyan reformers, the Methodist New Connexion. She persuaded Booth not only to pledge total abstinence from drink (which would later be mandatory for all Salvationists) but also to join her in taking their religious crusade to the street. The couple married in 1855, and despite her continual poor health and the interruptions of bearing eight children in quick succession, Catherine Booth took on a relentless program of social work, endless letter writing, and proselytizing.

Based on her careful study and understanding of the scriptures, Booth believed in egalitarianism in all public work and was ready to argue this point with any male preachers in her promotion of sexual equality within the Methodist movement. She outlined these ideas in her 1859 pamphlet, "Female Ministry: Or Women's Right to Preach the Gospel," a work she revised and republished in *Papers on Practical Religion* in 1879. Booth never wavered from her steadfast advocacy of women's right to be preachers and, having won over her husband, finally decided to defend her position in the pulpit herself, in 1860 at the Gateshead Bethesda, where her husband had been undertaking circuit work since 1858. She proved to be an exceptional orator and applied her as-yet-unexploited intellectual talents to speech making on social and moral reform. Booth was subsequently instrumental in molding Salvation Army policy on women's equality, ensuring that it enjoyed a high percentage of women officers. William Booth would later remark that the "best men in my Army are the women" (Helsinger, Sheets, and Veeder 1983, 183). Catherine Booth's advocacy of women's right to be preachers would also become an integral part of the Salvation Army's Women's Charter.

In 1861 Booth encouraged her husband to leave his post in Gateshead and become a full-time touring evangelist. For the next four years, they traveled around the country, living in Cornwall, Cardiff, Walsall, and Birmingham before settling back in London in 1864. There in 1865 they founded the Christian Revival Association (CRA) in Whitechapel (the precursor to their Christian Mission), which operated out of a marquee set up in an old Quaker burial ground. Their first premises, known as the People's Mission Hall, were opened in a building in the Whitechapel road in 1868; there they held all-night prayer vigils, known as the Midnight Meeting movement of the 1860s, and sold cheap food to the poor.

In its early guise, the East London Christian Mission (ELCM from 1867) operated as a charitable religious movement that set up a network of mission stations across London's East End to shelter and feed the destitute and spread the "good news" of God's word. By 1869 the original mission had established thirteen preaching stations, and Booth and her husband were holding open-air meetings where they regularly castigated drink and prostitution and in which music and song played an integral part. Catherine proved herself able to defend her beliefs in front of audiences full of hecklers at revival meetings and preached in some of the roughest parts of London, in and around the docklands of Rotherhithe and Bermondsey. She also wrote numerous tracts on temperance for the Temperance Society and oversaw the establishment of Food-for-the-Millions Shops, which offered hot dinners for sixpence. At the beginning of 1878, the ECLM was renamed the Salvation Army, with William Booth appointed its general. The organization relocated to larger premises on Queen Victoria Street, with the Booths now the acknowledged leaders, with Josephine Butler, of the social purity movement.

The Salvation Army's work was extended with the publication of its newspaper, the *War Cry,* which Catherine played a considerable role in running despite her frequent need to rest and recover her health. She conducted a series of highly successful public meetings during the 1880s in large London venues such as Exeter Hall and in major provincial cities, where she achieved dozens of converts at every session. The Salvation Army's "Hallelujah Bands" had become a familiar sight on the streets of many towns, and its anthem "Onward, Christian Soldiers" (an 1864 hymn set to music in 1872 by Arthur Sullivan of Gilbert and Sullivan fame) became a rallying cry for evangelizing reformers everywhere.

In 1885 the Booths joined with Josephine Butler and other social reformers in supporting the journalist William Thomas Stead's very public campaign against the white slave trade. The series of four articles he published in the *Pall Mall Gazette,* beginning with "The Maiden Tribute of Modern Babylon," gave impetus to campaigning to protect vulnerable young girls from being drawn into prostitution. The Booths' son Bramwell, who assisted Stead in the deliberate purchase of a thirteen-year-old girl for £5 in order to expose the trade in virgins, was prosecuted and acquitted. In the ensuing public furor over the articles, the Salvation Army was galvanized by Catherine's speeches on the subject and obtained 393,000 signatures on a petition demanding legislation to protect children from vice. In August 1885 the Criminal Law Amendment Act was passed, making procuring women and girls for prostitution a criminal offense and raising the age of consent to sixteen. Rebecca Jarrett, a former prostitute rescued by Bramwell Booth's wife Florence and Josephine Butler, who had acted as intermediary in the affair and had also been jailed, later worked as a brothel visitor for the Salvation Army (her story was told by Butler in her 1885 *Rebecca Jarrett).*

Aside from her work for temperance and against prostitution, Catherine Booth supported the suffrage campaign in the conviction that women with the vote would be a powerful force for good in the world. She also did valuable work in exposing the exploitation of cheap labor in the East End, in particular that of women, who were paid a fraction of the daily rate paid to men doing similar work. Like Annie Besant, Booth was particularly disturbed by the appalling conditions endured by women workers at Bryant and May's match factory. Here women frequently succumbed to the horrifying effects of "phossy jaw," a degenerative condition of the facial bones caused by constant exposure to noxious yellow phosphorus used in the manufacture of matches. Booth and Besant began campaigning to force the reluctant manufacturers to use the safer but more expensive red phosphorus, adopted long since in the industry in Europe.

Sadly, Catherine Booth did not live to see this campaign succeed. After her death, William Booth continued her fight against yellow phosphorus by establishing the Salvation Army's own match factory in direct competition with Bryant and May and offering better working conditions and rates of pay. So successful was the venture and the attendant publicity the factory received for its humane working practices that Bryant and May eventually was forced to capitulate in 1901 and abandon the use of yellow phosphorus.

Catherine Booth made her final public appearance before a large audience at the City Temple on 21 June 1888 and retired to the sea at Clacton. She died of cancer after a prolonged period of suffering at the age of sixty-one. Her funeral in London was attended by 36,000 people. By the time of her death in 1890, the Salvation Army had branches in Europe, India, South Africa, and South America; it had 45,000 full-time officers in Britain and about 9,416 officers worldwide. Its advocacy of social philanthropy was firmly established in William Booth's classic work, *In Darkest England and the Way Out* (1890), and it became one of the most successful and influential relief agencies in Britain. According to the *War Cry,* the army was rescuing up to 5,000 destitute women a year (Prochaska 1980, 190). In one way or another, all the Booth children became proselytizers for the "Sally Ann," as it was affectionately known as it extended its network across eighty countries and six continents. Catherine's daughter Evangeline eventually controlled the Salvation Army's operations throughout London, pioneered the movement in Canada, and went on to oversee its establishment throughout the United States. Her granddaughter Catherine Bramwell Booth, who lived to the age of 104, led important programs of social work in England in the 1920s and 1930s and was held in great affection by the British people.

See also Besant, Annie; Butler, Josephine.

References and Further Reading
Barnes, Cyril J. 1981. *Words of Catherine Booth.* London: Salvationist.
Bramwell-Booth, Catherine. 1970. *Catherine Booth: The Story of Her Loves.* London: Hodder and Stoughton.
Bristow, Edward J. 1977. *Vice and Vigilance: Purity Movements in Britain since 1700.* London: Gill and Macmillan.
Chappell, Jennie. 1910. *Noble Workers: Sketches of the Life-Work of Frances Willard, Agnes Weston, Sister Dora, Catherine Booth, the Baroness Burdett-Coutts, Lady Henry Somerset, Sarah Robinson, Mrs. Fawcett and Mrs. Gladstone.* London: S. W. Partridge.
Green, Roger J. 1996. *Catherine Booth: A Biography of the Co-founder of the Salvation Army.* Crowborough, Sussex: Monarch.
Hattersely, Roy. 1999. *Blood and Fire: William and Catherine Booth and Their Salvation Army.* London: Little, Brown.
Heasman, Kathleen. 1962. *Evangelicals in Action: An Appraisal of Social Work in the Victorian Era.* London: Geoffrey Bles.
Helsinger, Elizabeth K., Robin Lauterbach Sheets, and William Veeder. 1983. *The Woman Question: Social Issues, 1837–1883,* vol. 2, *Society and Literature in Britain and America, 1837–1883.* Manchester: Manchester University Press.
Prochaska, F. K. 1980. *Women and Philanthropy in Nineteenth-Century England.* Oxford: Clarendon Press.
Sandall, Robert, et al. 1955. *The History of the Salvation Army,* vol. 3, *Social Reform and Welfare Work.* London: T. Nelson.
Tucker, Frederick Booth. 1893. *The Life of Catherine Booth, the Mother of the Salvation Army.* New York: Fleming H. Revell.

Boucherett, Jessie
(1825–1905)
United Kingdom

A close colleague of Barbara Bodichon, the philanthropist and feminist Jessie Boucherett was one of the organizers of the women's suffrage petition of 1866 that was presented in Parliament. She made women's right to work a particular personal concern and assisted them in finding employment in respectable professions through the Society for Promoting the Employment of Women. Boucherett also freely gave from her own considerable wealth to various causes, selling her own diamonds to rescue the *English Woman's Journal* from closure in 1866.

Boucherett was descended from French Protestant refugees and grew up on an estate near Market Rasen in Lincolnshire, where her father was a landowner and high sheriff. Throughout her life, her views would reflect the conservative landowning tradition from which she had sprung and her own love of country life and hunting. In later years, she would recoil in horror at women's campaigning for the repeal of the Contagious Diseases Acts, and with Lydia Becker, she opposed the franchise being given to married women.

The story is told by Helen Blackburn (1902) that Boucherett was inspired to join the Langham Place Circle in 1858 after reading a copy of the *English Woman's Journal.* She enthusiastically presented herself at the journal's offices in June 1859, and soon after, encouraged by Harriet Martineau's 1859 tract "Female Industry," she mooted the idea of an employment agency for women, which she set up with Adelaide Procter and Bodichon in central London. Its object was "to help those who have been born and bred ladies to preserve the habits, the dress, and the countless moral and material associations of the rank to which they were born" (Perkin 1993, 166).

Boucherett and her colleagues were aware of the growing numbers of middle-class women in reduced circumstances who were desperate for work, and the agency was soon besieged by many such women, whom they assisted in obtaining clerical work, training for jobs in printing and lithography, and positions as shop girls, bookkeepers and cashiers, and legal copyists. Boucherett was highly resourceful in her suggestions for new areas of employment, arguing that women could be trained to hand-tint photographs, engrave on wood, decorate houses, carve ivory, and make shoes, and even asserting that they were more than capable of taking up poultry rearing and pig farming. Any profession that provided decent, honest work was in Boucherett's opinion better than lives lived on charity or in the workhouse. The society also acted as an agency referring women to potential employers, and it lasted into the twentieth century, referring women to new roles as telegraphers, telephonists, and type writers (as secretaries were first called). In addition, it went against prevailing opinions and urged women to enter nursing and the medical profession (Boucherett was a member of the first general committee of Elizabeth Garrett Anderson's St. Mary's Dispensary for Women and Children, later the New Hospital). In later years the society assisted women seeking to emigrate in search of greater opportunities in Canada and Australia, referring them to Maria Rye's Female Middle-Class Emigration Society. Boucherett also founded a school in nearby Charlotte Street that offered literacy classes to mature women seeking to improve their employment opportunities.

In 1863, impressed by Samuel Smiles's landmark 1859 work *Self-Help*, a collection of lectures on self-improvement, Boucherett published her own response, *Hints on Self-Help for Young Women*. She was one of a core of fifty women involved in the establishment of the Kensington Society in 1865, a discussion group that debated suffrage and other issues. A year later, she, Bodichon, and Emily Davies were involved in drafting the 1866 petition on women's suffrage that was submitted to Parliament by John Stuart Mill. Such was her commitment to the Langham Place Circle's work that in 1866

Boucherett sold some of her diamonds in order to revive the fortunes of the *English Woman's Journal*, which she relaunched as the *Englishwoman's Review*, remaining its editor until 1871 and frequently contributing articles of her own. The journal survived until 1903.

Boucherett published pamphlets on women's need for economic independence, such as "The Condition of Women in France" (1868) and her 1869 essays "The Employment of Women" and "How to Provide for Superfluous Women," which later appeared in a collection of essays edited by Josephine Butler and entitled *Woman's Work and Woman's Culture* (1869). But Boucherett opposed protective legislation for women, believing that such measures would reduce their earning power by limiting the professions that they could enter. She continued to support women's suffrage, in 1870 at a meeting of the National Association for the Promotion of Social Science reading a paper entitled "The Probable Use Women Would Make of the Political Franchise." She was a founding member of the Central Committee of the National Society for Women's Suffrage in 1871 but by 1884 was supporting William Woodhall's Representation of the People Bill, which called for a limited franchise for unmarried women and widows only. With her close colleague Helen Blackburn, Boucherett was also a member of the Liberty and Property Defence League and a founder of the Freedom of Labour Defence League (1899), both of which advocated women's self-employed labor.

With Helen Blackburn, Boucherett published *The Condition of Working Women and the Factory Acts* in 1896 and then retired to her family estate at Market Rasen, where she supported the work of its local cottage hospital. Boucherett's sister Louisa was also active in women's suffrage and reform and was an advocate of taking pauper children from workhouses and boarding them out with good families.

See also Anderson, Elizabeth Garrett; Becker, Lydia; Blackburn, Helen; Bodichon, Barbara; Davies, (Sarah) Emily; Martineau, Harriet.

References and Further Reading

Banks, Olive, ed. 1985, 1990. *The Biographical Dictionary of British Feminists*, vol. 1, *1800–1930*; vol. 2, *1900–1945*. Brighton: Harvester Wheatsheaf.

Baylen, J. O., and N. J. Gossman, eds. 1979–1984. *Biographical Dictionary of Modern British Radicals*. 3 vols. Hassocks, Sussex: Harvester Press.

Blackburn, Helen. 1902. *Women's Suffrage: A Record of the Women's Suffrage Movement in the British Isles.* London: Williams and Norgate.

Crawford, Elizabeth. 1999. *The Women's Suffrage Movement, 1866–1928: A Reference Guide.* London: University College of London Press.

Holcombe, Lee. 1983. *Wives and Property: Reform of the Married Women's Property Law in Nineteenth-Century England.* Toronto: University of Toronto Press.

Jordan, Ellen. 1997. *The Women's Movement and Women's Employment in Nineteenth-Century Britain.* London: Routledge.

Perkin, Joan. 1993. *Victorian Women.* London: John Murray.

Lily Braun (German Heritage Foundation)

Braun, Lily
(1865–1916)
Germany

A pacifist, feminist, and socialist who believed that motherhood was a "social function" that should be protected by the state through maternity insurance, Braun was one of the first German women to fight for the rights of working mothers and support the idea of communal living. As an independent thinker, she soon came into conflict with the militant socialist theoretician Clara Zetkin, who mistrusted Braun's bourgeois background. In their ensuing debate Zetkin labeled Braun one of the "perfumed salon socialists" (Quaterat 1979, 110). She abhorred Braun's move to assimilate middle-class women into the socialist movement as being indicative of her utopian objective of a gradual reform of society toward socialism rather than through outright class war.

Born into a rich, aristocratic landowning family in Halberstadt, then part of Prussia, Braun was the daughter of a distinguished general, and the family traveled a great deal. Educated in all the requisite skills of playing piano, drawing, cooking, sewing, and speaking French, Braun was brought up to expect little more from life than to marry well, once ruefully remarking that her life was "being arranged" for her. She was a sickly, lonely child, but her temperamental outbursts were such that she was sent away to an authoritarian aunt for a couple of years to be disciplined. There she read widely and on returning home became disenchanted with the social round. After the family's fortunes took a turn for the worse, she announced her determination to take control of her life and be useful to society. She settled in Berlin to continue her self-education, becoming a specialist in the work of Johann Wolfgang von Goethe and from 1893 publishing literary articles. Having entered the radical intellectual circuit in Berlin, Braun met and, much against her family's wishes, married the humanitarian and philosopher Georg von Gizycki (1851–1895). As a member of the Ethical Culture Society, he introduced her to ethical socialist theory, atheism, and feminism; tutored her; and brought her onto the board of his journal *Ethical Culture*. He also encouraged Braun to join the Berlin branch of the Women's Welfare Association in 1894. After Gizycki's death, Braun married socialist leader Heinrich Braun in 1896, inviting further criticism because he was twice divorced and also a Jew, but reaching a compromise with him over the balancing of both their commitments to work.

In 1895, having joined the Social Democratic Party, Braun collaborated with Minna Cauer to found the feminist newspaper the *Women's*

Movement (1895–1919), the organ of the Women's Welfare Association. A late convert to socialism (after her marriage to Braun), she declared that it was the only means whereby middle-class women reformers could get to the root of social ills, and she advocated cooperation by radicals with the majority conservative element of the feminist movement in the pursuit of their joint social objectives. This brought her into conflict with radical leader Clara Zetkin, who sought to bring the class struggle to the women's movement and restrict women's activities to direct action in support of the working classes only.

Braun valued motherhood as providing women with fulfillment of their true, biological nature, yet she saw marriage as subordinating woman and destroying love between couples. In the belief that marital monogamy would only survive if women agreed to subordinate themselves, she argued that the only option was for the state to provide financial protection of mothers, especially during pregnancy and their children's early years. This step would ensure that they remained independent of their male partners. In 1897 and again in 1901, she was the first woman to call for independent maternity insurance for women. She advocated raising insurance money by taxation to provide financial assistance during the crucial four weeks before and eight weeks after giving birth, so that mothers would be allowed some time with their new babies and have their jobs guaranteed for their return.

Despite becoming an excellent public speaker on social issues, Braun was never accepted by Clara Zetkin and, as a revisionist, came into open conflict with her when she set forth her own educational plan, published in the Social Democratic Party's journal *Equality* in 1897. She proposed the creation of four teams: to gather information on working women; to collect and publish data on women's employment in Germany and compare it with that in other European countries; to set up a legal team to monitor all legislation affecting women and offer advice; and finally, to establish a group to write articles and pamphlets for the socialist press. But Zetkin, mistrustful of the ability of an upper-class woman such as Braun to sufficiently understand the workers' struggle, condemned her plan, and Braun left the party.

In 1901 she turned to developing other ideas, publishing a pamphlet titled "Women's Labor and Household Cooperatives." Arguing that in-dustrialization had placed greater strains on the family and in particular working mothers, she advocated communal living as a way of minimizing the burden of domestic duties on women and continued to campaign for women to be awarded maternity insurance. Braun's arguments for this and a wide range of women's issues are encapsulated in her book *The Woman Question: Its Historical Development and Its Economic Aspect* (1901), in which she argued that capitalism destroys the family by taking women away from the family and into the workplace, thus paving the way for social upheaval. Her utopian ideal of a system of cooperatives in which men and women share work and child care would, she felt, lay the foundations for the peaceful, if gradual, transition to socialism. But Zetkin, who had no time for diversionary campaigns on women's issues, condemned Braun's ideas as the "latest blossoming of utopianism in its most dangerous, opportunistic form" (Boxer and Quaterat 1978, 130). She increasingly marginalized Braun for refusing to subordinate her feminist concerns for the well-being of women to the liberation of the proletariat. Braun's regular columns in *Equality* were whittled away so that by 1907, she was forced out of the movement altogether. Meanwhile, she had become involved in the establishment of Helene Stöcker's League for the Protection of Motherhood and Sexual Reform, attending its first convention in 1905 and helping to formulate its program of "new ethics" in support of sexual reform and the rights of unmarried mothers and illegitimate children. From 1909 to 1911, Braun published *Memoirs of a Socialist Woman,* her best-known published work.

See also Cauer, Minna; Stöcker, Helene; Zetkin, Clara.

References and Further Reading

Boxer, Marilyn, and Jean H. Quaterat. 1978. *Socialist Women: European Socialist Feminism in the Nineteenth and Twentieth Centuries.* New York: Isevier North-Holland.

Fout, John C. 1984. *German Women in the Nineteenth Century: A Social History.* New York: Holmes and Meier.

Meyer, Alfred G. 1985. *The Feminism and Socialism of Lily Braun.* Bloomington: Indiana University Press.

Quaterat, Jean H. 1979. *Reluctant Feminists in German Social Democracy 1885–1917.* Princeton: Princeton University Press.

Bremer, Fredrika
(1801–1865)
Sweden

The Swedish novelist, feminist, and peace campaigner Fredrika Bremer's tireless work for social and educational reform as a self-proclaimed "Christian socialist" came at a time when such activity by respectable women was not only frowned upon but strictly circumscribed by polite society in Sweden. In her outstanding social novels, she set out to enlighten society on the unjust sublimation of wives and daughters within the home.

Born in Åbo, Finland, the daughter of a wealthy merchant, Bremer's family moved to an estate at Årsta near Sweden in 1804. Despite being brought up in seclusion, as a strict Lutheran, on the family estate outside Stockholm, she received a good education. In 1820–1821 Fredrika enjoyed the privilege of being taken on a European grand tour, but by the time of her return, having seen something of the effects of poverty and social deprivation, she yearned for a constructive role in society and took up charity work. Her first book, *Sketches from Everyday Life*, was written to fund the good works she had begun undertaking on a limited scale among poor workers on her family's estate. As a woman, she was obliged to publish it anonymously in 1828; two further volumes of this work followed in 1832.

After her father's death in 1830, Bremer was released from many of the constraints that had limited her social work until then. Having resolved not to marry after turning down several proposals, she traveled widely and published several novels and short stories, adopting the style of the English social novel as her métier: *The Neighbours* (1837), *The Home, or Family Cares and Chores* (1843), and *Brothers and Sisters* (1850) all took family relationships and domestic life—and, in particular, the need women felt for some kind of useful occupation—as their theme. These novels became very popular both in Sweden and in England, where they were translated and promoted by Mary Howitt, an English poet and translator of Hans Andersen, in an eleven-volume sequence in 1844 and 1845. Howitt, an early British feminist and Unitarian, was one of many radicals in Britain who embraced Bremer's work; Howitt's friend, the writer Elizabeth Gaskell, read Bremer's works with ea-

Fredrika Bremer (Archive Photos)

ger interest. Bremer was also much admired by reformers such as Barbara Bodichon.

In 1831 and again in 1844, Bremer was awarded the Gold Medal by the Swedish Academy for her literary achievements. By this time, she had the public recognition and respect that enabled her to take an even more active role in calling for women's rights to education and training. She also led calls for the establishment of an age of majority at which young women could (or rather could not be compelled to) marry.

In 1849 Fredrika embarked on an ambitious trip to the United States in order to study social and political conditions there; en route, she stayed for two months in England. She spent two years in the United States, making a particular study of the status of women, and was heartened by inroads made into women's education there. She traveled extensively along the Atlantic Coast and in New England, where she made friends with abolitionists, and to the deep South and Minnesota. During her visit she met and earned the admiration of women such as Harriet Beecher Stowe, Lydia Maria Child, Lucy Stone, Dorothea Dix, Lucretia Mott, and Elizabeth Peabody. Her letters home to her sister Agatha were quickly translated and published as *The Homes of the New World: Impressions of America* in 1853. In them Bremer described many of the famous U.S. literati she had met in her travels, including Ralph Waldo Emerson, Nathaniel Hawthorne, and Henry Wadsworth Longfellow.

On her return to Stockholm, Bremer tried unsuccessfully to implement some of her new ideas but was thwarted in her desire to encourage women to set up groups to aid deprived children in Sweden's cities because the moral climate of the time precluded respectable women from leaving the home to do such work. Bremer refused to be daunted and turned her attention to nursing those who fell victim to a cholera epidemic in Stockholm in 1853, as well as founding an orphanage and a teacher-training school for women. During the Crimean War (1854–1856), Bremer was appalled by the battlefield stories being reported in the Swedish press and called on women to unite under the Christian principles of love and charity and use their "chain of healing, loving energies" to end the war (McFadden 1999, 157). She wrote an "Appeal to the Women of the World to Form an Alliance," which was published in *The Times* on 28 August 1854, but it was dismissed by the paper itself as the utopian idea of a "mere enthusiast." The concept of women acting as peace mediators resurfaced, however, during World War I when women pacifists held a peace conference in The Hague, at which copies of Bremer's speech, reprinted by members of the Swedish National Council of Women, were circulated to participants.

In 1856 Bremer published her best-known feminist novel, a thinly disguised social tract, *Hertha,* in which she argued strongly for women's emancipation. It was particularly pertinent for its time, for it criticized the outmoded Swedish Paternal Statutes of 1734 that persisted in depriving daughters of all rights over their persons and property by continuing to subordinate them to the control of fathers or male relatives. (*Hertha* later became the title of the journal of the Swedish women's movement.) The novel was influential in leading to debate over women's equality, resulting in legislative reform in 1858 in favor of women's rights, as was a subsequent Bremer novel, *Father and Daughter* (1858).

Despite the difficulties of foreign travel at that time, Bremer continued to make extensive trips to other parts of Europe, including Switzerland and Italy, and to the near East—and published the final book in her six-volume series *Life in the Old World* (1860–1862), in which she described these travels in detail. By the time of her death in 1865, Bremer's novels had established a new realist school of Swedish writing and paved the way for later feminist writers and campaigners. The first national women's society to be set up in Sweden, in 1885, was named the Fredrika Bremer Association after her, and its objective was to improve women's employment opportunities and lobby for higher salaries. The establishment of the International Committee of Women for Permanent Peace at The Hague conference in 1915 would also testify to the growing number of women expressing their dissent with man-made wars.

See also Bodichon, Barbara; Child, Lydia Maria; Dix, Dorothea Lynde; Gaskell, Elizabeth; Mott, Lucretia Coffin; Peabody, Elizabeth; Stone, Lucy; Stowe, Harriet Beecher.

References and Further Reading

Adams, W. H. Davenport. 1889. *Celebrated Women Travellers of the Nineteenth Century.* London: W. S. Sonnenschein.

Bremer, Charlotte, ed. 1868. *Life, Letters & Posthumous Works of Frederika Bremer.* Trans. Frederick Milow. London: Sampson Low.

Bremer, Frederika. 1968 [1853]. *The Homes of the New World: Impressions of America.* Trans. Mary Howitt. Reprint, New York: Negro University Press.

Howitt, Margaret. 1866. *Twelve Months with Fredrika Bremer in Sweden.* London: Jackson, Walford, and Hodder.

Josephson, Harold, Sandi Cooper, and Steven C. Hause et al., eds. 1985. *Biographical Dictionary of Modern Peace Leaders.* Westport, CT: Greenwood Press.

Kleman, Ellen. 1938. *Frederika Bremer and America.* Stockholm: Åhlén and Åkerlunds.

McFadden, Margaret. 1999. *Golden Cables of Sympathy: The Transatlantic Sources of Nineteenth Century Feminism.* Lexington: University Press of Kentucky.

Rooth, Alice Signe. 1955. *Seeress of the Northland: Frederika Bremer's American Journey 1849–1851.* Philadelphia: American Swedish Historical Foundation.

Stendhal, Brita K. 1994. *The Education of a Self-Made Woman: Frederika Bremer, 1801–1865.* Lewiston, Maine: Edwin Mellen Press.

Brittain, Vera
(1893–1970)
United Kingdom

The English socialist and feminist Vera Brittain has an enduring reputation as the author of one of the most moving accounts of the individual experience of war in *Testament of Youth* (1933). Her literary talents, however, were but one aspect of a life spent at the center of activism for social justice, for women's higher education, for entry into the professions, and for peace and independence movements in the Third World.

Brittain was born in Newcastle-under-Lyme in England's industrial heartland, where her father was a paper manufacturer. She grew up in Macclesfield and Buxton and, after a rudimentary education at home with governesses, was sent to school in Surrey. During her five years at St. Monica's, she showed great academic promise, and although her parents were against her entering higher education, she studied Latin and mathematics with her brother Edward's help in order to sit for a university scholarship. Further encouraged by the arguments on women's need for meaningful work in Olive Schreiner's 1911 book, *Woman and Labour,* she won a scholarship to Somerville College at Oxford University in 1914, just as war was breaking out. Unable to concentrate on her studies and enthused with a short-lived sense of patriotism, Brittain interrupted her studies in 1915 and offered herself as a Voluntary Aid Detachment nurse. After training in London and Malta, she was sent to a field hospital in France. Both her fiancé and brother, who had volunteered, perished: Roland Leighton was felled by a sniper in France in 1915, and Edward Brittain was killed on the Italian front in 1918. Brittain's harrowing firsthand experience of war in France and the loss of her loved ones would have a profound and disillusioning effect on her; she became a convinced pacifist and to the day she died remained a determined international critic of the arms race and the development of nuclear weapons.

Brittain resumed her studies in history after the war and joined the final days of campaigning for women's suffrage. After graduating in 1921, she taught for a while in Oxford and then moved to London in 1922 to take up journalism, sharing a flat with her college friend Winifred Holtby. In 1922 Brittain joined the radical Six-Point Group,

Vera Brittain (National Portrait Gallery)

a women's organization founded in 1921 and dedicated to meeting the following primary goals: equal pay and opportunities for women teachers and civil servants, widow's pensions, equal parental rights for women and men, and improvement of children's and unmarried mothers' lives through the introduction of family allowances. She began writing for the new feminist journal *Time and Tide,* founded by Lady Margaret Rhondda, which provided a forum for many of the group's ideas. In 1925 she married Cornell University academic and political philosopher George Catlin, but the relationship was conducted for most of the time on a "semi-detached" basis, as Brittain described it. She found campus life in the United States uncongenial and, frustrated by her inability to get published there, made the difficult choice of returning to England to pursue her career. Thereafter, Catlin spent the academic year in the United States, and Brittain brought up their two children in England. Meanwhile, her friendship with Holtby was deepened by their shared beliefs and their commitment to pacifism and feminism.

During the 1920s, Brittain published novels such as *The Dark Tide* (1923) and *Not without Honour* (1926), but it was her autobiographical work, *Testament of Youth* (1933), a eulogy to a "lost generation," that became a best-seller and established her enduring reputation. It is now regarded as a classic woman's account of the effects of war—not just on the soldiers who fought it but on the women left to bear the loss of a whole generation of young men who, as Brittain so poignantly remarked, "were swept from the threshold of life" (Liddington 1989, 158). The work is also a notable account of Brittain's struggle for admission into higher education. It is the first of a trilogy, with Brittain adding a second volume in 1940, *Testament of Friendship,* a moving tribute to her friend Winifred Holtby, who had died young in 1935. A final volume, *Testament of Experience* (1957), described her broader social concerns, particularly her pacifism, during the period 1925–1950.

After British women won the vote in 1918, Brittain, like many, was unsatisfied with the franchise being limited to women over age thirty and lobbied for changes through the Six-Point Group. She joined the Labour Party in 1924 and briefly contemplated standing for election to Parliament in support of social reforms relating to the introduction of a national maternity service, birth control clinics, and state nursery schools. She also attacked the double standard in sexual morality and defended the rights of homosexuals. She was one of several witnesses who testified in support of the lesbian writer Radclyffe Hall, when she was tried for obscenity after publishing her 1928 novel, *The Well of Loneliness.*

Between the wars, Brittain became prominent in the pacifist movement, undertaking three lecture tours in the United States. She supported the work of the League of Nations, founded in 1918 in the sincere hope that it could avert a second war, and volunteered as a speaker on its behalf in 1921, appearing in church halls and chapels across the United Kingdom and reporting on its activities in *Time and Tide.* She subsequently served as vice president of both the Women's International League for Peace and Freedom and the National Peace Council. In 1934 Brittain was a sponsor of the Paris conference of the Women's World Committee against War and Fascism. But by the mid-1930s, she had lost faith in the League of Nation's efficacy in promoting collective secu-rity. Convinced that there could be no political compromises on peace, in 1936 she joined the Christian pacifist group led by Anglican priest Dick Sheppard and known as the Peace Pledge Union. Brittain also wrote for its publication, *Peace News,* and during World War II established her own biweekly newsletter, *Letters to Peace-Lovers.* In her view, war could not be justified at any price, and she went so far as to speak out on effects of the Allies' devastating saturation bombing on Germany's civilian populations in her 1944 book, *Seed of Chaos: What Mass Bombing Really Means.* After the war, she was chair of the Peace Pledge Union from 1949 to 1951, and in 1957, true to character, she was a founding member of the Campaign for Nuclear Disarmament, taking part in many of its demonstrations.

Brittain wrote on many women's issues, notably in her books *Lady into Woman: A History of Women from Victoria to Elizabeth II* (1953) and *Women's Work in Modern England* (1928). She also used her journalistic skills in promoting her feminist beliefs in articles such as "The Whole Duty of Woman," published in *Time and Tide* in 1928, which exposed the male domination of all aspects of contemporary life and work and the usurpation by men of women's intellectual and physical resources. In this article and also in *Women's Work,* she argued against the traditional patriarchal structures that kept women in a subservient position and exposed the invidious choices women so often had to make between marriage and work. Men for too long had been disdainful of women's intellectual achievements, and clever women, she felt, had too often sacrificed themselves in order to care for and nurture others. Although she recognized that the additional domestic duties placed on women who try to pursue an intellectual life as well as run a home were spiritually and physically draining, in her own life Brittain fiercely defended her right to work despite her obligations as a mother. Her advocacy of women's equality in marriage and their right to careers and economic independence would be reflected in many of her novels, such as *Honourable Estate* (1936), although they never achieved the critical success of her autobiographical writings.

After World War II, Brittain made several extended lecture tours in Europe, the United States, India, and Pakistan, speaking on pacifism and in later years nuclear disarmament. As a humanist she continued to promote her own brand of "old feminism" based on her defense of equality for all in the cause of the common good. Brittain's daughter Shirley Williams became a leading Labour politician and a founder of the Social Democratic Party.

See also Holtby, Winifred; Schreiner, Olive.
References and Further Reading
Bailey, Hilary. 1987. *Vera Brittain: The Story of the Woman Who Wrote* Testament of Youth. Harmondsworth: Penguin.
Bennett, Yvonne. 1987. *Vera Brittain: Women and Peace.* London: Peace Pledge Union.
Berry, Paul, and Alan Bishop. 1985. *Testament of a Generation: The Journalism of Vera Brittain and Winifred Holtby.* London: Virago.
Berry, Paul, and Mark Bostridge. 1995. *Vera Brittain: A Life.* London: Chatto and Windus.
Brittain, Vera. 1981. *Chronicle of Youth: Vera Brittain's War Diary 1913–1917.* London: Victor Gollancz.
Brittain, Vera, and J. S. Reid, eds. 1960. *Selected Letters of Winifred Holtby and Vera Brittain.* London: A. Brown.
Gorham, Deborah. 1996. *Vera Brittain: A Feminist Life.* Oxford: Blackwell.
Josephson, Harold, Sandi Cooper, and Steven C. Hause et al., eds. 1985. *Biographical Dictionary of Modern Peace Leaders.* Westport, CT: Greenwood Press.
Kennard, Jean E. 1989. *Vera Brittain and Winifred Holtby: A Working Partnership.* Hanover: University Press of New England.
Liddington, Jill. 1989. *The Long Road to Greenham: Feminism and Anti-Militarism in Britain since 1820.* London: Virago.
Mellown, Muriel. 1983. "Vera Brittain: Feminist in a New Age." In Dale Spender, ed., *Feminist Theorists: Three Centuries of Women's Intellectual Traditions.* London: Women's Press.
Oldfield, Sybil, ed. 2001. *Women Humanitarians: A Biographical Dictionary of British Women Active between 1900 and 1950.* London: Continuum.

Brown, Charlotte Hawkins
(1883–1961)
United States

The black educator and religious and civic leader Charlotte Hawkins Brown, the granddaughter of slaves, established one of North Carolina's pioneering preparatory schools for black children. She nurtured her pupils on pride in their cultural and historical identity and paved the way for the institution of a state school system and with it considerable improvements to educational facilities.

Born in Henderson, North Carolina, Brown grew up in Cambridge, Massachusetts. After an education at the Cambridge English High and Latin School and Salem State Normal School (the latter studies funded by her patron Alice Freeman Palmer, the second president of Wellesley College), in 1901 she accepted a post from the American Missionary Association to return to her home state and teach. She quickly encountered the enormous deprivation of black children in a state that would provide no tax-supported public schools until 1937 and in which a few church-backed private schools could provide only the most rudimentary education. The little one-room rural school of the Bethany Congregational Church in Sedalia at which she taught fifteen children, spending most of her meager salary on equipment and clothes for its pupils, soon closed due to lack of funds. Brown resolved to raise funds to set up an establishment of her own.

A year later, having returned to Massachusetts, where she again obtained financial support from Alice Freeman Palmer and other patrons, she acquired a former blacksmith's workshop in Sedalia and 15 acres of land as school premises. Here, in October 1902 she opened the Palmer Institute, a day and boarding school for black children, initially without a salary. At first, the school concentrated on training black children for work in industry and agriculture and ran its own farm. In 1905, after further fund-raising, the school's Memorial Hall was constructed; after fires in 1917 and 1922 Brown again raised money to replace the lost wooden buildings with brick ones. A more academic curriculum was introduced during the 1920s, when the school was accredited by the Southern Association of Colleges and Secondary Schools and became known as the Palmer Memorial Institute, by which time it had 300 pupils.

During her long, fifty-year tenure at Palmer, Brown would see the campus grow to fourteen buildings covering 400 acres and offering unique educational opportunities to young blacks. She also turned to other social concerns, such as public health, child care, and the living conditions in prisons. She held various posts, including president of the General Federation of Women's Clubs in North Carolina and vice president of the National Association of Colored Women. In 1940 Brown was appointed to the State Council of Defense of North Carolina. As a devout Christian, she also worked for the Young Women's Christian Association (in 1921 becoming the first black woman appointed to its national board) and for racial integration, campaigning against lynching and segregation. As a member of the North Carolina State Federation of Negro Women's Clubs, she was involved in projects to help delinquent girls, such as the Efland Home for Wayward Girls and the Dobbs School for Girls. She collaborated with other civil rights activists such as Mary McCleod Bethune and Eleanor Roosevelt. Her humanitarianism and work for racial equality were recognized by the Council of Fair Play in 1944 with its Second Annual Award for Racial Understanding.

Brown became highly regarded as a public speaker on racial understanding and black education. Her published works include a short story about slavery, "Mammy: An Appeal to the Heart of the South" (1919), and a contribution to the collection *Rhetoric of Racial Revolt* (1964).

Brown retired from the Palmer Memorial Institute in 1952, and the school itself closed in 1971 after a devastating fire. But her work has continued with the establishment in 1983 of the Charlotte Hawkins Brown Historical Foundation on the school's old campus in North Carolina. It operates as a historical center and provides scholarships and research funds to preserve and promote the history of black people in North Carolina, on the web at http://www.netpath.net/ chb/.

See also Bethune, Mary McCleod; Roosevelt, (Anna) Eleanor.

References and Further Reading

Daniel, Sadie Iola. 1970. *Woman Builders.* Washington, DC: Associated Publishers.

Hine, Darlene Clarke, et al., eds. 1993. *Black Women in America: An Historical Encyclopedia.* 2 vols. Bloomington: Indiana University Press.

Marteena, Constance Hill. 1977. *The Lengthening Shadow of a Woman: A Biography of Charlotte Hawkins Brown.* Hicksville, NY: Exposition Press.

Ploski, Harry A., and James Williams, eds. 1989. *The Negro Almanac: A Reference Work on the African American.* 5th ed. Detroit: Gale.

Silcox-Jarrett, Diane. 1995. *Charlotte Hawkins Brown: One Woman's Dream.* Winston-Salem: Bandit Books.

Smith, Jessie Carney, ed. 1992. *Notable Black American Women.* Detroit: Gale.

Brown, Olympia
(1835–1926)
United States

Inspired by the ordination of Antoinette Brown Blackwell in 1853, Olympia Brown set out to become a preacher herself, achieving her goal in 1863 when she was ordained in the Universalist Church. She was also a leading suffragist and pacifist as a member of the Congressional Union and the Women's International League for Peace and Freedom.

Born in a rural backwater at Prairie Ronde, Michigan, Brown luckily had a reformist mother who encouraged her inquiring mind and her ambitions to study. At age fifteen, she taught school for a year and then attended Mount Holyoke Female Seminary. Disliking its authoritarian regime, she moved (with her entire family) to Yellow Springs, Ohio, in 1856, where she attended Antioch College, thanks to the visionary spirit of its administrator, the educator Horace Mann. There Brown challenged convention, turning up for lectures wearing the controversial new bloomers being championed at that time by feminists. She arranged a visit by the Unitarian preacher Antoinette Brown Blackwell in the winter of 1859–1860, and upon hearing Blackwell speak in church, Brown was uplifted and resolved to become a preacher. By the time she graduated from Antioch with a B.A. in 1860, she had also become active in the abolitionist movement.

Brown applied for training as a minister and was accepted at the Theological School of St. Lawrence University in New York state, one of only three such institutions in the United States that would admit women at that time. It did so reluctantly, being apprehensive about women ministers usurping the jobs of men. Ordained into the Northern Universalist Association in Malone, New York, in 1863, Brown studied elocution and took gymnastics in order to improve her performance in the pulpit. She had a succession of appointments, in Massachusetts (six years), Connecticut (eight years), and finally Wisconsin (nine years).

In 1866 Brown became interested in women's rights. She met Susan B. Anthony, and with her attended the eleventh national women's rights convention in New York at which the American Equal Rights Association was established. Having spoken at this meeting and being possessed of natural oratorical skills, Brown undertook an exhausting lecture tour on women's suffrage, traveling by horse and buggy around Kansas in 1867 when referendums on the award of suffrage to women and male blacks were being held there. Although the referendums failed, Brown gained useful experience from the 300 speeches she gave during this campaign. On her return to her ministry in New England, she was a founder, with Lucy Stone and others, of the New England Woman Suffrage Association in 1868, which inaugurated a campaign for women's suffrage at the federal level, as well as endorsing the award of the vote to black males.

In 1873 Brown married a newspaper proprietor, John Henry Willis, but retained her maiden name, insisting on being called Reverend Olympia Brown. In 1878 she took a post as pastor at the Church of the Good Shepherd in Racine, Wisconsin, where, after her husband's death in 1893, she also managed his newspaper, the *Racine Times,* and ran his Times Publishing Company until 1900. Having been appointed vice president of the National Woman Suffrage Association in 1869 and in 1884 president of the Wisconsin Woman's Suffrage Association, she invited leading women activists such as Anthony, Julia Ward Howe, and Mary Livermore to speak in her church at Racine. She also assisted Elizabeth Cady Stanton in writing her controversial *Woman's Bible* (published in two volumes in 1895 and 1898).

In 1887 Brown made the decision to give up her work as a minister at Racine in order to devote herself full-time to women's suffrage and the temperance campaign. By 1892 she had become increasingly dissatisfied with the disunity and lack of success of the campaign for women's suffrage at the state level run by the National American Woman Suffrage Association and also dismayed by the granting of voting rights to newly arrived immigrant males, and she helped form the Federal Suffrage Association in Chicago. Under Brown's presidency (1903–1920), this organization, renamed the Federal Equality Association in 1902, aimed at extending the national campaign for women's suffrage by working with various non-suffrage associations, but it remained relatively small and ineffectual. In 1913, Brown joined Alice Paul's militant Congressional Union for Woman Suffrage, which followed the lead of English militants and began picketing the White House and staging mass rallies and demonstrations.

In 1911 Brown published her memoirs, *Acquaintances, Old and New, among Reformers.* She also joined the American Civil Liberties Union and supported the pacifist movement during World War I. At the age of eighty-five, Brown joined the last great suffrage march—on the Republican Convention in Chicago in June 1920, just prior to the ratification of the Nineteenth Amendment. Brown spent her final years in Baltimore, undertaking a tour of Europe when she was ninety-one. She and her original mentor, Antoinette Brown Blackwell, were the sole survivors of the first generation of women suffragists who lived to witness the historic achievement of women's suffrage in 1920. In 1989 Brown's church at Racine was renamed the Olympia Brown Unitarian Universalist Church in her honor. For further information on Brown at Antioch college, see http://www.antioch-college.edu/ Antiochiana/.

See also Anthony, Susan B.; Blackwell, Antoinette Brown; Howe, Julia Ward; Livermore, Mary; Paul, Alice; Stanton, Elizabeth Cady.

References and Further Reading
Cole, Charlotte. 1989. *Olympia Brown: The Battle for Equality.* Racine, WI: Mother Courage Press.
Green, Diana, ed. 1983. *Suffrage and Religious Principle: Speeches and Writings of Olympia Brown.* Metuchen, NJ: Scarecrow Press.
Nichols, Claudia. 1992. *Olympia Brown: Minister of Social Reform.* Unitarian Universalist Women's Heritage Society.
Whitman, Alden, ed. 1988. *American Reformers: An H. W. Wilson Biographical Dictionary.* New York: H. W. Wilson.

Bukhari, Shahnaz
(active 1990s–)
Pakistan

Bukhari, a Pakistani activist who has campaigned for the female victims of domestic violence through the auspices of nongovernmental organizations (NGOs), has confronted in particular the question of religious-based laws that discriminate against women and children. More recently, she has drawn international attention to the plight of women who have suffered deliberate attacks by burning.

Bukhari trained as a clinical psychologist and

taught and practiced child psychology in Saudi Arabia before returning to Islamabad with her four children after her divorce. A member of the Pakistani senate and its standing committee on women's development, she is a prolific journalist and broadcaster and edits the English-Urdu-language magazine *Women's World,* which focuses on women's issues and aims in particular at raising the consciousness of Pakistani women themselves. She has also taken on the current military government by campaigning for it to restore parliamentary seats originally set aside for women that were withdrawn by a previous military government.

Bukhari now devotes herself to voluntary work in Islamabad as chief coordinator of the Progressive Women's Association (PWA), through which she campaigns against domestic violence and child abuse and supports the needs of women for educational and vocational training. In 1994 she announced on International Women's Day that women's NGOs would join together to raise public awareness of continuing domestic violence, most particularly the iniquitous practice of wife burning, which still persists as the result of disagreements over bridal dowries. Often called "stove burning," the groom's family resorts to this practice when the bride has failed to produce the promised large dowry. After being deliberately doused with kerosene, the young bride's clothes are set on fire, and she is burned to death. Afterward, the husband's family alleges that the burning happened accidentally while she was cooking. Bukhari has been monitoring this practice through the PWA and since 1994 has documented hundreds of cases of women being burned to death in this way.

The practice of wife burning, Bukhari alleges, has also been resorted to as the result of petty domestic quarrels, and its victims are not just Muslim and Christian wives in Pakistan but also Hindus in India. Only a handful of women have survived such attacks in Pakistan, but Bukhari has helped them obtain medical care and specialist plastic surgery, if necessary abroad, while raising both government and private financial support to do so. She also continues to take up the wider ramifications of domestic violence by promoting the activities of various pressure groups, organizing workshops, and liaising with police and judicial officials. Her ultimate objective is to set up a network of specialist crisis centers and refuges to help the victims of domestic violence and burning attacks as well as to offer counseling to those suffering other kinds of domestic violence. During the course of her crusade, Bukhari has received awards from both the Pakistani and French governments and a grant to take her workshops on domestic violence to the United States.

References and Further Reading
Curtiss, Richard H. "Shahnaz Bukhari—A Single-Minded Activist for Women's Rights," in "Washington Report on Middle East Affairs," www.washington-report.org/.

Burdett-Coutts, Angela
(1814–1906)
United Kingdom

In her lifetime and for many years after her death, the British philanthropist and social reformer Angela Burdett-Coutts was accorded the most excessive panegyrics and featured large in all biographical dictionaries of Victorian worthies. As "the richest heiress in Europe," she had poured much of her huge banking fortune into a great range of humanitarian causes in that noble Victorian tradition of benign (and some might say self-satisfied) benevolence. In her defense of children, the destitute, the homeless, animals, and good Christians in the Commonwealth, she was the kind of woman whom queens could safely admire—until, that is, she married beneath her. After her death, the British *Dictionary of National Biography* (DNB) devoted eight pages to Burdett-Coutts's life and work, while providing less than two pages on a far more important figure, the social purity reformer Josephine Butler—a reflection of the prevailing distaste, even in the 1900s, for women's work in controversial areas of social reform.

Burdett's father was the reformer and politician Sir Francis Burdett. Her young life was one of comfort and privilege; she received a relatively liberal education both at home and during travels on the Continent and mixed with famous figures of the day at her family's townhouse in St. James's Place, London. At the age of twenty-three, Burdett unexpectedly inherited the fortune of her banker grandfather, Thomas Coutts, through his second wife and her stepgrandmother, Harriot Mellon, a former actress. Mellon had developed a particular fondness for Burdett-Coutts and in her will ignored both her second husband, the duke of St. Albans, and all five of Angela's siblings, leaving her a fortune then worth something approaching £2 million. In 1838 Burdett-Coutts's high social status was acknowledged by an invitation to Queen Victoria's coronation at Westminster Abbey. By all accounts she was a charming, dignified woman, both learned and virtuous and thus, inevitably, the most sought-after marriage prospect in the land. There were many in the landed aristocracy who would have married her to retrieve their ailing fortunes, but Burdett remained resolutely single for forty years, eschewing the love and admiration of a husband for those of the thousands of grateful beneficiaries of her multitudinous acts of charity.

Burdett-Coutts became a friend of Charles Dickens, whom she had first met in 1835 and who introduced Burdett to some of the "more remediable evils in nineteenth-century London" (Ackroyd 1990, 404). Burdett shared his concern for many social causes and a genuine compassion for the poor. With Dickens acting as her unofficial agent, she began giving away her money to fund housing and education projects for the poor, such as the Field Lane ragged school at Saffron Hill and the model housing for the poor, built on the site of one of the Dickensian "dust heaps" described so vividly in *Our Mutual Friend,* at Nova Scotia Gardens, Bethnal Green. The four new tenement blocks raised there provided accommodation for 200 families and up-to-date laundry facilities and baths. With Dickens's encouragement, Burdett also built Columbia Market on Hackney Road in the East End to provide a cheaper and better-quality source of fish and vegetables for the poor. Their most noteworthy collaboration was the 1847 establishment of a home for fallen women at Urania Cottage in Shepherd's Bush, a notorious red-light district in West London. Dickens chose not to publicize this act of private philanthropy, perhaps not wishing to alienate his straitlaced readers. In 1844 Dickens dedicated his new novel, *Martin Chuzzlewit,* to Burdett-Coutts.

The DNB catalogs at length Burdett-Coutts's many humanitarian concerns and acts of charity. There were few good causes that did not benefit in some way from her undiscriminating generosity, ranging from the essential (model housing schemes) to the arcane (a topographical survey of Jerusalem) to the quixotic (goats for poor cottagers and drinking fountains for dogs) to philanthropy in the far-flung colonies of the British Empire (cotton gins for Nigeria). Burdett-Coutts created a shoeblack brigade to provide honest work for young working-class boys and a flower girls' brigade for the legions of London's Eliza Doolittles. Her money provided funds to protect aborigines in Australia and to relieve Irish people in Galway and Mayo suffering from another potato famine in 1880 (she gave £250,000 for the purchase of seed potatoes). She also funded more modest ventures, such as youth clubs and a sewing school in Spitalfields; a Destitute Children's Dinner Society, which provided nourishing meals for a penny each; and a factory for crippled girls in the East End. As a pillar of the established church, Burdett also built Anglican churches in Britain and the Commonwealth—South Africa, Canada, and Australia—where she endowed numerous bishoprics. With her money, even such a prosaic object as a public drinking fountain was erected in monumental high gothic style in the East End's Victoria Park. Needless to say, such was Burdett-Coutts's widespread reputation for generosity that the begging letters poured in; she is known to have received sometimes as many as 300–400 per day and made a point of trying to read them all.

During the severe winter of 1861, she gave financial assistance to the tanners of Bermondsey and to weavers in the East End and helped many weavers emigrate to Australia and Canada. Animal welfare was also high on her list, with Burdett-Coutts expressing her concern for overworked tram and bus horses, objecting to the popularity of feathers from exotic birds that were used on ladies' hats, and funding school prizes for essays on kindness to animals. Nor was Burdett-Coutts reticent about helping the victims of religious persecution: in 1877 during the Russo-Turkish War, her concern for the Muslim women and children being persecuted by the notoriously xenophobic Russian troops became so great that she founded the Turkish Compassionate Fund. The sultan returned the compliment by according her the unprecedented honor of the Order of Medjidie, the only woman to receive it. Other awards also singled Burdett-Coutts out as an exceptional woman of her day: in 1871 Queen Victoria made her a baroness (the female equivalent of a peerage), an honor only previously accorded by kings to their mistresses; and in 1872 Burdett-Coutts was the first woman to be given the Freedom of the City of London.

Burdett-Coutts proved to be a very good businesswoman and managed her own money with considerable acumen. She was also an excellent public speaker in the promotion of the causes she supported. Two of the most important and enduring reform movements to receive Burdett-Coutts's support were the Society for the Prevention of Cruelty to Animals and the National Society for the Prevention of Cruelty to Children. Burdett-Coutts also encouraged the Ragged School movement, endowing the Townshend Foundation Schools to provide elementary education and technical training for working-class children; she also set up science scholarships at Oxford. In all her campaigning, Burdett-Coutts remained self-effacing and modest; when she compiled a pamphlet on "Women's Work in England" for the 1893 Chicago World Fair, she did not mention her own contribution; nor did she in her work as editor of the *Year Book of Woman's Work,* which analyzed statistical information on women's philanthropy and described the reformist activities of many charities.

It seemed Burdett-Coutts could do no wrong—until she decided, at the age of sixty-seven, to get married. Queen Victoria was withering in her disapproval of this decision and did what she could to advise against such an ill-judged act that might damage that most precious of her possessions, her reputation. The groom was an American, William Ashmead Bartlett, who had been Burdett-Coutts's secretary for some time and who was thirty-seven years her junior. Victoria considered such an act demeaning in the extreme: "the poor foolish old woman . . . looked like his grandmother and was all decked out with jewels—not edifying" (Hibbert 2000, 315). Once married, however, Burdett-Coutts found herself a victim of the laws that then bound women's property to their husbands. It would be William Burdett-Coutts who not only took *her* name (in deference to her widely held reputation) but also, by legal right, control over her money, thus curtailing the freedom with which she could continue to give it away.

Upon her death in 1906, "the magical fairygodmother of philanthropy," as Ray Strachey described her (Strachey 1978, 83), who had, it is estimated, given away something between £3 and £4 million, lay in state so that 30,000 people should be able to pay their last respects. In her lifetime, Burdett-Coutts had come to be acknowledged as second in greatness in the land only to the queen herself. As David Owen (1965) points out, her lifespan almost matched that of the queen and both their lives encapsulated many of the qualities of the Victorian age. Burdett-Coutts was therefore considered worthy of burial in that Valhalla of the British great and good—Westminster Abbey. Together with Florence Nightingale (who turned the Abbey down), she was promoted well beyond the Victorian era as the acceptable public face of women's philanthropy in Britain.

See also Butler, Josephine.

References and Further Reading
Ackroyd, Peter. 1990. *Dickens.* London: Sinclair Stevenson.
Carey, Rosa Nouchette. 1899. *Twelve Notable Good Women.* London: Hutchinson.
Chappell, Jennie. 1910. *Noble Workers: Sketches of the Life-Work of Frances Willard, Agnes Weston, Sister Dora, Catherine Booth, the Baroness Burdett-Coutts, Lady Henry Somerset, Sarah Robinson, Mrs. Fawcett and Mrs. Gladstone.* London: S. W. Partridge.
Healey, Edna. 1978. *Lady Unknown: The Life of Angela Burdett-Coutts.* London: Sidgwick and Jackson.
Hibbert, Christopher. 2000. *Queen Victoria 2000.* London: HarperCollins.
Orton, D. 1980. *Made of Gold: A Biography of Angela Burdett-Coutts.* London: H. Hamilton.
Owen, David. 1965. *English Philanthropy 1660–1960.* Oxford: Oxford University Press.
Patterson, Clara Burdett. 1953. *Angela Burdett-Coutts and the Victorians.* London: John Murray.
Strachey, Ray. 1978 [1928]. *The Cause: A Brief History of the Women's Movement.* Reprint, London: Virago.

Buss, Frances
(1827–1894)
United Kingdom

The title of "headmistress," it is said, was coined by the pioneer educator Frances Buss in affirmation of women's dominant role in the education of their own sex. As the spinsterly female equivalent of the eternal schoolmaster, "Mr. Chips," her name was forever coupled with that of

Dorothea Beale, principal of Cheltenham Ladies' College. A popular verse underlined the public perception of the single-mindedness with which women such as Buss embraced public service in the Victorian era at the expense of an emotional life: "Miss Buss and Miss Beale / Cupid's darts do not feel. / How different from us, / Miss Beale and Miss Buss."

Buss was one of ten children. Her father's work as a painter and etcher earned insufficient money to support the family, and at the age of fourteen, after a rudimentary schooling, Buss began teaching at her mother's school. When she was eighteen, they moved to another school in Kentish Town in London. In addition to her teaching, Buss studied French, German, and geography at evening classes for a diploma in teaching at Queen's College for Ladies (1850). Despite the long walk to college and the extra hours involved, she had found a sense of mission in improving standards in girls' education and making it more widely available to women. She hoped, in her own small way, to "lighten, ever so little, the misery of women brought up 'to be married and taken care of' and left in the world destitute" (Strachey 1978, 127). In 1850 Buss transferred the school at Kentish Town to Camden, renaming it the North London Collegiate School for Ladies. It began modestly with only thirty-five pupils, but Buss insisted on high standards from the outset and employed only qualified teachers. She would remain headmistress for forty-four years, from 1850 to 1894, with the school's numbers rising to 500. The fees were kept low, at two guineas a term.

Buss's pupils were introduced to her advanced ideas and were expected to study the kind of subjects usually preserved for men, such as science and mathematics. Pupils also had to take healthy exercise in the form of walks and gentle calisthenics four times a week. In 1872 Buss instituted swimming lessons for her girls at the nearby St. Pancras Public Baths, and in 1879 the school was one of the first girls' schools to build a proper gymnasium and introduce daily physical education drills. Mindful that her girls should not overexert themselves, Buss appointed a part-time doctor to check the fitness of all those taking part in gymnastics, lessons that were taken in specially designed loose-fitting clothing. In 1892 the first proper gymnastics costume was introduced by Buss—the prototype of the school uniform.

In 1871 Buss changed the status of North London Collegiate School to that of an endowed grammar school controlled by a board of governors in order to ensure its financial future; a lower school, Camden School, was also founded in 1871 as a feeder for North London, with financial support from brewers' and clothworkers' companies. Although North London was an Anglican school, Buss was a stickler for religious tolerance and put up no barriers to religious practice, admitting Catholics, Jews, and nonconformists. The atmosphere at the school was noted for its lack of social competitiveness and snobbery and its emphasis on cooperation. Establishment of the Girls' Public Day School Company in London was inspired by Buss's efforts to educate girls to the same standards as those for boys in grammar schools, and by the mid-1880s there were twenty similar girls' schools in existence.

Academic excellence was emphasized by Buss as a prerequisite for taking the few examinations that were then open for girls. She was adamant that education was the only way for a woman to further her economic situation and personal independence, and she was steadfast in her belief that women teachers were far better equipped to instruct young girls than men. She became a close friend of educator Emily Davies and with her gave evidence to the government's Royal Commission on Endowed Schools, set up in 1864, which among other things investigated the low standards in girls' education.

Because Buss expected high standards of her teachers, she was also active in opening colleges and teacher-training establishments for women. She was a founding member of the Council for Teacher Training and in 1874 founded the Association of Headmistresses as an important venue for the exchange of ideas between teaching professionals. The presidency of the association was taken over on Buss's death by her friend Dorothea Beale.

With Davies, Buss defended women's ability to compete in examinations with men and campaigned for their admission to universities. She supported Davies's establishment of Girton College at Cambridge in 1873, and in 1885 she helped establish the Training College for Women Teachers at Cambridge to produce new women teachers for the two women's colleges that had been established there: Girton and Newnham. Buss's advocacy of women's entry into the medical profession was reflected in her role as a governor of the London School of Medicine for Women. She served on several school boards and boards of guardians and was a governor of University College.

Buss was a member of the group of feminists known as the Langham Place Circle, many of whom were involved in the foundation in 1865 of a women's discussion group, the Kensington Society. She gave her tacit moral support to Josephine Butler's campaign against the white slave trade and the Contagious Diseases Acts, but her position as a headmistress precluded her active support for fear of alienating parents. She was a signatory of the 1866 petition on women's suffrage presented by John Stuart Mill to Parliament but was an advocate of universal rather than exclusively women's suffrage.

See also Beale, Dorothea; Butler, Josephine; Davies, (Sarah) Emily.

References and Further Reading
Bryant, Margaret. 1979. *The Unexpected Revolution: A Study in the History of the Education of Women and Girls in the Nineteenth Century.* London: University of London Institute of Education.

Burstall, Sara. 1938. *Frances Mary Buss: An Educational Pioneer.* London: Society for Promoting Christian Knowledge.

Kamm, Josephine. 1958. *How Different from Us: A Biography of Miss Buss and Miss Beale.* London: Bodley Head.

McCrone, Kathleen E. 1988. *Sport and the Physical Emancipation of English Women 1870–1914.* London: Routledge.

Purvis, June. 1991. *A History of Women's Education in England.* Milton Keynes: Open University Press.

Ridley, Annie E. 1895. *Frances Mary Buss and Her Work for Education.* London: Longman's, Green.

Strachey, Ray. 1978 [1928]. *The Cause: A Brief History of the Women's Movement.* Reprint, London: Virago.

Butler, Josephine
(1828–1906)
United Kingdom

If any social reformer personified the Victorian epitome of womanly dignity, charity, and virtue it would be the charismatic Josephine Butler. A woman of singular beauty and of profound religious conviction, she devoted herself to the social reclamation of prostitutes as though it were a religious crusade. In her wide-reaching campaigning, she exposed the sexual and economic oppression of women in Victorian society, overcoming private grief and illness to lead one of the most hard-fought and controversial causes in nineteenth-century social reform—the repeal of the Contagious Diseases Acts. She took her battle to end the white slave trade and state-regulated prostitution to Europe, collaborating with other reformers such as Anna Maria Mozzoni in Italy and Mariya Trubnikova and Nadezhda Stasova in Russia in promoting the more compassionate care and rehabilitation of "fallen women." Butler did not become active in the women's suffrage or other feminist political movements of the nineteenth century, however, which has prompted considerable disagreement among commentators as to the true nature of her "feminism" and to assertions that the separateness of her own very personal campaign from the mainstream of the women's movement was ultimately divisive.

Butler was born on the family estate at Dilston in Northumberland, the seventh of nine children. She was educated at home and grew up in an evangelical environment that espoused enlightened reform. Her father, John Gray, an abolitionist, agricultural reformer of some international standing, and supporter of women's education, brought her up with liberal views and an advocacy of public works in an affectionate and open household that freely discussed social problems. Her education was completed by two years at boarding school in Newcastle-upon-Tyne.

In 1850 Josephine met George Butler, a tutor at Durham University, whom she married in 1852. They proved a most compatible and devoted couple; they were both keen supporters of women's education and shared the same ideas on social and moral reform. They settled in Oxford when George took a post as an examiner at the university, and there Butler helped him in the preparation of his various publications. But she disliked the isolation of the stultifying world of academia, and in 1857 George took the post as vice president of Cheltenham Boys' College. During the Civil War in the United States, the Butlers were socially ostracized for supporting the abolitionist North. The accidental death in 1864 of their only daughter Eva proved to be a turning point in Butler's life. After suffering agonies of grief for months, the family moved to Liverpool, where George taught at Liverpool College.

Butler soon found an outlet for her sense of loss in work for women's education, becoming president (1867–1873) of Anne Jemima Clough's North of England Council for Promoting the Higher Education of Women. She endorsed Jessie Boucherett's pioneering work in women's economic liberation through the Society for Promoting the Employment of Women (established in 1859) and was active in the feminist campaign for the Married Women's Property Acts of 1870, 1878, and 1882. Butler was one of many women to sign the 1866 petition on women's suffrage, but she did not enter the suffrage campaign.

Butler was first exposed to the plight of prostitutes when she took up work with the destitute and the poor in the 1860s in Liverpool. She became a visitor at the workhouse at Brownlow Hill, a grim institution housing hundreds of women and girls, many of them prostitutes. She discovered that many of these women had been forced into prostitution by economic necessity. Some were former domestic servants, sexually abused by their male employers and then dismissed; others had been seamstresses working at piece rates who took up prostitution in order to survive. Butler's visits to the slums, dives, and docklands of Liverpool revealed to her how widespread the problem of women's economic oppression was, and she began taking some of these women into her own home. With the help of her own family doctor, she established a home of rest for thirteen reformed prostitutes, and lobbied her friends for funds to help rehabilitate them. It was this element of Butler's redemptive Christian work, like the Good Samaritan who gave shelter to social outcasts, that would characterize the special spirituality of her nature. Her admirers looked upon Butler as a woman truly possessed of the spirit of God (and, indeed, she frequently experienced religious visions); she would be seen by them as a Victorian incarnation of Christlike compassion and charity, having almost divine gifts that set her outside the ranks of other mortals. As Eileen Yeo attests, her husband was one of many convinced of Butler's sainthood and, placing no limitations on her proselytizing activities, "patiently sat in railway stations for hours waiting for her return from speaking engagements" (1998, 132).

In 1869 when the Ladies' National Association for the Repeal of the Contagious Diseases Acts (generally known as the LNA) was established by Elizabeth Wolstenholme-Elmy and others, Butler was persuaded to take on its leadership. The acts, passed in 1864, extended in 1866 and 1869 and, defined by Dale Spender as "an archetype of sexual harassment" (1982, 343), had brought in licensing of prostitutes in state brothels in eleven garrison towns and ports in Britain where there was a high density of army and navy personnel. The women who serviced these men sexually were subjected to regular and often brutal physical examinations and were liable to prosecution if they refused. If found to be infected, they were confined to "lock hospitals" for treatment. However, the men who solicited their service were subject to neither moral condemnation nor prosecution, and it was this appalling double standard that incensed Butler and other reformers and galvanized them in the defense of the civil rights of women from the poorer classes at whom they saw the acts as being primarily targeted.

Despite her husband's poor health and the public antipathy toward any woman making public statements on sexuality, Butler bravely led the campaign, supported by many male reformers and other societies such as the National Vigilance Association for the Defence of Personal Rights, to have the acts repealed. She set out her own moral objections to the acts in the LNA's manifesto, basing her social philosophy on her conviction that the solution to prostitution lay not in its regulation through laws that penalized women but in the much more fundamental reform of the sexual habits of men. Asserting that "economics lie at the very root of practical morality" (Longford 1981, 115), Butler also identified the problem as an economic one that could be tackled only through improvements in the economic status of women. In turn, doing so required women's access to better education, which would enable them to obtain better-paid, legitimate employment.

Supported by Mary Carpenter, Harriet Martineau, Florence Nightingale, Lydia Becker, and a host of other eminent and worthy men and women, including many Quaker reformers, the LNA launched an intensive crusade against the Contagious Diseases Acts in major garrison towns. Before long, there was hardly a person in the land who had not been aroused by this contentious issue, even if, as the *Saturday Review* remarked in 1870, old maids were heard to ask if all this talk about the Contagious Diseases Acts had something to do with "cattle plague." On many occasions, Butler spoke to extremely hostile audiences where she had to contend with verbal abuse and constant threats of violence. She appealed to her listeners' consciences and religious faith and to the need for personal repentance, arguing that if legislation was ineffectual, then she had a better method: "I would sit on the steps of the brothel and pray the people out" (Pearsall 1969, 230). No wonder that later hagiographers such as Joseph Williamson looked upon her as a "forgotten saint."

A Royal Commission that reported its findings in 1871 upheld the legitimacy of the acts and exonerated men, famously pronouncing that "with the one sex [women] the offence is committed as a matter of gain; with the other [men] it is an irregular indulgence of a natural impulse" (Spender 1982, 340). By 1874 Butler was exhausted; she temporarily passed the leadership of the campaign to Sir James Stansfield and went to recuperate on the Continent. Having done so, she made good use of her time to tour state brothels and hospitals that treated prostitutes in France, Italy, and Switzerland, including the notorious St. Lazare prison-hospital in Paris. Returning to England in 1875, she wrote of the horrors she had encountered. Later that year she was one of the prime movers in the foundation of an international body, the British, Continental, and General Federation for the Abolition of Government Regulation of Prostitution, based in Geneva, and of which she became secretary. The federation held its first conference in Liverpool that year and in 1877 delegates from fifteen countries, including Russia, attended another in Geneva, at which 120 papers were read on hygiene, morality, social economy, preventive work, and legislation, after which the conference's resolutions were sent out to all European governments and the press, thus ensuring the high profile of the European campaign.

In 1883, after Butler and others had given evidence to another royal commission, the Contagious Diseases Acts were suspended. By the mid-1880s the Salvation Army had become a powerful force in the British social purity campaign, and in 1885 Butler and Salvation Army leader Catherine Booth helped journalist W. T. Stead in the preparation of a secret investigation into West End prostitution and the trade in underage girls. This was published as a series of exposé articles, beginning in the 6 July issue of the *Pall Mall Gazette* under the title "The Maiden Tribute of Babylon." The articles caused a public outcry, particularly in their revelations of the trade in child virgins for as little as £5, but as Ronald Pearsall points out, they were in themselves "using the weapons of pornography to right a wrong" (Pearsall 1969, 302). Stead was prosecuted and sent to prison, but the articles prompted immediate government action and the raising of the age of consent to sixteen in 1885 (under the Criminal Law Amendment Act).

The Contagious Diseases Acts were finally repealed in 1886 by royal assent. As Joan Perkin points out, England thus became the first European country to abolish state-regulated prostitution after having been the last in Europe to adopt it (1993, 230). By the late 1880s, the Butlers were living in Winchester, where George had a canonry. He retired in 1889 and died a few months later, leaving Josephine bereft. She remained unsettled for many years but finally returned to Cheltenham. Eventually, she also returned to the campaign against state-regulated prostitution—this time, in India—after discovering that it had been covertly revived there in the late 1890s despite the repeal of the Contagious Diseases Acts in 1886. She became a member of the British Committee for the Abolition of the State Regulation of Vice in India and the Dominions, showing a particular compassion for Indian prostitutes, whom she considered to be doubly disabled both as women and as oppressed colonial subjects. Her views on this subject were described in her 1893 pamphlet, "The Present Aspect of the Abolitionist Cause in Relation to British India."

Butler's arguments, not just on prostitution, vice, and social purity but across a wide range of topics including suffrage, Irish home rule, and slavery, were outlined in more than ninety published works, notably *The Education and Employment of Women* (1868); *Woman's Work and Woman's Culture,* which collected her essays and other seminal essays of the day (1869); and *Personal Reminiscences of a Great Crusade* (1896). She also wrote many articles for the LNA's journal, *The Shield* (1870–1886), as well as for the reformist journals the *Dawn* (1888–1896) and the *Storm-Bell* (1898–1900). Barbara Caine (1992) records that Butler's support for the Boer War of 1901 distanced her from former colleagues in the women's movement, many of whom were pacifists, although it would appear that Butler's support for the war stemmed not from any imperialist sentiments but from her revulsion for Boer maltreatment of black South Africans (see her book, *Native Races and the War,* published in 1900). In 1903 she returned to her home county of Northumberland, where she died in 1906.

In her study of Butler, Elizabeth Longford observes: "No one worked harder for women than Josephine Butler, not even famous suffragists like Millicent Fawcett and Elizabeth Garrett Anderson. Yet where are Mrs. Butler's honors? Mrs. Fawcett was created a Dame; Dr. Garrett Anderson has a hospital called after her, whereas Josephine Butler was . . . in danger of being forgotten" (1981, 109). It is Longford's view that because Butler "did not champion the right women," the Victorian reticence about public discussion of the sexual double standard prevented her ever from being accorded the otherwise high public profile she had earned as a moral and religious reformer.

The Fawcett Library in London contains the Josephine Butler Society library, a unique collection of books and documents on the history of prostitution and the white slave trade, with much material relating to Butler's campaign for the repeal of the Contagious Diseases Acts. The Josephine Butler Society (as the Association for Moral and Social Hygiene, the LNA's successor, was renamed in 1953) still campaigns for a single moral standard for both men and women and also exposes the sexual exploitation of children in the Third World. For further information on both, contact http://www.lgu.ac.uk/fawcett/butler.1.htm/ The website for the University of Liverpool's Josephine Butler Collections is also a source of much useful information, at http://sca.liv.ac.uk/collections/butler/butler1.htm. Jane Jordan's recent biography of Butler, the first since the 1960s, together with a definitive five-volume edition of many of Butler's letters and writings edited by Ingrid Sharp and Jordan, should greatly advance scholarship on this exceptional woman.

See also Becker, Lydia; Booth, Catherine; Boucherett, Jessie; Carpenter, Mary; Clough, Anne Jemima; Martineau, Harriet; Mozzoni, Anna Maria; Nightingale, Florence; Stasova, Nadezhda; Trubnikova, Mariya; Wolstenholme-Elmy, Elizabeth.

References and Further Reading

Bell, Enid Moberley. 1962 [1942]. *Josephine Butler: Flame of Fire.* Reprint, London: Constable.

Boyd, Nancy. 1982. *Josephine Butler, Octavia Hill, Florence Nightingale: Three Victorian Women Who Changed Their World.* London: Macmillan.

Burton, Antoinette. 1994. *Burdens of History: British Feminists, Indian Women and Imperial Culture 1865–1915.* Baltimore: Johns Hopkins University Press.

Butler, A. S. G. 1954. *Portrait of Josephine Butler.* London: Faber and Faber.

Caine, Barbara. 1992. *Victorian Feminists.* Oxford: Oxford University Press.

Chaudhuri, Nupur, and Margaret Strobel, eds. 1992. *Western Women and Imperialism: Complicity and Resistance.* Bloomington: Indiana University Press.

Fawcett, Millicent Garrett, and E. M. Turner. 1927. *Josephine Butler: Her Work and Principles, and Their Meaning for the Twentieth Century.* London: ASMH.

Forster, M. 1984. *Significant Sisters: The Grassroots of Active Feminism, 1839–1939.* London: Secker and Warburg.

Helsinger, Elizabeth K., Robin Lauterbach Sheets, and William Veeder. 1983. *The Woman Question: Social Issues, 1837–1883,* vol. 2, *Society and Literature in Britain and America, 1837–1883.* Manchester: Manchester University Press.

Jordan, Jane. 2001. *Josephine Butler.* London: John Murray.

Longford, Elizabeth. 1981. *Eminent Victorian Women.* London: Weidenfeld and Nicolson.

McDonald, Lynn, ed. 1998. *Women Theorists on Society and Politics.* Waterloo, Ontario: Wilfrid Laurier University Press.

Pearsall, Ronald. 1969. *The Worm in the Bud: The World of Victorian Sexuality.* London: Weidenfeld and Nicolson.

Perkin, Joan. 1993. *Victorian Women.* London: John Murray.

Petrie, Glen. 1971. *A Singular Iniquity: The Campaigns of Josephine Butler.* London: Macmillan.

Sharp, Ingrid, and Jane Jordan, eds. Forthcoming. *Diseases of the Body Politic: Josephine Butler and the Prostitution Campaigns.* 5 vols. London: Routledge.

Spender, Dale. 1982. *Women of Ideas, and What Men Have Done to Them.* London: Routledge and Kegan Paul.

Tuson, Penelope, ed. 1997. *The Queen's Daughters: An Anthology of Victorian Feminist Writings on India 1857–1900.* Reading, Berkshire, UK: Ithaca Press.

Uglow, Jenny. 1983. "Josephine Butler: From Sympathy to Theory." In Dale Spender, ed., *Feminist Theorists: Three Centuries of Women's Intellectual Traditions.* London: Women's Press.

Walkowitz, Judith. 1980. *Prostitution and Victorian*

Society: Women, Class and the State. Cambridge: Cambridge University Press.

———. 1992. *City of Dreadful Delight: Narratives of Sexual Danger in Late-Victorian London.* London: Virago.

Williamson, Joseph. 1977. *Josephine Butler: The Forgotten Saint.* Leighton Buzzard, UK: Faith Press.

Yeo, Eileen. 1998. *Radical Femininity: Women's Self-Representation in the Public Sphere.* Manchester: Manchester University Press.

Byrne, Lavinia
(1947–)
United Kingdom

As a radical feminist and liberation theologian, Lavinia Byrne has been an outspoken advocate of women's ordination into the Roman Catholic priesthood, through her career in broadcasting and journalism and in several books, notably *Woman at the Altar* (1994). However, her refusal to recant her perceived heresy and her continuing advocacy of birth control in contravention of Vatican rulings precipitated her departure from the Roman Catholic Church in 2000.

Byrne was born at Edgbaston in Birmingham and educated at Edgbaston's Holy Child Jesus Convent (1950–1958) and St. Mary's Convent in Shaftesbury (1958–1964). After entering religious life in 1964 at the Institute of the Blessed Virgin Mary, a noncontemplative order that has remained controversial since its establishment in 1606, she studied modern languages at the University of London and did postgraduate studies in education at Cambridge University. After graduating in 1971, she taught languages at a succession of convent schools (1971–1985) before working for the Institute of Spirituality at Heythrop College (part of the University of London). There she was involved in organizing retreats and spirituality training programs and taught a postgraduate course in pastoral studies. Further retreat work and the organization of training courses followed during 1991–1995 at the Council of Churches for Britain and Ireland, as associate secretary for the Community of Women and Men in the Church. During 1995–1996 Byrne ran postgraduate information studies at the University of North London.

Byrne's work in the media began in 1988 with regular contributions to the *Thought for the Day* slot on BBC Radio 3. From the mid-1990s, she was a presenter on its Daily Service. In 1997 she branched into television, working for BBC TV's Religious Programmes Department.

In 1988 Byrne first broached the subject of women's ordination—on theological grounds—in *Women before God.* In several follow-up works, culminating in 1994 with *Woman at the Altar,* she drew on her many subsequent encounters with ordained women across many denominations and elaborated on the cultural and historical significance of women in the priesthood, giving examples of their many and positive contributions to the life of the church. In noting the Roman Catholic Church's long-standing unwillingness to accept the female religious message and its continuing exclusion of women from spiritual life and the ministry, Byrne drew attention also to the suppression of many of their theological writings. She offered up fresh arguments in the ongoing debate on women's ordination and with it the changing role of Christians in the modern world. Religious women, she believed, had played a crucial role in social and philanthropic work among the poor and dispossessed. In a 1995 book, *The Hidden Voice,* Byrne retained her strong feminist position, affirming women's solidarity within the church and what she called the "commonality of the hidden tradition of women" (45), a tradition that she argues transcends religious denomination. In so doing, she cited many examples of women preachers—such as Catherine Booth and Maude Royden, the latter an important forerunner whom Byrne greatly admires—who had suffered prejudice, vilification, and oppression in their mission to preach the Gospel.

Woman at the Altar provoked an uproar in the Catholic Church, which shortly before its publication had brought out an "Apostolic Letter of His Holiness Pope John Paul II on Reserving Priestly Ordination to Men Alone." Much pressure was put on Byrne by the Vatican's Congregation for the Doctrine of the Faith (historically, the Holy Inquisition), which immediately banned the book, to repudiate it and also her position in support of birth control. As a feminist and an advocate of a woman's right to control her own fertility, Byrne had also repudiated the rulings of Pope Paul VI's *Humae Vitae* and Pope John Paul II's *Ordinato Sacerdotalis,* criticizing practicing Roman Catholics for their hypocrisy in privately practicing birth control while publicly supporting the Church's rulings.

Byrne was deeply saddened by the Church's response but unrepentant; for her women's admission into the priesthood was the fulfillment of centuries of church teaching and not, as church officials perceived it, an aberration. Unable to accede to the Vatican's demands and critical of its intimidation, she made the painful decision to remain true to her conscience and leave religious life, albeit much against her will. In January 2000 she left her order, the Institute of the Blessed Virgin, her home for twenty-five years, and requested dispensation from her vows. Although she has since begun giving religious instruction to male and female ordinands in the Church of England, she remains a Catholic by faith and retains her links with the Catholic Church, working with Catholic laywomen at the Cambridge Theological Foundation.

Byrne is the author of numerous works on religious figures, spirituality, and women's role in Christian ministry, including *The Hidden Tradition,* on women's spiritual writings (1989); *The Hidden Journey,* on women's missionary work (1991); *Traditions of Spiritual Guidance* (1990); *The Dome of Heaven* (1999); and *The Journey Is My Home* (2000). She has also published articles in *The Way, Review for Religious, The Tablet, The Universe,* and the *Church Times.* She has traveled widely, lecturing and running retreats in North America, Australia, and on the Continent. In 1997 she was made an honorary doctor of divinity by the University of Birmingham. She is theological adviser to the Churches Commission on Inter-Faith Relations and a trustee of the Catholic Media Trust.

See also Booth, Catherine; Royden, Maude.

References and Further Reading

Byrne, Lavinia. 1994. *Woman at the Altar.* London: Mowbray.

———. 1995. *The Hidden Voice: Christian Women and Social Change.* London: Society for Promoting Christian Knowledge.

———. 2000. *The Journey Is My Home.* London: Hodder and Stoughton.

C

Caballero de Castillo Ledón, Amalia Gonzalez
(1902–1986)
Mexico

A feminist writer, social activist, and later diplomat who was leader of the Mexican women's rights movement of the 1930s, Caballero disseminated the Latin American feminist viewpoint and experience at numerous international congresses. She was born in San Jerónimo, Tamaulipas, in northeastern Mexico. After completing her graduate studies in the humanities at the National University, she married a prominent historian, Luis Castillo Ledón. In 1933 Caballero founded the International Women's Club with other women activists from Switzerland, the Soviet Union, the Netherlands, and the United States.

Throughout the 1940s and 1950s, Caballero took part in several women's conferences as a Mexican representative. In 1945 she was the Mexican delegate for the Inter-American Commission of Women and acted as chairperson. Later she became vice president, and after the commission joined the Organization of American States in 1948, president (1949). At the inaugural UN conference in 1945 in San Francisco, Caballero was one of several female delegates who lobbied for the new UN Charter to include the phrase "the equal rights of men and women," a motion that was later carried. She took charge of the Sixth Committee at the First Congress of Women held in Guatemala in 1947, which included in its agenda a discussion of the topic "The Civil and Political Rights of Woman, and Her Access to Posts of Responsibility."

Not until 1953 were Mexican women given equal rights with men in politics, and Caballero was the first woman to address the Mexican Senate on women's suffrage. She represented Mexico at the UN Commission on the Status of Women and became the first Mexican woman to serve as a diplomat—taking up posts in Sweden, Finland, and Switzerland in the 1950s. At the end of her diplomatic career, she held several government posts: from 1958 to 1964 she was undersecretary for cultural affairs in the Ministry of Education. She also served as a member of the board of directors of the National Association of Children's Welfare and as a leader of the Pan American Women's League.

See also Carrillo Puerto, Elvia; García, María del Refugio; Gutiérrez de Mendoza, Juana Belén; Jiménez y Muro, Dolores.

References and Further Reading

Soto, Shirlene. 1990. *Emergence of the Modern Mexican Woman: Her Participation in Revolution and Struggle for Equality, 1910–1940.* Denver: Arden Press.
Tenenbaum, Barbara A., ed. 1996. *Encyclopedia of Latin American History and Culture.* Vol. 2. New York: Charles Scribner's Sons.

Cai Chang
(1900–1990)
China

Along with Xiang Jingyu, another outstanding leader of the Chinese women's movement in its first phase and, like her, a first-generation communist activist, Cai was one of the first women to take part in Mao Zedong's New People's Study Society and the May Fourth Movement in 1919, from which sprang several early leaders of the women's movement in China. She was, from 1949 to 1956, the lone woman's voice on the

Central Committee of the Chinese Communist Party (CCP).

Cai came from an impoverished middle-class family; her mother had left her husband and sold her possessions to send her children to school and had helped Cai avoid an arranged marriage. In any case, Cai had resolved to renounce marriage and remain celibate, believing in the liberating power of women's education. She attended the progressive Zhunan Girls' Middle School at Changsha. After she left in 1916, she was one of the first women involved in the New People's Study Society, a work-study movement set up by Mao Zedong and her brother Cai Hesen in the winter of 1917–1918, which encouraged women to set up self-help groups and take an active role in political change. She went to Europe with her mother and Cai Hesen, later to be joined in the work-study group by Xiang Jingyu, who became her sister-in-law when she married Cai Hesen. Cai Chang remained abroad for five years, working in factories and studying anarchism and Marxism in France, collaborating with other Chinese feminist and socialist students in exile and studying Leninism at the University of the Toilers of the East in Moscow. On her return to China in 1921, Cai trained to teach physical education and taught at the Zhunan Girls' School for four years. In 1923 she joined the CCP.

In 1925 Cai began working in the Central Women's Department of the Nationalist Party, and in 1927 she became a member of the Central Women's Committee, which she ran while its head, Xiang Jingyu, was away studying in Moscow. In this capacity, she had a role in the drafting of the Marriage Decree of 1930 and the Constitution of 1931. As the wife of a communist leader, Li Fuchun (whom she had married in 1922), she was one of an elite group of around fifty women who took part in the Long March of 1934–1935.

After 1949, Cai had a high profile in the new People's Republic of China. As chair of the All-China Democratic Women's Federation, she headed a program to train elite women to spearhead scientific and cultural change. This plan would, however, relegate the mass of Chinese women who had served the revolution with tremendous self-sacrifice to their old subordinate roles, working in service industries as road sweepers and shop assistants and primarily rearing and caring for children. Because of her involvement, Cai has earned criticism for condoning the CCP's official, chauvinistic view of women, a view based on cultivating the elite few for skilled work while placing a greater emphasis on technological advances and economic change, which would soon sideline issues of women's liberation.

See also Xiang Jingyu.

References and Further Reading

Andors, Phyllis. 1983. *The Unfinished Liberation of Chinese Women, 1949–1980*. Bloomington: Indiana University Press.

Fan Hong. 1997. *Footbinding, Feminism and Freedom*. Portland, OR: Frank Cass.

Gilmartin, Christina Kelly. 1995. *Engendering the Chinese Revolution: Radical Women, Communist Politics and Mass Movements in the 1920s*. Berkeley: University of California Press.

Caird, Mona
(Alice Mona Henryson)
(1854–1932)
United Kingdom

Thanks to recent scholarship, the work of the radical feminist novelist Mona Caird is at long last enjoying a revival of interest. With Sarah Grand and Eliza Lynn Linton, she is one of several English women writers of the late nineteenth century who were central to the debate on the "new woman," with Caird contributing one of the first and most challenging discourses on mother-daughter relationships to come out of that era. Less well known and equally important, however, is her groundbreaking and outspoken campaign on antivivisection, in support of which Caird produced several important tracts. Together with Frances Power Cobbe and Anna Kingsford, she reflected in her writings the growing concern of many feminists and suffragists for animal rights and vegetarianism, drawing close parallels between the abuses and subjugation of women and the treatment meted out to animals, particularly in the course of scientific experimentation.

Born into a wealthy family on the Isle of Wight, Caird spent some of her early life in Australia, but the details have yet to be uncovered. In 1874 she published her first novel, *Lady Hetty*, anonymously, after which she adopted the pseudonym G. Noel Hatton for *Whom Nature Leadeth* (1883) and *One That Wins* (1887). All three failed to sell. In 1877 she married a Scottish landowner, James Alexander Henryson-Caird, but although their marriage produced a son, Alister, in 1884, it was from the start a marriage-at-a-distance. Caird spent little time on the family estate at Cassencary, in Dumfries and Galloway. Preferring to remain in London, she began earning her own living from journalism and making frequent trips abroad. Nor was she ever close to her son, Alister. In adulthood, he disappointed Caird by becoming fiercely gung-ho and volunteering during World War I (while she remained a pacifist); more disturbingly (from Caird's viewpoint), Alister was a lover of the English country pursuits of hunting, shooting, and fishing, which Caird as an antivivisectionist and vegetarian abhorred.

It was not until she published the somewhat lurid and sensational *Wing of Azrael* in 1889 that Caird's writing caught the public imagination, with its story of Viola Sedley's murder of her sadistic husband and her subsequent death by suicide in order to avoid prosecution. In her next and most famous novel, *The Daughters of Danaus* (1894), Caird laid out many of her most important ideas on women's rights and their domestic duties. Although little is known of the true nature of Caird's own marriage, her antipathy to the institution and its inhibiting effects on women's development are patently clear in this, her best-selling novel. As a fiercely argued polemic on women's need for creative fulfillment in the face of the constraints of domestic life and filial duty, Caird depicts her heroine Hadira's attempts to escape the confines of the home, leaving behind her sons, and make her own choices by adopting a daughter and attempting to establish an artistic life in Paris. Caird thus suggested an alternative to the traditional domestic milieu for independently minded women, based on a network of feminist support and sisterhood through which they might focus on their own development.

In 1888 Caird's journalism sparked heated debate in the British press and with it the discussion of the nature of the "new woman" when she published two articles, "Marriage" and "Ideal Marriage," in the August and November issues of the *Westminster Review*. In them, she boldly challenged the sacred cow of domesticity—a Victorian ideal perpetuated in the public imagination by imagery of Queen Victoria as matriarch of her own considerable brood. The articles provoked an unprecedented, voluminous correspondence on the subject in the *Daily Telegraph*, under the heading "Is Marriage a Failure?" The newspaper received an estimated 27,000 letters. These and Caird's other essays on marriage (for the *Fortnightly Review*) were subsequently republished as *The Morality of Marriage and Other Essays* in 1897.

Caird published two more novels, *The Pathway of the Gods* (1898) and *The Stones of Sacrifice* (1915), the latter a further discourse on the conflict in women's lives between domestic duty and the desire for self-improvement, but much of her time from the late 1890s was given over to a passionate campaign for animal rights. In it, she was as characteristically outspoken and uncompromising as she was in her views on women's rights. She believed, as did many other feminists who loathed vivisection and supported animal rights, that animals, like women, were oppressed and subjugated by men and by the male-dominated world of science. The barbarity of men was also symbolized in the slaughtering of animals for food. Seeing women as innately pacific and altruistic and occupying the moral high ground, she invested them with the task of setting an example for men. It was, she felt, a primary duty of mothers to educate their children to feel sensitivity and compassion toward animals, and she urged women to consult only those male doctors who were against antivivisection. She was also extremely vocal in her criticism of the fashion of using exotic birds' feathers in women's dress. Hand in hand with her hatred of vivisection went her distaste for blood sports and an advocacy of vegetarianism; the latter became a cornerstone of her promotion of a healthier lifestyle based on exercise, rational dress, and the casting aside of tight corsets.

Caird's moral discourse on vivisection, replete as it is with individual case histories and containing horrific descriptions of the brutalization of animals, often without use of any anesthetics, does not make for an easy read. It appeared in three major pamphlets: "A Sentimental View of Vivisection" (1894), "Beyond the Pale: An Appeal on Behalf of the Victims of Vivisection" (1896), and "The Inquisition of Science" (1903). These tracts provide a chilling account of the arbitrariness of man's power over the animal kingdom and call into question what Victorian society perceived as being its "civilizing" influence in the world. By making only too clear the atrocities committed in the name of science, Caird presented a compelling argument on how moral and ethical standards all too easily "dwindle down in regard to the less powerful, and disappear altogether as soon as we reach the utterly defenceless" (1896, 64).

See also Cobbe, Frances Power; Grand, Sarah; Kingsford, Anna; Linton, Eliza Lynn.

References and Further Reading

Bland, Lucy. 1996. *Banishing the Beast: English Feminism and Sexual Morality, 1885–1914.* Harmondsworth: Penguin.

Caird, Mona. 1896. "Beyond the Pale: An Appeal on Behalf of the Victims of Vivisection." London: Bijou Library.

Crawford, Elizabeth. 1999. *The Women's Suffrage Movement, 1866–1928: A Reference Guide.* London: University College of London Press.

Gullette, Margaret Morganroth. 1989 [1894]. Afterword. In Mona Caird, *Daughters of Danaus.* Reprint, New York: Feminist Press.

Heilmann, Ann. 1995. "Mona Caird (1854–1932): Wild Woman, New Woman, and Early Radical Feminist Critic of Marriage and Motherhood." *Women's History Review* 5, no. 1: 67–95.

———. 1998. *The Late-Victorian Marriage Question: A Collection of Key New Woman Texts.* 5 vols. London: Routledge Thoemmes Press.

———. Forthcoming. *New Woman Strategies: Sarah Grand, Olive Schreiner, Mona Caird.* Manchester: Manchester University Press.

Sage, Lorna, ed. 1999. *The Cambridge Guide to Women's Writing.* Cambridge: Cambridge University Press.

Schlueter, Paul, and June Schlueter. 1998. *An Encylopedia of British Women Writers.* London: St. James Press.

Shattock, Joanne, ed. 1993. *Oxford Guide to British Women Writers.* Oxford: Oxford University Press.

Todd, Janet, ed. 1989. *Dictionary of British Women Writers.* London: Routledge.

Caldicott, Helen
(1938–)
Australia/United States

Since the mid-1970s, the Australian activist Helen Caldicott has been a leading international antinuclear protester who has persistently warned of the dangers to health from nuclear fallout and radiation. Born in Melbourne, she decided she wanted to be a doctor at the age of eleven and studied at the medical school of the University of Adelaide (1956–1961). After her marriage and the birth of three children, Caldicott moved to the United States to take up a fellowship in pediatrics at the Harvard Medical School (1966–1969) and work at the Children's Hospital Medical Center.

After returning to Australia, she specialized in pediatrics at the Queen Elizabeth Hospital in Adelaide in 1971, especially the treatment of cystic fibrosis in the young, and in 1975 founded the Cystic Fibrosis Clinic at the Children's Hospital there. Inspired by the empowering feminist message of Germaine Greer's *Female Eunuch,* she decided to take a stand against French atmospheric nuclear testing on the Mururoa Atoll in the South Pacific and launched a major campaign for a nuclear test ban in the area. As a doctor mindful of the terrifying genetic defects and cancers caused by radiation, she investigated the health threats from radioactive fallout in Adelaide, particularly in the food and water supply, and began raising awareness among trade unionists on the dangers of uranium mining for the manufacture of nuclear warheads. She orchestrated a series of demonstrations and boycotts of French goods. Her political lobbying on nuclear weapons helped to elect a Labour government sympathetic to the cause in 1972. A ban by the International Court of Justice ended atmospheric nuclear testing in the Pacific in 1975.

Subsequently, Caldicott headed a high-profile campaign in the press and on television and radio and returned to the United States in 1977 to lobby for controls on the nuclear power industry. She taught pediatrics at Harvard Medical School until 1980. In 1979 she published her influential book, *Nuclear Madness: What You Can Do!,* and was much in demand as a public speaker, visiting Europe and Japan, where she lectured on the effects of radiation on the human body. Her lectures to doctors led to the revival in 1979 of the Society of Physicians for Social Responsibility (SPSR), of which Caldicott was president until 1983, when she resigned to take an independent stand favoring abolition of nuclear power as well as weapons. She was also a founder of Women's Action for Nuclear Disarmament, based in Washington, D.C., and became a member of the SPSR's successor, the International Physicians for the Prevention of Nuclear War, a nonpartisan umbrella group of 135,000 members worldwide dedicated to the prevention of nuclear war. In 1985, this group was awarded the Nobel Peace Prize for its promotion of peace education. Caldicott returned once more to Australia in 1987 and stood for election to Parliament on an independent ticket but was narrowly defeated. In 1990–1991, when the Soviet Union collapsed and the Cold War ended, Caldicott's mission was partially accomplished as the threat of global nuclear war receded. After living in Leongatha, Victoria, for two years, she again spent time in the United States after 1995, where she resumed her work in pediatrics as well as continuing a career in broadcasting, broadening her activism to cover environmental issues. She returned to New South Wales and in 1998 became patron of Parents Protecting Our Children Against Radiation. In 1999 she was founder and president of the Star Foundation (Standing for Truth About Radiation) and, to promote her concern about the ravaging of the world's natural resources, a founder of the Our Common Future Political Party.

Caldicott has received many honors for her distinguished career in antinuclear activism, including nomination for a Nobel Peace Prize, the Gandhi Peace Prize in 1981, and the distinguished Peace Leadership Award of the Nuclear Age Peace Foundation in 1994. Her antinuclear campaigning was the subject of a documentary film by the National Film Board of Canada, *If You Love This Planet,* which won an Academy Award in 1983. Her published works include *Missile Envy: The Arms Race and Nuclear War* (1984) and a book based on the documentary, *If You Love This Planet: A Plan to Heal the Earth* (1992). A website on Caldicott, with links to many other sites about her life and work, can be found at http://www.macronet.org/women/helen.html. See also the International Physicians for the Prevention of Nuclear War website, http://www.ippnw.org.

See also Greer, Germaine.

References and Further Reading

Caldicott, Helen. 1997. *A Desperate Passion: An Autobiography.* New York: W. W. Norton.
Uglow, Jennifer, ed. 1998. *Macmillan Dictionary of Women's Biography.* 3d ed. Basingstoke: Macmillan.
Who's Who in Australia. 2001. Melbourne: Herald and Weekly Times.

Campoamor, Clara
(1888–1972)
Spain

As a radical lawyer and penologist and one of the first women to be admitted to the bar in Spain, Clara Campoamor was an outspoken defender of women's rights and suffrage during the drafting of the constitution of Republican Spain in 1931. She later became director of public welfare in 1933–1934 before being forced into exile by the outbreak of the Spanish Civil War.

Born into a working-class family in Madrid, Campoamor went out to work at the age of thirteen and studied part-time for the qualifications that enabled her to enter the University of Madrid to study law. After gaining her degree in 1924 she became a member of the Royal Academy of Jurisprudence and Legislation and was active in the Lawyers' Association of Madrid, as well as becoming a regular participant in intellectual and debating societies such as the Athenaeum and the Lyceum Club. In 1927 she pioneered new children's laws and changes to the electoral law of 1907. In 1931 the law was amended to allow women to stand as candidates for the first constituent assembly of the Second Republic, even though they were not allowed to vote. Campoamor was, with Victoria Kent, elected in June (Margarita Nelken joined them in October) as a representative of the Radical Party. On 1 October 1931, she became the first woman in Spain to address the constituent assembly. In her speech, she reminded the assembled male politicians that although they might hold political power, their right to do so while continuing to exclude women by denying them suffrage was not endorsed by natural law, which respected men and women equally. Furthermore, Campoamor felt that their actions contravened the basic democratic principles of the republic.

Her call for sexual equality and women's suffrage was greeted with hostility by conservative and Catholic elements who opposed women's emancipation and even by male activists on the left, who doubted women's ability to think rationally. She found herself fighting not just male prejudice but also the indifference of many Spanish women to suffrage and women's rights in general, partly as a result of their poor education. Worse still, Campoamor found herself in open opposition to Victoria Kent, herself also a trained lawyer, who did not favor women's immediate enfranchisement, since she felt that Spanish women were ill-prepared to use the vote judiciously.

Opposition from right-wing Catholic elements was finally overcome by Campoamor and her supporters when Article 36 of the new constitution was passed, giving Spanish women over the age of twenty-three the vote in October 1931 (ratified in December).

During the 1930s, Campoamor wrote extensively on women's rights and founded the Republican Feminine Union (one of five women's organizations she set up), which later ran under the name Women's Heritage. Alarmed at the rise of fascism in Spain and Italy, she was one of several Spanish activists who joined with Frenchwomen in 1933 to set up the Worldwide Committee of Women Against War and Fascism. But in 1933 a right-wing government ousted the socialists and republicans and banned the group's activities. Having lost her seat in the assembly, Campoamor turned to activism among the working classes. In 1934, during a general strike in Asturias led by a mixture of socialists and anarchists, Campoamor helped found Pro Infancia Obrera, a society to relieve the sufferings of the children in the region.

In her book *My Mortal Sin: Women's Vote and Me* (1936), Campoamor described her private conflict in reconciling her feminist and reformist concerns with her commitment to Socialist Party politics. After the Spanish Civil War and the establishment of the fascist regime of General Francisco Franco, Campoamor went into exile, first in France, and then in 1938 settled in Buenos Aires, Argentina. Meanwhile, in Spain General Franco suppressed women's suffrage during the Spanish Civil War; it was not fully restored in Spain until after his death, in 1975. In 1955, Campoamor moved back to Europe and lived in Lausanne, Switzerland. She wrote a notable monograph on the Spanish poet Sor Juana Inés de la Cruz, which was published in 1983. Like all too many other reformers of her time, she died forgotten; her work remains untranslated.

See also Nelken i Mausberger, Margarita.
References and Further Reading
Hannam, June, Mitzi Auchterlonie, and Katherine Holden. 2000. *International Encyclopedia of Women's Suffrage*. Santa Barbara: ABC-CLIO.

Keene, Judith. 1999. "'Into the Clean Air of the Plaza': Spanish Women Achieve the Vote in 1931." In Victoria Lorée Enders and Pamels Beth Radcliff, eds., *Constructing Spanish Womanhood: Female Identity in Modern Spain*. Albany: State University of New York Press.

Offen, Karen. 2000. *European Feminisms 1700-1950: A Political History*. Stanford: Stanford University Press.

Carmichael, Amy Wilson
(1867–1971)
Ireland

The Northern Irish evangelist Amy Carmichael went as a missionary to southern India, where she devoted herself to campaigning against child marriage, the ill treatment of widows, and temple prostitution. Born in County Down, the daughter of a mill owner, Carmichael was brought up as a strict Presbyterian. She defied convention and religious propriety in 1887 by living with fellow widowed evangelist Robert Wilson as his daughter. In 1893 she left Northern Ireland with Wilson and spent two years as a missionary in Japan and Sri Lanka before traveling to India in 1895 to join in the work of the Church of England Zenana Missionary Society.

Never one to be reticent in expressing her views, Carmichael quickly stirred up controversy among the British expatriate community still steeped in the ways of the old Raj. She took powerful, controversial stands on many issues involving the British administration in India, criticizing the complacency of the resident Anglican community, among whom she soon caused gossip and scandal when she took to wearing a sari and traveling around evangelizing with her group of followers, known as "The Woman's Band," in a bullock cart. Although her primary concern was the plight of Indian women, Carmichael constantly had to fight prejudice among other white missionaries and colonial officials toward her own activities.

In 1901, having based herself at Dohnavur, Carmichael founded the Dohnavur Fellowship to fund the education of Indian girls and boys who had been sold into prostitution, and in 1926 the Dohnavur Fellowship became a mission in its own right. In 1903 Carmichael's reputation reached a wider audience with the publication of *Things as They Are*, her account of her travels proselytizing among villagers in southern India.

Carmichael had begun taking in destitute women and children in the late 1890s. In 1900, establishing herself at Dohnavur, she founded a mission and orphanage that eventually became known as the Dohnavur Fellowship, where she raised funds to provide for the education of Indian girls and boys whom she had rescued from temple prostitution, several of whom converted to Christianity under her influence. Meanwhile, Carmichael had been publishing a stream of religious and evangelizing tracts and books to support and publicize her work, the most well-known of which are *Things as They Are,* which aroused public interest back home in Britain, and a discourse on her religious faith in *Overweights of Joy* (1906). In 1912, after years of being marginalized by British officialdom, which disapproved of her insistence on "going native" in order to further her campaigning, Carmichael's work achieved greater respectability when it was acknowledged by Queen Mary. In 1916 Carmichael founded the Sisters of the Common Life, a hands-on group of like-minded missionaries and reformers, and removed herself to a remote retreat, known as "Gray Jungle," where she began taking in orphaned and destitute children and in 1929 added a hospital.

In 1919 Carmichael was awarded the Kaiser-i-Hind Medal for her service to India. But despite her good works and humanitarian concerns, her reputation has been somewhat tarnished by her vehement dislike of Hinduism and her somewhat lurid descriptions of those aspects of Hindu practice, particularly child marriage, of which she disapproved in her own moral terms. Carmichael described the work of the Dohnavur Fellowship in her 1932 book *Gold Cord.*

She remained in India until her death, surrounded at Dohnavur by her devoted Indian followers, many of them rehabilitated prostitutes who revered her as "amma" (Mother).

References and Further Reading
Carmichael, Amy. 1903. *Things as They Are: Mission Work in Southern India.* New York: Fleming H. Revell.
Elliot, Elisabeth. 1987. *A Chance to Die—the Life and Legacy of Amy Carmichael.* New Jersey: Fleming H. Revell.
Houghton, Frank. 1954. *Amy Carmichael of Dohnavur: The Story of a Lover and Her Beloved.* London: SPCK.
Jayawardena, Kumari. 1995. *The White Woman's Other Burden: Western Women and South Asia During British Rule.* London: Routledge.
Skoglund, Elizabeth R. *Amma: The Life and Words of Amy Carmichael.* Grand Rapids, MI: Baker Books.
Wellman, Sam. 1998. *Amy Carmichael: A Life Abandoned to God.* Uhrichville, OH: Barbour Publishing.

Carpenter, Mary
(1807–1877)
United Kingdom

The English Unitarian reformer and educator Mary Carpenter was a pioneer of the ragged schools in Britain and the establishment of reformatories for juvenile offenders. Her philanthropic concerns also took her to the United States, where she supported the abolitionist cause, and to India, where she undertook pioneer work in education. As the eldest of the six children of an eminent Unitarian minister, Dr. Lant Carpenter, she enjoyed the rare privilege of being brought up in a family atmosphere where learning and scientific and philosophical debate were positively encouraged. Thus it is no accident that her brother William later became an eminent biologist, zoologist, and neurologist.

Carpenter was born in Exeter, Devon, and received an education at the school run by her father there. The family moved to Bristol, a notable center of radicalism and nonconformity, where Dr. Carpenter founded a local philosophical society and literary institution and with his wife ran a boarding school for boys. Carpenter took full advantage of any opportunities for education there with the direct encouragement of her father, who was a staunch supporter of education for girls. Contemporary accounts describe her as an earnest little girl who joined in on lessons with a seriousness and concentration that belied her young age. Her dedication is unsurprising considering the subjects she was already tackling, such as Latin, Greek, science, natural history, and mathematics—this at a time when most young women were being instructed in little more than the less strenuous arts of sewing, dancing, and singing.

All her life, Carpenter would remain devoutly religious and dedicated to good works (she never married). Inspired by her father's example, she soon began teaching in Dr. Carpenter's Sunday school, and in 1829, together with her mother and sister Anna, set up a school for girls in order to provide an income for the family after her father was forced to retire due to ill health. As a superintendent for the Lewin's Mead Sunday School, in 1835 Carpenter set up a Working and Visiting Society to visit the homes of poor children in the Bristol slums. She was distressed by the dismal conditions in which they lived and the devastating effects of cholera epidemics brought on by overcrowding. Her resolution to devote herself to working with the poor took on the complexion of a religious crusade, in which she saw education and enlightenment as the route to salvation from both moral depravity and social oppression. In particular, she chose to address the problems of those rejected even by conventional Victorian charities—juvenile delinquents.

In 1846 the founding of the Ragged School Union gave Carpenter the impetus to set up her own school in the slums of Bristol, with a roll call of twenty mostly homeless, barefoot boys. She was gratified by the response she received; soon her school was welcoming up to 200 children a week into its doors, and Carpenter set up a night school for another 160 pupils. In 1849 she published an account of her work in the pamphlet "Ragged Schools: Their Principles and Modes of Operation." Carpenter henceforward campaigned vigorously for the establishment of special schools for delinquent children and the rehabilitation of young criminals, by lobbying in Parliament and visiting prison chaplains and magistrates. She argued her case in her 1851 tract, "Reformatory Schools for the Children of the Perishing and Dangerous Classes, and for Juvenile Offenders" and "Juvenile Delinquents: Their Condition and Treatment" (1953), advocating the early and humane rehabilitation of child criminals in order to save them from becoming persistent offenders.

In 1852 Carpenter used much of her own money to found the Kingswood Industrial School for Boys and Girls. After a change in the law in 1854, she was able to convert this establishment into a reformatory for boys (known simply as the Boys' Reformatory) and simultaneously establish the first reformatory for girls. The famous Red Lodge Reformatory, as the latter was known, was housed in premises purchased in Bristol by philanthropist Lady Noel Byron—who had also funded Kingswood—"for the purpose of rescuing young girls from sin and misery, and

bringing them back to the paths of holiness," as the commemorative tablet there describes it (Mayne 1929, 427). Kingswood and the Red Lodge would become models for many similar establishments set up throughout Britain. In 1859 Carpenter also founded the Park Row Certified Industrial School for boys; a Workmen's Hall followed in 1865, where young working men and boys could gather for leisure activities (Carpenter hoped that this would keep them out of the public houses).

In all her schools, Carpenter not only addressed the discipline and rehabilitation of her pupils with compassion and a minimum of coercion but also placed considerable emphasis on the quality of the teaching, insisting on hiring trained teachers. The regime she set up was based on what she considered to be the three key qualities: love, faith, and obedience, with considerable attention paid to teaching the children some kind of trade and finding them suitable employment. Carpenter's tireless work in this area was directly influential in the passing of the Youthful Offenders Act of 1854, which sanctioned the establishment of reformatory schools run by volunteers under government supervision, and the Industrial Schools Acts of 1857, 1861, and 1866. In 1858–1859 Carpenter was assisted in her work at Red Lodge by Frances Power Cobbe, but the women proved incompatible, and Cobbe, unable to cope with Carpenter's self-denying lifestyle and the frugal diet she provided, left after a few months.

Since the 1830s, Carpenter had been impressed by the work of the Unitarian minister, social pioneer, and philanthropist Dr. Joseph Tuckerman in the United States. He had drawn her attention to the issue of abolition (a cause she long supported) and to the desperate need for welfare for destitute children. In the 1860s after slavery had been ended, Carpenter turned her attention to the plight of the destitute in India and the work being done there by the reformer Rajah Rammohun Roy, who had visited Britain in 1831 and had stayed with the Carpenters in Bristol. Carpenter had long nursed an ambition of traveling to India, which she finally achieved in 1866, and returned there on three further occasions (until 1876). During these visits, she set up the Model High School for Hindu Girls from her own finances, campaigned on behalf of women and child workers in Indian cotton mills (which led in part to the passing of the Indian Factory Act after her death), and lectured in support of women's education and prison reform. She was unable, however, to overcome caste prejudices and establish a teachers' training college.

Carpenter published accounts of her work in *Six Months in India* (1868), in which she detailed her visits to girls' schools, prisons, and mental asylums in several cities, describing her abhorrence of child marriage and calling on other English radicals to help raise the social consciousness of Indian women. She met and collaborated with Florence Nightingale, whose work for public health in India, as well as sanitary reforms in the British Army there, she supported. During her visits to India, Carpenter gave numerous public lectures on women's education (particularly on the merits of secular schools for girls), juvenile offenders, prison reform, and public health. In December 1866 she addressed the Bengal Social Science Association. In 1870 she set up the National Indian Association in Britain, to disseminate information about India and forge closer links between England and the subcontinent; her series of popular lectures in India was published as *Addresses to the Hindoos*. Not content with doing good works in India, Carpenter also visited the United States, Canada, and France, where she threw her energy into the reform of their prison systems. Although she was never involved in the general campaign for women's rights and suffrage in Britain, Carpenter supported the expansion of women's education and was an active member and speaker for the National Association for the Promotion of Social Science, established in 1856.

See also Cobbe, Frances Power; Nightingale, Florence.

References and Further Reading
Burton, Antoinette. 1994. *Burdens of History: British Feminists, Indian Women and Imperial Culture 1865–1915*. Baltimore: Johns Hopkins University Press.

———. 1995. "Fearful Bodies into Disciplined Subjects: Pleasure, Romance and the Family Drama of Colonial Reform in Mary Carpenter's *Six Months in India*." *Signs* 20(3): 545–574.

Carpenter, J. Estlin. 1879. *The Life and Work of Mary Carpenter*. London: Macmillan.

Chaudhuri, Nupur, and Margaret Strobel, eds. 1992. *Western Women and Imperialism: Complicity and Resistance*. Bloomington: Indiana University Press.

Gardner, P. 1984. *The Lost Elementary Schools of Victorian England*. London: Croom Helm.

Hollis, Patricia, ed. 1979. *Women in Public: The Women's Movement 1850–1900*. London: Allen and Unwin.

Jayawardena, Kumari. 1995. *The White Woman's Other Burden: Western Women and South Asia during British Rule*. London: Routledge.

Manton, Jo. 1976. *Mary Carpenter and the Children of the Streets*. London: Heinemann.

Mayne, Ethel Colburne. 1929. *Life and Letters of Lady Byron*. London: Constable.

Parker, Julia. 1988. *Women and Welfare*. London: Macmillan.

Saywell, Ruby J. 1964. *Mary Carpenter of Bristol*. Bristol: Historical Association.

Schupf, Harriet Warm. 1974. "Single Women and Social Reform in Mid-Nineteenth Century England: The Case of Mary Carpenter." *Victorian Studies* 17(2): 307–319.

Tobias, J. J. *Crime and Industrial Society in the Nineteenth Century*. London: Batsford.

Tuson, Penelope, ed. 1997. *The Queen's Daughters: An Anthology of Victorian Feminist Writings on India 1857–1900*. Reading, Berkshire, UK: Ithaca Press.

Carrillo Puerto, Elvia
(1878–1965)
Mexico

Carrillo was one of a group of radical women active in the Yucatán in the 1920s who initiated campaigns for birth control, sex education, and the rights of illegitimate children. As a socialist, she insisted on a sound economic basis for all reform relating to women's rights. As sister of the president of the Socialist Party of the Yucatán, Felipe Carrillo Puerto, who governed the province from 1922 to 1924 and endorsed women's rights to initiate divorce, use birth control, and have a life beyond the domestic one, Carrillo was instrumental in lobbying him to grant the vote to women in the Yucatán and allow them to stand for public office.

The Yucatán peninsula where Carrillo grew up is a remote rural area in southeastern Mexico. She married at the age of thirteen and was widowed by the age of twenty-one. Her second marriage ended in early separation, after which she worked as a schoolteacher in the Yucatán. She began to take an interest in women's issues and in 1912 founded an organization for peasant women.

In 1919 Carrillo set up a Feminist League at Mérida, named after the poet and teacher Rita Cetina Gutiérrez, and encouraged the establishment of a network of other leagues. Despite its geographical isolation, the Yucatán was, for a brief period, a region that pioneered social reform and feminist activities, with one of its most active leaders being Gutiérrez (1846–1908). The Feminist League took part in campaigning for local and national elections as well as helping to set up education programs.

Carrillo's most socially active phase came during her brother's governorship of the Yucatán. She represented its progressive government not only in Mexican state affairs but also at national and international feminist congresses, such as the 1922 Pan American Conference of Women, held in Baltimore, and the first international women's congress in Mexico, held in Mexico City the following year. In 1922 the Feminist League became involved in setting up a school, and Carrillo encouraged teachers to take on the challenge of teaching groups of twenty illiterate peasants to read and write in three months by offering a cash prize. The league brought out the monthly magazine *Feminism,* which Carrillo edited.

While setting up branches of the Feminist League, Carrillo was able to extend her activities, helping to set up conferences and meetings that would educate women about improving their lives through greater awareness about hygiene, child care, birth control, and the dangers of alcoholism. She also offered literacy classes and discussion of women's rights, suffrage, and the eradication of traditional superstitious practices. During her time in the Yucatán, she had made a personal crusade of her concern for the rights of illegitimate children and had encouraged her brother the governor to introduce a program aimed at giving them the same rights as their legitimate counterparts.

In 1923 Carrillo was one of the first women to be elected to the state legislature (at the age of twenty-eight) for the fifth district of the Yucatán, with a majority of more than 5,000 votes. That same year she was one of three outspoken women delegates from the Yucatán to attend the first international women's congress mentioned earlier and campaign on issues such as birth control, despite being met with hostility from the predominantly conservative, middle-class delegates.

When her brother was assassinated in 1924, Carrillo, who for several years had been paying regular visits to Mexico City to meet with other feminist and socialist leaders, extended her activities to campaigning for women's greater involvement in all aspects of government. She moved her activities to the state of San Luis Potosí in response to a program of limited suffrage reform that had been introduced there in 1923. Taking advantage of the law allowing literate women to vote in local elections, she stood as a deputy for the fourth district. In the ensuing election she won a seat but was barred from taking it by the new military junta, which had taken over in Mexico in 1925 and had rescinded the suffrage law of 1923. Faced with the lack of constitutional backing for her campaign, she returned to the Yucatán.

Carrillo now faced growing opposition to her feminist activities, not only from government but also from conservative, Roman Catholic women activists who took exception to her critical stance on the church's opposition to birth control and her views on "free love" and set up a rival Yucatán Women's Protective Association. Undeterred, and by now one of the few early feminists in Mexico to still be active, she petitioned the government in 1926 to introduce universal women's suffrage. She became a founding member of the Feminist Socialist Guiding League, set up in 1927 as a forum for employees in the Ministry of Agriculture, and, in 1932, of the Feminine Action Guiding League, which that year demonstrated at the opening of Congress in February and petitioned in November in an attempt to try to persuade the Chamber of Deputies to accord full political rights to women. By the 1930s, women's suffrage had been granted in Spain, but this step did not influence events in Mexico, to the disappointment of Mexican campaigners. The struggle for suffrage would continue throughout the 1930s and women would not achieve full suffrage until 1958.

By 1938, sick and reduced to poverty, Carrillo retired from activism. Although she was awarded the Legion of Honour by Mexican president Ruiz Cortinas in 1952 for her services to the nation, as Shirlene Soto points out, she died lonely, destitute, and "largely forgotten" in Mexico City in 1965.

References and Further Reading

Macías, Anna. 1983. *Against All Odds: The Feminist Movement in Mexico to 1940*. Westport, CT: Greenwood Press.

Soto, Shirlene. 1990. *Emergence of the Modern Mexican Woman: Her Participation in Revolution and Struggle for Equality, 1910–1940*. Denver: Arden Press.

Tenenbaum, Barbara A., ed. 1996. *Encyclopedia of Latin American History and Culture*. Vol. 2. New York: Charles Scribner's Sons.

Carson, Rachel
(1907–1964)
United States

Few women in history can have had a more far-reaching influence on the way people view the world in which they live and the way they have thoughtlessly destroyed it than the biologist Rachel Carson. In 1962, after she alerted the American people to the increasingly destructive long-term effects on wildlife and humanity of the unrestrained use of synthetic pesticides—what she called "the elixirs of death"—American agriculture was forced to accept accountability for its widespread use of 600 million pounds of pesticides per annum. It was Carson's seminal book *Silent Spring*, probably one of the most influential in the second half of the twentieth century, that laid the foundations of the environmental movement that grew up during the 1970s and ensured that both governments and individuals would henceforth have a greater sense of humility toward the natural environment, which they had assumed was theirs to control.

Carson was born in a farmhouse in rural Springdale in the Allegheny Valley of Pennsylvania. A naturally solitary and intellectual child, she grew up with a deep love for nature and the wildlife of the nearby river. By the age of ten, she had begun writing, and she went on to study English at Pennsylvania College for Women (now Chatham College), soon changing subjects to major in zoology and graduating in 1929. She conducted postgraduate research at the Marine Biological Laboratory at Woods Hole in Massachusetts and was awarded an M.A. in zoology at Johns Hopkins University in 1932. For the next

five years, she struggled with financial difficulties, supporting her widowed mother and her nieces (her sister had died in 1936) and teaching zoology at the University of Maryland (1931–1936). She then managed to secure a better salary as a marine biologist in the U.S. Bureau of Fisheries (1936–1952) (one of the first women to achieve a nonclerical appointment there), where she wrote a series of radio programs. During the war, she published bulletins on conservation for the government and in 1949 became editor-in-chief of publications for the U.S. Fish and Wildlife Service.

In 1937 after publishing an article titled "Undersea" in *Atlantic Monthly*, Carson was encouraged to write a full-length study, publishing *Under the Sea-Wind: A Naturalist's Picture of Ocean Life* in 1941. This book would be the first of a trilogy of books about the complex ecology of the sea and the delicate balance maintained between marine species; it was followed by a best-selling book on oceanography, *The Sea around Us* (1951), which had been serialized in the *New Yorker* and won several literary prizes. Carson was financially secure enough to retire from her government post in 1952. She bought a seashore retreat on the coast of Maine, where she wrote a book about its marine life, *The Edge of the Sea* (1955), combining scientific erudition with her unique literary skill for evoking the beauty of nature. In doing so she also conveyed a powerful underlying message about the pollution of the sea and the urgent need for the preservation of its ecology.

During the 1950s, Carson became alarmed at the sophisticated new technologies that were producing a wide range of synthetic chemicals and pesticides, particularly the increasing use of the wartime miracle cure-all, DDT, which had proved highly effective in the eradication of the body lice that spread typhus fever among troops. From 1956 to 1958, after being alerted to the destruction of the bird life at her friend Olga Owens Huckins's private bird sanctuary in Duxbury, Massachusetts, as a result of DDT spraying, Carson took upon herself a mission to warn the public of the dangers of chemical poisons used in agriculture and, in particular, the use of DDT sprays to combat mosquitoes. With the help of an assistant, Carson spent several years assembling painstaking research in the United States and in Europe on the effect of tox-

Rachel Carson (Library of Congress)

ins, both on land and in the water supply. With relentless precision, she catalogued the disappearance of fish from the rivers; of birds such as the robin, dove, and jay from gardens; and the frightening correlation between the rise of leukemia in areas where pesticides were heavily used and the threat of pesticides to human health through the food chain.

During her research, Carson often found that people were reluctant to talk to her or to openly condemn widespread federal agricultural programs. She then faced the obstacle of finding a publisher prepared to publish her controversial findings. The *Readers Digest* declined, but Carson was subsequently encouraged by the editor of the *New Yorker,* William Shawn, who published extracts from the book beginning in June 1962. Rejected by several publishers, the book *Silent Spring* was published by Houghton Mifflin in September of that year. But even after it was published and became an instant best-seller, Carson found herself up against the big guns of the U.S. chemical giants, who, with access to unlimited funds and astute lawyers, did everything they could to undermine and discredit her and

her work. Even eminent scientists doubted the wisdom of what they perceived as Carson's alarmist, if not hysterical, message and were prepared to publicly aver in support of the chemical companies that pesticides did not harm either wildlife or humans. Meanwhile, Carson was vilified and accused of fear-mongering.

By the time the book was published, Carson was terminally ill with breast and bone cancer and, having undergone a mastectomy, was facing her critics between debilitating courses of radiation treatment. But she lived long enough to see forty U.S. states introduce some form of pesticide control by the end of the year. Such was the widespread interest in her case and the high media profile given it, with *Silent Spring* eventually being translated into twenty-two languages, that Carson was called to testify before Congress on her findings. President John F. Kennedy's science advisory committee was appointed to investigate Carson's claims and eventually endorsed her arguments on the high toxicity of chemical pesticides, advocating a tough new federal pesticide policy, which was introduced to curb the use of toxic agricultural chemicals. In 1970 the Environmental Protection Agency was established, but it was not until ten years after the publication of *Silent Spring* that the final ban on DDT use in the United States came into force.

Carson never married but during her life showed a compassionate concern for children, helping to raise her nieces after her sister died and in 1955, at the age of forty-eight, adopting the five-year-old son of one of them. She lived long enough to receive numerous awards: in 1956 she was awarded the Literary Award of the Council of Women of the United States and in 1963 the Albert Schweitzer Prize for Animal Welfare (*Silent Spring* was dedicated to Schweitzer), the Audubon Medal, and the Cullen Medal of the American Geographical Society, as well as election to the American Academy of Arts and Sciences and the Conservationist Award from the National Wildlife Federation. She was also posthumously awarded the President's Medal of Freedom by President Jimmy Carter in 1980. Carson's untimely death at the age of fifty-six robbed the burgeoning environmental movement of a key prophetic figure, but thanks to her work and that of others, humankind has come to realize that it arrogantly abuses its natural environment at its peril. More important, governments have also had to learn that a healthy, unpolluted environment is as much a human right as any other, one upon which ordinary citizens are entitled to insist. The Rachel Carson Organization can be found online at http://www.rachelcarson.org/.

References and Further Reading

Brooks, Paul. 1972. *The House of Life: Rachel Carson at Work*. Boston: Houghton Mifflin.

Graham, Frank, Jr. 1970. *Since Silent Spring*. Boston: Houghton Mifflin.

Hendricksson, John. 1991. *Rachel Carson: The Environmental Movement*. Brookfield, CT: Millbrook Press.

Lear, Linda J. 1998. *Rachel Carson: Witness for Nature*. London: Allen Lane.

McKay, Mary. 1993. *Rachel Carson*. Boston: Twayne Publishers.

Waddell, Craig, ed. 2000. *And No Birds Sing: Rhetorical Analyses of Rachel Carson's* Silent Spring. Carbondale: Southern Illinois University Press.

Wadsworth, Ginger. 1991. *Rachel Carson: Voice of the Earth*. New York: Lerner Publications.

Wheeler, Leslie. 1991. *Rachel Carson*. Englewood Cliffs, NJ: Silver Burdett Press.

Cary, Mary Ann Shadd
(1823–1893)
United States/Canada

One of the first to resettle escaped American slaves in Canada was Mary Shadd Cary, a free black from Delaware. A combative and hardworking woman, she founded the *Provincial Freeman* to promote this work and advocated the full integration of immigrants into Canadian society.

Cary grew up in Wilmington, Delaware. One of thirteen children of a freed slave and notable abolitionist, she inherited her father's forthrightness in promoting a sense of pride in their own worth among blacks. She attended a Quaker school for the children of free blacks in Westchester, Pennsylvania, and, at the age of sixteen, back in Wilmington, established her own school for black children. She spent the next eleven years teaching there and in New York, New Jersey, and Pennsylvania.

In 1849 she published a pamphlet, "Hints to the Colored People of the North," extolling the virtues of hard work among black people and cautioning them against seeking to imitate the profligacy of whites. She decided to do something positive for her people when she moved to Windsor, Ontario, in 1851 to avoid the possibility of being enslaved under the Fugitive Slave Act, passed the previous year. Arriving in Canada, she used funding from the American Mission Association (AMA) to set up a school for the children of free black emigrants and those of escaped slaves coming into Canada on the Underground Railroad from the United States.

After publishing her call to free blacks to emigrate from the United States to Canada in "A Plea for Emigration: Or, Notes of Canada West, in Its Moral, Social and Political Aspect . . . for the Information of Colored Emigrants" in 1852, Cary also founded a nonsectarian black newspaper, the *Provincial Freeman* (1853–1859), in which she published antislavery editorials, accentuated women's work in safeguarding the welfare of escaped slaves, and advocated the integration of blacks into Canadian society. These activities brought her into conflict with other male activists who, more reliant on donations from patrons and well-wishers, sought to ghettoize blacks by settling them in their own separate communities. A very public controversy erupted between segregationists and integrationists, particularly black activist Henry Bibb, a supporter of settlements founded by the Refugee Home Society, which ended with the AMA, rattled by Cary's outspokenness, withdrawing its financial support for her school. Despite these developments, Cary continued to condemn black separatism, where some of her people chose to live in special settlements.

Also in the 1850s, Cary returned to the United States to raise funds to keep her school and newspaper going through lecturing, and she returned to Canada in early 1854 to bring the paper out more frequently from its new premises in Toronto. It struggled on through numerous financial crises for another five years, moving again to Chatham. Cary married in 1856 and had two children, but her husband died in 1860. Despite her loss, she was buoyed up by hopes of an end to slavery after meeting John Brown in Canada in 1858. During the years 1859–1864, Cary went back to running her own school in Chatham. Anxious to play her part after the American Civil War broke out in 1861, she returned to the United States in 1863 to encourage black recruitment in the Union Army in Indiana, Michigan, Pennsylvania, and Ohio. After the war was over, Cary decided to stay in the United States to take up much-needed work in the resettlement and education of its emancipated slaves.

She studied for a teaching qualification and in 1868 returned to teaching, first in Detroit and then in several public schools in Washington, D.C., during 1872–1874 serving as principal of a grammar school. In 1869 when she was forty-six, she decided to take up the law, studying until 1871 at Howard University; but her studies were interrupted for some time. It was not until 1883 that she finally received her law degree. In the meantime, she had become engaged in activism for women's suffrage and promoting better education facilities for blacks. It is not known whether she ever practiced as a lawyer.

References and Further Reading

Bearden, Jim, and Linda Jean Butler. 1977. *Shadd: The Life and Times of Mary Shadd Cary.* Toronto: NC Press.

Hill, Daniel G. 1981. *The Freedom-Seekers: Blacks in Early Canada.* Agincourt: Book Society of Canada.

Litwack, Leon, and August Meier. 1988. *Black Leaders of the Nineteenth Century.* Urbana: University of Illinois Press.

Pease, William H., and Jane H. Pease. 1963. *Black Utopia: Negro Communal Experiments in America.* Madison: State Historical Society of Wisconsin.

Quarles, Benjamin. 1969. *Black Abolitionists.* New York: Oxford University Press.

Sadleir, Rosemary. 1994. *Leading the War: Black Women in Canada.* Toronto: Umbrella Press.

Winks, Robin. 1971. *The Blacks in Canada: A History.* Montreal: McGill-Queen's University Press.

Casely Hayford, Adelaide Smith
(1868–1960)
Sierra Leone

One of the first black women in Africa to pioneer women's education that rejected colonial methods, emphasized African talents, and nurtured a pride in traditional culture, Adelaide Casely Hayford was also the first African woman to make a lecture tour of the United States.

One of seven children, Adelaide Smith moved with her family to London in 1872. Later she was sent to study at the Ladies College on the island of Jersey and at the age of seventeen went to Germany to study music. Returning to Freetown in 1892, she became a teacher at a Methodist school and in 1897 set up an elementary girls' school with her sister Emma.

Adelaide returned to London in 1900, where after three years she met and married J. E. Casely Hayford, a lawyer and leading Ghanaian nationalist. In 1907 Adelaide joined her husband on the Gold Coast, but the marriage ended in 1914 (although they never divorced), and she returned to Sierra Leone to take up local community work in Freetown. In 1915 she expressed her interest in women's education in a speech she gave as president of the Young Women's Christian Association, entitled "The Rights of Women and Christian Marriage," elaborating on her vision of an African-run school for girls that emphasized traditional African culture and arts and provided vocational training.

In 1923 in Freetown, she finally began fundraising for her Girls' Vocational and Industrial Training School, assisted by her niece Kathleen Easmon. In 1920–1923 and again in 1926–1927 she also toured the United States, speaking at Radcliffe and Bryn Mawr Colleges, visiting black schools in Alabama and Georgia, and raising more money for her own school. The school opened in 1926, with Casely Hayford affirming its objectives as being to offer "an education which would instill into us a love of country, a pride of race, an enthusiasm for a black man's capabilities, and a genuine admiration for Africa's wonderful art work" (Cromwell 1986, 102). Casely Hayford was assisted in school administration by her daughter Gladys, but in 1940, a combination of age, insufficient funding, and the difficulties of educating children during wartime forced Casely Hayford to close the school down.

Casely Hayford was made a Member of the Order of the British Empire (MBE) in 1949. Through her work as president of the women's section of the Universal Negro Improvement Association, formed by Marcus Garvey in the 1910s Casely Hayford had throughout her life encouraged black people to take pride in their color and their culture.

References and Further Reading
Cromwell, Adelaide M. 1986. *An African Victorian Feminist: The Life and Times of Adelaide Smith Casely Hayford 1868–1960*. London: Frank Cass.

Casgrain, Thérèse
(1896–1981)
Canada

The Québecois suffrage leader and preeminent woman politician Thérèse Casgrain was the first female leader of a political party in that province and headed a twelve-year fight for women to be granted the provincial vote, which was finally achieved in 1940. Revered by English- and French-speaking Canadians alike, she went on to become the first woman promoted to the Senate of the Canadian federal government. In later years, she was a leading Canadian pacifist.

Casgrain was born into a wealthy Montreal family, the daughter of a conservative politician, Rodolphe Forget, himself a lawyer and notable philanthropist. She was educated at the Convent des Dames du Sacré-Coeur in Sault-aux-Récollets and married in 1916. Her husband, Pierre François Casgrain, was a liberal politician and lawyer.

In 1918 women in Canada were awarded the vote in federal elections, but they were still excluded from provincial elections in Quebec, even after all other Canadian provinces had awarded suffrage to women by 1922. She took up work for

her husband's 1921 election campaign when he was sidelined by illness, where she discovered her talents for public speaking and became active in promoting the suffrage cause in Quebec, in 1922 being a founding member of the Provincial Franchise Committee (PFC). After a split in the PFC's leadership in 1927, Casgrain became sole president. In November 1929, the PFC changed its name to the League for the Rights of Women and launched a long, concerted battle to win voting rights for women in provincial elections in Quebec. It would take twelve years to wear down the opposition to women's suffrage in the ultra-conservative provincial legislature, and Casgrain worked hard to involve women in remote rural parts of Quebec to support the campaign, achieving a high profile for campaigning through her regular radio program *Femina* during the 1930s.

Casgrain also devoted much energy to her many social concerns as a member of the National Health Council and the National Welfare Council. She lobbied in particular for legal changes relating to the position of women. In November 1929 she gave evidence to the Dorion Commission on reform of the civil code, arguing in particular for married women's control of their own earnings, their right to bring lawsuits without their husband's permission, and their right of consent to the marriage of daughters who were minors. Sixteen changes were subsequently recommended to the Canadian legislature, some of which were enacted in 1931.

The Quebec movement for women's provincial suffrage encountered endless disappointments and the rejection of its annual petitions to government, but it was greatly aided by Casgrain's spirit, wit, and dedication. During 1936–1940, when her husband was serving as speaker of the Federal House of Commons, she became a high-profile figure. In 1936 she helped organize a petition to King George V on the provincial vote and did much to defuse antisuffragist criticism as a mother of four children—proving thereby, she argued, that suffragists were not embittered spinsters. On 25 April 1940, Québecois women finally won the vote.

Casgrain continued her work for the Liberal Party of Canada, lobbying for child protection laws and reform of the civil code and the prison system. In 1942, after her husband had left Parliament to become a judge, she stood unsuccessfully as a Liberal candidate for the Canadian federal Parliament in her husband's seat of Charlevoix-Saguenay, the first woman to do so. Undeterred by defeat, she stood unsuccessfully for provincial and federal elections nine times in all from 1942 to 1962. Such determination demonstrated the depth of her conviction that the presence of more women in government would transform traditional power politics. She constantly argued that women would provide government with a more compassionate face in addressing the plight of the exploited and dispossessed.

During World War II, Casgrain organized the Women's Surveillance Committee of the Wartime Prices and Trade Board and also its Consumer Branch, receiving an Order of the British Empire for her wartime services. In 1946 she finally abandoned the Liberals, joined the socialist Co-operative Commonwealth Federation (from 1955 the National Democratic Party [NDP]), and was elected one of its national vice chairs in 1948. In 1951 she became leader of the NDP's Quebec branch—the first woman party leader in Canada—and was reelected to that office twice more until she stood down in 1957.

In her later years Casgrain gave up more and more time to the pacifist movement. In 1961 she established the Quebec branch of the Voice of Women peace group (founded in 1960) and, as its national president from 1962, led opposition to Canada's acquisition of nuclear missiles. She resigned after a year to stand unsuccessfully as an NDP candidate on a pacifist ticket in the 1963 federal election. For the rest of her career, Casgrain remained an international peace campaigner and was a regular delegate at conferences. She took a strong stand against U.S. intervention in Vietnam and served as president of the Quebec Medical Aid to Vietnam Committee.

Casgrain's wide-ranging interests prompted her involvement in 1967 in the founding of the Federation of Women of Quebec, an umbrella organization for various women's groups established during the UN Year for the Celebration of Human Rights. She also served as president of the League of the Rights of Man, the Canadian Consumers Association for Quebec, and the French section of the Canadian Adult Education Association, and was a founder of the French Junior League and the French Federated Charities. In 1967 Casgrain was nominated Woman of the Century by the National Council of Jewish Women of Canada; in 1974 she was made a Companion of the Order of Canada.

In 1970, in recognition of Casgrain's status as elder stateswoman, Canadian prime minister Pierre Trudeau called her to the Senate, where she took the opportunity of opposing the supply of Canadian-manufactured napalm and agent orange for U.S. use in Vietnam. Forced by law to retire nine months later, she went out fighting—to formally oppose compulsory retirement.

Shortly after her death, a Thérèse Casgrain Foundation was established in 1982 to further the ideals and objectives that Casgrain had espoused, particularly relating to the advancement of women. It now offers a fellowship for research on women and social change in Canada under the auspices of the Social Sciences and Humanities Research Council of Canada. For information, contact http://.www.sshrc.ca/english.

References and Further Reading
Brown, George W., et al., eds. 1966. *Dictionary of Canadian Biography.* Toronto: University of Toronto Press.
Casgrain, Thérèse. 1972. *A Woman in a Man's World.* Toronto: McClelland and Stewart.
Cleverdon, Catherine Lyle. 1950. *The Woman Suffrage Movement in Canada.* Toronto: University of Toronto Press.
Dadson, True. 1973. *The Golden Strings.* Toronto: Griffin House.
Josephson, Harold, Sandi Cooper, and Steven C. Hause et al., eds. 1985. *Biographical Dictionary of Modern Peace Leaders.* Westport, CT: Greenwood Press.
Lazarus, Morden. 1983. *Six Women Who Dared.* Toronto: CPA Publishers.
Munnings, Gladys. 1993. *Canadian Women of Distinction: Emily Ferguson Murphy, Agnes Campbell, Thérèse Casgrain, Molly (Mary) Brant, Frances Anne Hopkins.* Newmarket, ON: Quaker Press.

Castle, Barbara (Baroness Castle of Blackburn)
(1910–)
United Kingdom

During her long life in public service as the "First Lady of Socialism," the indomitable Labour politician Barbara Castle has been a passionate advocate of the welfare state, public health care and pensions, and women's equality. In the words of fellow member of Parliament (MP) Shirley Williams, "The words social justice are written on her heart" (BBC Radio 4, *Any Questions,* 1998). Castle's espousal of the idealism of the Bevanite vision of social reform and public welfare allowed no compromise. She became legendary, not just for her passion but also for her stubbornness with regard to the causes in which she believed, a fact that would lead to her reputation as the eternal maverick of Labour politics.

As Anne Perkins points out (1999), the story of Castle's life parallels the rise and changing fortunes of the Labour Party in Britain, stretching from her election campaigning in 1931 through close involvement in the establishment of the building blocks of the welfare state under Labour governments. The title of Castle's autobiography, *Fighting All the Way,* attests to her long career in activism. She was born in Chesterfield, the daughter of a tax inspector who was editor of the Independent Labour Party's newspaper, the *Pioneer.* Her mother was also a socialist and a Labour councilor in Bradford. Educated at Bradford Girls Grammar School, Castle won a scholarship to St. Hugh's College at Oxford University.

Castle began her career in public service by working for St. Pancras Borough Council in London from 1937 to 1945 and for the Metropolitan Water Board from 1940 to 1945. During World War II, she was an administrative officer at the Ministry of Food (1941–1944). In 1943, she backed Labour MPs who attacked Winston Churchill's wartime government for postponing the implementation of proposals for social welfare reform under the 1942 Beveridge Report on Social Insurance and Allied Services (Castle had worked behind the scenes on its preparation). The report contained the guiding principles of the new postwar Labour government, which won a landslide victory in the 1945 elections and in which Castle would be a leading light as MP for Blackburn. Elected in 1945, she would remain in Parliament for thirty-four years and undoubtedly was one of the leading Labour politicians of her generation. As a dedicated Bevanite—a group of left-wing MPs in the Labour Party who supported Minister of Health Aneurin Bevan's introduction of the National Health Service and new housing programs—Castle would criticize escalating government expenditure on the arms race during the Cold War, which was funded by cutbacks in expenditure on welfare programs;

she also opposed the introduction of health service charges.

From 1950 to 1979, Castle was a member of the National Executive of the Labour Party and subsequently held important government posts. She became the fourth woman in British history to attain cabinet rank, when she was appointed minister of overseas development (1964–1965), during which time she injected new energy into its programs. Subsequently, as minister of transport (1965–1968), she pushed through a 70-mile-per-hour speed limit and breathalyzer tests. In the newly created post of secretary of state for employment and productivity (1968–1970), Castle had to deal with an unpopular prices and incomes policy, producing a controversial policy document on trade union reform, *In Place of Strife.* In 1970 she succeeded in getting the Equal Pay Bill through Parliament, which was finally ratified in 1975 as part of the Sex Discrimination Act. In her last major post, as secretary of state for social services in 1974–1976, Castle introduced legislation to improve wage-linked pensions, to have child benefits paid directly to mothers (replacing the payment of family allowances in men's wage packets), and to ensure equal pay for women. When the Labour moderate James Callaghan took over the leadership of the Labour Party from Harold Wilson (who described Castle as his best minister), she was sacked, just before she was due to introduce a bill to phase out private pay beds in national health hospitals.

In 1979, having retired from Parliament, Castle stood for election as a member of the European Parliament for Greater Manchester North, remaining in that position until 1989. She was also vice chair of the Socialist Group within the European Economic Community (1979–1986) and leader of the British Labour Group (1979–1985).

After finally retiring from political life, Castle was made a life peer in 1990. But she still kept on campaigning, concentrating her efforts on the rights of the elderly and for the continued linkage of wages with old-age pensions. *The Castle Diaries,* covering her time in office from 1974 to 1976 (vol. 1) and from 1964 to 1970 (vol. 2), were published in 1980 and 1984. Castle is also the author of *The NHS Revisited* (1976), *Pensions as of Right for All* (1999), and *We Can Afford the Welfare State* (1996). In 1987 she published a vivid biography of the Pankhurst sisters, Sylvia and Christabel.

Throughout her long defense of women's equal rights in the workplace, Castle has been adamantly opposed to any promotion of a sex war, herself combining femininity with steely resourcefulness and political acumen. She has long argued that women do not need to be man haters in order to compete successfully alongside them, nor did she ever exploit her sexuality when in government, averring that she had too much respect for her male colleagues. Even in her late eighties, Castle was still writing articles and addressing Labour constituency party meetings, insisting that despite the hard times, she had enjoyed the challenges and responsibilities of being in government.

When the twenty-fifth anniversary of the passing of the 1975 Sex Discrimination Act, which she introduced in Parliament, was marked in 2001, Castle had lost none of her passion, arguing at the age of ninety that the battle for sexual equality was still not over and that "women have to do more to help themselves. If there is no fire in women's bellies it will all become a very dainty process. Organize yourselves and speak out" (*Independent on Sunday,* 21 January 2001). A small and feisty woman renowned for her mesmerizing powers of oratory, her intelligence, and determination, Barbara Castle remains one of the great movers and shakers of British social activism of the twentieth century.

References and Further Reading

Castle, Barbara. 1993. *Fighting All the Way.* London: Macmillan.
De'Ath, Wilfred. 1970. *Barbara Castle: A Portrait from Life.* London: Clifton.
Martineau, Lisa. 2000. *Barbara Castle: Politics and Power.* London: Andre Deutsch.
Perkins, Anne. 1999. "Red Queen in the Pink." [The *Guardian* profile.] *Guardian,* 25 September: 6–7.

Catt, Carrie Chapman
(1859–1947)
United States

The central figure in the final years of the American suffrage campaign, Carrie Chapman Catt was a leading moderate feminist with innate qualities of leadership, public oratory, and statesmanship. She worked hard for unity, training women to take up direct political action and bringing the American movement into close contact with suffragists around the world through her presidency of the International Woman Suffrage Alliance (IWSA). Her political acumen and powers as an organizer prompted her to reorganize the suffrage movement on political district lines during 1905–1915, between her two presidencies of the National American Woman Suffrage Association (NAWSA) from 1900 to 1904 and 1916 to 1920.

Born in Ripon, Wisconsin, Catt grew up on a remote prairie farm near Charles City, Iowa. Her early life in this frontier area taught her independence and a tough-mindedness that would stand her in good stead in her later life as an activist. After graduating from Iowa State College in 1880, she considered entering law school but instead accepted a post as high school principal in Mason City, Iowa, in 1881, becoming one of the first female school superintendents in the state in 1883. She married the newspaper proprietor Leo Chapman in 1885 and helped edit his *Mason City Republican.* But he died of typhoid fever the following year, and she returned to Charles City, trying to come to terms with her grief by devoting herself to women's suffrage. From 1887 to 1890 she was an active member of the Iowa Woman Suffrage Association, joining NAWSA in 1890.

When Carrie remarried in 1890, she and her husband signed a prenuptial agreement allowing her to spend four months of every year working for suffrage. Indeed, George William Catt was a considerable encouragement to Carrie in her suffrage work. They settled in New York, where Catt soon lent her skills to the administration of the organizational committee in charge of fieldwork for the NAWSA, beginning in 1895. Although Catt succeeded Susan B. Anthony as its president in 1900, the ill health of her husband forced her to abandon the post in 1904. His death in 1905 dealt Catt another severe emotional blow, but it left her financially secure so that she could once more devote her energies to women's suffrage, which she did with great energy and efficiency.

Catt became a familiar figure in the international women's movement as a founding member and president of the IWSA, which she served from 1902 to 1923, regularly attending congresses in Europe. A powerful presence and dignified speaker, she lent great weight and social acceptability to the public face of the international and U.S. suffrage movements. In 1911–1912 she undertook an ambitious fact-finding world tour in support of women's suffrage in the company of the leading Dutch suffragist Aletta Jacobs. Together they visited Egypt, Palestine, India, Burma, China, Japan, Java, the Philippines, and Hawaii. In 1922–1923 during another tour to South America, Catt offered considerable moral support to the yet-to-be-enfranchised women of that continent.

In 1913–1914 Catt led a high-profile suffrage campaign in New York state, working for a state referendum on votes for women, and a year later she resumed the presidency of NAWSA. In 1915 she set about reorganizing and galvanizing the suffrage movement, which had in her absence become polarized between Alice Paul's militants in the Congressional Union, who sought suffrage at the federal level, and the moderates. Catt's so-called winning plan attempted to combine campaigns at both the federal and state levels. She believed that state campaigns were more likely to succeed in the political climate of the 1910s. In 1915 she also headed an ambitious and vigorous campaign for the vote in New York state, which, despite its failure, provided Catt with valuable organizational experience preparatory to the final onslaught for women's suffrage, launched in 1917.

As a pacifist, Catt had attended the women's peace convention in Washington, D.C., in January 1915 at which the Woman's Peace Party had been founded. The entry of the United States into the war in 1917 prompted Catt to make a pragmatic compromise of her beliefs and lend her support to the war effort. Like suffragists in other countries, such as Christabel and Sylvia Pankhurst, Catt saw the war as offering a prime opportunity for women to prove their worthiness of the vote, with women's suffrage following as a natural democratic progression of the ideals of the wartime allies. She served on the Woman's Committee of the Council of National Defense during the war while adamantly refusing to succumb to pressure to abandon the suffrage campaign altogether during the war—a fact that precipitated regular attacks on her for being insufficiently patriotic and even accusations of her having communist leanings. At the end of the war she was, however, presented with the prestigious national civilian honor, the Distinguished Service Medal.

Once President Woodrow Wilson's support for a federal amendment had been won, particularly after several American states passed suffrage bills in 1917–1918, Catt had to face a tough fourteen-month battle for final ratification of the Nineteenth Amendment across the remaining states, from June 1919 until the final nail-biting conclusion in the summer of 1920, when Tennessee was the last state to decide the matter. She wrote an account with Nettie R. Shuler, *Woman Suffrage and Politics: The Inner Story of the Suffrage Movement* (1923), and thereafter supported the establishment of a League of Women Voters, based on the 2-million-strong membership of the NAWSA, which continued to lobby for progressive reforms and give women electors impartial information on political candidates in elections. After Catt's death in 1947, the league set up a Carrie Chapman Catt Memorial Foundation in her honor to encourage women's participation in political life through the exercise of their vote.

By the early 1920s, having already devoted forty years to women's suffrage, Catt felt that the time had come to pass the torch of women's work on to a new generation of women activists, preferring to devote her time instead to the peace movement and disarmament, although she remained honorary president of NAWSA until her death. In 1924, with the backing of several national women's organizations, Catt began planning the Conference on the Cause and Cure of War. This was held the following year in Washington, where Catt was a founding member and was elected chair of the Committee for the Cause and Cure of War (in which she remained active till 1932). As an amalgam of eleven national women's organizations, the committee was dedicated to peace and the establishment of an international body to promote it. Catt also endorsed the work for peace mediation and the peaceful coexistence of member states of the League of Nations and its successor the United Nations, where she was influential in securing the appointments of women to important commissions. In 1935 she published *Why Wars Must Cease.*

During the 1930s Catt became aware, through her European contacts in the IWSA, of the persecution of the Jews in Hitler's Germany. Some of her Jewish colleagues, such as Rosa Manus (who died in Auschwitz) and Rosika Schwimmer (who fled to the United States), had appealed to Catt to help Jewish refugees, which she did by founding the Protest Committee of Non-Jewish Women against the Persecution of Jews in Germany, work for which in 1933 she received the American Hebrew Medal. She would continue her work for Jewish refugees until her death.

Catt's commitment to playing the role of conciliator within the women's suffrage movement and her instincts as a subtle political strategist were at the root of her reluctance to prejudice unity by resorting to militancy in a belief that "organization is the only assurance of final triumph of any cause" (Van Voris 1987, vii). She refused to kowtow to more radical activists who might alienate male liberal support (although in the end she did concede that their direct action had helped the cause); nor did she openly criticize the racism and elitism of right-wing elements within NAWSA in the South. These decisions have led to criticism of her political leadership, in particular her willingness to accept partial suffrage at the state level rather than holding out for full federal suffrage alone. Her backing for U.S. entry into World War I while herself remaining an avowed pacifist has also come under fire. Nevertheless, Catt's commitment to the overriding objective of the cause above personal political differences and prejudices could not have allowed her to adopt a different position. As a persuasive speaker and revered international figure, she lent a dignity to the suffrage movement both at home and abroad and ensured her own immortality as one of its major icons alongside Susan B. Anthony and Elizabeth Cady Stanton.

Catt's childhood home in Charles City, Iowa, is now on the National Register of Historic Places and is currently being restored as the Carrie Chapman Catt Museum. Information on the museum and on Catt's life and works can be found on its website at http://www.catt.org/.

See also Anthony, Susan B.; Jacobs, Aletta; Manus, Rosa; Pankhurst, Christabel; Pankhurst, (Estelle) Sylvia; Paul, Alice; Schwimmer, Rosika.

References and Further Reading
Bolt, Christine. 1995. *Feminist Ferment: The Woman Question in the USA and Britain 1870–1940*. London: University College of London Press.
Flexner, Eleanor. 1975 [1959]. *A Century of Struggle: The Woman's Rights Movement in the United States*. Rev. ed. Cambridge, MA: Belknap Press of Harvard University Press.
Fowler, Robert Booth. 1986. *Carrie Catt: Feminist Politician*. Boston: Northeastern University Press.
Jacobs, Aletta. 1996. *Memories: My Life as an International Leader in Health, Suffrage, and Peace*. New York: Feminist Press.
Kraditor, Aileen. 1981 [1965]. *The Ideas of the Woman Suffrage Movement 1890–1920*. Reprint, New York: W. W. Norton.
O'Neill, William L. 1989. *Feminism in America: A History*. 2d ed. New Brunswick, NJ: Transaction.
Peck, Mary Gray. 1944. *Carrie Chapman Catt: A Biography*. New York: H. W. Wilson.
Rupp, Leila J. 1997. *Worlds of Women: The Making of an International Women's Movement*. Princeton: Princeton University Press.
Van Voris, Jacqueline. 1987. *Carrie Chapman Catt: A Public Life*. New York: Feminist Press.
Weatherford, Doris. 1998. *A History of the American Suffragist Movement*. Santa Barbara, CA: ABC-CLIO.

Cauer, Minna
(1841–1922)
Germany

Minna Cauer was an energetic woman of many talents: feminist, publisher, educator, and suffragist. Through her leadership of the Women's Welfare Association she enlisted German women in a wide range of social work and represented the interests of working women as leader of the Commercial Union of Female Salaried Employees, founded in 1889. As a radical, she felt let down by male liberal and social democratic politicians because of the insufficient emphasis they gave to women's suffrage and from 1902 devoted her energies to the fight for the vote within the women's movement.

Born in Freyenstein (Osprignitz), the daughter of a pastor, Cauer married the left-wing educator August Latzel in 1862. Widowed in 1866, she trained as a teacher and worked in Paris for a year, before marrying school inspector Eduard Cauer, a fellow advocate of women's higher education, in 1869. The couple moved to Berlin.

Widowed again in 1881, Cauer resumed work as a teacher and began studying women's history. In 1889 she joined with Helene Lange and medical pioneer Franziska Tiburtius in enlisting support for the establishment of the Realkurse girls' high school in Berlin, which opened in October

1889 with 214 students, offering a two-year course in mathematics, science, history, economics, Latin, and modern languages.

As a founding member, in 1888, and later president of the Women's Welfare Association, Cauer was a firm believer that women should work for their own emancipation. She wanted women's education to be valued as a means of growth and self-improvement, not just in terms of making better mothers. She endorsed the association's provision of education and vocational training opportunities for women as well as its encouragement of their participation in charity and social work, such as running homes for the blind and day nurseries, in the belief that female activism in social welfare and reform played a crucial role in nation building. In 1889 Cauer established one of the first nonpolitical women's trade unions when she formed the Commercial Union of Female Salaried Employees, which by the time of her death would represent over 100,000 female members in 400 local branches.

In the 1890s Cauer took on a range of roles that sought to bring women into social activism. In 1893 she was cofounder of the Girls' and Women's Groups for Social Assistance Work and an organizer of the German delegation to the World's Fair in Chicago. She presided over the International Congress of Women's Work and Women's Endeavors in Berlin in 1896, the first international conference of women to be staged in Germany, attended by 1,700 delegates from Europe and the United States. In 1894, in a major step forward for the German women's movement, Cauer, Anita Augspurg, and Marie Stritt established the Federation of German Women's Associations (FGWA) to unite German women's groups in a joint campaign for improvements to women's legal, economic, and social position; to strive for suffrage and changes to those elements of the civil code that favored men; and to abolish state-regulated prostitution. The reinvigorated women's movement was well served by Cauer's establishment of, with Lily Braun, and her editorship of, a new journal, the *Women's Movement* (1895-1919).

But Cauer soon became frustrated at the domination of the movement by moderates and with Augspurg founded the Union of Progressive Women's Associations in 1898, with a more radical program on women's rights, serving as its president until 1907. Although Cauer remained

Minna Cauer (German Heritage Foundation)

in the FGWA, the Women's Welfare Association and the Commercial Union of Female Salaried Employees, both of which she supported, also joined the union.

Cauer had long been an advocate of women's suffrage, but it was not until 1902 that the suffrage movement in Germany finally gained headway with the backing of the FGWA. As cofounder that year of the German Union for Women's Suffrage with Anita Augspurg, Lida Gustava Heymann, and Marie Stritt, Cauer combined lobbying for the vote with a moral crusade that sought to regenerate society under the guiding influence of women. In 1903 the union affiliated itself with the FGWA. Operating from Hamburg, where the law of association permitted women to be politically active (elsewhere in Germany, women's political activities were illegal until 1908), the union campaigned strenuously for the abolition of state-regulated prostitution, with Cauer being fined for defying the ban on speaking at public meetings. In an attempt to further challenge the government on female suffrage, she tried in 1906 to have herself added to the electoral roll in Berlin by challenging ambiguities in the law that referred to those eligible to vote as "persons"—that is, not specifying men only.

By 1908 Cauer had become disenchanted with attempts by the union to gain support for suffrage from male politicians in the Liberal People's Party, which after long prevarication ultimately refused to add votes for women to its program. She therefore founded a more radical group, the Prussian Union for Women's Suffrage, in Berlin. Becoming increasingly militant as the mainstream of the suffrage movement fragmented, she eventually joined the Democratic Alliance, a left-liberal splinter group. When in 1912 leaders of the suffrage union were poised to amend their demands to women's suffrage rather than universal suffrage, Cauer resigned. In 1914 she joined other radicals who had established a new German Women's Suffrage League. But with three different groups now in conflict with each other, the women's suffrage movement in Germany disintegrated on the eve of World War I.

Having worked with Bertha von Suttner in the German Peace Society in 1892, Cauer turned to pacifist activities during the war and supported international women's groups such as the International Council of Women and the International Committee of Women for Permanent Peace. After World War I Cauer retired from her various official posts but continued to use much of her own money to fund and edit the journal *Women's Movement* until 1919. She worked for greater international understanding, collaborating with Augspurg and Heymann on the pacifist journal *Woman in the State* (1919–1933) and joining them in their support for the establishment of the League of Nations.

See also Augspurg, Anita; Lange, Helene; Stritt, Marie; Suttner, Bertha Félice Sophie von; Tiburtius, Franziska.

References and Further Reading
Evans, Richard. 1973. *The Feminist Movement in Germany 1894–1933*. London: Sage.
Sklar, Kathryn Kish. 1998. *Social Justice Feminists in the United States and Germany: A Dialogue in Documents 1885–1933*. Ithaca: Cornell University Press.

Chattopadhyaya, Kamaladevi
(1903–1990)
India

Born into a wealthy, cultured family in Mangalore, India, the socialist and reformer Kamaladevi Chattopadhyaya retained a strong interest in the promotion of Indian arts and culture throughout her life. She did so in her capacity as chair of the All-India Handicrafts Board, under whose auspices she encouraged cottage industries that supported poor women throughout the country.

Chattopadhyaya grew up under the feminist, Westernized influences of her parents. Her mother, herself an admirer of Pandita Ramabai and Annie Besant, fostered in Chattopadhyaya a love of Indian arts and crafts at a time when social conventions restricted women's pursuit of such activities. Despite entering an arranged marriage, according to custom, and being widowed while very young, Chattopadhyaya continued her education in Madras and later at the London School of Economics. In 1920 she defied tradition by getting remarried against caste to Harindranath Chattopadhyaya, the brother of the leading Indian poet and feminist Sarojini Naidu. Her husband was also a poet and dramatist. Although they later divorced (1933), the couple worked together in producing and performing plays and set up branches of the Theatre Centre of India all over the country. Chattopadhyaya later served as its president.

Chattopadhyaya's interest in women's education and emancipation was fostered by her meeting with Margaret Cousins at school in Madras. Chattopadhyaya would later take on voluntary social work with Cousins, her acknowledged "guru," under the auspices of the All-India Women's Conference (AIWC). She also developed a close friendship with Annie Besant after her mother, who was a devoted admirer of the English Theosophist and reformer, donated her mansion in Mangalore to her for use as a girls' school. Inevitably, as a reformer and patriot Chattopadhyaya came under the influence of Mahatma Gandhi and Jawaharlalal Nehru and joined the Indian nationalist movement.

In 1926 Chattopadhyaya became the first woman to stand for election to government as a candidate for South Kanara. Despite vigorous canvassing on her behalf from feminists such as Margaret Cousins, the campaign failed, but it prompted other women to take up the challenge of running for public office. The following year, Chattopadhyaya won a seat in the legislative assembly.

In the 1920s Chattopadhyaya also took an active part in Gandhi's *satyagraha* (civil disobedience) movement, making speeches and picketing foreign shops at a time when Indians were boycotting imported goods in favor of *swadeshi* (indigenous) goods. In April 1930, she was one of the first to break the salt law in Bombay in open defiance of the British government's monopoly on the industry, and she witnessed with pride the strength of the female, nonviolent support for the movement: "thousands of women strode down to the sea like proud warriors. But instead of weapons, they bore pitchers of clay, brass and copper; and, instead of uniforms, the simple cotton saris of village India. One watched them fascinated and awestruck. How had they broken their age-old shell of social seclusion and burst into this fierce light of open warfare? What had stirred their ancient quietude and turned them into militant rebels? Undoubtedly the women turned this struggle into a beautiful epic" (Nanda 1976, 25).

When she was arrested and put on trial for her involvement in the salt campaign, Chattopadhyaya even attempted to enlist the judge in the movement. After her imprisonment ended, she began setting up women's branches of the Hindustani cooperative organization, the Seva Dal, which taught young women Indian history and geography, as well as training them in domestic hygiene, child care, sewing, and spinning. Arrested again in 1932, Chattopadhyaya served a year in prison, but her sentence only reinforced her increasingly radical position on Indian independence. In 1934 she joined the Congress Socialist Party and during the 1930s traveled extensively abroad, becoming known as a leading spokesperson on Indian independence. She continued her association with the AIWC, serving as its president in 1944–1945. In 1946 Jawaharlal Nehru invited her to serve as a member of the Congress Party's Working Committee.

In 1948, in the wake of violence and social upheaval after the partition of India, Chattopadhyaya set up the Indian Cooperative Union (ICU) to help the flood of Hindu refugees entering India after the creation of a separate state for Muslims—Pakistan. The union aided in the development of the city of Faridabad in northwestern India as a resettlement center for the accommodation of many thousands of these refugees and helped them set up new light industries there. With Indian independence achieved, her attention returned to her early interest in Indian

arts and crafts, and she helped set up hand loom cooperatives as a way of both promoting indigenous crafts and creating employment for many refugees. In 1952 she became chair of the All-India Handicrafts Board. The Cottage Industries Emporium that she founded also provided a valuable sales outlet for the goods produced in the ICU's many cooperatives. In 1966 Chattopadhyaya was awarded the Ramón Magsaysay Award for Community Leadership.

See also Besant, Annie; Cousins, Margaret; Ramabai, Pandita Saraswati.

References and Further Reading

Bhushan, Jamila Brij. 1976. *Kamaladevi Chattopadhyaya: Portrait of a Rebel.* New Delhi: Abhinav.

Chattopadhyaya, Kamala Devi [sic]. 1937. *The Awakening of Indian Women.* Madras: Everyman's Press.

———. 1983. *Indian Women's Battle for Freedom.* New Delhi: Abhinav.

Nanda, B. R., ed. 1976. *Indian Women: From Purdah to Modernity.* New Delhi: Vikas.

Chaudharani, Saraladevi
(1872–1945)
India

The niece of the Indian poet and mystic Rabindranath Tagore, Chaudharani was the daughter of Swarnakumari Devi, a leading activist for the *swadeshi* (indigenous) and Indian nationalist movements. A Brahmin feminist and Theosophist, as a young woman she had been inspired by the resurgence in Indian cultural pride stimulated by her uncle and herself developed gifts in music and poetry.

Chaudharani studied at home with private tutors before attending the Bethune College, where she took her B.A. in English in 1890. She continued her education at home, learning Sanskrit, Persian, and French, and resisted the traditional path of early marriage. Instead, she became a teacher at the maharani's school in Mysore, the beginning of a lifetime commitment to education.

From 1897 to 1899 she took over the editorship of her parents' Bengali journal *Bharti,* in which she called for unity among Hindus and Muslims. Beginning in the 1900s, she was active in the *swadeshi* movement, which promoted the purchase of indigenous Indian goods. She also helped to organize agricultural projects in the provinces, where many of the impressionable young people involved fell under the influence of the Indian nationalist movement.

In 1905 Chaudharani finally married, but only in order to fulfill her mother's last wish. Her husband, Rambhuj Dutt, was a well-known nationalist leader, and she transferred her activities from Bengal to his native state of the Punjab. She toured the Punjab giving speeches and writing patriotic songs and eventually found herself under surveillance by the British government.

Chaudharani was one of the first Indian women to call for their own, separate political association rather than continue cooperating with male-dominated organizations. In 1910 she achieved her objective when the Great Circle of Indian Women (Bharat Stri Maha Mandal) was founded in Allahabad. As its secretary, Chaudharani organized its proselytizing activities among Indian women of all castes and creeds across the subcontinent. In cases where women could not or would not leave purdah (seclusion) in order to attend classes, members of organizations taught them in their own homes. In particular, Chaudharani encouraged physical exercise for women living lives of forced indolence.

During the 1917 visit of British secretary of state for India Edwin Montagu on a fact-finding mission on Indian self-government, Chaudharani asked that the Great Circle of Women be allowed to meet him to discuss the extension of women's education in India, but Montagu would only accept a deputation to discuss political demands. At the thirty-third session of the Indian National Congress in Delhi in 1918, Chaudharani spoke in support of the resolution to give women the vote, taking a more radical position than many of her contemporaries by refusing to acknowledge a degree of female subservience to the male political cause and by insisting that women were men's physical and intellectual equals. The next year she worked for Mahatma Gandhi's political campaign and took part in Margaret Cousins's drive to win the vote for Indian women. In 1930 she opened a girls' school, the Shri Shiksha Sadan, in Calcutta. In 1935, discouraged by the lack of political progress in India, Chaudharani became a spiritualist; during her later years she turned increasingly to pacifism.

See also Cousins, Margaret.

There is, as yet, no single source on Chaudharani. Biographical information is scattered and fragmentary.

Chertkoff de Repetto, Fenia
(1869–1928)
Argentina

The Argentine socialist and founder of the Feminist Socialist Center Fenia Chertkoff de Repetto came from an immigrant Russian-Jewish family that had fled czarist pogroms and settled in Argentina in 1895. Together with her sisters Adela and Mariana, Chertkoff became a leading figure in the Argentine socialist movement: Mariana became the first wife of the president, Juan B. Justo (his second wife was Alicia Moreau de Justo), and Adela married socialist theorist Adolfo Dickman.

When Fenia arrived in Argentina, she was already a widow with a small child (her socialist husband, Gabriel Gukovsky, had died in Europe). She took refuge at an agricultural colony at Santa Clara established by émigré eastern European Jews. There she founded a primary school and put together a library. In 1897–1898 on a trip back to Europe to visit her sister-in-law in Switzerland, she met other European feminists and took the opportunity to study the pioneering methods of the German educator Friedrich Froebel, who had founded kindergarten education.

On her return to Argentina, Chertkoff married fellow socialist Nicolas Repetto. Such was her concern about the dangerous, unsavory working conditions endured by women that she founded an organization in Buenos Aires to represent their interests, the Women's Labor Union, and volunteered to visit factories. She reported her findings to the Labor Department and made recommendations for labor legislation. She also organized women workers, particularly in the clothing industry, to resist management malpractice and published articles on her trade union work in the leading socialist journals the *Vanguard* and *Protest*.

In 1903 Chertkoff was the only female delegate to the Fifth Congress of the Socialist Party; that August she was appointed a delegate to the National Party Council. In 1910 she helped organize the First International Women's Congress in Argentina with her brother-in-law's sister, Sara Justo, and other leading Argentine feminists such as Julieta Lanteri-Renshaw, Elvira Rawson de Dellepiane, and Cecilia Grierson. Until 1916, Chertkoff devoted herself to work in Buenos Aires for the Feminist Socialist Center established by Gabriela Laperrière in 1902, and its special welfare programs for women and child workers, introducing child care facilities for working mothers. She was joined in much of her work by her sisters Mariana and Adela. Eventually, Chertkoff was bedridden by illness. She spent the last twenty years of her life as a valetudinarian yet produced many articles and essays on child development, the rights of working women, and feminism.

See also Grierson, Cecilia; Lanteri-Renshaw, Julieta; Laperrière du Coni, Gabriela; Moreau de Justo, Alicia; Rawson de Dellepiane, Elvira.

References and Further Reading

Carlson, Narifran. 1988. *Feminismo! The Woman's Movement in Argentina from Its Beginnings to Eva Perón.* Chicago: Academy Chicago Publications.

Lavrin, Asunción. 1995. *Women, Feminism, and Social Change in Argentina, Chile, and Uruguay 1890–1940.* Lincoln: University of Nebraska Press.

Chew, Ada Nield
(1870–1945)
United Kingdom

In a British suffrage movement dominated by middle-class women, Ada Nield Chew made her mark as an outspoken working woman who went from trade union activist in the north of England to forceful advocate of adult suffrage. For decades, her story and those of other working-class women who played a significant role in the winning of women's suffrage in Britain remained entirely neglected, until groundbreaking research by Jill Liddington and Jill Norris uncovered their stories in the seminal book, *One Hand Tied behind Us* (originally published in 1978).

One of thirteen children, Chew grew up in poverty on a smallholding in north Staffordshire. Her life followed a pattern shared by so many working-class girls of her time: Chew's brief and inadequate schooling was cut short at the age of eleven by the exigencies of having to help look after her many siblings. At the age of seventeen, she began work as a seamstress and

later took a job as a tailoress in a clothing factory in Crewe that specialized in uniforms. Here, her social conscience aroused, she began fighting against bad working conditions and long hours in her industry, publishing a series of letters in the *Crewe Chronicle* in 1894. Chew pointed out the exploitation of such women's labor by factory management and the total lack of public interest in the plight of overworked women such as herself.

In making her criticisms, Chew had to retain her anonymity in order to preserve her job, but she bravely catalogued the injustices suffered by women finishers such as herself, who were paid per garment and had to count themselves lucky if they earned threepence an hour. If they worked a ten-hour day, their weekly wage averaged eight shillings, which was not a living wage. Many such women, as Chew pointed out, had to take on additional work at home in the evenings in order to have enough money to survive and to pay board and lodging to the factory owners. Thousands of them were thus condemned to lives of exhausting drudgery, fifty-two weeks a year, with no hope of a holiday. Although little known for so long, Chew's contribution was historic in being one of the first by a working woman who risked her job to argue publicly—or, as she put it in a 19 May letter to the *Crewe Chronicle,* to "butt her head against the stone wall of public ignorance"—for a living wage for factory girls and to express the faint hope that one day, just possibly, they might see the advent of the eight-hour working day.

After publishing her letters, Chew was invited to join the Crewe branch of the Independent Labour Party, and her letters received a wider audience when they were reprinted in the socialist journal the *Clarion.* She revealed her identity, launched a "Crewe Factory Girl" campaign in support of women in the industry, and began touring the north of England and Scotland in horse-drawn campaign vans funded by the *Clarion,* making a point of visiting workers in remote areas. In 1900 she became a full-time organizer for the Women's Trade Union League and dedicated the next twelve years to tireless campaigning. Continuing her campaign for the Crewe factory girls, she argued that their low wages would not improve while they lacked the political power—the vote—to change things. She believed that it was essential for women to be less dependent economically on men but was not optimistic about galvanizing them for the fight, when so many were weighed down with work as well as their domestic and family responsibilities. Chew did not accept the traditional division of labor between the sexes or the conviction of some reformers that women should receive state benefits to stay at home with the children. Women, she felt, were not always the best people to take care of children, and therefore she was all in favor of the establishment of nurseries and co-operative living and cooking schemes (along the lines of those advocated by Charlotte Perkins Gilman, whom Chew greatly admired) that would enable women to enter the workplace and improve their economic position: "You can not breed a free people from slave mothers, and husband-kept or state-kept women can never know the meaning of liberty" (Yeo 1998, 190).

In the early 1900s Chew had supported full adult suffrage, believing that the introduction of a limited form of suffrage for women would benefit only women of the middle and upper classes, leaving working women without suffrage and reducing the political power of many working men. She entered into a fierce debate with Christabel Pankhurst on the subject when a limited suffrage bill was introduced in Parliament but came to shift her position on women's suffrage, reducing her trade union activities by 1910 and becoming a radical suffragist and organizer for the National Union of Women's Suffrage Societies (NUWSS) from 1911 to 1914. From 1912 to 1914, she and Selina Cooper were familiar campaigners for the NUWSS and Independent Labour Party in by-elections. During World War I, Chew was also active in the Manchester branch of the International Committee of Women for Permanent Peace (later the Women's International League for Peace and Freedom). She wrote suffrage articles for women's rights publications such as the *Freewoman,* the *Englishwoman,* and the *Common Cause;* her daughter Doris published many of these, along with an autobiographical sketch in 1982.

See also Cooper, Selina; Gilman, Charlotte Perkins; Pankhurst, Christabel.

References and Further Reading

Banks, Olive, ed. 1985, 1990. *The Biographical Dictionary of British Feminists,* vol. 1, *1800–1930;* vol. 2, *1900–1945.* Brighton: Harvester Wheatsheaf.
Bellamy, Joyce M., and John Saville. 1982. *Dictionary of Labour Biography.* London: Macmillan.
Chew, Doris Nield. 1982. *Ada Nield Chew: The Life and Writings of a Working Woman.* London: Virago.
Crawford, Elizabeth. 1999. *The Women's Suffrage Movement, 1866–1928: A Reference Guide.* London: University College of London Press.
Liddington, Jill, and Jill Norris. 2000 [1978]. *One Hand Tied behind Us.* Rev. ed. London: Virago.
Yeo, Eileen. 1998. *Radical Femininity: Women's Self-Representation in the Public Sphere.* Manchester: Manchester University Press.

Child, Lydia Maria
(1802–1880)
United States

As an advocate of the emancipation of women and slaves and a defender of the rights of Native Americans, Lydia Maria Child abandoned a successful literary career for the challenges and controversies of a life devoted to the support of minority rights. She produced several important tracts in which she explored the social issues of her day and, through her voluminous correspondence with abolitionists in England, helped to establish closer links between its women's movement and that in the United States.

Born in Medford, Massachusetts, Child was the daughter of a baker noted for his best-selling crackers. She briefly taught school before moving to Maine to live with her brother, Convers, a Unitarian pastor. There she began writing historical novels such as *Hobomok: A Tale of Early Times* (1824), a sympathetic and controversial portrait of Native Americans that depicts a Puritan white woman's love for and eventual marriage to a native Pequot man in Massachusetts. *The Rebels, or Boston before the Revolution* followed in 1825, and *Philothea: A Romance of Classical Greece* was published in 1836. In *A Romance of the Republic* (1837), she dealt with slavery. By the late 1820s, during which time she was also editing the first, and extremely popular, children's monthly journal in the United States, *Juvenile Miscellany* (1826–1834), Child turned to social concerns and in the process courted considerable loss of favor among her readership because of her radical position.

From 1825 to 1828, Child supported herself by running a small private school in Watertown. She began moving in literary circles in Boston, associating with women reformers such as the educator Elizabeth Peabody and becoming drawn to the

Transcendentalist ideas of Margaret Fuller. After her marriage in 1828 to Boston lawyer and reformer David Lee Child, she continued to write to support them financially. As a member of the New England Anti-Slavery Society, her husband encouraged her activism in the abolitionist campaign, and after meeting William Lloyd Garrison in 1831, Child became active in the movement. She embarked on the writing of a major antislavery tract: "An Appeal in Favor of the Class of Americans Called Africans." Published in 1833, it first described the horrors of slavery and its history, condemned racial prejudice in the North, and argued for blacks to be given equal access to education and employment.

Horrified by Child's wide-reaching attack, polite society in Boston turned its back on her. The Boston Athenaeum no longer welcomed her as a member, and her readers cancelled their subscriptions to the *Juvenile Miscellany,* pushing her to bankruptcy. Undaunted, in 1834 Child joined the Boston Female Anti-Slavery Society and published *Anti-slavery Catechism* (1836). Her home was used as a refuge for slaves on the Underground Railroad, and in 1840 she was elected to the executive committee of the American Anti-Slavery Society. During 1841–1844, she edited the society's weekly New York journal, the *National Anti-Slavery Standard,* producing numerous editorials on freedom of worship, capital punishment, slavery, and women's rights.

In 1829, with an eye to a good financial return in the light of her husband's unsuccessful utopian business ventures, Child had published a book on domestic skills and economic household management, *The Frugal Housewife* (which predated the better-known 1841 *Treatise on Domestic Economy* by Catharine Beecher), which was so successful that it ran to twenty-one editions in ten years. In 1837 Child again found herself having to deal with a financial crisis when her husband's scheme for manufacturing beet sugar failed. Over the next twelve years, the couple spent much time apart, with the irredeemably improvident David Lee Child taking a succession of jobs, including working for a while in Washington, D.C., as a journalist.

In 1841 Child moved to New York, where she lived with Quaker friends and took up journalism for the *Boston Courier* (her articles, later collected as the two-volume *Letters from New York* and published in 1843–1845, proved extremely

Lydia Maria Child (Library of Congress)

popular). She continued to work on the *Standard,* but after a disagreement with William Lloyd Garrison, the abolitionist movement's leader, she gave up her editorial work and returned to writing. In 1855, she reunited with her husband; the couple finally settled in Wayland, near Boston, where Child had inherited her father's farm. She turned to religious interests and eventually spiritualism, the product of which was an ambitious three-volume work, *The Progress of Religious Ideas, through Successive Ages,* in 1855. She attracted renewed public attention when in 1859 the *New York Times* revealed that she had written to the abolitionist leader John Brown, volunteering to nurse him in prison after he had been wounded at the raid on Harpers Ferry. Their correspondence, although provoking criticism of Child, also provided excellent material for the abolitionist cause and was published as a pamphlet in 1860 as "Correspondence between Lydia Maria Child and Governor Wise and Mrs. Mason of Virginia."

Child produced several more abolitionist tracts during the early 1860s and in 1861 edited *Incidents in the Life of a Slave Girl* by former slave Harriet Jacobs. After the slaves were freed at the end of the Civil War, she edited *The Freedmen's Book* (1865), a self-help manual for newly liberated slaves. Having first written about the indigenous peoples of the United States in her 1820s work, *The First Settlers of New England,* she returned to the subject in her 1868 book, *An Appeal for the Indians.*

Throughout her life, Child was a strong believer in peace and nonresistance; was active in the Massachusetts Peace Society, the League of Universal Brotherhood, and the New England Non-Resistance Society; and published articles in the pacifist journals *Advocate of Peace* and *Universal Brotherhood.* Although she never joined any women's organizations, she entered into debates of the issues of her time and lent her support to the movements for moral reform and women's emancipation through her writings. In stories collected as *Fact and Fiction* (1846), she appealed for greater compassion toward women who had fallen into prostitution, exposing the double moral standard that condemned women for the loss of their virtue while never questioning the sexual behavior of men. In her 1835 work, *The History of the Condition of Women in Various Ages and Nations,* Child argued for women's ability to be the equal of men in the workplace, a fact that she had proved only too well in her own married life by frequently being the primary breadwinner.

See also Beecher, Catharine Esther; Fuller, (Sarah) Margaret; Peabody, Elizabeth.

References and Further Reading
Clifford, Deborah Pinkman. 1992. *Crusader for Freedom: A Life of Lydia Maria Child.* Boston: Beacon Press.
Hersch, Blanche G. 1978. *Slavery of Sex: Feminist Abolitionists in America.* Urbana: University of Illinois Press.
Holland, P. G., M. Meltzer, and F. Krasno, eds. 1982. *Lydia Maria Child: Selected Letters 1817–1880.* Amherst: University of Massachusetts Press.
Karcher, Karen L. 1995. *The First Woman in the Republic: A Cultural Biography of Lydia Maria Child.* Durham, NC: Duke University Press.
Leach, William. 1981. *True Love and Perfect Union: The Feminist Reform of Sex and Society.* London: Routledge and Kegan Paul.
Melder, Keith E. 1977. *The Beginnings of Sisterhood: The American Woman's Rights Movement, 1800–1850.* New York: Schocken.
Meltzer, Milton. 1965. *Tongue of Flame: The Life of Lydia Maria Child.* New York: Crowell.
Mills, Bruce. 1994. *Cultural Reformations: Lydia Maria Child and the Literature of Reform.* Athens: University of Georgia Press.
Osborne, William S. 1980. *Lydia Maria Child.* Boston: Twayne.
Yellen, Jean Fagan. 1989. *Women and Sisters: The Antislavery Feminists in American Culture.* New Haven: Yale University Press.

Chisholm, Caroline
(1808–1877)
United Kingdom/Australia

A legendary pioneer of emigration to Australia, first by women and then by whole families, Caroline Chisholm was popularly known as "the emigrant's friend" for her work in helping destitute new arrivals and in setting up a scheme to provide loans for their sea passage. Born in Wootton, Northamptonshire, in England, Chisholm was the daughter of a well-off yeoman farmer. Her background was evangelical, but after her marriage to Scotsman Archibald Chisholm in 1830, she converted to Roman Catholicism. In 1832 she accompanied him to Madras, India, where he was posted as a captain in the army of the East India Company. Having insisted upon her marriage that she should be allowed to continue with charitable work, on her arrival in India, Chisholm soon became alarmed at the poor living conditions of soldiers' families in Madras. She set up a school for their children and orphans, which became known as the Female School of Industry for the Daughters of European Soldiers.

In September 1838, suffering the debilitating effects of the Indian climate on their health, the Chisholms went on leave to Australia, settling at Windsor, New South Wales, where Chisholm remained with their three sons after her husband returned to duty in India in 1840. By this time, her compassion had been aroused for the many impoverished and destitute immigrant women she saw in the port of Sydney, which at that time was still very much a place of convicts. Chisholm set about meeting every immigrant ship that arrived there. Such was her concern for the welfare of the destitute immigrant women, many of whom had been forced into prostitution, that Chisholm often took them into her own home. In 1841 she approached the New South Wales legislature and lobbied Governor George Gipps to provide premises for her to take up work with new arrivals in Sydney. In response, officials provided a filthy, rat-infested, disused immigrants' barracks, which was refurbished as the Female Immigrants' Home, able to accommodate ninety-six women.

Chisholm often interviewed new arrivals, drawing on their stories in pamphlets she published to promote her work, such as "Female Immigration, Considered in a Brief Account of the Sydney Immigrants' Home" (1842)—the first tract published by a woman in Australia. Over the next five years she helped many new arrivals find jobs by setting up a free employment agency in Sydney. She even escorted many of them on horseback into the outback, where they went to take up domestic employment on farms. In addition, she set up other employment agencies, and staging posts, where immigrants could rest on their journey.

Soon Chisholm no longer limited herself to working with women but assisted all unemployed immigrants arriving in Sydney, including families, believing that by helping them disperse from the city to take up leases of land or jobs on farms in the interior, she would help resolve the acute accommodation problems in the city. During the 1840s, it is estimated that Chisholm helped around 11,000 women and children, and by the middle of the decade, her original scheme had broadened into a program promoting family colonization in Australia.

In 1846 Chisholm decided to return to the United Kingdom with her husband, who had now retired from the army, to promote the scheme. Once there, she raised funds and lobbied influential figures such Home Secretary Earl Grey and Sir James Stephen, permanent secretary at the Colonial Office, for government financial support for the migration of whole families to Australia; she also set out to encourage small farmers to emigrate. Chisholm argued that the authorities should provide free passage to the dependents of transported convicts at the end of their term, so that they could settle with them in Australia. From a moral and social viewpoint, she also sought to address the demographic problem created in Australia by a lack of women, whose greater presence, she felt, would have a reformist effect on the rough and ready lifestyle of male emigrants. Chisholm's specialist knowledge of life in Australia soon made her an important source

of information to prospective investors and migrants to the country. Even the government consulted her in April 1847, when she was asked to give evidence to the House of Lords Committee on the Execution of the Criminal Laws.

The next important step for Chisholm was to establish a Family Colonization Loan Society, founded in 1849 and underwritten by philanthropist Angela Burdett-Coutts's family bank, under which loans were repaid by migrants in small installments at no interest. In 1852 its funds were greatly enlarged by an injection of £10,000 from the New South Wales government. Meanwhile, Chisholm had continued to publicize her work, remaining critical of the inadequacies of existing government emigration schemes in "Emigration and Transportation Relatively Considered" (1847) and "The ABC of Colonisation" (1850). By 1850 she had gathered around her a circle of rich and influential supporters, such as Charles Dickens, Burdett-Coutts, and Harriet Martineau, who backed her newly founded society. Dickens in particular promoted her work during 1851–1852 in his journal *Household Words,* and disseminated the idea of emigration in *David Copperfield* (serialized 1849–1850), in which the improvident Mr. Micawber finally seeks an escape from perennial debt by emigrating with his family to Australia. Less flattering was his parody of Chisholm herself as the philanthropist Mrs. Jellyby in *Bleak House* (serialized 1852–1853). Although he was deeply impressed with Chisholm herself, on visiting her home Dickens had noted that she was so caught up in her philanthropic concerns that she neglected her own children (she had nine eventually): "I dream of Mrs. Chisholm and her housekeeping," he wrote to Burdett-Coutts in February 1850. "The dirty faces of her children are my continual companions" (Ackroyd 1990, 586).

In 1853 such was the demand for information on Australia that Chisholm published *The Emigrants' Guide to Australia* to help new emigrants in settling there, but the discovery of gold in the state of Victoria a year later did much in itself to encourage a flood of new emigrants. The gold rush created yet more destitution in Australia, especially for those living in primitive camp conditions in the goldfields. In 1854 Chisholm returned to Australia and carried on her work for emigrants. Although she had become something of a celebrity, both in England and in Australia, she lived in straitened circumstances. Well-wishers helped her set up in business, and she continued to make public speeches on emigration and land reform, until she was forced by illness to move to Kyneton in 1857. Still in financial difficulty, she established a small girls' school in 1862. In 1866 she and her husband returned to the United Kingdom, where they were given a government pension of £100 a year. Chisholm, reluctant always to accept financial reward for her work, lived out her days in poverty and obscurity, first in Liverpool and then in London, lending her support to the growing movement for women's suffrage. In Australia she was honored with depiction on its five-dollar note.

See also Burdett-Coutts, Angela; Martineau, Harriet.

References and Further Reading
Ackroyd, Peter. 1990. *Dickens.* London: Sinclair Stevenson.
Bogle, Joanna. 1993. *Caroline Chisholm: The Emigrant's Friend.* Leominster: Gracewing.
Hoban, Mary. 1973. *Fifty-One Pieces of Wedding Cake: A Biography of Caroline Chisholm.* Kilmore, Victoria: Lowden.
Holcombe, Lee. 1983. *Wives and Property: Reform of the Married Women's Property Law in Nineteenth-Century England.* Toronto: University of Toronto Press.
Kiddle, Margaret L. 1957. *Caroline Chisholm.* Melbourne: Melbourne University Press.
Pratt, Edwin. A. 1897. *Pioneering Women in Victoria's Reign.* London: George Newnes.
Robertson, Priscilla. 1982. *An Experience of Women: Pattern and Change in Nineteenth-Century Europe.* Philadelphia: Temple University Press.

Chisholm, Shirley
(1924–)
United States

The United States' first black congresswoman and revered elder stateswoman Shirley Chisholm is a renowned expert in the education of the young. During her long career in the House of Representatives, she sought to further racial and sexual equality and defended the rights of deprived inner-city ethnic groups to greater work opportunities and welfare programs.

Chisholm was born to West Indian immigrants who had settled in Brooklyn, New York. She grew up in Barbados with her grandmother, while her parents struggled to save the money to

pay for her education. She returned to Brooklyn when she was eleven and, after attending high school, studied for a B.A. in sociology at Brooklyn College (1946) and took an M.A. in elementary education at Columbia University in 1952. Specializing in the education of young children, she worked at the Mount Calvary Child Care Center (1946–1952) and was director of the Friend in Need Day Nursery in Brooklyn. From 1953 to 1959, she directed the Hamilton-Madison Child Care Center in New York before being appointed to the day care division of the New York Bureau of Child Welfare (1959–1964). During 1964–1968, she served in the New York State Assembly, representing the Fifty-fifth District, during which time she lobbied for a minimum wage for domestic workers. She was also active in the National Association for the Advancement of Colored People.

In 1968 Chisholm was the first black woman elected to the U.S. House of Representatives, as a Democrat from the Twelfth District in Brooklyn; she remained in office for seven terms (1968–1983). Soon after her arrival, she rejected what she saw as an unsuitable appointment to the Committee on Agriculture because she wished to serve the inner-city interests of her electorate. She subsequently served on the Veterans' Affairs, Rules, Education, and Labor Committees during her years in office. From the late 1960s, she became a powerful voice in Congress in support of the growing women's rights movement.

In 1969 Chisholm made a landmark address to the House of Representatives on women's rights when she introduced the Equal Rights Amendment. In her speech, she argued against male perceptions of women's sphere of activity and of the limitations on their working capabilities, suggesting that women enjoyed the same inherent leadership skills as men. They too could be efficient administrators, managers in industry, doctors, lawyers, and members of Congress, in her view, yet they held only about 2 percent of such positions. Chisholm also emphasized the double difficulty encountered by black women, for although racial prejudice was being eroded, that against women in the workplace was still firmly entrenched. She argued forcefully against protective legislation for women, urging instead that laws should be introduced to protect all working people from exploitation and provide fair rates of pay for both sexes. (A similar bill on women's equal pay would be introduced in the British Parliament in 1970 by another redoubtable woman politician, Barbara Castle.)

Chisholm was in the forefront of the pioneering women's liberation movement of the 1970s. In August 1970 she took part in the women's strike for equality, to celebrate fifty years since the vote for women was won in the United States. A year later, Chisholm was a founding member, with Gloria Steinem and Betty Friedan, of the National Women's Political Caucus, which had as its objective reform of the legal and political position of women through the introduction of the Equal Rights Amendment.

During her time in Congress, Chisholm criticized militarism and arms development. She campaigned to ban arms sales to South Africa and opposed the Vietnam War, in 1971 supporting a bipartisan coalition that sought to end the draft. She responded continuously to the particular problems of the deprived inner-city areas of Bedford-Stuyvesant and Bushwick in Brooklyn, which she represented, supporting the development of day care centers for the elderly and child care centers for working mothers and lobbying for unemployment insurance to be given to low-paid domestic workers. Her other areas of interest were urban poverty, consumer protection, fair housing, and the problems encountered by Brooklyn's large black and Hispanic communities. She also was critical of the seniority system of the House of Representatives, observing how U.S. politics was dominated by elderly men, and insufficient opportunity was being given to young people to make their way in politics.

Chisholm described her campaigning in her 1970 book, *Unbought and Unbossed* (the book's title had been her electoral campaign slogan), in which she referred to U.S. politics as a "beautiful fraud" whereby politicians offered "gilded promises" in return for votes, and in *The Good Fight* (1973), in which she argued for greater racial harmony. During 1972–1976 she served on the Democratic National Committee, and in 1972, with the endorsement of the president of the National Organization for Women (and despite the reservations of its membership, who didn't think the country was ready for a woman candidate and wouldn't take her seriously), was the first black person—male or female—to stand for nomination for president, but garnered, as her detractors predicted, only about 7 percent of the vote.

In 1983 Chisholm retired from Congress, disillusioned by the cuts in welfare and education programs of the Reagan administration. During her retirement, she maintained the political connections she had made as a member of the House Rules Committee and secretary of the House Democratic Caucus. In 1983 she accepted the Purington Chair at Mount Holyoke College in Massachusetts, remaining there until 1987.

See also Castle, Barbara; Friedan, Betty; Steinem, Gloria.

References and Further Reading

Brownmiller, Susan. 1970. *Shirley Chisholm: A Biography.* Garden City, NY: Doubleday.

Chisholm, Shirley. 1970. *Unbought and Unbossed.* Boston: Houghton Mifflin.

Kaptur, Marcy. 1996. *Women of Congress: A Twentieth-century Odyssey.* Washington, D.C.: Congressional Quarterly.

Marshall, White, Eleanor. 1991. *Women: Catalysts for Change. Interpretative Biographies of Shirley St. Hill Chisholm, Sandra Day O'Connor, and Nancy Landon Kassebaum.* New York: Vantage Press.

Morin, Isobel V. 1994. *Women of the United States Congress.* Minneapolis: Oliver Press.

Pollack, Jill S. 1994. *Shirley Chisholm.* New York: F. Watts.

Clough, Anne Jemima
(1820–1892)
United Kingdom

The educationist and founder of Newnham College at Cambridge University, Anne Jemima Clough was a leading figure in the women's higher education movement in Britain, along with Emily Davies. They were, however, poles apart in the tenor of their different aspirations. Clough wanted a modified form of university examinations that would at least allow women access to university study, albeit at a lower academic level, whereas the unrelenting Davies fiercely defended women's right to study under nothing less than the same rigorous standards as men.

Clough was born in Liverpool, where her father was a wealthy cotton importer. His business took the family to the cotton plantations of Charleston, South Carolina, in 1822, but after the family returned to Liverpool in 1836, her father's business failed, and he died in 1841. During her young life, Clough's brother, the poet Arthur Clough, was an influential figure and the source of much intellectual stimulation. After their father's death, Arthur encouraged Anne to take up teaching in a school for poor children in Liverpool, a post she held until 1846. After obtaining some training at the Home and Colonial School and privately studying educational methods, Clough moved to the Lake District with her mother in 1852, where they set up a school in Ambleside. However, Clough was forced to abandon the venture because of family illnesses. She moved to London in 1861 and lived with her sister.

In the capital, she became friendly with Barbara Bodichon, Emily Davies, and Frances Buss of the Langham Place Circle, who encouraged her desire to establish a college of higher education for women. Although she would be an innovator in her work for women's education, Clough did not involve herself in the mainstream of the women's movement. In 1866 she attended the inaugural meeting of the Schoolmistresses' Association founded by Davies and went back to Liverpool to set up a branch there. She solicited the support of schoolmistresses and enlightened friends such as Josephine Butler and her husband, who were living in Liverpool at the time. That same year, she also published an article in *Macmillan's Magazine* advocating the establishment of a board to regulate the secondary education of girls. As part of her scheme to improve women's education, Clough suggested that a series of university lectures be set up in four neighboring northern towns for the benefit of interested senior schoolgirls, in order to instruct them in new subjects and to provide an opportunity for teachers seeking to be updated in teaching methods. The request was largely fulfilled by Cambridge don James Stuart through what would become known as the University Extension movement. He was assisted by the North of England Council for Promoting the Higher Education of Women, established in 1867 under Butler's presidency and with Clough as secretary (until 1870; she was president in 1873–1874); another founder and leading member of the council would be Elizabeth Wolstenholme-Elmy.

The course of lectures began with a series on astronomy by Stuart in October 1867 and proved hugely successful. Stuart received some 300 written questions in response (it was considered improper for him to enter into question-and-answer sessions in person with the young women who attended the lectures). By 1870 Clough and her colleagues had established twenty-five lecture centers, and eventually these became part of a preparatory scheme that Stuart incorporated into the University Extension scheme for both men and women and that resulted in the admission of the first women to the colleges at Manchester and Newcastle.

Galvanized by the popularity of the lectures, Clough petitioned in 1868 for Cambridge University to devise special local examinations that could be sat by women but that were at a lower academic level than university degrees. When Cambridge acceded to this request in 1870, lectures in science, philosophy, history, and economics were attended by eighty women. Soon women from outside the area were clamoring to attend, and in the summer of 1871 the educator Henry Sidgwick, an advocate of reform of the entrance examination system at Cambridge University, purchased a townhouse in Cambridge as a residence for such women, initially attracting five students. Clough was appointed to run it and soon relocated to larger premises known as Merton Hall. There was considerable public suspicion of such a venture and Clough had to ensure that strict standards of propriety were adhered to and that her residents were closely chaperoned.

By 1874, with more and more women students desperate to enter the University Extension scheme, it was decided to build a residence hall specifically for the purpose, and in 1875 Newnham Hall was opened. Suggestions were made that this should be joined with Emily Davies's newly established Girton College, but by this time the two women found themselves in opposition to each other, offering quite different schemes for women's college education. Davies, disdaining the softer option of the Newnham courses and demanding absolute academic parity for women with men in order to prove they were their intellectual equals, fought hard against what she saw as the undermining effects of Clough's University Extension scheme. The pragmatist Clough accepted specially tailored courses for women students that were less academically rigorous than those for male students, but Davies insisted that her students should take on the Greek and Tripos examinations and the rigors of mathematics and classics. In 1880 Newnham Hall became a college at Cambridge with Clough as first principal. She held that position until her death, during which time she was noted for her devotion to and pastoral care of her students, similar to a mother hen who worried "over their health, diet, hours of sleep and exposure to draughts" (Perkin 1993, 43). The extension courses attended by her residents produced many excellent teachers through the less academically challenging local examinations, but as Christine Bolt (1993) points out, the "animosity" between Clough and Davies, with her purist approach at Girton College, continued (162).

See also Bodichon, Barbara; Buss, Frances; Butler, Josephine; Davies, (Sarah) Emily; Wolstenholme-Elmy, Elizabeth.

References and Further Reading

Banks, Olive, ed. 1985, 1990. *The Biographical Dictionary of British Feminists*, vol. 1, *1800–1930*; vol. 2, *1900–1945*. Brighton: Harvester Wheatsheaf.

Bolt, Christine. 1993. *The Women's Movements in the United States and Britain from the 1790s to the 1920s*. London: Harvester Wheatsheaf.

Clough, Blanche A. 1903. *Memoir of Annie Jemima Clough, First Principal of Newnham College*. 2d ed. London: Edward Arnold.

Hamilton, M. A. 1936. *Newnham: An Informal Biography*. London: Faber and Faber.

McWilliams-Tullberg, Rita. 1975. *Women at Cambridge: A Men's University—Though of a Mixed Type*. London: Gollancz.

Perkin, Joan. 1993. *Victorian Women*. London: John Murray.

Rothblatt, Sheldon. 1968. *The Revolution of the Dons: Cambridge and Society in Victorian England*. London: Faber and Faber.

Simey, Margaret B. 1951. *Charitable Effort in Liverpool in the Nineteenth Century*. Liverpool: Liverpool University Press.

Strachey, Ray. 1978 [1928]. *The Cause: A Brief History of the Women's Movement*. Reprint, London: Virago.

Stuart, James. 1911. *Reminiscences*. Printed privately.

Cobbe, Frances Power
(1822–1904)
Ireland/United Kingdom

The Anglo-Irish feminist and social reformer, who was also a founder of the antivivisection movement in Britain, retained a wit and humanity in all her many lucid writings on moral and philosophical topics and the rights of women.

Despite the fact that she was never a militant campaigner and never married, she was one of the first women to discuss the controversial issues of sexual exploitation and physical abuse of wives by husbands.

Born into a landowning family in Newbridge near Dublin, Cobbe was educated, as fitted her station, at home by governesses and for two years at a private girls' school in Brighton. She developed wide and eclectic interests at an early age, studying Greek, history, astronomy, geometry and the sciences as well as German philosophy. As a young woman during the Irish potato famine of 1845–1846, Cobbe helped her father set up schools for local tenants and teach reading and writing to their children. But she felt frustratingly constrained by the evangelical Protestant milieu in which she was raised. Having been forced by illness to spend much time inactive, she read a great deal and discovered the philosophy of Immanuel Kant. After suffering a crisis in her religious views, she rejected orthodox Christian teaching and adopted theism, through which she developed her own ideas on what was morally right and just. She became a follower of the thinking of the American Unitarian social reformer Theodore Parker, a man ahead of his time whom she met in Italy and whose fourteen volumes of works she later edited. It was Parker's work that further stimulated Cobbe's natural rejection of the patriarchy of organized religion and the traditional idea of a cruel and vengeful God. Instead, in all her writings Cobbe stressed the importance of intuition rather than blind acceptance in matters of religious faith and promoted the idea of a rational and just God possessed of a compassionate, gentle and feminine side.

Despite the objections of her authoritarian father regarding her change in religious faith, Cobbe challenged him further by anonymously publishing "Essay on Intuitive Morals" in 1855. In this book she attempted an exposition of her views on morality, which ironically were later commended by a critic from the *Caledonian Mercury* for being the work of a "lofty masculine mind" (Buck 1992, 428). But eventually, like her contemporary, the Swedish writer and reformer Fredrika Bremer (who had also been confined by a strict father), Cobbe found herself liberated by the death of her father in 1856 and with it from the stultifying role of housekeeper and companion (he had been widowed some years earlier) on

Frances Power Cobbe (Archive Photos)

suited to utilizing her undoubted talents in writing about reform. Cobbe would, however, always acknowledge the impetus she had gained from Carpenter in her pursuit of women's rights and her respect for the progressive reformist movements that Carpenter encouraged in India.

Cobbe therefore moved into other areas of welfare: the reform of workhouses, the care of sick and unemployed young girls, and improvements in the treatment and care of lunatics and the terminally ill. All her life she would remain an active supporter of the Workhouse Visiting Society and the Societies for Friendless Girls. Meanwhile, she was increasingly earning an income from writing—she proved to be a prolific professional journalist—with hundreds of articles published in journals, newspapers, and magazines on a wide range of topics. Much of the money she made was donated to her many social causes, from women's rights to antivivisection.

In the 1860s Cobbe also turned her attention to women's education, suffrage, and the thorny issue of the rights of married women. Along with Emily Davies, who was also tackling this issue at the same time, Cobbe was one of the first feminists to initiate the public debate on women's education. In 1862 she read a paper on the subject at the annual congress of the National Association for the Promotion of Social Science. Subsequently published as "The Education of Women, and How It Would Be Affected by University Examinations," the article advocated the admission of women to university degree courses and argued that they deserved the full benefits of education in order to feel themselves socially useful. It was Cobbe's fundamental belief that women needed to be trained to use their reason over their intuition, in order to open their minds to a wide range of social issues and be able to stand up for their rights. But although her feminist beliefs were deeply held, she disliked the idea of joining in a large and increasingly combative suffrage campaign. Her membership in the London National Society for Women's Suffrage lasted only a few weeks; for its own part, the suffrage movement at times found itself embarrassed by Cobbe's obvious Tory leanings—a legacy, no doubt, of her privileged background as a member of the gentry.

the family estate. Now provided at the age of thirty-four with a small private income of £200 per year, which allowed her the freedom to travel, in 1856–1858 Cobbe toured Europe and the Near East, where her feminist consciousness was further stimulated by her meetings with several extraordinary British and American female expatriates in Italy. *The Cities of the Past* (1864) and *Italics* (1864) were the product of these travels, and she would frequently return to the subject of Italy—her great love—in articles for the British national newspaper, the *Daily News.*

Returning to England, Cobbe threw herself into philanthropic work. In 1858 she joined the reformer Mary Carpenter in her social work in the "ragged schools" (for vagrant children, or those wearing "rags") and reformatories of Bristol and took great inspiration from her example of "teaching, singing and praying with the wild street-boys" (Perkin 1993, 207–208). But confronting juvenile delinquency soon became too trying for Cobbe and the conditions in which Carpenter lived and worked too spartan. Carpenter herself felt that Cobbe would be better

Throughout her long life, Cobbe's campaigning was primarily conducted through the written word in some thirty major published works (although this number excludes the literally hundreds of pamphlets she wrote on many issues). She preferred that her philanthropic works speak for themselves, being of the opinion that such activity should be undertaken by women voluntarily, without the constraints of organized and often dictatorial leadership (as in the case of the suffrage movement); nor, equally, should women be led by men in the fulfillment of good works. She also underlined the fact that unmarried, celibate women such as herself should not think themselves redundant members of society; they had a useful contribution to make, as she argued with ironic wit in her essay "What Shall We Do with Our Old Maids?"

In 1878, having been horrified by the increasing incidence of domestic assaults on women, Cobbe produced her most famous and politically provocative piece of writing, "Wife Torture in England." In it she examined the issue of women's economic dependence on men and their right to separate from violent and abusive husbands. She also savagely attacked the legalized theft of women's own property and inheritance that was effectively sanctioned by existing laws penalizing married women. Cobbe argued not only for the provision of financial maintenance to separated wives but also that they should receive custody of all children under the age of ten. She was one of a group of British feminists who through their writings directly brought about a change in the law, culminating in the introduction of the Married Women's Property Act of 1882 and the Matrimonial Causes Act in 1884.

Cobbe was greatly concerned with women's health and well-being. In "Wife Torture," she not only raised the issue of physical abuse by husbands of their wives but also described with horror the physical harm suffered by women at the hands of unsympathetic, incompetent doctors. Cobbe herself remained resolutely single and, while underlining the immorality of servitude and obedience required of women within marriage, made a point in her writings of contrasting the married state with the happiness of the unmarried, celibate life and the opportunities for freedom and self-fulfillment it provided.

Cobbe never ceased to write eloquently in support of all her social concerns. Her book *The Duties of Women* (1881) was looked upon as one of the more "philosophical" discussions of the subject, with its cogent argument that women must first be emancipated in order to be freed from any constraint in playing their full part in philanthropic and social good works. But it also exposed the underlying conventionality of Cobbe's attitude toward women's moral duty as wives and mothers. Her attitude did not prevent her, however, from emphasizing the right to self-determination of daughters obliged to remain at home and care for sick and elderly parents. For although Cobbe accepted the primary duty of daughters in this regard, she objected to their exclusion from social contact and education as a result of the fulfillment of that duty.

Cobbe's most passionate concern, and one that dominated her later life, was for animal welfare, and this aspect of her reformist activities is now being given the attention it deserves. It was born in part of her inherent mistrust of the medical profession, its misogyny and abuse of women patients (notable in the then current practice of removing women's ovaries in an attempt to control forms of hysteria—as PMT was then perceived). Animals, even more so than women, were, in Cobbe's view, at the mercy of cynical male experimenters. She had espoused anti-vivisection campaigning while in Italy in 1863, where she had staged protests by members of the English community in Florence against the medical experimentation carried out on animals at the Royal Superior Institute by its professor of physiology, Moritz Schiff.

Although Cobbe supported the work in Britain of the Royal Society for the Prevention of Cruelty to Animals (RSPCA) she persistently urged it to take a decisive stand against vivisection—a step it could not and would not take because of its significant backing by members of the medical and scientific professions. In 1875, therefore, she abandoned her long commitment to independent campaigning, having come to the conclusion that "the authority of a formally constituted society was needed to make headway against an evil which daily revealed itself as more formidable" (Cobbe 1894, 586). She founded the Victoria Street Society for the Protection of Animals Liable to Vivisection (popularly known as the Victoria Street Society) in 1875, to which she attracted many eminent personalities, including Lord Shaftesbury—its first president—as well as the tacit support of Queen Victoria (herself a great animal-lover). As honorary secretary

(1876–1884) and later president, Cobbe threw her energies into an exhausting round of writing, speechmaking, and lobbying, turning out dozens of anti-vivisection pamphlets—most notably the moving and eloquent "Light in Dark Places" (1885), which was subsequently translated into French and German by sympathizers in Europe. The rise of the Victoria Street Society prompted the proliferation of other anti-vivisection and animal rights groups, dominated by a female membership that was often as high as 70 percent—and many of these conservative women who would never ordinarily have taken up public campaigning. For Cobbe the huge and compassionate response of women to the suffering of animals was a vindication of her belief that they would be the moral and spiritual regenerators of society—a society that should cease to degrade itself by the deliberate infliction of cruelty on animals.

However, Cobbe's tireless work against vivisection wore down her health and strength and at the end of the 1880s she left London for the rural seclusion of Wales, where she lived with her lifelong, self-effacing friend and companion, Mary Lloyd, until Lloyd's death in 1896. In 1898 after the Victoria Street Society voiced its willingness to compromise on vivisection issues and condone limited experimentation on animals under anesthetic, Cobbe formed the British Union for the Abolition of Vivisection, which was adamant in its total rejection of all forms of experimentation. As a result of her uncompromising stance on this issue, Cobbe fell out with her old friend and campaigner on women's education, Emily Davies, who allowed her science students at Girton College, Cambridge, to witness (although they did not take part in) experiments on living animals.

Among Cobbe's other published works, the most notable are *The Scientific Spirit of the Age* (1888), *Essays on the Pursuits of Women* (1863), *Darwinism in Morals and Other Essays* (1872), and *The Moral Aspects of Vivisection* (1875).

See also Blackwell, Elizabeth; Bremer, Fredrika; Davies, (Sarah) Emily.

References and Further Reading

Buck, Claire, ed. 1992. *Bloomsbury Guide to Women's Literature.* London: Bloomsbury.

Caine, Barbara. 1992. *Victorian Feminists.* Oxford: Oxford University Press.

Cobbe, Frances Power. 1894. *The Life of Frances Power Cobbe.* 2 vols. London: Allen and Unwin.

Cullen, Mary, and Maria Luddy. 1995. *Women: Power and Consciousness in Nineteenth-Century Ireland. Eight Biographical Studies.* Dublin: Attic Press.

French, R. D. 1975. *Anti-Vivisection and Medical Science in Victorian Britain.* Princeton: Princeton University Press.

Perkin, Joan. 1993. *Victorian Women.* London: John Murray.

Spender, Dale. 1982. *Women of Ideas and What Men Have Done to Them.* London: Routledge and Kegan Paul.

Williamson, Lori. 2001. *Power and Protest: Frances Power Cobbe and Victorian Society.* London: Rivers Oram Press.

Collado, María
(1899–?)
Cuba

A poet and reformer, Collado became prominent through her leadership of the Democratic Suffragist Party (DSP), which committed itself not only to working for women's suffrage but also to protecting the rights of working women. Described as a "radical conservative" by K. Lynn Stoner (1991), Collado opposed militancy, and her support for reform was limited to that which preserved the interests of property owners and by association gave tacit support to capitalism. She was criticized by other Cuban socialist feminists because of her privileged background, but in fact Collado made no issue of her class; indeed, it was precisely this bête noire that she felt got in the way of reformist activity.

Born into a wealthy upper-class Havana family, Collado never needed to work but devoted herself to protecting the rights of those who did. She became a leading writer on women's issues in the journal *Protective Review of the Woman* and in the Havana newspaper *The Discussion*. In 1924 she began writing regular columns in the dailies *Cuba* and *The Night*.

Like many of her feminist contemporaries, Collado was active in the Women's Club of Cuba, founded in 1917, and became its director of publicity. In 1924 she was elected vice president of the National Suffragist Party, but she left this organization to found the less radical Democratic Suffragist Party, which favored cooperating with the government of President Gerardo Machado y Morales. When Machado failed to implement his 1925 promise to give the vote to women, the DSP lost popular support, and Collado was criticized for her conservatism. Nevertheless, in 1929 Collado founded and edited the DSP's official journal, *The Woman,* which ran until 1942, thus becoming the most successful, long-running feminist journal in Cuba before the revolution led by Fidel Castro. In her regular articles in *The Woman,* Collado continued to press for women to forget the class differences that divided them and join forces to campaign against traditional patriarchy and for women's equal rights with men.

In 1925 Collado volunteered to serve as an investigator for the Department of Agriculture, Industry and Commerce, inspecting workplaces and making a study of the exploitation of women workers by private business and providing the authorities with the evidence to prosecute those businesses that failed to meet safety standards. She published her findings on the inspections she had made. In December 1929 she took a major role in the "ten cent" strike by Woolworths' employees; after conducting interviews with workers and management, she came to the conclusion that there was no case against management in terms of unsanitary working conditions or low wages.

From the late 1920s until 1937, Collado became caught up in an increasingly heated rivalry with the socialist feminist women's rights campaigner Ofelia Domínguez Navarro, whom Collado considered an extremist. Collado became highly critical of women's organizations on the left and tried to persuade members of the DSP to boycott the organization led by Domínguez, the Women's Labor Union. As with all organizations on the left, including the Feminist University Union, which she also attacked, Collado felt that Domínguez's group dissipated its energies in fueling class antipathy rather than getting down to the issues of reform. She felt it was better that elite and conservative political groups should cooperate with the Machado regime (which lasted from 1925 to 1933) in order to effect some degree of reform, including suffrage, rather than none at all. But all the time that Machado remained in power and Collado continued to support his regime (mainly because of its anticommunist stance), she lost support in the mainstream of the feminist movement.

Despite left-wing and Marxist opposition, Collado continued to lobby for her own brand of reform, based primarily on male-female equality as a precursor to women's liberation and through means that avoided violence and confrontation over class issues. Although she supported abortion rights, liberalization of divorce laws, and the rights of illegitimate children and undertook charity work for orphans, her attitudes were prompted primarily by a belief in the social control that such things effected—that is, limitation of the numbers of unwanted children—rather than out of a concern for the sexual liberation of the woman. She has been seen as nursing the naive belief that the preservation of old class values and the administration of public acts of charity by upper-class women philanthropists were sufficient; that by "looking after" the welfare of poor and colored working women, the status quo could be preserved through a program of benign and middle-of-the-road social reform. Inevitably, her position was looked upon as arrogant and narrow.

During Machado's regime, Collado came out strongly against the growing influence of Marxism in the women's movement in Cuba, particularly when public protest by radical groups against the regime had prompted Machado to suspend the nation's constitutional rights in November 1930. This action resulted in three years of political turmoil and undeclared civil war that ended with Machado's ouster by an army coup in August 1933.

After the resolution of the political situation in 1933, the antipathy between the left and right wings of the Cuban feminist movement receded. Collado did not change her position and continued to call for unity in the women's movement, remaining convinced that "class and race divisions among women could be resolved as long as women honored biological ties and ignored class and ethnic origins" (Stoner 1991, 139).

See also Domínguez Navarro, Ofelia; Rodríguez Acosta, Ofelia; Sabas Alomá, Mariblanca.

References and Further Reading

Stoner, K. Lynn. 1991. *From the House to the Streets: The Cuban Woman's Movement for Legal Reform 1898—1940.* Durham, NC: Duke University Press.

Collett, Camilla
(1813–1895)
Norway

The feminist essayist and novelist Camilla Collett stands alone in Norwegian women's history of the early nineteenth century as a woman who, like her contemporary Fredrika Bremer in Sweden, initiated the debate on the position of women through her social novels. Thirty years before the organized movement for women's emancipation got under way in Norway, Collett's determined advocacy of women's equality and her own liberated and unconventional lifestyle prompted her to write the first novel in that country to address the subject of the subjugation of women within the family and the legal constraints placed upon them in marriage. It was a novel that would have a profound effect on later writers, including Henrik Ibsen.

The daughter of a minister, Collett was born in Kristiansand. The family moved nearer to Oslo in 1817, and Collett enjoyed a cultured education at home and in private schools. Her brother, Henrik Wergeland, became a national figure and poet in the Byronic mold. In 1830 at the age of seventeen, Collett fell in love with the poet Johan Sebastian Welhaven, a conservative to whom her revolutionary and deeply nationalist brother was bitterly opposed. The relationship ended unhappily in 1836, after Collett had spent some time grappling with her divided loyalties. In 1841 she married a lawyer, Peter Jonas Collett, who encouraged her literary endeavors, but it was only after she was widowed with four sons at the age of forty-eight that she assumed her position as a writer and cultural critic for the next thirty years.

After the deaths of her parents and her husband, Collett published her outstanding social novel *Amtmandens døttre,* translated later as *The District Governor's Daughters* in installments from 1854 to 1855. It appeared anonymously because her father was a state official, although it was widely known that its author was a woman. With its plea for the recognition and respect of women's intellectual and emotional capacities as individuals, their dignity, and their need for love, it broke the silence on women's subjugation in marriage and established Collett's reputation. It was the first novel in Norway to depict the misery endured by young women condemned by religion and social convention to interminable domestic lives under the thumbs of tyrannical fathers, only to have no choice in whom they subsequently married. With its questioning of traditional education and marriage and its suggestion that if women had freedom of choice in marriage they would be better people, it attempted to lead Norwegian women out of the darkness of their traditional submissiveness and aroused considerable controversy.

Collett published a series of short stories between 1861 and 1873, and her memoirs, *Through the Long Nights,* in 1863. She further discussed the emancipation of women in six volumes of essays—*Last Pages* (1868, 1872, 1873), *From the Camp of the Mute* (1877), and *Against the Stream* (1879, 1885). In 1873 she had abandoned her anonymity to write under her own name. Although Collett's life and work remained outside the emergent Norwegian women's movement, its participants nevertheless took inspiration from her writings on sexual equality and the movement finally took root when Collett's heir, Gina Krog, established the first Norwegian women's society in 1885. Collett's preeminence in Scandinavia was also acknowledged by Theodore Stanton, who invited her to contribute a section on Norway for his landmark 1884 book *The Woman Question in Europe: A Series of Original Essays.*

See also Bremer, Fredrika; Krog, Gina.

References and Further Reading
Collett, Camilla. 1991. *The District Governors' Daughters.* Trans. Kirsten Seaver. Norwich: Norvik Press.
O'Leary, Margaret Hayford. 1993. "Norwegian Women Writers." In Harald S. Naess, ed., *A History of Norwegian Literature.* Lincoln: University of Nebraska Press in cooperation with the American-Scandinavian Foundation.
Wergeland, Agnes Mathilde, and Katharine Merrill. 1916. "Camilla Collett: A Centenary Tribute, January 23, 1813–January 23, 1914." *Leaders in Norway and Other Essays.* Menasha, WI: Banta.

Cooper, Selina
(1864–1946)
United Kingdom

Along with Ada Nield Chew, Selina Cooper was an outstanding radical leader of working women in the north of England. She was a very vocal working-class presence in the National Union of Women's Suffrage Societies (NUWSS) as well as a notable local preacher at her hometown in Lancashire. Like Chew, her contribution as a socialist feminist and as a suffragist has been largely neglected in favor of an emphasis on the more prominent middle-class figures, such as NUWSS leader Millicent Garrett Fawcett, herself an admirer of Cooper's work.

Cooper was born in Cornwall, but her father's death took the family north in search of work, which for Cooper began at the age of eleven in a cotton mill at Brierfield, near Nelson, Lancashire. When her mother became disabled by rheumatism, she had to leave her mill job to take care of her and was forced to take in washing to eke out a living. She went back to working as a winder at the mill after her mother's death in 1889. Selina joined the Independent Labour Party (ILP) when it established a branch in Nelson in 1892, where she met Robert Cooper, a cotton weaver whom she married in 1896. Her early activism was as a member of the winders' committee of her local branch of the weavers' union. After becoming active in the Women's Cooperative Guild, where she was encouraged to improve her literacy levels by attending classes, she also developed an interest in politics, hygiene and health care, and birth control.

In 1900 the couple moved to Nelson, where Cooper was one of several Lancashire textile workers to be drawn into the women's suffrage campaign as organizers of a petition on that subject, led by Eva Gore-Booth of the North of England Society for Women's Suffrage. They obtained the signatures of many female cotton-mill workers, and Cooper later traveled to London to present the petition to Parliament. As a working woman, Cooper viewed the issue of women's suffrage not merely as a theoretical argument about women's equality with men but as the essential basis for welfare and maternity reforms that would improve the lot of working women everywhere. In 1901 she was invited by the ILP to become one of its candidates for Poor Law Guardian elections in Burnley in 1901. During her term of office, she fought to have the butter allowance of children in the workhouse doubled. By 1903 she had begun giving speeches on women's suffrage locally for the North of England Society for Women's Suffrage and in 1904 was a founder of the Nelson and Colne local suffrage committee. With Isabella Ford, she was one of several women's labor activists who tried to establish closer links between the suffrage and labor movements. But after attending the Labour Representation Committee Conference in Liverpool in 1905, she became increasingly disenchanted with the ILP's refusal to fully endorse women's suffrage. Although she remained a socialist and never abandoned the labor movement entirely, by 1907, realizing that the ILP would not change its position, Cooper became a full-time paid organizer for the NUWSS.

Cooper proved to be a gifted public speaker and toured the country on behalf of the NUWSS, lecturing on women's suffrage and speaking at by-elections, where she continued to support Labour candidates through the NUWSS's Election Fighting Fund. In 1913 she scored a notable success in convincing the Miner's Federation to support women's suffrage. Campaigning for the Labour candidate in the Keighley by-election that year, Cooper refused to be intimidated by a hostile crowd at the Yorkshire village of Haworth and carried on speaking through a hail of rotten eggs and tomatoes, reminding her detractors that "this blooming village would never have been known about but for three women—the Brontës" (the Brontë sisters' father had been the local vicar) (Liddington and Norris 2000, 248).

During World War I, Cooper remained firmly committed to pacifism, despite antipathy from her colleagues in the ILP, and, with her husband, opposed conscription in her hometown. In August 1917 she helped stage the Nelson Women's Peace Crusade, in which more than 1,000 women marched through the town and which culminated in Cooper giving a speech before the crowd at the Methodist Sunday School. Refusing herself to support the war effort, although she reluctantly served on the local Munitions Tribunal, which monitored women's work in the industry, she helped run relief committees and a new maternity center in Nelson (having taught herself midwifery from medical books). After the war, she was a supporter of the Women's International League for Peace and Freedom.

With the fight for women's suffrage won in 1918, Cooper joined Eleanor Rathbone in the National Union of Societies for Equal Citizenship and remained active in local politics as a town councilor and magistrate. In the latter capacity, she showed a particular concern for the female victims of domestic violence and was sympathetic toward the Burnley weavers involved in violent demonstrations against increased working hours. Having given up all her trade union activism by 1923, Cooper gave her campaigning energies to the birth control movement. During the rise of Adolf Hitler to power in the 1930s, she visited Germany as a delegate of The Women's World Committee Against War and Fascism, but her continuing pacifism and her communist sympathies resulted in her expulsion from the Labour Party when World War II broke out.

See also Chew, Ada Nield; Fawcett, Millicent Garrett; Ford, Isabella; Gore-Booth, Eva; Rathbone, Eleanor.

References and Further Reading
Banks, Olive, ed. 1985, 1990. *The Biographical Dictionary of British Feminists*, vol. 1, *1800–1930*; vol. 2, *1900–1945*. Brighton: Harvester Wheatsheaf.
Crawford, Elizabeth. 1999. *The Women's Suffrage Movement, 1866–1928: A Reference Guide.* London: University College of London Press.
Liddington, Jill. 1984. *The Life and Times of a Respectable Rebel: Selina Cooper 1864–1946.* London: Virago.
Liddington, Jill, and Jill Norris. 2000 [1978]. *One Hand Tied behind Us.* Rev. ed. London: Virago.
Oldfield, Sybil, ed. 2001. *Women Humanitarians: A Biographical Dictionary of British Women Active between 1900 and 1950.* London: Continuum.
Roberts, E. 1984. *Woman's Place: An Oral History of Working Class Women 1890–1940.* Oxford: Blackwell.

Cornelius, Johanna
(1912–1974)
South Africa

The work of the Afrikaner radical and trade unionist Johanna Cornelius, who dedicated herself to the rights of South African garment workers in the Transvaal, has yet to be properly documented. Together with her sister Hester (1907–1978), she was one of only a handful of Afrikaner women who overcame inbred Boer prejudices (reaching back to their Dutch Protestant roots) to voice a social awareness that went beyond the bounds of her own narrow group.

Cornelius was one of nine children and grew up on the family farm in the western Transvaal. She and her older sister Hester went to Johannesburg in the 1920s to escape the hardships of rural life and in 1930 obtained work at a garment factory. Cornelius soon became involved in the activities of the mainly Afrikaner Garment Workers' Union (GWU) led by Solly Sachs, and in 1932 she was arrested for taking part in agitation during a general strike by the GWU, which resulted in capitulation by the union and a reduction in wages. The experience served only to fire Cornelius's determination to campaign for a living wage and to build the union into an effective force in support of improved living conditions for its workers. In 1933 she went to the Soviet Union as a member of a workers' delegation and on her return became a full-time organizer for the GWU at its office in Germiston. In 1935–1937 she served as GWU president, during which time the union succeeded in getting working hours reduced and wages increased.

In 1938 Cornelius fought off attempts by Afrikaner nationalists to hijack control of the union in the face of a vilification campaign against her for her communist connections. She lent her support to other unions, continuing to emphasize the fundamental class struggle between rich and poor. She dissociated herself from ingrained Afrikaner prejudice, not just against blacks but also against the British: "It took me years to get used to the notion that even the English—let alone the natives—were human beings" (Berger 1992, 124). Under Cornelius, the women of the GWU drew inspiration from the pioneering spirit of the original Afrikaner settlers and viewed their own struggle to feed their families as being worthy of the same respect.

In 1938 Cornelius was a founding figure in the National Union of Cigarette and Tobacco Workers and in September 1940 led a two-week strike of tobacco workers at Rustenberg. She became a member of the executive of the Trade Union Council of South Africa in 1955. When she stood as an Independent Labor Party candidate in 1943, her attempt at a political career failed, however. After Solly Sachs was exiled from South Africa in 1952, Cornelius replaced him as general secretary of the GWU, a post she retained until her death. During this time, she saw wages plummet as the industry ruthlessly exploited lower-paid black workers, and she was forced to negotiate different wage agreements for black and white workers when the South African government prohibited mixed-race trade unions in 1953. Cornelius was justifiably criticized for this action by the African National Congress but continued to struggle against wage cutbacks and the erosion of union rights until her death.

References and Further Reading

Berger, Iris. 1992. *Threads of Solidarity: Women in South African Industry, 1900–1980.* Bloomington: Indiana University Press.

Uerwey, E. J., ed. 1995. *New Dictionary of South African Biography.* Pretoria: HSRC Publishers.

Courtney, Kathleen D'Olier
(1878–1974)
United Kingdom

The humanitarian Kathleen Courtney was one of a generation of middle-class British women who rejected their comfortable backgrounds for a life of activism. She learned the ropes of political campaigning in the suffrage movement, but with the outbreak of war in 1914 she devoted herself to pacifism and became an influential figure behind the scenes in the international peace movement and in support of collective security.

Courtney's family came from the Anglo-Irish gentry. She was born in Chatham, Kent, where her father was a major in the Royal engineers. She received a genteel education at an Anglo-French school in Kensington and a boarding school in Malvern and studied German in Dresden before going to Lady Margaret Hall at Oxford University to study languages.

Courtney took up voluntary settlement work at the Lambeth Girls' Club after graduating in 1900 and returned to Oxford University as an administrator for the University Extension scheme. In 1908 she went north to work as secretary of the North of England Society for Women's Suffrage, based in Manchester, where she collaborated with Helena Swanwick. In 1911 Courtney moved back to London after being elected honorary secretary of Millicent Garrett Fawcett's National Union of Women's Suffrage Societies (NUWSS), a post she held until 1915. Courtney's work for the NUWSS came to a somewhat bitter end in 1915, when she resigned in protest at its insufficient commitment to peace and as a result of leader Fawcett's denunciation of women who did not support the war effort as traitors. Courtney was one of several peace advocates in the suffrage movement who left when war broke out, sharing the belief with her friends Maude Royden, Helena Swanwick, and Catherine

Marshall that the NUWSS should link its activities not just with suffrage but also, as Courtney put it, with "the advocacy of the deeper principles which underlie it" (Hannam 1989, 170).

During the war, Courtney began encouraging influential women to collectively call for an end to the fighting. In February 1915 she traveled to Europe, where she and other women called a meeting in support of a women's peace congress to be held in the Netherlands later that year. Courtney and Chrystal MacMillan were the only English delegates able to attend the congress in The Hague in April because they were already in Europe (Emmeline Pethick-Lawrence joined them from the United States); the others were not allowed out of England. At the congress, Courtney was one of the prime movers behind the establishment of a women's peace organization, the International Committee of Women for Permanent Peace (which established the Women's International League, renamed the Women's International League for Peace and Freedom [WILPF] in 1919). It had its first meeting in Britain that autumn, at which Courtney was elected one of its vice chairs.

In 1916 Courtney worked as a volunteer for the Serbian Relief Fund with refugees in Salonika and later in a refugee camp for Serbs in Corsica. After the war, she headed the British section of the WILPF for ten years (1923–1933) and then resigned, feeling that peace campaigning should apply not just to stopping wars that had already broken out but also to working for collective security in the prevention of future ones. She supported the continuing efforts of the League of Nations, and in 1926 was an organizer of the Manchester venue for the women's Pilgrimage for Peace, held in England in support of peace arbitration and disarmament.

Courtney never made up her rift with Fawcett, although she accepted reelection to the NUWSS in 1918 and, after suffrage was won, joined its successor, the National Union of Societies for Equal Citizenship. She acted as delegate to the Paris conference of the International Woman Suffrage Alliance in 1923. As a member of the committee of the Family Endowment Council, she lobbied with Eleanor Rathbone for the government introduction of family allowances.

In 1928 Courtney became an executive member of the British League of Nations Union and in 1939 vice chair, roles that required her to travel to many international conferences to give lectures. She worked for the women's disarmament committee in Geneva in the early 1930s and organized a 1932 petition to the disarmament conference. During World War II, she undertook the dangerous sea crossing to the United States, where she lectured on behalf of the British government's Ministry of Information on collective security. She was in San Francisco in 1945 for the historic founding congress of the United Nations at which the UN Charter was drawn up. She was nominated to be vice chair of the British branch of the UN Association in 1945 and served as chair from 1949 to 1951. Courtney was made a Commander of the Order of the British Empire (CBE) in 1946 and a Dame Commander of the Order of the British Empire (DBE) in 1952. Shortly before her death at the age of ninety-six, she was the recipient of the UN Peace Medal in 1972.

See also Fawcett, Millicent Garrett; MacMillan, Chrystal; Marshall, Catherine; Pethick-Lawrence, Emmeline; Rathbone, Eleanor; Royden, Maude; Swanwick, Helena.

References and Further Reading
Alberti, Johanna. 1989. *Beyond Suffrage: Feminists in War and Peace.* London: Macmillan.
Banks, Olive, ed. 1985, 1990. *The Biographical Dictionary of British Feminists,* vol. 1, *1800–1930;* vol. 2, *1900–1945.* Brighton: Harvester Wheatsheaf.
Crawford, Elizabeth. 1999. *The Women's Suffrage Movement, 1866–1928: A Reference Guide.* London: University College of London Press.
Hannam, June. 1989. *Isabella Ford.* Oxford: Blackwell.
Holton, Sandra Stanley. 1986. *Feminism and Democracy: Women's Suffrage and Reform Politics in Britain, 1900–1918.* Cambridge: Cambridge University Press.
Liddington, Jill. 1984. *The Life and Times of a Respectable Rebel: Selina Cooper 1864–1946.* London: Virago.
Nicholls, C. S., ed. 1993. *Dictionary of National Biography: Missing Persons.* Oxford: Oxford University Press.
Oldfield, Sybil. 1989. *Women against the Iron Fist: Alternatives to Militarism 1900–1989.* Oxford: Basil Blackwell.
Wiltsher, Anne. 1985. *Most Dangerous Women: Feminist Peace Campaigners of the Great War.* London: Pandora, and Westport, CT: Greenwood Press.

Cousins, Margaret
(1878–1954)
Ireland

The Irish educationist, suffragist, and Theosophist Margaret Cousins was a founder of the Irish Women's Franchise League (IWFL) in 1908 and later carried her campaign for women's rights into India, where she worked closely with leading Indian suffragists and Mahatma Gandhi.

Born Margaret Gillespie into a Protestant family from County Roscommon, Cousins studied music from 1898 to 1902 at Dublin's Royal Irish Academy and the University of Ireland and went on to teach music at the primary school level. At an early age, she had begun to rebel against inequalities between the sexes and took a passionate interest in women's rights. In 1903 she married James Cousins, a socialist writer and poet. The couple moved in Dublin's fin-de-siècle literary circles (whose leading lights were people such as James Joyce, W. B. Yeats, and George Bernard Shaw), and Margaret became caught up in the highly fashionable preoccupation of the time—psychic experimentation—acting as a medium in séances. She was unorthodox in her many other pursuits as well: as a passionate anti-vivisectionist, she opposed the use of feathers and fur in ladies' fashions, and belonged to the Irish Vegetarian Society. Believing that a simple vegetarian diet based on whole and raw foods would save women the grisly task of dealing with raw meat and having to "disgorge the entrails of fowl, game and fish" (*Vegetarian Messenger and Health Review* 1907 [4]: 296), Cousins was also convinced that it would relieve them from unnecessary labor in the kitchen and give them "more time to think"—particularly about their rights. Cousins ran a vegetarian food factory and restaurant in Dublin; she also took a combative stance on compulsory inoculation and smoking.

In 1907, like many other socialist and feminist women of her time who rebelled against the established church and patriarchal religion in general, Cousins explored the alternatives of Eastern religion, studying works such as the *Bhagavad Gita* and becoming deeply involved with Theosophy. With her husband she helped found the Irish Theosophical Society, but her political consciousness had also been raised when she attended the National Conference of Women in Manchester in 1906, where she met leading

British suffragists. That same year she organized a meeting on suffrage in Dublin in response to the ineligibility of Irish women to sit on county and borough councils (whereas Scotswomen and Englishwomen were eligible). This effort led to the founding in 1908 of the Irish Women's Franchise League, which she set up together with her husband and the socialists Frank and Hannah Sheehy-Skeffington and of which Cousins became its treasurer. The IWFL campaigned among Irish members of Parliament for support for suffrage as part of any future agreement with the British government on Irish home rule. With a £200 donation from sympathizers, Emmeline and Frederick Pethick-Lawrence, the league also later set up its own newspaper, the *Irish Citizen* (1912–1920), devoted to the suffrage cause.

Having spent time in 1909 working with the Women's Social and Political Union in London, Cousins became more militant in her activities, touring Ireland and speaking at rallies. She also helped to organize a visit by Christabel Pankhurst, during which 3,000 people crowded into the Rotunda in Dublin to hear her suffrage message. Late in 1910 Cousins traveled to London in an Irish delegation invited by Pankhurst to take part in lobbying at Parliament on women's suffrage. This "parliament of women," which comprised 400 suffragists, took a petition to Prime Minister Herbert Asquith at the House of Commons. As a result of a series of rowdy demonstrations and scuffles outside No. 10 Downing Street that ended in stone throwing, Cousins was arrested for hurling a missile and spent a month in Holloway Prison.

A further period in jail in Dublin followed, when Cousins once again was arrested after breaking windows at Dublin Castle in January 1913 during an Irish debate on the second reading of the Home Rule Bill. Sentenced to one month in prison, she went on a hunger strike in Tullamore jail in order to be classified as a political prisoner. Upon her release, Cousins undertook further propaganda tours on behalf of the suffrage movement in Ireland, but her growing commitment to Theosophy, impelled by a recent psychic message that it was her true path, led her and her husband James to volunteer themselves to movement leader Annie Besant, who now lived in India. They set sail for Madras, India, in October 1915 to work at the movement's headquarters, where James was a literary editor on

Besant's publication, the fiercely anticolonial *New India*. However, it quickly became apparent to Besant that Cousins did not take a militant enough position. He resigned and the couple moved to Madanapalle, where Margaret was hired to teach English at a high school affiliated with the local Theosophical College where James had a lectureship. She also developed an interest in Indian arts and crafts as a way of creating a more positive role for women and promoted their work in rattan weaving through meetings of the local Weaker Sex Improvement Society (Abala Abhivardini Samaj). This society, with its self-deprecating title, would be the springboard for the Women's Indian Association (WIA), of which Cousins became the first non-Indian member in 1917 at Poona.

Within the WIA, Cousins voiced her strong opinions on women's rights, visiting many of the movement's forty or more branches and writing regularly in the association's journal, *Stri Dharma*. She was particularly critical of the traditional male oppression of women in India and the practice of child marriage, which brought with it the hazards of premature motherhood, and used the WIA as the channel for her campaigns for free primary education and equality of education for girls, better health care facilities, and the creation of institutions to train and educate women, such as teacher-training schools and medical colleges. She also initiated the first deputation of women from the Indian Women's University to Edwin Montagu, the British secretary of state for India, in support of women's education and suffrage. But it was not until 1929 that Indian women finally could be elected to provincial legislatures and 1949 before universal adult suffrage for Indian women became law. During all this time Cousins continued to campaign and lobby tirelessly on behalf of women's suffrage, despite opposition from Annie Besant, her spiritual leader, who would not include women's suffrage in her own campaign for Indian home rule.

From 1919 to 1920 Cousins was the first headmistress of the National Girls' School in Mangalore, after the Madanapalle school was closed by the government. In 1920 she became the first female honorary bench magistrate in India while also continuing to organize suffrage campaigns. She proved to be a very efficient administrator, and other posts followed, culminating in 1926 in her work as the driving force behind the foundation of the All-India Women's Conference. In preparation for the conference, she appealed to women throughout the Indian provinces to discuss and draw up resolutions on education, moral training, early marriage, and the age of consent. The conference itself called for an extension of education opportunities for women to higher education in law, medicine, social science, and fine arts. In 1931 Cousins organized Indian women's groups to take part in the first All-Asia Women's Conference, held at Lahore. The conference had as its central theme equal opportunities for women and sought to do away with traditional practices such as polygamy and child labor. It also drew up resolutions on working hours and conditions for women and encouraged family planning.

Indian nationalist politics increasingly took over Cousins's attention during the 1930s. In 1932 her support for Gandhi's program of civil disobedience resulted in a yearlong jail sentence after she appeared at protest meetings and attacked the British government's proposed emergency measures, which banned freedom of speech. Sentenced to prison for a year, Cousins remained defiant, stating at her trial: "I am proud to stand here in support of free speech and Indian national freedom and I am ashamed that English idealism has fallen to the present depths of oppression and suppression" (Cousins and Cousins 1950, 582–583). She served her year in prison in Vellore, where she taught the other inmates, and was given a hero's welcome on her release.

Cousins returned to political life with undimmed vigor. She joined electioneering campaigns for women candidates to the Congress Party, rejoined the Women's Indian Association in 1933, and in 1936 served as president of the All-India Women's Conference. Her leadership of the AIWC was inspirational, according to Kamaladevi Chattopadhyaya: "She imbued the very basis of the cause with an element of humanitarianism and turned it into a mission of social service" (1983, 84). Cousins was left paralyzed by a brain hemorrhage from 1943 until her death but was given considerable financial support by Indian friends, the Madras government, and even Motilal Nehru for her services to India and lived to see Indian independence granted in 1947.

See also Besant, Annie; Chattopadhyaya, Kamaladevi; Sheehy-Skeffington, Hannah.

References and Further Reading

Candy, Catherine. 1994. "Relating Feminisms, Nationalism, and Imperialisms: Ireland, India, and Margaret Cousins' Sexual Politics." *Women's History Review* 3(4): 581–594.

Chattopadhaya, K. S. D. 1983. *Indian Women's Battle for Freedom.* New Delhi: Abhinav.

Cousins, James, and Margaret Cousins. 1950. *We Two Together.* Madras: Ganesh.

Jayawardena, Kumari. 1995. *The White Woman's Other Burden: Western Women and South Asia during British Rule.* London: Routledge.

Ó Céirín, Kit, and Cyril Ó Céirín. 1996. *Women of Ireland: A Biographic Dictionary.* Kinvara, County Galway: Tír Eolas.

Cunard, Nancy
(1896–1965)
United Kingdom

The details of the misspent youth and wasted years of professional rebel Nancy Cunard have been well-catalogued in both the memoirs and fiction of many of her contemporaries, notably her incarnation as Margot Beste-Chetwynde in Evelyn Waugh's *Decline and Fall.* Together with the Mitford sisters, she was one of the notorious upper-class dropouts of her generation. In the 1920s, as a well-known figure in the fast set and the bohemian avant-garde, she lived a life of destructive self-interest. But Cunard, like others of her generation who cast themselves adrift from their aristocratic roots, was also a woman in search of a cause. She found one as an outspoken advocate of racial justice and a campaigner against lynching. In the 1930s, Cunard also defended the civil liberties of those persecuted by General Francisco Franco's fascist regime during and after the Spanish Civil War.

Cunard was born into the wealthy Anglo-American shipping family that ran the famous Cunard transatlantic liners. Her mother Emerald was a well-known socialite, outrageous snob, and wit, famous for her put-downs. As a child, Cunard was educated by governesses and developed an interest in poetry and literature after being allowed to mix with literary and artistic guests at the family home. Her parents separated when she was fourteen, and Cunard lived with her mother in London, from where she was sent to expensive private finishing schools in Germany and France. By the time she had completed her education in

Paris in 1916, she had begun writing poetry and mixing in Parisian bohemian circles. Cunard's taste for bohemianism did not extend, however, to her choice of husband. Her marriage to a rather conventional guards officer in 1916 was a disaster, and the couple separated after twenty months and divorced in 1925. Her life thereafter, divided between artistic circles in London and Paris, took a downturn, with Cunard becoming heavily dependent on drink and drugs.

In London, she disdained the formality of the social scene among the British upper classes to frequent places such as the Eiffel Tower restaurant in Bloomsbury, the hangout, or as Cunard called it, "our carnal-spiritual home," of the artistic Fitzrovia or Higher Bohemia set (Pearson 1978, 100). This group included other socialites such as Lady Diana Manners and Iris Beerbohm Tree and, later on, artistic luminaries such as Augustus John and Dylan Thomas. At the Eiffel Tower, Cunard became famous for her outrageous opinions and talk. She continued to write poetry and became friendly with the literary lioness and poet Edith Sitwell, publishing her poems in Sitwell's magazine *Wheels: An Anthology of Verse,* which first appeared in 1916. Cunard published three volumes of poetry during the 1920s: *Outlaws* (1921), *Sublunary* (1923), and *Parallax* (1925), the latter published by her friend Virginia Woolf.

In 1927 Cunard bought a printing press and set herself up as a publisher in a rented farmhouse at La Chapelle-Réanville, in Normandy. Her imprint, the Hours Press, would publish the work of Ezra Pound and Samuel Beckett, and she later described her experience of these years in her posthumously published memoir, *These Were the Hours* (1969). In 1928 Cunard's life took on a dramatic new direction when, in blatant defiance of her own social background, she began a relationship with a black American jazz musician, Henry Crowder, whom she had met in Venice in 1926. As her biographer, Anne Chisholm, remarks, she found not just a lover in Crowder but "a cause, a symbol, a weapon, a victim" (1979, 128). Socially ostracized in Britain, the couple spent most of their time in Europe, living openly together for the next two years, and moving the Hours Press to Paris until Crowder finally returned to his wife in the United States. The relationship provoked a final and irrevocable falling-out with her mother in December

1930, who promptly halved Cunard's personal allowance and threatened to cut her out of her will. Cunard wryly observed: "The black man is a well-known factor in the changing of testaments" (Cunard 1931, 2). In contrast, family friend, conductor Sir Thomas Beecham, opined with typical British bluster that Cunard should be "tarred and feathered" (Chisholm 1979, 231) for the sin of interracial sex.

In April 1931, Cunard published a bitter attack on the ignorance and racial prejudice she had encountered in Britain in the *New Review.* It was a vitriolic account of the white supremacy and upper-class snobbery of her mother and a condemnation of her mother's class for its profligacy, sybaritic lifestyle, and unrepentant racism. In a follow-up essay, Cunard presented a condensed history of the injustices of slavery and the long abuse of black people, detailing the spate of lynchings then current in the United States and the particular injustices of the Scottsboro case. Printed at Cunard's own expense in 1931 and circulated in hundreds of copies among friends and sympathizers, the essay, entitled "Black Man and White Ladyship: An Anniversary," demolished long-entrenched British prejudices and popular superstitions about black people and condemned the narrow-mindedness of social stereotyping. Cunard was adamant: "The days of Rastus and Sambo are long gone" (1931, 9); black people, she argued, were no longer prepared to be put upon by whites.

In 1931 Cunard had become closely involved in the case of the Scottsboro boys, nine young black men from Scottsboro, Alabama, who had been condemned to death for an alleged sexual assault on two white women. Having been told about it by Crowder, she felt that this case epitomized the evils of racism. The case became a cause célèbre among civil rights campaigners such as Jessie Daniel Ames, and Cunard became involved in fund-raising for the defendants' U.S. Supreme Court appeal, in 1932 organizing a mixed-race ball. In the Supreme Court decision, some of the original indictments were eventually overturned and the death sentences commuted to life imprisonment. It later became clear that the young women involved had perjured themselves, but the Scottsboro boys nevertheless spent many long years in jail before their release.

In 1931 and 1932 Cunard made several visits to the United States, living in Harlem, where she wrote articles for the Associated Negro Press and collected material for an ambitious anthology she was preparing of black history and culture inspired by the Harlem Renaissance. Her continuing support for the Scottsboro boys, through financial assistance to their families and as honorary treasurer of the British Scottsboro Defence Committee, had led to threats from the Ku Klux Klan. Even Crowder, who assisted her in editing and publishing the anthology, could not tolerate the constant glare of publicity they had to endure, not to mention the constant battle with discriminatory hotel managers over their sharing a room. Their on-off relationship would eventually founder when in 1935 he returned to the United States. In 1933, unable to find a publisher to take it on, Cunard published the 855-page *Negro: An Anthology Collected and Edited by Nancy Cunard,* at her own expense. In this innovative and exceptional work, published in a limited printrun of 1,000 copies, she celebrated the many achievements of black art, sculpture, music, and literature, calling for black civil liberties and greater racial tolerance. The anthology also contained articles by Cunard herself: "The American Moron and the American of Sense—Letters on the Negro," "Scottsboro—and Other Scottsboros," and "Colour Bar." *Negro* quickly became "fashionable" reading among the bohemian set and literati who admired black artistry; for Cunard, who had worked tirelessly in its preparation, it marked a contribution to racial understanding that perhaps, she felt, went some way toward redeeming her early wasted years. Extraordinary for its time, despite receiving favorable reviews, the book was large and unwieldy and did not sell well; Cunard would publish an edited-down version five years before her death.

Cunard announced her intention to "devote the rest of my life to work on behalf of the coloured race" (Chisholm 1979, 231), by this time convinced that the only solution to the race problem was communism and the overthrow of capitalist society. In 1935, therefore, she set out for a visit to the Soviet Union, where talk of a Russian edition of *Negro* came to nothing. In 1936, however, Cunard was caught up in a new cause with the outbreak of the Spanish Civil War. She joined the International Brigade, and went to Spain. She worked as a freelance journalist, writing a stream of antifascist articles for British newspapers, including the *News Chronicle* and

Sylvia Pankhurst's *New Times,* as well as sending reports to the Associated Negro Press in the United States. She lobbied for better treatment of Spanish refugees in France, visiting refugee camps and appealing for relief supplies to be sent to feed the half million people who had fled Spain. After the war, she continued to support exiled antifascist Spaniards, again bombarding friends and sympathizers for support, money, clothes, and food and writing articles and letters of complaint about their poor treatment in France. She also edited a collection of articles on the subject, *Authors Take Sides on the Spanish War* (1937). Throughout the 1930s, Cunard traveled continually in South America, the Caribbean, and North Africa. She joined with Una Marson and Pankhurst in expressing her concern at the 1935–1936 Ethiopian crisis in reports to the Associated Negro Press and observed with dismay the negative effects of British colonialism on black society and culture in Africa in articles such as "The White Man's Duty" (1943). In it she argued that if blacks from Britain's colonies were willing to fight on Britain's behalf during World War II, then they had a right to their independence.

In the years after World War II, Cunard continued to challenge British society on the operation of the color bar, particularly when the first wave of black immigrants began arriving from the West Indies, but by that time her physical and mental health was in sharp decline, and her increasing eccentricity (manifested, for example, in a bizarre campaign on the wage rights of Venetian gondoliers, whom she considered were underpaid) provoked extremes of behavior that gradually alienated many of her friends. In the end, she was taken into a sanatorium for psychiatric treatment. Throughout her life, the birdlike Cunard had eaten sparingly and had drunk and smoked to excess, and soon her body gave out. Crippled with emphysema, she died alone and forgotten in the public ward of a charity hospital in Paris.

See also Ames, Jessie Daniel; Marson, Una; Pankhurst, (Estelle) Sylvia.

References and Further Reading

Bush, Barbara. 1998. "Britain's Conscience on Africa: White Women, Race, and Imperial Politics in Inter-War Britain." In Clare Midgeley, ed., *Gender and Imperialism.* Manchester: Manchester University Press.

Chisholm, Anne. 1979. *Nancy Cunard: A Biography.* New York: Alfred A. Knopf.

Cunard, Nancy. 1931. "Black Man and White Ladyship: An Anniversary." Privately printed.

———. 1996 [1934]. *Negro: An Anthology Collected and Edited by Nancy Cunard.* Reprint, New York: Continuum.

Ford, Hugh D., ed. 1968. *Nancy Cunard: Brave Poet, Indomitable Rebel, 1896–1965.* Philadelphia: Chilton.

Pearson, John. 1978. *Facades.* London: Macmillan.

Schlueter, Paul, and June Schlueter. 1988. *Encyclopedia of British Women Writers.* London: St James Press.

D

Daulatabadi, Sadiqa
(1881–1961)
Iran

An early promoter of women's education and a writer on women's issues in prerevolutionary Iran, Daulatabadi was also the first woman to run a leading woman's publication, *Woman's Voice* (*Zaban Zanan*), which became a forum for the debate of many women's issues under the shahs. Daulatabadi was the daughter of an eminent Shi'ite clergyman and was brought up in a strict religious household, although she received some education at home from tutors. It is said that such was her desire to learn that she dressed as a boy in order to sneak into lessons at her brother's school. But before long she was confronted with the inevitability of early marriage; at the age of sixteen she was married to a much older man. Despite family disapproval, she took the bold step of opening the first girls' school in Esfahan, but her family forbade her from running it herself. The school was closed down after three months, and Daulatabadi suffered physical attacks as a demonstration of hostility to the venture.

In 1906, after the new constitution failed to give women the vote, Daulatabadi became a leading member of several illicit women's groups that called for secondary education for girls and for reform of child marriage. In 1907 she was one of sixty women to set up the Women's Freedom Society, a focus group for women's issues that in 1910 changed its name to the National Ladies Society. The membership were all fiercely patriotic, and as one of the society's executive committee members, Daulatabadi organized its participation in the nationalist campaign and boycott of foreign goods, which took place at the time of the 1907 Anglo-Russian treaty. This treaty divided Persia (as it was then called) into Russian and British spheres of influence, leading to Russian incursions into northern Iran in 1909–1911, which were the cause of much public protest in the capital.

The National Ladies Society also set up an orphanage at this time and in 1910 held a conference in Tehran to discuss women's education. Throughout her life, Daulatabadi would use the society as a forum for her campaign on many women's issues. Undeterred by official disapproval of her activities, she set up the Esfahan Ladies Association in her hometown and, in 1910, started the *Women's Voice*. Both were subsequently banned, and Daulatabadi was exiled from Esfahan. The chief of police told her at the time of her exile that her activities were ahead of their time and that she had been "born a hundred years too early." Daulatabadi's response was to aver that she had, in fact, been born 100 years too late, for she would not otherwise have allowed her sex to become "so enchained by men today" (Paidar 1995, 93).

Daulatabadi promoted numerous women's issues in articles she published in *Women's Voice*. She wrote against veiling and the enforced early marriage of girls as young as eight and nine years of age, but her activities and her writing constantly brought with them abuse and physical threats in retaliation for her perceived irreverence and immodesty. *Women's Voice* took a strong position against Iran's treaty with Britain in 1919, but despite the fact that the publication was not anti-Islamic, it aroused hostility from fundamentalists, who threw stones at the office windows, broke in, and looted it. (The publication survived, only to be closed down again after thirteen months for its critical stance.) Meanwhile, Daulatabadi took time to help a group of forty women weavers set themselves up in cooperative workshops in Yazd, Kerman, and Esfahan.

By now, with her brother having become a mullah, Daulatabadi had been forced to cut herself off from her family because of their continuing opposition to her political activities. She moved to Tehran and there resumed publication of *Women's Voice,* which over the following months saw its circulation rise to more than 2,000, no doubt the result of Daulatabadi's trenchant editorials on not only women's issues but other national concerns.

In 1921 *Women's Voice* was banned again, and a year later Daulatabadi left for France to study psychology and educational training methods at the Sorbonne, making use of her time abroad to attend international women's conferences. She also published articles on women in Iran in French journals, such as one that discussed the right of Iranian women to control their own property. But she remained convinced of the fundamental tenets of Islam, which in her estimation accorded greater status to women in Iran than was given to many women in Western society. When she returned to Iran in 1927, however, after gaining her degree in psychology in Paris, Daulatabadi now appeared thoroughly Westernized, wearing European clothes and eschewing a veil. She became a government girls' schools inspector and once again gave up much time to her various social concerns.

When the Patriotic Women's League, established in 1922, was disbanded by the government of Iran in 1932 because of its socialist connections (along with other women's organizations prohibited by the shah), it was replaced with the government-backed Women's Center, set up in 1934 to serve as a multipurpose, pro-establishment forum supplanting all former groups. Daulatabadi was asked by the Ministry of Education to become the center's president. She took up this role in 1937, which involved inaugurating a program of women's activities, including "mental and moral education," instruction in domestic tasks and child care, physical fitness, the creation of charitable relief for poor mothers and their children, and the promotion of the use of indigenous products. By the early 1940s, it was clear that the Women's Center had limited scope, with its emphasis on literacy and training in home-based crafts serving only to reinforce traditional domestic roles and with its mainly up-

per-class members not seeking to challenge the authority of the state. It was closed down after the removal of Reza Shah Pahlavi from power in 1941. In 1942 Daulatabadi boldly resumed publication of *Women's Voice.* The government yet again attempted to ban it, but she petitioned to have the ban revoked. Ten issues later the journal was finally suppressed, after calling during World War II for the Allies to leave Iranian territory.

Within the limitations of her pro-monarchy, nationalist position, Daulatabadi was able to back and promote a limited program of women's emancipation under the shahs, convinced that more could be achieved through legitimate channels than through open dissent. In 1955 she founded the New Path League, one of her last acts in promoting the improved status of Iranian women. She continued to speak out against veiling and the seclusion of women throughout her life, and her final critical act was to ask, when she died, that women not veil themselves either at her burial or when visiting her grave. Her tomb was destroyed during the 1979 Islamic Revolution.

References and Further Reading

Afshar, Haleh. 1998. *Islam and Feminisms: An Iranian Case Study.* Basingstoke: Macmillan.

Bamdad, B. 1977. *From Darkness into Light: Women's Emancipation in Iran.* Hicksville, NY: Exposition Press.

Jayawardena, K. 1986. *Feminism and Nationalism in the Third World.* London: Zed Books.

Paidar, Parvin. 1995. *Women and the Political Process in Twentieth-Century Iran.* Cambridge: Cambridge University Press.

Davies, (Sarah) Emily
(1830–1921)
United Kingdom

Quiet and sober, Emily Davies dedicated herself to the furthering of women's university education in Britain. She did so with an exceptional single-mindedness and obstinacy that brooked no compromise. She was a stickler for academic excellence and discipline, setting the most rigorous standards for the women who entered Girton College at Cambridge, the first women's college in Britain, which she founded in 1869. Davies was also a prominent figure in the developing women's suffrage movement in Britain, and in 1918, after the Representation of the People Act finally granted suffrage to British women over thirty, she cast her vote at the age of eighty-eight, one of the few initiators of the campaign who lived to see their dream of women's political emancipation finally come true.

Davies was born in Southampton, the daughter of the Reverend John Davies, an evangelical clergyman and writer who was the author of high-minded texts such as *Splendid Sins and Other Hellfire and Brimstone Tracts.* Like many Victorian daughters of respectable families, Emily Davies was forced to suppress her intellectual interests and vocational aspirations throughout the many long years she was confined to the home. She was educated by her mother, denied even the most lighthearted private entertainments, and obliged merely to share in domestic duties, as expected of any dutiful daughter.

After the family settled in Gateshead in Northumberland, Davies continued to have it impressed upon her that she was a member of the weaker sex, incapable of embracing intellectual thought or of indulging in any kind of strenuous physical labor. Her father even refused to allow her to sit in on her brothers' lessons with their tutors. Having had no formal education, she later recalled: "Our education answered to the description of clergymen's daughters. . . . They have lessons and get on as well as they can" (Bennett 1990, 7–8). After helping to teach at a girls' school in Gateshead, Emily accompanied her brother to Algiers in search of a cure for his tuberculosis. Here she met Nannie Leigh Smith, the sister of English feminist Barbara Bodichon, who introduced her to the Langham Place Circle on Davies's return. Under Bodichon's guidance and inspiration, Davies's narrow existence rapidly changed.

Davies's first self-liberating act was taking up parish work in Gateshead. In London in the spring of 1859, she visited her brother John Llewelyn, a notable theologian and supporter of women's education, and Elizabeth Garrett Anderson (to whom she had been introduced in 1854) and attended lectures given by Elizabeth Blackwell (the first woman to qualify as a doctor in the United States), briefly entertaining the idea of taking up medicine herself. Upon her return up north, Davies founded a Northumberland and Durham branch of the Society for Promoting the Employment of Women and set up a

(Sarah) Emily Davies (The Mistress and Fellows, Girton College, Cambridge)

register to find positions for governesses. She discussed the problems women had in trying to find respectable employment in letters to the local paper in Newcastle and also observed working conditions for women in sweatshop labor in local factories. After her father died in 1862, Davies and her mother moved to London, living not far from the Garrett family. Together with Elizabeth Garrett Anderson, Davies began campaigning for women to become doctors, lobbying the University of London to allow women into medical training programs. As a member of her brother's organization, the National Association for the Promotion of Social Science, she wrote a landmark paper titled "Medicine as a Profession for Women" in 1862.

In December 1862 Davies began working part-time on the *English Woman's Journal,* run by Bodichon, but it folded a few months later (to be revived in 1865 as the *Englishwoman's Review*). Inspired by the campaigning of Frances Power Cobbe, she began to develop an interest in education for girls and the promotion of better access to learning for older women. By this time having decided that marriage was a form of institutionalized slavery for women, Davies devoted the rest of her life to women's education. She discussed the subject with other campaigners, decided upon a campaign for university-sponsored school examinations to be thrown open to girls as well as boys, and wrote to the Oxford and Cambridge University examination boards, urging them to change their policy excluding women. Various friends and colleagues joined in, including the famous educators Dorothea Beale and Frances Buss, although there was still considerable opposition from Victorian women at large, who thought their sex should confine themselves to music and sewing in the belief that political campaigning of any kind would divert them from their domestic duties.

After much persistent lobbying from Davies, Cambridge eventually agreed in 1863 to allow an experimental examination for girls: ninety-one entered, and only six of them failed. Support for Davies's cause was also forthcoming from other eminent Victorian women such as Octavia Hill and Harriet Martineau, but she had to face constant ignorance and prejudice on all sides, despite the success of the trial examination. She was determined to continue to fight against the deadening effects of the repressed environment in which women such as she herself had grown up, which she saw as breeding dullness into them as individuals and sterility into their everyday lives.

In the 1860s, Davies became the first woman to be involved in a royal commission—in this case, the Royal Commission on Endowed Schools that was set up in 1865 to look into boys' schools. She organized her own, similar investigation into girls' schools, preparing a dossier on their dreadful inadequacies. The commissioners finally agreed, at Davies's urging, to extend the focus of their commission to cover girls' schools and entrusted a leading role to her. This in itself was a major step forward for women's education. Davies's report, when it was published in 1868, was damning: it exposed the appalling conditions in girls' schools and the diversion of public money away from girls' education into boys'. London University offered a possible compromise—a special women's examination set at a lower academic level than that sat by men—but Davies rejected such an option outright; similarly, she later refused to collaborate with Anne Jemima Clough and the University Extension scheme, which later offered such modified

courses at Newnham. The whole point of Davies's campaigning was that she wanted no discrimination to be exercised with regard to women students and no "special" courses adapted to the supposed inferior abilities of women. Women, she believed, should be admitted to degree courses on the same level as men and allowed to prove their intellectual equality with them.

Meanwhile, in 1865 Davies had been a founding member and secretary of a new women's discussion group, the Kensington Society, which proved to be an important springboard for the campaigns for suffrage and women's education. After publishing *The Higher Education of Women* and founding the Association of Schoolmistresses in 1866, Davies set up the association's London branch and decided to concentrate her attentions on further education for women and a campaign to persuade London University to allow women to matriculate as members. *Higher Education* proved to be an important, groundbreaking argument against prevailing perceptions of sexual difference, with Davies arguing that traditional Church of England teachings allowed for no differentiation between the sexes and that the arguments in support of women's inferior intellectual capacities, many of them perpetuated by the medical establishment, were unfounded.

Once again, Davies came up against a wall of opposition in her drive for women's admission to the universities; she decided to circumvent the problem by herself establishing a college for women. Barbara Bodichon shared her enthusiasm for the project but insisted that women's suffrage should come before educational reform, and Davies agreed to postpone her campaign, despite the fact that doing so went against her fundamental belief that improvements to women's education should come before the vote.

In 1866 John Stuart Mill, on being elected to Parliament, had raised the debate on women's emancipation. Davies, Bodichon, and others formed the Women's Suffrage Petition Committee to raise a petition for Mill to present to Parliament on women's suffrage. Although she worked hard on the project and organized the distribution of thousands of leaflets, Davies privately believed the petition would not succeed. And indeed, the movement did fail—partly because it could not raise the support of ordinary women, many of whom did not view suffrage as a moral cause. By the end of 1866 Davies, having accepted the nominal role of secretary of the Enfranchisement of Women Committee (under the strict understanding that it would not be announced publicly in case this might affect her education campaigning), had fallen back on her fundamental belief that nothing would change until women had the right to a university education.

Davies set up two committees to launch her scheme for women's higher education, but when these failed she embarked on a far more ambitious campaign, planning to raise £30,000 to set up her own college at Cambridge. She lobbied friends and sympathizers for donations, one of the first (for £1,000) coming from Barbara Bodichon, and organized a college committee to draw up a constitution and plan the curriculum. After Cambridge University made its opposition to her efforts clear, in 1868 Davies was offered the possibility of taking over a suitable premises, Benslow House in Hitchin Herts, which was 20 miles from Cambridge. Once again her plans came under attack, when *The Times* featured an article about the dangers of education for women at the university level, insisting that the female brain could not cope with the strain of such rigorous academic study. But Davies battled on. In October 1869 her college at Hitchin opened with five students, all of whom passed the examination in classics with two of them also passing mathematics. To achieve this goal, they had had to endure a strictly supervised, chaperoned life at Hitchin, very much on the periphery of the real university life of the city.

When the lease on Benslow House came to an end in 1872, Davies raised the initial money to buy a piece of land at Girton in Cambridge and a further £7,000 to get the building work started. Girton College, Cambridge—the first women's institution of higher education in Britain—was opened in the fall of 1873, despite being only half built, cold, and drafty. In November, Davies's first three candidates sat the Classical Tripos, as the Cambridge degree examination was known. In 1877, twenty-three Cambridge dons announced that they would open their lectures to women—even allowing them to attend medical lectures and anatomy classes—but it was not until 1884 that Cambridge University opened all its examinations to women. The regime that Davies introduced at Girton College allowed for no slackening in its high standards

but did include exercise. Country walks and croquet were encouraged, and within ten years women students were also playing racquets (an early form of squash), badminton, and tennis and enjoying the benefits of a gymnasium built in 1877.

Davies retired as mistress of Girton in 1875. A legacy of £19,000 left to the college in 1879 ensured its future, and by 1895, thirty-five to forty students a year were entering. With one of her two primary objectives now achieved—admission to degree courses for women—she went back to campaigning for women's suffrage in the mid-1880s, convinced that women had proved through their ability to educate themselves that they also had the right to the vote. She rejoined the London branch of the National Society for Women's Suffrage in 1890 and became a member of its executive committee, taking on the role of reorganizing some thirty disparate women's suffrage societies around the country and working closely with Millicent Garrett Fawcett. From 1900 to 1906, Davies also served on the executive committee of the Central National Society for Women's Suffrage (and its successor, the London Society for Women's Suffrage), for which she published a pamphlet titled "The Women's Suffrage Movement: I. Why Should We Care for It? II. How Can We Help It Further?"

After finally resigning from the executive committee at Girton in 1904, Davies gave even more of her time to the suffrage cause. In 1910 she published a collection of her writings as *Thoughts on Some Questions Relating to Women, 1860–1908*. However, by 1912, as a staunch Tory who disliked the campaigning of suffragists in the National Union of Women's Suffrage Societies on behalf of Labour Party candidates, she joined the more moderate Conservative and Unionist Women's Franchise League, becoming vice president. Alarmed by the violent new turn in women's suffrage campaigning, as led by the militant Women's Social and Political Union of Emmeline and Christabel Pankhurst, and rejecting their tactics and their hatred of men, Davies felt that they misrepresented the general tone of the movement. During World War I, Davies encouraged women to prove their worthiness for the vote by helping the war effort as nurses (she herself helped set up a hospital in France), running schools, and working in munitions factories. Davies's determined and unobtrusive campaigning was vindicated, when at the end of 1918, women over thirty were finally given the right to vote.

See also Anderson, Elizabeth Garrett; Beale, Dorothea; Blackwell, Elizabeth; Bodichon, Barbara; Buss, Frances; Clough, Anne Jemima; Cobbe, Frances Power; Fawcett, Millicent Garrett; Hill, Octavia; Martineau, Harriet; Pankhurst, Christabel; Pankhurst, Emmeline.

References and Further Reading
Bennett, Daphne. 1990. *Emily Davies and the Liberation of Women 1830–1921*. London: André Deutsch.
Blake, Catriona. 1990. *The Charge of the Parasols: Women's Entry to the Medical Profession*. London: Women's Press.
Burstyn, Joan N. 1980. *Victorian Education and the Ideal of Womanhood*. London: Croom Helm.
Caine, Barbara. 1992. *Victorian Feminists*. Oxford: Oxford University Press.
Fawcett, Millicent. 1924. *What I Remember*. London: T. Fisher Unwin.
Forster, M. 1984. *Significant Sisters: The Grassroots of Active Feminism, 1839–1939*. London: Secker and Warburg.
Stephen, Barbara Nightingale. 1976. *Emily Davies and Girton College*. Westport, CT: Hyperion Press.
Strachey, Ray. 1978 [1928]. *The Cause: A Brief History of the Women's Movement*. Reprint, London: Virago.

Davison, Emily Wilding
(1872–1913)
United Kingdom

In 1913 the violent death of suffragette Emily Wilding Davison under the feet of a horse on Derby Day was recorded in all its vivid horror by the film camera. Seen in Gaumont Graphic cinema newsreels all around Britain, it brought home to public audiences the intensity of feeling with which the militant phase of the suffrage campaign was being embraced. In a reckless moment of protest ending in death, Davison ensured her immortalization as a feminist icon, but as Elizabeth Crawford (1999) points out, it would become impossible thereafter to strip away the layers of hagiography to find the true woman and real motives lying beneath.

Davison was one of three children of her businessman father's second marriage. She was educated at Kensington High School in 1885–1891

and studied literature at Royal Holloway College, but she had to leave before completing her course, when her father died in 1893. Her mother moved to Morpeth in Northumberland, but Davison remained in London, taking work as a governess (1893–1895) and teaching at Edgbaston and West Worthing (1895–1898). In her spare time, she studied at London University for a degree in English, for which she took the examination at Oxford University in 1897, passing with first-class honors. For six years (1900–1906), Davison was governess to a family in Berkshire.

In 1906 she joined the Women's Social and Political Union (WSPU). By the end of 1909, she gave up teaching to become a full-time organizer, being paid for a while after 1910 and subsidizing herself with articles for journals such as *Votes for Women*. During this time she took part in numerous violent demonstrations. Under the leadership of the Pankhursts, members of the WSPU had resorted to breaking windows, throwing stones (in Davison's case, at the car of Prime Minister David Lloyd George in Newcastle), setting fire to postboxes, and other acts of civil disobedience, with Davison herself whipping a man whom she wrongly identified as Lloyd George.

Davison's militancy resulted in regular arrests and imprisonment on eight occasions. During her final term at Holloway prison in 1911–1912, she was force-fed. Her incarceration did not prevent her from making impetuous, self-dramatizing acts of protest, even in prison. Once, having barricaded herself in her cell against the prospect of being force-fed, she was hosed with ice-cold water (after her release, she successfully sued for assault and won damages of forty shillings). In 1911 she staged a protest by throwing herself over the landing railings onto wire netting at Holloway, and in the process, permanently damaging her spine. Davison's well-documented propensity for self-destructive protest has left historians uncertain as to whether her final act— recorded by the coroner as "misadventure"—had been intended to bring about her death.

In May 1913, with Emmeline Pankhurst dangerously weak on a hunger and thirst strike in prison, Davison decided to draw attention to her case by trying to stop the king's horse on Derby Day, a high point in the British racing calendar guaranteed to attract huge public attendance. She made no mention of this to her friends beforehand and left no "suicide" note, and it is argued that she had never intended to kill herself but rather had failed to realize how fast the horses would be moving. Stepping out in front of the king's horse at Tattenham Corner and shouting "Votes for Women!," Davison was knocked over as she tried to grab the horse's rein. The horse turned a somersault and trampled her. Davison died of head injuries three days later without regaining consciousness. The WSPU ensured that their unexpected martyr received a suitably somber and very public funeral on 14 June, with 2,000 suffragettes as escort. In the event, it would be "the last large demonstration organized by the WSPU" (Vicinus 1985, 278). The outbreak of war the following year put the suffrage campaign on hold. Those WSPU members leading the funeral cortege and holding aloft a banner with the words "Fight On and God Will Give the Victory," were dressed in white with black armbands and held laurel wreaths. Others responded to calls by the WSPU leadership to wear black and carry purple irises or wear purple with crimson peonies. Marching with them in silent sympathy were trade unionists, members of the clergy, and representatives from many other suffrage societies; looking on were huge and mainly silent crowds lining the streets.

In a masterpiece of WSPU organizing, the suffrage militants thus obtained huge political capital from the act of a woman who had actually been seen by the leadership very much as a dangerously unpredictable maverick. Eulogies in the WSPU journal the *Suffragette* praised Davison's "supreme sacrifice" as a gallant and warlike fighter who had laid down her life for the cause. Meanwhile, suffragist Mary Stocks recorded her own account of the funeral, admitting her bafflement at the public response: "What a strange thing the London public is! It breaks up meetings and throws clods of earth at unoffending law-abiding National Unionists, and it turns out in its thousands, with its hat in its hand and tears in its eye, to watch the funeral of the most destructive militant who ever milled" (Stocks 1970, 66–67).

An article by Davison, entitled "The Price of Liberty," was published posthumously in the June 1914 issue of the *Suffragette*. In it, prefiguring her own martyrdom and equating it with that of Christ, she talked of personal sacrifice in the fight for women's suffrage, attesting in highly religious tones that to "re-enact the tragedy of Calvary for generations yet unborn, that is the last consummate sacrifice of the Militant!" (Vicinus 1985, 277). An Emily Wilding Davison Club was established in her memory in London, and during World War I a group of pacifist suffragettes within the WSPU who were against the jingoism of the British war effort established an Emily Wilding Davison fellowship.

Wilding's gravestone at the family plot in Morpeth has as its epitaph "Deeds not Words," in affirmation of Davison's own belief that nothing less than the ultimate personal sacrifice would persuade men that women's suffrage was a just cause. It is still a place of feminist pilgrimage. The Labour Group, located in Davison's home at Morpeth, is today appealing for funds to restore the now overgrown site as a permanent memorial.

See also Pankhurst, Christabel; Pankhurst, Emmeline; Pankhurst, (Estelle) Sylvia.

References and Further Reading
Colmore, Gertrude. 1988. "The Life of Emily Wilding Davison." In Ann Morley and Liz Stanley, *The Life and Death of Emily Wilding Davison*. London: Woman's Press.
Crawford, Elizabeth. 1999. *The Women's Suffrage Movement, 1866–1928: A Reference Guide*. London: University College of London Press.
Mackenzie, Midge. 1975. *Shoulder to Shoulder*. London: Penguin.
Stocks, Mary. 1970. *My Commonplace Book*. London: Peter Davies.
Tickner, L. 1987. *The Spectacle of Women: Imagery of the Suffrage Campaign 1907–1914*. London: Chatto and Windus.
Vicinus, Martha. 1985. *Independent Women, Work and Community for Single Women, 1850–1920*. London: Virago.
West, Rebecca. 1913. "The Life of Emily Davison." In J. Marcus, ed., *The Young Rebecca: Writings of Rebecca West 1911–17*. London: Virago.

Day, Dorothy
(1897–1980)
United States

An ardent pacifist, humanitarian, and administrator of welfare for the poor and a lay leader of the Catholic worker movement, Dorothy Day was arrested and imprisoned on several occasions because of her radicalism and her opposition to militarism. Yet there was much about

Day's character and her special brand of "Christian anarchism" that seemed highly contradictory: as a radical social activist, she combined her work with a deep religious faith that accepted traditional Catholic dogma. For Day, the role of the individual in social activism within the community was crucial: "We have all known the long loneliness and we have learned that the only solution is love and that love comes with community" (Day 1952, 286).

The daughter of a sports journalist, Day was born in Brooklyn, New York, and grew up in a Protestant household in California. She attended high school in Chicago and won a scholarship to Urbana College at the University of Illinois, but left before graduating to follow her father into journalism. When the family moved to New York in 1916, she took up reporting on social deprivation on Manhattan's Lower East Side. As a committed socialist, she gravitated to left-wing and intellectual circles in Greenwich Village, associating with radicals such as John Reed and Louise Bryant and being influenced by the social writing of Leo Tolstoy, Upton Sinclair, and Jack London. She worked as a reporter from 1917 on left-wing, Marxist journals such as the *Call*—for which she reported on industrial and trade union issues— Max Eastman's pacifist socialist journal, the *Masses* (assistant editor, 1917–1919); and Crystal and Max Eastman's *Liberator* (1918; assistant editor, 1923). She was a member of the militant group the Industrial Workers of the World (known as the "Wobblies") and the Socialist Party.

Day was also active in the women's movement, supporting free love (she had common-law unions and an illegitimate child) and birth control. She joined the militants of Alice Paul's Congressional Union for Woman Suffrage and was arrested for demonstrating at the White House in November 1917. Sentenced to thirty days in Occoquan workhouse, she went on a hunger strike for ten days, demanding to be given the status of a political prisoner. Ironically, although Day defended the right of the individual to suffrage, her personal mistrust of government was such that she never voted.

At the end of World War I, Day worked as probationary nurse in the King's County Hospital during the devastating influenza epidemic of 1918 and then traveled in Europe for some time. In 1924 she published an autobiographical novel, *The Eleventh Virgin*. During the 1920s, Day's so-

cialism became closely intertwined with her religious beliefs and commitment to pacifism. She lived with the anarchist Forster Batterham, giving birth to their daughter, Tamar Theresa, in 1927, but the relationship ended when Day converted to Catholicism and had the child baptized a Catholic, a fact that Batterham could not reconcile with his own atheism. Day took up writing for the liberal-Catholic journal, *Commonweal*, until 1932, when she met one of the guiding influences in her life, the French priest Peter Maurin. She espoused his Catholic ideals of social reconstruction, and together they founded the penny monthly, the *Catholic Worker*, in May 1933 (to which Day would contribute more than 1,000 articles and which she edited until her death). The journal was pacifist in tone and urged the Roman Catholic Church to take a stance against war and militarism and play a greater role in social programs. Its objective was to promote "the green revolution," which rejected capitalism in favor of cooperation and community, brought workers and socialists together in communities of voluntary poverty, and improved conditions for farmworkers and educational opportunities for the working classes. By 1936, its circulation had risen from its initial 2,500 to 150,000.

Day's Catholic worker movement founded its first refuge, the St. Joseph's House of Hospitality in New York's Bowery, in 1934, a district notorious for its drunks and down-and-outs. Starting out with about twenty volunteers, this shelter (later known as Catholic Workers House) was the first of several established to help counteract the homelessness and destitution suffered by the unemployed during the Great Depression with similar ventures soon following in Boston, Rochester, and Milwaukee. The movement also set up a farm community at Tivoli in New York state to create work for those who had lost their jobs. Day would later describe these and her activities in the Catholic worker movement in her 1939 book, *House of Hospitality*.

During World War I, Day had been adamant in her strong moral position on pacifism, basing her principles on the teachings of the Sermon on the Mount. She became a member of the Anti-Conscription League and during World War I was active in the establishment of the Association of Catholic Conscientious Objectors. During the Spanish Civil War (1936–1939), the

Catholic Worker lost readers because Day insisted on absolute neutrality and refused to accede to the pro-Franco sympathies of most American Catholics, which she saw as endorsing the fascist regime. The houses of hospitality were also affected by a loss of volunteer support, and fifteen were forced to close down. In the 1950s, Day joined the civil disobedience activities of the antinuclear movement. She was imprisoned for demonstrating in 1955 and three more times between then and 1959. During the Cuban missile crisis in 1962, she went on a peace mission to Cuba. She also demonstrated for racial equality, by joining civil rights marches in the South, and against the Vietnam War, and she frequently came up against the Catholic establishment for her uncompromising stand on nuclear weapons and her support of draft dodgers. Even in her mid-seventies, Day was still campaigning—this time in support of Cesar Chavez and Dolores Huerta, the leaders of the United Farm Workers of America (UFWA), in the fight to protect the rights of migrant Mexican workers. She ended up in jail at age seventy-six for illegal picketing.

Day published several works exploring her amalgam of socialist and Catholic belief, including *From Union Square to Rome* (1938), *On Pilgrimage* (1948), *The Long Loneliness* (1952), and *On Pilgrimage: The Sixties* (1972). In 1972 she was awarded the Laetare Medal by Notre Dame University in recognition of her work for the poor. In old age, she retreated from her earlier, more libertarian ideas and opposed the new youth culture of sex and drugs of the 1960s onward. It is fitting that Day, who lived and worked among the poor and espoused voluntary poverty, died in one of the Catholic Worker houses for homeless women that she had established. Moves to have her canonized as a Catholic saint began soon after her death at the request of Cardinal John Connor, although critics have argued against Day's suitability, asserting that she would much rather have had the money required to fund such a campaign to be spent on the poor. Further information on Day's life and the Catholic worker movement is available at http://www.catholicworker.org/dorothyday/.

See also Eastman, Crystal; Paul, Alice.

References and Further Reading
Coles, Robert. 1987. *Dorothy Day: A Radical Devotion.* Reading, MA: Addison-Wesley.
Day, Dorothy. 1952. *The Long Loneliness: The Autobiography of Dorothy Day.* New York: Harper.
Ellsberg, Robert, ed. 1983. *By Little and by Little: The Selected Writings of Dorothy Day.* New York: Knopf.
Forest, Jim. 1986. *Love Is the Measure: A Biography of Dorothy Day.* New York: Paulist.
Miller, William. 1974. *A Harsh and Dreadful Love: Dorothy Day and the Catholic Worker Movement.* Garden City, NY: Doubleday.
———. 1982. *Dorothy Day: A Biography.* San Francisco: Harper and Row.
Piehl, Mel. 1982. *Breaking Bread: The Catholic Workers and the Origin of Catholic Radicalism in America.* Philadelphia: Temple University Press.

de Silva, Agnes
(1885–1961)
Sri Lanka

Few facts can be found about the life of the foremost pioneer for women's suffrage in colonial Ceylon (Sri Lanka), who acted as secretary of the Women's Franchise Union, founded in 1927 by women of the middle and professional classes. De Silva was the niece of a pioneering women's doctor, Winifred Nell. In 1908 she married Sinhalese lawyer George de Silva—a leading liberal politician, social reformer, and supporter of women's suffrage. Agnes organized a deputation of women members of the franchise union to give evidence at the 1928 Donoughmore Commission on Constitutional Reform set up by the British government (which at that time ruled Ceylon), which recommended limiting the franchise to women over thirty. That same year she accompanied her husband on a visit to Britain in his mission to campaign for suffrage and other reforms, which were later incorporated into a new constitution for Ceylon that became law in 1931.

The 1931 constitution extended the franchise to all women over age twenty-one. De Silva stood in the ensuing general election as Labour Party candidate for the Galagedera seat on a ticket calling for universal suffrage, but she was not elected. She also served on the Executive Committee of the Labour Party.

References and Further Reading
Jayawardena, K. 1986. *Feminism and Nationalism in the Third World.* London: Zed Books.
Russell, Jane. 1981. *Our George: A Biography of F. E. De Silva.* Colombo: Times of Ceylon.

Deng Yingchao
(1904–1992)
China

An early activist in the Chinese women's movement, Deng later became vice president of the newly established All-China Women's Federation in 1949 and played an important role in the economic reconstruction of China. A product of the blossoming of Chinese intellectual and political activity inspired by the May Fourth Movement of 1919, Deng was brought up by her widowed mother who worked as a teacher. She was educated at the Beiyang First Girls' Normal School in Tianjin and helped set up the Tianjin Association of Women Patriotic Comrades, a short-lived organization superseded by the Tianjin Student Union, a mixed-sex group that discussed sexual relationships, women's emancipation and freedom in choice of marriage partner, and equality in education and employment. Deng wrote articles on feminist issues and social reform, such as the outlawing of arranged marriages, for its *Journal of the Student Union*. The magazine was hugely influential, and its calls for social reform led to the establishment of the Awakening Society, of which Deng became a leading member. In 1923 Deng married Zhou Enlai, the journal's editor and secretary of the European branch of the Chinese Communist Youth Corps.

Deng went on to edit the only women's newspapers in China at that time, the *Women's Daily* in Tianjin and the *Women's Star,* and in 1925 became a member of the women's committee that called for women's participation in the National Assembly. She joined the Chinese Communist Party (CCP) that same year and took a role in the Nationalist Central Women's Department then being run by He Xiangning (in the absence abroad of its head, Xiang Jingyu). As secretary of the Guangdong Provincial Women's Department, Deng organized women's support for the Chinese revolution, seeking to unite peasants and workers in a countrywide campaign. She wrote on women's issues for the CCP publication *The Voice of Women* and was a delegate at its Second Party Congress in 1926.

In 1934, suffering from tuberculosis, Deng nevertheless joined her husband on the Long March and endured the arduous 9,600-kilometer journey to the communist enclave in northern Shanxi province. There she worked at raising the consciousness of local peasant women, encouraging them to take part in the communist revolution. She organized women's cadres that helped these women set up their own local women's associations to call for their liberation from patriarchal customs.

In 1949, as a senior official in the CCP, Deng wrote a report on the future strategy of the Chinese women's movement, taking into account the unique problems facing China in its reconstruction. This report was taken up at the first congress of Chinese women, which, although it discussed women's rights to freedom and equality, sidelined the more personal issues revolving around their roles as wives and mothers in favor of discussing their enlistment in the construction of the new socialist state. As a leading voice on women's issues, Deng was also appointed vice president of the All-China Women's Federation in 1949. In 1956 she joined another legendary figure, Cai Chang, as one of three women on the Central Committee of the CCP (the other was Chen Shaoming).

See also Cai Chang; He Xiangning; Xiang Jingyu.
References and Further Reading
Croll, Elizabeth. 1978. *Feminism and Socialism in China.* New York: Schocken Books.
Gilmartin, Christina Kelly. 1995. *Engendering the Chinese Revolution: Radical Women, Communist Politics and Mass Movements in the 1920s.* Berkeley: University of California Press.
Ono Kazuko. 1978. *Chinese Women in a Century of Revolution.* Stanford: Stanford University Press.
Spence, Jonathan D. 1982. *The Gate of Heavenly Peace: The Chinese and Their Revolution, 1895–1980.* London: Faber and Faber
Wang Zheng. 1999. *Women in the Chinese Enlightenment: Oral and Textual Histories.* Berkeley: University of California Press.

Deng Yuzhi (Cora Deng)
(1900–1996)
China

A forgotten Chinese Christian who set up the Labor Bureau of the Chinese Young Women's Christian Association (YMCA) and later became its general secretary, Deng was one of several Chinese female reformers who took up the cause of women factory workers in the 1930s. Theirs was an underrated campaign of social activism that has been overshadowed by the more high-profile activities of women in the revolutionary movement. Deng's work for the YWCA helped inspire women to take part in the wider communist revolution and earned her the respect of the outstanding women's leader Xiang Jingyu.

Born in Shashi in the province of Hubei, Deng grew up in Changsha, where she attended the progressive Zhunan Girls' Middle School (also attended by activists such as Xiang Jingyu, Cai Chang, and Ding Ling). After the death of her parents, her grandmother, a Christian convert, sent her to the Fuxiang School for Girls—a missionary school—to complete her education. After leaving school and hoping to continue her education, Deng was forced to accept the arranged marriage her parents had made for her many years before. But in 1921 she ran away to Shanghai when her husband's family prohibited her from practicing as a Christian and blocked her attempts to go to college. Having joined the groundswell of young Chinese women inspired by the May Fourth Movement of 1919 when she was still at school, she was determined to take part in the movement's widespread activities for political and social change, including its campaign to end the age-old oppression of women. She studied sociology at Jinling College in Nanjing and spent a year at the London School of Economics (1929) in between taking up work for the Chinese YWCA.

Deng's commitment to the YWCA's welfare program was nurtured by its American secretary in China, Maud Russell, whom Deng had met in 1922 and who taught her English and enrolled her as a student member of the YWCA. Originally established in China in 1890 by Western missionaries, the YWCA changed dramatically in character during the 1920s as a result of the night schools it began running for working women in Shanghai and its numerous social projects among the urban poor. Deng's studies at Jingling involved writing a report on a children's home and conducting a survey of tapestry industry workers in Nanjing. After graduating from Jingling College, she had intended to become a teacher but instead took up Maud Russell's offer of working for the Student Department of the YWCA. In 1928, however, she rejected this proselytizing role in favor of pursuing grassroots social work.

In 1930 Deng became head of the YWCA's Labor Bureau and redirected her efforts toward a growing support for the social ideals of communism. She spearheaded a program of research among Chinese factory girls, studying conditions in factories and taking down detailed oral histories of their working lives. In her studies of women cotton mill workers during the 1930s, Deng reported on the inferior status of women from the northern province of Subei and on the primitive conditions in which many workers lived on *sampans* (Chinese fishing boats). She fought to penetrate a wall of management resistance in her efforts to expose the system by which girls as young as eleven or twelve were brought into the city from rural areas as contract labor and housed in overcrowded dormitories, sharing beds on a rotating basis. From the many hundreds of interviews with working women that she conducted, she ascertained that many of these girls had been dragooned into slavery in the factories not just by the mill owners but by their own poor families. They were sent to these factories so that they could raise the money needed to pay for their brothers to be taught a trade, which in turn would improve the family income.

Deng's other major project at this time was to set up night schools for women in major factory districts where working women could gain literacy skills and possibly become more socially aware. Thus, her schools offered a curriculum that included study of trade unionism and labor legislation in addition to traditional subjects such as the three R's, history, and geography. Political radicalization and patriotic consciousness-raising increased during the troubles with Japan that led to war in 1937. The changing political climate also challenged Deng to find a satisfactory compromise between her Christian beliefs and her growing support for a communist revolution in China.

Deng managed to sidestep being enlisted by Song Meiling (Madame Chiang Kai-shek) into official Guomindang (Nationalist Party) women's activities by traveling to the United States in 1939 to study for her master's degree at New York University. Her years of research were published by the university in 1941 as "The Economic Status of Women in Industry in China: With Special Reference to a Group in Shanghai." When the People's Republic of China came into being in 1949, Deng was asked to be a cofounder of the

All-China Women's Federation and to take a more prominent role in communist politics, representing Chinese Christians. In 1949 she became general secretary of the Chinese YWCA and in 1953 represented Chinese Christians at the World Peace Conference in Warsaw. With great skill and integrity, Deng continued to blend her Christian and communist ideals, liaising between the Chinese communist government and many international organizations. For information on the YWCA in China, contact www.worldywca.org.

See also Cai Chang; Ding Ling; Xiang Jingyu.
References and Further Reading
Honig, Emily. 1986. *Sisters and Strangers: Women in the Shanghai Cotton Mills 1919–1949*. Stanford: Stanford University Press.
———. 1992. "Christianity, Feminism, and Communism: The Life and Times of Deng Yuzhi (Cora Deng)." In Cheryl Johnson-Odim and Margaret Strobel, *Expanding the Boundaries of Women's History: Essays on Women in the Third World*. Bloomington: Indiana University Press.

Dennett, Mary Ware
(1872–1947)
United States

At the beginning of the twentieth century, the U.S. birth control movement was dominated by the combative, radical figure of Margaret Sanger, while the work of another important activist, the humanist Mary Ware Dennett, was relegated to a secondary position. Part of the reason for the long neglect of Dennett's work is that she came into conflict with the flamboyant Sanger over tactics. Sanger was prepared to flout the laws and establish birth control clinics to promote the cause, but Dennett preferred to fight for legal change. Ultimately, she suffered the same vilification as Sanger when she was prosecuted for sending birth control literature through the post. Dennett was also active in the suffrage, labor, and pacifist movements, in later life supporting the concept of a world federation.

Dennett was born into an old New England family in Worcester, Massachusetts. She began her career as an artist after studying at Boston's Museum of Fine Arts and was inspired by the British arts and crafts movement led by William Morris. She held the position of head of the School of Design and Decoration at the Drexel Institute in Philadelphia (1894–1897) and developed a specialized skill for tapestry making, as well as rediscovering the age-old Spanish technique of making Cordoval leather wall hangings. She moved back to Boston in 1898 and opened her own handicraft shop with her sister Clara. In 1900 Dennett married an architect and had two sons. She worked for a while as an interior designer before becoming involved in the suffrage movement, joining the Massachusetts Woman Suffrage Association in 1908. With her marriage in trouble because of her husband's adultery, Dennett accepted the appointment as corresponding secretary of the National American Woman Suffrage Association in 1910 and moved to New York, divorcing her husband in 1913. But she found the organization too conservative and in 1914 resigned to work for the pacifist and socialist movements. During World War I, she joined the U.S. Woman's Peace Party (which in 1919 became the U.S. branch of the Women's International League for Peace and Freedom), worked as field secretary of the American Union Against Militarism, and was a founding member of an antimilitarist group, the People's Council.

In 1914 Dennett had written her first pamphlet on sex education in the belief that the population explosion fueled military expansionism. Disliking the militancy of direct action that Sanger advocated, Dennett established the National Birth Control League in 1915. With more moderate objectives, the league campaigned to have the definition of birth control as obscene removed from the New York state statutes and to organize lobbying for its legalization. But the league quickly ran into financial difficulties, and with the birth control movement divided (because Dennett would not support Sanger's Brownsville Clinic), the league was disbanded in 1919. The problem, as ever, for Dennett would be that Sanger's more charismatic personality and well-developed political skills would always overshadow her own and those of others in the movement.

In 1919 Dennett formed a new group, the Voluntary Parenthood League, asserting that parenthood, like freedom of speech, was a fundamental civil liberty and a matter of individual choice. Dennett elaborated on her arguments as editor of the *Birth Control Herald* (1922–1925), her primary objective being to achieve the abolition of the 1873 Comstock law, which defined contraceptives as illegal. This new league began campaigning for changes to the postal code, which classified literature on birth control as obscene, and suggested its reclassification as "scientific" material, which would then allow it to be sent through the post. Changing the federal law would result in birth control's wider dissemination across many U.S. states. In order to make the law palatable to more conservative opponents, Dennett suggested in 1924 that the new law should stipulate that all birth control material be vetted by a medical board for its suitability.

During 1919–1920, Dennett had attempted a rapprochement with Sanger and did serve on the board of Sanger's *Birth Control Review* for a while. But she was unable to reconcile herself to Sanger's more radical activism, and the divisions between them were further exacerbated by Sanger's formation in 1921 of the American Birth Control League, which was committed to making it legal for doctors to administer birth control. Dennett felt that such a move would greatly restrict women's access to contraception and birth control advice if they were only made available to those who could afford to obtain it through doctors and not via the mail or through free clinics. The relationship between the two campaigners became pointed and often antagonistic, based in part on Sanger's overriding desire to maintain total control over the movement. In 1925, when the Voluntary Parenthood League finally accepted that the provision of contraceptive devices would only be legalized if they were administered by doctors, it merged with Sanger's American Birth Control League. Because this was a fundamental point on which Dennett firmly disagreed, she resigned. The documented story of the rivalry between Mary Ware Dennett and Margaret Sanger in the American birth control movement can be found online at http://www.womhist.binghamton.edu/birth/intro.htm.

In 1918, with her two young sons in mind, Dennett had produced an important essay on sexuality, republished as a pamphlet titled "The Sex Side of Life: An Explanation for Young People." She was deluged with more than 25,000 requests for copies in the first few years, but in 1922 the pamphlet was declared obscene by the postmaster general, thus initiating a long battle with the legal system for the right to disseminate such literature through the post that culminated in her prosecution in 1929. In *Birth Control Laws: Shall We Keep Them, Change Them, or Abolish Them?* (1926), Dennett emphasized that birth control was a civil liberty, and the American Civil Liberties Union (ACLU) came to her defense. In 1928 the U.S. Postal Service set in motion its plan to prosecute Dennett's pamphlet as being "lewd, lascivious, filthy, vile and indecent" (Reynolds 1994, 91). But it soon became clear that what Dennett's conservative opponents really objected to in "The Sex Side of Life" was her assertion that not only could sexual intercourse be pleasurable for women as well as men, but also that masturbation would not turn those who practiced it into mental degenerates. In 1929 the case finally came to court, and Dennett was convicted and fined $300. With the support of the ACLU, she appealed, and the ruling was overturned in 1930, when the appeal judge concluded that Dennett was providing serious and accurate information on sex education. Soon after, she published her own account of the trial, *Who's Obscene?*

Besides her important work for birth control, in which her objectives remained closer to those of the British pioneer Marie Stopes, Dennett was also active in the pacifist movement and supported free trade, consumer protection, and the single-tax movement. In 1941 she was a cofounder of the World Federalist Group, which sought to bring greater economic and political unity throughout the world by peaceful means. A description by Linda Gordon of Dennett's papers relating to the birth control movement in the Schlesinger Library, Radcliffe College, can be found online at http://www.lexis-nexis.com/cispubs/guides/womens_studies/.

See also Sanger, Margaret; Stopes, Marie.

References and Further Reading

Chen, Constance C. 1996. *The Sex Side of Life: Mary Ware Dennett's Pioneering Battle for Birth Control and Sex Education.* New York: New Press.

Gordon, Linda. 1976. *Woman's Body, Woman's Right: A Social History of Birth Control in America.* New York: Grossman.

Reynolds, Moira Davison. 1994. *Women Advocates of Reproductive Rights: Eleven Who Led the Struggle in the United States and Great Britain.* Jefferson, NC: McFarland.

Whitman, Alden, ed. 1988. *American Reformers: An H. W. Wilson Biographical Dictionary.* New York: H. W. Wilson.

Deraismes, Marie
(1828–1894)
France

An outstanding public speaker on women's rights, Marie Deraismes began her activities running a republican salon in Paris in the 1860s. She was also one of the first Frenchwomen to fight for women to be admitted to the closed world of freemasonry. As a secularist, orator, and leading figure in the revival of feminism in France during the 1860s and 1870s, she was founder of the women's group the Society for the Improvement of the Condition of Women and the magazine *Women's Rights.*

Born into a wealthy, enlightened Protestant family, Deraismes grew up in Pontoise. She was well educated, studying Greek, Latin, and philosophy, and the early death of both parents left her an ample income. During the early 1860s, she took to writing undistinguished comedies of feminist content as well as literary criticism and also published two feminist pamphlets ("To Rich Women" and "Theresa and Her Epoch"). From the mid-1860s she worked as a journalist for the *National* and the *Epoch,* developing her themes of women in society.

Deraismes rejected free love, advocated by other French feminists, many of whom were followers of social reformer Henri de Saint-Simon, as allowing men to perpetuate a sexual double standard and wrote openly about women's right to passion and sexual fulfillment within marriage. Although she chose to remain unmarried, she staunchly defended the family as the cornerstone of social and moral order, provided that husbands and wives enjoyed equality within it: "This miniature society—the family—prepares for the larger one. It contains all the seeds of society: justice, equality, right, freedom, solidarity. Here we have a ready-made school: a strong nation will come from it" (Moses 1993, 184). But this ideal family could only be achieved if women were able to acquire greater intellectual skills on a par with men through access to education. In regard to women's suffrage, although Deraismes believed in it as a fundamental right for women, in terms of activism she approached the subject with caution, believing that if women were enfranchised too soon, the majority of them would be likely to support the Catholic and pro-royalist establishment rather than republicanism and with it democratic rights for all.

In 1866 Deraismes joined the moderate Society for the Demand of the Rights of Women, a group dedicated particularly to establishing girls' schools. She funded the group with much of her own money, but the members were dispersed during the upheavals of the Franco-Prussian War (1870–1871) and the Commune of Paris of 1871. In 1866, with the encouragement of Léon Richer, she gave a lecture on women's rights at a Sunday "philosophical conference" organized at the Grand Orient Lodge, in so doing becoming the first woman to address male freemasons. In 1870 Richer and Deraismes founded a new society, the moderate Association for the Rights of Women, which in 1874 changed its name to the Society for the Improvement of the Condition of Women. Its objective was the emancipation of women, understood as the attainment of social and civil equality before political equality and the vote, and its precepts were framed by Deraismes in its weekly journal *Women's Rights,* founded in 1869, for which she wrote during the 1870s.

Deraismes was a pioneer in international cooperation among feminists, and in 1878 and again in 1889 she helped set up the first two feminist congresses ever held in France, using her own money to help fund them. But attendance at both was barely more than 200, with only a handful of countries represented, although Deraismes herself was a powerful presence at the second of the two, the French and First International Congress on Women's Rights held in Paris at the time of the Paris Exposition. In 1881 Deraismes's association with Richer ended when he left the Society for the Improvement of the Condition of Women after a disagreement with her. The society combined forces with the remnants of the Society for the Demand of the Rights of Women to become the Society for the Improvement of the Condition of Women and the Demand for Their Rights. Under Deraismes's presidency, which lasted from 1881 until her death, the new society continued to advocate educating women and reforming the civil code. Deraismes also took up new causes, attempting to inaugurate the moral regeneration of France by working in the French section of Josephine Butler's burgeoning campaign against state-regulated prostitution; she also became an ardent antivivisectionist.

During the 1880s Deraismes adjusted her gradualist views on the achievement of women's political rights, particularly suffrage, as the more radical campaigning of Hubertine Auclert's Women's Suffrage group gained ground from 1883. Nevertheless, she still feared that male republican politicians were not yet ready to give women's suffrage their full support.

From 1881 to 1885 from her family estate at Pontoise, Deraismes ran the newspaper *The Republican of Seine-et-Oise.* She took part in antichurch activities, calling for the separation of church and state and in 1881 presiding at the first anticlerical congress in France. In 1885 she was honorary president of the French Federation of Freethinking Groups of Seine-et-Oise. Such activities, combined with her support for the republicans, led her to challenge the male bastion of freemasonry when in 1882 she went through the initiation ceremony of a freethinker freemason's lodge. Her initiation was declared invalid by the Masonic hierarchy in 1893. However, later that year, Deraismes was finally allowed to found Human Right, the first mixed lodge that endorsed sexual equality.

Deraimes's involvement in the pacifist cause grew naturally from her social and political concerns, as a fundamental component of the moral regeneration of society. She believed that women's qualities of "sagacity, perseverance, abnegation" (Josephson et al. 1985, 208) made them the natural defenders of peace and morality, and she elaborated on women's virtues as peacemakers and moral guardians in feminist works such as the 1868 tract "Our Principles and Morals." In 1872 she published *Eve against Mr. Dumas, Son,* a collection of her series of public speeches entitled "The Bluestockings," in which she criticized male writers such as Dumas for denigrating women as the inferior sex. Other notable works were *The Rights of Children* (1886) and her major feminist essays, collected in *Eve in Humanity* (1891).

See also Auclert, Hubertine.

References and Further Reading

Bidelman, Patrick Kay. 1982. *Pariahs Stand Up! The Founding of the Liberal Feminist Movement in France 1858–1889.* Westport, CT: Greenwood Press.

Evans, Richard. 1977. *The Feminists: Women's Emancipation Movement in Europe, America and Australasia 1840–1920.* London: Croom Helm.

Josephson, Harold, Sandi Cooper, and Steven C. Hause et al., eds. 1985. *Biographical Dictionary of Modern Peace Leaders.* Westport, CT: Greenwood Press.

Moses, Claire Goldberg. 1993. *Feminism, Socialism, and French Romanticism.* Bloomington: Indiana University Press.

Offen, Karen. 2000. *European Feminisms 1700–1950: A Political History.* Stanford: Stanford University Press.

Sowerwine, Charles. 1982. *Sisters or Citizens? Women and Socialism in France since 1876.* Cambridge: Cambridge University Press.

Deroin, Jeanne
(1805–1894)
France

Building on her working-class roots as an embroiderer and inspired by the views on women's emancipation of the St. Simonian social movement of the 1830s, Jeanne Deroin would become a leading feminist during the 1848 revolution, along with Pauline Roland and Eugénie Niboyet. A fierce critic of the bondage of marriage and a campaigner for women's self-emancipation both as mothers and workers, Deroin believed that "man is able to establish order only by despotism; woman is able to organise only through the power of maternal love; the two united will be able to reconcile order and liberty" (Rendall 1987, 294–295). With this idea in mind, she dedicated herself to obtaining the liberation of working women by establishing a union of cooperatives that would ensure their equal rights with men.

Deroin was self-educated and grew up in poverty, earning her living as a laundress. She married the bursar of an old people's home in a civil ceremony in 1832 but refused to use her husband's surname (Desroches). She began contributing to the St. Simonian journal the *Free Woman* (later known as the *Women's Tribune*) in the early 1830s. Aware of the lack of educational opportunity for working-class children such as her own, she trained as a teacher and obtained her certificate, although she was barely literate, and opened a school in the 1840s.

Deroin embraced the upheavals of 1848 when King Louis-Philippe was overthrown by the radical movement, attended many meetings at revolutionary clubs, and wrote petitions and journal articles. She produced a pamphlet on women's oppression, "A Course in Social Law for Women," in which she illustrated how the proper recognition of women's contribution to society within the sphere of motherhood was an essential component of any new society. With women forbidden by law from public speaking, Deroin contributed to the feminist socialist newspaper *Women's Voice* run by Eugénie Niboyet (closed down in June 1848). She also set up her own short-lived Women's Emancipation Club and cofounded with Desirée Gay a Women's Mutual Education Society dedicated to the struggle of working-class women. She contributed to the society's journal *Women's Politics,* changing its title soon after to *Women's Opinion,* and struggled to keep the journal going until August 1849.

Deroin believed that women could only be emancipated in the wake of the liberation of the working classes and wider social change and should therefore take an active part in effecting this goal. As a follower of the ideas of Henri St. Simon (the social reformer who advocated cooperation between the sexes), she believed that the maternal role of women should be given equal weight in any new society. Because women had a natural talent for cooperation, according to her, they could "organize with love" the transformation of society into mutually supportive communities. In her editorials and articles, she encouraged women's solidarity in self-help groups and proposed that poorer female workers should be assisted in training and marketing by those who made greater profits.

In May 1849, determined to "strike at every closed door" (Rowbotham 1999, 219), Deroin interpreted the reference to "citizens" in the constitution of 1848 as meaning both men and women and stood for election to the National Assembly. She called for support from the revolutionary clubs and among feminists such as the novelist George Sand and Pauline Roland, both of whom declined to stand with her. Her demand that the French National Assembly allow both workers and women to participate in politics on an equal footing with middle-class men was soundly rejected: Deroin received only fifteen votes.

In the final issue of *Women's Opinion* in August 1849, Deroin laid out her Project for the Union of Workers' Associations, a network of national workshops that would promote sexual equality and set up cooperatives to provide employment. Her objective was also jointly to establish a central commission that would monitor the balance of supply and demand of goods, raise credit where needed, and ensure the even distribution of workers across key industries. At a meeting in

August 1849, 400 cooperative associations came together under this banner, and at year's end Deroin was elected to its central committee.

During 1850 the work of the Union of Workers' Associations came under increasing surveillance, and its supporters were rounded up by the police. Deroin was put on trial for conspiracy to subvert society in November but acceded to a plea from male members of the union to keep silent about her central role in it for the sake of unity. In court, insisting on being cross-examined under her own and not her married name, she eloquently defended her social principles and the Union of Workers' Associations' idea of a free interchange of goods and services that would eliminate the capitalist principle of profit.

She was held in St. Lazare prison for six months, from where, with Pauline Roland, she gave her enthusiastic endorsement of the 1851 U.S. women's rights convention and appealed for support from American women for the plight of women in France who had seen democracy slip away from them with the failure of the 1848 revolution. Upon her release, Deroin worked as a teacher. After Louis Napoleon's coup in December 1851, Deroin helped organize support for the families of prisoners, but in August 1852 she fled into exile in London, where she attempted to establish a mutual aid society for French exiles and a school for their children. She published the journal *The Women's Almanach* (1854) in both French and English and a *Letter to Workers* (1856). In the 1880s her letters on the rights of illegitimate children were published in the French journal *The Rights of Women.* The French government awarded her a pension, which enabled her to care properly for her mentally retarded son, but she never returned to France. In December 1882, the caring and compassionate Elizabeth Cady Stanton, who had not forgotten Deroin's brave support for U.S. suffrage from her prison cell and who had published her letter in her *History of Woman Suffrage,* sought Deroin out during a visit to her daughter in England. She found her "living in great poverty and obscurity at Shepherd's Bush" and noted how physically Deroin had greatly aged. "She is a little, dried-up woman, though her face still beams with intelligence" (Stanton 1922, vol. 2, 201). When Deroin died in 1894, such was the respect for her in British socialist circles that her English friend and supporter

William Morris (a founder of the Socialist League) gave a eulogy at her funeral.

See also Niboyet, Eugénie; Roland, Pauline.
References and Further Reading
Gordon, Felicia, and Máire Cross. 1996. *Early French Feminism, 1830–1940: A Passion for Liberty.* Cheltenham: Edward Elgar.
Moses, Claire Goldberg. 1984. *French Feminism in the Nineteenth Century.* Albany: State University of New York Press.
Offen, Karen. 2000. *European Feminisms 1700–1950: A Political History.* Stanford: Stanford University Press.
Rendall, J. 1987. *Equal or Different: Women's Politics 1800–1914.* Oxford: Blackwell.
Rowbotham, Sheila. 1999. *Threads through Time: Writings on History and Autobiography.* London: Penguin.
Scott, Joan Wallach. 1996. *Only Paradoxes to Offer: French Feminists and the Rights of Man.* Cambridge, MA: Harvard University Press.
Stanton, Theodore, and Harriot Stanton Blatch, eds. 1922. *Elizabeth Cady Stanton, as Revealed in Her Letters, Diary, and Reminiscences.* New York: Arno Press.

Charlotte Despard (National Portrait Gallery)

Despard, Charlotte
(1844–1939)
United Kingdom/Ireland

The Anglo-Irish suffragette, pacifist, and social campaigner Charlotte Despard was a striking and eccentric figure, famous for her thin, wiry frame, steely gray hair, and black widow's weeds. She proved a fearsome adversary in political debate throughout an extraordinary career of social and political campaigning. In later years, she was often seen in tandem with the redoubtable Maud Gonne campaigning for Irish political prisoners, activities that earned them the sobriquet of "Maud Gonne Mad and Mrs. Desperate." Like Gonne, Despard was not actually born in Ireland, and later, like both Gonne and Constance de Markievicz, she converted to Catholicism. All three in many ways proved to be more Irish than the Irish in their commitment to Irish independence and imbued the movement with a unique romantic fire and feminine passion.

Born in Kent, England, Despard was educated at boarding school. She lost her father at a young age, and when her mother was pronounced insane, Despard was sent to relatives who brought her up as a strict Presbyterian. She was a natural rebel and had a strong social conscience. She longed to do something useful with her life and soon balked at the idea of doing what all genteel middle-class young ladies were expected to do— sit idly by, waiting for the right husband to present himself.

Despard witnessed poverty early in her life when she settled in London in 1862. She left England in 1866 on a three-year European tour, during which she met and, in 1870, married a fellow radical, the Frenchman Maximilien Despard. For the next twenty years, until her husband's death in 1890, Despard pursued her social concerns solely through the medium of the ten novels she wrote. These romantic works had titles such as *Chaste as Ice, Pure as Snow* (1874), although *A Voice from the Dim Millions,* an unpublished novel written in the 1880s, was a genuine attempt to tackle the subjects that most concerned her: poverty, disease, and premature death among factory workers. In the 1880s Despard voiced her support for the national campaign for the Married Women's Property

Act, but it was not until she was widowed in 1890 that she finally felt she could give her full commitment to activism and began working with the poor. She did so in the grim Nine Elms district of London. There during the 1890s she became a familiar figure, dressed in her black lace mantilla and open sandals as she worked among destitute street children. She bought a house in the area, where she opened one of the first child welfare centers in England, offering nursing care and subsidized meals of soup and milk pudding as part of her drive to deal with the effects of malnutrition. She also regularly took parties of poor children on trips to the countryside. In 1895 Despard expanded her activities and opened a boys' club. Such was the esteem in which her work was held that it was commented upon in Charles Booth's classic seventeen-volume study of the living conditions of the London poor, *Life and Labour of the People in London* (1889–1902).

Despard undertook an important new role when she became a workhouse visitor for the Kingston Poor Law Board in 1892. In 1894 she was elected a poor law guardian for Vauxhall and for the next nine years did social work in Lambeth. The abuses and shortcomings of the antiquated system appalled and outraged her. She so despised its cruelties—made manifest to her by the punitive regime at the Renfrew Road Workhouse—that she began actively campaigning for reform of the Poor Laws so that the poor could receive relief without having to be incarcerated in such degrading institutions. She even traveled to Canada to gain firsthand experience of how the system of sending young and destitute unemployed children to that country worked and was again horrified at the exploitation she witnessed.

By the time of her journey, Despard had discovered her talent for public speaking, and her compassion and sense of moral outrage would characterize all her many appearances on the podium right into her nineties. During the course of her long career she befriended many socialist and trade union leaders, including Keir Hardie. She joined the Social Democratic Federation and put her boys' club hall in Wandsworth at its disposal. But she later became dissatisfied with the federation's level of support for women's rights and in 1902 transferred her activities to the Independent Labour Party, which seemed to her to offer a greater commitment to women's suffrage.

Despard had first become interested in women's rights when she witnessed the plight of single working mothers caused by the punitive workings of the poor laws, but she never embraced suffrage as a single issue, viewing all the social evils suffered by both men and women as stemming from the capitalist system. For her, suffrage was but one milestone on the road to the achievement of a noble socialist utopia built on the tenets of Marxism. In 1903 she joined Emmeline Pankhurst's Women's Social and Political Union (WSPU) and took part in more militant campaigning for suffrage, trying very hard to get herself arrested. The British police duly obliged in 1907, when she spent twenty-one days in Holloway jail after brandishing her umbrella during a rowdy suffrage demonstration outside the House of Commons. But Despard soon came to dislike the increasingly dictatorial leadership of Emmeline Pankhurst and her daughter Christabel and later in 1907 attempted, along with Teresa Billington-Greig, Edith How-Martyn, and other moderates to get the organization to reform itself. When this effort failed, Despard and seventy other suffragists broke away and with others of similar mind formed the Women's Freedom League to campaign on wider issues than purely that of suffrage, including better working conditions for women in sweatshops and other issues such as prostitution and infanticide.

Events would eventually prove Despard right when she remarked that the "history of the twentieth century will show the rise of two great movements—women and labour" (Linklater 1980, 101). Inspired by the work of Mahatma Gandhi in India (whom she met in 1909) and under Despard's driving influence, the Women's Freedom League espoused the Indian concept of *satyagraha,* which employed nonviolent methods of civil disobedience and spiritual resistance by refusing to pay taxes and boycotting the 1911 census. The failure of the electoral reform bill in 1912 to introduce women's suffrage galvanized Despard into increasing militancy, and by then she had also come under the influence of the Theosophy movement, on which she wrote numerous pamphlets.

As a humanitarian and pacifist, Despard opposed war when it broke out in 1914 and gave her support to the Irish Women's Peace Committee. She was also dismayed at the decision of the British members of the National Union of Women's Suffrage Societies and the WSPU to halt their suffragist activities for the duration of the war. Outspoken as ever, she criticized the British government for its misplaced social concerns, averring that it should "take over the milk as you have taken over the munitions" (Linklater 1980, 183). This was at a time when her brother, Field Marshall John French, was chief of staff of the British army. She turned her attention to organizing relief through the National Aid Corps, which trained women police volunteers as special constables, and herself provided free meals and a nursery in Nine Elms for sick mothers whose husbands were away fighting.

Now in her seventies, Despard seemed unstoppable, her energies limitless. As her biographers have observed, in 1916–1917 she was serving simultaneously on the councils of the Women's Freedom League (as president, 1909–1918), the Women's International League, the No-Conscription Fellowship (Battersea branch), the National Council for Civil Liberties, the Theosophical Society, the London Vegetarian Society, The National Canine Defence League, the Battersea Labour Party, the Women's Labour League, the Home Rule for India Committee, and the Women's Peace Crusade—all of which involved her in as many as thirty meetings a month—and this on top of her charitable work in Nine Elms, the writing of pamphlets, and endless public speech making. In 1918, after women won the vote, she stood as a Labour Party candidate in Battersea, but her pacifist views ran counter to the current climate of British jingoism, and she failed to win election.

At the end of the war, Despard undertook relief work and fund-raised to send food to central Europe, but in these final twenty years of her life, she became passionately caught up in the cause of Irish separatism and human rights. At a time when her brother, as lord lieutenant of Ireland from 1918 to 1921, was recruiting the notorious Black and Tan troops to quell civil unrest in Ireland, Despard settled in Dublin and did everything she could to embarrass her brother's administration.

In the 1920s she sponsored an Irish Workers' College in a building she owned on Eccles Street. On the eve of the Irish Civil War of 1922–1923, she joined forces with Maud Gonne in support of Sinn Féin, setting up a refuge for victims of the violence and forming the Women's Prisoners' Defence League to offer help to the families of imprisoned men. The house they set up for this purpose became a meeting place for Republicans and fugitives, and Despard donated much of her own money toward providing help to those who asked for it. When Gonne was later arrested and jailed, the small, frail figure of Charlotte Despard—now "as old as the hills and twice as wrinkled," as Margaret Cousins described her (Cousins and Cousins 1950, 170), could be seen keeping vigil for two weeks outside Kilmainham Jail.

For long a communist sympathizer, Despard founded the Friends of Soviet Russia and traveled to the Soviet Union in 1930, when other Western supporters of the regime (including Beatrice and Sidney Webb and George Bernard Shaw) had also felt compelled personally to verify the "success" of the Soviet experiment. Having been totally taken in by the carefully controlled, cosmetic version of Soviet reality with which she had been presented, she came back content, but the trip had its repercussions. Soon after, Despard was forced to move north to Belfast, after being criticized for her support of communism and for joining the Communist Party. Undaunted, she defied her critics at the age of ninety by donating her Eccles Street house in Dublin to the Friends of Soviet Russia, one of her last philanthropic acts. In 1935 she set about helping Catholic victims of the sectarian troubles in Belfast.

Despite her conversion to Catholicism and her passionate commitment to Ireland in her latter years, there was a quality about Despard that remained defiantly and bulldoggishly British in its blend of stubborn gentility and indignant opprobrium. Observers have commented on her having the physical appearance of a prophet or Cassandra figure and on her simultaneous and voracious espousal of a myriad of good causes. Andre Linklater has pointed out the conundrum of the "silver-haired lady, with a fine educated English accent, talking of revolution and the overthrow of government to an audience of shipyard and linen-mill workers, police spies and trade-union leaders, most of whom regarded her with either embarrassment or incomprehension" (Linklater 1980, 15). For her own part, Despard frequently reminisced on the long struggle of all her many social campaigns as being "impossible dreams," but during the course of her extraordinary life she had remained, as her close friend Maud Gonne described her, "like a white flame in the defence of prisoners and the oppressed" (Linklater 1980, 257).

See also Billington-Greig, Teresa; Cousins, Margaret; Gonne, Maud; How-Martyn, Edith; Markievicz, Constance de; Pankhurst, Emmeline; Webb, Beatrice.

References and Further Reading

Cousins, James, and Margaret Cousins. 1950. *We Two Together*. Madras: Ganesh.

Crawford, Elizabeth. 1999. *The Women's Suffrage Movement, 1866–1928: A Reference Guide.* London: University College of London Press.

Hollis, Patricia., ed. 1987. *Ladies Elect: Women in English Local Government 1865–1914*. Oxford: Clarendon Press.

Linklater, Andro. 1980. *An Unhusbanded Life: Charlotte Despard, Suffragette, Socialist, and Sinn Feiner*. London: Hutchinson.

Mulvihill, Margaret. 1989. *Charlotte Despard*. London: Pandora.

Ó Céirín, Kit, and Cyril Ó Céirín, eds. 1996. *Women of Ireland: A Biographic Dictionary*. Kinvara, Co. Galway: Tír Éolas.

Diana, Princess of Wales
(1961–1997)
United Kingdom

Few personalities in the twentieth century who campaigned on social and humanitarian issues were able to attract attention to their causes on such a universal and unprecedented scale as was the princess of Wales, during her all too brief lifetime as a public figure. Although purists might discount the validity of her contribution as a "serious" social reformer, Princess Diana's particular contribution to the demystification of acquired immunodeficiency syndrome (AIDS) was achieved at the grassroots level by the manner in which she showed unqualified warmth and empathy toward its victims. In so doing, she attracted widespread media and public attention and helped promote both a better understanding of the disease and a greater tolerance for gays. Indeed, she had a rare gift for instilling compassion in people for the innocent victims not only of disease but also of war, as she did most notably in her work for the Red Cross in the campaign against the use of antipersonnel mines in the months before her death.

Until Princess Diana found a channel for her natural compassion and love of children in her work for the many charities that she supported as the wife of the heir to the British throne, the facts of her life had been unremarkable. Born into one of England's great aristocratic families, as Lady Diana Spencer she received a conventional private education and attended finishing school in Switzerland, before taking a job at an upmarket kindergarten in London's West End. She might have been set for a life in comfortable obscurity had she not met Prince Charles and become engaged to him in February 1981. Lady Di, as she was then referred to by the press (and this tag persisted even after she became Princess of Wales), was rapidly propelled from shy kindergarten assistant to the mother of the two heirs to the throne—William, born in 1982, and Harry, in 1984. Her natural beauty, winning smile, and superlative dress sense soon saw her promoted to world media star and incomparable fashion icon.

Princess Diana's adoption into the British royal family marked the beginning of a seventeen-year love-hate relationship with the press and also with the royal family itself. Adrift in a world of royal protocol and formality that stifled her naturally boisterous and demonstrative personality, she gradually learned to use the press to her own advantage by providing photo opportunities that drew the world's attention to the things she cared so passionately about. And none more so than AIDS. In 1987, at a time when the paranoia about the disease was at its height, with people calling for the virtual quarantining of those who tested positive for the human immunodeficiency virus (HIV) and some religious groups proclaiming that AIDS was "God's visitation on sexual deviants," Princess Diana had her photograph taken shaking hands with a gay man who was HIV-positive. The encounter, which took place at a pioneering AIDS clinic at London's Middlesex Hospital, was shown on television and syndicated in press photographs around the world. It did more than the princess's many unpublicized and private visits to AIDS hospices combined to raise public awareness about the disease and to modulate the escalating climate of homophobia. It also dissipated the hysterical rumors that the AIDS virus could be transmitted by touch. Similarly, in later years Princess Diana went out of her way to be seen touching and comforting people with leprosy and children with cancer and to be photographed with the mutilated victims of landmine explosions in Angola and Bosnia, although this latter campaigning provoked controversial, with the princess being accused of meddling in political matters.

Princess Diana also campaigned vigorously for greater tolerance for many other underprivileged and marginalized groups, in particular the homeless, in her work for London's Centrepoint charity. Herself the child of a broken marriage (her parents divorced when she was six), she spoke frankly about her personal experiences of anorexia, bulimia, and postpartum depression in a book by Andrew Morton, *Diana: Her True Story* (1992). A BBC television interview in 1996—for all its controversy and Diana's very patent exploitation of her new and very public role as victim—enabled her to speak on a personal level to many other women who had suffered similar problems in their own lives.

When her marriage to Prince Charles, which had foundered in the mid-1980s, ended in a formal separation in 1992 and divorce in 1996, Princess Diana withdrew from some of her charity work. However, she remained an important communicator across many creeds and cultures, averring: "I'm not a political figure. . . . I'm a humanitarian figure. I always have been and I always will be" (*Daily Telegraph,* 17 January 1997). In this guise, the last and most public cause she was to adopt was that of banning antipersonnel mines worldwide.

Diana, Princess of Wales, died tragically young, shortly after being involved in a car crash in Paris, at a time when rumors abounded on the nature of her relationship with international playboy Dodi Fayed. She died before seeing the inauguration of the anti-landmine treaty of September 1997, which banned the use, production, stockpiling, and transfer of antipersonnel mines. This treaty opened for signature in Ottawa on 3 December 1998 and was subsequently signed by 139 countries; it has now been fully ratified by 111. For further information on this issue, contact the International Campaign to Ban Landmines at http://www.icbl. org.

The princess's life and many charitable concerns are now commemorated by the Diana, Princess of Wales Memorial Fund, an independent organization that makes grants to dozens of charities all over the world, as well as continuing to support the six charities that were closest to her own heart: Centrepoint, the English National Ballet, Great Ormond Street Hospital for Children, the Leprosy Mission (begun by the late Mother Teresa, a woman the princess greatly admired), the National AIDS Trust, and the Royal Marsden National Health Service Hospital Trust. For further information on the princess's life, access the official royal website at http://www.royal.gov.uk/main.

References and Further Reading
Burchill, Julie. 1998. *Diana.* London: Weidenfeld and Nicolson.
Campbell, Beatrix. 1998. *Diana: How Sexual Politics Shook the Monarchy.* London: Women's Press.
MacArthur, Brian. 1998. *Requiem: Diana, Princess of Wales 1961–1997.* London: Pavilion.
Morton, Andrew. 1997. *Diana: Her True Story, in Her Own Words,* London: Michael O'Mara.
Smith, Sally Bedell. 2000. *Diana in Search of Herself: Portrait of a Troubled Princess.* London: Signet.

Dilke, Emilia
(1840–1904)
United Kingdom

The English trade union leader Emilia Dilke was also one of the first and most influential female art critics of her generation. As a leading advocate of women's unionization, she cultivated the support of the Trades Union Congress and worked closely with her second husband, Sir Charles Dilke, for protective legislation for women factory workers and shop assistants. She and her husband advocated the introduction of a minimum wage and pioneered the rise of the lady factory inspector.

Christened Emily Frances Strong, Dilke was called Frances for much of her young life. Her father was an army officer who had served in the Raj and retired to Ilfracombe in Devon. Dilke grew up in Oxfordshire and was allowed to study art at South Kensington Art School from 1859 to 1861. Throughout her life as an art critic, publishing under the name E. F. S. Pattison, she would be an admirer of John Ruskin, who was also her friend and mentor. Her work would also be deeply influenced by her own mix of mystical and ethical Christian beliefs and a strong sense of the need for public service.

Shortly after leaving art school in 1861, Dilke married Mark Pattison, the rector of Lincoln College at Oxford University, a man twenty-seven years older than she who was noted for his academic rigor and neuroses. The couple were friendly with George Eliot, whose relationship with Dilke deepened after she visited Lincoln

College in 1871. The marriage proved a difficult and unhappy one for Dilke, and many have commented on the similarities between the Pattisons and the characters of Dorothea Brooke and Edward Casaubon in George Eliot's novel *Middlemarch*. Eliot's biographer, Kathryn Hughes, argues: "There were certain details about Emilia's intense Anglo-Catholic adolescence which found their way into the description of the Evangelical Dorothea Brooke, including a propensity to fast and to pray simultaneously for the souls of the astonished poor" (1998, 287).

In the 1870s the Pattisons gave their support to the women's suffrage movement, and from 1872 Dilke was honorary secretary of the Oxford branch of the National Society for Women's Suffrage. After the Women's Protective and Provident League (WPPL) was founded in 1874, the Pattisons set up an Oxford branch. In 1878 Dilke became active in the Radical Club. Much of her life was spent abroad in the years 1879–1884, during which time she became established as a writer and critic, in particular a specialist on French art, publishing journal articles and works such as *The Renaissance of Art in France* (1879). *French Painters of the Eighteenth Century* followed much later, in 1899.

In 1886 Mark Pattison died, and soon after, Emilia remarried. Her second husband was Sir Charles Dilke, a prominent Liberal politician and probable successor to William Gladstone as party leader, who had been cited as co-respondent in a high-society divorce case that kept the gutter press busy for months. Dilke spent years gathering evidence to prove that the accusations against her husband were false but nevertheless suffered frequent social ostracism as a result. For example, although her husband offered his support to the Women's Franchise League, the suffrage movement in general was reluctant to have their cause tainted by links to him.

In the mid-1880s, Emilia Dilke undertook a series of lecture tours in England and Scotland in support of women's trade unions, at a time when the movement was growing fast and there was a marked upsurge in militancy. After the death of WPPL leader Emma Paterson in 1886, Dilke took over the leadership, making it her primary objective to achieve closer links between the women's and men's trade union movements in order to build political muscle in women's trade unionism in its arguments for equal pay for equal work. From 1889 until her death in 1904, she regularly attended trade union congresses, consolidating her leadership throughout the 1890s. Although she took a concerted stand on equal pay for women, she remained sympathetic to the plight of women who would prefer to be at home with their families but who were forced by economic necessity to take work, often at a much lower rate than men. In April 1891 the WPPL, now renamed the Women's Trade Union League (WTUL), supported protective legislation for laundresses who held mass demonstrations in London's Hyde Park against the damp and unsanitary conditions in which they worked. In 1892 Dilke liaised with the Manchester Trades Council in the organization of women in that city while continuing to work with her husband for the unionization of shop assistants and in support of better working conditions for those in sweatshops. Legislation in their favor was partially achieved in the year of Dilke's death with the passing of the 1904 Shops Act.

During this time, however, Dilke and leaders of the General Union of Textile Workers criticized married women with families who went out to work when they did not need to do so—arguments expressed in her 1890 article in the *New Review*, "Trade Unionism for Women." Unlike most of the members of the WTUL, she did not need to work for pay and, in fact, injected much of her own money into the league. Under its auspices, Dilke initiated investigations of the use of chemicals in dangerous trades, such as white lead used in glazing pottery and carpet dyeing, insisting that legislation be introduced to protect such workers. With Annie Besant she championed the cause of East End matchgirls and in 1890 even entertained 300 of them at tea in her own home.

Shortly before her death, Lady Dilke became a member of the Labour Party. Over the years, she wrote numerous pamphlets for the WTUL and contributed articles on trade unionism, in particular the welfare of women and juvenile workers, to the *New Review, Fortnightly Review,* and the *North American Review*.

See also Besant, Annie; Paterson, Emma.

References and Further Reading

Askwith, Betty E. 1969. *Lady Dilke: A Biography.* London: Chatto and Windus.

Banks, Olive, ed. 1985, 1990. *The Biographical Dictionary of British Feminists,* vol. 1, *1800–1930;*

vol. 2, *1900–1945*. Brighton: Harvester Wheatsheaf.

Baylen, J. O., and N. J. Gossman. 1979–1984. *Biographical Dictionary of Modern British Radicals*. 3 vols. Hassocks, Sussex: Harvester Press.

Hamilton, Mary. 1941. *Women at Work: A Brief Introduction to Trade Unionism for Women*. London: Routledge & Sons.

Hughes, Kathryn. 1998. *George Eliot: The Last Victorian*. London: Fourth Estate.

Israel, Kali. 1998. *Names and Stories: Emilia Dilke and Victorian Culture*. Oxford: Oxford University Press.

Jenkins, Ray. 1968. *Sir Charles Dilke: A Victorian Tragedy*. London: Collins.

McFeely, Mary Drake. 1998. *Lady Inspectors: The Campaign for a Better Workplace 1893–1921*. Oxford: Blackwell.

Ding Ling (Chiang Ping-tzu)
(1906–1986)
China

Ding Ling (Library of Congress)

An outstanding Chinese feminist writer who was repressed by both the nationalist and communist governments for her outspoken views, Ding Ling was one of the first novelists to explore the changing position of women in China and challenge the old patriarchal society based on Confucian values. Ding was born (as Chiang Ping-tzu) in Hunan province into a family of impoverished feudal gentry. Her liberally minded mother, who had become a teacher to support her family after her husband's death, educated Ding and her sister at the girls' school in Changsha where she taught. Ding earned high grades but was prohibited from going to France to study with other Chinese students as she had wished. Inspired by the reformist fervor of the 1919 May Fourth Movement, she led demonstrations by pupils at her Zhunan Girls' Middle School calling for equal rights for women. Together with five other girls, she defied convention and entered a boys' middle school in Changsha, which with its broader curriculum offered her more scope in her studies, and in 1921 she transferred to the progressive Common People's Girls' School in Shanghai. In 1922 she was one of a handful of female students to offer support to female mill workers on strike for improved conditions in Pootung.

In Shanghai Ding joined intellectual and anarchist circles and developed her interests in social issues. She studied literature at Shanghai University for two years and in 1924 transferred to Beijing National University. She tried and failed to pursue an acting career in the film industry and eventually began writing short stories under the pen name by which she is known. Works such as "Diary of Miss Sophie" (1927; the story that brought her first major literary success) demonstrated her ability to create strong, independent heroines and broke new ground in its controversial exploration of women's sexuality. Ding remained determinedly individualistic, believing in the need for women to gain political and economic independence. She was convinced that women's emancipation in these terms, and not through love and marriage, was the only way in which they could hope to free themselves and gain real equality with men. In her own life she practiced free love; she lived with the poet Hu Yepin from 1925, became caught up in a love triangle, and eventually married Hu and had a son by him. The couple lived in poverty, attempting to scrape a living from their writing and running literary journals, but Hu was arrested by the Guomindang and executed in February 1931.

In 1930 Ding joined the League of Leftist Writers and became editor of its journal *The Great Dipper*. Her condemnation of women's oppression by traditional Chinese patriarchy is most notable in her novel *Mother* (1932), in which she expounded on the limitations placed on Chinese women by strict social and religious conventions that kept them in servitude. By then she was also writing on wider social issues, and her increasing activism led to a newfound Marxist, proletarian orientation in her work, which was influenced by Soviet socialist realism. She finally joined the Chinese Communist Party (CCP) in 1933 but disappeared later that year—having been captured by nationalist agents—and was imprisoned in Nanjing. She escaped from house arrest there in 1936 and, disguised as a soldier, made her way to Mao Zedong's Red Army forces at Yenan in Shensi province.

Her alignment with the communists did not prevent Ding, on International Women's Day, 8 March 1942, from attacking the CCP for its male chauvinism, in her essay "Thoughts on March 8." Women were still suffering oppression and exploitation, she felt, only this time at the hands of the CCP. For not only were they being expected to support the revolution by taking over the farms and manning industry while men went off to fight, but also they still had to fulfill the traditional domestic duties that continued to belittle and oppress them. The party's response was to condemn Ding's ideas as "outmoded"—for had not the revolution already established equality among the sexes? During the ensuing "rectification" campaign, pressure was put upon Ding to conform.

After World War II Ding taught at Yenan and North China Universities and in 1948 produced what the authorities wanted—a major socialist-realist novel, *The Sun Shines over the Saggan River* (probably inspired by Mikhail Sholokhov's similar 1934 epic novel, *Quiet Flows the Don*). With its theme of the exploitation of poor peasants and attempts at land reform in rural China, it became the first Chinese novel to win a Stalin Prize for literature (1951) and was translated into thirteen languages.

After the establishment of the People's Republic of China in 1949, Ding was honored with several official posts on cultural bodies, becoming vice chair of the Union of Chinese Writers. But when she joined the Hundred Flowers Campaign of 1956–1957, which called for the relaxation of ideological control on writers and intellectuals and openly criticized the CCP, she was hounded for her outspokenness as a subversive "rightist." Looked upon as an incorrigible "anti-element," she was expelled from the CCP and dismissed from her all posts. With her writings banned, she was sent into obscurity to be ideologically reeducated and worked as a peasant farmer in northern Manchuria. After the 1966 Cultural Revolution, she again fell victim to ideology and was imprisoned during 1970–1975 in solitary confinement, followed by exile in the mountains until 1978.

Ding was finally rehabilitated in 1979 and elected to the Executive Committee of the Chinese Literary Association. A fierce and unbowed individualist, she defended women's right to autonomy at a time when the CCP demanded the subordination of the individual to the needs of the masses and when it was promoting an ideal of womanhood that drew strongly on the traditional stereotype of the dutiful and silent wife and mother.

References and Further Reading

Barlow, Tani, ed. 1989. *I Myself Am a Woman: Selected Writings of Ding Ling.* Boston: Beacon Press.

Ding Ling. 1985. *Miss Sophie's Diary and Other Stories.* Trans. W. J. F. Jenner. Beijing: China International Book Trading Corporation.

Gilmartin, Christina Kelly. 1995. *Engendering the Chinese Revolution: Radical Women, Communist Politics and Mass Movements in the 1920s.* Berkeley: University of California Press.

Snow, Helen Foster. 1967. *Women in Modern China.* The Hague: Mouton.

Spence, Jonathan D. 1982. *The Gate of Heavenly Peace: The Chinese and Their Revolution, 1895–1980.* London: Faber and Faber.

Dirie, Waris
(1970–)
Somalia

As UN Special Ambassador for the Elimination of Female Genital Mutilation and an international campaigner on the subject, Waris Dirie has brought worldwide attention to one of the most horrifying acts of physical abuse against young girls, still practiced in twenty-eight countries on the African continent. Dirie was born in the desert of Somalia, one of a family of twelve children. For her first thirteen years she lived a traditional, nomadic life, until she ran away to avoid being traded in marriage by her father for five camels. She made her way across the desert to Mogadishu, where she worked carrying loads of sand on building sites and cleaned houses. In Addis Ababa she was taken in by an uncle, who took her to England in 1981 when he was appointed Somali ambassador. For a while, she worked for the family as a maid, and then cleaning the kitchens at a McDonald's while rooming in a nearby Young Women's Christian Association (YWCA) dormitory. A chance meeting with a fashion photographer led to a successful modeling career in Europe and the United States.

At the age of five, Dirie had endured circumcision (in her case, infibulation—the removal of all external genitalia and the stitching of the vaginal opening) under the most primitive of circumstances. As a result, like many other Somali girls, she experienced the recurring aftermath of pain and disfigurement. After undergoing an operation to reconstruct her genitals, she resolved to take up the plight of those less fortunate women who still suffered the agonies of botched circumcisions, which frequently caused them severe pain in childbirth. She returned to Somalia in 1995 to make a documentary with the British Broadcasting Corporation (BBC), *The Day That Changed My Life*. After that, in a groundbreaking article in the magazine *Marie Claire* titled "The Tragedy of Female Circumcision," she graphically brought the full terror of the experience to a wider audience. A news item on Dirie on Barbara Walters's influential U.S. television show *20/20*, entitled "A Healing Journey," resulted in Dirie's being contacted by the United Nations and asked to join the campaign to bring a worldwide end to female circumcision, a practice undergone by as many as 2 million young girls a year that kills many thousands of them. The difficulty in eradicating the practice is compounded by the fact that for many African societies it is a religious and social rite of passage that cannot be overturned without offending traditional belief. Dirie argues, however, as do many other campaigners in the field, that there is no support for this, a mainly Muslim rite, in the Qur'an, and that the practice has been perpetuated by male tribal society in order to keep women subservient. In addition, it deprives them of much sexual pleasure and denies their right to gender equality.

As UN Special Ambassador for the Elimination of Female Genital Mutilation since 1997, Dirie has traveled to many countries in her campaign to change the cultural mindset at the root of the practice that in Somalia alone affects 98 percent of women, and where the rate of infibulation is much higher than in other African countries. She acknowledges that eliminating it will require far more than legislation alone, including an end to the dislocations of war. For information on the UN campaign against FGM, contact www.unfpa.org.

References and Further Reading
Dirie, Waris, and Cathleen Miller. 1999. *Desert Flower: The Extraordinary Life of a Desert Nomad*. London: Virago.

Dix, Dorothea Lynde
(1802–1887)
United States

A lone and persistent female voice for reform of the mental health system in the United States—both for the more humane treatment of the institutionalized and incurably insane and for the development of new techniques in psychotherapy—Dorothea Dix argued for such care to be removed from its traditional dependence on acts of private charity and for provisions to be made available at the federal level. During the Civil War, Dix's tenacity and determination were exercised to the utmost in overcoming the hostility of the male medical establishment when she oversaw the nurses of the Union Army's Sanitary Commission. Like her British counterpart Florence Nightingale, she had an iron will and an extraordinarily thick skin, and she was not afraid of confronting and alienating people by being tough—so much so that she was nicknamed "Dragon Dix." For this reason, she and another equally strong-willed U.S. Civil War nurse, Clara Barton, took care to work in separate spheres from each other.

Born in Hampden, Maine, the daughter of a farmer who was also an itinerant Methodist lay preacher, Dix was consigned to looking after her younger siblings. She suffered neglect as a child as a result of her mother's ill health and her father's alcoholism and was eventually sent to live with her wealthy grandmother and then her great-aunt in Boston. At only fifteen years of age, she began teaching at her own dame school for girls in Worcester, Massachusetts, while continu-

Dorothea Lynde Dix (Library of Congress)

damp, dark, and cold conditions endured by the women, many of whom were not criminals but insane, having been confined in prison for want of an alternative institution in which to house them. On questioning such inhumane treatment of the insane, Dix was told that they, unlike normal sentient human beings, had no awareness of cold or the squalor of their surroundings and that since they would never recover or be cured, there was little point in making life more comfortable for them. Dix was appalled at their maltreatment and the indiscriminate use of corporal punishment: the insane were often kept in cages or fetters and chains and also suffered sexual abuse by their jailers. With a small legacy from her grandmother, Dix was able to spend the next eighteen months visiting insane asylums, brothels, workhouses, and jails in Massachusetts and saw firsthand how widespread was the practice of keeping the mentally ill cooped up alongside common criminals. She prepared a report of her findings, the "Memorial to the Legislature of Massachusetts," which she submitted in 1843. In it she argued that the insane should be separated from criminals. As result of her report, the Massachusetts legislature initiated improvements at the state insane asylum in Worcester.

Dix then took up campaigning with a vengeance, despite her continuing feeble health. From 1843 to 1845, she traveled 10,000 miles by every means of available transport, from Rhode Island through New York, Pennsylvania, Kentucky, Maryland, Ohio, Illinois, Mississippi, Alabama, Tennessee, and North Carolina, inspecting prisons, almshouses, and mental asylums. In 1844, while in New Jersey, she lobbied for the construction of a proper mental asylum; funds were raised to construct the New Jersey State Lunatic Asylum in Trenton. It was only one of thirty-two mental asylums and fifteen schools for the feebleminded established in fifteen states as a result of Dix's efforts, at the end of which she published her detailed observations in *Remarks on Prisons and Prison Discipline in the United States* (1845).

By this time armed with a wealth of persuasive detail advocating reform, Dix marched on Washington in 1848 to launch a campaign at the federal level. She presented her "Memorial of D. L. Dix Praying a Grant of Land for the Relief and Support of the Indigent Curable and Incurable Insane in the United States, June 23, 1848," in which she argued for a bill to extend public ser-

ing to educate herself by reading books from her Harvard-educated grandfather's library. In 1821 she broke off her engagement to her second cousin, Edward Bangs, and opened a school for young ladies at her grandparents' home in Boston. But by 1836, when she had to nurse her sick grandmother, Dix began suffering recurring bouts of ill health that turned out to be tuberculosis and gave up her school. For a while, she concentrated on writing moral tales for children, a Unitarian hymnbook, and a science textbook, *Conversations on Common Things* (1824), while living the confined life of a semi-invalid. Having been ordered to rest by her doctor, she traveled to England and for eighteen months stayed in Liverpool with the family of the Unitarian reformer William Rathbone (grandfather of Eleanor Rathbone), who introduced her to other English social reformers.

After returning to the United States in January 1841 but still not well enough to resume teaching, Dix turned to the only channel then available—philanthropic work. At the end of March, she began teaching a Sunday school class for women inmates of the House of Correction at East Cambridge. She was horrified by the filthy,

vices for the insane from the local to the state and even federal levels. In order to fund such a program, she appealed to the U.S. government for a grant of 5 million acres of public lands to provide tax revenues that would help support the indigent curable and incurable insane. Dix advocated the construction of new asylums, the reorganization of existing ones, and the retraining of their warders in more humane methods. She suggested the introduction of educational programs and the segregation of prisoners in separate groups according to the severity of their crimes. In the event, President Franklin Pierce vetoed Dix's bill in 1854, insisting that the care of the insane was the responsibility of public philanthropy. It would not be until 1933 that Franklin D. Roosevelt's Federal Emergency Relief Administration would grant government funds for direct services to such people.

Dix was broken by the ultimate failure of her campaign, and once again her health collapsed. She went on another convalescent trip to Europe in 1854, during which she appealed to the pope to intercede on behalf of the insane. She found it difficult to resist her natural campaigning urges and soon became caught up with visiting jails and asylums in Scotland and the Channel Islands before traveling in Europe, from Sweden in the north to Turkey in the south and east from Belgium across to Russia, everywhere lobbying officials to reform their prisons and insane asylums.

Once again back in the United States in 1856, Dix resumed her investigations of insane asylums but eventually found another cause when the Civil War broke out in April 1861. She volunteered herself to the Union Army as a nurse and in June was appointed superintendent of women nurses in charge of the military hospitals in the north (later known as the Army Nursing Corps of the Sanitary Commission). Working for no pay for the next five years, she applied her customary energy to converting public buildings into hospitals and imposing a strict regime, but her administration antagonized many, with Dix rapidly gaining notoriety as a martinet and autocrat. She dismissed any romantic notions her women volunteers might have about becoming ministering angels on the battlefield and refused to accept nuns or women under thirty, who were tersely informed that they "need not apply." And as for their mode of dress, "All nurses are required to be very plain-looking women. Their dresses must be brown or black, with no bows, no curls, no jewelry and no hoop skirts" (Ward 1990, 149). With the imposition of such strict regulations, it is not surprising that Dix's reputation went before her, for the equally indomitable Clara Barton—the more celebrated nursing pioneer of the Civil War—declined the offer of joining her nursing corps, thus avoiding an inevitable clash of personalities.

At the end of the Civil War, Dix returned to her interest in mental health reform in 1867 and also helped societies promoting charitable work for orphans; disaster victims; and the deaf, dumb, and blind. In 1881 she retired, having seen the number of mental asylums in the United States grow from 13 in 1841 to 123. She took up residence in guest quarters at the New Jersey State Lunatic Asylum in Trenton, her "firstborn child," as she called the first mental hospital built as a result of her crusading, no doubt content that she had fulfilled the objective laid out in a letter written to Lydia Maria Child on 31 December 1844: "In a world where there is so much to be done, I felt strongly impressed that there must be something for me to do" (Child 1845, Vol. 2). During her lifetime, Dix sought no honors or preferment for her work and declined the opportunity of having institutions named after her. A collection of her writings, *On Behalf of the Insane Poor: Selected Reports 1842–62,* was republished in 1975, and *Remarks on Prison and Prison Discipline* appeared in 1984.

See also Barton, Clara; Child, Lydia Maria; Rathbone, Eleanor.

References and Further Reading

Child, Lydia Maria. 1843, 1845. *Letters from New York.* Vol. 2. New York: C. S. Francis and Co.

Colman, Penny. 1992. *Breaking the Chains: The Crusade of Dorothea Lynde Dix.* White Hall, VA: Shoe Tree Press.

Gollaher, David. 1995. *A Voice for the Mad: The Life of Dorothea Dix.* New York: Free Press.

Hersteck, Amy Pualson. 2001. *Dorothea Dix: Crusader for the Mentally Ill.* Berkeley Heights, NJ: Enslow.

Malone, Mary. 1991. *Dorothea L. Dix: Hospital Founder.* New York: Chelsea House.

Marshall, Helen E. 1937. *Dorothea Dix: Forgotten Samaritan.* Chapel Hill: University of North Carolina Press.

Schlaifer, Charles, and Lucy Freeman. 1991. *Heart's Work: Civil War Heroine and Champion of the Mentally Ill Dorothea Lynde Dix.* New York: Paragon House.

Tiffany, Francis. 1992 [1891]. *Life of Dorothea Dix.* Reprint, Salem, MA: Higginson.

Ward, Geoffrey C. 1990. *The Civil War: An Illustrated History.* New York: Alfred A. Knopf.

Wilson, Dorothy Clarke. 1975. *Stranger and Traveler: The Story of Dorothea Dix, American Reformer.* Boston: Little, Brown.

Dodge, Grace
(1856–1914)
United States

The American philanthropist and educator Grace Dodge's own unpaid work in social welfare for working women and young girls was prompted by her deep religious beliefs. Born in New York City into a wealthy family, Dodge was educated privately at home until she was sixteen and then at a school in Connecticut for two years. After she finished school, she earnestly sought to do something useful with her time and in 1874 began teaching in Sunday schools and the industrial schools run by the Children's Aid Society. With her parents, she participated in the work of the New York State Charities Aid Association to improve tenement accommodations for the working classes and to teach domestic skills to working girls through the Kitchen Garden Association. At her family's summer home at Riverdale, New Jersey, Dodge also set up a local library, woman's club, and sewing school.

Having decided to dedicate herself to social service, throughout the 1880s and 1890s Dodge remained closely involved in the development of projects of the Kitchen Garden Association's successor, the Industrial Education Association, which extended its activities to offer training to young boys. In 1884 Dodge established the 38th Street Working Girls' Society in a slum district of New York, a discussion group for mainly female factory employees, that was the prototype for other clubs set up subsequently in the East and Midwest that would unite in 1885 as the Working Girls' Association of Clubs (WGAC), producing its own magazine, *Far and Near.* At 38th Street, Dodge promoted her own staunch beliefs in religious observance and social purity and placed the emphasis on "co-operation, self-government, self-reliance" (Pivar 1973, 179) and urged working girls to view the human body as the "Temple of God." Her homilies were published in pamphlet form as a series of "Talks to Busy Girls" and in

1885 Dodge reiterated her objectives in lectures such as that at the Woman's Christian Association in Cincinnati entitled "Practical Suggestions Relating to Moral Education and Preventive Work Among Girls." In 1887 Dodge's pamphlets were collected as *A Bundle of Letters to Busy Girls on Practical Matters.* In addition to discussion groups, venues of the WGAC offered their members library facilities, literacy classes, instruction in physical fitness, and lessons in cooking and sewing, as well as free medical care. But the long-term influence of the WGAC was limited and generally ineffectual in improving the lot of working women. It would take unionization and the advent of the Women's Trade Union League (WTUL) in 1903 before things would radically alter and the WTUL would absorb most of the clubs of the WGAC in the new century. Meanwhile, Dodge served as director of the WGAC until 1896, after which she left to pursue other interests.

Dodge had been greatly impressed with the work of the English social purity campaigner (Alice) Ellice Hopkins, whose religious and reformist tracts had been widely circulated in the USA. Taking an increasing interest in similar moral reform and social hygiene campaigns among working women in the USA, Dodge was closely involved in the foundation of the National Vigilance Committee in 1906, which in 1910 became a society and soon after was reorganizaed as the American Society for Sex Hygiene (ASSH). In 1913 Dodge was again instrumental in the consolidation of the ASSH and other similar groups into the American Social Hygiene Association.

Dodge was also active in several other strands of welfare and reform. In 1904 she was a founder in New York of the Travelers' Aid Alliance, set up to protect the chastity of women travellers. But it was to education that she also devoted much of her time and money, and Dodge worked with reformer Anna Garlin Spencer in raising the standards of teacher training. In 1886 she had joined the New York City Board of Education and gave much of her private wealth to fund the establishment in 1889 of the New York College for the Training of Teachers (she also generously contributed to the founding by Spencer of the New York School of Social Work). As treasurer of the New York College until 1911, Dodge took over responsibility for fund-raising and managing the college's budget when it moved to new premises in 1892. Eventually, it became the Teachers College of Columbia University.

Dodge also followed in the tradition of her family, which had supported the Young Men's Christian Association, in 1905 healing a rift in the Young Women's Christian Association (YWCA) between the evangelical and liberal wings and playing a leading role in creating the YWCA's National Board in 1906. She served as YWCA president from 1906 to 1914 and partially financed the construction of offices in New York in 1913. At the end of a life lived modestly as a devout Presbyterian, and having doggedly avoided the limelight, Dodge bequeathed $1.5 million to various charities.

See also Hopkins, (Alice) Ellice.

References and Further Reading
Graham, Abbie. 1926. *Grace H. Dodge: Merchant of Dreams.* New York: YWCA.
Lagemann, Ellen C. 1979. *A Generation of Women: Education in the Lives of Progressive Reformers.* Cambridge, MA: Harvard University Press.
Lasch, Christopher. 1965. *The New Radicalism, America 1889–1963: The Intellectual as Social Type.* New York: W. W. Norton.
Pivar, David J. 1973. *Purity Crusade: Sexual Morality and Social Control, 1868–1900.* Westport, CT: Greenwood Press.
Robinson, Marion O. 1966. *Eight Women of the YWCA.* New York: National Board of the Young Women's Christian Association of the U.S.A.
Stein, L., and A. Baxter. 1974. *Grace H. Dodge: Her Life and Work.* New York: Arno Press.

Dohm, Hedwig
(1833–1919)
Germany

The radical literary feminist and theorist Hedwig Dohm aroused controversy with her powerful polemics against the assumed superiority of men over women and her calls for women's education and their economic and psychological liberation. Although she defended women's rights through her prolific writings, averring that "everything I write is for the sake of women" (Duelli-Klein 1983, 166), Dohm never affiliated herself with any political group. Nevertheless, in 1873 she was well ahead of other German feminists in being the first to explicitly argue for women's suffrage and in more universal terms to frame her demands for women's equality as their inalienable right as individuals in any just society.

Dohm was one of eighteen children born into a Jewish family in Berlin. Her father was a tobacco merchant. She had an unhappy relationship with her mother, who subjected her to regular beatings, and this experience prompted her own later support for children's rights. Forced to leave school at the age of fifteen in 1848 to help her mother at home, Dohm deeply resented having her education cut short and in her writings bewailed the lost hours spent sewing "antimacassars, table covers and cushions" while waiting for parental permission to continue her education. Eighteen months later, her parents finally relented in the face of her repeated requests and allowed her to go to teacher-training college. But she was disappointed in the narrowness of its curriculum for women, much of it based on learning by rote and, disillusioned, sought release in an early marriage in 1852 at the age of nineteen. Her husband Ernst Dohm was the editor of the satirical journal *Crash-Bang-Wallop* (*Kladderadatsch*). While bringing up her four daughters, Dohm continued to educate herself. She absorbed the work of philosophers and feminist writers, and keeping abreast of the arguments of suffragists such as Elizabeth Cady Stanton, Susan B. Anthony, and Harriet Martineau, turned her home into a meeting place for Berlin intellectuals.

By the mid-1860s, frustrated by the lack of a women's movement in Germany, she began writing, first on Spanish literature (some of which she also translated), and then produced her first feminist tract in 1872, "What Clergymen Think of Women." This critique of the church's dogmatic attitude, and her calls for women's social, political, and economic independence, was followed by essays criticizing the subjection of women to a purely domestic role within the family. In 1874 Dohm published *The Scientific Emancipation of Women,* in which she challenged male scientific arguments on women's natural inferiority to men. She saw the problem as lying with men's ingrained attitudes and their unshakeable belief that women's lives were dependent upon them and urged women to seek fulfillment of their own needs. In 1876 in her treatise "Women's Nature and Privilege," she reiterated her support for women's suffrage and advocated the establishment of a German female suffrage society, a call rejected, however, by Luise

Otto-Peters, leader of the General German Women's Association.

For the next few years Dohm turned to plays and fiction, writing about women making the transition from the old world of their traditional subjection to a new one of emancipation and independence and fulfilling themselves in ways that allowed for differences in women's personal objectives. Her novella *How Women Are Made—Become the Woman You Are* and also the trilogy *Destinies of a Soul* (1896–1899) are expositions of the oppression of middle-class women within sterile marriages. It was Dohm's conclusion that the only happy marriages were those in which both partners were educated to the same level and could appreciate each other's right to equality and freedom. Her acerbic and provocative comments on sex roles and women's autonomy proved too radical for many in the German women's movement, and she would remain determinedly outside any recognized group.

In 1902 Dohm published an essay on Friedrich Nietzsche's antifeminism and a collection of essays attacking female supporters of male subjection of women, *The Antifeminists.* Her 1903 work *The Mother* argued against ageism and for the rights of older women to be upheld once they are no longer useful to society as breeders of children: "One day, women will be totally fed up with having babies if they are told over and over again that this is all they should expect of life" (Duelli-Klein 1983, 174). She also wrote an essay in 1912 on the rights of unborn children to state protection.

Dohm was disillusioned by the change in direction of the German women's movement in support of German militarism and remained a staunch pacifist during World War I, expressing her views in her essay "The Misuse of Death." A woman of genuine charm and affection, she was, according to Renate Duelli-Klein, the archetypal granny, "tiny, timid, lovably sweet," a physical appearance that belied the power of her intellect (1983, 177). Too shy to take up public speaking or activism and held in suspicion by women on both the left (too bourgeois) and right (too radical), she channeled her energies into producing an opus of feminist thought that remains underappreciated. Unwavering in her belief in women's suffrage as a basic human right, she wrote toward the end of her life: "Long after I am dead and burned, my ashes will glow when the portals of the Reichstag are opened to women" (Anthony 1915, 220).

See also Anthony, Susan B.; Martineau, Harriet; Otto-Peters, Luise; Stanton, Elizabeth Cady.

References and Further Reading

Anthony, Katherine S. 1915. *Feminism in Germany and Scandinavia.* New York: Henry Holt Co.

Dohm, Hedwig. 1976 [1896]. *Women's Nature and Privilege.* Trans. Constance Campbell. Reprint, Westport, CT: Hyperion.

Duelli-Klein, Renate. 1983. "Hedwig Dohm: Passionate Theorist." In Dale Spender, ed., *Feminist Theorists: Three Centuries of Women's Intellectual Traditions.* London: Women's Press.

Joeres, Ruth-Ellen B., and Mary Jo Maynes, eds. 1986. *German Women in the Eighteenth and Nineteenth Centuries:: A Social and Literary History.* Bloomington: Indiana University Press.

Singer, Sandra L. 1995. *Free Soul, Free Woman? A Study of Selected Fictional Works of Hedwig Dohm, Isolde Kurz, and Helen Böhlau.* New York: P. Lang.

Domínguez Navarro, Ofelia
(1894–1970s?)
Cuba

A powerful voice in support of what she saw as the sacred role of motherhood, Domínguez was a fervent campaigner for the rights of illegitimate children. Originally inspired by the North American model of social feminism, she later became critical of it and the more moderate feminist groups in Cuba, carving out her own path as a committed radical. As a lawyer, she was frequently called upon to defend activists arrested by the repressive government of General Gerardo Machado y Morales.

Domínguez was born in Mataquá in Las Villas, where both her parents had taken part in antigovernment revolutionary activities. For a time her father had been deported to a penal colony in Algiers, only to resume his activities on his return. In 1911 Domínguez became a teacher in the rural community of Jorobada in Las Villas, where she managed to construct a schoolroom of sorts and offered a curriculum that included the three R's plus singing and physical education, which even in its modest ambitions exceeded what was condoned by the church at that time. She ploughed much of her meager salary as a teacher back into the school to help improve its structure and also helped illiterate people in the town by reading letters and newspapers to them.

While she was still teaching, she studied for her high school diploma. She had decided upon a career in law and went on to study that subject through a correspondence course. Once qualified to practice, Domínguez moved to Havana, where she took up criminal law in the defense of many prostitutes and thieves who had been forced into a life of crime by poverty and were not accorded equal treatment under the law.

From 1917 on, women in Cuba became more vociferous in their demands for equal rights with men and founded the Women's Club of Cuba. Domínguez soon became a member and noticed the growing number of elite, highly educated, middle- and upper-class women in its ranks who were taking up programs of philanthropic reform, but from the outset she distanced herself from these groups, choosing to follow her own more radical path. She first came to public attention as a delegate to the 1923 national women's congress set up by the Women's Club of Cuba, where she gave a speech calling for a resolution on illegitimate children that would modify the civil code to give them the same rights as legitimate children. Domínguez urged that rather than being ostracized, children such as these should be accorded the economic and emotional security of the family circle. Her strong belief in the moral and nurturing value of the family lay at the root of her support for the civil status of all children, both legitimate and illegitimate. It was a subject on which she spoke out on numerous occasions, including a lecture at the University of Havana. All women, in her view, had the right to be mothers whether or not they were married, and illegitimate children had just as much claim to shelter within the home and a share of their parents' property.

In 1925 at the second national women's congress, Domínguez once again forced her audience to tackle the issue of equal status for *all* children by presenting evidence on the economic plight of unmarried mothers. When her proposal was defeated by the outraged religious moral majority at the congress who accused her of advocating free love, she walked out in protest. As time went on and she faced persistent hostility to her radical ideas, she detached herself more and more from the middle-of-the-road elements in the women's movement and took up her own cause of illegiti-

mate children, attending numerous national and international conferences between 1915 and 1928. In 1927 she was the cofounder of the National Feminist Alliance, which was set up as a political pressure group to promote cultural and recreational pursuits for women.

In 1925 Gerardo Machado became the fifth president of Cuba (which had gained its independence from Spain in 1898). Domínguez became a vociferous opponent of his brutal regime, which lasted until 1933, and became "perhaps the most effective feminist dissident" in Cuba during the 1930s (Stoner 1991, 71). For many years, the movement for civil rights in Cuba was blocked by the government, resulting in a turbulent period in the country's history punctuated by strikes, demonstrations, and student unrest. As a lawyer, Domínguez was frequently called on to defend radical activists who had been arrested and imprisoned by the authorities. When the communist activist Julio Antonio Mella was imprisoned for protesting against Machado's dictatorship, Domínguez organized protest marches and a vigil outside the jail and even enlisted the help of Machado's mother in interceding for the sick Mella to be released. In 1927 she appealed to Machado for a wide-ranging improvement of women's working conditions, calling for equal pay, maternity rights, and the protection of child workers.

During this period, she also worked with the Socialist Party in ameliorating the working conditions of cigar and sugar workers and underpaid teachers, bringing various groups of activists together under the umbrella of the National Feminist Alliance in September 1928. As the group's legal spokesperson, Domínguez wrote to Machado on behalf of the alliance, demanding basic legal changes to the civil code that would give women the vote, protect them as workers, and provide full citizenship for them. She also boldly criticized the government in journal and newspaper articles and radio broadcasts in Havana. But as ever, Domínguez found herself discouraged by the lack of involvement of poorer, working-class women in the movement, which was to a certain extent hamstrung by its ties to the religious establishment. In 1930 she withdrew to set up her own, more radical, nationalist, and anticapitalist organization, the Women's Labor Union (WLU), which set out to explore class and gender issues, promote the interests of working-class women, and fight for women's suffrage and education and the abolition of capital punishment. With the support of male radicals on the left, the WLU also had as its objective a more radical objective of overturning the old economic system in Cuba.

In 1931 when other leading Cuban feminists such as the conservative reformer María Collado had entered into a political compromise with Machado's government in hopes of his granting women's suffrage, Domínguez broke away from the mainstream, suspicious that Machado had no intention of delivering on his promise and convinced that many feminists were allowing themselves to be hoodwinked. She became a Marxist and devoted her energies to an open criticism of capitalism and, most especially, U.S. political and economic interests in Cuba. Her fierce opposition to Collado from the late 1920s onward increased her isolation, with Domínguez being accused of egotism and of becoming enslaved by the dogma of communism.

When it became clear that Domínguez's appeals to Machado's government to introduce constitutional reforms had failed and that he had reneged on his promises about suffrage, Domínguez called on women to join the revolutionary cause because to lend their support to Machado was to endorse a corrupt, brutal regime. Through the WLU, she began organizing strikes and demonstrations and helping workers to unionize. She soon came under police surveillance and was arrested on 3 January 1931. Held in a filthy, damp prison, she became ill and was released, but she immediately resumed her protest campaign, was arrested on several more occasions, and was imprisoned for a second time in March. She would later write a powerful account of her time in jail (*From 6 to 6*, 1937) in the company mainly of prostitutes, where she saw the terrible consequences of drug addiction and alcoholism. Aware that many of the prostitutes and the children they had with them were syphilitic, she encouraged her fellow prisoners to adopt better standards of personal hygiene.

Having spent seven months in prison, Domínguez was released in September 1931 to find undeclared civil war still rife in Cuba. For the next two years of the student-led revolution, she defended students and labor leaders at their trials, gave public speeches, and helped to keep the Marxist newspapers running when members of their editorial staff were imprisoned. At the end of the revolution in 1933, Domínguez was forced to flee to Mexico. For the next seven years, Cuba would endure continuing unrest and a succession of seven puppet presidents put in power by the military leader Fulgencio Batista y Zaldívar.

In 1934 the new regime of President Carlos Mendieta extended suffrage to women under the new provisions of the constitution. Domínguez continued to attack the right-wing feminists and philanthropists who had cooperated with the government on this issue, having now come to the conclusion that suffrage was not the answer for working women. Women's right to vote, she was convinced, would only be manipulated by male politicians in support of their own policies. She demanded an amnesty for all political opposition groups and opposed the use of emergency courts to try revolutionaries. She also revived the call for better working conditions and rates of pay for those in the tobacco and needleworking industries.

Jailed again twice in 1937 for her activities, Domínguez was deported to Mexico, where she lived in exile till 1939 and became a member of the Radical Union of Mexico. Here she took up work as a legal adviser and helped organize the nationalization of U.S. oil interests in Mexico. She also involved herself in setting up and running independent labor unions and wrote articles for radical journals. On her return to Cuba in 1939, inspired by the example of Mexico's progressive president Lázaro Cardenas and now less combative in her political attitudes, she took part in the third national women's congress, reopening the debate on equal rights for illegitimate children. She published articles, appeared on radio, and during the run-up to war denounced fascism. In 1946 she acted as secretary-general of the Cuban delegation to the United Nations planning meetings in San Francisco and held the post for the next sixteen years. She opposed the military coup and subsequent dictatorship of Fulgencio Batista in 1952 and continued her work with the United Nations until she was forced to resign by ill health. In 1971 Domínguez published her autobiography in Havana, titled *Fifty Years of a Life.*

See also Collado, María; Gómez de Avellaneda y Arteaga, Gertrudis; Rodríguez Acosta, Ofelia; Sabas Alomá, Mariblanca.

References and Further Reading

Beezley, William, and Judith Ewell. 1987. *The Human Tradition in Latin America: The Twentieth Century.* Wilmington, DE: Scholarly Resources.

Stoner, K. Lynn. 1991. *From the House to the Streets: The Cuban Woman's Movement for Legal Reform 1898–1940.* Durham, NC: Duke University Press.

Dorkenoo, Efua (Scilla McLean)
(1940s?–)
Ghana

A respected international campaigner against female genital mutilation (FGM) and for the treatment of women suffering the physical side effects of not only this practice but also early marriage and motherhood, Efua Dorkenoo has been promoting her work for African women and their children through the Foundation for Women's Health Research and Development (Forward) since 1983. Dorkenoo was working as a midwife when she realized the full impact on African women of FGM, which frequently causes complications in childbirth, particularly in those women who have suffered its most extreme form, infibulation. She researched the various aspects of its practice at the London School of Hygiene and Tropical Medicine and together with a group of supporters set up Forward, initially to promote women's health in general. Within two years of the organization's establishment in Britain, FGM was made illegal there, and with the weight of support from the World Health Organization (WHO) and the United Nations Dorkenoo has been able to concentrate campaigning in that area.

Forward has been used as a model by the WHO to promote an educational program, not just in Africa but in immigrant communities around the world where FGM is still practiced. From its base in London, it has promoted programs in the Gambia and Kenya and offers a training program backed by the British Department of Health to send specialist health workers into ethnic communities.

Because Forward's campaigning has become instrumental in the recognition of FGM as a violation of human rights, Dorkenoo has been appointed acting director of WHO's Department of Women's Health. In this capacity she coordinates regional action plans in six African countries: Burkina Faso (where FGM affects 70 per-

Efua Dorkenoo (Courtesy of Efua Dorkenoo)

cent of women), Ghana, Cameroon, Nigeria, Kenya, and the Sudan (where it affects 89 percent). She has also been sponsored by the British Commonwealth as an expert on FGM and has collaborated with various international nongovernmental organizations such as Amnesty International in working toward the elimination of FGM and other health-threatening traditional practices to which African women are subjected.

In 1994 Dorkenoo was made an Officer of the Order of the British Empire (OBE). Forward is currently collaborating with the Association of Church Development Projects in a consciousness-raising program on women's health in northern Ghana. It can be found on the Internet at www.forward.dircon.co.uk/.

References and Further Reading

Dorkenoo, Efua. 1992. *Female Genital Mutilation: Proposals for Change.* London: Minority Group.

———. 1994. *Cutting the Rose: Female Genital Mutilation: The Practice and Its Prevention.* London: Minority Rights Group.

Dreier, Mary Elisabeth
(1875–1963)
United States

A labor reformer and president of the Women's Trade Union League, Mary Elisabeth Dreier came from a distinguished family of evangelical social activists and was the younger sister of Margaret Dreier Robins. Born in Brooklyn, New York, the daughter of German immigrants, Dreier took up charitable work in 1899 at a Brooklyn settlement named Asacog House and attended courses at the New York School of Philanthropy in about 1904. Having developed an interest in the rights of working women in the garment industry, she became involved in the Women's Trade Union League (WTUL).

In 1906 Dreier became president of the New York branch of the WTUL and devoted her life to women's trade unionism, in particular the rights of the women workers in the sweatshops of New York. She was arrested on 4 November 1909 for picketing the Triangle Shirtwaist Company prior to one of the most famous strikes in women's labor history. By the end of November, Dreier was involved in planning the strike by Triangle's mainly immigrant female workers in protest at their employment on piece rates in freezing conditions. The strike lasted for thirteen weeks, during which Dreier overcame her natural shyness to become a powerful voice in the leadership of the 20,000 women strikers.

At the end of March 1911, after the devastation of the Triangle Shirtwaist Company fire of 25 March, during which 146 people were trapped in the inferno or died jumping from windows to escape it, the WTUL took center stage under Dreier in a campaign for protective legislation for women factory workers. A state Factory Investigating Commission was set up soon after, headed by Frances Coralie Perkins, which Dreier joined. During the years 1911–1915, Dreier headed a far-reaching investigation into working conditions and safety standards set by the commission that led to the reform of New York state industrial legislation, which included the introduction of the fifty-four-hour week. After her achievements in labor reform, Dreier remained committed to her work for the WTUL until it folded in 1950. She turned to the cause of women's suffrage, serving as chair of the New York Woman's Suffrage Party in the last days of campaigning leading to women's attainment of the franchise in 1920. As head of the party's Industrial Section, she advised on child labor legislation and supported the reformist work of the Progressive Party and, during the 1930s, Franklin D. Roosevelt's New Deal.

During World War I, Dreier had been active in the Advisory Commission of the Council of National Defense as president of its New York State Committee, and in 1942 she was appointed chair of the War Labor Standards Committee, but after World War II ended, she developed increasingly pacifist and socialist sympathies and supported rapprochement between the United States and the Soviet Union. Dismayed by the onslaught of the Cold War in the 1950s and the arms race, she campaigned against nuclear weapons, which led to her being investigated by the House Un-American Activities Committee.

In 1950 Dreier published a hagiography of her sister, *Margaret Dreier Robins: Her Life, Letters and Work*. She never married and used much of her inherited wealth of $600,000 to provide financial assistance to other social reformers. Quiet, modest, and God-fearing, Dreier became a Presbyterian in 1943 and worked for the National Board of the Young Women's Christian Association.

References and Further Reading
Adickes, Sandra. 1997. *To Be Young Was Very Heaven: Women in New York before the Great War.* Basingstoke: Macmillan.
Boone, Gladys. 1942. *The Women's Trade Union Leagues in Great Britain and the United States of America.* New York: Columbia University Press.
Dye, Nancy Schrom. 1980. *As Equals and as Sisters: Feminism, the Labor Movement and the Women's Trade Union League of New York.* Columbia: University of Missouri Press.
Orleck, Annelise. 1995. *Common Sense and a Little Fire: Women and Working-Class Politics in the United States, 1900–1965.* Chapel Hill: University of North Carolina Press.

Dugdale, Henrietta
(1826?–1918)
Australia

A leading campaigner for women's vote in the Australian state of Victoria and a radical, secularist, and uncompromising freethinker, Henrietta Dugdale claimed to be the first female suffragist in Australia. She was born in London and married at the age of fourteen. In 1852 she emigrated to Australia, where she married for a second time, to a clergyman named William Dugdale.

Little is known about her life before she began speaking in support of women's suffrage in the state of Victoria, Australia, in 1869. It would take fifteen years of concerted campaigning before the first official women's suffrage society was founded there in 1884, when Dugdale and Annie Lowe formed the Victorian Women's Suffrage Society (VWSS) in Melbourne. The society's establishment had been prompted not just by women's demand for the vote but also in order to organize women in defense of their rights after the state authorities had failed to respond to increasing acts of domestic and other violence against women. Dugdale was unequivocal when it came to the subject of the physical abuse of women: "Here in Australia it is considered more a crime to steal a horse than ruin a girl" (Lake 1999, 23). The perpetrators of rape, in her view, should be castrated. The element of moral crusade in the VWSS was augmented in 1887 by an influx of members from the powerful Woman's Christian Temperance Union (WCTU), which had spread from the United States to Australia and elsewhere.

Dugdale was one of the first women in Australia to advocate not just suffrage but also the sexual, political, and legal equality of women and men. She did so in an 1883 utopian tract, "A Few Hours in a Far Off Age," in which she attacked male ignorance and presented a vision of a new and enlightened Australian society free of inequality, prostitution, poverty, and crime, which would come into existence after women had been granted suffrage. She felt women's emancipation would counter the negative aspects of drunkenness in men and general levels of illiteracy. She sought women's social elevation through education and access to birth control and, speaking from her own bitter experiences, forcefully argued for the rights of married women to control their own property. It was her belief that the leveling of social and economic inequality must come through legal controls on the length of the working day and a fairer distribution of wealth across all classes.

Dugdale was a maverick in her many outspoken views, a fact reflected in her membership in the Australian Secular Association and a controversial group of freethinkers known as the Eclectics. She rejected colonial control and the British monarchy, which she viewed as corrupt and reactionary, and was equally dismissive of organized religion, which for her was the major source of women's age-old subordination. Such radical opinions proved problematic in her suffrage work, with many conservative suffragists (who were themselves dedicated members of the WCTU) objecting to her extreme views on religion. Equally, Dugdale's perceived eccentricity as an advocate of dress reform, vigorous physical exercise, and women's liberation from the corset was made use of by her detractors in the press, who ridiculed her adoption of bloomers and men's jackets.

In about 1905 Dugdale married for a third time in her seventies. A dedicated nonconformist in her social, political, and moral attitudes, she remained a colorful and feisty campaigner into her old age, living to cast her vote on several occasions before her death at the age of ninety-two.

References and Further Reading
Lake, Marilyn. 1999. *Getting Equal: The History of Australian Feminism.* London: Allen and Unwin.
Oldfield, Audrey. 1992. *Woman Suffrage in Australia: A Gift or a Struggle?* Melbourne: Cambridge University Press.
Pike, Douglas Henry, ed. 1966– . *Australian Dictionary of Biography.* Melbourne: Melbourne University Press.

Durand, Marguerite
(1864–1939)
France

A former actress with the Comédie Française, Marguerite Durand became a militant campaigner for suffrage primarily through her work as a journalist, running and funding *La Fronde* (*The Sling*), the seminal feminist daily newspaper written and produced by women for women. She was also an ardent antivivisectionist who established a famous pet cemetery north of Paris at Asnières.

The illegitimate daughter of a general, Durand was raised by her grandparents and sent to a convent. She left home when she was seventeen to go on the stage and became a leading performer at the Comédie Française. But in 1886 she gave up acting to marry the radical deputy Georges Laguerre and became drawn into political circles, soon hosting her own salons that became a meeting place for republicans.

After her divorce in 1891, Durand took up journalism and worked for the mainstream conservative daily newspaper, the *Figaro*. Her espousal of feminist concerns came late, in 1896, when she embraced women's rights after being assigned to report on the congress of the French League for the Defense of Women, held in Paris. The experience inspired Durand, by then a woman of some wealth, to use her personal fortune to establish *La Fronde* in December 1897, its title being a reference to a rebellion against the monarchy that took place in France during 1648–1653. The paper, the first of its kind run by and for women, was published daily from 1897 to 1903 and thereafter monthly until 1905. It built up a mass following, with a press run of 200,000, which was exceptional for such a publication. Under Durand's direction, the female staff of *La Fronde* pioneered women's feminist journalism, offering an alternative to then current women's magazines by seeking to engage women's interest in social issues and subjects beyond the domestic sphere. In particular, the intention was to engage the interest of working women in order to create a wide base of support for campaigning on women's issues. Eventually *La Fronde* became the repository of militant, republican action and demands for reform of the civil code, with writers such as Séverine becoming regular contributors.

In 1900 Durand helped arrange an international women's rights congress in Paris in the hope that a new socialist feminist movement might develop from a program of discussion of major reform. The congress was carefully prepared by Durand to attract working women to attend, with topics such as the eight-hour day and the minimum wage under discussion. But the congress failed to unite socialists and bourgeois feminists in the common cause; the middle-class women who comprised most of the delegates balked at debate of the suggestion of one day off per week for their domestic servants. This failure marked a turning point in the French movement, and by 1903 Durand abandoned campaigning on socialist-feminist issues. In 1905 she closed down *La Fronde* and narrowed her objectives to the suffrage campaign, founding the National League for Women's Vote and with it a new publication, *Action*. She launched a campaign for women's equality not just in the political sphere but in law and in the workplace, insisting that they should be paid for doing housework and that those who worked should be protected by maternity insurance. She also became involved with other social movements such as the campaigns for temperance, antivivisection, and social purity.

Durand returned to journalism in 1908 as codirector of the Paris evening paper the *News* and briefly revived *La Fronde* to galvanize French patriotism during World War I. She lent her support to a call for women to be allowed to serve in auxiliary forces; when this demand was rejected, she organized teams of women ambulance drivers to transport the wounded from the battlefields. After her death, the bequest by Durand of her extensive personal archive of posters, letters, books, and photographs became the basis of a new feminist library, the Bibliothèque Marguerite Durand, established in the Town Hall of Paris's fifth *arrondissement*.

See also Séverine.

References and Further Reading

Roberts, Mary Louise. 1996. "Acting Up: The Feminist Theatrics of Marguerite Durand." *French Historical Studies* 19(4): 1103–1138.

Sowerwine, Charles. 1982. *Sisters or Citizens? Women and Socialism in France since 1876*. Cambridge: Cambridge University Press.

Uglow, Jennifer, ed. 1998. *Macmillan Dictionary of Women's Biography*. 3d ed. Basingstoke: Macmillan.

Dutt, Saroj Nalini
(1887–1925)
India

In the sincere belief that her home country could never be strong until it provided better educational and economic opportunities for its women, Saroj Nalini Dutt set up a network of women's committees (*mahila samitis*) in Indian towns to provide a meeting place for women restricted by the rules of purdah, where they could learn new skills and as a result become more financially independent.

Dutt was the daughter of a high-caste civil servant of the British Raj and was educated at home by a governess. She married in 1906 but continued to take an interest in self-education and progressive ideas while retaining a respect for her traditional background. Despite the opprobrium of her contemporaries, she felt compelled to take up the cause of Indian women, particularly impoverished widows, by finding a means of offering them practical help and advice. She set up her first *mahila samiti* in 1913; another followed in 1916, and more in 1917, 1918, and 1921. During World War I, Dutt undertook humanitarian work for the Red Cross and in 1918 was made a Member of the Order of the British Empire (MBE) by King George V.

On a visit to England in 1921, Dutt was greatly impressed with the work of the Women's Institute and took it as the model for a more effective and centralized organization in Calcutta to oversee the work of the local women's committees, but she died prematurely before being able to put her plan into action. The Saroj Nalini Dutt Memorial Association was set up in her memory to carry out this project. Through a network of 400 *samitis,* facilities were developed to offer adult education and mother and baby care, to train women in first aid and home nursing, and to promote and exhibit local cottage industries and handicrafts. By the end of the 1920s, the association had extended its work across India, Burma, and Sri Lanka (Ceylon).

References and Further Reading
Dutt, Guru Sadaya. 1929. *A Woman of India: Being the Life of Sarojini Nalini.* London: Hogarth Press.

Dworkin, Andrea
(1946–)
United States

As an outspoken polemicist of the women's movement during the 1980s, Andrea Dworkin became a major if contentious voice in the debate over male exploitation of women through the use of pornography. Her view that male sexism and violence against women are aggravated by the dissemination of pornography, which debases women as "sexual fodder," has led Dworkin to demand the outlawing of such literature as a violation of the civil rights of women. Her contention has brought her into open and prolonged conflict with other feminists, who perceive pornography as merely a symptom of the wider cultural oppression of women. Dworkin's detractors continue to argue that to ban pornogra-

phy would be a breach of freedom of speech.

Born in Camden, New Jersey, Dworkin read and admired Fyodor Dostoevsky and the writings of the Brontë sisters, Virginia Woolf, and George Eliot as a young woman. She had already decided that she wanted to work for social change by the time she entered Bennington College in Vermont. After earning her B.A., in 1968 she went to Europe and lived in the Netherlands for three years, during which time she was briefly married. After leaving her husband when he subjected her to physical abuse, she remained in Europe until the mid-1970s and then returned to the United States. There, after making do through a succession of occasional jobs as waitress, receptionist, and factory worker, in 1974 she published her first book, *Woman Hating,* an unsettling discourse on the historical subjugation of women by men in which she sought to eradicate gender identity and "destroy the structure of culture as we know it" (*Current Biography* 1994, 148). At this point, Dworkin also made her mark as a compelling public speaker when she addressed a 1,000-strong audience at the Conference on Sexuality mounted by the National Organization of Women in New York.

Publication of her feminist essays, *Our Blood: Prophecies and Discourses on Sexual Politics,* followed in 1976, and a collection of short stories, *The New Woman's Broken Heart,* came out in 1980, both cataloguing the various long-standing methods by which Dworkin considers that men have ensured women's cultural and physical oppression. It was Dworkin's contribution to the collection *Take Back the Night: Women and Pornography* in 1981 and her publication soon after of *Pornography: Men Possessing Women* that established her position as a radical thinker of the women's movement. In this latter bleak assessment of male sexism and sadism, Dworkin presented a forceful argument in support of her belief that pornography is fundamentally misogynist, that it incites violence in the male, and thus provides men with the power of the rapist. The producers of pornography should thus, in her view, be held accountable for the sexual violence that it unleashes.

The book provoked a long-running, bitter debate among feminists and polarized opinion on pornography, with Dworkin's arguments accused of being naive and simplistic in their advocacy of censorship. The controversy was further exacerbated when in 1984 Dworkin and the feminist lawyer Catharine MacKinnon initiated a campaign in the courts to have pornography outlawed, by making it legal for women whose civil liberties were infringed as a result of its use to sue in the courts. Surprising support came from the right-wing Moral Majority, and anti-pornography laws were introduced in Indianapolis, Minneapolis, Los Angeles, and Washington, D.C. But like the court case, these laws failed, and in 1986 the Supreme Court ruled that Dworkin and MacKinnon's lawsuit was unconstitutional and a violation of freedom of speech under the First Amendment.

Many liberal feminists have consistently opposed such action by Dworkin as a contravention of the basic right of freedom of speech, arguing that pornography is but one aspect of women's oppression and that its prohibition would be as ineffectual as that of alcohol in the 1920s. With Catharine MacKinnon, Dworkin extended her argument in *Pornography and Civil Rights* (1988), in which she explored the persisting paradox raised precisely by sexual liberation: "The sexually liberated woman is the woman of pornography. . . . Freedom is the mass-marketing of woman as whore. Free sexuality for the woman is in being massively consumed, denied an individual nature, denied any sexual sensibility other than that which serves the male."

Dworkin's other publications include *Intercourse* (1987), a controversial discussion of the relationship between sexual intercourse and misogyny and a continuation of her analysis of women as victims; *Ice and Fire* (1986), a semiautobiographical novel; *Letters from a War Zone: Writings 1976–1987* (1988); and *Mercy,* a 1990 novel. She has also held various lecturing ap-

pointments, becoming renowned for her combative spirit and radicalism.

In 2000 Dworkin opened up a new debate with her controversial book *Scapegoat: The Jews, Israel and Women's Liberation.* A book in which she invested eight years of serious research and the accumulation of her thinking as a Jew, *Scapegoat* offers a polemical account of the history of anti-Semitism, the Holocaust, Zionism, and the establishment of Israel and women's relationship to contemporary Judaism. Dworkin concludes that just as the Jews were downtrodden over centuries and eventually fought back, so too should women in the new state of Israel, who have been debased by a militaristic state and are looked on, along with the Palestinians, as an internal enemy. The book testifies to Dworkin's undimmed commitment to the liberation of women as a continuing political struggle and to her refusal to moderate her always controversial position. Many of Dworkin's writings are accessible online via the Dworkin website at http://www.igc.org/womensnet/ dworkin/.

References and Further Reading

Current Biography. 1994. New York: H. W. Wilson.
"Feminism Revisited: A Symposium." *Times Literary Supplement* 4955 (1998): 3–7.
Jenefsky, Cindy, with Ann Russo. 1998. *Without Apology: Andrea Dworkin's Art and Politics.* Boulder: Westview Press.
MacKinnon, Catharine, and Andrew Dworkin. 1997. *In Harm's Way: The Pornography Civil Rights Hearings.* Cambridge, MA: Harvard University Press.
Rubin, S. A., and L. B. Alexander. 1998. "Regulating Pornography: The Feminist Influence." *Communications and the Law* 18(4): 73–94.

E

Eastman, Crystal
(1881–1928)
United States

A founder of the women's pacifist movement who emphasized the humanizing role of women in society, Crystal Eastman was a leading international socialist, feminist, and advocate of civil liberties. A believer in social revolution, she was convinced that women were physically able to take their place alongside men in the workplace without recourse to protective legislation that would set them apart from men. Eastman was a beautiful woman of great humanity and deep social conscience and during her short life was a charismatic figure in American women's activism, the value of whose contribution was all too easily lost between her death in 1928 and her rediscovery in the mid-1970s.

Born in Glenora, New York, Eastman was the daughter of Congregational ministers who worked as joint pastors of Park Church in Elmira, New York. Her mother, Annis Eastman, who had notably preached at the funeral of Mark Twain, was herself an outspoken women's rights campaigner and an influential figure in Crystal's early life. Eastman went to a local school in Elmira. By her teens, she was a committed feminist. She studied at Vassar until 1903 and, moving to Greenwich Village, lived in a socialist bohemian commune while studying for her M.A. in sociology at Columbia University, which she received in 1904. Tall, graceful, and athletic, she became a conspicuous figure, noted for her outspoken, "new woman" views. She took up law at New York University and obtained her L.L.B. in 1907. For a while, she worked on a voluntary basis in the New York settlement house movement, where she met Paul Kellogg, the editor of the so-

cial work journal *Charities and the Commons,* who invited her to join a research project funded by the Russell Sage Foundation. For this project, Eastman did a survey of 1,000 industrial accidents that had taken place in Pittsburgh and gathered details on the concomitant hardships suffered by the families of breadwinners who had been injured. On the strength of this work, she was invited to serve (1909–1911) as the only woman member of the New York State Commission on Employers' Liability and Causes of Industrial Accidents, Unemployment, and Lack of Farm Labor, which drafted a bill regarding workers' compensation and safety legislation for New York state that later became the model for similar legislation in other states. The results of Eastman's findings were published in *Work Accidents and the Law* (1910; reprinted in 1970). She followed it in 1911 with an article, "Three Essentials for Accident Prevention," and in 1913–1914 she took another appointment with the U.S. Commission on Industrial Relations.

In what seemed to be a contradictory act for someone as liberated as Eastman, she married an insurance salesman named Wallace Benedict in 1911 and moved west to Milwaukee. In 1909 she had encouraged her brother Max to establish a Men's League for Woman Suffrage at Columbia University and she now joined the suffrage movement in Wisconsin as a member of the Political Equality League, acting as campaign chair for Wisconsin's suffrage referendum, which was defeated in 1912. With her marriage a failure and life in Wisconsin stultifying, Eastman separated from her husband in 1913 and moved back to New York, where she was asked to help revitalize the flagging National American Woman Suffrage Association by joining its board. However, Eastman found its position insufficiently radical, and in

Crystal Eastman (Library of Congress)

1913, with Alice Paul and others, she helped found the radical Congressional Union for Woman Suffrage, the forerunner of the National Woman's Party. The party's main objective was to work for an Equal Rights Amendment, which it first introduced in 1923, calling for women to be granted the same rights to education and employment as men and to have equal legal status with them.

Eastman disagreed with moderate feminists who advocated protective legislation for women, arguing that it would only limit their opportunities to compete with men on an equal basis in the workplace. She also adamantly rejected the idea of alimony, averring that "no self-respecting feminist" would accept what was tantamount to a woman's "confession that she could not take care of herself" (Niess 1977, 87). For Eastman, as Spender illustrates, *equal* meant "the same" (Spender 1982, 382)—not just in sexual terms but also in manners and in morals, in the workplace, in the home, and in education.

Eastman had long been an advocate of pacifism, and in 1913 at an International Woman Suffrage Alliance congress in Budapest, she met many international feminists and pacifists, including Emmeline Pethick-Lawrence, who later came to New York to support Eastman in her call

to establish a Woman's Peace Party (WPP) in Washington in November 1914. The beginning of the war in Europe fortified Eastman's belief that women had a natural instinct for the preservation of life and would therefore be more determined in suing for peace, and she was vindicated when 25,000 women joined the ranks of the WPP during its first year. In 1915 she attended the first women's peace congress at The Hague and in November took on the WPP's "Truth about Preparedness Campaign" in direct opposition to the U.S. government's military buildup, in her argument exposing the greed of the capitalist interests that lay behind increased military spending. During the war Eastman wrote regular articles for the WPP newsletter the *Four Lights* and continued to serve as the main organizer and chair of its New York branch until 1919.

As a pacifist, Eastman opposed conscription and pressure from the Allies that the United States should enter the war in Europe, serving as executive director of the American Union Against Militarism, which in 1916 attempted to defuse antagonism between the United States and Mexico that might have led to fighting in the Caribbean and Latin America. But her tireless lobbying for peace failed to keep the United States out of the war, which it entered in 1917. As a member of the newly established National Civil Liberties Bureau (later the American Civil Liberties Union), Eastman was unshakably dedicated to upholding freedom of speech and helping conscientious objectors. She also contributed pacifist articles to her brother Max's journal *The Masses,* and after it was banned, the two of them established a similar new journal, the *Liberator,* which she helped run from 1918 to 1921 (it folded in 1922). These were difficult years for a woman as uncompromising as Eastman, for she was frequently confronted with disapproval of her radicalism by moderate women in the WPP, who disliked her socialist beliefs and her support for the 1917 Russian Revolution. She also invited criticism from suffragists because of her refusal to place suffrage first and temporarily abandon her pacifism to support the war effort, with a view to buying the subsequent postwar support of male politicians for suffrage. Even stalwarts such as Jane Addams, with whom Eastman had been a cofounder of the national Woman's Peace Party, had a distaste for her reputation for bohemianism and her advocacy of free love and birth control.

After the war, Eastman returned to women's campaigning as an organizer of the First Feminist Congress, which was staged in New York City in 1919, under the auspices of the New York branch of the WPP, to discuss equal rights issues. In her opening address, she illustrated the continuing exclusion of women from political and government office throughout the United States; the denial of equal pay, trade union rights, and access to birth control; and the discrimination women encountered in marriage laws. In an ambitious vision of social reform that broke down gender roles, she advocated changes to divorce and marriage laws, the introduction of wages for housework, and state benefits for mothers. She argued that if women opted to stay at home and rear children, then that work should be recognized as a social service and be duly remunerated—thus releasing women from their economic dependence on men. For Eastman, economic issues were central to women's autonomy. She also advocated that men learn domestic skills, especially in support of working wives, thus releasing women from their traditional roles as cooks and needlewomen at home. As Sheila Rowbotham has illustrated, what distinguishes Eastman from other proponents of an "egalitarian feminist strategy" was her assertion that it should be part of a much wider program of social reform, rather than reform only "within the existing society" (1992, 243). Eastman also supported the work of birth control pioneer Margaret Sanger and wrote in support of sex education in the *Birth Control Review,* arguing for women's right to choose when to have their children rather than having them when they were physically or financially ill-equipped to do so.

Eastman's first marriage had not been a happy one, and she divorced Wallace Benedict in 1919 and shortly afterward remarried the pacifist and poet Walter Fuller. From 1919 to 1921, Eastman and her husband both found it difficult to get work in the politically constricting atmosphere of conservative postwar America, in which many American socialists had been blacklisted as a result of the "Red Scare." By this time, Eastman's work on the *Liberator,* to which she had contributed numerous articles on socialism and Bolshevik Russia, had drawn attention to her unrepentant left-wing sympathies, resulting in regular surveillance by the Federal Bureau of Investigation (FBI) and harassment of both herself and her husband. The couple spent much of the years 1921–1927 traveling back and forth between England and New York in search of work. While in England, Eastman joined the suffrage campaign. In London, she established a branch of the U.S. Woman's Peace Party, was active in the Birmingham Conference of Labour Women, and associated with radical women such as Rebecca West, Vera Brittain, and Winifred Holtby. She earned an erratic income from her journalism, writing articles for Lady Margaret Rhondda's militant socialist newspaper, *Time and Tide,* as well as Alice Paul's journal *Equal Rights,* but remained in considerable financial difficulty. Eastman was never happy in England, and when her husband died in 1927, she returned to the United States. She died there ten months later of kidney disease at the age of forty-six.

The work of Crystal Eastman, the sister of the better-known socialist writer and editor Max Eastman, is all too often acknowledged only in tandem with his work, and she has yet to find a biographer, although historian Blanche Wiesen Cook has, since the mid-1970s, done much to revive interest in the charisma, passion, vitality, and breadth of vision of a woman who devoted herself always to peaceful social revolution.

See also Brittain, Vera; Holtby, Winifred; Paul, Alice; Pethick-Lawrence, Emmeline; Sanger, Margaret.

References and Further Reading

Adickes, Sandra. 1997. *To Be Young Was Very Heaven: Women in New York before the Great War.* Basingstoke: Macmillan.

Cook, Blanche Wiesen, ed. 1976. *Toward the Great Change: Crystal and Max Eastman on Feminism, Antimilitarism, and Revolution.* New York: Garland.

———. 1978. *Crystal Eastman on Women and Revolution.* New York: Oxford University Press.

———. 1993. "Radical Women of Greenwich Village." In Rick Beard and Leslie Cohen Berlowitz, eds., *Greenwich Village.* Newark, NJ: Rutgers University Press.

Josephson, Harold, Sandi Cooper, and Steven C. Hause et al., eds. 1985. *Biographical Dictionary of Modern Peace Leaders.* Westport, CT: Greenwood Press.

Kerber, Linda K., and Jane DeHart-Mathews. 2000. *Women's America: Refocusing the Past.* New York: Oxford University Press.

Niess, Judith. 1977. *Seven Women: Portraits from the American Radical Tradition.* New York: Viking Press.

O'Neill, William L. 1978. *The Last Romantic: A Life of Max Eastman.* New York: Oxford University Press.

Rowbotham, Sheila. 1992. *Women in Movement: Feminism and Social Action.* New York: Routledge.

Sochen, June. 1972. *The New Woman: Feminism in Greenwich Village 1910–1920.* New York: Quadrangle.

Spender, Dale. 1982. *Women of Ideas, and What Men Have Done to Them.* London: Routledge and Kegan Paul.

Edelman, Marian Wright
(1939–)
United States

Marian Wright Edelman (Associated Press AP)

An eminent campaigner for children's rights, Marian Wright Edelman has from an early age been driven by her passionate sense of social justice and a desire, expressed as long ago as 1958, to "fight for the moral and political health of America as a whole" (Smith 1992, 310). She founded the Children's Defense Fund (CDF) in 1973 to help counteract the deprivation and suffering encountered by U.S. children across all ethnic and minority groups. With 1999 census records revealing that in the United States 12.1 million children (one in six) live below the poverty line, the work of the CDF has become indispensable in raising public and governmental awareness of the social problems that such deprivation creates.

Edelman was born into a Baptist family in Benettsville, South Carolina. In addition to rearing five children of her own, her mother took in foster children, and her preacher-father encouraged his children and congregation to combat the segregation laws and set up their own self-help schemes. Edelman studied at Spelman College in Atlanta from 1956 to 1960, where she won a Merrill Scholarship to study in Paris and Geneva and a Lisle Scholarship to study in Moscow.

After graduating from Spelman in 1960, Edelman studied law at Yale University on a John Hay Whitney Fellowship. In her final year at Spelman College, she had become active in the civil rights movement, and at Yale University, she became involved in student sit-ins for civil rights and took part in a drive to encourage black voters to register in Mississippi. After gaining her law degree in 1963, she joined the Legal Defense and Educational Fund of the National Association for the Advancement of Colored People (NAACP) in New York. A year later, after transferring to the NAACP's branch in Jackson, Mississippi, she developed her skills as a civil rights lawyer, often representing the black victims of racial hatred and Ku Klux Klan attacks. In 1966 she was the first black woman admitted to the bar in Mississippi.

During the late 1960s, Edelman became increasingly aware of the economic deprivation that so often went hand in hand with the civil rights abuses of black people in the South. She alerted Senator Robert Kennedy to increasing levels of widespread poverty among black families, many of whom were losing their traditional jobs as cotton pickers in the widespread changeover to machinery. In Jackson, she took part in developing community programs for the Child Development Group of Mississippi, which provided funding to set up a Head Start Program in Mississippi to work with underprivileged preschool children.

In 1968, after marrying Robert Kennedy's legislative assistant, Peter B. Edelman, Marian moved to Washington, where she took a role as legal counsel to the Baptist civil rights leader Ralph Abernathy's Poor People's Campaign, which Martin Luther King, Jr., founded before his death, and which was aimed at calling a mass rally of America's poor to Washington that May to lobby Congress for government aid to the poor and unemployed. She also began exploring child care legislation with a view to the introduction of federal schemes to help minority groups. From 1968 to 1973, with the award of a grant by the Field Foundation, she became a member of the Washington Research Project of the Southern Center for Public Policy, during which time (1971) she investigated protective legislation for the poor and first developed the idea of the Children's Defense Fund. Shortly after completing two years at Harvard as director of the Center for Law and Education, she founded the CDF in 1973 as a nonprofit organization that helps deprived children of all creeds and colors by studying their living conditions and environment.

Statistical breakdowns provided the proof of worrying increases in the rates of neglect and deprivation, particularly among black children. Edelman's objective was to work with federal agencies and lobby for legislation to help improve the quality of life of such children. The CDF promoted health care and sex education programs to combat high rates of infant mortality, teenage pregnancy, and juvenile crime and to reduce the numbers of high school dropouts. Since 1973, it has greatly extended its activities to encourage reform of foster care and child care regulations, and initiate affordable child care and low-cost health insurance for low-paid working parents. It set up vaccination programs and in 1990 achieved the passage of the first bill on child care in the United States for nearly twenty years. In a vigorous advertising campaign during the 1992 presidential elections, the CDF stated its major objectives for children: "a healthy start," "a head start," and "a fair start," to which it later added "a safe start" and "a moral start"—all five concepts covering its major arenas of activity in protecting the lives of youth. In 2000 the CDF's newest campaign was to draw public attention to the escalating numbers of children dying as the result of the widespread availability of firearms.

A well-known public speaker and seasoned Washington lobbyist, Edelman has been lauded as one of the most influential women in the United States. She has served on innumerable legal and official bodies, many of them relating to the rights and welfare of children (such as the Carnegie Council on Children, 1971–1977), and is the recipient of a great many honorary law degrees. Her regular contributions of newspaper and journal articles and appearances on TV chat shows and current affairs programs such as *60 Minutes* continue to promote the work of the CDF. Her numerous published works cover many of the issues raised by the work of the CDF and include *Children Out of School in America* (1974); *Portrait of Inequality: Black and White Children in America* (1980); *Families in Peril: An Agenda for Social Change,* a collection of lectures given at Harvard in 1986 (1987); the 1992 bestseller, *The Measure of Our Success: A Letter to My Children and Yours;* and *Lanterns: A Memoir of Mentors* (1999).

Edelman's many awards include a 1985 MacArthur Foundation Fellowship (which she donated to the CDF), the Rockefeller Public Service Award, and the award in August 2000 of the Presidential Freedom Medal, on which occasion President Bill Clinton commended her work as a "crusader of conscience." The CDF now proclaims "Leave No Child Behind" as its official motto, and Edelman has seen her organization grow into a highly influential body. A mark of Edelman's considerable successes came in May 2001, when, together with Senator Chris Dodd and Congressman George Miller, she announced plans to introduce a bill to protect the health, safety, and welfare of all of America's children. At a press conference at Capitol Hill she spoke of an ambitious new twelve-point piece of legislation, designated the Act to Leave No Child Behind, with the united backing of many welfare and youth organizations as well as churches and civil rights groups. It was, she said, a bill for the new millennium, which would be the most comprehensive attempt yet to combat child poverty and hunger, improve literacy levels, and provide better health insurance and after-school care for children. Edelman's objective was also to ensure the protection of all children against violence, abuse, and neglect—both in and out of the home. Further details on this new act and the campaign to promote it can be found on the CDF's website at www.childrensdefense.org/.

References and Further Reading
Burch, Joann Johansen. 1994. *Marian Wright Edelman, Children's Champion.* Brookfield, CT: Millbrook Press.

Collopy, Michael, and Jason Gardner. 2000. *Architects of Peace: Visions of Hope in Words and Images.* Novato, CA: New World Library.

Current Biography. 1992. New York: H. W. Wilson.

Edelman, Marian Wright. 1992. *The Measure of Our Success: A Letter to My Children and Yours.* Boston: Beacon Press.

Old, Wendie. C. 1995. *Marian Wright Edelman: Fighting for Children's Rights.* Springfield, NJ: Enslow Publishers.

Otfinoski, Steve. 1991 *Marian Wright Edelman: Defender of Children's Rights.* Blackbirch Press.

Smith, Jessie Carney. 1992. *Notable Black American Women.* Detroit: Gale.

Edgeworth, Maria
(1767–1849)
Ireland

Irish writer, moralist, and educator Maria Edgeworth was born in Oxfordshire but from the age of fifteen lived in Ireland on the family estate at Edgeworthstown, County Longford. Here she spent much of her adult life as an unpaid factotum to her father, member of Parliament Richard Edgeworth. Very much a man of the Enlightenment and something of an inventor, Edgeworth was responsible for innovations as diverse as a turnip cutter and a velocipede. As an unmarried elder daughter, Maria was obliged to be governess to her various younger siblings (eighteen in all, the product of Richard's four different wives), but she was also very much an intellectual guiding force in her father's life (as he was in hers), and she assisted him in his literary ventures and managed his estates with considerable skill.

In between projects, under her father's influence, Edgeworth began to write her own didactic novels and stories in which she attempted to break with the prevalent patronizing, parodic literary conventions in the depiction of Ireland and the Irish. But she finally abandoned her mission in 1834, admitting: "It is impossible to draw Ireland as she is now in a book of fiction—realities are too strong—party passions are too violent to bear to see, or care to look at, their faces in a looking glass. The people would only break the glass and curse the fool who held the mirror up to nature" (Foster 1989, 306–307).

Maria Edgeworth's interests in women's education began with a passionate defense of the subject in *Letters to Literary Ladies,* published in 1795 after she was criticized for undertaking work translating a French novel. She further developed her ideas on education as a result of her collaboration on her father's book on educational methods, *Practical Education* (1798). With its method of studying children's reasoning through their dialogues with adults, Edgeworth and her father described an educational method that was innovative for its time and that favored an extraordinarily benign approach based on teacher vocation and an encouragement of the child's natural spontaneity. They recommended patience, kindness, and lessons of short duration by which "a young child may be initiated in the mysteries of learning, and in the first principles of knowledge without fatigue, or punishment, or tears" (Uglow 1993, 27). The work eventually became accepted as an educational standard across Napoleonic Europe. Richard Edgeworth's utilitarian ethics and ideas on the moral reform and improvement of children through education also inspired Maria to reflect on the subject in a series of edifying tales that called for social improvement, *Moral Tales for Young People* (1801).

In her "Big House" novels of life on Irish landed estates, such as *Castle Rackrent* (1800), *The Absentee* (1812), and *Ormond* (1817), Edgeworth's skill in writing in dialect helped her depict the decline of the seventeenth-century Irish landed gentry and expose its exploitation of the local peasantry. Again, her approach was inspired by her father's own passionate belief that the Irish peasantry should be treated with respect. *Castle Rackrent* was extremely successful in its day and did much to inspire the regional novel as a genre that was later developed by writers such as Elizabeth Gaskell, with whom Edgeworth became close friends and corresponded from 1813 to 1849. *Castle Rackrent* made Edgeworth a household name and also secured her fortune; between 1800 and 1814 her earnings as an author were far in excess of the modest sales of her contemporary, Jane Austen. On a visit to London in 1803, she was much feted and met several eminent writers of the time, including Sir Walter Scott, who became an admirer of her work and acknowledged its inspiration in his own historical novels, such as *Waverley.*

But Edgeworth eschewed the life of literary celebrity as also she did marriage. She made several trips abroad, including one to Paris in

1802–1803 during which she turned down a marriage proposal from a Swedish count, but out of devotion to her family she continued to manage the family estate after her father's death in 1817. Although she wrote little after this date, in her final years she devoted considerable time and energy to helping the starving people in her local community during the potato famine of 1845–1847 and providing education for the children of her estate workers. Although never an active campaigner, Edgeworth was a strong believer in the importance of a woman's right to independent thought and action in the creation of her own self-sufficiency, as demonstrated in her novels *Belinda* (1801) and *The Wanderer* (1814). Her devotion to Ireland and the preservation of her home country's cultural, linguistic, and historical identity did much to inspire later generations of Irish writers and activists.

See also Gaskell, Elizabeth.
References and Further Reading
Butler, Marilyn. 1972. *Maria Edgeworth: A Literary Biography.* Oxford: Clarendon Press.
Foster, R. F., ed. 1989. *The Oxford Illustrated History of Ireland.* Oxford: Oxford University Press.
Hurst, Michael. 1969. *Maria Edgeworth and the Public Scene: Intellect, Fine Feeling and Landlordism in the Age of Reform.* London: Macmillan.
Inglis-Jones, Elisabeth. 1959. *The Great Maria: A Portrait of Maria Edgeworth.* Westport, CT: Greenwood Press.
Kowaleski-Wallace, Elizabeth. 1991. *Their Father's Daughters: Hannah More, Maria Edgeworth, and Patriarchal Complicity.* New York: Oxford University Press.
Ó Ceirnín, Kit, and Cyril Ó Cirnín, eds. 1996. *Women of Ireland: A Historical Dictionary.* Kinvara: Tír Eolas.
Uglow, Jennifer. 1993. *Elizabeth Gaskell: A Habit of Stories.* London: Faber and Faber.

Edip, Halide (known as Halide Salih from 1901 to 1910; also Halide Adivar)
(1883–1964)
Turkey

An influential writer, reformer, and nationalist, Halide Edip was the first Turkish Muslim girl to study at the American College for Girls in Scutari. She was also the first female professor at the University of Istanbul. In her time she was referred to as "the woman who stands behind Kemal" because of her close association with the Turkish leader during the war of liberation. Her major work was in the extension of primary school education in Turkey and Syria during Ottoman rule.

From a wealthy family of the old aristocracy, Edip was born in Istanbul (then known as Constantinople), where her father was a palace official and secretary to the reactionary sultan Abdülhamid II. Her mother died when she was very young, and Edip was kept in seclusion and was brought up by her maternal grandparents until the age of four. She was educated at home by governesses and then became the first Turkish girl to study at the American College for Girls, where she excelled at mathematics. She was forced to withdraw from the school by the weight of public and family opinion that opposed her education, however. Nevertheless, she continued her studies in secret on visits to London and Paris. Her perfect English prompted her to retain a keen interest in the English language and even to write some of her own books in that language. At sixteen she wrote her first book on Turkish life, in which she described the life of seclusion lived by women in the harem. In 1901 she married her tutor, Salih Zeki Bey.

As supporters of the Young Turk revolution of 1908 (which in 1909 finally ousted the sultan), Edip and her husband moved in revolutionary and intellectual circles. She began writing articles on women's rights for publications such as the liberal newspaper *Tanine*. She helped organize the Society for the Advancement of Women, which provided educational courses and conferences for women in Istanbul, and eventually she became the first Turkish woman to lecture at the university.

After her divorce in 1910 (she rebelled when her husband took a second wife), she took a more prominent role as a public speaker and supporter of women's education, urging women also to discard the veil. During the period 1910–1912, she became involved in clandestine political activities for the fiercely patriotic nationalist movement as the only female member of the Ojak (Turkish hearth), a network of nationalist clubs that set out to improve standards of literacy and encourage social reforms.

Edip witnessed the chaos and suffering of the Balkan wars of 1912–1913 and wrote about the Turkish nationalist movement in *The New Turan* and a novel, *Handan* (both published in 1912), which describes a woman's love affair with a socialist intellectual. The two volumes of her memoirs, *Memoirs of Halide Edip* (1926) and *The Turkish Ordeal* (1928), were written in English and describe her firsthand experience of the nationalist struggle.

During World War I, Edip developed a reputation as a Turkish Florence Nightingale when she undertook relief work in Syria and Lebanon and set up Turkish schools and orphanages for refugee children in Damascus and Beirut. She also taught Turkish women nursing, despite government disapproval. In 1916 she joined the educator Bayan Nakiye in the reorganization of the Mosque Foundation Schools, which were brought together under the control of the Ministry of Public Instruction.

In 1917 she was married for the second time to Adnan Adivar, a fellow supporter of the Turkish independence movement. Together the couple took a prominent role in the nationalist movement.

In 1918 Edip was voted onto the Ojak's eleven-person-strong council by the Ojak congress and saw a new mission for herself in the rebuilding of the Turkish nation. On 6 June 1919, she gave a famous public speech, unveiled, in Istanbul's Sultanahmet Square, urging resistance to Greek attempts to invade Smyrna. By then she had become an outstanding female public speaker and, by association, a leading national figure.

Edip and her husband joined Mustafa Kemal's (later known as Atatürk) resistance forces during the Turkish War of Liberation in Anatolia of 1919–1923. She worked as a writer and translator for Atatürk, accompanying him on military expeditions to the front lines and at times taking part in the fighting. Eventually, she was promoted from the military rank of corporal to major by Atatürk, who also encouraged her in her pedagogic work.

After the proclamation of a new Turkish republic by Kemal, Edip was sentenced to death by the deposed sultan's government as a rebel. Kemal appointed her minister of education in the first nationalist ministry established in Istanbul, but Edip and her husband severed their links with Atatürk after he imposed a virtual dictatorship on Turkey in 1924, introducing draconian reforms such as the abolition of the Muslim caliphate. They gave up their political causes. Edip retired from social campaigning and left Turkey in 1925, spending the next thirteen years teaching and lecturing in North America and India and living for a time in England and France. During this time she wrote articles for newspapers in Europe and the United States. After Kemal's death in 1938, the couple returned to Turkey. A year later, Edip became professor of English at the University of Istanbul, and in 1950 she was elected to the Turkish parliament as the member for Izmir (formerly Smyrna) (1950–1954).

Edip wrote several important and popular novels about the Turkish way of life in which she discussed nationalism, women's position in society, and the need for social reform. Her most well-known novel was *The Daughter of Smyrna* (1922), about a female freedom fighter. She also wrote *The Clown and His Daughter* (1935), which blends Turkish nationalism with Westernized ideals; *Family* (1912), which analyzes the problems facing Turkish women who desired to obtain an education; and several other books on Turkish politics, notably *Turkey Faces West: A Turkish View of Recent Changes and Their Origins* (1930).

References and Further Reading

Adivar, Halide Edip. 1926. *Memoirs of Halide Edip.* Chicago: Century Company.

———. 1981 [1928]. *The Turkish Ordeal: Being the Further Memoirs of Halide Edip.* Reprint, Westport, CT: Hyperion.

Avakian, Monique. 2000. *Reformers, Activists, Educators, Religious Leaders.* Austin, TX: Raintree Steck-Vaughn.

Badran, Margot, and Margaret Cooke, eds. 1990. *Opening the Gates: A Century of Arab Feminist Writing.* London: Virago.

Beck, L., and N. Keddie, eds. 1978. *Women in the Muslim World.* Cambridge, MA: Harvard University Press.

Buck, Claire, ed. 1992. *Bloomsbury Guide to Women's Literature.* London: Bloomsbury.

Davis, Fanny. 1986. *The Ottoman Lady: A Social History from 1718 to 1918.* Westport, CT: Greenwood Press.

Roberts, Frank C., ed. 1964. *Obituaries from* The Times. Vol 2. Reading: Newspaper Archive Developments.

F

Farnham, Eliza Wood (Eliza Wood Burhans)
(1815–1864)
United States

In the 1840s, the American freethinker and prison reformer Eliza Farnham was the first woman to head a state prison, following in that great tradition of female Quaker prison reformers established by Elizabeth Fry. As the author of *Woman and Her Era* (1864), she also acquired a reputation as an eccentric feminist figure, notable for her strange brand of "apocalyptic feminism" (Helsinger, Sheets, and Veeder 1983, xv), which Helsinger asserts "pushed woman-worship to its logical conclusion—that women rely upon their superiority and become literally the sovereigns of society" (196). Together with early feminist writers such as Lydia Maria Child and Catharine Beecher and the Grimké sisters, she propagated the idea that women's moral superiority better equipped them to reform society.

Her Quaker mother died five years after Farnham was born in Rensselaerville, New York, and she was sent to live with relatives at Maple Springs, enduring a strict regime under her ill-tempered aunt until in 1830 she went to live with an uncle. After attending Quaker boarding school for a year, she transferred to the Albany Female Academy but soon after fell ill with overwork. In 1836 Farnham married a lawyer and pioneer settler and moved out west to Illinois, later describing her life in this frontier area in *Life in Prairie Land* (1846).

Returning to New York in 1840 without her husband (who had gone to California), Farnham published an essay on women's role in the magazine *Brother Jonathan*, in which she argued that women should take greater care in their respon-

sibilities as wives and mothers to set a moral example for society. In 1844, inspired by the work of the English prison reformer Elizabeth Fry, she succeeded in persuading the all-male Quaker board of Sing Sing prison in Ossining, New York, to appoint her matron of its adjacent women's prison, Mount Pleasant. Her introduction of methods of prisoner rehabilitation and incentives for good behavior during her administration there was a considerable success. In January 1846, Farnham made concessions to the old and much-hated "silent system" prohibiting prisoners from talking to each other, by allowing conversation at certain times daily. She instituted numerous changes that improved the quality of life of the inmates, set up a nursery for prisoners' children, gave them lessons, obtained donations of books from friends and well-wishers (including Margaret Fuller), and even introduced curtains and flowers to enliven the drab surroundings. A piano was brought into the prison, the women were encouraged to sing and read, and the younger ones were provided with dolls.

By 1846 Farnham had become interested in the fashionable practice of phrenology, which linked character traits with the shape of the skull, and she edited the U.S. edition of the *Rationale of Crime* by the English phrenologist Marmaduke B. Sampson. Two years later, continuing official male antipathy to Farnham's innovations at Sing Sing resulted in Farnham's dismissal early in 1848, after the prison's administration had changed. Farnham later took up other prison work, making a critique of the conditions at San Quentin prison and working for a year as matron of the Female Department of Stockton Insane Asylum, when she was in California from 1861 to 1862.

Farnham moved to Boston in the late 1840s after leaving Sing Sing and worked at Samuel

Gridley Howe's pioneering Perkins Institution for the blind, where she taught Laura Bridgman, the first deaf, dumb, and blind girl in the United States to be educated using new techniques by Howe. After her husband's death in California in 1848, she traveled there to settle his estate, taking the sea route via South America and eventually arriving after several months in late 1849. Having bought a farm in Santa Cruz County, she wrote down her impressions of life in the land of the Gold Rush, *California, In-doors and Out* (1856). While in California, Farnham remarried, but the relationship foundered after four years, and the couple divorced in 1856.

After returning to New York, Farnham took up the private study of medicine from 1856 through 1858 and published her autobiography, *My Early Days,* in 1859. She set up a society to help poor women resettle out west and accompanied several groups of female migrants to California. Although she opposed women's suffrage and their involvement in politics, in a speech made at the national women's rights convention held in New York in 1858, she endorsed abolition. In 1863, as a member of the Woman's National Loyal League, she collected signatures for a petition to Congress on abolition. She volunteered as a nurse at Gettysburg, but died of tuberculosis in 1864, the year in which she published her best-known work, the two-volume *Woman and Her Era*, a radical, mystical view of women's biological and moral superiority and leadership qualities.

In this work, Farnham echoed the sentiments expressed earlier in Margaret Fuller's *Woman in the Nineteenth Century* (1845; a work that has greatly overshadowed Farnham's), like Fuller drawing on a wide range of cultural and historical sources in asserting women's moral and spiritual superiority over men. Both Farnham and Fuller believed that the time had come for women to extend their intellectual capabilities and their civilizing influence beyond the domestic sphere. In exalted, religious tones, Farnham invested the procreative role of women with a messianic quality: "Life is exalted in proportion to its Organic and Functional Complexity; Woman's Organism is more complex and her totality of Function larger than those of any other being inhabiting our earth. Therefore her position in the scale of Life is the most exalted—the Sovereign one" (Helsinger, Sheets, and Veeder

1983, 76). Her abstruse arguments, based on a vision of the Virgin Mary as the spiritual redeemer of humanity alongside Christ, failed to have any impact, however, partly due no doubt to their complex grammatical and technical structure and Farnham's highly rarefied style. Their major legacy would lie in giving added impetus to the "new abolitionism" movement of the second half of the nineteenth century, which sought to bring an end to prostitution through the reform of men's immorality, and the social purity movement, which sought to eliminate the sexual double standard. Farnham's further thoughts on the roles of men and women can be found in her autobiographical fiction, *Eliza Woodson, or, The Early Days of One of the World's Workers* (1859), and the posthumous discussion of gender roles, *The Ideal Attained* (1865).

See also Beecher, Catharine Esther; Child, Lydia Maria; Fry, Elizabeth; Fuller, (Sarah) Margaret; Grimké, Angelina Emily and Sarah Moore.

References and Further Reading

Farnham, Eliza. 1972 [1846]. *Life in Prairie Land.* Reprint, New York: Arno Press.

———. 1972 [1856]. *California In-doors and Out.* Reprint, Nieuwkoop: De Graaf.

Freedman, Estelle. 1980. *Their Sisters' Keepers: Women's Prison Reform in America, 1830–1930.* Ann Arbor: University of Michigan Press.

Helsinger, Elizabeth K., Robin Lauterbach Sheets, and William Veeder. 1983. *The Woman Question: Social Issues, 1837–1883,* vol. 2, *Society and Literature in Britain and America, 1837–1883.* Manchester: Manchester University Press.

Lewis, David. 1965. *From Newgate to Dannemore: The Rise of the Penitentiary in New York, 1796–1848.* Ithaca: Cornell University Press.

Fawcett, Millicent Garrett
(1847–1929)
United Kingdom

Like her contemporary, the disarmingly gentle-faced Josephine Butler, Millicent Garrett Fawcett had a physical delicacy and demeanor that belied the underlying doggedness and resilience that would keep her at the helm of the moderate, constitutional wing of the British suffrage movement for over half a century. Obituary tributes to her "sweet reasonableness" (Oakley 1983, 20) categorized her as the antithesis of the Pankhurst-led militants, and for this reason Fawcett's patient campaigning for women's enfranchisement by legal methods was for long overshadowed by that of the much more voluble and volatile figures in the Women's Social and Political Union (WSPU). Remaining an uncontroversial and, some have said, unemotional figure, Fawcett was lauded as a paragon of the "womanly" campaigner: self-controlled, feminine, dutiful, and patient. She was also, however, a skillful administrator and astute propagandist who never allowed her commitment to what she saw as an overridingly moral cause be undermined by her private doubts about whether women would be enfranchised in her own lifetime. In the event, she lived not only to celebrate women winning the vote in 1918 but to see their voting age reduced from thirty to twenty-one in 1928.

Fawcett was born and grew up in Aldeburgh, on the Suffolk coast, one of ten children of a comfortably off malter, brewer, and ship-owner. She enjoyed a particularly close relationship with her father, Newson Garrett, a notable radical who inspired a sense of social justice in both her and her older sister, Elizabeth Garrett Anderson, who would go on to become the pioneer of women's medicine in Britain. After attending Miss Browning's school in Blackheath, London (1859–1862), Fawcett spent much of her time in London with her elder sisters, Elizabeth and Louise, through whom she met the radical member of Parliament, John Stuart Mill, and her husband Henry Fawcett. At the age of twenty, she married Henry, a Liberal MP and reformer who was a professor of economics at Cambridge University. He had been blinded in a shooting accident in 1858, and much of Millicent's time was taken up with the roles of supportive wife, political secretary, amanuensis, and companion to Henry. As an advocate of women's emancipation, he encouraged her feminist interests.

Through Mill and her friend Clementia Taylor, Fawcett met women of the Langham Place Circle, who were laying the foundations of the British suffrage movement. In 1866, led by Barbara Bodichon, they had collected signatures for a petition on women's franchise that was introduced in Parliament by John Stuart Mill. Fawcett was able to witness the eventual debate on women's suffrage in Parliament in May 1967 from her seat in the visitors' gallery. In July she joined the executive committee of the London National Society for Women's Suffrage and soon

Millicent Garrett Fawcett (Library of Congress)

overcame her reticence to give her first public speech on suffrage in July 1868, a fact noted in Parliament as disgraceful, coming as it did from the wife of an MP. In 1871 Fawcett had acquired sufficient confidence to conduct a speaking tour of the west of England. During this period, she also endorsed the movement for the Married Women's Property Act (a reaction to widespread disappointment at the issue not being addressed in the provisions of the 1857 Matrimonial Causes Act) and supported Anne Jemima Clough's University Extension scheme at Newnham Hall, Cambridge. Her daughter Philippa would be one of the first women to study at Newnham when it was promoted to a college.

During the 1870s, Fawcett gave strong moral approval to Josephine Butler's campaigns for repeal of the Contagious Diseases Acts. However, she took no part in the public campaign, partly out of her own aversion to discussing sexual matters but also because she feared that doing so would damage her work for suffrage. Nevertheless, she was an unswerving supporter of the social purity campaign and had a genuine concern that legal steps be taken to protect young girls from sexual exploitation. Her husband was also an advocate of social reform in India and introduced her to issues such as child marriage.

In 1878 Fawcett joined the Central Committee of the National Society for Women's Suffrage, but her campaigning for suffrage and the other causes that interested her, particularly outside London, was most effective after her husband's death in 1884. Only thirty-seven when she was widowed, Fawcett turned down the offer of becoming mistress of Girton College at Cambridge University to devote her time to suffrage and the social purity movement. Along with many other reformers, such as Butler and Catherine Booth, she supported W. T. Stead's exposé of the white slave trade. In 1886 she was a founding member of the National Vigilance Association for the Repression of Criminal Vice and Immorality and was elected chair of one of its subcommittees, remaining active in the association until 1926. During the period 1887–1903, Fawcett was sidetracked by the intense debate in Parliament over Irish home rule. She joined the Liberal Unionist group, as a committee member of the Women's Liberal Unionist Association, in opposition to home rule and toured Ireland regularly from 1887 to 1895 in support of the campaign. In 1888 Fawcett finally became a central figure in the suffrage movement when she took control of the Central Committee of the National Society for Women's Suffrage, after a split in the group over its proposed affiliation with women's Liberal associations. Fawcett wanted the suffrage movement to remain nonpartisan and with Lydia Becker defended the Central Committee's position of nonalignment. When Becker died in 1890, Fawcett set about reuniting the suffrage movement. In 1897, she was a leading organizer of a new umbrella coalition, the National Union of Women's Suffrage Societies (NUWSS), and as a member of its parliamentary committee, took on the considerable task of helping to coordinate the propaganda work, tactics, and activities of two London and eighteen provincial suffrage societies throughout Britain over the next twenty-two years. During this time, she accepted the presidency with the adoption of a new NUWSS constitution in 1907 and became an important political figure who consistently offered well-balanced, lucid arguments in support of women's suffrage and who was prepared to stick to patient lobbying to achieve it. As Mary Stocks remarks on Fawcett, "being wholly reasonable herself, she

never doubted that reasonable methods would triumph, and her service to women's suffrage was thoughtful, persistent and dogged" (1970, 71).

In 1901, such was Fawcett's acknowledged preeminence in British political life that after Emily Hobhouse's damning unofficial report on the British concentration camps in South Africa during the Boer War had caused a public outcry, she was asked to conduct an official inquiry. She sailed for South Africa at the head of a Ladies Commission of Enquiry and during August and September of that year toured thirty-three camps and inspected the conditions, confirming Hobhouse's conclusions in a detailed and balanced report to Parliament in December 1901.

At the turn of the twentieth century, Fawcett was initially encouraged by the high public profile achieved for women's suffrage by the militant campaigning inaugurated by the Pankhursts through the Women's Social and Political Union (WSPU). She admired their courage and congratulated hunger strikers on their release from prison in December 1906. But, when acts of violence by the WSPU escalated, as a constitutionalist Fawcett became increasingly concerned that these actions would alienate potential supporters of women's franchise among male politicians, and she became estranged from the militant wing. As a conciliator, she was ever ready to make compromises and in 1910 collaborated with journalist Henry Brailsford in framing the Conciliation Bill, which introduced the franchise for single women and widows who were heads of households. But three failed attempts to get the bill through Parliament in 1910–1912, during Liberal prime minister Herbert Asquith's government, disappointed Fawcett deeply, and she was forced to reappraise her long-held views on the nonalignment of the NUWSS. Although she was a long-standing Liberal, she made the pragmatic decision to formally ally the society with the Labour Party in May 1912 because it was the only political party that had declared its open support for female suffrage. This move created dissent in the NUWSS—an organization by that time composed of 411 disparate and self-supporting societies—leading to an exodus of members. Meanwhile, Fawcett oversaw the establishment of the NUWSS's Election Fighting Fund to promote Labour Party candidates in parliamentary by-elections.

Further antipathies in the suffrage movement were kindled by Fawcett's adoption of a "your country needs you" attitude toward the war effort. This came once her and Chrystal MacMillan's official appeal in July 1914 on behalf of British women for the government to seek peace mediation had failed to prevent Britain from entering World War I. Although she had been active in the International Woman Suffrage Alliance since 1904, like many of its members Fawcett left the international stage and concentrated on the national war effort. Her criticism of pacifist suffragists who called for international peace mediation at a meeting at The Hague in 1915 led to a walkout by many pacifist women on her executive committee. But Fawcett, having agreed to suspend her work for suffrage to support wartime propaganda, remained convinced that the crucial role played by women during the war would validate their moral right to suffrage and full citizenship. Behind the scenes, she continued to press for women's enfranchisement to be put before Parliament again as soon as the war was over.

In 1919, after the passage of the Representation of the People Act had given the vote to British women over the age of thirty, Fawcett resigned from the presidency of the NUWSS. She continued to advocate reforms promoting sexual equality and was active in the London and National Society for Women's Service, which strove to open up more professions to women. She also supported the NUWSS, in its new guise as the National Union of Societies for Equal Citizenship (NUSEC) and now led by Eleanor Rathbone, in its continuing battle for the franchise age for women to be lowered from thirty to twenty-one. But her disagreement with Rathbone's advocacy of family allowances and pensions for mothers in 1925 caused Fawcett to resign from NUSEC's board of directors.

Fawcett published many pamphlets on women's rights and suffrage during her long career. Early in her marriage, she assisted her husband in revising his *Manual of Political Economy,* becoming something of an expert on the subject in the process. In 1870 she published a school textbook, *Political Economy for Beginners,* that was translated into several languages and remained a standard text until her death. She also wrote two novels and a eulogistic *Life of Queen Victoria* (1895) and collaborated with E. M. Turner on a 1927 biography of Josephine Butler (*Josephine Butler: Her Work and Principles, and Their Meaning for the Twentieth Century*). Her own account of

the suffrage campaign, *The Women's Victory—and After,* was published in 1920 and her reminiscences, *What I Remember,* in 1924. She was made a Dame of the British Empire in 1925.

In 1919 the London Society for Women's Suffrage was renamed the Fawcett Society in support of an ongoing campaign for equal rights and responsibilities for all citizens. It continues to lobby against sexual inequality, focusing on equal opportunities in work and education for women. The Fawcett Library, named in her honor and relocated to newly built premises in October 2001, is the primary repository in Britain of a considerable archive of feminist and suffrage material and is dedicated to continuing to document the changing role of women in society. The Fawcett Library's website is http:// www.lgu.ac.uk/fawcett/ main.htm. The Fawcett Society's website is http:// www. gn.apc.org/fawcett/.

See also Anderson, Elizabeth Garrett; Becker, Lydia; Bodichon, Barbara; Butler, Josephine; Clough, Anne Jemima; Hobhouse, Emily; MacMillan, Chrystal; Pankhurst, Christabel; Pankhurst, Emmeline; Pankhurst, (Estelle) Sylvia; Rathbone, Eleanor.

References and Further Reading

Bland, Lucy. 1996. *Banishing the Beast: English Feminism and Sexual Morality, 1885–1914.* Harmondsworth: Penguin.

Caine, Barbara. 1992. *Victorian Feminists.* Oxford: Oxford University Press.

Crawford, Elizabeth. 1999. *The Women's Suffrage Movement, 1866–1928: A Reference Guide.* London: University College of London Press.

Harrison, Brian. 1987. *Prudent Revolutionaries: Portraits of British Feminists between the Wars.* Oxford: Clarendon Press.

Holton, Sandra Stanley. 1986. *Feminism and Democracy: Women's Suffrage and Reform Politics in Britain, 1900–1918.* Cambridge: Cambridge University Press.

Jeffreys, Sheila. 1985. *The Spinster and Her Enemies: Feminism and Sexuality 1880–1930.* London: Pandora.

Oakley, Ann. 1983. "Millicent Garrett Fawcett: Duty and Determination." In Dale Spender, ed., *Feminist Theorists: Three Centuries of Women's Intellectual Traditions.* London: Women's Press.

Purvis, June, and Sandra Stanley Holton, eds. 2000. *Votes for Women.* London and New York: Routledge.

Rover, Constance. 1967. *Women's Suffrage and Party Politics in Britain 1866–1914.* London: Routledge and Kegan Paul.

Rubinstein, David. 1986. *Before the Suffragettes: Women's Emancipation in the 1890s.* Brighton: Harvester Press.

———. 1991. *A Different World for Women: The Life of Millicent Garrett Fawcett.* Brighton: Harvester Wheatsheaf.

Stocks, Mary. 1970. *My Commonplace Book.* London: Peter Davies.

Strachey, Ray. 1931. *Millicent Garrett Fawcett.* London: John Murray.

Felix, Concepción
(active 1900s–1930s)
Philippines

Concepción Felix was a pioneer suffragist and social reformer in the Philippines who challenged the conventional view of women as inherently domestic, capable only of sitting at home cooking or sewing or taking on menial work as typists, nurses, or schoolteachers. During a 1912 visit to the Philippines by the leaders of the International Woman Suffrage Alliance, Carrie Chapman Catt and Aletta Jacobs, local women campaigners were encouraged by them to organize. Felix had already founded an organization in 1905, the Philippine Feminist Association, but had been reluctant to campaign for women's suffrage at that time. But after Catt and Jacobs's visit, she was encouraged to enlist others to found the Society for the Advancement of Women, which became the Women's Club of Manila. Its members supported a suffrage bill in 1912 and another in 1918, the latter also supported by the U.S. governor-general, but both failed to pass in the Philippine legislature. In 1920 a more combative, broader-based organization, the National League of Filipino Women, was established to fight primarily for suffrage throughout the entire country, not just the capital, Manila. It was joined in its campaigning by the Women Citizens' League, established in 1928 by a pioneer doctor, Maria Paz Mendoza-Guazon, which had a greater appeal to working-class and poorer women.

In 1934 when the Commonwealth of the Philippines was established by the United States in preparation for the granting of independence, a Constitutional Convention was set up to draft a new Constitution. At the same time, a General Council of Women was formed to unite several suffrage groups in a concerted effort to obtain the franchise for women. Its members gave evidence to the convention and subsequently mounted a national campaign to get women to support the idea of suffrage. Felix and her colleagues toured the Philippines, holding rallies and giving speeches, and enlisted the support of 447,725 women who endorsed the "yes" vote for women's suffrage. In 1937 legislation was finally passed giving women equal voting rights with men.

See also Catt, Carrie Chapman; Jacobs, Aletta.
References and Further Reading
Jayawardena, Kumari. 1986. *Feminism and Nationalism in the Third World.* London: Zed Books.

Subido, Tarroso. 1955. *The Feminist Movement in the Philippines 1905–1955.* Manila. (This appears to be the only English-language source available on Felix.)

Filosova, Anna
(1837–1912)
Russia

Anna Filosova was a pioneer of women's philanthropic work in nineteenth-century Russia. Although the charitable work undertaken by women such as her made only tiny inroads into improving the pitiful lives of the urban working classes in Russia's major cities, it provided a springboard for later campaigns to improve women's higher education and obtain them the vote. In 1885 Filosova was a cofounder of the Russian Women's Mutual Philanthropic Society, which began modestly as a women's reading circle and later ran housing projects for working women and day care facilities for their children. The society quickly lost much of its restless young blood, however, who embraced the more far-reaching objectives of the Russian revolutionary movement.

Filosova came from a comfortable background: she was born into the famous old Diaghilev family in Moscow, which had connections at court. (The founder of the Ballets Russes, the art critic and impresario Serge Diaghilev, was her nephew.) She received the traditional narrow education at home from governesses, learning "French, German and curtseying" as she put it (Porter 1976, 86), until the age of sixteen. In 1855 she married a high-ranking government official, Vladimir Filosov, by whom she had nine children. Bored with court life and seeking social challenges, she took up charitable work in 1859 after meeting Mariya Trubnikova. Together with Nadezhda Stasova, they founded the Society to Provide Cheap Lodgings and Other Benefits for the Citizens of St. Petersburg in 1859, and it received official approval in 1861. The society's initial objective was to provide clean and cheap accommodations for twenty-three indigent women and children in a house that also provided hot meals and a communal laundry. An attempt was also made to find suitable, respectable work, such as dressmaking for the women, many of whom were widows or wives who had been abandoned. Members of the society also volunteered to run day care facilities and give lessons to children whose mothers were at work. Such activity went to the limits of respectable social activism allowed women by the tsarist authorities at the time, but over the next twenty years the society expanded its range of activities, opening further cheap lodgings, canteens, workshops, and eventually some schools.

Filosova was also involved in the establishment of a Women's Publishing Cooperative in 1863, which aimed to provide work for better-educated women in copying, editing, and translating published books suitable for women. The cooperative of forty women made a great success of the venture, in the process refining their own skills and discovering a sense of self-worth.

In 1865 Filosova supported the idea of a more wide-reaching Society for Women's Labor posited by male activists including Peter Lavrov, which would serve as an employment agency that would not only place women in a wider range of work but also train them and offer financial support when unemployed. But the society, fraught with dissent among its founding members, who were polarized into two camps—bourgeois moderates versus radicals—never got off the ground. Women such as Filosova stuck to the middle ground of conventional good works and lent their energies to the major cause that would preoccupy Russian women from the late 1860s, women's further education.

In 1868 Filosova was one of several hundred women in St. Petersburg and Moscow who began serious campaigning for university courses for women. She used her family connections at court personally to lobby Count Dmitry Tolstoy, the minister for public instruction (1866–1880), but he (as a well-known misogynist) rejected all appeals for women's higher education. Although he allowed women to be admitted as auditors to a limited curriculum of public lectures held in Moscow and St. Petersburg from 1869, it would be another seven years before Tolstoy would see that his refusal was only forcing Russian women to study abroad in Switzerland, where they were rapidly becoming radicalized. Thereafter, women's university courses were founded in Kazan (1876) and St. Petersburg and Kiev (1878), the most popular being the Bestuzhev higher courses for women in St. Petersburg. There was a tremendous hunger for learning among young Russian women of this period, a desire that drove them to live in penury to the point of starvation in order to be able to study. Filosova, Stasova, and Trubnikova, recognizing the desperate need these women had for financial assistance, set up a Society to Provide Means of Support for the Women's Higher Courses in 1883, fund-raising for support among their rich, aristocratic friends and staging benefit concerts, lotteries, and lectures. The society eventually became the main benefactor of women taking the Bestuzhev courses.

During the 1870s, with the arrest and incarceration of many young radicals, Filosova raised funds for political prisoners and underground groups and allowed them to deliver illegal literature to her family home. Eventually, her increasingly political activities affected her husband's position at court, and she lived outside Russia from 1879 to 1881. After the 1881 assassination of Tsar Alexander II, all the early gains in women's education came to an abrupt end, with a reversal of official policy under the reactionary administration of Konstantin Pobedonostsev, who strongly opposed women's emancipation. The women's medical courses and other higher educational courses were all closed down by the mid-1880s, and those Russian women who were determined to pursue their studies had to do so once again abroad, in Switzerland and Germany. Eventually, under Nicholas II, women were allowed back into higher education, when, following the previous pattern, the government realized that women studying abroad were becoming increasingly involved in political activism. But by then, it was too late. The revolutionary movement that would bring down the empire had been born, and women played a central part in it.

In 1893 Filosova and Stasova announced the

projected establishment of a new charitable society in the journal *New Times*. In 1895 the society was finally launched with the support of other older-generation, moderate pioneers such as Trubnikova and Anna Shabanova under the necessarily rather tepid name the Russian Women's Mutual Philanthropic Society. But younger members found it too reticent in its approach to reform, and many turned their attention to socialism and anarchism. During the final years of her life, Filosova became well-known in the international women's and pacifist movements and hoped to see Russian women's societies united under the umbrella of the International Council of Women. In 1899 she and Shabanova failed in their attempt to set up a women's committee of the Russian League of Peace. That same year, Filosova attended a congress of the International Council of Women in London, the first of its kind to be held in Europe, where she met international suffragists such as Aletta Jacobs, Susan B. Anthony, and Anna Howard Shaw and was elected one of the organization's vice presidents.

The Society to Provide Means of Support for the Women's Higher Courses continued into the new century, and in 1904 Filosova was congratulated by the tsar for her twenty-five years of dedicated work for it. During the upheavals of the 1905 Revolution, the Mutual Philanthropic Society lost ground as the women's suffrage movement emerged. With her friends Stasova and Trubnikova now dead, Filosova remained committed to peaceful change and supported the constitutional democrats in the Duma. Her last public appearance came as chair in 1908 of the first All-Russian Women's Congress held in St. Petersburg, at which she also gave the opening speech. But her sense of achievement was marred by the mockery afforded the congress by male reactionaries, one of whom dubbed it an "assembly of whores." Five years after Filosova's death, Shabanova succeeded in establishing a Russian affiliate of the International Council of Women in early 1917, but the events of the October Revolution soon swept away this and all other feminist remnants of the old prerevolutionary order.

See also Anthony, Susan B.; Jacobs, Aletta; Shabanova, Anna; Shaw, Anna Howard; Stasova, Nadezhda; Trubnikova, Mariya.

References and Further Reading

Edmondson, Linda. 1984. *Feminism in Russia, 1900–1917*. London: Heinemann.
Engel, Barbara Alpern. 1983. *Mothers and Daughters: Women of the Intelligentsia in Nineteenth-Century Russia*. Cambridge: Cambridge University Press.
Evans, Richard. 1977. *The Feminists: Women's Emancipation Movements in Europe, America and Australasia 1840–1920*. London: Croom Helm.
Porter, Cathy. 1976. *Fathers and Daughters: Russian Women in Revolution*. London: Virago.
Stites, Richard. 1991 [1978]. *The Women's Liberation Movement in Russia: Feminism, Nihilism, and Bolshevism, 1860–1930*. Reprint, Princeton: Princeton University Press.

First, Ruth
(1925–1982)
South Africa

One of the most distinguished white members of the African National Congress (ANC), who paid with her life for her fearless campaigning against apartheid, Ruth First was killed by a letter bomb in September 1982. As a Marxist, feminist, sociologist, and human rights campaigner, she was invaluable to the cause of black African civil rights, and the loss was immense.

First's parents were Jewish socialist immigrants from the Baltic with a strong sense of racial justice, who had become founding members of the Communist Party of South Africa. She was educated at Jeppe High School and joined the Communist Party while she was a student at Witwatersrand University (1942–1946). She became a familiar figure at political rallies and took the post of secretary of the Young Communist League, as well as cofounding the Federation of Progressive Students.

After leaving the university, First worked briefly for the Johannesburg City Council and taught politics at night schools for blacks before taking up investigative journalism as an editor for the weekly radical newspaper, the *Guardian*. She helped found the Congress of Democrats in 1953 and edited its literary magazine *Fighting Talk*. Her work soon became familiar for its perceptive coverage of labor issues, the women's anti–Pass Law campaign, and exposés of the abuse of blacks under the judicial system. In particular, First drew attention to the arduous working conditions of black miners (she supported their strike in 1946) and the exploitation of black migrant farmworkers. First's powerful indictment of the cruel treatment of migrant

Ruth First (AP/Wide World Photos)

potato pickers at Bethal prompted the ANC to call for a monthlong boycott of potatoes. First also supported bus boycotts and the passive resistance campaign of the country's minority group from the Indian subcontinent.

In 1949 First married Joe Slovo, a leading journalist, trade unionist, and civil rights activist. Their home in Roosevelt Park quickly became a rallying point for other activists, including their close friends Nelson Mandela and Walter Sisulu. With the Communist Party banned in 1950 and First and Slovo's activities monitored, they had to channel their activities through the Congress Alliance and the ANC. Along with many ANC members, including Mandela and Sisulu, First and Slovo were arraigned in the four-year-long treason trial that began in 1956, after being involved in drafting the ANC's famous Freedom Charter. First and Slovo were finally acquitted. But after the 1960 Sharpeville Massacre, with many activists again being rounded up, First fled to Swaziland with her three daughters. She returned to South Africa six months later to continue with underground

activities and took up the editorship of the Congress Alliance's journal *New Age*.

But First was arrested again in 1963 in the wake of a roundup of underground ANC activists, not long after she had published *South West Africa: Travesty of Trust,* a critique of South African colonial involvement in what is now Namibia. She was held in solitary confinement for 117 days (under the 90-day detention clause of the General Law Amendment Act) and was also tortured. When she was placed under a strict banning order after her release, First decided to leave South Africa, writing about her imprisonment in *117 Days* (1965).

First joined Slovo in England, where they retained their vigorous support for the anti-apartheid movement, with First representing the ANC at international conferences and researching and editing Nelson Mandela's *No Easy Walk to Freedom* (1967). In 1972 she became Simon Research Fellow at Manchester University before taking a lectureship in development theory and the sociology of underdeveloped societies at Durham University (1973–1979). First's published works during this period include *The South African Connection: Western Involvement in Apartheid* (1972) and *The Barrel of a Gun: A Study of Military Rule in Africa* (1970). With Ann Scott, she wrote a biography of the pioneer South African feminist Olive Schreiner (1980).

In 1977 First spent a year's sabbatical at the Research Centre of African Studies at Eduardo Mondlane University in newly independent Mozambique, where she studied the lives of migrant workers. She took a particular interest in the hardships endured by black migrant miners in South Africa who worked in the gold and diamond mines, and her study was published as *Black Gold: The Mozambique Miner, Proletarian, and Peasant* (1983).

First stayed on as director of the center, where she was killed by a letter bomb in 1982 not long after the center hosted a United Nations Educational, Scientific, and Cultural Organization conference. The South African Bureau of State Security has long been implicated in her death, but nothing has been conclusively proved. Ruth First's story became the basis of a film scripted by her daughter Shawn, *A World Apart* (1988).

See also Schreiner, Olive.

References and Further Reading
The Annual Obituary. 1982. New York: St. Martin's Press.
Pinnock, Don. 1995. *Ruth First.* Cape Town: Maskew Miller Longman.
———. 1997. *Ruth First: Voices of Liberation,* vol. 2. Pretoria: HSRC Publishers.
Uerwey, E. J., ed. 1995. *New Dictionary of South African Biography.* Pretoria: HSRC Publishers.
Uweche, Raph, ed. 1996. *Makers of Modern Africa.* 3d ed. London: Africa Books.

Flynn, Elizabeth Gurley
(1890–1964)
United States

Popularly immortalized as the "rebel girl," Elizabeth Gurley Flynn was one of the most notable U.S. female labor organizers. In her work for the Industrial Workers of the World, she led some of the most highly charged trade union demonstrations and strikes in the United States. As a communist activist and unshakable idealist with great natural gifts for oratory, she bravely spoke out on social injustice, political oppression, and the economic slavery of the working classes. Her uncompromising political views led to persecution and imprisonment during the McCarthy era in the 1950s.

Born in Concord, New Hampshire, Flynn grew up in the mill towns of New England, where her father, a socialist engineer, had gone from one job to another. The family finally settled in New York at her mother's insistence, and it was Annie Flynn's Irish nationalist sympathies and sense of social justice that would have a lasting impression on the young Elizabeth. Growing up in the South Bronx, she began attending socialist meetings as a teenager and reading the writings of feminists Mary Wollstonecraft and Emma Goldman and the social treatises of August Bebel, Friedrich Engels, and William Morris.

After leaving school, Gurley joined the Industrial Workers of the World (IWW), better known as the "Wobblies," in 1906. The year 1906 also marked her baptism into a life of radical action: she gave her first speech at Harlem Socialist Club, entitled "What Socialism Will Do for Women," and was arrested for the first time for impeding the traffic on Broadway during an impromptu soapbox address on socialism. Thereafter she adopted her mother's maiden name, and as Elizabeth Gurley Flynn, she became a familiar public speaker in and around New York for both the IWW and the Socialist Party.

In 1907 Flynn took part in her first strike, among metalworkers in Bridgeport, Connecticut, and a year later married miner and labor activist Jack Jones. Soon after the birth of their second child in 1910 (the first baby had died), the couple finally separated and were divorced in 1920. In the meantime, Flynn had become a leading figure in the IWW, organizing free speech campaigns in Montana and Washington state in 1908–1910 after they had banned IWW public meetings. During the course of these activities, she was twice arrested and jailed in Spokane, Washington.

In January 1912 Flynn and Margaret Sanger organized 14,000 women woolen mill workers in the famous "Bread and Roses" strike in Lawrence, Massachusetts. Carrying banners with the message "We want bread and roses too," the demonstrators were mainly immigrant women from as many as twenty-five different nationalities. Flynn joined them on the picket lines in the bitter cold in their bid to secure equal pay with men. Eventually, the three-month strike culminated in machine smashing and violence, and the mill owners acceded grudgingly to most demands, with workers receiving as the minimum a 5 percent wage increase.

From Lawrence, Flynn organized a strike by 25,000 silk workers in Paterson, New Jersey, against the introduction of new machinery that would eliminate many jobs. The strike began in February 1913 and lasted for five months, during which time Flynn addressed mass rallies and was arrested, but the strike collapsed in August when IWW funds ran out. In 1915 Flynn was a defiant supporter of the trade unionist Joe Hill, joining the campaign for his reprieve from a death sentence after he had been found guilty of murder in Utah. She visited him in jail and created a lasting impression, with Hill dedicating his song "The Rebel Girl" to her before his execution.

During World War I, Flynn was a staunch pacifist and supported IWW conscientious objectors and pacifists imprisoned on antiwar charges. In 1916, after a rift with IWW secretary William D. Haywood, Flynn gravitated toward work for the U.S. Communist Party. At war's end, with industrial unrest once more raising its head, she helped organize the Workers' Defense Union in December 1918, which provided legal help and financial support to socialist immigrants being hounded in the hysterical postwar political climate of the "red scare." In 1920 Flynn joined the revamped National Civil Liberties Bureau, renamed the American Civil Liberties Union (ACLU), and worked with Jane Addams, Crystal Eastman, Helen Keller, and other women to protect political "undesirables" from unjustified deportation. In 1926, after the Workers' Defense Union amalgamated with International Labor Defense, Flynn was appointed chair and served until 1930. Through these legal defense organizations, she doggedly campaigned from 1920–1927 in support of the Italian-born anarchists Nicola Sacco and Bartolomeo Vanzetti, who had been condemned to death for their supposed part in a murder in Massachusetts.

In her personal life, Flynn had entered into a long affair with the Italian anarchist Carlo Tresca, whom she had met during the 1912 strike in Lawrence. In 1913 he moved into her apartment in New York, and they remained together until 1925. Shortly after they separated, Flynn became dangerously ill with heart disease and for the next ten years was forced to cut back drastically on her activities. But the life of an invalid made her restless, and in 1936 she returned to high-profile political activism as a full member of the U.S. Communist Party, giving her first speech in this capacity at Madison Square Garden in 1937 and becoming an important female figure in the movement. She also wrote regular articles on women's issues for the Communist Party's newspaper, the *Daily Worker,* and in 1938 was elected to the Communist Party's national committee. But the changing political climate, together with heightened anticommunist feeling at the time of the 1939 Nazi-Soviet pact, led to Flynn's expulsion from the ACLU in 1940, on which occasion she lamented the dilution of the organization's radicalism and its descent into respectability. Flynn's many radical friends and supporters also deplored this blatant violation of Flynn's right to freedom of conscience by an organization purporting to be the defender of civil liberties. And, indeed, the fears of the ACLU were soon overturned after the Soviet Union joined the Allied cause in World War II. It would not be until 1978, however, that Flynn would be posthumously rehabilitated by the board of the ACLU.

In 1942 Flynn ran for Congress on a variety of women's issues and garnered 50,000 votes. She supported the recruitment of women into the Women's Army Corps, published *Women in the War* (1942), and underscored women's contribution to industry and the economy during World War II in both this work and her 1947 book, *Women's Place in the Fight for a Better World.* During the ensuing Cold War, Flynn supported U.S. communist leaders suffering persecution for their political beliefs and in June 1951 became a victim herself, when she was tried under the Smith Act for conspiring to incite the overthrow of the U.S. government. After a protracted nine-month trial, she was sentenced to three years' imprisonment. In 1955 Flynn published her autobiography up to the year 1925, *I Speak My Own Piece: Autobiography of "The Rebel Girl,"* and began serving her sentence at the Federal Reformatory for Women in Alderson, West Virginia. Throughout the two years and five months that she spent in jail, Flynn retained a sense of indomitable pride at being a "political prisoner" and averred in her memoir of that time, *The Alderson Story* (1963), that she looked upon her prison number 11710 as a "badge of honor."

During her imprisonment, Flynn maintained her support for the U.S. Communist Party and after her release in 1957 returned to New York, determined to fight for the party's right to free speech. In 1961 she became the first woman to be appointed chair of the party's national committee. In 1962, with historian Herbert Aptheker, she brought a civil rights test case to the Supreme Court in protest of the government practice, under the National Security (McCarran) Act of 1950, of denying passports to members of the Communist Party and other radical organizations. (She had had her own passport revoked for attending the recent Twenty-second Congress of the Communist Party in the Soviet Union. In 1964 the U.S. Supreme Court ruled on appeal that Flynn had been wrongfully denied due process of the law and her passport was restored.) Meanwhile, she had been invited to visit the communist bloc countries in Eastern Europe. One month after her arrival in Moscow in 1964, she became seriously ill and died in a hospital there. Her death was a great propaganda coup for the Soviets, who gave her an official lying-in-state at the Hall of Columns (reserved only for top party bigwigs such as Vladimir Ilyich Lenin and Joseph Stalin) and a state funeral service in Red Square in Moscow, before her body was flown home for burial.

See also Addams, Jane; Eastman, Crystal; Goldman, Emma; Keller, Helen; Wollstonecraft, Mary.

References and Further Reading
Adickes, Sandra. 1997. *To Be Young Was Very Heaven: Women in New York before the Great War.* Basingstoke: Macmillan.
Baxandall, Rosalyn Fraad. 1987. *Words on Fire: The Life and Writings of Elizabeth Gurley Flynn.* New Brunswick, NJ: Rutgers University Press.
Camp, Helen C. 1995. *Iron in Her Soul: Elizabeth Gurley Flynn and the American Left.* Pullman: Washington State University Press.
Dubofsky, Melvyn. 2000 [1969]. *We Shall Be All: A History of the Industrial Workers of the World.* Reprint, Urbana: University of Illinois Press.
Foner, Philip. 1979. *Women and the American Labor Movement,* vol. 1: *From Colonial Times to the Eve of World War I.* New York: Free Press.
Lamont, Corliss, ed. 1968. *The Trial of Elizabeth Gurley Flynn by the American Civil Liberties Union.* New York: Monthly Review Press.

Ford, Isabella
(1855–1924)
United Kingdom

The Leeds-based socialist feminist Isabella Ford was a dynamic force in the north of England labor and suffrage movements as a founding member of the Leeds branch of the Independent Labour Party in 1893 and a regional leader of the National Union of Women's Suffrage Societies (NUWSS). Having grown up in the heart of the clothing industry in Yorkshire, she was convinced of the rights of working women and their need to organize, and worked hard to establish links between the suffrage and labor movements in mutually supportive ways that would further this end. Her arguments were laid out in her important 1904 pamphlet, "Women and Socialism," which suggested that the "Socialist movement . . . and the Woman's movement are but different aspects of the same great force which has been, all through the ages, gradually pushing its way upwards, making for the reconstruction and regeneration of Society" (Hannam 1989, 6).

Ford was born into an upper-middle-class Quaker family in Leeds. Her father was a landowner and local solicitor with radical liberal sympathies; her mother had been active in the antislavery movement. The family home was a meeting place for local humanitarians, socialists, and trade unionists and it was here that Ford was introduced to socialist ideas after meeting the radical Edward Carpenter, with whom she joined the Fabian Society in 1883.

In 1885 Ford began associating with women workers in the Leeds and Bradford clothing industries and collaborating with Emma Paterson, president of the Women's Protective and Provident League. She attended meetings of tailoresses in Leeds and helped them establish a Machinists' Society with members of the Leeds Trades Council. Growing ever more sympathetic to the difficulties of working women's lives and their need for unionization, in 1886 she founded a Workwomen's Society for tailoresses and textile workers in Leeds and eventually, in 1889, helped establish the Leeds Tailoresses' Union. She associated closely with activists in the Leeds Socialist League and became a leading organizer of women textile workers and tailoresses in the large clothing industry based in the West Riding area of Yorkshire. Ford had been involved in strikes by 200 women weavers in 1888, who were protesting a new management system of fining, and in 1889 organized 700 machinists who were striking at the deduction from their wage packets of charges (one penny in every shilling) for the electricity used to run their machines. The management responded to the strike by giving the work to home workers, an area of women's unionization in which Ford was never able to achieve any success, although she would preside over the Leeds Tailoresses' Union from 1890 to 1899. In 1891 Ford was involved in the defense of another long strike, this time by workers at the Manningham mills in Bradford.

After joining the Independent Labour Party in 1893, Ford became one of its leading propagandists and speakers, acted as a delegate to various trade union and socialist congresses at home and abroad, and wrote articles on labor issues for socialist and feminist newspapers, including her 1893 book *Women's Wages*. In 1896 she founded the Women's Trade Union Club in Leeds. In 1901 Ford produced her most important pamphlet, entitled "Industrial Women and How to Help Them," in which she criticized the traditional education of girls to be passive and unquestioning. She urged working women to rise in defense of their rights, arguing that real progress in improving working women's lives would not come until women had obtained the vote, and she now devoted herself increasingly to political campaigning to secure women's suffrage.

With her sister and sister-in-law, in 1890 Ford had established the Leeds Women's Suffrage Society; she was also active in the Manchester National Society for Women's Suffrage and was a friend of suffrage leader Millicent Garrett Fawcett. During the years 1903–1907, as a member of the National Administrative Council of the Independent Labour Party, Ford used this platform to promote collaboration between women activists and the labor movement, encouraging male Labour members of Parliament to advocate women's suffrage. In 1903 she was the first woman to speak at a Labour Party conference; becoming a parish councilor soon after, she was probably also the first woman in Britain to hold that post who was also a member of the Labour Party. In her 1904 pamphlet, "Women and Socialism," Ford recognized that the labor and suffrage movements were now inextricably linked. June Hannam points out that this publication

proved to be a wide-reaching examination of women's rights that went beyond the narrow debate on suffrage. Ford was convinced that "dependence on the owner of property is at the bottom of the woman's question as much as it is at the bottom of the labour question" (Hannam 1989, 6). For years thereafter, Ford doggedly lobbied the Independent Labour Party at annual conferences of the Labour Representation Committee and trade union congresses to commit itself to an official policy on women's suffrage. After the split between moderates and militants in the suffrage campaign in 1907, Ford aligned herself with the NUWSS under Fawcett. She joined its executive committee that year, hoping to persuade a reluctant Fawcett of the need for the NUWSS to throw in its lot with the Labour Party, which it did in 1912. After the NUWSS set up an Election Fighting Fund in support of Labour Party candidates for Parliament, Ford began electioneering in by-elections all over the country.

From 1908 Ford was drawn into the International Woman Suffrage Alliance and became friendly with many European feminists and pacifists, such as Rosika Schwimmer. Upon the outbreak of World War I, she strongly believed that suffragists everywhere should support peace mediation and organized a peace rally in London. She resigned from the executive committee of the NUWSS in 1915 when Fawcett took a strongly patriotic line in defense of the war effort and joined the Women's International League, for which she disseminated pacifist propaganda during the war. Ford turned down the chance to run for a Labour seat in the 1918 general election, choosing instead to join with other leading international feminists and pacifists such as Kate Courtney and Catherine Marshall in the postwar establishment of the Women's International League for Peace and Freedom (1919), the successor of the Women's International League, attending its annual conferences from 1919 to 1922. She was also a supporter of the work of the League of Nations.

Ford had renewed her campaigning for women's suffrage toward the end of the war but was dissatisfied with its eventual award only to women over the age of thirty. Throughout the 1920s, she regularly attended peace and women's rights congresses and continued to campaign for the Labour Party. She was the author of three novels, notably a "new woman" novel in 1895, *On the Threshold,* which explored contemporary social problems such as marriage and women's role in a society that was rapidly changing and in which Ford presented the benefits to be gained if women embraced socialism. In this and her many articles and pamphlets, she set out always to encourage "intelligent discontent" among her readers, in the hopes that working women in particular would enter into a "discriminating and well-organized rebellion" against the constraints placed on them (Rubinstein 1986, 98). Ford's biographer, June Hannam, attests to the difficulty in reconstructing the details of Ford's life in the absence of personal papers, diaries, and letters—a fact that underlines Ford's long neglect as an important figure in women's trade union history and in the rise of the Independent Labour Party.

See also Courtney, Kathleen D'Olier; Fawcett, Millicent Garrett; Marshall, Catherine; Schwimmer, Rosika.

References and Further Reading
Banks, Olive, ed. 1985, 1990. *The Biographical Dictionary of British Feminists,* vol. 1, *1800–1930;* vol. 2, *1900–1945.* Brighton: Harvester Wheatsheaf.
Crawford, Elizabeth. 1999. *The Women's Suffrage Movement, 1866–1928: A Reference Guide.* London: University College of London Press.
Ford, Isabella. 1993. "Women and Socialism." In Marie Mulvay Roberts and Tamae Mizuta, eds., *Sources of British Feminism,* vol. 2, *The Reformers: Socialist Feminism.* London: Routledge.
Hannam, June. 1989. *Isabella Ford 1855–1924.* Oxford: Blackwell.
Ingram, Angela, and Daphne Patai, eds. 1993. *Rediscovering Forgotten Radicals: British Women Writers, 1889–1939.* Chapel Hill: University of North Carolina Press.
Liddington, Jill. 1989. *The Long Road to Greenham: Feminism and Anti-Militarism in Britain since 1820.* London: Virago.
Pankhurst, E. Sylvia. 1977 [1931]. *The Suffrage Movement: An Intimate Account of Persons and Ideals.* Reprint, London: Virago.
Rubinstein, David. 1986. *Before the Suffragettes: Women's Emancipation in the 1890s.* Brighton: Harvester Press.
Wiltsher, Anne. 1985. *Most Dangerous Women: Feminist Peace Campaigners of the Great War.* London: Pandora, and Westport, CT: Greenwood Press.

Foster, Abby (Abigail) Kelley
(1810–1887)
United States

A pioneer abolitionist, freethinker, and feminist who with quiet modesty dressed and lived according to Quaker tenets, Abby Foster believed that women, like slaves, were denied their equal rights. Foster not only passionately defended her beliefs in public, frequently encountering virulent antagonism, but also fought against chauvinism within the abolitionist movement itself. She embraced a range of social issues from dress reform to temperance, seeing all her humanitarian concerns as being "bound up in one great bundle" (Bacon 1986, 201).

Foster grew up on a farm in Worcester, Massachusetts, and became a teacher in the early 1830s. During this time, she was inspired by the writings of the abolitionist William Lloyd Garrison, published in his journal the *Liberator,* and took up work for the abolitionist cause, at first as secretary of the Lynn Female Anti-Slavery Society. By the end of 1838, she had given up her teaching post at the Quaker school at Lynn, after attending the Boston Peace Convention that September when she joined a Quaker organization, the New England Non-Resistance Society. As a vehicle for pacifist ideals, the society attracted numerous other women members, including Lucretia Mott, Lydia Maria Child, and the Grimké sisters. Foster was also active in the American Anti-Slavery Society (AASS), a national organization established by William Lloyd Garrison in 1833. Along with Garrison, she argued persuasively for women to be given equal status in the society, which agreed in 1839 that they should be allowed to lecture for it.

Immediately, and much to her widowed mother's dismay, Foster embarked on a vigorous lecture tour at a time when simply the sight of a woman lecturing to mixed-sex audiences was considered scandalous by many. Until 1860, she traveled extensively in New England, Pennsylvania, Michigan, Indiana, and Ohio, lecturing on both antislavery and women's rights. By the end of her travels, she had earned a degree of fame, if not notoriety, achieved by few women of her time, and like another prominent female abolitionist, Angelina Grimké, she found herself having to face accusations of being a "Jezebel" for her public appearances, despite the care she had taken to have a chaperone at all times. However, Foster's anticlericalism and the attacks she made on evangelicals in New York state and Ohio for supporting slavery frequently resulted in her being blocked from speaking in certain churches, for example, the Presbyterian church in Seneca Falls, New York. Nevertheless, Foster steadily enlisted new women supporters wherever she went, including Lucy Stone and Susan B. Anthony, the latter becoming a regular on the abolitionist lecture circuit with Foster during 1857–1861. In 1841, however, Foster reluctantly resigned from her own church, the Society of Friends, because of its continuing criticism of the antislavery activities of some members and its refusal to allow her to use its meeting houses for her lectures.

Garrison, meanwhile, had placed great confidence in Foster's administrative skills, appointing her to the business committee of the American Anti-Slavery Society in May 1840 and an official AASS delegate to the World Anti-Slavery Convention in London that summer. But opposition persisted among the male membership to Foster's having a hand in running the society's finances, and some conservative and clerical male members left in protest. Eventually, a profound division developed over the role of women in the society, which ended with the formation of a splinter group, the American and Foreign Anti-Slavery Society.

In 1845, after a long engagement, Abby married fellow abolitionist Stephen Symonds Foster, who was equally radical in his advocacy of social justice and would support her later work for women's rights. In their marriage they respected each other as equal partners, with Stephen taking turns with Abby to go out lecturing, while the other looked after their farm and children.

In 1850, when the newly introduced Fugitive Slave Act demanded the return of escaped slaves, Abby upheld the right of slaves to resist oppression and urged abolitionists in Ohio (a well-known stop on the Underground Railroad) to defy the law and help them escape to the North. In October 1850, after helping plan a women's rights convention held at Worcester, Massachusetts, Foster turned increasingly to lecturing on women's rights and suffrage, urging young women to become financially self-supporting.

By the time the Civil War broke out in 1861, Foster was worn out and did not contribute to the war effort. Despite being an ardent suffragist,

Abby (Abigail) Kelley Foster (North Wind Picture Archive)

she supported those petitioning for the Fifteenth Amendment, which in 1870 eliminated race as a criterion in having the right to vote. Foster was greatly saddened by the profound split in the suffrage movement in 1869 caused by the earlier decision by some activists to support suffrage for black men ahead of that for women, and she responded to the call of Stone's moderate group to establish an American Woman Suffrage Association. During the 1870s, Foster campaigned for temperance and in 1880 attended the thirtieth-anniversary celebrations of the Worcester women's rights convention of 1850 as one of its keynote speakers. On that occasion, she denounced the moves by some suffragists to settle for partial suffrage at state level—for example, in the case of school board elections, for which women in Massachusetts were now allowed to be nominated—being of the opinion that "half a vote" was worse than none at all (Weatherford 1998, 144).

Foster and her husband refused to pay their taxes between 1874 and 1878, arguing that since she had no right to vote, she should not therefore be liable for taxation, thus echoing the calls for "no taxation without representation" that had been the slogan of the American Revolution. As a result, the Fosters' farm in Connecticut was sold by the authorities. But the couple's supporters, who backed their symbolic gesture, later secured the return of the deeds. The Fosters subsequently called a convention on taxation without representation and continued refusing to pay their taxes until 1880, when they finally settled with the revenue authorities.

Foster spent her remaining years as an invalid, retaining her absolute moral integrity to the end. Perhaps the finest tribute to her work can be found in a letter written to her in July 1859 by William Lloyd Garrison, who commented: "Of all the women who have appeared upon the historic stage, I have always regarded you as peerless—the moral Joan of Arc of the world" (Bolt 1993, 65).

See also Anthony, Susan B., Child, Lydia Maria; Grimké, Angelina Emily and Sarah Moore; Mott, Lucretia Coffin; Stone, Lucy.

References and Further Reading

Bacon, Margaret Hope. 1976. *I Speak for My Slave Sister: The Life of Abby Kelley Foster.* New York: Thomas Y. Crowell.
———. 1986. *Mothers of Feminism: The Story of Quaker Women in America.* San Francisco: Harper and Row.
Bolt, Christine. 1993. *The Women's Movements in the United States and Britain from the 1790s to the 1920s.* London: Harvester Wheatsheaf.
Hersch, Blanche G. 1978. *Slavery of Sex: Feminist Abolitionists in America.* Urbana: University of Illinois Press.
Josephson, Harold, Sandi Cooper, and Steven C. Hause et al., eds., 1985. *Biographical Dictionary of Modern Peace Leaders.* Westport, CT: Greenwood Press.
Sterling, Dorothy. 1991. *Ahead of Her Time: Abby Kelley and the Politics of Antislavery.* New York: Norton.
Weatherford, Doris. 1998. *A History of the American Suffragist Movement.* Santa Barbara, CA: ABC-CLIO.

Friedan, Betty
(Elizabeth Naomi Goldstein)
(1921–)
United States

As author of *The Feminine Mystique,* which shattered the traditional myth of women's domestic contentment, the feminist and social psychologist Betty Friedan contributed one of the seminal and most enduring texts of the second wave of American feminism. As founder of the National Organization for Women and a cofounder of the National Women's Political Caucus, Friedan has since the mid-1960s explored at length what she defined as "the problem that has no name"— women's dissatisfaction with their limited sphere of activity and their need to balance fulfillment in their working careers with their biological instincts as mothers.

Born in Peoria, Illinois, the daughter of a Jewish jeweler and a mother who had given up journalism to be a homemaker, Friedan studied psychology and sociology at Smith College in Northampton, Massachusetts. After graduating in 1942, she won a research fellowship in psychology at the University of California at Berkeley, afterwards moving to New York and working as a journalist for a news service. But work gradually yielded to the demands of bringing up her three children after she married in 1947. Eventually, she lost her reporting job when her employers refused to grant her maternity leave during her second pregnancy. (She divorced her husband in 1969, after suffering years of physical abuse.)

By 1957, finding her life at home in suburbia stultifying, Friedan became interested in finding out how other similar women felt and to what degree further education had or had not been beneficial to them. She drew up a questionnaire and circulated it to her friends from Smith College, in it asking about their aspirations and working lives since college. Detecting an underlying note of depression and loss of self-esteem that she considered to be a widespread social phenomenon among many middle-class women, she took the research further through a series of similar questionnaires. During John F. Kennedy's presidency, she established links with women in his administration involved in federal investigations into the status of women. From these and other research findings a picture emerged: since the 1950s, women had lost all the gains of the war years, when they had taken over men's jobs to aid the war effort. They were now backsliding into unchallenging domestic and subservient roles. Friedan detected a wide-reaching and growing sense of dissatisfaction among women at the limitations of these traditional "feminine" roles. She first published an article in *Good*

Housekeeping in 1960 entitled "Women Are People Too!" and went on to discuss the results of her investigations in her 1963 book, *The Feminine Mystique.* It proved to be a serious study of the social and cultural prejudices operating against women in U.S. society, which had forced so many of them into conformist roles as wives, mothers, and homemakers. In describing the increasing sense of malaise and dissatisfaction among middle-class housewives, Friedan argued that such was their lack of self-esteem that many women had come to accept that the domestic sphere was the best and only one to which they could aspire in life. And what is more, women were constantly being warned that those who sought independent careers outside the home in male spheres such as politics would remain miserable and frustrated.

Friedan went on to lecture and give radio talks and TV interviews on the arguments contained in *The Feminine Mystique,* which, along with Germaine Greer's book *The Female Eunuch,* had a lasting influence on the women's movement. She also took up lecturing posts at New York University and the New School for Social Research. In June 1966, during a conference of the Equal Employment Opportunity Commission, Friedan and a group of other women agreed to make the issue of women's rights a matter of basic civil liberty. Inspired by the 1964 passage of the Civil Rights Act, they set out to defend women's rights along the lines of Title VII of the act, which banned sexual as well as racial discrimination. Inspired too by the work of the National Association for the Advancement of Colored People, Friedan and her associates founded the National Organization for Women (NOW) in October 1966—the first official women's organization of the second wave of the women's movement—dedicated to achieving women's full equality, to bringing them "into the mainstream of American society now, exercising all privileges and responsibilities thereof, in truly equal partnership with men" (Cullen-Dupont 2000, 78). Friedan served as its first president until 1970, initiating a program of concerted lobbying in Washington, D.C., followed by picketing of the Equal Employment Opportunity Commission. Campaigns were also launched to eliminate sexual discrimination and inequalities in the workplace, prohibit sex discrimination in employment advertisements, and ban sexist advertising.

Betty Friedan (Library of Congress)

NOW also sought reform of the Social Security laws, the legalization of abortion, and an increase in the provision of day care facilities for working mothers.

In 1970 Friedan was a leader of the national women's strike for equality, which on 26 August marched down New York's Fifth Avenue in celebration of the fiftieth anniversary of the winning of women's suffrage in the United States and the recent passage of the Equal Rights Amendment by the House of Representatives, although Congress as a whole did not pass the ERA until 1972, when it was sent to the states for ratification. Meanwhile, NOW found itself mired in controversy, first for its exclusion of lesbian activists until 1971, when it voted to change its policies and include lesbian and gay rights in its feminist agenda, and second when the movement split over the issue of abortion.

In 1971 Friedan left NOW, finding its position on lesbian rights and the exclusion of and hostility toward men too extreme. That year, she was a founding member of the National Women's Political Caucus (NWPC) with Bella Abzug and Shirley Chisholm, which brought women of all political persuasions together and committed itself to campaigning for political and legal reform and the appointment of women to positions where they could defend the rights of women and minorities. NWPC leaders stressed at all times the need for the women's movement to retain the support of the moderate majority.

Friedan was a convener of the international feminist congress in 1973 and cofounder of the First Women's Bank. She also accepted academic appointments at Yale and Temple Universities and at Queens College, New York. In 1976 she published her account of the early years of the women's movement and took stock of the progress made in *It Changed My Life: Writings on the Women's Movement*. From the late 1970s, she campaigned for ratification of the Equal Rights Amendment, which ultimately failed in 1982, three states short of the number needed for ratification.

The appearance of Friedan's book *The Second Stage* in 1981 was a very disconcerting moment for her feminist supporters. In her discussion of women's old and new roles in society, Friedan emphasized the relevance of both and seemed to her critics to be backpedaling by arguing that the women's movement had been too quick to dismiss women's natural and nurturing roles. Many, she argued, were emotionally unsuited to the competitive workplace, where too many women were now trying to take on male roles, juggling career and home to the detriment of their emotional well-being. Friedan also now eschewed the confrontational politics of the early days of the women's movement and the advocacy of an out-and-out sex war, claiming that the stridency of demands for liberation made women feel guilty if they loved their husbands and enjoyed being mothers. Instead, she advocated the "human liberation" of both sexes from stereotyped roles.

Since modifying her position on women's liberation, Friedan has gone on to argue for women's rights within the Democratic Party, insisting that half of its delegates should be women. Upon her appointment in 1988 as visiting distinguished professor at the school of journalism and the Institute for the Study of Women and Men at the University of Southern California (USC), she began to make a study of the elderly.

In 1989 Friedan conducted research at the Andrus Gerontology Center at USC on the prejudices and difficulties encountered by elderly women, publishing the results of her study as *The Fountain of Age* in 1993. In this work she discussed the positive aspects of aging, as well as warning against the many predators on the elderly in big business, attacking their exploitation of the sick and vulnerable through inflated insurance and health care schemes. She has also recently held posts at the Smithsonian Institution and Mount Vernon College. In 2000 Friedan published her autobiography, *Life So Far*, and was granted $1 million by the Ford Foundation to conduct research on the changing roles of men and women in the workplace.

See also Greer, Germaine.
References and Further Reading

Attallah, Naim. 1998. *In Conversation with Naim Attallah*. London: Quartet Books.

Cullen-Dupont, Kathryn, ed. 2000. *Encyclopedia of Women's History in America*. New York: Facts on File.

Falk, Gerhard. 1998. *Sex, Gender, and Social Change: The Great Revolution*. Lanham, MD: University Press of America.

Friedan, Betty. 1998 [1976]. *It Changed My Life: Writings on the Women's Movement*. Reprint, Cambridge, MA: Harvard University Press.

———. 2000. *Life So Far*. New York: Simon and Schuster.

Hennessee, Judith Adler. 1999. *Betty Friedan: A Biography*. New York: Random House.

Horowitz, Daniel. 2000. *Betty Friedan and the Making of the Feminine Mystique: The American Left, the Cold War, and Modern Feminism*. Amherst: University of Massachusetts Press.

Kerber, Linda K., and Jane DeHart-Mathews. 2000. *Women's America: Refocusing the Past*. New York: Oxford University Press.

Mitchell, Susan. 1997. *Icons, Saints & Divas: Intimate Conversations with Women Who Changed the World*. London: Pandora.

Reynolds, Moira Davison. 1994. *Women Advocates of Reproductive Rights: 11 Who Led the Struggle in the United States and Great Britain*. Jefferson, NC: McFarland.

Rountree, Cathleen. 1999. *On Women Turning 70: Honoring the Voices of Wisdom*. San Francisco: Jossey-Bass Publishers.

Walker, Martin. 2000. *America Reborn: A Twentieth-Century Narrative in Twenty-Six Lives*. "Betty Friedan and the American Woman." New York: Knopf.

Wolfe, Alan. 1999. "The Mystique of Betty Friedan—Looking Back at the Foundations of Friedan's Theory." *The Atlantic* 284(3): 98–105.

Fry, Elizabeth
(1780–1845)
United Kingdom

One of the most widely disseminated didactic stories of social reform in Britain is that of the Quaker prison reformer Elizabeth Fry. Her edifying story became a catechism of religious philanthropy in Victorian schools, ensuring that if children grew up knowing the names of any social reformers, they would probably be those of Fry and Florence Nightingale. Promoted as the "Angel of the Prisons" (by one biographer) to rival Nightingale as "the Lady with the Lamp," Fry was raised to the status of secular saint. As a pious woman and mother of many children, she herself remained ambivalent about having taken on public campaigning. Many of her suggestions for radical penal reform would be ignored, and the power of her evangelical style of proselytizing was overtaken in the second half of the nineteenth century by the rhetoric of the more vocal and flamboyant figures in the suffrage and feminist movements.

Elizabeth Fry was born into a prosperous Quaker family in Norwich, Norfolk, where her father was a successful wool merchant and banker. She grew up imbued with the Quaker abhorrence for slavery and her family's advocacy of social reform and philanthropy. Seeking some kind of social vocation, she began collecting clothes for the destitute, teaching poor children to read, and visiting the squalid homes in which they lived. But her activities were curtailed by marriage in 1800 to a Quaker banker, Joseph Fry, and a succession of ten pregnancies between 1801 and 1816 (an eleventh child was born in 1822). She continued to do a limited amount of charity work as a workhouse visitor in Islington, in London, but it was not until 1809, after the death of her father, that she began preaching at Quaker meetings. In 1811 she was formally acknowledged by the Society of Friends as a minister.

Having heard in 1813 from family friend Stephen Grellet, an American Quaker prison reformer and evangelist, that conditions in London's Newgate Prison were worse than any he had seen on the Continent, Fry found the cause for which she had been searching. She became a prison visitor to the "female side" of Newgate, where 300 filthy, hungry, and often drunk women (they were allowed access to cheap gin)

Elizabeth Fry (Library of Congress)

were crowded together thirty at a time in large communal cells and were forced to sleep on cold stone floors without bedding, along with many of their own children.

After being forced by a downturn in her husband's business affairs to farm some of her children out among relatives, in 1817 Fry turned to regular prison visiting and serious reform of conditions at Newgate. Although her primary intentions as a woman of deep religious faith were to save such women from eternal damnation, she was also determined to reduce the overcrowding and introduce programs of social rehabilitation for the women prisoners. She persuaded the prison governor to provide a room for use as a school, which offered sewing and literacy classes and regular injections of Bible reading and religious worship. Fry and her helpers brought in fresh clothes for the bedraggled women as part of their plan to revive in prisoners a sense of self-respect. In 1817 Fry was one of a group of Quaker prison reformers who founded the Association for the Improvement of the Female Prisoners in Newgate, and their advocacy of reform was promoted by member of Parliament Thomas Fowell Buxton.

In 1818 Fry was asked to give evidence to a Select Committee on the Prisons of the Metropolis (London). She made use of the opportunity to voice her opposition to capital punishment, arguing that it made human life valueless. In England at that time, the criminal justice system was based on draconian punishment rather than rehabilitation or compassion, and criminals could be executed for a wide range of misdemeanors. Fry was instrumental in having some of these, such as pocket-picking and petty theft, removed from the list of capital offenses when legislation in 1837 reduced the list from thirty-seven to sixteen. She made numerous serious recommendations for reform at Newgate (not all of them taken seriously by the authorities), advocating an end to mixed-sex cells, the classification of prisoners according to seriousness of crime, the introduction of women warders for female prisoners, access to religious worship and basic literacy lessons, and useful rather than humiliating employment for prisoners while in jail.

This work continued with the establishment in 1821 of the British Society of Ladies for Promoting the Reformation of Female Prisoners, which published guidelines on the standards of behavior to be set among prisoners. The recommendations, extended to cover inmates of other institutions, involved a system of self-discipline over gambling and bad language, the observance of regular washing, and religious devotions. After writing a report on her visits to prisons in Scotland and the north of England in 1821 with her brother Joseph Gurney, Fry received requests for information from prisons in Italy, Denmark, and Russia. In these countries and elsewhere, many of Fry's suggestions for prison reform were also taken up, particularly after she made a tour of prisons on the Continent in 1843 (visiting France, Switzerland, Germany, Belgium, Denmark, and the Netherlands). Fry's example also did much to inspire Quaker women in the United States, such as Eliza Wood Farnham, to take up prison work.

Fry published accounts of her prison inspections in *Notes on a Visit to Some Prisons in Scotland and the North of England in Company with E. Fry*, by J. J. Gurney, in 1819. A summary of her ideas on penal reform and a justification of her work made in response to criticism for having supposedly abandoned her domestic duties was also published in Fry's 1827 book, *Observations on the Visiting, Superintendence and Government of Female Prisoners*. In later years, she would be one of the first reformers to voice serious objection to the new practice of solitary confinement as a punishment in prisons.

Fry did not confine her concern for convicts just to the prisons in which they were held. She was also deeply concerned about the appalling unsanitary and overcrowded conditions on board the convict ships that transported so many of them on the long journey to the penal colonies of New South Wales. She personally inspected 106 convict ships between 1818 and 1843 and also corresponded with Lady Jane Franklin, wife of the explorer Sir John Franklin, who was later governor of the penal colony at Van Diemen's Land. Lady Franklin sent Fry detailed reports of life there, in which she raised the issue of the welfare of women convicts often forced into prostitution. Inspired by Fry's work, Lady Franklin established a Tasmanian Ladies' Society for the Reformation of Female Prisoners.

During the 1820s, Fry promoted a range of other welfare projects, taking her reforming activities to hospitals and mental institutions, where she worked for more humane treatment of the mentally ill and better nursing care. It was always her great regret that her prison work had kept her away from another major concern—improvements to nursing standards in hospitals, which she had touched upon in her 1827 book, *Observations*. In 1834 Fry was visited by a German clergyman, Pastor Theodore Fliedner, who was impressed with her work in prisoner welfare at Newgate. She shared with him her long-held desire to establish proper training for women nurses, which inspired Fliedner to found the Institution of Protestant Deaconesses at Kaiserwerth in 1836, which, although it did not offer formal training, established principles of hospice care. Fry visited the institution in May 1840, delighted to see women at last given an outlet for vocational work. More significantly, the institution would provide Florence Nightingale, who expressed her admiration of Fry's work by letter, with her first valuable nursing experience. After reading about the work at Kaiserwerth in a copy of its yearbook sent to her by a friend in 1846, Nightingale badgered her parents until she was allowed to spend time there in 1851.

Fry's other plans for enhancing welfare among the poor extended to the establishment of low-cost housing schemes and soup kitchens and night shelters for the homeless in London during winter. She arranged networks of district visitors to the sick and poor through the establishment of the Brighton District Visiting Society (which was the impetus for similar organizations throughout Britain), and at her suggestion even traveling libraries were provided for isolated coast guard stations. In May 1840, after returning from Kaiserwerth, Fry finally founded an institution to train nurses, known as the Protestant Sisters of Charity (whose trainees were later popularly referred to as "Fry sisters"), to provide respectable nursing training to middle-class women; the first eight received their training at Guy's Hospital in London. A few of the Fry sisters would work with Florence Nightingale in the Crimean War, but as is the case with Fry's own groundbreaking work for nursing, their contribution would be obliterated by the vast god-building industry that surrounded Nightingale after her return from the Crimea.

In 1828 Fry's husband went bankrupt. Thereafter the couple had to live in greatly reduced circumstances, which not only affected Fry's credibility as a fund-raiser for many charities but also limited her campaigning activities until her brother Joseph provided her with an income. From 1838 to 1843, she made five tours of prisons on the Continent. Fry also advocated workhouse reform, and in 1829 she joined other reformers in lobbying successfully for the British government to ban the practice of suttee in India. In 1847 a two-volume *Memoir of Elizabeth Fry with Extracts from her Journal and Letters* was published by two of her daughters. A website devoted to Fry's life and work can be found at http://www.elizabethfry.net.

See also Farnham, Eliza Wood; Nightingale, Florence.

References and Further Reading
Abbot, Willis J. 1913. *Notable Women in History.* London: Greening.
Carey, Rosa Nouchette. 1899. *Twelve Notable Good Women.* London: Hutchinson.
Johnson, B. R., ed. 1931. *Elizabeth Fry's Journeys on the Continent 1840–1841, from a Diary Kept by Her Niece Elizabeth Gurney.* London: John Lane.
Kent, John. 1962. *Elizabeth Fry.* London: B. T. Batsford.
Prochaska, F. K. 1980. *Women and Philanthropy in Nineteenth-Century England.* Oxford: Clarendon Press.
Rose, June. 1994 [1980]. *Elizabeth Fry.* Reprint, London: Macmillan.
Van Drenth, A., and F. de Haan. 1999. *The Rise of Caring Power: Elizabeth Fry and Josephine Butler in Britain and the Netherlands.* Amsterdam: Amsterdam University Press.
Whitney, Janet. 1936. *Elizabeth Fry, Quaker Heroine.* Boston: Little, Brown.

Fukuda Hideko
(Kageyama Hideko)
(1865–1927)
Japan

A leading socialist feminist in the Japanese Liberal Party, Fukuda was inspired by the work of Kishida Toshiko. She attempted to promote women's issues during the reformist period in Meiji Japan (1868–1912), a time when women's democratic rights were addressed by both male and female activists eager to see an end to feudal practices that disempowered women and contributed to the continuing backwardness of Japanese society.

Born in Okoyama, Fukuda attended an elementary girls' school run by her mother and, after graduating at the top of her class, became an assistant teacher there at the age of fifteen. Fukuda balked at the idea of learning the niceties of flower arranging, sewing, and serving tea in preparation for an early arranged marriage, and because she was earning the then princely sum of three yen a month, she was able to offer to work to support her impoverished family instead. In 1881, after hearing Kishida Toshiko speak on women's rights, she was drawn into the popular rights movement that was spreading across Japan and joined the Okoyama Women's Lecture Society, which was dedicated to liberating women from their state of feudal oppression.

In 1883, with the help of her mother, who was an inspirational figure in her life, and her older brother, Fukuda established a private school. It took in female pupils between the ages of six and sixty and boys aged six to ten but was soon closed down because of Fukuda's activities in setting up a women's social group for the Liberal Party. Fukuda went to Tokyo, where with the help of the head of the Liberal Party she was introduced to a philanthropist who provided the money for her to continue her education at Shinsakae

Women's School. With a friend, she set up the Society for the Liberation of Women and in 1885 began taking part in Liberal Party activities in opposition to the foreign policy of the Meiji government, which involved the establishment of a reformist, constitutional Japanese government in exile in Korea. The resulting failed coup, known as the "Osaka incident," led to Fukuda's arrest in November 1885 for bomb making. She was sent to prison on the Ise Peninsula, the first Japanese woman to be imprisoned for a political crime.

After her early release on amnesty in February 1889, Fukuda began to look beyond purely nationalistic concerns to socialism and women's rights. The Meiji Constitution of 1889 was a great disappointment to reformers, for it not only denied women the vote but also enacted a new law excluding women from inheriting the throne of Japan. Along with other feminists, Fukuda protested the enactment of Article 5 of the Police Security Regulations of 1890, which prohibited women from joining political parties and from organizing meetings of a political nature or attending them.

After being involved in a common-law relationship with Oi Kentaro and giving birth to a son, Fukuda left the relationship in 1891 to set up a school in Tokyo for working women and their children with her father and grandmother, but she had to close it when they died. A year later she met and eventually (in 1898) married Fukuda Yusaku and had two sons by him. But he died in 1900, leaving her destitute. Struggling to remain self-sufficient, in 1901 Fukuda set up a girls' technological school. Japan was now heading toward conflict with Russia, and Fukuda led other socialist women in condemning the Russo-Japanese war when it broke out in 1904. She voiced her views in the liberal paper *Commoner's News*. At this time, she also became involved in an environmental campaign against the pollution of rivers by the Ashio Copper Mine.

In 1904 Fukuda became the first Japanese woman to publish her autobiography, *Half of My Life,* in which she recounted her involvement in the Osaka incident and her prison experiences. A year later, she published a novel entitled *My Reminiscences,* which with her previous book established her as a public figure. In 1907 she founded the socialist women's journal *Women of the World,* through which she continued to advocate women's political rights. She also ran her

antipollution campaign, exposing the appalling working conditions in textile factories, and promoted the Society for the Reinstatement of Women's Rights, an organization inspired by the memory of Chinese heroine Qiu Jin.

The society wanted women to emancipate themselves by forming their own movement for social reform. Women, Fukuda felt, must rediscover their moral dignity by refusing to become concubines and resisting traditional practices that kept them subordinate. Fukuda's journal also gave voice to the continuing campaign against Article 5, the Police Security Regulations of 1890, revised in 1900, banning women from political organizations, with Fukuda herself condemning a Japanese legal system that she felt had a contemptuous attitude toward the rights of women. Through her association with Japanese Christians, she also took part in welfare schemes and the training of poor girls in order to give them greater economic independence, setting up a handicraft school in Tokyo to help women find ways of supporting themselves.

In August 1909 *Women of the World* was closed down by the authorities, after thirty-seven issues that had provided an important outlet for female political thinkers. Fukuda's writing activities decreased after this setback, although she published occasional articles on social and political issues in other journals, such as her February 1913 essay "A Solution to the Woman's Problem," which appeared in the magazine *Bluestocking*. It offered a socialist perspective on the movement for women's rights and marked a shift in emphasis among some Japanese reformers away from purely feminist issues toward a wider drive for social justice. It aroused much controversy with its call for nothing short of social and economic revolution in Japan. For Fukuda, the liberation of women would only be achieved through the adoption of the socialist system, and to achieve that end women would inevitably have to fight elitism within their own ranks. The article, not only ahead of its time but politically dangerous within the context of conservative Japanese society, led to the issue of the magazine in which it appeared being banned. Fukuda herself lived on in very straitened circumstances, forced to sell clothes to support her three sons.

See also Kishida Toshiko; Qiu Jin.

References and Further Reading

Conroy, Hilary, Sandra T. Davis, and Wayne Peterson. 1984. *Japan in Transition: Thought and Action in the Meiji Era 1868–1912.* Toronto: Farleigh Dickinson University Press.

Hane, Mikiso, ed. 1988. *Reflections on the Way to the Gallows: Rebel Women in Prewar Japan.* Berkeley: University of California Press and Pantheon Books.

Jayawardena, Kumari. 1986. *Feminism and Nationalism in the Third World.* London: Zed Books.

Sievers, Sharon. 1983. *Flowers in Salt: The Beginnings of Feminist Consciousness in Modern Japan.* Stanford: Stanford University Press.

Fuller, (Sarah) Margaret (Marchesa d'Ossoli)
(1810–1850)
United States

In 1845 the American feminist writer and journalist Margaret Fuller, an imposing and idiosyncratic intellectual figure in literary circles in New England, published an important early contribution to the history of American feminism. Her discussions of women's roles and their need for an independent life in *Woman in the Nineteenth Century* would make it one of the most influential works of its time and add impetus to the call in 1848 for the first women's rights convention in Seneca Falls, New York.

Certain aspects of Fuller's character—her reputation for excessive self-regard and grandness of manner, coupled with her unconventionality—unfortunately resulted in exaggerated and often extremely biased (male) accounts of her by contemporaries. Since Fuller's rediscovery with the coming of the second wave of the women's movement in the 1970s, a surfeit of scholarship and criticism on her testify (in their subtitles) to a newfound if sometimes excessive regard for her work as "visionary of a new age," "whetstone of genius," "citizen of the world," and the archetypal "American romantic," a woman who had traveled the intellectual road "from Transcendentalism to revolution."

Born in Cambridgeport, Massachusetts, Fuller was educated by her demanding and domineering lawyer father. A strict Calvinist, he kept her on a treadmill of self-improvement that involved getting up at five in the morning, after which Fuller would walk, practice the piano, and study

(Sarah) Margaret Fuller (Library of Congress)

French and philosophy—all before 9:30 A.M. Further intense study would follow into the evening, until Fuller fell into her bed exhausted at 11 P.M. She was soon set apart from her peers as an extraordinary, precocious child who studied Greek, Latin, and Italian and read classics and Shakespeare from a young age. Such was the force-feeding of Fuller's undoubted critical and analytical powers that she ultimately paid the price for her academic brilliance by suffering permanent damage to her health. When Fuller was sent to a local school at the age of fourteen, she was ostracized for her strangeness. Painfully aware of her "otherness," she later ruefully observed of her early years: "My book life and lonely habits had given a cold aloofness to my whole expression and veiled my manner with a *hauteur* which turned all hearts away" (Abbott 1913, 388).

During the 1820s, word spread in Harvard intellectual society about her prodigious talents, but in 1833 Fuller moved back to the countryside on her father's retirement, and when he died in 1835 she was obliged to teach to help support her family. She accepted a post from the Transcendentalist Bronson Alcott, the father of the writer Louisa May Alcott, at his progressive Temple School in Boston (1836–1837). There Fuller became friendly with the educationist Elizabeth Peabody and in 1837 left to set up a school of her own similar to Alcott's, the Greene School, in Providence (1837–1839).

During this time, Fuller continued with her own private study, turning to German literature—translating Johann Eckermann's *Conversations with Goethe* (1839)—and philosophy, in particular the work of Immanuel Kant. On moving to Jamaica Plain near Boston in 1839, Fuller became friendly with the essayist and poet Ralph Waldo Emerson, who invited her to join discussions of the German and French philosophers with members of a small, select group of Transcendentalist intellectuals who gravitated around Emerson in Concord, Massachusetts. These included Walt Whitman and Henry David Thoreau, with Elizabeth Peabody the only other woman invited to join. Peabody's biographer, Louise Hall Tharp, records that Fuller soon had a reputation for being a formidable debater "with her 'man's logic' and her 'woman's tongue'" (1950, 140).

During the period 1839–1844, in an attempt to encourage women to educate themselves and learn to debate and speak in public, Fuller convened a series of Wednesday afternoon "conversations" for women on sexual equality and women's rights. Cultural subjects such as philosophy, mythology, education, and art were also discussed. Taking place at Elizabeth Peabody's bookshop on Boston's West Street, Fuller's gatherings were soon unkindly nicknamed the "Babel of talkers" by Thoreau (Tharp 1950, 143), and even Peabody herself described them as often degenerating from "conversations" into audiences at which "Queen Margaret" (as Peabody later referred to Fuller) held forth with great eloquence to an awestruck audience on subjects such as "The Great Lawsuit—Man versus Men. Woman versus Women." This essay was published by Fuller, along with several others, in the Transcendentalist quarterly journal *The Dial*, which she founded with Emerson in 1840 and which she and Peabody edited over the next two years.

Having garnered a considerable reputation as an intellectual, in 1844 Fuller published her first book, *Summer on the Lakes in 1843*, recording a trip she had made to Chicago and her impressions of pioneering out west. She moved to New York in 1844, where for the first time she witnessed the life of the poor in the city's tenement buildings. She took up journalism, writing on charitable work in the city, including the creation of a Women's Prison Association, and began her own analysis of the economic and social ills that beset the United States. She also became a book reviewer and before long was considered a major literary critic of her day, publishing in the *New York Tribune* from 1844 to 1846.

In 1845 Fuller produced an exposition of her feminist ideas in *Woman in the Nineteenth Century and Kindred Papers Relating to the Sphere, Condition and Duties of Woman*. Despite a certain lack of unity in its subject matter and arguments, its arcane references, and the mystical and religious overtones of its literary language, the book is a penetrating study of the far-reaching consequences of women's traditional submissiveness and their unquestioning acceptance of their own inequality. Emphasizing women's need for inner growth, Fuller urged them not to be inhibited by their physical weakness. They should embark on their own self-discovery and self-liberation on the basis of their accepted difference from—but not inequality with—men. Thus, Fuller encouraged her readers to act independently of men, instead of being led by them and continuing to accept their view of the world. It was only then, in her view, that women would be able to unite in what she saw as their sacred duty and a great spiritual and moral crusade—collective social action to help other underprivileged and oppressed women such as prostitutes, seamstresses, and poor laundry women. In urging women to reject traditional sexual stereotyping and secure their free access to the professions and employment, Fuller famously advocated, "Let them be Sea-Captains if they will" (Fuller 1998, 102). For her, women's self-liberation was all part of the greater cosmic purpose of human existence, in which the complementary natures of men and women should work in harmony toward the achievement of their divine purpose on Earth.

In 1846, the year that she published *Papers on Literature and Art*, Fuller became the first American woman to be appointed a foreign correspondent when Horace Greeley, proprietor of the *New York Tribune*, gave her a front-page column, to which she contributed regular letters during a trip to Europe. In London Fuller was feted as an intellectual celebrity and became friends with Harriet Martineau, as well as meeting the poet William Wordsworth and the historian Thomas Carlyle. In her reports home, however, she registered her shock at the poverty and deprivation she encountered in London and in the industrial north. Traveling on to Paris, Fuller met the lioness of French literature, George Sand, and her lover Frédéric Chopin. With revolutionary activity boiling all over Europe, she traveled to Rome in 1847, where she interviewed the Italian nationalist leader Giuseppe Mazzini after his return to Italy in 1848.

In Italy, at last, Fuller finally found love when she met one of Mazzini's followers, Giovanni Angelo, the Marchese Ossoli. She had a son by him, Angelo, in 1848 and married him in secret in the summer of 1849, after living with him for two years. With Ossoli, Fuller joined republicans fighting in the Italian war of liberation against the papal government. At the siege of Rome by the French in February 1849, she nursed the wounded in the makeshift Fate Bene Fratelli hospital. But the couple were forced to flee to Florence when the republic collapsed. There, for a while, Fuller became friendly with the English poet Elizabeth Barrett Browning and settled down to write what she considered her magnum opus, a history of the Italian Revolution of 1848–1849. In 1850, because of financial difficulties and continuing police harassment for their participation in the revolution, the Ossolis decided to sail for the United States. But Margaret, her husband, and baby son were all drowned and the manuscript of her Italian history lost, when the ship on which they sailed from Leghorn was wrecked at Fire Island, in sight of the coast of New York.

Two collections of Fuller's writings were published shortly after her death, as *At Home and Abroad* (1856) and *Life Without and Life Within* (1860). The poet and reformer Julia Ward Howe edited *Love-Letters of Margaret Fuller, 1845–1846* in 1903, and her complete letters were published in four volumes in 1983. Dale Spender contends that the posthumous *Memoirs of Margaret Fuller Ossoli* of 1852, selectively edited by Emerson and others (and including rewrites of Fuller's own original words), laid the foundation for the later distortion if not "blatant misrepresentation" of Fuller's personality and the descriptions of her physical unattractiveness. It is said that the character of the doomed suicide Zenobia in Nathaniel Hawthorne's novel *The Blithedale Ro-*

mance was based on Fuller, as were, allegedly, the eponymous heroine of Oliver Wendell Holmes's *Elsie Venner,* Verbena Tarrant in Henry James's *Bostonians,* and Miranda in James Russell Lowell's poetry collection, *A Fable for Critics.* In their collective belittlement of Fuller's extraordinary intellect, Fuller's erstwhile male admirers transformed her into the kind of arrogant feminist bluestocking that misogynists love to hate (Spender 1982, 147) and contributed in no small part toward her disappearance into obscurity for over a century.

See also Howe, Julia Ward; Martineau, Harriet; Peabody, Elizabeth.

References and Further Reading

Abbott, Willis J. 1913. *Notable Women in History.* London: Greening.

Blanchard, Paula. 1987. *Margaret Fuller: From Transcendentalism to Revolution.* New York: Delacorte Press.

Cappa, Charles. 1992. *Margaret Fuller: An American Romantic Life.* New York: Oxford University Press.

Chevigny, Belle Gale. 1976. *The Woman and the Myth: Margaret Fuller's Life and Writings.* Old Westbury, NY: Feminist Press.

Fuller, Margaret. 1998 [1845]. *Woman in the Nineteenth Century.* Reprint, Norton Critical Edition, edited by Larry J. Reynolds. New York: W. W. Norton.

Melder, Keith E. 1977. *The Beginnings of Sisterhood: The American Woman's Rights Movement, 1800–1850.* New York: Schocken.

Reynolds, Larry J., and Susan B. Smith, eds. *"These Sad but Glorious Days": Dispatches from Europe 1846–1850.* New Haven: Yale University Press.

Spender, Dale. 1982. *Women of Ideas, and What Men Have Done to Them.* London: Routledge and Kegan Paul.

Tharp, Louise Hall. 1950. *The Peabody Sisters of Salem.* Boston: Little, Brown.

Urbanski, Marie Mitchell Olesen. 1980. *Margaret Fuller's "Woman in the Nineteenth Century": A Literary Study of Form and Content, of Sources and Influence.* Westport, CT: Greenwood Press.

———. 1983. "Margaret Fuller: Feminist Writer and Revolutionary." In Dale Spender, ed., *Feminist Theorists: Three Centuries of Women's Intellectual Traditions.* London: Women's Press.

Wade, Mason. 1940. *Margaret Fuller: Whetstone of Genius.* New York: Viking.

Watson, David. 1988. *Margaret Fuller: An American Romantic.* New York and Oxford: St. Martin's Press and Berg.

Furujhelm, Annie
(1860–1937)
Finland

The Finnish suffragist and politician Annie Furujhelm had the good fortune to be one of the first fully enfranchised women in Europe when her country, newly independent of the Russian Empire, granted women the vote in 1906. Thereafter, she took a leading role in the international suffrage movement as a greatly respected second vice president of the International Woman Suffrage Alliance (IWSA).

Furujhelm was born in Rekoor Castle, at Sitka on Baranof Island. One of the most remote spots in the former Russian Empire, it is situated on the Gulf of Alaska. Her father, Admiral Johan Hampus Furujhelm, was serving there as the last Russian-appointed governor of Alaska; the family left in 1867 after five years at Sitka, when Alaska was sold by Russia to the United States. Admiral Furjhelm was appointed governor of far eastern Siberia, and after six years in Nikolaevsk on the Pacific coast, the family made the greater part of the long journey home to Helsinki overland, across Russia, covering 6,000 miles of Siberia's snowy wastes by carriage.

At age eleven, Furujhelm was taken to Dresden to be educated before returning to Helsinki. She went to live on the family estate, where she later founded a school. For many years she remained there, working as a nurse among the local villagers, but eventually her dislike of rural isolation and a burning desire to be a writer took her to journalism. Furujhelm was a highly cultured woman and an extremely talented linguist, speaking seven languages. She was also passionately interested in politics and had a fervent desire to see Finland gain its independence from Russia (two of her brothers became involved in the independence movement). She began working for women's rights, entering journalism in 1890 and setting up her own newspaper, *New Tide*, which became the organ of the Finnish women's movement. From 1907 she also edited the women's magazine *Astra*.

Finnish feminists had first petitioned the Diet on women's suffrage as early as 1879, but they lacked a cohesive movement. In 1904 Furujhelm traveled to Berlin to attend the quinquennial congress of the International Council of Women (ICW). She appealed to its members to support the establishment of a Finnish suffrage organization. Although the ICW refused because Finland was still part of the Russian Empire, Furujhelm was encouraged by Carrie Chapman Catt of the International Woman Suffrage Alliance, who agreed that a Finnish organization would be able to affiliate with the IWSA. Fired with enthusiasm, Furujhelm returned home and called a women's suffrage congress in November, which was attended by 1,000 women. In 1905 the Central Committee for Woman Suffrage was established in Finland under her presidency. After a general strike during the winter of 1905, Finland was given its independence from the Russian Empire, and a new constitution awarded universal suffrage to men and women over the age of twenty-four. Thus, in the world's shortest suffrage campaign by any organized group, women in Finland achieved the vote on 28 May 1906, whereas many of their sisters would have to wait until the end of World War I or even longer to be enfranchised. In 1906 at a congress of the IWSA held in Copenhagen, Furujhelm was a keynote speaker and received a standing oration for the "fiery eloquence" with which she described the events of 1905, after which women's enfranchisement had quickly followed.

In 1907 Furujhelm was elected president of the newly established Swedish Women's Association of Finland (Sweden and Finland had been closely linked for hundreds of years and Swedish remained the official language in all political processes and government), a role she retained until her death in 1937. With suffrage in her own country achieved, Furujhelm devoted herself to the international campaign, becoming a contributor of regular reports on the women's movement in Finland to the IWSA journal *Jus Suffragii*. She served as a member of the board of the IWSA from 1909 to 1920 and attended all its congresses from 1906 to 1929. She became a friend of Carrie Chapman Catt and accompanied her to England in 1913, where they stayed in London during the militant suffrage campaigns of the Pankhursts' Women's Social and Political Union and even visited activist Annie Kenney, who was being held at Bow St. Police Station.

During another trip to England the following year, Furujhelm accompanied Catt to the Houses of Parliament and on 14 July 1914 gave a landmark address to the House of Commons on women's suffrage, the first woman parliamentarian to do so. In 1913 Furujhelm had become one of the first twenty-one female members elected to the Russian-controlled Finnish Diet. (Finland did not achieve full independence from Russia until after the 1917 Russian Revolution.) She went on to serve for five three-year terms until 1929 and during this time pressed for many social reforms, becoming one of the longest-serving women legislators of her day. Such was the influence of women in the new Finnish government that at their request the word *man* in the constitution was altered to *person* to reflect the high level of political equality enjoyed by women in Finland.

In the 1917 parliament, Furujhelm was a member of the law committee, helped in the elections that briefly restored the monarchy, and then voted in the country's first president. Defeated in elections of 1924, Furujhelm was re-elected in 1925 as a candidate of the Swedish National Party. At the Paris congress of the IWSA in 1926, she chaired a sesson of the Enfranchised Women's Committee of the IWSA.

In 1929, Furjhelm decided that the time had come for her to leave Finnish politics and to devote more time to the international women's movement. Upon her retirement from politics at the age of seventy, she was awarded the Order of the White Rose of Finland. In her remaining years of activism, she continued to chair or serve as a member of many organizations working for political, social, and women's rights. At the twenty-fifth-anniversary congress of the IWSA, held in 1929 in Berlin, Furjhelm spoke with great pleasure on the years of progress in the movement for women's suffrage. By the time of her death on 17 July 1937, shortly before which she published two large volumes of memoirs, she was remembered with great affection as the "Grand Old Lady of Finland."

See also Catt, Carrie Chapman; Kenney, Annie; Pankhurst, Christabel; Pankhurst, Emmeline; Pankhurst, (Estelle) Sylvia.

References and Further Reading

Bosch, Mineke. 1990. *Politics and Friendship: Letters from the International Woman Suffrage Alliance, 1902–42.* Columbus: Ohio State University Press.

Evans, Richard. 1977. *The Feminists: Women's Emancipation Movements in Europe, America and Australasia 1840–1920.* London: Croom Helm.

Jallinoja, Riitta. 1980. "The Women's Liberation Movement in Finland." *Scandinavian Journal of History* 5: 37–49.

Jus Suffragii (later *International Woman Suffrage News*) from 1913 to 1937.

Offen, Karen. 2000. *European Feminisms 1700–1950: A Political History.* Stanford: Stanford University Press.

G

Gage, Matilda Joslyn
(1826–1898)
United States

The theoretical contribution to the U.S. women's rights movement by radical feminist Matilda Joslyn Gage was for many years neglected in favor of that of the better-known Elizabeth Cady Stanton and Susan B. Anthony, with whom she collaborated on the publication of the first three volumes of the *History of Woman Suffrage* (1881–1886), with Stanton writing most of the chapters. In her day, Gage applied her considerable analytical skills and extensive scholarship to an appraisal of the historical contribution of women in science, politics, and the arts. In rediscovering the underappreciated or deliberately suppressed contribution of women throughout history, she provided a cogent critique of traditional male patriarchy eighty years ahead of the discourses of the second wave of the women's movement. Her lapse into obscurity after her death is as much the result of her unconscionable neglect by her female contemporaries as it is a manifestation of Gage's own self-effacing nature, which ensured a paucity of available biographical facts about her.

Existing brief accounts of Gage's early life place considerable emphasis on the influence of her father, a doctor, on Gage's intellectual development and her lifelong and consuming love of history. Born in Cicero, New York, she was encouraged by her father to study subjects such as physiology, anatomy, Greek, mathematics, and physics and later attended the Clinton Seminary. Because of her father's support of abolition, she learned of the work of abolitionists such as Abby Kelley Foster and William Lloyd Garrison and assisted her father in gathering antislavery petitions. The family home was often used as a place of refuge for slaves escaping to Canada on the Underground Railroad. At age eighteen, she married a wealthy merchant, Henry Gage, and settled in Fayetteville, New York, where she continued to work for the abolitionist cause while developing a growing admiration for the women's rights movement that began with the 1848 convention in Seneca Falls.

When Gage first entered the women's rights movement, much more was made of her elegant dress sense than of her oratory. Yet in 1852, as a complete newcomer to the suffragist cause, she had plucked up the courage to speak at the national woman's rights convention, held in Syracuse, New York. At twenty-six, she was the youngest woman ever to speak in public on the subject. So impressive was her speech, in which she described the diversity of women's intellectual and cultural achievements throughout history and their ability to play a part in government, that at the behest of Lucretia Mott it was issued soon after as a pamphlet. Almost immediately, Gage's outspokenness was condemned by the local clergy.

Thereafter, Gage became a close associate of Stanton and Anthony, in 1854 donating money to fund Anthony's lecture tour and joining her on the lecture circuit as a speaker on women's suffrage. In 1869 she was a founder of the National Woman Suffrage Association (NWSA) and its New York state and Virginia branches, serving as secretary and vice president of NWSA from 1869 to 1875 and briefly as president from 1875 to 1876, during which time she edited its newspaper, *The Revolution*.

In 1871–1872 Gage lent her unqualified support to Anthony's policy of civil disobedience, attempting to vote in elections in Rochester, New

York, but being turned away. When Anthony faced prosecution for voting, Gage gave public lectures entitled "The United States on Trial, Not Susan B. Anthony," in every postal district of Ontario County, decrying the deliberate exclusion of women by men from full citizenship. On 4 July 1876, she again joined Anthony and three other suffragists in staging a demonstration during official celebrations of the centennial of the signing of the Declaration of Independence in Philadelphia, where they handed out copies to those assembled, including the acting vice president of the United States, of the "Declaration of Rights of the Women of the United States," which Gage and Stanton had recently composed. In 1877 Gage contested the right of convicted male criminals to petition Congress for their voting rights to be restored by petitioning for her own voting rights as a citizen. She persisted in her challenges to state and federal laws on suffrage, in 1893 initiating a test case on women's right to be elected to school boards.

During 1878–1881 Gage edited and published the official newspaper of the National Woman Suffrage Association, the *National Citizen and Ballot Box,* in which she published articles on various aspects of suffrage, women's labor rights, and prison reform. She also wrote articles promoting the idea of cooperatives and argued for the civil rights of Native Americans. A little-known aspect of Gage's scholarship is her deep respect for the ancient matriarchies of some Native American cultures, which Gage expressed in a series of articles written during the 1870s. Gage was an admirer of the Iroquois Confederacy in New York state, also known as the "Six Nations," for its respect for the rights of women and its democratic principles, and criticized the destruction of their traditional native communities by the encroachment of white people and the Native Americans' forced settlement on reservations.

Gage resigned in protest from NWSA when it joined forces with the moderate American Woman Suffrage Association to become the National American Woman Suffrage Association in 1890, drawing in with it the conservative and moral forces of the Woman's Christian Temperance Union (WCTU). She had long since come to the conclusion that suffrage alone would not effect women's liberation in a male-dominated world, nor did she share the view of other suffragists that women had to "earn" the right to the

vote by resigning themselves to steady but limited progress on women's rights. In her view, the effectiveness of the American women's movement was rapidly becoming diluted and was losing its way by also trying to obtain suffrage at the state level. She asserted that women throughout history had more than proved their worthiness of equal citizenship with men and that nothing less was required than a profound restructuring of the whole social and economic fabric, which was too heavily based on the unrewarded labor of women and too tightly controlled by the church.

Gage's response to her disillusionment with the mainstream suffrage movement was to found her own radical, antichurch group, the Woman's National Liberal Union, which sought to end the combined domination over women of church and state and achieve their separation. She elaborated on this view in her groundbreaking 1893 work, *Woman, Church and State: The Original Exposé of Male Collaboration against the Female Sex* (which was not reprinted until 1980). In this extensively researched historical treatise, admired by Stanton and others for its serious and scientific approach, she described how organized religion (and Christianity in particular) had colluded with the patriarchy of the state in perpetuating the subjection of women. Women's exclusion from the process of lawmaking meant that they remained political slaves in a country where, Gage asserted, "man has assumed the right to think for woman" (1980, 239), an argument she later reiterated when she collaborated with Stanton on *The Woman's Bible* (1895). What is more, in *Woman, Church and State,* Gage illustrated that in the past, women had on occasion (and particularly in the eighteenth century) enjoyed greater political freedom and a role in government that was now denied them, and in the many examples she cited from history, she not only underlined the centuries-old exploitation of women's unpaid labor but went so far as to argue that men had blatantly plundered women's intellectual and creative contributions and consistently denied them the opportunity of education.

Such a controversial and radical piece of work, which was in many respects a forerunner to Charlotte Perkins Gilman's 1898 study, *Women and Economics,* was disowned by many suffragists, particularly the moral crusaders of the WCTU, because of its condemnation of the enduring conspiracy between church and state to keep women in a subservient position. If anything, Gage became even more radical in her views, continuing to urge women to resist the exploitation by men of their physical and intellectual powers, a fact that contributed to her increasing isolation in the women's movement during the remaining years of her life.

As has been pointed out in Dale Spender's landmark 1982 work in rehabilitating feminist thinkers, *Women of Ideas and What Men Have Done to Them,* the honesty and intellectual power of Gage's argument failed to be exploited by the women's movement of her day. Such was her subsequent disappearance from women's history that it would be the task of a later generation of feminists in the 1970s and beyond to reconstruct the ideas that Gage had so lucidly posited in the 1890s. Gage has yet to be accorded sufficient recognition in many essential works on the history of the U.S. women's movement, although her neglect is now being redressed by the feminist historian Sally Roesch Wagner, who edited the 1980 and 1998 reissues of *Woman, Church and State* and has posted an account of Gage's work and extracts from her major writings on a website dedicated to Gage at http://www.pinn.net/~sunshine/gage/mjg.html.

See also Anthony, Susan B.; Foster, Abby (Abigail) Kelley; Gilman, Charlotte Perkins; Mott, Lucretia Coffin; Stanton, Elizabeth Cady.

References and Further Reading
Brammer, Leila R. 2000. *Excluded from Suffrage History: Matilda Joslyn Gage, Nineteenth Century American Feminist.* Westport, CT: Greenwood Press.
Daly, Mary. 1978. *Gyn/Ecology: The Metaethics of Radical Feminism.* Boston: Beacon Press.
Gage, Matilda Joslyn. 1980 [1893]. *Woman, Church and State: The Original Exposé of Male Collaboration against the Female Sex.* Reprint, Watertown, MA: Persephone Press.
———. 1998 [1893]. *Woman, Church and State.* Edited by Sally Roesch Wagner. Aberdeen, SD: Sky Carrier Press.
Leach, William. 1981. *True Love and Perfect Union: The Feminist Reform of Sex and Society.* London: Routledge and Kegan Paul.
Spender, Dale. 1982. *Women of Ideas, and What Men Have Done to Them.* London: Routledge and Kegan Paul.
Spender, Lynne. 1983. "Matilda Joslyn Gage: Active Intellectual." In Dale Spender, ed., *Feminist Theorists: Three Centuries of Women's Intellectual Traditions.* London: Women's Press.
Wagner, Sally Roesch. 1992. "The Iroquois Influence on Women's Rights." In Jose Barreiro, ed., *Indian Roots of American Democracy.* Fairfax, VA: Falmouth Institute.
———. 1994. *Matilda Joslyn Gage: Forgotten Feminist.* Aberdeen, SD: Sky Carrier Press.
———. 1998. *She Who Holds the Sky: Matilda Joslyn Gage.* Aberdeen, SD: Sky Carrier Press.
Waters, Kristin. 2000. *Women and Men Political Theorists: Enlightened Conversations.* Malden, MA: Blackwell.

García, Maria del Refugio
(ca. 1898/1900–1970s)
Mexico

As secretary-general of the largest and most influential Mexican women's organization, the Sole Front for Women's Rights, García became a crucial figure in the early struggle for not only women's emancipation but also the protection of peasant lands and the rights of indigenous Mexican people. A committed and inexhaustible revolutionary known to her friends as "Cuca," she looked upon feminist activity for suffrage as diverting women activists away from the real issue—that of the working-class struggle against capitalism.

The daughter of a village doctor, García was born in the lake region of Uruápan. In 1913 she became a member of the Michoacán Revolutionary Movement in Mexico City and in 1920 helped set up the Mexican Feminist Council and expanded on its program of political, economic, and social reform in its journal *Woman.* García became active organizing women government employees. She also endorsed the rights of rural peasants to the land and better wages; at a 1931 women's congress she accused the military regime of murdering peasants who were fighting to protect their own land and was subsequently jailed.

In 1934 García and other Marxist dissidents took a strong position on the social origins of prostitution. At the first Mexican congress of intellectuals and professionals, held in Mexico City that year to study the social problems of prostitution, deep divisions arose between reformists and communists. García endorsed Marxist thinking that prostitution was caused by poverty and would never be eradicated while a capitalist system prevailed in Mexico. She therefore called for state-registered prostitution to be abandoned in favor of grassroots campaigning to ameliorate the conditions of poverty in which people lived and educate them out of their ignorance. She believed that self-respect could only be gained through equal pay for equal work and that women would not need to turn to prostitution if they had access to cheaper food, state housing, child care facilities, free school textbooks, and school meals.

García contributed regularly to the *Machete,* the journal of the Mexican Communist Party. In 1935 she was cofounder of the Sole Front for Women's Rights, which worked with radical groups on the left for women's suffrage and the right to stand for office. It called for amendments to the civil code that would allow women equal political rights with men; it also argued for the agrarian code to be modified to allow women the right to apply for government land grants. Workers' rights were also addressed with calls for all women to be allowed maternity rights, for indigenous women to be encouraged to take their place in society and politics, and for unemployed women to be helped through the establishment of work centers. At the height of its activities, the Sole Front had a membership of 50,000 women, taking in over 800 women's groups and including many native people.

In 1937, when Mexican feminists decided to challenge the wording of the Constitution over precisely who was eligible for citizenship (it did not specify "men and women") and therefore to vote, García stood for election as a Sole Front candidate for her home district of Uruápan to the Mexican Chamber of Deputies. García won by a huge margin of 10,000 votes but was not allowed to take her seat by the government because to allow her to do so would have involved amending the Constitution. In response, García went on a hunger strike outside President Lázaro Cárdenas's residence in Mexico City for eleven days in August 1937. Cárdenas responded by promising to change Article 34 of the Constitution that September. By December the amendment had been passed by congress, and women were granted full citizenship. It would be a long wait for the vote, however—women were not granted this right until 1958.

As "one of the most genuinely popular women in Mexico," according to Anna Macías, García eventually recognized the power for social regeneration that women's organizations such as her Sole Front for Women's Rights could achieve. But despite her high-profile campaigning, she died—probably destitute—sometime in the 1970s, and her name figures only in specialist books on Mexican history of this period.

References and Further Reading

Macías, Anna. 1983. *Against All Odds: The Feminist Movement in Mexico to 1940.* Westport, CT: Greenwood Press.

Morton, Ward D. 1962. *Woman Suffrage in Mexico.* Gainesville: University of Florida Press.

Soto, Shirlene. 1990. *Emergence of the Modern Mexican Woman: Her Participation in Revolution and Struggle for Equality, 1910–1940.* Denver: Arden Press.

Gaskell, Elizabeth
(1810–1865)
United Kingdom

Together with the novelist Charles Dickens, Elizabeth Gaskell was a leading exponent of the "interventionist" school of realistic writing in Victorian England, playing a central role in arousing British public opinion from its laissez-faire attitude toward social evils and presenting a compassionate, humane, and vivid depiction of life among the oppressed in the rapidly industrializing north.

Born in Chelsea, London, where her father was keeper of records to the Treasury, Gaskell grew up with her aunt Hannah Lumb in Knutsford, Cheshire, after her mother died when she was only a year old. After some basic schooling at home, she was sent to a school in Barford, Warwickshire, which was later relocated to Avonbank School in Stratford-upon-Avon, where Gaskell boarded until 1827. She lived with her father after his remarriage (her unease with her new stepmother was later reflected in the 1866 novel *Wives and Daughters*), but after his death in 1829 and the loss of her only and much-loved brother, she returned to Knutsford.

In 1832 Elizabeth married Unitarian minister William Gaskell, whose parish was based at Cross Street in a poor district of Manchester. Here as a young wife, Elizabeth was confronted on all sides by the problems of the urban poor—hunger and disease and frequent outbreaks of cholera in the slums. It was also a time of considerable social unrest in Britain, of escalating confrontations between discontented workers and management as well as popular demonstrations against the Corn Laws, all of which would later serve as a backdrop to Gaskell's novels. For most of the next fifteen years, however, she was confined by her domestic duties as the mother of five surviving children. Her growing empathy with the poor was expressed through her charitable work for her husband's church. She wrote some poetry but did not begin to write in earnest until after losing her only son to diphtheria in 1845. *Mary Barton: A Tale of Manchester Life* was published anonymously in 1848 after Gaskell encountered some difficulty in securing a publisher. Written as a "social problem" novel, it set out to condemn precisely those self-seeking Manchester manufacturers who populated her husband's own congregation.

Gaskell's novel broke new ground in its depiction of working-class characters and was imbued with a strong sense of social purpose in exposing inequalities and attempting to reconcile social antipathies. In her descriptions of the hardships endured by the Barton family and other northern millworkers during the period of economic decline known as "the hungry forties," Gaskell dealt controversially with their exploitation by the new and ruthless breed of self-made industrialists. With its central tormented hero, the weaver John Barton, who lashes out against the suffering and poverty of his own family, the novel shocked Victorian middle-class sensibilities. Its flair for realistic description and local dialect (she had always enjoyed the bold and cheery conversation of Lancashire mill girls), scrupulous honesty, hatred of hypocrisy, and compassion for the socially deprived set the standard for Gaskell's later work.

Together with that of Dickens, Gaskell's work would take center stage in the exposure of the deepening social and economic divide between rich and poor in Britain that became known as the "condition of England" novel, a literary genre that described the pitiable lives of the nation's urban underclasses and the problems of unemployment created by the Industrial Revolution. The success of *Mary Barton* led to a meeting between Gaskell and Dickens and a commission to write a novel to be serialized in his journal, *Household Words*. In the novel she produced,

Cranford (published in book form in 1853), a gentle and affectionate social satire, Gaskell fell back on safer territory. As a collection of sketches of genteel life in a small county town, based on Knutsford where she had grown up, *Cranford* represented for Gaskell the safe and unchallenging old world from which she had sprung. It would remain her least controversial and most popular novel, popular no doubt because of the charm with which it immortalized a rapidly vanishing world of rural eccentrics and gossips.

In 1853 Gaskell braved public opinion with the publication of her "fallen woman" novel, *Ruth,* which was filled with her own deeply held Christian belief in the forgiveness of sin. It was based in part on the story of a young prostitute whom Gaskell had met in 1849 as a prison visitor at the New Bailey in Manchester and for whom, with the help of Dickens and Angela Burdett-Coutts, she had obtained an emigration passage to South Africa upon her release. The novel centers on the seduction of seamstress Ruth Hilton by a landowner, Henry Bellingham. She is dismissed after discovering that she is pregnant but redeems herself by later selflessly nursing the victims of a cholera epidemic, after which she herself succumbs to the disease. In raising the problem of the unmarried mother and ethical questions about the double sexual standard, Gaskell exposed the hypocrisy of a society forever ready to condemn the seduced and never the seducer—an exposé that predates Thomas Hardy's *Tess of the d'Urbervilles* (1891) by forty years. *Ruth* caused considerable controversy and debate: copies were taken out of libraries and destroyed, many of Gaskell's own friends were appalled by its subject matter, and members of her husband's congregation burned it or forbade their wives to read it. Such was the critical response that Gaskell described herself as being shot with arrows like "St. Sebastian tied to a tree" (Uglow 1993, 338). But she was unrepentant about writing the novel, insisting that she had felt compelled to speak out. If nothing else, Gaskell argued, *Ruth* had prompted readers to "talk and think a little on a subject which is so painful that it requires all one's bravery not to hide one's head like an ostrich and try by doing so to forget that the evil exists" (Uglow 1993, 339). In the end, other prominent people such as Dickens and Florence Nightingale approved of the novel, and women writers responded with their own examination of the issue (e.g., George Eliot in *Adam Bede* in 1859). The novel also would be influential in the lives of other women social reformers such as Josephine Butler, who led a long campaign against the sexual double standard later in the century.

Gaskell's next major novel, *North and South,* was again written in serial form for publication in 1854 in *Household Words,* and published as a book in 1855. (Dickens himself also produced a work, *Hard Times,* that same year on a similar industrial theme.) The story centers on a love affair between a man and a woman from different ends of the social scale, setting in opposition, as the title suggests, the differing qualities and values of contemporary British society. Gaskell counterpoints the complacency of the middle-class rural south, home of the heroine Margaret Hale, with the vigor of the forward-looking, working-class industrial north in the figure of her lover, John Thornton. In her depiction of trade unionism and industrial conflict as the social backdrop to her story, which is set in the northern city of Manchester, Gaskell set out to underline the urgent need for reconciliation between the classes.

Shortly after the death of her friend, the novelist Charlotte Brontë, in 1855, Gaskell was commissioned by Brontë's father and her husband, Arthur Bell Nicholls, to write her biography. She spent two years in its preparation, publishing *The Life of Charlotte Brontë* in 1857, a work unique for its time and long considered a landmark text in the art of the literary biography. But again there were complaints and even threats of libel action over its content, and Gaskell fled to Rome until the situation died down. However, the royalties from this book and her other bestselling novels allowed Gaskell to live a comfortable lifestyle and to travel in her final years. In the late 1850s, Gaskell produced collections of short stories, returning to the novel with *Sylvia's Lovers* (1863), set during the Napoleonic Wars, and publishing the novella *Cousin Phillis: A Tale* (1864), considered by many to be a masterpiece. Gaskell collapsed and died of heart failure before completing *Wives and Daughters: An Every-Day Story,* published posthumously in 1866.

Although Gaskell was never active in the women's rights movement, in January 1856 she was a signatory of Barbara Bodichon's petition on the reform of laws concerning married women's right to their property and she supported women's right to a better education. Throughout her life, she was involved in humanitarian work among the poor in her husband's parish, and during the 1860s cotton famine, she and her daughters undertook exhausting relief work in Manchester. Gaskell's Unitarian instincts ensured that she would always speak out against social injustices, just as she was also prompted to acknowledge women's need for economic independence through work. Throughout her life, she remained torn between her literary craft and her duties to family and sympathized with other women writers seeking to reconcile these two spheres of activity. In the end, Gaskell agreed with the view of Charlotte Brontë that for a woman, writing should remain a pursuit entered into not out of financial need but "out of the fulness of one's heart, spontaneously" (Uglow 1993, 312). There is a vast body of scholarship available on Gaskell, and the reading list that follows is highly selective. A first-class website devoted to Gaskell, her life and her work, with links to many other sites such as the Gaskell Society, can be found at http://www.lang.nagoya-u.ac.jp/~matsuoka/Gaskell.html.

See also Bodichon, Barbara; Burdett-Coutts, Angela; Butler, Josephine; Nightingale, Florence.

References and Further Reading

Allott, M. 1960. *Elizabeth Gaskell.* London: Longman's Green.

Cazamian, Louis. 1973. *The Social Novel in England 1830–1850: Dickens, Disraeli, Mrs. Gaskell, Kingsley.* London: Routledge and Kegan Paul.

Chapple, J. B. V., and Arthur Pollard. 1966. *The Letters of Mrs. Gaskell.* Manchester: Manchester University Press.

Guérin, Winifred. 1976. *Elizabeth Gaskell: A Biography.* Oxford: Oxford Univesity Press.

Hopkins, Annette Brown. 1952. *Elizabeth Gaskell: Her Life and Work.* London: Lehmann.

Krueger, Christine L. 1992. *The Reader's Repentance: Women Preachers, Women Writers, and Nineteenth-Century Social Discourse.* Chicago: University of Chicago Press.

Lansbury, Coral. 1975. *Elizabeth Gaskell: The Novel of Social Crisis.* New York: Barnes and Noble.

Pollard, Arthur. 1965. *Mrs. Gaskell: Novelist and Biographer.* Manchester: Manchester University Press.

Spencer, Jane. 1993. *Elizabeth Gaskell.* Basingstoke: Macmillan.

Stoneman, Patsy. 1987. *Elizabeth Gaskell.* Brighton: Harvester.

Uglow, Jenny. 1993. *Elizabeth Gaskell: A Habit of Stories.* London: Faber and Faber.

al-Ghazali, Zeinab
(1918–)
Egypt

A radical Islamist fundamentalist reformer, al-Ghazali has sought to improve women's social position in Egypt through a return to Islam as the true path and through the reaffirmation of women's primary role as wives and mothers. One of eleven children of a cotton merchant, al-Ghazali grew up in a village outside Cairo. She was brought up to study Islamic culture by her father, who was convinced that a historic role awaited her. For this reason, he allowed her to be educated and study religious texts. In so doing, he instilled in her a messianic vision, which she felt compelled to follow and later fulfilled as founder of the Muslim Women's Society (MWS).

At the age of seventeen, an eager al-Ghazali joined Huda Sha'rawi's Egyptian Feminist Union (EFU), but she soon rejected what she perceived as Sha'rawi's Westernized form of feminism as being too secular and out of touch with the roots of Islam. In her view, the "Egyptian Feminist Union wanted to establish the civilization of the Western Woman in Egypt, the Arab world, and the Islamic world" (Moghadam 1994, 209). Instead, al-Ghazali sought to create a Muslim form of feminism that affirmed women's social and legal rights but did not reject the traditional, religious, and cultural background or seek "women's liberation" in a form that was threatening or contrary to Islam.

After leaving the EFU in 1936, at the age of eighteen al-Ghazali founded the MWS, which based its principles on *shari'ah,* or Islamic law, upheld by a belief in the fundamental equality between men and women as originally described in sacred texts. For her, there is no "woman's question" within Islam. Muslim women should behave with decorum and respect toward their elders and betters and dress according to tradition; al-Ghazali has sought their liberation strictly within that selfsame religious framework, with the accent on the traditional qualities of passivity and obedience in the context of women's duties as wives and mothers. Her association works primarily to encourage women to enlighten themselves through the study of Islam so that they are then able to recognize the values and freedoms it offers and realize that they have no need to be "liberated." Similarly, a return to the fundamental principles of Islam and the

Qu'ran will, in al-Ghazali's view, lead to a resurgence of Islamic culture and theocratic statehood in oppressed Muslim societies torn apart by religious factionalism—countries such as Israel, the Palestinian National Authority, and Afghanistan.

Over the years, al-Ghazali has initiated numerous welfare activities, setting up an orphanage, providing economic relief to poor families, and assisting unemployed men and women in finding work. She recognized women's rights to a profession and a role in political life but, again, within the confines of her own interpretation of Islamic law. During the late 1940s, al-Ghazali resisted a government order to dissolve the MWS, which had liaised with nationalist groups such as the Wafd and the Muslim Brothers during the dissident movement against British rule. In 1948 the MWS joined forces with the outlawed Muslim Brothers, renaming itself the Society of the Muslim Sisters, thereby indicating that they too had become "soldiers" in the struggle for the rebirth of the Islamic state. The sisters gave humanitarian aid and support to the families of those activists who were imprisoned and helped them after their release.

Herself married twice, al-Ghazali has lived up to her father's expectation of her becoming an Islamic leader, in so doing claiming her own situation to be an exception to her general view of women's role in Islam. In the matter of her own two divorces (something that, for Muslim women in general, she insists is a crime worthy of punishment), she announced that both her husbands had had to accede to the greater demands of her work for Islam, which took priority over her duties as a wife, averring: "I had decided to cancel the matter of marriage from my life, in order to devote myself completely to the mission" (Ahmed 1992, 200). Throughout her long political career, she has been very active, collaborating with male Muslim activists to promote Islamic society (rather than religion) as a driving national force in the world. "We Muslims only carry arms in order to spread peace. We want to purify the world of unbelief, atheism, oppression, and persecution" (201). She has taken her message far and wide, giving lectures across the Muslim world—in Egypt, Pakistan, and Saudi Arabia—and also in the United States.

After Gamal Abdel Nasser came to power in 1956, al-Ghazali's activities led to a clash with the authorities, and she was arrested and sentenced to death. When riots took place in reaction to the verdict, the sentence was commuted to twenty-five years in jail in Cairo. During her incarceration, she was tortured for several months during the period 1965–1972 as a result of her association with the Muslim Brothers. In 1986 she published *Days of My Life,* an extremely disturbing account of her time in jail in which she described how she was hung up by her hands for hours at a time and often kept in a very small cell with no room to move. Sometimes ravenous dogs were let loose in the cell with her. Meanwhile, the Muslim Sisters was banned in 1965, and all other women's organizations were outlawed by Nasser.

On Nasser's death in 1970, the Saudi Arabian king petitioned Egypt's new president, Anwar Sadat, for al-Ghazali to be released, and she resumed her activities at the head of the Muslim Sisters in 1971. She also gave lectures on the Qu'ran and in 1979 published an article condemning feminists who encourage women to undertake public roles unprepared for the problems that they will encounter in doing so. However, al-Ghazali's own very public activities and also her ambivalent attitude toward divorce have led to accusations of hypocrisy.

In 1985 al-Ghazali presented the paper "The Role of Women in the Building of Society" to a conference of Muslim women in Lahore, Pakistan, in which she further underlined her hostility to women seeking political roles and criticized women's involvement in politics in the West, insisting: "Woman's skill in the rearing of her sons and preparing them for their leading and productive roles in society is far more valuable and useful" (Karam 1998, 210). This is but one aspect of the generally idealistic nature of much of al-Ghazali's attachment to traditional Islamic values, which at times makes many of them seem contradictory, if not antagonistic, to the goals of achieving women's basic civil and human rights. More recently, al-Ghazali showed signs of developing a more compassionate attitude toward other women and an affirmation of their right to autonomy—insofar as their exercise of personal choice remains contained, as ever, within their inherent duty to Islam.

References and Further Reading

Ahmed, Leila. 1992. *Women and Gender in Islam: Historical Roots of a Modern Debate.* New Haven: Yale University Press.

Hoffman, V. J. 1985. "An Islamic Activist: Zeinab al Ghazali." In Elizabeth Fernea, ed., *Women and the Family in the Middle East.* Austin: University of Texas Press.

Karam, Azza M. 1998. *Women, Islamism and the State: Contemporary Feminism in Egypt.* London: Macmillan.

Moghadam, Valerie M., ed. 1994. *Identity, Politics and Women: Cultural Reassertions and Feminisms in International Perspective.* Boulder, CO: Westview Press.

Gibbons, Abigail Hopper
(1801–1893)
United States

The American abolitionist, Civil War nurse, and prison reformer Abigail Gibbons, a pioneer of the rehabilitation of women prisoners, became head of the Female Department of the Prison Association of New York in 1845. In this capacity, she worked toward the social rehabilitation of women prisoners and for the reeducation of their keepers into adopting more humane methods of treatment. In so doing, she was instrumental in the creation of a women's prison system, run by women, that shifted its attitude from moral condemnation and punishment to a more compassionate concern for prisoners' welfare, during and after their term of sentence.

Gibbons's father, Isaac Tatem Hopper, was a Quaker abolitionist and prison reformer who believed in women's equality with men. As a member of the Hicksite faction of liberal Quakers who had broken away during the schism of 1827–1828, he was a vigorous supporter of abolitionism and made his home a stop on the Underground Railroad, which assisted runaway slaves in getting north to Canada.

Gibbons grew up in Philadelphia and was educated in Quaker schools, between 1821 and 1831 running a small school of her own to assist her parents in supporting their other nine children. After moving to New York, where she ran a Quaker school from 1830, she met and married a Quaker businessman and later banker, James Gibbons, in 1833. After two years in Philadelphia, the couple returned to New York, where, as leading members of the Manhattan Anti-Slavery Society, they raised funds among sympathizers. Their home became renowned as a stop on the Underground Railroad and a meeting place of abolitionists, including Lydia Maria Child and Sarah Moore Grimké, following in Gibbons's father's tradition. In 1842 both her father and husband were disowned by the New York Yearly Meeting of the Quakers for their militancy over abolition, and she resigned her membership in protest, although she retained her Hicksite Quaker beliefs for the rest of her life.

In New York, she became involved in welfare work among the poor in the city's tenements and slums. She became a prison visitor, working with her father after he founded the Prison Association of New York in December 1844. Early the following year, the association established a Female Department, with Gibbons appointed to lead a team of female volunteer workers.

In the summer of 1845, the Female Department founded a halfway house to aid former women prisoners in their voluntary rehabilitation after their discharge from prison. The women who lived there took in work as laundresses and needlewomen to help pay for their keep and were assisted in finding jobs in domestic service. Known as the Home for Discharged Female Convicts, it was probably the first institution of its kind in the world. But the regime was spartan; the women were obliged to rise early and attend morning service, afterwards occupying themselves during the day with literacy classes and sewing administered by Gibbons and her team, who also took every opportunity to provide moral guidance against the dangers of alcohol, vagrancy, and prostitution that awaited women upon their release into the wicked outside world. According to Margaret Bacon (1986), over a period of eight years, 300 out of 900 inmates had successfully settled into jobs found for them by the home.

In 1853 Gibbons's Female Department was given its autonomy and renamed the Women's Prison Association (WPA); its institution was renamed the Isaac Hopper House after her father. Soon after, Gibbons obtained a New York State Charter, which enabled her to introduce reforms, most notably the training of female prison warders. Along with another prison reformer, Josephine Shaw Lowell, she felt women prisoners would be better served if they were not held, segregated, within men's prisons, and she advocated the establishment of separate women's reformatories run by women. Gibbons also retained her interests in education, in 1859 setting up a German Industrial School for the welfare of homeless German immigrant children and remaining its director until 1871.

When the Civil War broke out in 1861, Gibbons volunteered her services to the U.S. Sanitary Commission. After training at David's Island Hospital in New York, she went to Washington, D.C., with her daughter Sarah and niece Maria Hopper. There they worked on and off for the next four years as nurses, first at the Washington Office Hospital. Gibbons organized the distribution of supplies donated by the New York Relief Agency and went on to set up two field hospitals at Strasburg and Falls Church, Virginia. Sent to nurse at Hammond General Hospital in Point Lookout, Maryland, she encountered the sharp tongue and domineering personality of the Sanitary Commission's superintendent of nurses, Dorothea Dix. It is a mark of Gibbons's strength of character that she succeeded in securing the post as matron at Hammond General, where she took full advantage of her position to ensure that wounded "contrabands" (runaway slaves who had volunteered for the Union Army) who arrived for treatment retained their liberty. Like Dix, Gibbons was outspoken in her criticism of the brutal medical methods of U.S. Army doctors and the mismanagement of supplies by its male administrators.

When the war ended, Gibbons established the Labor and Aid Society to help in the rehabilitation of war veterans and the relief of their families, but it failed to take off. She returned to her work for the WPA in New York and the many other reformist activities she had embraced in the 1850s—improvements in the care of the mentally ill and conditions in mental asylums, temperance, and the abolition of the death penalty. She also worked for blind and disabled children in the local poorhouse at West Farms (later the Randall's Island Children's Asylum). She founded the New York Diet Kitchen Association in 1873 to offer nutritious meals to children, the sick, and the poor and joined the moral campaign of the New York Committee for the Prevention of State Regulation of Vice, serving as its president.

In 1877 Gibbons became president of the WPA and pressed hard for further prison reform. In 1890, after many years of lobbying, she saw the introduction of women matrons to manage the women held in police custody. In 1892, at age ninety-one, Gibbons gave evidence before the New York legislature that resulted in the passage of a bill shortly before her death establishing a reformatory for women and girls to serve New York and Westchester.

The spirit of Gibbons's pioneering work on behalf of women prisoners is continued today by the Women's Prison Association in institutions such as the Hopper Home and its Alternative to Incarceration Program in New York, which enables women offenders to remain in the community with their children. The Transitional Services Unit offers counseling and training in parenting skills, as well as rehabilitation programs designed to help women released from prison avoid reoffending. For an account of the work of the WPA, Gibbons's contribution, and its ongoing projects provided by the New York Correction History Society, see "150 Years in the Forefront" at http://www.correctionhistory.org/html/chronicl/wpa/html.

See also Child, Lydia Maria; Dix, Dorothe Lynde; Grimké, Angelina Emily and Sarah Moore; Lowell, Josephine Shaw.

References and Further Reading
Bacon, Margaret Hope. 1986. *Mothers of Feminism: The Story of Quaker Women in America.* San Francisco: Harper and Row.
Emerson, Sarah Hopper. 1896. *The Life of Abby Hopper Gibbons, Told Chiefly through Her Correspondence.* 2 vols. New York: Putnam.
Ginzberg, Lori D. 1990. *Women and the Work of Benevolence: Morality, Politics, and Class in the Nineteenth-Century United States.* New Haven, CT: Yale University Press.
Lewis, David. 1965. *From Newgate to Dannemore: The Rise of the Penitentiary in New York, 1796–1848.* Ithaca: Cornell University Press.
Pivar, David J. 1973. *Purity Crusade: Sexual Morality and Social Control, 1868–1900.* Westport, CT: Greenwood Press.

Gilman, Charlotte Perkins
(1860–1935)
United States

Charlotte Perkins Gilman, feminist theorist, economist, and poet, is now an icon in the pantheon of U.S. women writers, most widely known for her extraordinary account of a woman's descent into insanity in her short story "The Yellow Wall-Paper." Less well known and long neglected is her 1898 historical and social study of women's status and economic oppression, *Women and Economics.* Written with consuming energy in a fifty-eight-day period of intense creativity, it argues the need for women's economic independence from men as a prerequisite for improving their civil status, over and above the winning of suffrage. In its description of the deadening effect of the bondage of domestic duty on women's morale and intellect, it is a powerful indictment of patriarchal society and the attendant atrophying of women's sense of personal aspiration and self-worth.

Gilman's father, Frederick Beecher Perkins (a great-nephew of Harriet Beecher Stowe), deserted his family not long after Charlotte's birth in Hartford, Connecticut, in 1860. The years of struggle endured by her mother, left to bring up Charlotte alone, led to growing embitterment and a withdrawal of maternal affection that would have a lasting effect on the impressionable young Charlotte. Isolated at home with her uncommunicative mother, Perkins took up her own private study of anthropology, sociology, and economics and became interested in health and dress reform. Having displayed considerable artistic skills, at eighteen she entered the Rhode Island School of Design and after her training worked as a commercial artist and also taught art.

Her brief marriage to the painter Charles Walter Stetson, after a persistent courtship on his part, ended in separation in 1888. Oppressed by the routine of domestic life, Gilman had suffered a bout of severe postpartum depression after giving birth to a daughter, Katharine, in 1885. The exhortations of her neurologist, S. Weir Mitchell, to reject the artistic life for the domestic in order to regain her mental well-being served only to make matters worse. An enforced and prolonged rest cure aggravated Gilman's precarious mental state and precipitated total nervous collapse, the experience of which would later provide the basis for Gilman's most widely known and haunting work, "The Yellow Wall-Paper," published in the *New England Magazine* in 1892.

After her marriage broke up, Gilman settled in Pasadena, California, where she supported herself and her daughter, first by running a boardinghouse and then through her writing. She and her husband were eventually divorced in 1894. Gilman published a collection of poetry, *In This Our World,* in 1893, as well as several short stories. In 1894 she and Helen Campbell coedited *Impress: A Journal of the Pacific Coast Women's Association*. In the mid-1890s, she became increasingly politically active, taking an interest in women's suffrage, trade unionism, and social reform. After long years of illness and emotional turmoil, she finally rediscovered her equilibrium in work, which she later described as "the normal life of every human being, which is joy and growth and service, without which one is a pauper and a parasite" (Lane 1983, 208).

Gilman began a new career as an itinerant lecturer, speaking at labor and women's associations. Having agreed that her daughter should go to live with her ex-husband and his new wife, she found herself the subject of considerable criticism for supposedly rejecting her maternal role. In 1895 she helped organize the California Women's Congress, where she met Jane Addams, after which she spent time at Hull House in Chicago. In 1896 she traveled to London for the International Socialist and Labour Congress, where she mixed with Fabians George Bernard Shaw and Beatrice and Sidney Webb, and in 1899 she returned to London for the congress of the International Council of Women. Gilman's contact with socialist activists both at home and abroad and her interest in then-current ideas on social Darwinism of the pioneer sociologist Lester Ward provided the impetus to the major work that would prove to be her enduring intellectual achievement. Published in 1898, *Women and Economics: A Study of the Economic Relation between Men and Women as a Factor in Social Evolution* was a reworking of her earlier California lectures. Arguing that not only women's intellectual capacity but also their ability to contribute fully to social progress had been stunted by their dependence on men, she emphasized the urgency of women achieving financial autonomy. She set out alternative ways whereby women could command a central, not a peripheral, role in the reshaping of society through the establishment of a new economic structure that was based neither on the capitalist profit motive nor on Marxist theories of destructive class warfare.

Fundamental to her view of a new society was women's cultural and civilizing role, which she argued could be enhanced by their collective rearing and socializing of the next generation of children. Establishing cooperative day care facilities would enable mothers to enter employment, and setting up cooperative household services could offset the time and energy they spent on domestic duties. Thus in Gilman's view, communal apartments and kitchens where women could share the cooking, washing, sewing, cleaning, and child care provided a more efficient and scientific management of domestic chores. She also argued that men should play a greater role in the education and upbringing of their children, thus enabling their wives to take up professions, because it was precisely the continuing exclusion of women from professional and public life that impeded social and economic progress.

Women and Economics was promptly embraced by suffragist leaders, with Carrie Chapman Catt acclaiming Gilman a feminist heroine and applauding the book for "utterly revolutionizing the attitude of mind in the entire country, indeed of other countries, as to woman's place" (Van Voris 1987, 62). It proved to be a seminal feminist work and was translated into seven languages, with leading feminists of the time serving as translators: the German version was undertaken by Marie Stritt, the Dutch version by Aletta Jacobs, and the Hungarian one by Rosika Schwimmer.

In 1900 Gilman remarried and settled in New York. Her second husband was her cousin George Gilman, and despite the continuing precariousness of her mental health, the partnership would prove a happy one until George's death in 1934. During this period, Gilman extended the sociological arguments of *Women and Economics* in *Concerning Children* (1900), *The Home: Its Work and Influence* (1903), *Human Work* (1904), and *His Religion and Hers: A Study of the Faith of Our Fathers and the Work of Our Mothers* (1923). From 1909 to 1916, she edited and contributed to her own feminist-socialist monthly journal, the *Forerunner*, in which she serialized her novel *Herland* in 1915, a satire of male-dominated society that posits the idea of a separatist woman-led utopia in which the role of motherhood is the foundation of a new culture.

Gilman's pacifist views were expounded in her 1911 book, *The Man-Made World* (originally serialized in the *Forerunner*), a eugenics-inspired argument against male militarism advocating improvement of the human race, not through man-made wars, which serve only to eliminate the physically fit, but through the liberation of women from their enslavement as domestic drudges. Once given the autonomy to reject the long-dominant male values that destroy the fabric of society, women would be able to assert their moral superiority as peacemakers in building a new world; in addition, Gilman believed that this new freedom would encourage them to be selective in their choice of fathers for their children, a reflection of her advocacy of sexual restraint and her growing distaste for the postwar sexual revolution of the 1920s. As she grew older, Gilman invested hopes in a future society that would not place so great an emphasis on sexuality (a fact she had explored in the replacement of heterosexual procreation by parthenogenesis in *Herland*). Sex, in her view, was too often the cause of women's misery and enslavement to men, but despite her misgivings about contraception encouraging sexual license, in 1932 she gave her formal support to the birth control movement. Gilman's espousal of eugenics in *The Man-Made World* would, however, mark the onset of an increasingly racist tone to her writing that aroused disquiet among her feminist supporters and colleagues and remains a problem for her many modern-day admirers. After her husband's sudden death in 1934, Gilman returned to Pasadena, where she committed suicide a year later by taking chloroform rather than face an agonizing death from the breast cancer from which she had been suffering for several years.

See also Addams, Jane; Catt, Carrie Chapman; Jacobs, Aletta; Schwimmer, Rosika; Stowe, Harriet Beecher; Stritt, Marie; Webb, Beatrice.

References and Further Reading
Adickes, Sandra. 1997. *To Be Young Was Very Heaven: Women in New York before the Great War.* Basingstoke: Macmillan.
Gilman, Charlotte Perkins. 1935. *The Living of Charlotte Perkins Gilman: An Autobiography.* New York: Appleton-Century.
Golden, Catherine J., and Joanna Zangrado, eds. 2000. *The Mixed Legacy of Charlotte Perkins Gilman.* Cranbury, NJ: University of Delaware Press.
Hill, Mary Armfield. 1980. *Charlotte Perkins Gilman: The Making of a Radical Feminist, 1860–1896.* Philadelphia: Temple University Press.
Kessler, Carol Farley. 1995. *Charlotte Perkins Gilman: Her Progress Toward Utopia with Selected Writings.* Liverpool: Liverpool University Press.
Lane, Ann J. 1983. "Charlotte Perkins Gilman: The Personal Is Political." In Dale Spender, ed., *Feminist Theorists: Three Centuries of Women's Intellectual Traditions.* London: Women's Press.
———. 1990. *To Herland and Beyond: The Life and Work of Charlotte Perkins Gilman.* New York: Pantheon Books.
Niess, Judith. 1977. *Seven Women: Portraits from the American Radical Tradition.* New York: Viking Press.
O'Neill, William L. 1969. *The Women's Movement: Feminism in the United States and England.* London: George Allen and Unwin.
Scharnhorst, Gary. 1985. *Charlotte Perkins Gilman.* Boston: Twayne.
Spender, Dale. 1982. *Women of Ideas and What Men Have Done to Them.* London: Routledge and Kegan Paul.
Van Voris, Jacqueline. 1987. *Carrie Chapman Catt: A Public Life.* New York: Feminist Press.

Glücklich, Vilma
(1872–1927)
Hungary

The Jewish educational reformer and pacifist Vilma Glücklich was seen by her friends and admirers in the international women's movement as a tragic Antigone figure, who always held out the hand of friendship and love wherever she encountered hatred and violence. The laudatory tributes to her devotion and self-sacrifice reflect the genuine compassion and courage of a woman who, with Rosika Schwimmer, pioneered the women's movement in Hungary.

Glücklich studied at a teacher training school in Budapest before becoming, in 1896, the first woman in Hungary to be admitted to a university, where she studied physics and mathematics. She was also the first to acquire her M.A., as a result suffering, in her modest view, an unnecessary amount of public attention. She taught in a Budapest high school before becoming active in trade union work in 1902 as a member of the board of the National Association of Women Office Workers, an organization with which she remained closely associated. In 1904 she and Rosika Schwimmer founded the Hungarian Feminist Association (HFA), which as an auxiliary of the International Woman Suffrage Alliance became a surprisingly powerful force in the international women's movement. Glücklich headed the association with her characteristic efficiency until the end of her life. With Rosika Schwimmer, she served as a major link between Hungarian activists and women's suffrage and

Vilma Glücklich (German Heritage Foundation)

peace societies around the world, and in 1913 Glücklich and Schwimmer successfully organized the staging of the seventh congress of the International Woman Suffrage Alliance in Budapest—the first major women's conference of its kind to be held in Hungary.

As a gentle, sensitive person imbued with patience and modesty, Glücklich was violently opposed to militarism and was dismayed by the outbreak of war in 1914. She organized members of the HFU to undertake relief work for the displaced and destitute and wrote editorials on pacifism and other issues, particularly on women's higher education, in the HFU's journal, *Woman*. With Schwimmer, in 1915 she headed the Hungarian delegation to the international women's peace congress at The Hague, which called for neutral countries to mediate between warring parties, and created the International Committee of Women for Permanent Peace. She remained at the head of the Hungarian section of the committee at war's end, and in 1919 Glücklich was again in the vanguard of women who attended the Zurich congress, at which the organization's name was changed to the Women's International League for Peace and Freedom

(WILPF). But she lost her teaching job as a result of her pacifist activities. She therefore took the appointment as international secretary of the WILPF and lived in Geneva from 1922 to 1925, when she was forced to retire from her international activities because of ill health. Meanwhile, the Hungarian government had deemed that she should forfeit her pension because of her refusal to give up pacifist work.

By all accounts exemplary in her altruism (she had never married or had children), Glücklich refused special treatment when she became seriously ill. By now having lost many friends in Hungary's political upheavals (most particularly her close friend Rosika Schwimmer, who had been forced into exile in the United States), she died a lonely and painful death in the large ward of a public hospital. Glücklich was posthumously decorated for her heroism by the short-lived Hungarian republic at the end of World War II. The Hungarian branch of the WILPF for which Glücklich had worked so tirelessly was dissolved by the Soviets in 1949.

See also Schwimmer, Rosika.

References and Further Reading

Bosch, Mineke. 1990. *Politics and Friendship: Letters from the International Woman Suffrage Alliance, 1902–42.* Columbus: Ohio State University Press.

"In Memoriam: Vilma Glücklich." 1927. *Jus Suffragii/ International Woman Suffrage News* (27 December).

Josephson, Harold, Sandi Cooper, and Steven C. Hause et al., eds. 1985. *Biographical Dictionary of Modern Peace Leaders.* Westport, CT: Greenwood Press.

Goegg, Marie Pouchoulin
(1826–1899)
Switzerland

Marie Pouchoulin Goegg was, in her time, greatly respected for being a pioneer of women's rights and the women's peace movement in Switzerland. So much so, that for his 1884 landmark work, *The Woman Question in Europe: A Series of Original Essays,* Theodore Stanton invited her to write the entry on Switzerland. As a founder of the Geneva-based International Association of Women (*Association Internationale des Femmes*—not to be confused with later, similarly named bodies) she was a central figure in Continental activism for women's equal rights and better education.

The daughter of a clockmaker, Goegg was born in Geneva. Her family were Huguenot refugees who had settled in Germany in the eighteenth century. She attended elementary school until the age of thirteen, when she had to give up her education to work in her father's shop, but she continued to read literature and history. In 1845 she married her first husband. Divorced in 1856, she married a German, Armand Goegg, who had fled to Switzerland after taking part in unsuccessful revolutionary activities in Baden during the upheavals of 1848. The couple lived in exile in London for a while before returning to Switzerland. They separated in 1874 but never divorced.

In 1867 Goegg attended the first peace congress of the newly formed International League for Peace and Freedom (ILPF) in Geneva, which had been organized by a loose grouping of European radicals of various political persuasions that included her husband. But she was immediately critical of the league's lack of encouragement for women to join. The congress, and women's lack of participation in it, provided Goegg with the impetus to set up her own organization in Geneva, the International Association of Women (IAW). At the ILPF's annual conference a year later in Bern, Goegg made one of the first public speeches by a European woman. In it, she emphasized the importance of women's role in political life and described how even the male leaders of the French Revolution had failed to confront the issue of women's rights and incorporate them in the spirit of their triple demand for "liberty, equality, and fraternity." Social progress, she argued, had stagnated because women were still denied equality with men. She believed they had an important function as mothers in bringing up their children with greater pacifist rather than militaristic instincts. The IAW staged its own meeting during the 1868 congress and Goegg published an article in the March 1868 of the ILPF's journal, the *United States of Europe,* in which she argued that without the support of women, the league's pacifist objectives would not be achieved. The ILPF subsequently added women's emancipation to its program of demands.

Goegg's IAW staged its own first congress in March 1870, attended by fifteen member nations,

and was affiliated with the ILPF through its shared pacifist objectives. It also played a short-term but important role in striving to unite women across all countries and social classes in the struggle for their social and political rights. It soon drew into it other member associations, some from the Swiss cantons, others from elsewhere in Europe, the United States (through Elizabeth Cady Stanton's staunch support), and the United Kingdom (through Josephine Butler). Thus, motivated by Goegg's argument that "the source of the majority of evils of the feminine sex stems from its dependence on the masculine sex" (Cooper 1991, 41), the IAW formed a network of women's groups that corresponded with each other and campaigned against state-regulated prostitution, for women's rights and education, and the extension of women's role in the public sphere—all some years before the advent of the International Council of Women (1888) and the International Woman Suffrage Association (1904). The IAW also lent much support in Butler's work for repeal of the Contagious Diseases Acts in Britain. Many IAW members would later (1875) find their way into campaigning for social purity through their national branches of Butler's British, Continental, and General Federation for the Abolition of State Regulation of Vice.

In 1870 the outbreak of the Franco-Prussian War and the ensuing political upheavals in Switzerland underlined Goegg's arguments that women should have a greater voice in the public sphere in order to avert military conflicts. With the need for women's education and emancipation even more pressing, in her estimation, she resigned from the IAW, which in any event fell into disarray after the collapse of the Paris Commune in 1871 because the IAW's name had suggested links with the Communist International. Goegg retained her role on the board of the IAW and wrote for its *Women's Journal,* which later amalgamated with Marie Deraismes's journal, *Rights of Women.* In general, though, her later campaigning was confined to more narrow, Swiss issues on women's rights—such as the 1872 campaign for revision of the civil codes and improvements to education for women. As a native of the French-speaking part of Switzerland, Goegg was involved in the Association for the Defense of the Rights of Women—a French-based group founded in the late 1860s by the feminist novelist and later communard (1871)

André Leo (Léodile Bara de Champeix) and others, and that was controlled increasingly by Marie Deraismes. Through this assocation Goegg successfully led calls for the University of Geneva to join that in Zurich in opening its doors to women, thus reinforcing the Swiss tradition of being the first European country to offer university education to women.

See also Butler, Josephine; Stanton, Elizabeth Cady.
References and Further Reading
Cooper, Sandi E. 1991. *Patriotic Pacifism: Waging War on War in Europe, 1815–1914*. Oxford: Oxford University Press.
Josephson, Harold, Sandi Cooper, and Steven C. Hause et al., eds. 1985. *Biographical Dictionary of Modern Peace Leaders*. Westport, CT: Greenwood Press.
Offen, Karen. 2000. *European Feminism 1700–1950*. Stanford: Stanford University Press.
Pierson, Ruth Roach, ed. 1987. *Woman and Peace: Theoretical, Historical and Practical Perspectives*. London: Croom Helm.
Ruser, Urusla-Maria. 1993. *Bertha von Suttner (1843–1914) and Other Women in Pursuit of Peace*. Geneva: United Nations Office at Geneva.

Emma Goldman (Library of Congress)

Goldman, Emma
(1869–1940)
Lithuania/United States

"Red Emma," the archetypal anarchist rebel best known for her defense of individual freedom and the rights of workers, became one of the most reviled women of her time. Much was made of Goldman's perceived "infamy" as a female political firebrand and her many colorful affairs as an advocate of free love. With the U.S. authorities doing their best to discredit her activities at every turn, an undue emphasis was placed on her political extremism, and little attention was paid to her reformist beliefs until the revival of interest in her that came with the second wave of the feminist movement in the 1970s. Although Goldman rejected the work of bourgeois feminists and suffrage organizations, as a leading figure in the U.S. birth control movement, she was dedicated to the idea of women's sexual freedom, their liberation from the institution of marriage, and their control over their reproductive roles.

After her birth in Kovno (now Kaunas), Lithuania (which was then part of the Russian Empire), Goldman's Orthodox Jewish family moved to St. Petersburg in 1882. She received an education only until age thirteen, when she began working in a glove factory to help the family finances and came into contact with Russian radicals. In 1885 she emigrated to the United States to join her half sister Lena in order to avoid an arranged marriage. The sisters settled in Rochester, New York, where they were befriended by German Jewish anarchists. There Emma was forced to find underpaid work, sewing for ten hours a day in a sweatshop. A brief marriage to a fellow immigrant, Jacob Kerchner, ended in divorce after three months because of Goldman's sexual frustration at his impotence.

Vowing never to subject herself to the humiliation of marriage again, in August 1889, Goldman took herself and her sewing machine to New York and joined a community of émigré Russian anarchists. She became involved with the revolutionary Alexander Berkman and, together with him, his cousin Fedya, and another woman, set up a commune. Goldman soon began having an affair with Fedya too. She met and debated with other anarchists and bohemians in clubs and cafés around Greenwich Village and began giving political lectures while continuing to support herself as a dressmaker. Meanwhile, Berkman was plotting to assassinate steel magnate Henry Frick in retaliation for the death of steelworkers during a strike at Frick's steelworks in Pennsylvania. When his attempt in 1892 failed, he was imprisoned, and Goldman was implicated; forever after, she would be deemed a political bogeyman.

With an industrial crisis looming in New York in 1892, Goldman threw herself into direct action in support of trade unions and organized food supplies for the families of striking workers. In 1893 she was sent to prison for one year for incitement to riot, making good use of her time there by learning some rudimentary nursing as assistant to a prison doctor. Defiant and unrepentant, she emerged from jail to find herself labeled as a public enemy, but she immediately went on the fund-raising and lecture circuit in continuation of her work for labor, suffering repeated intimidation and surveillance. In 1895 she traveled to Europe (and again in 1899–1900) on a lecture tour, during the course of which she trained as a midwife and nurse in Vienna, where she also attended lectures by the celebrated psychoanalyst Sigmund Freud. Upon her return to the United States, what she had learned at a neo-Malthusian conference in Paris in 1900 inspired her to join the campaign for birth control, and she worked in New York's slums as a nurse. She resumed her impassioned political speaking and writing and ran a series of lectures on the plays of George Bernard Shaw, August Strindberg, and Henrik Ibsen, which became the basis of her 1914 book, *The Significance of Modern Drama.*

After the assassination of President William McKinley in 1901 by a professed anarchist, Goldman, because of her declared political beliefs, was assumed to be involved. But a case could not be made against her, and she was released from custody after two weeks. Such was the heightened public hostility toward extremists in the wake of this event that Goldman was obliged to maintain a low political profile after her release from prison, gradually returning to public lecturing on social rather than political issues. In March 1906 she founded a feminist and anarchist magazine, *Mother Earth,* in which, until its suppression in 1917, she published articles on her political ideas, as well as on social issues such as birth control, the reform of laws affecting

marriage, women's sexual freedom, and the upbringing of children. Goldman was assisted in running the magazine by Berkman, who had been released after serving fourteen years in prison.

Goldman was utterly scornful in her rejection of the U.S. suffrage movement. She had no time for the predominantly middle-class, conservative membership, the majority of whom patently abhorred her extremism and her sexual libertarianism. As Alix Shulman argues, Goldman viewed the suffrage campaign as ineffectual and the majority of its membership as conformist supporters of the political establishment, arguing: "True emancipation begins neither at the polls nor in courts. It begins in a woman's soul" (Shulman 1983, 227). Nothing would change, she felt, if women were given the vote, because women as voters would be ineffectual in ending the continuing corruption of government and its coercion of the individual. Goldman's views on this subject inevitably alienated many would-be feminist supporters, and indeed, her failure either to criticize the patriarchy that perpetuated women's subjection or to embrace the sisterhood of female activists, preferring instead the male-dominated spheres of political activism, has contributed to her remaining an isolated figure who stands outside the mainstream of the U.S. women's movement of the nineteenth century.

In 1910 many of Goldman's seminal writings were collected in *Anarchism and Other Essays,* including five essays on women, such as "Marriage and Love" and "The Tragedy of Women's Emancipation." In the latter, she highlighted the limitations of the "emancipation" achieved by women so far, and how, in moving into the workplace, they had exchanged domestic enslavement for long hours working for low pay in factory and department stores or, worse still, had had their workload doubled by having to do both. A lesser-known aspect of Goldman's radicalism was her twenty years' work for birth control in support of the rights of freedom of speech and conscience. Her campaigning was also bound up in her advocacy of women's right to freely express themselves sexually, and Goldman herself practiced what she preached by having many sexual affairs. She wanted women to be able to enjoy their sexuality instead of being enslaved by it through unwanted pregnancies (the results of which she had witnessed too many times as a midwife). She joined Margaret Sanger, whom she had first met in 1910, in being the first women to speak publicly on the subject. She contributed to Sanger's short-lived magazine, *The Woman Rebel,* and embarked on fund-raising lecture tours on birth control during 1915–1916. Goldman openly discussed the use of contraceptives during Yiddish-language lectures to Jewish immigrant women on the Lower East Side, and in April 1916 she was given a fifteen-day prison sentence under the Comstock Law banning the dissemination of contraceptive literature, for lecturing on "The Social Aspects of Birth Control."

As a pacifist, Goldman was dismayed by the outbreak of war in Europe in 1914. Appalled by the escalation of militarism in the United States, in 1916 she toured with a lecture entitled "Preparedness, the Road to Universal Slaughter," later published as a pamphlet, in which she opposed U.S. entry into the war. In 1917 she was sentenced to two years in the Missouri Penitentiary for opposing the draft, by channeling her activities through the No-Conscription League that she had founded. Goldman served eighteen months in jail and was deported after her release in 1919, along with Berkman and over 200 other "undesirable aliens." It was the height of the "red scare" in the United States, but Goldman held her head high, stating that she had considered it "an honor to be the first political agitator deported from the United States" (Spender 1982, 364). She placed her hope for a better life in the Soviet Union. Her disillusion with the realities of life there would be bitter. She and Berkman were dismayed at the widespread hunger they witnessed, resulting from the arbitrary nature of Lenin's "war communism," which ensured that the fat cats of the Communist Party were well provided for while others starved. She also was dismayed at the abuse of civil liberties by the Bolshevik leaders (in particular, their persecution of Russian anarchists), concluding that they had betrayed the ideals of communism through their establishment of an increasingly centralized and authoritarian government. After the brutal government suppression at Kronstadt of a mutiny by workers and sailors protesting the erosion of freedom of speech, she and Berkman left the Soviet Union in 1921. They went to Berlin, where Goldman wrote *My Disillusionment in Russia* (1923) and *My Further Disillusionment in Russia* (1924).

In 1924 Goldman went to England in an attempt to galvanize radical support for an anti-Soviet campaign. In order to obtain a passport, she made a marriage of convenience to a Scottish anarchist and miner, James Colton, in 1925 and left England soon after to be reunited with Berkman in France, where she wrote her autobiography, *Living My Life* (1931). Goldman was never allowed to resettle in the United States, revisiting only briefly in 1934 before going to Spain on three occasions during the civil war of 1936–1939 to support anarchists opposing General Franco's forces and raise funds for refugees. She died in Toronto during a fund-raising trip. The U.S. authorities finally allowed her to return—in death—to be buried alongside anarchist martyrs in a plot in Chicago's Waldheim Cemetery.

See also Sanger, Margaret.

References and Further Reading

Adickes, Sandra. 1997. *To Be Young Was Very Heaven: Women in New York before the Great War.* Basingstoke: Macmillan.

Buhle, Mari Jo. 1981. *Women and American Socialism, 1870–1920.* Urbana: University of Illinois Press.

Drinnan, Richard. 1961. *Rebel in Paradise: A Biography of Emma Goldman.* Chicago: University of Chicago Press.

Falk, Candace. 1984. *Love, Anarchy and Emma Goldman.* New York: Holt, Rinehart, and Winston.

Forster, M. 1984. *Significant Sisters: The Grassroots of Active Feminism, 1839–1939.* London: Secker and Warburg.

Goldman, Emma. 1931. *Living My Life: An Autobiography of Emma Goldman.* Salt Lake City, UT: G. M. Smith.

Goldsmith, Margaret. 1935. *Seven Women against the World.* London: Methuen.

Gordon, Ann D., et al. 1997. *African American Women and the Vote 1837–1965.* Amherst: University of Massachusetts Press.

Morton, Marian J. 1992. *Emma Goldman and the American Left: "Nowhere at Home."* New York: Twayne.

Reynolds, Moira Davison. 1994. *Women Advocates of Reproductive Rights: 11 Who Led the Struggle in the United States and Great Britain.* Jefferson, NC: McFarland.

Rowbotham, Sheila. 1999. *Threads through Time: Writings on History and Autobiography.* London: Penguin.

Sanger, Margaret. 1931. *My Fight for Birth Control.* New York: Farrar and Rinehart.

Shulman, Alix Kates, ed. 1971. *To the Barricades: The Anarchist Life of Emma Goldman.* New York: Crowell.

———. 1972. *Red Emma Speaks: Selected Writings and Speeches by Emma Goldman.* New York: Vintage Books.

———. 1983. "Emma Goldman: Anarchist Queen." In Dale Spender, ed., *Feminist Theorists: Three Centuries of Women's Intellectual Traditions.* London: Women's Press.

Spender, Dale. 1982. *Women of Ideas, and What Men Have Done to Them.* London: Routledge and Kegan Paul.

Watson, Martha. 1987. *Emma Goldman.* Boston: Twayne.

Wexler, Alice. 1984. *Emma Goldman: An Intimate Life.* New York: Pantheon.

———. 1989. *Emma Goldman in Exile.* Boston: Beacon Press.

Goldstein, Vida
(1869–1949)
Australia

An outstanding feminist and suffragist leader who was uncompromising in her radical socialist and pacifist beliefs, the combative Vida Goldstein had as many detractors as admirers. She rose to prominence in the late stages of the campaign for women's suffrage in Australia, which granted the federal vote to women in 1902. She was the first woman in Australia to stand in nationwide elections—running for office unsuccessfully five times between 1903 and 1917—and became an international figure, retaining a determined antiparty position in the belief that women should work for social change unbiased by party loyalties.

Goldstein enjoyed the advantage of being born to a mother with progressive ideas who was an active suffragist herself; her father, too, was noted for his philanthropy and charitable work. Born in Portland, Victoria, Vida was educated at home by governesses and grew up at Warrnambool. The family moved back to Melbourne in 1877, where she studied at the Ladies Presbyterian College (1884–1886). A regular attendee at her Australian Church, a breakaway of the Scottish Presbyterian church, she became, with her mother, involved in the church's social movement. They took up volunteer work in the Melbourne slums under the guidance of their priest, Dr. Charles Strong, protesting the exploitation of workers in sweatshops and running crèches for their children. In 1891 Goldstein was one of the organizers of a massive suffrage petition that gained 30,000 signatures and was sent to the parliament of Victoria.

Other philanthropy undertaken by Goldstein during the 1890s in tandem with her mother included work for the National Anti-Sweating League and the Criminology Society and the organization of a fund-raising appeal during Queen Victoria's Jubilee in 1897 for the Queen Victoria Hospital for Women and Children, of which her mother had been a founder. In addition, when the family suffered financial losses in 1893, Goldstein and her sisters, finding themselves obliged to find paid employment, had established a coeducational preparatory school at East St. Kilda, Melbourne.

Goldstein gave more and more time to suffrage campaigning, encouraged by the suffrage leader Annette Bear, a founder of the United Council for Women's Suffrage (UCWS). When Bear died suddenly in 1899, Goldstein, who had been working as a paid organizer of the UCWS, took over the leadership and closed her school to concentrate on the campaign for women's enfranchisement for the next nine years. She took her role very seriously, studying parliamentary procedure and reading up on legislative and economic reform. In September 1900 she established a monthly feminist journal, the *Australian Woman's Sphere,* which tackled both local and women's issues and often featured articles from Lucy's Stone's U.S. publication, the *Woman's Journal.*

In 1902 Australian women were granted full suffrage at the federal level, but the fight for the state vote had yet to be won in Tasmania, Queensland, and Goldstein's state of Victoria. That year Goldstein was the Australian and New Zealand representative to an international women's conference held in Washington, D.C., which led to the founding of the International Woman Suffrage Alliance in 1904; Goldstein served as corresponding secretary. She remained in the United States for six months, observing the suffrage campaign there and giving public lectures. She was also invited to give evidence on suffrage to a U.S. House of Representatives Committee on the Judiciary.

Galvanized by her experiences in the United States, Goldstein returned to Australia in 1903 and kick-started a new phase of campaigning by founding the Women's Federal Political Association (changed to the Women's Political Association, or WPA, soon after). Elected the WPA's president, Goldstein stood as an independent candidate in the first Australian federal elections in which women voted. She was the first woman in the British Empire to take this new political step, and during her nonaligned political campaign, she concentrated strongly on promoting feminist issues and winning the new female vote. She encountered much hostility from the male electorate but nevertheless gained 51,497 votes—not enough to elect her but enough to encourage her to found a Men's League for Woman's Suffrage, to join in campaigning with the WPA. She stood again in federal elections in 1910, 1913, 1914, and 1917 but was defeated every time, much of her opposition within the women's movement coming from the right-wing majority of Woman's Christian Temperance Union (WCTU) members.

In 1905 Goldstein closed the *Australian Woman's Sphere* to concentrate on the campaign for suffrage in Victoria, which was achieved in 1908. In 1909 she set up a new weekly paper, the *Woman Voter,* to further the reform of federal marriage and divorce laws and to advocate equal rights in many areas, particularly pay and the employment of women in official posts. Dedicated to the principles of socialism and trade unionism, Goldstein supported arbitration and conciliation in labor disputes and the more equitable distribution of wealth through profit sharing and the nationalization of key industries. She wanted the age of marriage and consent raised and campaigned for more thorough inspection of food for contamination. Most important, she worked to protect young offenders by helping to draft the 1906 Children's Court Act. But her refusal to align herself politically prejudiced support for her from other male politicians and women voters, and she continued to be the butt of frequent press hostility.

In 1911 Goldstein visited the United Kingdom under the auspices of the Pankhursts' Women's Social and Political Union. She published articles in its journal, *Votes for Women,* during her eight-month stay, completed a much-trumpeted speaking tour, and joined English suffragettes on marches and at rallies. While in Britain, she cofounded the Australian and New Zealand Voters' Association to provide a forum for expatriates to register their support for the suffrage campaign back in Australia. She also met and helped arrange for Emmeline Pankhurst's youngest daughter, Adela, to emigrate to Australia.

After her return to Australia, there was a marked change in Goldstein's views, which became increasingly reactionary. She had become a devotee of Christian Science, and the tone of her articles in the *Woman Voter* grew more overtly antimale. Continuing to resist party alignment in the belief that social issues transcended political argument, she promoted her views from a purely feminist position, attacking the double sexual standard, advocating sexual restraint and social purity, and repudiating the free love practiced by some feminists. She also began voicing her opposition to indiscriminate assisted emigration.

When war broke out in Europe in the summer of 1914, Goldstein's strong pacifist sympathies influenced the position of the WPA and the editorial slant of the *Woman Voter,* which featured pacifist articles. She was elected chair of the Australian Peace Alliance, and in 1915 founded the Women's Peace Army with Adela Pankhurst. She set up and helped run a Women's Unemployment Bureau during 1915–1916 in an attempt to alleviate the economic hardship of women whose men were away fighting and led an anti-conscription campaign during 1916–1917. Her pacifism further compounded male hostility toward her and led to accusations of a lack of patriotism; the WPA came under police surveillance and official censorship.

In 1919 Goldstein accepted the offer to be one of three Australian women delegates to the International Congress of Women in Zurich, at which the International Committee of Women for Permanent Peace, founded in 1915, became the Women's International League for Peace and Freedom. She remained abroad for three years, traveling around Europe. By the time she returned, her support base had waned, and the WPA and the *Woman Voter* had folded. By then seeing the best hopes for social reform lying in the spiritual rehabilitation of the individual, Goldstein effectively withdrew from public activism to devote herself to the Christian Scientist church. Although she would lend her support later to the birth control, disarmament, and antinuclear movements and would advocate changes to the naturalization laws, she faded out of view, espousing a new quasi-religious utopian vision of a future society based on Christian socialism and the natural, civilizing influences of women.

Goldstein's suffrage writings are relatively few, but see the pamphlets "The Senate Election—Manifesto to the Electors of Victoria" (1903) and "Parliament for Involved Women" (1914). She was also active in the National Council of Women, the Victorian Women's Public Servants' Association, and the Women Writers' Club.

See also Pankhurst, Christabel; Pankhurst, Emmeline; Pankhurst, (Estelle) Sylvia; Stone, Lucy.

References and Further Reading

Bomford, Janet. 1993. *That Dangerous Persuasive Woman: A Life of Vida Goldstein.* Carlton, Victoria: Melbourne University Press.

Caine, Barbara. 1993. "Vida Goldstein and the English Militant Campaign." *Women's History Review* 2(3): 363–376.

Daley, Caroline, and Melanie Nolan. 1994. *Suffrage and Beyond: International Feminist Perspectives.* New York: New York University Press.

Henderson, Leslie M. 1973. *The Goldstein Story.* Melbourne: Stockland Press.

Lake, Marilyn. 1999. *Getting Equal: The History of Australian Feminism.* London: Allen and Unwin.

MacKenzie, Norman. 1960. "Vida Goldstein: The Australian Suffragette." *Australian Journal of Politics and History* 6: 190–204.

Oldfield, Audrey. 1992. *Woman Suffrage in Australia: A Gift or a Struggle?* Melbourne: Cambridge University Press.

Weiner, Gaby. 1983. "Vida Goldstein: The Women's Candidate (1869–1949)." In Dale Spender, ed., *Feminist Theorists: Three Centuries of Women's Intellectual Traditions.* London: Women's Press.

Gómez de Avellaneda y Arteaga, Gertrudis
(1814–1873)
Cuba/Spain

The Cuban writer Gertrudis Gómez de Avellaneda, who made her reputation in Spain, has the distinction of tackling the subject of slavery in fiction eleven years before Harriet Beecher Stowe did so in her far more widely known novel, *Uncle Tom's Cabin* (1851–1852). Although Gómez was primarily a poet, historical dramatist, and leading woman of letters in the Spanish elite, recognition is long overdue for her bold exploration of the issue of racial oppression at a time when the majority of women did not even dare publish under their own names.

Gómez was born in Puerto Principe, Cuba, of mixed Spanish and Cuban parentage. Her father, a Spanish naval officer, died when she was nine. In 1836, during a period of social unrest in Cuba, the family returned to Spain and settled in Seville. Gómez later moved to Madrid and remained there for the next twenty years, becoming the leading female literary lion of her day. She also embarked on numerous love affairs, had an illegitimate daughter by a poet, and became a notorious figure much in the style of French novelist George Sand, whom she admired—a reflection of the less restrictive social mores of Cuban life with which Gómez had grown up.

The first of Gómez's many plays, *Leoncia,* was staged in Seville in 1840 (another eight would be staged in Madrid from 1849 to 1853). She also wrote romantic poetry and novels, such as *Two Women* (1842), in which she challenged social convention, marriage, and women's position in society. Such was her preeminent position in Spanish letters that in 1852 Gómez called on the Spanish Royal Academy to admit her. She was, of course, rejected because of her sex.

It was in 1841 that Gómez published her powerful, and for its time remarkable, antislavery novel, *Sab the Mulatto,* which sees not only the black slaves of Cuba's plantations but also women as victims of society. In drawing obvious parallels between the subjection of women and of slaves, Gómez demanded basic human rights for both. As the first abolitionist novel written in Spanish, it would also be the first of many attacks she would make on slavery, prisons, and the criminal justice system in her work. Because of its powerful indictment of the plantation-based economy in Cuba (where 40 precent of the population was slaves), the novel was banned there in 1844.

In 1846 Gómez finally married but was widowed only three months later. As a devout Catholic, she considered entering a convent and spent some time in retreat in Bordeaux, where she wrote a prayer book. In 1854 she remarried; her husband, the Spanish courtier Colonel Domingo Verdugo, was posted to Cuba in 1859, and upon their return in 1860, Gómez was awarded the country's highest literary honors. In Havana she founded the first journal in Cuba edited by a woman, the *Cuban Album of the Good and the Beautiful.* In a series of four articles on women's position that she wrote for it, Gómez lauded the moral superiority of women, their natural charity and compassion, and their instinctive altruism. She encouraged them to reject the traditional patriarchal view of their intellectual inferiority. Believing that they had the ability to take on challenging roles in government, science, and the arts, Gómez urged women to fight for integration into those spheres from which they had for so long been excluded. Their inclusion, she felt, would be the true mark of a civilized society.

In 1863, Gómez returned to Madrid and later visited the United States, England, and France. She became more conservative in her views as she grew older, but within the limitations of her passionate Christian reformist concerns, she was an important forerunner in the quest for racial and sexual equality in the Spanish-speaking world.

See also Stowe, Harriet Beecher.

References and Further Reading

Davies, Catherine. 1998. *Spanish Women's Writing 1849–1996.* London: Athlone Press.

Gómez de Avellaneda, Gertrudis. 1992. *Sab, and Autobiography.* Trans. Nina M. Scott. Austin: University of Texas Press.

———. 2001. *Sab.* Spanish text, with notes and introduction by Catherine Davies. Manchester: Manchester University Press.

Harter, Hugh. 1981. *Gertrudis Goméz de Avellaneda.* Boston: Twayne.

Pastor, Brigida. 1995. "Cuba's Covert Cultural Critic: The Feminist Writings of Gertrudis Gómez de Avellaneda." *Romance Quarterly* 42(3): 178–190.

Tenenbaum, Barbara A., ed. 1996. *Encyclopedia of Latin American History and Culture,* vol. 3. New York: Charles Scribner's Sons.

Williams, Edwin Bucher. 1924. *The Life and Dramatic Works of Gertrudis Gomez de Avellaneda.* Philadelphia: n.p.

Gonne, Maud
(1866–1953)
Ireland

The indomitable Maud Gonne, in her day one of Ireland's great beauties and famously loved by the poet W. B. Yeats, was one of the most charismatic figures in the long struggle for Irish independence. The cult of adoration surrounding her

Maud Gonne (Bettmann/Corbis)

later led to many sobriquets regarding her legendary beauty and the view many had of her as the incarnation of the spirit of "Mother Ireland." Some even alluded to her as "Ireland's Joan of Arc," but she was not a militaristic figure; she loathed violence and devoted much of her life to the support and rehabilitation of Irish political prisoners.

Gonne was born in Aldershot, England, the daughter of a British army colonel of Irish descent and of some wealth. Her father had been posted to army duty in Dublin in 1867, and she spent her childhood there until her mother died when she was four. At this time, however, Maud showed signs of having weak lungs and was sent to France, where she and sister were educated by a governess.

Gonne joined her father back in Dublin in 1882, was presented to the prince of Wales in Dublin Castle, and became something of a society hostess on her father's behalf. Her father, who was sympathetic to the cause of the Irish Land League, considered standing as a home rule candidate for Parliament but died prematurely of typhoid. At the age of twenty-one, provided for by a trust fund, Gonne found herself with sufficient income to pursue her own interests, which already included the Irish cause and social justice for the unemployed.

She became an actress, but lung trouble again forced her back to France. While recuperating in the Auvergne, she met Lucien Millevoye, a French politician and journalist. Together they began campaigning for the restoration of the province of Alsace-Lorraine to France and from a distance, supported the ongoing campaign for independence for Ireland. Returning to Dublin in 1888, Gonne met with Irish nationalist and republican activists, who enlisted her help in protests against the mass evictions of Irish tenant farmers in Donegal. Gonne's natural passions were aroused by the sight of homeless, destitute families left stranded by the roadside; such sights changed her attitude toward her own privileged class forever. She helped collect money and donated some of her own to relieve suffering in the local community and build "Land League huts" for the dispossessed. She also lent her support to twenty-seven Irish political prisoners being held in foul conditions in Portland prison in Dorset. From these events stemmed her lifelong campaign for the welfare of not just political but also ordinary prisoners, particularly those who were badly treated and often left for long periods in solitary confinement.

Soon Gonne found her activities were attracting official attention and that she was in danger of arrest by the British. She returned to France in 1890, where she resumed her relationship with Millevoye and had two children by him (her son died a few months after his birth in 1891; her daughter Iseult was born in 1895). In Paris she wrote for and edited a French newspaper, *Free Ireland,* in which she spoke of the need for Irish separatism. Such became her consuming commitment to Irish independence that in 1895 she began traveling back and forth across the English Channel to take up the case of Irish political prisoners through her work for the Amnesty Association, as well as embarking on fund-raising lecture tours to Irish-American enclaves in the United States.

In 1898 Gonne, now a figure of some eminence in the Irish national movement, was asked by the Irish socialist leader James Connolly to go to County Mayo to report on the near-famine conditions prevailing there as a result of the failure of the potato crop. She wrote to the Dublin newspapers about the terrible conditions she witnessed, raised subscriptions and put up her own money to buy relief supplies, and successfully confronted the local Board of Guardians to get workers' relief payments increased. She arranged school meals and the care of the sick, and not surprisingly, local people looked on her as something of a miracle worker.

By 1899 it had become clear that Gonne's commitment to Ireland was greater than that to her relationship with Millevoye, and she left France to devote herself to campaigning in Ireland for home rule. She now turned her sights to involving more women in the cause of Irish independence, and in 1900 founded the Daughters of Ireland. The organization sought to foster an Irish revival by teaching the Gaelic language and Irish history, and Gonne wrote many feminist and political articles for its journal, the *Irish Woman.* In October 1898 Gonne and Arthur Griffith had cofounded the Transvaal Committee to support Afrikaners against the British in the Boer War. Members of the Daughters of Ireland later joined the campaign to persuade Irishmen not to enlist in the British army. Such was the drive at that time to encourage Irish recruitment to the British armed forces that Queen Victoria was persuaded to visit Ireland, prompting Gonne to publish her most passionate article, in *Free Ireland,* in which she condemned Queen Victoria in its title as "The Famine Queen." Needless to say, publication of the article was swiftly suppressed by the British authorities. The occasion of Queen Victoria's state visit to Ireland also gave Gonne the opportunity to stage a subversive protest in the wake of the official celebrations by arranging an "Irish Patriotic Children's Treat" in July for 30,000 Dublin children, an event that outrivaled the official Phoenix Park treat staged by the British government for a mere 5,000 earlier that year during the queen's visit.

In 1889 Gonne had met the poet W. B. Yeats and became involved in his Irish theater movement, helping him found the National Literary Society in Dublin in 1892 while actively seeking his influential support for Irish nationalism. But despite his abiding passion for her, she turned down Yeats's marriage proposal in 1891 (and another, some ten years later). She did, however, find herself drawn into Yeats's experimentation with the mystical and occult through the somewhat risible activities of the Order of the Golden Dawn.

In 1902 Gonne took to the stage to perform in Yeats's *Cathleen ni Houlihan,* written especially for her, in which she seemed to many to be the romantic incarnation of Mother Ireland, and which her fellow nationalist Constance Markievicz and others took as an inspiration in the fight for Irish independence. Statuesque and beautiful and by then a Roman Catholic convert, Gonne represented the long-repressed spiritual qualities of Ireland, as Yeats confirmed: "When women did her bidding they did it not only because she was beautiful, but because that beauty suggested joy and freedom" (Coxhead 1965, 49).

Back in Paris in 1903, Gonne met and married the Irish Republican major John MacBride, who had fought with the Afrikaners in South Africa and was recruiting for an Irish regiment. But the marriage was a disaster. The couple separated, but Gonne stayed in Paris for the most part until 1918 with their son, Sean. In Dublin in 1910, Gonne resumed her philanthropic work and in the pages of the *Irish Woman* wrote about the terrible conditions in the Dublin slums, the plight of poor Irish children, and the pitiful wages of working-class women. The members of the journal worked to raise money to help slum children and organize the provision of hot lunches for them. During World War I, Gonne undertook work for the Red Cross in France and, at the time of the 1916 Easter Rising in Dublin, adopted her husband's name after his execution as one of the ringleaders, even though the couple had long been separated. Despite being banned from returning to Ireland, in 1918 she returned in disguise with the help of Yeats, who procured a passport for her. She was soon arrested and imprisoned in Holloway jail in London for campaigning against military conscription, supposedly all part of an Irish plot with the Germans against the British authorities. Her health failed, and Yeats managed to get her moved to a hospital, from where she escaped and made her way back to Dublin.

During the Irish War of Independence of 1919–1921 and the ensuing Civil War of 1922–1923, Gonne did not engage in acts of violence (which she hated but saw as a necessary evil) but devoted herself to relief work through the auspices of the White Cross, helping victims of the war and their dependents by cooking, sewing, and feeding children. She led a delegation of women to Arthur Griffith (in 1922 elected president of the Dáil Eireann) to find a way of reconciling the Irish Free State and Republicans and avoid bloodshed. With Charlotte Despard, Gonne founded the Women's Prisoners' Defence League (WPDL), setting up in a house they bought in Cork a cottage industry for families of Republican fighters who had been killed or were prisoners.

Together Despard and Gonne held regular public protest meetings against the Irish Free State. The sight of the now sunken-cheeked and gaunt Gonne alongside the wizened figure of Despard, both in their black widows' weeds, was an emotive image that always attracted attention, and their activities irritated the Free State government to such an extent that in 1923 Gonne was arrested and jailed. In prison she went on hunger strike and was released when once again Yeats came to her rescue. In 1935 Gonne again joined with the WPDL in support of Republican prisoners—this time those jailed by the new Fianna Fáil government. Like Despard she was indefatigable in her campaigning, making speeches and writing endless letters of protest to the press in her agitation for prison reform and the rehabilitation of prisoners. In 1938 she finally found time to write her autobiography, with deliberate irony subtitled *A Servant of the Queen.*

Despite her weak constitution, Gonne lived to the age of eighty-six, a much venerated figure in Ireland who was accorded burial in the Republican plot in Dublin's Glasnevin cemetery when she died in 1953. By this time, Ireland's great patriot had become the stuff of legend through the magic of Yeats's poetry:

How many loved your movements of glad
    grace,
And loved your beauty with love false or
    true;
But one man loved the pilgrim soul in you,
And loved the sorrows of your changing face.
("When You Are Old")

See also Despard, Charlotte; Markievicz, Constance de.

References and Further Reading

Cardozo, Nancy. 1979. *Maud Gonne: Lucky Eyes and a High Heart.* London: Gollancz.

Coxhead, Elizabeth. 1965. *Daughters of Erin: Five Women of the Irish Renaissance.* London: Secker & Warburg.

Levenson, Sam. 1977. *Maud Gonne.* London: Cassell.

MacBride, Maud Gonne. 1995 [1938]. *The Autobiography of Maud Gonne: A Servant of the Queen.* Reprint, Chicago: University of Chicago Press.

Ó Céirín, Kit, and Cyril Ó Céirín, eds. 1996. *Women of Ireland: A Biographic Dictionary.* Kinvara, County Galway: Tír Eolas.

Ward, Margaret. 1990. *Maud Gonne: Ireland's Joan of Arc.* London: Pandora.

Gore-Booth, Eva
(1870–1926)
Ireland

Eva Gore-Booth was the antithesis of her flamboyant sister, the Irish nationalist Constance de Markievicz, with whom she shared a passionate sense of social justice. Despite the admiration of men such as the poet W. B. Yeats, who immortalized her gazellelike beauty in his poetry, Eva Gore-Booth eschewed the life of a wealthy socialite and exacerbated her poor health by choosing to live in the industrial heartland of the north of England, where she supported trade unions for working women.

Born into Anglo-Irish gentry in Lissadell, County Sligo, Gore-Booth and her sister were interested in women's rights from an early age, when she and Constance had both helped their philanthropic father, Sir Henry Gore-Booth, distribute food and clothing to the poor on their estate. In 1897 she exchanged the lyrically beautiful Irish setting of her childhood (although she would continue to celebrate it in her poetry) for a poky terraced house in a working-class slum district of Manchester, which she shared with the English socialist Esther Roper.

The move was inspired by Gore-Booth's meeting in Italy the previous year with Roper, who was secretary of the Manchester National Society for Women's Suffrage (later known as the North of England Society for Women's Suffrage) and who was also active in the campaign for the unionization of working women. Suffering from weak lungs, Gore-Booth had traveled to Europe for a much-needed respite from the English climate. She and Roper (who was one of the first women to graduate from Manchester University) became a devoted couple, albeit celibate—they had separate bedrooms, and were looked upon as something of an oddity by the suffrage movement, which they both espoused with their work for the North of England Society for Women's Suffrage. Their joint work for women's causes over the next eight years had a considerable influence in Lancashire, where they proselytized among female textile workers in the cotton mills. As keen supporters of the unionization of women and protective legislation to defend them against exploitation, they founded a trade union for barmaids (in 1908) and supported the employment rights of London flower sellers and other female workers such as circus performers and pit-brow workers (women who worked at the "heads" of mines, not underground). The 1907 campaign in support of barmaids not being required to work after 8 P.M. had its detractors, and Gore-Booth lost some support from temperance activists as a result.

Gore-Booth also worked for women's education through the Manchester Education Committee, arguing against the exclusion of girls from colleges. She wrote for feminist journals such as *Woman's Labour News* and *The Common Cause,* the journal of the National Union of Women's Suffrage Societies (NUWSS), and, as a natural speaker and organizer, lent her support to many ventures. She took to running poetry circles at the university and classes on Shakespeare for working women in the evenings, and in 1900 she became joint secretary of the Manchester and Salford Women's Trade Union Council. In 1901 Gore-Booth organized a petition in support of the franchise that was signed by 67,000 textile workers and also campaigned for the local Labour candidate in a by-election in 1902.

For a while Gore-Booth collaborated with Christabel Pankhurst (with whom Roper was friendly and whom she had encouraged to study law), but she remained a loyal supporter of the more moderate views on suffrage of Millicent Fawcett's NUWSS. Pankhurst worked with Gore-Booth and Roper in the North of England Society for Women's Suffrage and the Women's Trade Union Council (WTUC), but by 1904 Gore-Booth had become alienated from the militancy of the Pankhursts and their new suffrage organization, the Women's Social and Political Union (WSPU), as well as by Christabel's interference in the workings of the WTUC. Seeking to distance herself from Pankhurst's domination, Gore-Booth resigned from the WTUC in 1904 to help establish the Manchester and Salford Women's Trade and Labour Council.

Inevitably, Gore-Booth's fragile health collapsed (she had been diagnosed with tuberculosis in 1895). In her later hagiography of women in the suffrage movement, Sylvia Pankhurst depicted Gore-Booth as a frail and beautiful martyr of consumption. In 1913 she and Roper moved to Hampstead in London, away from the harsher environment of the industrial north. In later life Gore-Booth became a Theosophist and antivivisectionist, and after the execution of the Irish patriot Roger Casement in 1916, she supported the League for the Abolition of Capital Punishment. In 1916, together with other feminists, she founded an esoteric journal named *Urania,* which propagated a rejection of the animality of sex and the promotion of the spiritual life. During World War I, in addition to continuing to support the suffrage campaign, Gore-Booth and Roper joined the Women's Peace Crusade and the No-Conscription Fellowship, helping victims of the war, including the families of English conscientious objectors and German nationals who had been interned. In the process, Gore-Booth frequently donated funds from her own private income.

Throughout her life, Gore-Booth continued to write poetry, publishing collections such as *The One and Many* in 1904 and two more in 1905 and 1912; Roper wrote a biographical introduction to *The Poems of Eva Gore-Booth,* published posthumously in 1929. Gore-Booth's poetry reflected not only her innate social awareness but also her romantic utopian concepts and preoccupation with the mystical qualities of the Irish landscape and Celtic tradition. A gentle beauty who was a fervent pacifist and used her position of privilege to fulfill her own sense of a moral duty to society, Gore-Booth died prematurely of cancer of the colon at the age of fifty-six, leaving everything to her companion, Roper.

See also Fawcett, Millicent Garrett; Markievicz, Constance de; Pankhurst, Christabel.

References and Further Reading

Crawford, Elizabeth. 1999. *The Women's Suffrage Movement, 1866–1928: A Reference Guide.* London: University College of London Press.

Lewis, Gifford. 1988. *Eva Gore-Booth and Esther Roper.* London: Pandora.

Liddington, Jill, and J. Norris. 2000 [1978]. *One Hand Tied behind Us.* Rev. ed. London: Virago.

Ó Céirin, Kit, and Cyril Ó Céirin, eds. 1996. *Women of Ireland: A Biographical Dictionary.* Kinvara, County Galway: Tír Eolas.

Gouges, Olympe de (Marie-Olympe Gouze)
(1755–1793)
France

The feminist and pamphleteer Olympe de Gouges is probably the best known of a number of radical women campaigning for equal rights with men during the French Revolution (1789–1794). As one of the first martyrs of French feminism, her assertion that "woman has the right to mount the scaffold; she has equally the right to mount the rostrum" soon became all too terrifyingly real when she herself fell victim to the guillotine in 1793 (Applewhite et al. 1979, 91).

Born illegitimate in Montauban, Marie Gouze was convinced that her real father had been a nobleman-poet, Jean-Jacques Lefranc, the marquis de Pompignan, not the humble butcher who had brought her up. Later she changed her name to give herself an air of social status. She married young to French officer Louis Aubury and had two children. But after two years, de Gouges ran away to Paris and, while working as an actress and playwright, became a professional courtesan, thus acquiring her longed-for social status via the bedroom. She lived a life of sybaritic abandon until she reached her forties, when with her looks fading, she reinvented herself, embracing the revolution and the cause of social justice. Previously, de Gouges had written plays on women's issues, such as *A Generous Man* (1786), about women being denied political power, and *The Convent* (1792), about women forced into nunneries, but the Théâtre Français had refused to stage all except one, the abolitionist play *Black Slavery* (1792).

During the French Revolution, de Gouges began producing hastily put together and misspelled political tracts and pamphlets. In them, she outlined her own ideas on constitutional monarchy, reform of the tax system, and social welfare, including the introduction of state-run workshops to help the unemployed, a tax on luxuries to fund better maternity care, and homes for orphans and the elderly. But little notice was taken of her work, a fact that she bemoaned as demonstrating the indifference to women's ideas.

De Gouges's central work, the *Declaration of the Rights of Woman and Citizen,* which was written in 1791 as a response to the seventeen articles of the *Declaration of the Rights of Man* adopted by the French National Assembly in 1789, was also ignored in its day. Written only a year before Mary Wollstonecraft's *Vindication of the Rights of Woman* (1792), it is a more formal exposition of women's rights, calling for universal suffrage and equality for women as citizens alongside men in taxation, property ownership within marriage, education, and employment. Rejecting conventional marriage and demanding the abolition of the dowry system, de Gouges argued for a "social contract" between men and women to replace it and was also one of the first women in France to argue for the rights of illegitimate children by suggesting the introduction of a law to establish their paternity.

As the revolution progressed, de Gouges called for women to be allowed to take part in political life, going so far as to argue that they should be allowed to fight for their country. She also took it upon herself to plead for the life of the deposed king, Louis XVI, who she felt had fallen prey to corrupt courtiers and deserved only to be exiled. Defiant, she took the Girondist side in condemnation of the excesses of Maximilien de Robespierre and Jean-Paul Marat and called for the re-unification of France's warring factions. She demanded guarantees of the rights of women under a new Constitution that had been promised by the Jacobins but had not materialized. A reform of the divorce law in September 1792 was welcomed by de Gouges, but she cared more passionately, by that point, about seeing her country reunited behind a monarchy and a federal government. She was arrested soon after and taken to the prison of L'Abbaye, from where she continued vehemently to denounce the Jacobins.

By now de Gouges was looked upon by the revolutionary National Convention as a self-destructive, eccentric troublemaker. Held in prison for three months, she had refused the chance of escape while ill in the infirmary. On 2 November, she conducted her own defense with theatrical flair when she was put on trial for sedition in her appeal against Louis XVI's execu-

tion and for slandering the Jacobin leaders. In an attempt to evade a death sentence, she claimed she was pregnant, but examination by doctors refuted this assertion. She was executed the following day.

See also Wollstonecraft, Mary.

References and References and Further Reading

Applewhite, H. B., M. D. Johnson, and D. G. Levy, 1979. *Women in Revolutionary Paris.* Urbana: University of Illinois Press.

Kelly, Linda. 1987. *Women of the French Revolution.* London: Hamish Hamilton.

Maza, Sara. 2001. "French Feminists and the Rights of 'Man.' Olympe de Gouges's Declarations." In Ronald Schechter, ed., *The French Revolution: The Essential Readings.* Oxford: Blackwell.

Rowbotham, Sheila. 1992. *Women in Movement: Feminism and Social Action.* New York: Routledge.

Spender, Dale. 1982. *Women of Ideas, and What Men Have Done to Them.* London: Routledge and Kegan Paul.

Grand, Sarah (Frances McFall)
(1854–1943)
United Kingdom

The now considerable feminist interest in the Victorian novelist Sarah Grand, doyenne of the "new woman" novel of the 1890s (a term that critics long believed she had coined in 1894), rests primarily on her two most controversial novels in which she confronted the topical and vexed issues of the constraints of marriage, women's right to an independent life, and the moral reform of the male sex. In what became an all-too-familiar pattern affecting many women writers of the Victorian period, Grand went from considerable fame and notoriety in her day through a long period of literary obscurity, until she was rediscovered by feminists in the 1970s. Her works were, for their time, a bold and uncompromising attempt to confront Victorian society with its hypocrisy and tolerance of the sexual double standard, an issue that had long been under attack by women in the social purity movement, led by Josephine Butler. But where Butler spent years campaigning doggedly for legal changes, Grand used the pen to address a potentially huge reading audience on the same uncomfortable issues—venereal disease, the male medical establishment's oppression of women, adultery, and sexual violence. In so doing, she also presented powerful arguments in support of a woman's right to an independent, self-supporting lifestyle.

The daughter of an English naval officer, Grand was born in Donaghdee, in County Down, Northern Ireland. The family returned to England in 1861 after her father died, and Grand was sent to live with relatives in Yorkshire, where she endured several miserable years in boarding schools. She married in haste in 1870, at the age of sixteen, to escape from her stultifying milieu. Her husband, Major David McFall, was an army surgeon; he was twenty-three years older and a widower with two children. The McFalls spent five years traveling in the Far East, returning to settle in Norfolk and later Lancashire. During the 1880s, Grand began writing her first novel, *Ideala: A Study for Life,* published at her own expense in 1888 and reissued anonymously in 1889. By this time, she had become estranged from her husband, and, deeply averse to his drinking and smoking. Stifled by his controlling nature, Grand left him in about 1890. With the royalties from her book, she earned enough to settle in her own flat in London in 1891, where in 1893 she adopted the literary pseudonym Sarah Grand to emphasize her newfound sense of independence and self-worth.

Grand became a familiar figure in feminist and literary circles. Her 1891 novel, *A Domestic Experiment,* approached the subject of adultery, but it was her fourth and best-known novel, *The Heavenly Twins* (1893), the second in a trilogy with *Ideala,* that attracted wide public attention. The work contained a frank discussion of the sexual irresponsibility of men and their infection of unwitting women with venereal disease and reflected the inspiration of Butler's campaigning, which Grand had first come to admire in the 1870s. Centering on a "new woman"—Evadne—and her adoption of progressive views, the novel describes her refusal to sleep with her husband, after discovering he has an immoral past, and her subsequent mental collapse. Much was made at the time of one of the novel's subplots, in which Evadne's friend Edith dies after giving birth to a syphilitic baby.

Present-day feminist interest in *The Heavenly Twins* has focused on it as a groundbreaking study in female psychology: in a further subplot about the other "heavenly twin" Angelica, Grand

offers a subversive depiction of cross-dressing and repressed lesbian desire (which 1890s readers completely failed to recognize). In its unshrinking discussion of syphilis, the novel inevitably attracted howls of public disgust and considerable debate and moral consternation. But, naturally enough, as a controversial book it also sold extremely well, running through 20,000 copies and six reprints in its first year. Such huge sales helped disseminate a wider public awareness on the issue of sexuality and other aspects of the "new woman" debate, and Grand was much in demand thereafter as a public speaker on social purity and women's issues.

Grand was also a prolific writer of journal articles and in 1894 published her now famous "new woman" article in the *North American Review,* "The New Aspect of the Woman Question." For a long time, this article was considered to be the source of the term, a fact that Grand herself claimed, although research now suggests that the concept, if the not the term itself, had had some currency in English literature since the 1860s. It rapidly became the buzzword of the times, a catchall conveniently fallen back on by the press for the indiscriminate labeling of all women who sought to be independent and sexually liberated; it also attached itself to those women in the suffrage movement who were now adopting a far more radical identity. Whether the term was new or Grand's invention, in many ways it merely reflected the growing sensitivities to the long oppression of their sex of a succession of English women writers, reaching back to the Brontës in the late 1840s and 1850s. Much as the term *permissive society* was hotly debated in 1960s, followed by the bandying about of the word *feminist* from the 1970s, so the term *new woman* would, in the Victorian era, encapsulate many issues and become the focus for contentious debates over women's rights. Equally, just as the rise of the feminist movement of the 1970s provoked a moral backlash, so too did the new woman writing in the 1890s. Reaction manifested itself not just among men but also among other women, notably in the journalism of that archreactionary, Eliza Lynn Linton, who would launch numerous attacks on Grand's writing.

In 1897 Grand published *The Beth Book: Being a Study from the Life of Elizabeth Caldwell Machure, a Woman of Genius,* the final part of what would become her seminal "new woman" trilogy. It depicts the liberation and politicization of a woman who turns her back on a domineering husband, seeking an independent life outside marriage as a creative artist. Strongly autobiographical in tone, much of this rites-of-passage novel is taken up with describing the heroine Beth's early life in parochial Northern Ireland. It also charts her subsequent unhappy marriage, with much of her husband Dan's character based on the unattractive side of Grand's own husband's personality. It also served as a vehicle for Grand's own strong feelings on the sexual abuse of women; as Ann Heilmann points out (2000, 93–95), Grand draws strong allegorical links between the vivisectionist activities of Beth's husband, a lock hospital doctor (prostitutes with venereal disease were held in lock hospitals by force), and Beth's own sexual degradation at his hands.

Throughout the 1890s, Grand was a staunch advocate of women's suffrage and a member of the Pioneer Club, an organization for professional women that held regular social and political debates on subjects such as coeducation, vivisection, and women's suffrage. She settled in Tunbridge Wells in 1898, where she became president of the local branch of the National Union of Women's Suffrage Societies. She was also a Member of the Women Writers Suffrage League and lectured continuously, both in Britain and in the United States, on various women's issues. As a committee member of the Rational Dress Society during the 1890s, Grand was also a passionate believer in women's physical liberation from conventional modes of dress and opposed the constraining effects of tight corsets; she was a leading advocate of the woman's bicycle, proclaiming cycling's recuperative effects for those occupied in taxing intellectual pursuits.

After publishing the first two novels in another planned trilogy, *Adam's Orchard* (1912) and *The Winged Victory* (1916), followed by the short story collection *Variety* in 1922, Grand disappeared from the literary and feminist scene on the eve of women's enfranchisement (1918). She moved to Bath in 1920, and her life now took on an oddly matronly and conventional tone in contrast with her early career. The inherently conservative elements in her character came to the fore, and Grand was elevated as a pillar of the local community, becoming mayoress of Bath (to fulfill civic duties in tandem with its widowed mayor)

in 1923 and 1925–1929, seeming content to play the role of "provincial Lady Bountiful opening the chrysanthemum show" (Showalter 1999, 210). Her later literary efforts failed to capture an audience, and by the time of her death in 1943, Grand's powerful feminist rhetoric had become unfashionable and the bulk of her writing, aside from *The Heavenly Twins,* was long forgotten.

See also Butler, Josephine; Linton, Eliza Lynn.

References and Further Reading
Bland, Lucy. 1996. *Banishing the Beast: English Feminism and Sexual Morality, 1885–1914.* Harmondsworth: Penguin.
Cunningham, Gail. 1978. *The New Woman and the Victorian Novel.* London: Macmillan.
Grand, Sarah. 2000. *Sex, Social Purity and Sarah Grand.* London: Routledge.
Harman, Barbara Leah, and Susan Meyer, eds. 1996. *The New Nineteenth Century: Feminist Readings of Underread Victorian Fiction.* New York: Garland.
Heilmann, Ann. 2000. *New Woman Fiction: Women Writing First-Wave Feminism.* Basingstoke: Macmillan.
———. Forthcoming. *New Woman Strategies: Sarah Grand, Olive Schreiner, Mona Caird.* Manchester: Manchester University Press.
Kersley, Gillian. 1983. *Darling Madame: Sarah Grand and Devoted Friend.* London: Virago.
Ledger, Sally. 1997. *The New Woman: Fiction and Feminism at the Fin de Siècle.* Manchester: Manchester University Press.
Mangum, Teresa. 1998. *Married, Middle-Brow, and Militant: Sarah Grand and the New Woman Novel.* Ann Arbor: University of Michigan Press.
Shanley, Mary Lyndon. 1989. *Feminism, Marriage, and the Law in Victorian England, 1850–1895.* Princeton: Princeton University Press.
Showalter, Elaine. 1999 [1977]. *A Literature of Their Own: British Women Novelists from Bronte to Lessing.* Reprint, London: Virago.
Willis, Chris, and Angelique Richardson, eds. 1999. *The New Woman in Fiction and in Fact.* Basingstoke: Macmillan.

Greer, Germaine
(1939–)
Australia/United Kingdom

The feminist writer, critic, and journalist Germaine Greer confronted male chauvinism head-on in her 1970 book *The Female Eunuch,* one of the works that inaugurated the second wave of the women's movement in Britain. She also challenged women's perception of the male sex by controversially alleging, in this and her other writings, that women were unaware of the real levels of male antagonism toward them. A charismatic woman of formidable intellect, ferocious combative spirit, and provocative language, she became one of the key polemicists of the women's movement. In later years, she was denounced by feminists for backpedaling on the original message of *The Female Eunuch.*

Greer was born in the Melbourne suburb of Elwood and educated at the Star of the Sea Convent School at Gardenvale. Although she soon rebelled against this narrow, restrictive world, she would remain grateful that the nuns recognized her intellectual gifts and talent for languages and encouraged her academic aspirations. The absence of a cultural life at home was stultifying, and she left for good when she was seventeen, when she won a scholarship to study at the University of Melbourne. She obtained a B.A. in English and French literature in 1959 and an M.A. in English in 1961 at the University of Sydney. After teaching in a girls' school and tutoring at Sydney University, Greer was awarded a Commonwealth scholarship in 1964 to study for a Ph.D. in English literature at Newnham College, Cambridge. She was awarded her degree in 1967 for a dissertation on the early comedies of Shakespeare.

A five-year lectureship (1967–1972) in English at the University of Warwick followed, during which Greer married in 1968 and separated only three weeks later. By that time she was becoming known for her TV appearances and her journalism, writing for publications as dramatically different as the BBC's the *Listener,* the left-wing journal the *Spectator,* and underground publications such as *Oz* and *Suck*—the latter featuring a notoriously "gynecological" self-portrait that provoked huge controversy.

While still lecturing at Warwick, Greer began working on the book that, overnight, would bring her both fame and infamy—*The Female Eunuch.* Probably the most talked-about book of the second half of the twentieth century, it presented an analysis of the ways in which women have been misrepresented and stereotyped sexually and intellectually—in the media, literature, and society—and how traditional patriarchal practices have conspired to effectively castrate women and stereotype them as the "eternal feminine" by making them meek and submissive without drive or ambition. She was, she declared, "sick of the powder room. I'm sick of belying my own intelligence, my own reason. I'm sick of pretending some fatuous male's self-important pronouncements are objects of my undivided attention. I am a woman, not a castrate" (Greer 1970, 61–62).

Marriage, Greer averred, was nothing but legalized slavery and child rearing a burden. Neither of these arguments was in itself innovative; in fact they reached back through two centuries of feminist writing that had begun with women such as Mary Wollstonecraft. Greer's message to women was simple: reject passivity and the life of the castrate and demand sexual and personal liberation. She believed that women could not effectively reclaim their identity without learning to love and respect themselves and abandon their neediness, particularly their emotional dependency on their male partners. *The Female Eunuch* was translated into twelve languages and sold over a million copies. But although it was successful in the United States, many American feminists took offense at Greer's criticism of their own movement and the National Women's Political Caucus, established by Gloria Steinem, Betty Friedan, and others. They also objected to her contention that the campaign for an Equal Rights Amendment in the United States was an act of tokenism on the part of middle-class feminists.

The bawdy language, explicit sexual descriptions, and forthright style of *The Female Eunuch* shocked many and laid down the verbal style for which Greer would be both admired and vilified over the years. In itself, it provoked fierce arguments among couples who read it. Greer rapidly became a leading celebrity and feminist pundit in the United Kingdom, who in her articles in *Private Eye, Spare Rib, Esquire,* and the *Sunday Times* courted controversy and brought with her an element of healthy sexuality and irreverence that enlivened a sometimes overly serious and humorless women's movement. At all times she enjoyed the fray, conducting a much publicized and highly charged public debate on women's liberation with Norman Mailer at New York's Town Hall during her 1971 U.S. tour.

The huge royalties from *The Female Eunuch* allowed Greer to buy properties in London and Tuscany. In 1979 she published *The Obstacle Race: The Fortunes of Women Painters and Their Works.* In this pioneering book, the result of eight years of research in European art galleries, she sought to uncover the buried histories of women artists but was finally forced to concede that there was no single, great woman artist of the caliber of Leonardo da Vinci, a fact she put down to women's age-old social and cultural oppression.

In 1979 Greer was invited to Oklahoma to set up the Tulsa Center for the Study of Women's Literature at the University of Tulsa, remaining until 1983 as professor of modern letters. After returning to Britain, she returned to sexual politics with her 1984 book, *Sex and Destiny: The Politics of Human Fertility,* which was in part the product of her observations of family structures and human fertility during her travels since the 1970s in India, Africa, and the Third World. Seen as regressive and antifeminist by many of Greer's erstwhile admirers, the book detailed her loss of faith in the sexual revolution and warned of its destructive elements. Greer felt that sex had come to so dominate life and culture that people indulged in it without really wanting it. By seeking mere sexual gratification above all else, she argued, people had ceased to value the family and children. She advocated that women should have no sex at all rather than unsatisfactory sex; what was important, in her view, was that women should enjoy *better,* rather than unlimited, sex. Greer also allowed that motherhood was important to some women, and as an admirer of the archetypal Third World earth mother, she advocated a return to the large, extended family. She criticized Western pressures on Third World women to control the size of their families, favoring natural methods of contraception over the imposition on such cultures of artificial devices like the IUD and the cap. Her critics, however, would question to what extent these amended views were colored by her own embittered position on sexual relations.

During the 1980s, Greer produced a variety of writing: *Shakespeare,* a volume of literary criticism (1986); *The Madwoman's Underclothes: Essays and Occasional Writings* (1987); her collected journalism (1968–1985); and in 1989, her acclaimed *Daddy: We Hardly Knew You.* In this obsessive genealogical quest for the truth about her lost father, she uncovered the painful truth that he had been a compulsive liar and not the man she had thought he was. An important book on women's coming to terms with middle age, *The Change: Women, Aging and the Menopause*

(1991), went some way toward approaching the subject positively, viewing menopause as a liberating experience, with Greer arguing that sex was not a necessity for women in middle age.

A talented self-publicist, Greer has remained in the public eye as a pundit on feminist issues while others of her second-wave contemporaries have since disappeared from view. She became the highest-paid feminist writer, when she was offered a rumored £500,000 advance to write a reassessment of *The Female Eunuch,* which appeared in 1999 as *The Whole Woman.* It was a book she had vowed would never happen, but in the event she came out fighting with the catch phrase "It's time to get angry again." Her anger was directed at the failures of the modern-day feminist movement, with Greer berating Western "lifestyle feminists" for misconstruing the real point about women's liberation. In becoming obsessed with sexual equality and role reversal at the expense of true sexual liberation, they were, she argued, still acceding to males' rules in the workplace and in society by attempting to gain admittance to the masculine elite. Through their preoccupations with money, fashion, and the fruitless quest for beauty, contemporary women were perpetuating their own sense of insecurity. More important, Greer believed that in their self-obsession they had failed to offer feminine solidarity to underprivileged women in the Third World.

The book received considerable criticism for its hectoring—some said "bullying"—tone. Some feminists perceived an increasing element of misogyny in its content, despite the fact that Greer continued to lambaste men for their brutality, their lack of emotional commitment, and their sexual selfishness. Others saw Greer's entire argument as being overstated and often contradictory, containing dangerous generalizations and exaggerations.

Greer is now a part-time professor at Warwick University, dividing her time there between the English Department and the Centres for British and Cultural Studies and for Women and Gender. She continues to appear regularly on review and discussion programs, such as *Newsnight's Late Review,* and has established her own imprint, Stump Cross Books, to publish books by women, particularly poetry. She admits to the private pleasures of gardening and cooking at her farmhouse in Essex, where she lives alone, surrounded by dogs, cats, and geese. Her greatest personal sadness was the abortions she had when young, which damaged her fallopian tubes and prevented her from having children later. In 2000 she was attacked and tied up in her home by an obsessed female admirer but refused to be fazed, once again asserting the self-reliance she had preached since the days of *The Female Eunuch:* "the self-reliant woman is always loved, . . . she cannot be lonely as long as there are people in the world who need her joy and strength" (Greer 1970, 244). In her seventh decade, she refuses to mellow and remains as unrepentant, sharp-witted, and rebellious as ever. She will no doubt continue to exasperate, enrage, and entertain with her passionately felt and challenging polemics, which have made many people seriously reappraise their own sexual attitudes.

See also Friedan, Betty; Steinem, Gloria; Wollstonecraft, Mary.

References and Further Reading

Current Biography. 1988. New York: W. W. Norton.

Greer, Germaine. 1970. *The Female Eunuch.* London: MacGibbon and Kee.

———. 1986. *The Madwoman's Underclothes: Essays and Occasional Writings 1968–85.* London: Pan Books.

———. 1989. *Daddy We Hardly Knew You.* London: Hamish Hamilton.

———. 1997. "Serenity and Power." In Marilyn Pearsall, ed., *The Other Within Us: Feminist Explorations of Women and Aging.* Boulder, CO: Westview Press.

Mitchell, Susan. 1997. *Icons, Saints & Divas: Intimate Conversations with Women Who Changed the World.* London: Pandora.

Plante, David. 1983. *Difficult Women: A Memoir of Three.* London: Victor Gollancz.

Todd, Janet. 1983. *Women Writers Talking.* New York: Holmes & Meier.

Wallace, Christine. 1999. *Germaine Greer: Untamed Shrew.* London: Richard Cohen Books.

Grierson, Cecilia
(1859–1934)
Argentina

The first woman doctor to qualify for and obtain a license in Latin America, in 1889, and a founding member of the Argentine National Council of Women, Grierson was driven by a commitment to social welfare, health care, and the liberation of women from sexual exploitation. Part of her broader mission was to see women given a greater role in the betterment of society.

Grierson came from Scottish immigrant stock. Her parents farmed on a ranch at Entre Ríos, where her father was later killed during a political revolt. The Grierson women contributed significantly to the local community in Entre Ríos; some worked as midwives and sought to raise awareness among local women about standards of hygiene in childbirth and the care of their children. Others taught, as did Grierson herself, who helped her mother from the age of thirteen in the local primary school that she had established. When she was fifteen, Grierson went to Buenos Aires to attend the secondary school established by Emma Nicolay de Caprile, graduating in 1878. It was the crusading spirit of her female relatives that propelled Grierson to take up the challenge of studying medicine at the University of Buenos Aires, which she did as the only woman—it is said she had to dress as a man in order to evade notice—and in the face of considerable public disapproval.

The depths of Grierson's dedication to serving women's health were tested by the long battle she had to fight to be allowed to practice as a doctor; she was finally granted a license to practice in 1889, when she was thirty-nine. She began her career by serving as a medical intern at Rivadavia Hospital, a women's hospital in Buenos Aires funded and run by the Society for the Well-being of the Capital. With time, she developed a considerable reputation for herself as a doctor, teacher of obstetrics (at the obstetrical school of the University of Buenos Aires from 1905) and physical therapy (she established a course for undergraduates in 1903), founder of the National Obstetrical Association, and supporter of women's education. Eventually, she founded a professional training school for nurses, which was named after her, and the first association of obstetricians and obstetrical nurses. She traveled to Europe to study medical techniques, particularly in gynecology, and also became an expert in the treatment of blindness and hearing problems. Upon her return to Argentina she also pioneered work in the education of children with mental disabilities and founded an academy for its study.

Grierson had committed herself to women's rights and the campaign for suffrage from its inception. In 1899 she attended the second congress of the International Council of Women in London, as a result of which, on her return to Argentina, she set out in 1900 to establish an affiliated women's organization there, with its prime objective being social and moral reform as a prelude to the campaign for suffrage. After much canvassing, and with the support of a leading charity, the Beneficent Society, Grierson succeeded in persuading thirty-three Argentine charitable and other organizations to send delegates to an inaugural National Council of Women (NCW), held in September 1900, at which she was elected one of five vice presidents. In 1901 this group was affiliated with the International Council of Women. However, the elitist makeup of the NCW's membership, many of whom were foreign expatriates living in Argentina, left it open to criticism for not being sufficiently representative of Argentine women.

By the early 1900s it had become clear that mere isolated philanthropic acts by an enlightened few were insufficient to meet the need for widespread education programs in Argentina in preparation for women's suffrage. A concerted campaign in government and in the press was needed to arouse women's interest in the broad objective of the elevation of women's status through greater access to education. The NCW thus set about initiating the construction of libraries at Rosario and La Plata, where women could improve their literacy levels and undertake courses in child care, health care, and first aid.

Because reform of the civil code was, Grierson believed, a prerequisite for women's suffrage, in 1902 she began studying it to prepare a report on women's civil rights in Argentina (her report was delivered in 1906). In 1902, together with other female professionals such as Elvira Rawson de Dellepiane and Sara de Justo, Grierson set up the Argentine Association of University Women (AAUW), which aimed to dilute the elitism of the hardcore membership of the NCW by attracting predominantly middle-class, educated women members. It administered its own free social welfare programs from its headquarters and planned a training school to teach poor women domestic and other technical skills so that they could support themselves and not succumb to prostitution. Grierson's work in the NCW was hampered, however, by exactly the problems she had set out to circumvent in the AAUW, in the form of a powerful clash of personalities between herself

and the organization's president, Alvina Van Praet de Sala. The conflict became symptomatic of the difference in approach and objectives between well-connected, upper-class philanthropists of the old Argentine oligarchy, such as de Sala, and the new grassroots activists from the middle and working classes, such as Grierson, who felt that individual egos should not play a part in campaigning. Despite these difficulties and the limited outlook of de Sala and her kind, the NCW by 1905 had brought together 100 societies and 300 working members.

Grierson continued to address a wide range of social issues: in 1905 she drafted a government proposal to grant maternity leave and provide benefits and welfare services for pregnant women (rejected by congress in 1906). She also endorsed the establishment of the Argentine Association of Free Thought, which set out to achieve women's equal civil status with men. In 1910 she was made honorary president of the Pan-American Women's League. That same year, Grierson helped plan and acted as president of the First International Women's Congress in Argentina, held in Buenos Aires, in which more than 200 women delegates from Argentina, Chile, Paraguay, Peru, and Uruguay took part, as well as some delegates from beyond South America. Discussions at the congress covered a wide spectrum of issues relating to women's legal rights, the conditions in which women worked, and their health care. By that time, however, the ongoing conflict with the elite, conservative element in the NCW had become even more pronounced, as they continued to resist Grierson's exhortations to initiate and take part in more radical and politicized programs of social reform. When a conference of the NCW called that year to discuss social issues degenerated into what Grierson saw as an occasion for ineffectual socializing rather than vigorous campaigning, Grierson resigned, and the AAUW also withdrew from the NCW. In what became a malicious campaign of tit for tat, de Sala responded by sacking Grierson from the vice presidency and withdrawing funding for her School for Domestic and Technical Training, which she had set up in 1906. Grierson in turn published a scathing pamphlet, "The Decadence of the Argentine National Council of Women," in which she criticized de Sala and her supporters for their lack of commitment to important social issues.

By the close of her colorful and vigorous career, Grierson had made health care and child care issues of political and public importance in Argentina, not merely matters dependent on acts of philanthropy. She had greatly advanced medical science, writing numerous learned papers and encouraging other women to take up medicine, and also retained a keen interest in the fine arts, donating land at Los Cocos, Córdoba, Argentina, for the establishment of a residence for convalescent artists.

See also Rawson de Dellepiane, Elvira.

References and Further Reading

Carlson, Narifran. 1988. *Feminismo! The Woman's Movement in Argentina from Its Beginnings to Eva Perón.* Chicago: Academy Chicago Publications.

Lavrin, Asunción. 1995. *Women, Feminism, and Social Change in Argentina, Chile, and Uruguay 1890–1940.* Lincoln: University of Nebraska Press.

Grimké, Angelina Emily and Sarah Moore
(1805–1879) and (1792–1873)
United States

The Grimké sisters of South Carolina bravely broke new ground in the history of the U.S. abolitionist movement by being the first southern women, and the daughters of a plantation owner to boot, to publicly speak out against slavery. During the course of their highly unorthodox public careers, they caused controversy with their outspoken views on women's emancipation and the direct links they drew between the bondage of the black slave and the domestic enslavement of women. Although their service to the cause of women's emancipation remained essentially an intellectual and moral one, closely bound up with their religious faith and their belief in women as the moral superiors of men, the propagandist writings of the Grimkés would provide the first and most enduring moral arguments against slavery contributed by American women in the early nineteenth century.

Born into a family of wealthy Episcopalian southern slave owners, the Grimkés grew up in a family of fourteen children on their father's plantation in Charleston, South Carolina, and were educated at home by private tutors. Such was Sarah's hatred for slavery, which she had witnessed firsthand, coupled with her desire for a wider education and independence, that she rejected her Episcopalian faith and joined the Society of Friends. She left home in 1821 and settled in Philadelphia. She would spend the rest of her life regretting that she had never had an opportunity to study subjects as challenging as Greek, Latin, philosophy, and most particularly her father's profession, law, which she felt might have enabled her to be more useful to society. She had once entertained hopes of becoming a minister and remained deeply committed to women's liberation through education. Throughout her life Sarah, who was given to bouts of introspection, would lament the shortcomings of her own education and what she termed the "terrible eclipse of those intellectual powers which in early life seemed prophetic of usefulness and happiness" (Trager 1994, 260).

Sarah's younger sister Angelina was even more haunted by the abuses of slavery than her sister; of the two, she would always be the more proactive and outspoken. She joined Sarah in Philadelphia in 1829 and, having earlier converted to Presbyterianism, became a Quaker. Together the sisters began undertaking charity work and developing a growing commitment to the abolitionist movement. In 1833 they attended the Female Anti-Slavery Society's first meeting, held in Philadelphia. Two years later, Angelina was the first to enter the public debate on slavery when she wrote a letter of support to William Lloyd Garrison's abolitionist journal, *The Liberator.* She followed this letter in September 1836 with *An Appeal to the Christian Women of the South,* which, after publication in the *Anti-Slavery Examiner,* aroused considerable controversy in its plea to southern women slaveowners to liberate their slaves. (In 1838 both sisters would free the slaves who were their share of their late father's estate.) Such was the outrage in the South to this publication that Angelina was threatened with imprisonment if ever she returned home.

Angelina was invited soon after to lecture to female audiences of the American Anti-Slavery Society. She and Sarah settled in New York, where Sarah decided to add her own voice to the abolitionist cause after being prevented from speaking on slavery at a Quaker meeting. *An Epistle to the Clergy of the Southern States* (1836) was an attempt to counter the official religious arguments in support of slavery. Both Angelina

Angelina Emily Grimké (Library of Congress)

Sarah Moore Grimké (Library of Congress)

and Sarah undertook a short period of training as official abolitionist speakers before embarking early in 1837 on a twenty-three-week lecture tour around New England, at first addressing small, female-only groups. Later they spoke to mixed audiences of 300 or so in public lecture halls and churches and audiences of 1,000 at an open-air meeting in Lynn and 1,500 in Lowell, Massachusetts. Wherever they went, they inspired more people to enlist in the movement and set up societies in support of the abolitionist cause.

The sisters rapidly achieved notoriety for their public appearances and were quickly criticized in the press and in a pastoral letter by the Massachusetts Council of Congregationalist Ministers in July 1837, which railed against "females who itinerate" (Bacon 1986, 105). Even their own friends criticized the Grimkés for what they deemed unladylike behavior. The entry of the sisters into public life provoked criticism, too, from other female reformers such as the educator Catharine Beecher, a conservative who opposed women's public campaigning, and with whom they debated the issue of women's appropriate spheres of activity over many years. Angelina published a defense of her work for aboli-

tionism in *Letters to Catharine Beecher* in 1838, and Beecher's response was published in 1845, in the form of "An Essay on Slavery and Abolitionism with Reference to the Duty of American Women to Their Country," which she addressed to Angelina.

However, the criticism with which the Grimkés were assaulted on all sides served only to reinforce their belief that the fight for women's freedom of speech in support of abolition was inextricably tied to the winning of their wider civil rights as men's equals in the public and political sphere. But their comparison of slavery with the oppression of women caused profound divisions in the abolitionist movement, between those led by William Lloyd Garrison who supported women's rights and those who felt that linking them with abolitionism would endanger the success of the abolitionist campaign. Eventually, the sisters' continuing distaste for male religious authority and the elements of racial prejudice and opposition to their radicalism they encountered within their Quaker meetings would lead to their alienation from the Society of Friends.

Further discussions by letter on the inequality of the sexes, which Sarah had originally published in the *New England Spectator* and *The Lib-*

erator, were collected by her in *Letters on the Equality of the Sexes, and The Condition of Woman* (1838). In this work, Sarah argued in support of women's right to speak in public on issues of morality and in so doing provided the first major discussion in print of women's rights by an American woman. Sarah's descriptions of the diminution of woman's status through marriage and the narrowness of the purely domestic sphere of activity were damning. She believed that the loss of individual identity and independence resulting from women's lack of education and sexual and economic oppression reduced them to adjuncts of their husbands, and she made the now legendary statement: "I ask no favors for my sex. I surrender not our claim to equality. All I ask of our brethren is that they will take their feet from off our necks, and permit us to stand upright on the ground which God has designed for us to occupy" (Lerner 1971, 192).

In 1837 Angelina produced another pamphlet, *An Appeal to the Women of the Nominally Free States,* in which she reminded women that they shared the responsibility for the continuation of slavery. In calling for emancipation she reminded the church that it should not differentiate between male and female rights but should recognize only human rights, arguing that until it ceased to discriminate between the sexes, it would remain ineffectual in inspiring social change. On 21 February 1938, Angelina demonstrated her commanding presence when she presented an appeal on abolition signed by 20,000 women to a committee of the Massachusetts legislature; the dignity and conviction with which she gave her speech on this occasion were likened by Harriet Martineau, in an 1835 essay on abolition, "to the appeal of Hortensia to the Roman Senate" (McDonald 1998, 141).

In May 1838 Angelina married a leading abolitionist, Theodore Weld, but his opposition to her public speaking compelled her to withdraw from the lecture circuit. After making a final speech the day after her marriage at an antislavery convention of American women held in the Pennsylvania Hall in Philadelphia, she promptly withdrew from public speaking and thereafter confined herself to writing. Sarah too retreated from activism and joined her sister in New Jersey, where, on their farm at Belleville, she helped Angelina run a small boarding school. The family eventually settled in Hyde Park, Boston, in 1864, where

the sisters taught in a progressive school. Notwithstanding their absence from the public platform, they continued to lend their support to abolitionism and temperance and to moral and dress reform, in the mid-1850s briefly wearing the bloomers adopted by New England feminists. The spirit of their work against slavery was continued by other women reformers such as Abby Kelley Foster, Lucy Stone, and Lucretia Mott.

The sisters' remaining published work was a collaboration with Theodore Weld, *Slavery as It Is: Testimony of a Thousand Witnesses* (1839), which provided valuable background on the suffering of U.S. slaves to Harriet Beecher Stowe in the writing of *Uncle Tom's Cabin.* In it, they expressed their particular concern at the sexual exploitation of female slaves by white men, and the reality of this practice soon came all too painfully to light when they discovered that their brother Henry had fathered two sons by a slave woman. Having retired from teaching in 1867, they acknowledged their two newly discovered nephews in 1868 and sponsored their education. (Archibald Grimké would become a lawyer and a leader of the National Association for the Advancement of Colored People.) Sarah and Angelina reemerged briefly in 1870 to join women suffragists in a token attempt to vote in elections held in March of that year in Massachusetts.

See also Beecher, Catharine Esther; Foster, Abby (Abigail) Kelley; Mott, Lucretia Coffin; Stone, Lucy; Stowe, Harriet Beecher.

References and Further Reading

Bacon, Margaret Hope. 1986. *Mothers of Feminism: The Story of Quaker Women in America.* San Francisco: Harper and Row.

Barnes, Gilbert H., and Dwight L. Dumond. 1934. The *Letters of Theodore Dwight Weld, Angelina Grimké Weld, and Sarah Grimké 1822–1844.* New York: D. Appleton-Century.

Birney, Catherine H. 1969 [1885]. *Sarah and Angelina Grimké: The First American Women Advocates of Abolition and Women's Rights.* Reprint, Westport, CT: Greenwood Press.

Ceplair, Larry, ed. 1989. *The Public Years of Sarah and Angelina Grimké: Selected Writings, 1835–1839.* New York: Columbia University Press.

Hersch, Blanche G. 1978. *Slavery of Sex: Feminist Abolitionists in America.* Urbana: University of Illinois Press.

Kerber, Linda K., and Jane DeHart-Mathews. 2000. *Women's America: Refocusing the Past.* New York: Oxford University Press.

Kraditor, Aileen. 1969. *Means and Ends in American Abolitionism: Garrison and His Critics on Strategy and Tactics, 1834–50.* New York: Pantheon.

Lerner, Gerda. 1971 [1967]. *The Grimké Sisters from South Carolina: Rebels against Slavery.* Reprint, New York: Schocken Books.

———. 1998. "The Feminist Thought of Sarah Grimké." In Lynn McDonald, ed., *Women Theorists on Society and Politics.* Waterloo, Ontario: Wilfrid Laurier University Press.

Lumpkin, Katherine Du Pré. 1974. *The Emancipation of Angelina Grimké.* Chapel Hill: University of North Carolina Press.

McDonald, Lynn, ed. 1998. *Women Theorists on Society and Politics.* Waterloo, ON: Wilfred Laurier University Press.

Melder, Keith E. 1977. *The Beginnings of Sisterhood: The American Woman's Rights Movement, 1800–1850.* New York: Schocken.

Niess, Judith. 1977. *Seven Women: Portraits from the American Radical Tradition.* New York: Viking Press.

Taylor, Clare. 1974. *British and American Abolitionists: An Episode in Transatlantic Understanding.* Edinburgh: Edinburgh University Press.

Trager, James. 1994. *The Women's Chronology: A Year-by-Year Record, from Prehistory to the Present.* London: Aurum Press.

Yellen, Jean Fagan. 1989. *Women and Sisters: The Antislavery Feminists in American Culture.* New Haven: Yale University Press.

Gutiérrez de Mendoza, Juana Belén
(1875–1942)
Mexico

Journalist, teacher, feminist, and socialist Gutiérrez took part in the resistance campaign of the Mexican Liberal Party against the regime of Porfirio Díaz from 1909. As the founder of numerous feminist and socialist journals, she spoke out against injustice in all its manifestations and supported women's suffrage and their equal rights with men.

Gutiérrez was born in Durango into a working-class family of mixed native blood. She left home at the age of fifteen after having had a basic education, trained as a typographer, and married a miner. The couple lived at Palomas Negras in Coahuila, where Gutiérrez became alarmed at the appalling conditions in which miners worked. She wrote an article for the liberal publication *The Newspaper of the Home* (*El Diario del Hogar*). Although only eighteen at the time, she suffered three months' imprisonment for having the temerity to write this article. Serving time in prison did nothing to dampen her social conscience, and before long Gutiérrez was openly criticizing the whole sociopolitical system in Mexico.

In 1900 she met with other liberal reformers opposed to Díaz's regime in San Luis Potosí and founded a liberal club. A year later Gutiérrez and her husband, now committed to an anticapitalist revolt against the government by peasants and workers, sold their goats to raise the money to go to southern Mexico. There they set up an anti-Díaz newspaper, *Vesper: Justice and Liberty,* in 1901, in which they attacked not only the brutal, corrupt government for failing to fulfill its promises to the people but also the mine owners, who blatantly exploited their workers. Gutiérrez took the political lead in a new and uncharacteristically female way that prompted one (male) commentator to note that "she had trousers in her style" (Macías 1983, 26). She called upon the people to fight for their rights and for workers to resist the foreign takeover of Mexico's mines, banks, railroads, and industries.

Meanwhile, her publication *Vesper,* which grew to a circulation of 8,000 weekly, regularly ran into trouble with the government. It was frequently censored, its printing press was confiscated, and the editorial employees were persecuted. In 1903 *Vesper* was temporarily closed down, and its contributors and editors, including Gutiérrez, were interned in Belén prison in Mexico City. It was one of several jail sentences she would endure from that year until 1920. Gutiérrez would receive several death threats in an attempt to silence her, but fiercely combative and forthright by nature, she continued fighting till her death in 1942.

Gutiérrez further enraged the authorities by collaborating on another publication in opposition to Porfirio Díaz's regime, the newspaper *Anáhuac* (named after the homeland of Mexico's Aztecs). Once again, several of its women employees were arrested and imprisoned. While devoting her energy to numerous demonstrations in support of suffrage from 1910 to 1920, Gutiérrez also became involved in several revolutionary organizations. In 1911, she supported an army-backed plot known as the "Complot de Tacubaya" to supplant President Díaz with Francisco Madero. In June 1911 she organized a group known as the Female Friends of the People (which she had founded in 1909) to join forces with other feminist groups to petition Madero, by then the new president, for women's suffrage. Also in 1911 she joined the Zapatistas, a rebel group fighting in southwestern Mexico, and by 1914 had become a colonel in a Zapatista regiment while still keeping up her journalistic work on *Vesper,* which continued to be subject to regular censorship and shutdowns, writing in support of indigenous Mexicans and the need for rural education. In 1914 she founded a new publication called *Reform,* which with its banner of "For the Land and for the People" concentrated its campaigning efforts on defending the rights of Mexico's indigenous peoples.

In 1915 Gutiérrez was arrested and imprisoned by the military. After revolutionary leader Emiliano Zapata's assassination in 1919, she began publication of the newspaper *El Desmonte* (The Leveling) in Mexico City, in support of social and economic reforms in the wake of the Mexican Revolution. But the 1910s were a difficult, disillusioning period for her, with the country's infrastructure weakened by years of upheaval, the people hungry, and their political leadership in tatters after the death of Zapata.

Gutiérrez continued to plug away at the causes she believed in with her journalistic work. In the 1920s she contributed a series of articles on women's education and the need for schools in rural areas to the Mexico City daily the *Herald of Mexico* as part of the reconstruction program going on after the revolution. She served on many bodies, becoming president in 1919 of the National Council of Mexican Women, which worked for women's rights as well as offering support to miners and their families. In the early 1920s she helped run a rural school and in 1922 set up an experimental agricultural colony in the state of Morelos, but the latter failed because of Gutiérrez's resistance to interference from the church. She also, somehow, found time to study anthropology to better understand and promote Mexico's indigenous culture, advocating welfare schemes and remaining constantly alert to the exploitation of indigenous peoples by U.S.-backed capitalist interests.

In 1933 she was still campaigning—this time, at the second National Congress of Women Workers and Peasants held in Mexico City, calling for women peasants to be eligible to acquire land in a newly introduced agrarian reform program. She also returned to journalism: *Vesper* resurfaced in 1932, and Gutiérrez contributed to a magazine discussing women's issues (*Revolutionary X-Rays*) as well as starting another feminist journal of her own, *The Source.* She continued to tackle issues ranging from education to constitutional reform. She took a particularly radical line in 1936, suggesting that communities of women peasants, with their own self-supporting network of child care facilities, communal land, and banks, be set up in south-central Mexico. That same year she took over the directorship of a girls' school in Morelia, but by the end of the decade, she had worn herself out and was forced to reduce her activities. She had also become disenchanted with her colleagues in the Communist Party and alarmed at their dogmatic attitudes, and she was equally depressed about the upper-class, elitist leadership of the feminist movement, which she felt was bourgeois and did not set enough store by indigenous Mexican culture. She preferred to devote much of her time to her journalism and writing, in 1935 setting up another biweekly publication with the characteristic title of *Mexican Heart: For the Land and for the People.*

Despite all her many activities and commitments, Gutiérrez managed to bring up her three children alone after being widowed. Although she was eventually granted a small pension in recognition of her work for the revolution, she lived the rest of her life in poverty and with a growing feeling of disappointment that so many of the things she had fought for had not been achieved, writing: "My sixty years have not served me for anything. I can't use them to make a blindfold for my eyes or a shroud for my conscience" (Soto 1990, 134). Like her compatriot, Elvía Carrillo Puerto, Gutiérrez's lifetime of struggle on behalf of the working classes and peasants of Mexico received only token recognition and was soon forgotten after her death. Shirlene Soto describes the poignancy of her final years: almost destitute, she was obliged to burn her private papers in order to fuel a cooking stove to heat the food she sold on the streets. When she died, her family was so poor they had to sell her typewriter in order to pay for her burial. Gutiérrez's story, like that of so many other women reformers in Latin America, has yet to be fully told in English or to reach a wider audience.

See also Carrillo Puerto, Elvia.
References and Further Reading
Adams, Jerome R. 1991. *Liberators and Patriots of Latin America: Biographies of 23 Leaders from Doña Marina (1505–1530) to Bishop Romero (1917–1980).* Jefferson, NC: McFarland & Co.
Macías, Anna. 1983. *Against All Odds: The Feminist Movement in Mexico to 1940.* Westport, CT: Greenwood Press.
Soto, Shirlene. 1990. *Emergence of the Modern Mexican Woman: Her Participation in Revolution and Struggle for Equality, 1910–1940.* Denver: Arden Press.

Gwis-Adami, Rosalia
(1880–1930)
Italy

Like many figures in the history of women's activism in Italy at the turn of the twentieth century, Rosalia Gwis-Adami languishes in obscurity. A leading pacifist and moderate as well as a social novelist, she sought to organize women in support of the peace movement, which she considered to be more pressing than other social and human rights campaigning at the time, including women's suffrage.

Gwis-Adami grew up in a family of *Risorgimento* patriots who nurtured her on the democratic ideals of Giuseppe Mazzini and Giuseppe Garibaldi. She began her professional life as a social writer, publishing her first novel, *Conscience,* in 1905. She joined the Italian peace movement in 1908 and soon proved herself to be an indispensable contributor to the Italian pacifist journal *International Life.* Also that year, she published the novel *Outside the Nest: The Golden Virgin,* a novel that discussed women's social problems, in 1914.

In 1909 Gwis-Adami was a cofounder in Milan of the Italian Young Women's Society for Peace, an organization aimed at female high school students and teachers, with the objective of teaching young women to differentiate between positive patriotism and the kind that supported the destruction of another country. She thus sought to bring the youthful membership to a greater awareness of the need for international cooperation in the achievement of arms reduction in Europe. On this basis, the society raised funds to foster student and teacher exchange programs that would enable Italian women to study abroad. During this time, Gwis-Adami also worked with the leading Italian pacifist Ernesto Teodoro Moneta, both in Milan and for the Bern office of the International Peace Bureau.

In 1911 Gwis-Adami abandoned her pacifism to support the Italian invasion of Libya-Cyrenaica, insisting that Italian national independence was paramount if her country was to play its true international role and that it was doing no more than assert its colonial rights, as France and England did. Others in the Italian pacifist movement, such as Alma Dolens, were unable to square their patriotic feeling with their commitment to pacifism and refused to support the war.

In 1912 Gwis-Adami represented Italy at the Geneva Universal Peace Congress and resumed her support for European unity. She was also present at a pacifist meeting in Brussels in July 1914, but by autumn she found herself questioning her country's continuing neutrality after the outbreak of World War I. During the war, Gwis-Adami wrote articles on women's patriotic support for the war effort in pamphlets such as "In the Fray" (1917). She hoped that women's support would win them greater political rights at war's end, and she continued to raise the issues of women's political and legal rights until her death, also supporting the work of the League of Nations.

See also Alma Dolens.
References and Further Reading
Josephson, Harold, Sandi Cooper, and Steven C. Hause et al., eds. 1985. *Biographical Dictionary of Modern Peace Leaders.* Westport, CT: Greenwood Press.
Pierson, Ruth Roach, ed. 1987. *Woman and Peace: Theoretical, Historical and Practical Perspectives.* London: Croom Helm.

H

Hale, Clara ("Mother Hale")
(1905–1992)
United States

Clara Hale pioneered a new area of social welfare among the most helpless of social outcasts—drug-addicted babies—when she established the first voluntary child care institution for black children in the United States, in Harlem, to foster the infants of local drug addicts. Known as Hale House, this institution in later years established rehabilitation programs for pregnant addicts and provided care for babies infected with acquired immunodeficiency syndrome (AIDS), as well as supporting government schemes to prevent infant addiction to nicotine and alcohol.

Born in Philadelphia, Hale was orphaned at sixteen and went to New York, where she worked in domestic service. Widowed at the age of twenty-seven with three children to support, she found it impossible to hold down her cleaning jobs without leaving her children unsupervised and so began minding children and eventually took in foster children.

In 1969, after thirty years spent caring for other people's children, Hale retired, only to find herself drawn into a new and challenging venture when her daughter Lorraine rescued a two-month-old baby from a homeless drug addict she encountered on the street and suggested it be left in Hale's care while the mother underwent a drug rehabilitation program. Hale soon set about making space in her apartment for more babies and within weeks was looking after twenty similar babies, some suffering withdrawal symptoms because they had been born drug-addicted.

In 1975, with government funding from the Office of Economic Opportunity, Hale and her daughter Lorraine established a home in a rented five-story brownstone in Harlem, which was given the official title of the Center for the Promotion of Human Potential. Such was the success of the venture that even after government funding was withdrawn in 1989, Hale House was able to continue its work on private donations and fund-raising. Hale concentrated on the training of more volunteer caretakers, and her daughter took over the day-to-day administration of the house. By the time of Mother Hale's death, Hale House had taken in about 800 babies, and the original project had been extended to provide accommodation and rehabilitation for drug addict mothers and care for mothers and babies with AIDS. The work continues under the direction of Hale's daughter Lorraine.

Hale was honored for her work on numerous occasions. In 1985 President Reagan awarded her the Presidential Medal of Freedom and invited her to take part in his American Commission on Drug Free Schools; in 1987 she received the Leonard H. Carter Humanitarian Award and in 1990 the Booth Community Service Award from the Salvation Army. A year after Hale's death, the Women's International Center dedicated its Living Legacy Awards to her memory. A woman of simplicity, quiet religious faith, and compassion, Hale's life and work were a testament to the Christian tenets of love and charity in which she so unswervingly believed. For further information on Hale House, contact http://www.halehouse.org/.

References and Further Reading
Current Biography. 1985. New York: H. W. Wilson.
Hale, Clara. 1993. *Mother to Those Who Needed One.* Edited by Bob Italia. Edina, MN: Abdo & Daughters.
Hine, Darlene Clarke, et al., eds. 1993. *Black Women in America: An Historical Encyclopedia.* 2 vols. Bloomington: Indiana University Press.

Lanker, Brian. 1989. *I Dream a World.* New York: Stewart, Tabori and Chang.

Penguin Biographical Dictionary of Women. 1998. Harmondsworth: Penguin.

Smith, Jessie Carney, ed. 1992. *Notable Black American Women.* Detroit: Gale.

Hamer, Fanny Lou
(1917–1977)
United States

One of twenty children, Fanny Lou Hamer grew up in grinding poverty and spent the greater part of her life in financial and physical hardship, working in the cotton fields of the Mississippi Delta before joining the civil rights movement in the early 1960s. Like Ella Baker, Hamer worked for voter registration, and her assistance to poor blacks in the South inspired a cooperative movement in Sunflower County. A charismatic public speaker whose inimitable style, punctuated by bursts of civil rights songs such as her favorite, "This Little Light of Mine," was admired for its honesty, forthright homespun philosophy, and down-to-earth tone, Hamer insisted that black women work *together* with, not against, black men in liberating people of all colors from destitution and oppression.

Born in Montgomery County, Mississippi, Hamer was the daughter of poor sharecroppers and after six years' basic education had to join her family in the fields. She married a plantation tractor driver in 1944 and settled in Ruleville but did not become politically active until 1961. After being given a hysterectomy without her consent while undergoing hospital treatment, she was prompted to defend her civil rights and registered for the vote at the age of forty-five. After failing the literacy tests for black voters on her first two attempts, in 1962 she joined the southern campaign for black voter registration led by the Student Nonviolent Coordinating Committee (SNCC). This action cost her a job as a timekeeper on the plantation where she had worked for many years and the home that came with it. A year later, she finally registered, but soon after she suffered an appalling beating after being arrested in Winona for taking part in a civil rights workshop.

As a field secretary for SNCC, Hamer began holding workshops for young black volunteers. But her civil rights activities would bring constant harassment, threats, arrests, and permanent injury from the beating she received in 1963. In 1971 her house was firebombed. In order to provide an alternative for black voters to the official, white-dominated Democratic Party in elections, in 1964 Hamer cofounded the Mississippi Freedom Democratic Party and spoke out on racial discrimination before the Credentials Committee of the Democratic Party's national convention that August. She was a member of the Democratic National Committee from 1968 to 1971.

Hamer also worked for her local black community in Mississippi, assisting poor black families in claiming welfare benefits and supporting a strike by black cotton workers in 1965. In the last years of her life, she worked toward desegregation of Mississippi's schools. She decried the vast sums being spent on munitions for the Vietnam War, while poor people in the South remained hungry and without decent homes and took part in War on Poverty programs. In 1968, under the auspices of the National Council of Negro Women, she founded a livestock cooperative, the Pig Bank, to produce cheap meat and a year later set up the Freedom Farm Cooperative in Sunflower County, one of the poorest parts of Mississippi. There she encouraged a community of poor black families to farm 40 acres as a nonprofit enterprise, which was soon producing food for 1,500 people. In 1970, the Young World Developers organization bought another 640 acres of land, where homes were built not only for poor black families but also for poor white ones. Hamer also initiated the construction of a clothing factory in Ruleville to bring work to the area.

In 1971 Hamer gave a speech to the Legal Defense Fund of the National Association for the Advancement of Colored People, in which she reiterated her lifelong insistence on fighting to liberate all people from oppression. It was a belief she reiterated as a founding member of the Central Committee of the National Women's Political Caucus. She regretted the growing antagonism of some feminists toward men, which she considered served only to divide women's aspirations for liberation, and wanted to see both sexes work together toward the political and economic liberation of all oppressed people—male and female, black and white. Before her premature death from cancer at the age of fifty-nine, Hamer was awarded several honorary degrees.

See also Baker, Ella.

References and Further Reading

Carson, Clayborn. 1981. *In Struggle: SNCC and the Black Awakening of the 1960s.* Cambridge, MA: Harvard University Press.

Colman, Penny. 1993. *Fannie Lou Hamer and the Fight for the Vote.* Brookfield, CT: Millbrook Press.

Crawford, Vicki L., Jacqueline Anne Rouse, and Barbara Woods, eds. 1990. *Women in the Civil Rights Movement: Trailblazers and Torchbearers.* Brooklyn: Carlson Publishing.

Giddings, Paula. 1984. *When and Where I Enter: The Impact of Black Women on Race and Sex in America.* New York: W. W. Norton.

Hamer, Fannie Lou. 1967. *To Praise Our Bridges: The Autobiography of Fannie Lou Hamer.* Jackson, MS: KIPCO.

Harmon, Rod. 2000. *American Civil Rights Leaders.* Berkeley Heights, NJ: Enslow.

Jordan, June. 1972. *Fannie Lou Hamer.* New York: Crowell.

Lee, Chana Kai. 1999. *For Freedom's Sake: The Life of Fannie Hamer.* Urbana: University of Illiinois Press.

Mills, Kay. 1993. *This Little Light of Mine: Fannie Lou Hamer.* New York: E. P. Dutton.

Rubel, David. 1990. *Fannie Lou Hamer: From Sharecropping to Politics.* Englewood Cliffs, NJ: Silver Burdett.

Alice Hamilton (Library of Congress)

Hamilton, Alice
(1869–1970)
United States

A female pioneer in the male-dominated field of industrial toxicology, U.S. doctor Alice Hamilton fought discrimination in the medical profession to further the scientific study of occupational disease. She advised government on improvements to worker safety standards in industry and the payment of compensation for injury at work. Her work in correlating the widespread use of chemicals such as lead and mercury with the high levels of industrial disease among workers in dangerous industries prefigured the later far-reaching conclusions on the unbridled use of chemicals in the natural environment by Rachel Carson. Hamilton was also an advocate of birth control, was active in the National Consumers' League and women's suffrage movement, and supported the mother and baby health programs of the Children's Bureau.

Born in New York City, Hamilton received a limited education at home on the family estate in Fort Wayne, Indiana, and then, from 1886 to 1888 studying at Miss Porter's School in Farmington, Connecticut. Resolved to be independent and enter social service as a doctor, she studied medicine, first at Fort Wayne Medical College and then at the University of Michigan, graduating in 1893. She served an internship at the Northwestern Hospital for Women and Children in Minneapolis and at the New England Hospital for Women and Children in Boston. By this time, however, she had decided upon a career in medical research rather than as a doctor. In the autumn of 1895, Alice went to Europe with her sister Edith and managed to gain admittance to lectures on pathology and bacteriology at the universities of Leipzig and Munich at a time when women's admittance into medical studies was still frowned upon. After another year of postgraduate work at Johns Hopkins Medical School, Hamilton took a post in Chicago in 1897 as professor of pathology at the Woman's Medical School of Northwestern University.

During this period, Hamilton combined her teaching with work as a volunteer at Jane Addams's Hull House in Chicago, with which she retained a close connection until 1919. She established a well-baby clinic and health education classes for poor immigrants. Coming into regular contact with the sick and underprivileged, she investigated their susceptibility to typhoid and tuberculosis in the unsanitary environment in which they lived and first became aware of the incidence among workers of various types of occupational illnesses. Many of them suffered from the effects of inhalation of fumes in Chicago's steel mills and exposure to lead dust in various industries.

In 1902, when the Woman's Medical School closed, Hamilton began working as a bacteriologist at the Memorial Institute for Infectious Diseases. But by the turn of the century, her activities at Hull House and the publication in 1902 of Sir Thomas Oliver's groundbreaking *Dangerous Trades: The Historical, Social, and Legal Aspects of Industrial Occupation as Affecting Health* had drawn her increasingly to the health problems facing workers in dangerous industries. She made a comparison of safety provisions and the compensation given to workers in Germany, England, and the United States, which revealed to her how little legislative provision there was for workers' health in her own country. Through Hull House, she obtained an appointment in 1908 to the Illinois Commission on Occupational Diseases, which resulted in her being asked two years later to head a detailed field study of industrial poisons in copper mines and steel mills. In particular, Hamilton investigated the high incidences of lead poisoning among workers performing seventy-seven industrial processes.

Hamilton rapidly became a major authority on industrial diseases and in 1911 was appointed a special investigator for the U.S. Bureau of Labor. Maintaining a scrupulous professional approach in her research and avoiding the lure of sensationalist exposés, over the next ten years she set up further surveys on the negative health effects suffered by workers in the lead, rubber, and munitions industries, which not only directly influenced the raising of health standards in industry but finally convinced the government of the necessity of the long-overdue introduction of workers' compensation.

Hamilton's research into the high-risk munitions industry before and during World War I served to reinforce her long commitment to pacifism. She opposed U.S. entry into the war and in 1915 joined U.S. pacifist leaders Emily Greene Balch and Jane Addams in attending the international congress of women held at The Hague, which attempted to promote peace mediation by neutral nations and formed the International Committee of Women for Permanent Peace to further that effort. During the war, Hamilton continued to monitor the dangers to health for workers in the munitions industry, in particular the effects of nitrous fume poisoning, and drew attention to the wider medical consequences of the more sophisticated weapons of war being developed in the United States at the time.

Hamilton was in Europe again at war's end to attend the 1919 peace congress in Zurich, at which the committee was reborn as the Women's International League for Peace and Freedom. With Addams, Dutch reformer Aletta Jacobs, and Carolina Wood, Hamilton went on a mission to postwar Germany to study food shortages. They attempted to alleviate the widespread suffering of children by distributing clothing and food on behalf of the American Friends Service Committee, a Quaker pacifist group set up in 1917 to administer relief work in Europe. Later Hamilton modified her pacifism because of the rise of fascism in Germany, eventually conceding that the war against Adolf Hitler was a necessary one.

On her return from Europe in 1919, Hamilton was invited to become the first woman professor at Harvard Medical School and to head a degree course in industrial medicine. She agreed to work part-time while retaining her commitment to issues of industrial health and safety and cooperating with both industrial managers and health inspectors to suggest improvements in factory working conditions. Much of her work was incorporated into her groundbreaking 1925 text, *Industrial Poisons in the United States,* which she followed in 1934 with *Industrial Toxicology.*

Throughout her life, Hamilton retained a close interest in the problems faced by women workers. She published an official pamphlet for the Department of Labor on "Women Workers and Industrial Poisons" but did not support the 1920s campaign for women's equality under the Equal Rights Amendment because she favored protective legislation for women in industry. In 1924 she visited the Soviet Union, where despite her distaste for the clampdown on civil liberties, she was impressed with moves toward improving women's equality and the standards of industrial hygiene observed there.

Hamilton's commitment to a wide range of social activism eventually alienated the male academic establishment at Harvard University, and she was forced out of her job in 1935. She became a consultant to the Division of Labor Standards at the U.S. Department of Labor, initiating an important investigation into the viscose rayon industry before retiring to Connecticut, where she wrote her autobiography, *Exploring the Dangerous Trades* (1943), and served as president of the National Consumers' League (1944–1949). Her other official posts included service on the Health Committee of the League of Nations (1924–1930) and on the President's Research Committee on Social Trends (1930–1932). In her old age, she defended freedom of speech and civil liberties during the McCarthy era and lived until she was 100, long enough to protest U.S. involvement in the Vietnam War.

During her long career, Hamilton cast her investigative net far and wide, uncovering the toxic effects of dyes, acids, radium, and deadly poisons such as arsenic in manufacturing processes. She described the prevalence among women workers in the safety match manufacturing industry of "phossy jaw," the painful degeneration of facial bones caused by white phosphorus, the use of which was eventually outlawed. Hamilton also described the dangers to health from carbon disulphide used in manufacturing, which could result in mental illness, paralysis, and blindness, and was one of the first to document the incidence of silicosis among miners. The results of her findings led eventually to the introduction of laws in several states to set safety standards and impose regular medical checks of workers exposed to dangerous substances, as well as the first compensation provisions for workers in dangerous trades.

Hamilton was the first woman to receive the Lasker Award of the U.S. Public Health Association. In February 1988 an Alice Hamilton Science Award for Occupational Safety and Health was established by the National Institute for Occupational Safety and Health. The Alice Hamilton Occupational Health Center continues Hamilton's work, offering training in environmental health and safety. For further information about Hamilton's work, contact http://www.alicehamilton.org/english/.

See also Addams, Jane; Balch, Emily Greene; Carson, Rachel; Jacobs, Aletta.

References and Further Reading
Current Biography. 1946. New York: H. W. Wilson.
Frankel, Noralee, and Nancy S. Dye. 1991. *Gender, Class, Race, and Reform in the Progressive Era.* Lexington: University of Kentucky Press.
Grant, Madeline P. 1967. *Alice Hamilton: Pioneer Doctor in Industrial Medicine.* New York: Abelard-Shuman.
Hamilton, Alice. 1943. *Exploring the Dangerous Trades: The Autobiography of Alice Hamilton.* Boston: Little, Brown.
Josephson, Harold, Sandi Cooper, and Steven C. Hause et al., eds. 1985. *Biographical Dictionary of Modern Peace Leaders.* Westport, CT: Greenwood Press.
Kass-Simon, G., and Patricia Farnes. 1993. *Women of Science: Righting the Record.* Bloomington: Indiana University Press.
Sicherman, Barbara. 1984. *Alice Hamilton: A Life in Letters.* Cambridge, MA: Harvard University Press.
Sklar, Kathryn Kish. 1998. *Social Justice Feminists in the United States and Germany: A Dialogue in Documents 1885–1933.* Ithaca: Cornell University Press.

Hani Motoko
(1873–1957)
Japan

One of the pioneering group of women allowed to study at Tokyo's First Higher Women's School under the terms of the 1872 Education Act, the Japanese educator Hani Motoko was one of the country's first female journalists. She was a central voice in the women's movement through her long-running magazine *Women's Friend* and later founded a progressive private high school for girls, the Freedom School (Jiyu Gakuen). Throughout her career, she testified to her own firmly held belief that women were capable of combining a happy personal life with the challenges of a career.

Hani's samurai family had become relatively well-off landowners in northeastern Japan during the Meiji period (1868–1911). She was brought up by her grandfather, who allowed her an exceptional education for a woman at that time, and went on to attend Tokyo's First Higher Women's School as one of only a few hundred female students educated in secondary school across the whole of Japan. Indeed, Hani's school had been one of the first to take government financing to admit women, in 1889, the year Hani entered it. After graduating in 1891 and having been baptized in 1890, Hani entered the Meiji Women's Christian School, run by foreign-educated Japanese, which allowed students to study until age twenty. Founded on Christian principles, the school placed great emphasis on the pastoral care of students in preparation for their roles in society as responsible, self-reliant individuals. The principal of the Meiji School, Iwamoto Yoshiharu, also gave Hani an editing role on his journal *Women's Learning* in return for her board and tuition.

Hani left the school in 1892 and taught at an elementary school in Hachinohe and after that at a Catholic girls' school in Morioka. Her 1895 marriage proved a disaster, and she soon left for Tokyo where she worked as a maid in the home of a pioneering female doctor, Yoshioka Yayoi, who ran the Tokyo Women's Medical Institute and encouraged Hani's intellectual interests. In 1897 she succeeded in obtaining a post on the *Information Newspaper* (*Hochi Shimbun*) as one of Japan's first female copyeditors and, later, reporters. The paper, which was known for its human rights campaigning and prided itself on its high principles and its universality, concluded that having a woman on the editorial board would enhance its appeal to its readership. Over the next few years, Hani published numerous articles on women's employment and careers, such as her 1905 piece, "New Professions for Women," in which she remarked that the average Japanese woman was not educationally equipped to pursue a career such as hers. And so she would remain, argued Hani, all the time that women's education was so sorely neglected in Japan. Another article by Hani on the Okayama Orphanage, which argued against the traditional Japanese resistance to the idea of adoption, earned the praise of the president of the House of Peers.

Hani remarried in 1901 and established a long, happy union with fellow journalist Hani Yoshikazu, who supported her in her work. Hani left her job and went to work on the journal of the Women's Education Association. She set up her own journal, *Friend of the Home*, in 1903, and in 1908 with her husband she founded the longest-running women's periodical in Japan, *Women's Friend*, which had as its motto, "Daily life in itself is education." The magazine embraced a wide spectrum of issues, such as women's emancipation, their right to employment, and their emotional well-being. It also supported women's suffrage and helped readers in dealing with everyday management of their homes and finances, health care, and the future marriage and education of their children. The Freedom School that Motoko and her husband founded in 1921 with just twenty-six pupils was an extension of these concerns, based on a synthesis of "Protestant and Confucian ideals of self-sufficiency, hard work, and proud independence" (Mulhern 1991, 231). In the 1920s even to suggest that women should be able to do their own cooking and cleaning, instead of depending on servants to do it for them, was in itself a step forward in changing conventional attitudes. The school proved so successful that in 1932 Hani was selected to represent Japanese educators at the World New Education Conference in Nice. In 1928 she published her autobiography, *Speaking of Myself*, in which she tackled social issues and relationships within the family.

References and Further Reading

Fujimura-Fanselow, Kumiko, and Atsuko Kameda. 1995. *Japanese Women: New Feminist Perspectives on the Past, Present, and Future.* New York: Feminist Press.

Mulhern, Chieko Irie. 1991. *Heroic with Grace: Legendary Women of Japan.* Armonk, NY: M. E. Sharpe.

Haslam, Anna
(1829–1922)
Ireland

The Quaker and feminist Anna Haslam from County Cork, who was one of the founders of the Irish suffrage movement, also worked with Roman Catholics in the cause of women's education and emancipation in Ireland for more than sixty years. Yet she remains one of many women reformers in nineteenth-century Ireland whose contribution has yet to be recognized in a wider context. As a female Quaker reformer, like her friend the American pioneer Susan B. Anthony, Haslam was brought up not only to believe in the fundamental equality of men and women but also to support the campaigns against slavery and for temperance and pacifism.

Born in Youghal, County Cork, Anna Maria Fisher, as she was then known, was educated at Quaker boarding schools in County Waterford and Ackworth, Yorkshire. She joined her parents in their philanthropic activities in Cork during the Irish potato famine of 1845–1847 and helped in soup kitchens. At this time, she first became involved in alleviating the plight of unemployed women, when she set up cottage industries for local girls in lace making, crocheting, and knitting. In 1849 Haslam helped found the Olive Leaf Circle of Quaker pacifists, and her commitment to pacifism brought her into contact with the work of female Quaker activists in the United States such as Anthony and Lucretia Mott.

In 1854 Anna married a fellow teacher, Thomas Haslam, after returning to teach at her old school at Ackworth. Haslam had the good fortune to find in her husband a partner who shared her belief in the equality of men and women and who, throughout their long marriage, would lend his unqualified support (mainly via the written word) to all her various social campaigns. Although she remained modest about her many achievements, Haslam would eventually become the breadwinner after her husband was incapacitated by illness in 1866. She set up her own stationer's business in Rathmines Road, Dublin, which supported the couple for the next forty years.

In the early 1860s, Haslam collaborated on various projects with other Irish women reformers. She supported Isabella Tod's welfare work on behalf of factory girls and Anne Jellicoe's establishment of an Irish Society for the Trade and Employment of Educated Women. Haslam also contributed to Jellicoe's establishment of the Queen's Institute in 1861 and endorsed her calls for women's further education, which resulted in the Intermediate Education Act of 1878 and the Royal University Act of 1879.

In 1866, Haslam was one of twenty-five Irishwomen who signed John Stuart Mill's petition to Parliament on female suffrage, and she took part in the first public meeting on women's suffrage, held in Dublin in 1870. Her activities rapidly extended to include involvement in the major feminist campaigns in Britain for women's medical training, for their rights to control their own property, and for repeal of the Contagious Diseases Acts. Throughout the 1860s and 1870s, she endorsed the attempts of women to be accepted into medical schools. In 1874 this goal was achieved when the London School of Medicine for Women was established. In 1869, she and Isabella Tod helped found numerous Irish branches of the Ladies National Association, which campaigned for the repeal of the Contagious Diseases Acts, a campaign for which Haslam's husband wrote pamphlets, including some of the first on birth control. (In 1870 he had even gone so far, in a pamphlet on prostitution, as to castigate his fellow men for its perpetuation by making victims of women through their own "licentiousness.") Eventually, Anna Haslam was accepted into the inner sanctum of the male-run National Association for the Repeal of the Contagious Diseases Acts as a council member. She also served as a member of the Dublin support committee for the Married Women's Property Act campaign and as a committee member for the Philanthropic Reform Association, the Irish Workhouse Association, and the Irish Schoolmistresses Association. As a committed Christian, Haslam also joined in the social purity campaign as a member of the Women's Vigilance Committee.

In 1874 the Haslams set up a feminist journal, the *Women's Advocate,* the first publication in Ireland to advocate women's suffrage. Two years later, with the support of several Dublin Quakers, they founded the Dublin Women's Suffrage Association (which, after several name changes, in 1901 became known as the Irish Women's Suffrage and Local Government Association, or IWSLGA). Because of its strong Quaker background, the society remained relatively small—with only forty-three members listed in 1896—and fundamentally nonmilitant. It placed a great emphasis on women's education, producing many pamphlets and petitions and sponsoring lectures in support of its concerted drive to raise public awareness on women's issues on the local as well as the national level. It later absorbed the talents of other leading Irish feminist campaigners such as Hannah Sheehy-Skeffington and Margaret Cousins, and Haslam tried hard to extend its welcome to Roman Catholic women as well. However, it soon lost the support of more radical campaigners such as Cousins and Skeffington because of its refusal to take a more militant position and also because of its traditional sympathies with the Unionist cause. Eventually the work of Haslam's IWSLGA was eclipsed by the more strident and militant Irish Women's Franchise League. Meanwhile, Haslam remained a loyal secretary of the IWSLGA from 1876 to 1913 (until she was in her eighties), after which she became its life president.

In 1889 Haslam replaced Isabella Tod, the founding mother of Irish suffrage, on the London Committee of the Ladies National Association. Her energetic campaigning remained undimmed during the 1890s, as she took on involvement in the cause of Irish working women. Although she did not support Irish home rule, she helped found the Dublin branch of the Women's Liberal Unionist Association and encouraged the work of other Unionist associations opposed to the act. When the IWSLGA failed to gain a broad base of support because of its Unionist affiliation, she encouraged its involvement in local affairs on urban and rural councils and the work of the Poor Law Guardians in the relief of poverty. She recognized that local government, particularly after the passing of the Local Government (Ireland) Act of 1898, offered women the chance to extend their activities, whereas national campaigns such as that for suffrage were constantly being frustrated by lack of political progress.

Well into their eighties, both the Haslams were still campaigning. In 1916 Thomas produced his swan song, "Some Last Words on Women's Suffrage," a year before his death. To the last, Anna carried on her campaigning and invaluable administrative work in the many societies she supported with grace and good humor. She lived to cast her vote in December 1918 at her polling station on St. Stephen's Green, Dublin, in the first general election at which Irish women were entitled to vote.

See also Anthony, Susan B.; Cousins, Margaret; Jellicoe, Anne; Mott, Lucretia Coffin; Sheehy-Skeffington, Hannah; Stanton, Elizabeth Cady; Tod, Isabella.

References and Further Reading

Cullen, Mary. 1995. "Anna Maria Haslam." In Mary Cullen and Maria Luddy, *Women: Power and Consciousness in Nineteenth-Century Ireland: Eight Biographical Studies*. Dublin: Attic Press.

Cullen, Mary, and Maria Luddy. 1995. *Women: Power and Consciousness in Nineteenth-Century Ireland: Eight Biographical Studies*. Dublin: Attic Press.

Murphy, Cliona, ed. 1989. *The Women's Suffrage Movement and Irish Society in the Early Twentieth Century*. London: Harvester Wheatsheaf.

Ó Céirin, Kit, and Cyril Ó Céirin, eds. 1996. *Women of Ireland: A Historical Dictionary*. Kinvara, County Galway: Tír Eolas.

Owens, Rosemary Cullen. 1984. *Smashing Times: A History of the Irish Women's Suffrage Movement 1889–1922*. Dublin: Attic Press.

He Xiangning
(1878–1972)
China

He Xiangning played a leading role in the Central Women's Department of the Nationalist Party (Guomindang) established by Sun Yat-sen in 1924, which aimed to raise the consciousness of the mass of Chinese women in support of revolutionary social change. A determined feminist from a young age, she resisted traditional practices and refused to have her feet bound. She married a Westernized Chinese and in 1902 sold off her trousseau to raise funds to go with him to Tokyo and join other Chinese radicals studying there. She entered Tokyo Women's Art School and in 1905 joined Sun Yat-sen's Revolutionary Alliance without first obtaining her husband's permission.

He Xiangning lived in exile in Japan and returned to China in 1923. Her husband, Liao Zhongkai, a close and trusted associate of Sun Yat-sen, was given a leading role in the nationalist government in 1924. Along with Song Qingling, she was elected to the Guomindang's Central Executive Committee and was also appointed to a prestigious post in the Central Women's Department, where she worked on women's rights and the encouragement of their participation in the revolution. She also organized cooperation between the department and other anti-imperialist associations such as the communist-led Women's Suffrage Association. Liaising between various peasant associations, she attempted to unify women in the cause of their own emancipation, although this goal would have to wait until after the Chinese Revolution and the reunification of the country. With funds from the Soviet Comintern during 1924–1925, He's department enlisted the help of leading feminist activists Cai Chang and Deng Yingchao. Such a disparate mix of people led to inevitable difficulties, however, and a lack of consensus on the major gender issues that He wished to challenge, such as women's free choice in marriage, their right to divorce, and the abolition of the traditional practices of polygamy and concubinage. With this conflict in mind, He emphasized programs that would encourage women of all political persuasions to work together. For example, she set up literacy schools, which would help women learn new skills, encourage them to teach, and perhaps eventually lead them to support reform of the legal codes. In everything, her aim was to unite women against their age-old subordination and in support of nationalist ideals and revolutionary change.

In 1926 He organized peasant and working women into Red Cross units in support of the Northern Expedition campaign led by Sun Yat-sen's successor, Chang Kai-shek, against the warlords. She took a group of women with her to Wuhan and there gave them training. During the bitter fighting between communists and nationalists that broke out in 1927, many of these radical women were hunted down and killed. During the following twenty years, He Xiangning kept away from mainstream politics. By the end of her life, she was looked upon as one of the great Chinese role models, along with Cai Chang, Xiang Jingyu, Song Qingling, and Qiu Jin. Revered as an elder stateswoman, she was given several honorary roles in the People's Republic of China, including that of chair of the All-China Women's Federation.

See also Cai Chang; Deng Yingchao; Qiu Jin; Song Qingling; Xiang Jingyu.

References and Further Reading

Gilmartin, Christina Kelly. 1995. *Engendering the Chinese Revolution: Radical Women, Communist Politics and Mass Movements in the 1920s.* Berkeley: University of California Press.

Wang Zheng. 1999. *Women in the Chinese Enlightenment: An Illustrated History.* New York: Alfred A. Knopf.

Heymann, Lida Gustava
(1867–1943)
Germany

The feminist, suffragist, and social reformer Lida Gustava Heymann worked closely with Anita Augspurg, her friend and companion, for forty years. Both were dedicated antivivisectionists and vegetarians and were leading figures in the German suffrage movement until nationalist interests prevailed over those of women's suffrage at the outbreak of war in 1914. Disillusioned, Heymann diverted her energies thereafter into the international pacifist movement.

Heymann was born into a wealthy Protestant family in Hamburg. Her father was a coffee importer, and after her education at a girls' school, Heymann lived at home until her father's death in 1896. Then financially independent, she was able freely to take up philanthropic work and, impressed by the work of the U.S. settlement movement of Jane Addams, she involved herself in numerous humanitarian enterprises. She helped set up a soup kitchen; founded a day nursery, a lunch club for single women, an actresses' benevolent society, a women's home, and a society for female clerical workers; she also supported dress reform. In 1896, at a women's conference in Berlin, she met Anita Augspurg, who would become her lifetime companion. In 1898 Heymann joined the reformer Minna Cauer in the campaign against state-regulated prostitution as a member of the Women's Welfare Association in Hamburg, but persistent police repression of the association's meetings led her to take legal action in 1900.

In 1902 with thirteen other women, Heymann founded the German Association for Women's Suffrage, which combined the campaign for the vote with a moral crusade for temperance, the protection of the dignity of women, and the continued campaign against state-regulated prostitution. In 1907 the association moved to Munich, and in 1913 when the left and right wings could no longer work together, Heymann, Augspurg, and Minna Cauer joined the more militant German Women's Suffrage Association (established in 1912 by Johanna Elberskirchen) and took part in numerous demonstrations and marches.

From 1904 to 1909, Heymann had worked with Augspurg on the establishment of the International Woman Suffrage Alliance. During World War I, Heymann withdrew to concentrate on the pacifist activities that she had been working on since 1899. In 1915 she published an impassioned appeal, "Women of Europe, When Will Your Call Ring Out?," urging women everywhere to speak out against the massacre going on in the trenches of France and Flanders. In April she Attended the congress of pacifist women held in The Hague at which the International Committee of Women for Permanent Peace (which in 1919 became the Women's International League for Peace and Freedom) was established, acting as an interpreter and demonstrating, with other pacifist women, that the international women's movement should attempt reconciliation between the warring sides.

After the congress, Augspurg founded the German Women's Committee for a Permanent Peace with Heymann. Like many other feminist pacifists, Heymann saw war as a peculiarly male pursuit in which male-run states fought each other, whereas women's qualities of cooperation and understanding were thus innately pacifist. She was, however, banned from making speeches in November 1915. Her activities were further suppressed when the militant German Women's Suffrage League was dissolved in 1916 by the government. In February 1917 Heymann, who with Augspurg was fiercely anti-Prussian, was forced to go into hiding because of her support for a Bavarian republic. But in 1919 Bavaria was incorporated into the new Weimar Republic, and after women in Germany won the vote in 1918, Heymann stood (unsuccessfully) as a social democratic candidate for the Weimar national assembly. As a radical and a pacifist, her activities would be closely monitored by the Nazis in later years, during which, for the most part, she and Augspurg were inseparable and lived on a farm outside Munich with female-only farmhands. In 1919 she and Augspurg began publishing the journal *Woman in the State* (to 1932) in Munich, but as a pacifist Heymann disassociated herself from the mainstream German women's movement because of its increasingly nationalistic and militaristic stance during the rise of Nazism. She concentrated her energies instead on working for the Women's International League for Peace and Freedom, serving as its vice president from 1919 to 1924, during which time she organized its German branch in Switzerland and afterward served as its honorary chair. On holiday in Mallorca in Italy when the Nazis came to power in 1933, she went into exile with Augspurg and spent the rest of her life sharing a home with her in Zurich. Their joint memoirs, *Erlebtes-Erschautes* (Experienced and Seen), were published in 1972.

See also Addams, Jane; Augspurg, Anita; Cauer, Minna.

References and Further Reading
Braker, Regina. 1995. "Bertha von Suttner's Spiritual Daughters: The Feminist Pacifism of Anita Augspurg, Lida Gustava Heymann, and Helene Stöcker at the International Congress of Women at the Hague, 1915." *Women's Studies International Forum* 18(2): 103–111.
Bussey, Gertrude, and Margaret Tims. 1980 [1960]. *Pioneers for Peace: Women's International League for Peace and Freedom 1915–1965*. Reprint, London: George Allen and Unwin.
Evans, Richard. 1973. *The Feminist Movement in Germany 1894–1933*. London: Sage.
Josephson, Harold, Sandi Cooper, and Steven C. Hause et al., eds. 1985. *Biographical Dictionary of Modern Peace Leaders*. Westport, CT: Greenwood Press.
Rupp, Leila J. 1997. *Worlds of Women: The Making of an International Women's Movement*. Princeton: Princeton University Press.
Sklar, Kathryn Kish. 1998. *Social Justice Feminists in the United States and Germany: A Dialogue in Documents 1885–1933*. Ithaca: Cornell University Press.

Heyrick, Elizabeth
(1769–1831)
United Kingdom

The English Quaker abolitionist Elizabeth Heyrick was the author of more than twenty tracts and pamphlets between 1815 and 1830 on a range of social, political, and economic issues that were exceptional subjects for a woman of her time to consider. In her writings, she tackled not only slavery but also penal reform, including corporal punishment and the abolition of the death penalty, cruelty to animals, the injustices of the corn laws and the high price of bread, Catholic emancipation, vagrancy, and the economic distress of the Leicestershire framework-knitters. In her written contributions, Heyrick was undoubtedly one of the most persuasive voices in the women's antislavery movement in Britain. It was she who, by demanding the immediate liberation of all the British Empire's slaves—a view supported by the mainstream of a surprisingly radical female abolitionist movement in Britain—challenged the cautious, gradualist approach to abolition of the male-led Anti-Slavery Society. But in Heyrick's case, as with so many other unappreciated women reformers who worked in male-dominated movements, her contribution was marginalized in subsequent histories and memoirs written by men, with Heyrick often frowned upon for her extremism as a "fanatic."

Heyrick grew up in a Unitarian family of prosperous hosiery manufacturers in Leicester. As a young woman, she developed a reputation for compassion and charity and was guided in her religious faith by a belief in the sinfulness of slavery. She married when she was nineteen in 1787, and after her husband took up a career in the army, her life was a continuous round of shifting from one army billet to another, both in England and in Ireland. After being widowed in 1797 and having no children, Heyrick went back to Leicestershire to live with her family. She became a Quaker in about 1798 and decided to devote her life to social causes. Heyrick was greatly inspired by the writings of the English radical Thomas Paine on liberty and abolition, and, liberated by widowhood from a highly circumscribed life, began pouring out her views in a stream of literature. She saw all social ills as emanating from the same essential sin—the "lust of wealth"—combined with the punitive effects on the poor of protectionist legislation such as the corn laws. In her writings, she exposed the deleterious effects on the human psyche of economic misery and in particular condemned the exploitation of the working masses by the new manufacturing industries of the Industrial Revolution. In her advocacy of a proper respect for the labor of the poor and for protective legislation including a maximum twelve-hour day and the institution of a minimum wage, she also supported the laborers' right to strike. Heyrick sympathized with the bitter campaign of the Luddites, who had wrecked machinery in Leicester in 1817 in protest at the threat it posed to their livelihoods, a protest that had ended with the execution of six of their leaders. In 1825 she actively supported a strike by Leicestershire framework knitters against a reduction in their earnings to less than a living wage.

In the first years of the nineteenth century, Heyrick had published a pacifist tract, "The Warning: Recommended to the Serious Attention of All Christians and Lovers of Their Country." In her early years of activism, she undertook charitable voluntary work as a prison visitor and even attempted to stop the cruel practice of bull baiting, when in 1809 at Bonsall in Derbyshire she ended such a contest by intervening and buying the bull. That same year she published two tracts on the subject: "A Christmas Box for the Advocates of Bull-Baiting" and "Bull Baiting: A

Village Dialogue between Tom Brown and John Simms." Other tracts on Christian morality, the virtues of honest toil, the relief of distress among the unemployed in the manufacturing industries, the cruelties of the meat trade at Smithfield Market, and legislation against vagrants followed between 1811 and 1824, by which time she had taken up her concerted campaign for the abolition of slavery.

Heyrick was a founding member and district treasurer of the Birmingham Ladies Society for the Relief of Negro Slaves, established in 1825 (later known as the Female Society for the Relief of British Negro Slaves), as well as leading the Leicester Ladies' Anti-Slavery Society in her home county. Although the *trade* in slaves had been abolished in Britain in 1807, the slaves in Britain's colonies, many of them in the economically crucial sugar-producing plantations of the West Indies, had not been emancipated. Heyrick's first public act on behalf of the British abolitionist campaign came in 1824 when, after conducting a door-to-door survey in her home city of Leicester, she called for consumers to boycott West Indian sugar in the optimistic hope that they could be persuaded to opt for the much more expensive free-grown sugar from the East Indies. She had come to the conclusion that nothing less than the immediate, wholesale liberation of the slaves in Britain's colonies was necessary, a belief that placed her in direct opposition to the gradualist approach adopted by the male members of the Anti-Slavery Society led by William Wilberforce, who had settled for its piecemeal eradication.

Heyrick laid out her principles on abolition and the boycott of West Indian sugar in four pamphlets published in 1824, most notably the landmark text "Immediate, Not Gradual Abolition of Slavery." The impact of this tract on the abolitionist movement in Britain was unprecedented. "Hurled like a bomb in the midst of battle" (Ware 1992, 71), it provoked considerable debate on the tactics of the abolitionist campaign and was also widely circulated in the United States. Indeed, its argument was so powerfully stated that many assumed the tract had been written by a man. Such was the alarm with which Heyrick's radical argument was viewed by Wilberforce and the male leadership of the abolitionist movement, which disapproved of a woman taking such an outspoken and public position on abolition, that attempts were made to suppress it.

In an uncharacteristic move considering the social climate of the times, women supporters of the antislavery movement in Britain did not oblige the male leadership by kowtowing to their more conservative approach. By 1831, the year of Heyrick's death, there were forty-seven such women's societies in existence, and many of their members agreed with Heyrick's far-reaching calls for nothing less than immediate abolition. Her abolitionist pamphlets, such as "No British Slavery" (1827), were widely circulated by these women's groups, which also organized sugar boycotts in cities such as Worcester, Colchester, London, and Edinburgh. In 1826 Heyrick went so far as to call for male electors to vote only for parliamentary candidates who announced their commitment to abolition. And in 1830 the Female Society for the Relief of British Negro Slaves in Birmingham submitted a resolution to the Anti-Slavery Society urging it to call for immediate abolition, at Heyrick's instigation threatening to withdraw its financial support from the society if it did not. Because the Anti-Slavery Society was heavily reliant on its many female fund-raisers, it conceded and at its May 1830 conference agreed to remove references to "gradual abolition" from its literature.

Heyrick remained an influential figure until her death, which sadly came two years before all British slaves were emancipated, in 1833. Although two hagiographic accounts of her life were published in 1862 and 1895, she was quickly forgotten and disappeared into obscurity. However, according to Kenneth Corfield's illuminating essay (Corfield 1986), her work was an inspiration to U.S. abolitionists such as Lucretia Mott and William Lloyd Garrison, and the black abolitionist Frederick Douglass was unequivocal in his praise, lauding Heyrick as "the woman to whom I owe everything" (Corfield 1986, 49). Although there were limitations to Heyrick's reformist principles, and she never went so far as to demand changes to the franchise leading to women's political emancipation, in her fusion of her Christian beliefs in righteousness and justice with her egalitarian principles, she demonstrated to other women that they were capable of a constructive social mission outside the domestic sphere.

See also Mott, Lucretia Coffin.

References and Further Reading
A Brief Sketch of the Life and Labours of Mrs. Elizabeth Heyrick. 1862. Leicester: n.p.
Corfield, Kenneth. 1986. "Elizabeth Heyrick: Radical Quaker." In Gail Malmgreen, ed., *Religion in the Lives of English Women, 1760–1930.* London: Croom Helm.
Fladeland, Betty. 1972. *Men and Brothers: Anglo-American Antislavery Cooperation.* Chicago: University of Illinois Press.
Gleadle, Kathryn. 1995. *The Early Feminists: Radical Unitarians and the Emergence of the Women's Rights Movement, 1831–1851.* London: Macmillan.
Halbersleben, Karen I. 1993. *Women's Participation in the British Antislavery Movement 1824–1865.* Lewiston: Edwin Mellen Press.
Midgely, Clare. 1992. *Women against Slavery: The British Campaigns 1780–1870.* London: Routledge.
Nicholls, C. S., ed. 1993. *Dictionary of National Biography: Missing Persons.* Oxford: Oxford University Press.
Ware, Vron. 1992. *Beyond the Pale: White Women, Racism, and History.* London: Verso.

Hill, Octavia
(1838–1912)
United Kingdom

The outstanding British pioneer for housing reform Octavia Hill set standards for the renovation and management of dwellings for the poor that were adopted throughout the Continent and United States. In the belief that it was of fundamental importance to establish a relationship of mutual trust and respect between slum tenants and their landlords, she introduced a network of more sympathetic volunteer rent collectors and set about the refurbishment of rented accommodation for the poor that would discourage vandalism and defaulting on payment of rents. From these reforming activities sprung up a system of social work among the poor based on Hill's belief that they should be assisted in the recovery of their self-respect, not through indiscriminate handouts but through retraining and rehabilitation into the workplace. Hill was also a pioneer of the open space movement that led to the founding of the National Trust for Places of Historic Interest or Natural Beauty.

Hill was born into a family of reformers, in Wisbech, Cambridgeshire. Her grandfather Thomas Southwood Smith had been a sanitary reformer, and her father had had a long interest in penal reform, with his wife at one stage running a progressive school for infants in Wisbech based on the principles of educational pioneer Johann Pestalozzi. When her father's banking business failed, however, he suffered a nervous breakdown, and the family was split up, with Octavia being sent to take up paid work for the Ladies' Co-operative Guild in London in 1851. Set up as a Christian socialist project, the co-operative was managed by her mother, and at the age of only fourteen, Hill was entrusted with teaching the younger girls how to make toy dolls in the guild's crafts workshop for working-class women and girls. It was there that she met the art critic and socialist John Ruskin in 1853 and the Christian socialist Frederick Maurice, under whose influence she gave up her Unitarian faith.

Hill's early years in London were spent in Russell Square, where she had her first indelible memories of watching out of her window "the London poor pass in rain and fog" and "Tottenham Court Road on Saturday night, with its haggard faces" (Bell 1943, 19). After studying art under Ruskin, Hill earned a living as a copyist, but she was soon drawn into her lifetime of social activism, when in 1856 she was appointed secretary of the women's classes run by Maurice at his Working Men's College. At this time, she became a close friend of the medical pioneer Sophia Jex-Blake and was involved in the organization in 1866 of Barbara Bodichon's petition on women's suffrage in Britain, as well as supporting the Married Women's Property Act campaign and Bodichon's petition for London University to establish local examinations for girls. For a while, Hill taught French and drawing lessons at Bodichon's pioneering Portman Hall school, as did her sister Miranda. But Hill's support for women's emancipation did not extend to a belief in women's suffrage, and she remained firmly convinced that "political power would militate against women's usefulness in the large field of public work" (Perkin 1993, 217).

It was in 1864 that Hill took up her pioneering housing project in Marylebone. With the support of Ruskin, she bought three houses in Nottingham Place, in a squalid slum district, and experimented with a new style of housing management. Disliking the oppression of the poor by uncaring rent collectors, Hill replaced them with personal visitors, initially collecting

Octavia Hill (National Portrait Gallery)

the rent herself in order to become acquainted with the tenants, who were also offered rewards for paying on time and helped by Hill with obtaining work or apprenticeships for their children. Hill took her work very seriously; she made a study of building and banking practices in order to establish fair practices, and by 1866, when she bought six more houses and her scheme expanded, she had introduced a new element to attract other landlords, guaranteeing them a 5 percent financial return on their investment in new model housing. As housing for the poor was refurbished, Hill encouraged the families themselves to clean up the adjoining passageways and staircases, and unemployed tenants were enlisted in much of the repair work. Hill trained teams of volunteer rent collectors and housing managers, established the Society of Women Housing Managers, and designed training courses leading to a diploma from the National Association of Housing Managers. By the early 1880s, some 2,000 people had been rehoused under Hill's scheme.

In 1869 Hill founded the Charity Organisation Society (COS), an umbrella organization for London charities that would be a leading voice in Victorian philanthropy, and became a member of the Marylebone District Relief Committee, which was responsible for outdoor relief (i.e., not in a workhouse) of the destitute. Under its auspices, she organized a team of volunteer women visitors, whose numbers had risen to thirty by 1874. Hill gave them training, advocating that they work for other charities in order to broaden their experience. Central to her methods was the keeping of proper, detailed case notes on the economic status of the families visited and the exchanging of information with local Poor Law officials of the St. Mary's Poor Law District, during which Hill insisted that the privacy of applicants be respected. Once each case had been evaluated, based on the merits of the individual characters of applicants, and help administered, their progress was monitored. There were, however, many deserving poor who would have no truck with the system because they disliked its intrusive practices.

Thus Hill's methods became the prototype for social work. But on one issue, Hill was adamant and would remain so all her life: at all times she maintained a clear distinction between her rehabilitation work among the poor and that of the antiquated poor law system, which, she felt, baled out charity willy-nilly to many undeserving cases. Believing as she did, in that diehard Victorian tradition, that there were two types of poor people—the deserving and the undeserving—Hill became a leading advocate of self-help schemes for the poor that circumvented indiscriminate and sentimental acts of charity, such as handouts by the Salvation Army. She believed that solicitation by the poor of public charity was demeaning and also corrupting, observing (in a typical paper read at the COS in February 1889): "I am quite awed when I think what our impatient charity is doing to the poor of London. Men who should hold up their heads as self-respecting fathers of families, learning to sing like beggars in the streets—all because we give pennies" (Boyd 1982). Such beliefs would also lead to extremism, with Hill going so far as to argue against old-age pensions for the same reason. As with her housing management scheme, Hill's principles on the relief of poverty would spread later to Europe and the United States.

By 1874, such had been the importance attached to Hill's work that her friends raised a fund so that she could stop teaching art and give her time to housing reform. She published two accounts of her theories, *Homes of the London Poor* (1875) and *Our Common Land* (1878), in the latter outlining her belief in the preservation of open spaces in the inner cities.

In 1884 Hill effected a personal triumph when she managed to persuade the Ecclesiastic Commissioners to allow her to manage their rented property in Southwark and Deptford, which greatly enhanced the prestige of her work. The work of the COS also was greatly extended, from individual casework to major campaigns for sanitary reforms, lobbied for by special sanitary aid committees set up to combat infectious diseases. The COS also organized volunteer health visitors, health education programs, and assisted emigration. In 1886 the Invalid Children's Aid Association was established as the result of a COS-led project set up to visit crippled and sick children. Other important community services proliferated, including the first dispensary to counteract tuberculosis, work with the blind and mentally ill, and a network of hospital almoners.

After the founding of the Women's University Settlement in an area of model housing in Southwark in 1887, Hill somewhat reluctantly agreed to be on its executive committee. She was initially skeptical of the social acceptability of a gaggle of women removing themselves from their homes and families to live together in an artificial community. She soon changed her mind, however, becoming convinced that settlement work provided new opportunities for public service for respectable middle-class women in poor areas where they would normally never have set foot. Hill also discovered that such work provided a perfect opportunity for the development of that essential sense of relationship between the rich and the poor that she believed was the foundation of social work. Hill later established a scholarship fund appeal to give financial assistance to women wishing to take up social work training through the settlement. One of the first to benefit was reformer Mary Sheepshanks, who later worked for the Morley Memorial College for Working Men and Women, a pioneering adult education institution that received much support from Hill.

The other essential building block of Hill's work in rehabilitating the poor was to provide places of recreation for them that gave welcome relief from the drabness of their daily lives in the slums. In essence, Hill was one of the first women eco-campaigners in her drive to preserve open spaces and establish what she called "open air sitting rooms for the poor" (Owen 1965, 495). In the 1870s she had tried and failed to save the Swiss Cottage Fields from developers, and she joined with her sister Miranda in founding the Kyrle Society in 1877 to carry out tree-planting schemes in inner cities in an attempt to improve run-down urban environments. Concerned at how the London school board closed all its many playgrounds across London in the evenings and on Saturdays, Hill argued for greater access to them for poor children in her 1877 book, *Our Common Land*. In 1884 she set up a committee to raise the then-enormous sum of £70,000 to buy Parliament Hill Fields, which in 1889 were successfully purchased and incorporated into that much-loved great open space of north London—Hampstead Heath. In 1895 Hill was involved in the establishment of one of her most enduring legacies, the National Trust for Places of Historic Interest or Natural Beauty, which plays a crucial role today in the preservation of the British landscape. In a forward-thinking essay of 1899, "The Open Spaces of the Future," published in the *Nineteenth Century*, Hill urged that greater attention be paid to preserving greenbelts in urban areas.

Hill was still active in many causes in the twentieth century. During 1905–1908, she served on the Royal Commission on the Poor Laws and the Relief of Distress from Unemployment with Beatrice Webb, but was not at her best in such work, remaining constrained by her personal concerns that free relief of poverty would discourage the working classes from getting honest work or putting money by for time of trouble. Even the provision of free school meals, in her estimation, discouraged the responsibility of working-class parents to make adequate provisions for their children.

Octavia Hill spent her life surrounded by middle-aged women, many of them spinsters like herself who, as Sybil Oldfield has pointed out in *Spinsters of This Parish* (1984), had dedicated their lives to the feminine sphere of duty and were the backbone of Victorian philanthropic activity in the nineteenth century. In *English Philanthropy, 1660–1960*, David Owen paints a picture of a woman who could be both brusque and supremely bossy in her paternalistic no-nonsense approach to humanitarian work, one of history's many benevolent despots who was convinced that the eradication of social deprivation often boiled down to a matter of individual resolve and strength of character. She was not a beautiful woman but was most certainly impressive; in the words of Mary Stocks she was "supreme, imaginative, original, and in the best sense of the word, charitable" (Stocks 1970, 55). Octavia Hill displayed an intense and unflagging degree of self-devotion to the betterment of society and a desire to see the poor rediscover their own "spark of nobleness" (Maurice 1913, 61). The Octavia Hill Housing Trust continues to support affordable housing schemes to this day in the spirit of Octavia Hill's vision, and can be contacted at http://www.octaviahill.co.uk/trust.

See also Bodichon, Barbara; Jex-Blake, Sophia; Webb, Beatrice.

References and Further Reading
Bell, Enid Moberley. 1943. *Octavia Hill*. London: Constable.

Boyd, Nancy. 1982. *Josephine Butler, Octavia Hill, Florence Nightingale: Three Victorian Women Who Changed Their World*. London: Macmillan.

Darley, Gillian. 1990. *Octavia Hill: A Life*. London: Constable.

Hill, William Thompson. 1956. *Octavia Hill: Pioneer of the National Trust and Housing Reformer*. London: Hutchins.

Lewis, Jane. 1991. *Women and Social Action in Victorian and Edwardian England*. Aldershot: Elgar.

Maurice, C. Edmund, ed. 1913. *Life of Octavia Hill as Told in Her Letters*. London: Macmillan.

Morris, Emily, ed. 1928. *Octavia Hill: Early Ideals*. London: Allen and Unwin.

Mowat, Charles Loch. 1961. *The Charity Organisation Society, 1869–1913: Its Ideas and Work*. London: Methuen.

Oldfield, Sybil. 1984. *Spinsters of This Parish: The Life and Times of F. M. Mayor and Mary Sheepshanks*. London: Virago.

Owen, David. 1965. *English Philanthropy 1660–1960*. Oxford: Oxford University Press.

Perkin, Joan. 1993. *Victorian Women*. London: John Murray.

Prochaska, F. K. 1980. *Women and Philanthropy in Nineteenth-Century England*. Oxford: Clarendon Press.

Stocks, Mary. 1970. *My Commonplace Book*. London: Peter Davies.

Walton, Ronald G. 1975. *Women in Social Work*. London: Routledge and Kegan Paul.

Hiratsuka Raicho
(Hiratsuka Haruko)
(1886–1971)
Japan

Hiratsuka Raicho's activities as the inspiration of Japan's "new women," through her innovative Bluestocking Society and magazine of the same name, revived feminist activity in Japan after the Meiji Constitution of 1889 had curtailed women's political activities. Originally founded in 1911 to promote women's writing and literary interests, the Bluestocking Society inspired a brief flowering of feminist writing in Japan and the dissemination of feminist ideas from the West. Japanese women were encouraged to become involved in issues such as abortion, birth control, and, in the case of Hiratsuka, a reaffirmation of their indispensable roles as mothers.

Born in Tokyo, Hiratsuka enjoyed the benefits of an intellectual, albeit conservative upbringing. She studied at the Ochanomizu Girls' High School in Tokyo and disregarded her father's wishes, continuing her education in 1903 at the Japan Women's University. After graduating in 1906, she studied Zen Buddhism, learned English, and joined a literary group.

With financial help from her mother, who offered the use of Hiratsuka's dowry money as well as other supporters in the literary milieu, in 1911 Hiratsuka founded the magazine *Bluestocking*, which gave its name to the feminist group it inspired. Hiratsuka, for long revered as the guiding influence on the movement, would later express in a famous essay the yearnings of the Japanese new woman awakening and rising up like a sun to challenge old male-dominated conventions and seeking "to create a new kingdom, where a new religion, new morality, and new laws are carried out, based on the spiritual values and surpassing the brilliance of the sun" (Sievers 1983, 176).

In the pages of *Bluestocking*, in addition to printing fiction and poetry that explored love, women's sexuality, and their need for self-expression, Hiratsuka's magazine set out to promote general interest among women in literature, culture, and their own creativity. Hiratsuka and her contemporaries became very interested in the work of Henrik Ibsen and in particular his play *A Doll's House. Bluestocking* debated the choices faced by many "Japanese Noras" who found themselves in a similar predicament, raising the question of what happens after the independent-minded Nora rejects her marriage and leaves home. Hiratsuka also translated the feminist writings of the Swedish reformer Ellen Key, as well as work by Emma Goldman and Olive Schreiner, and published articles on sexual behavior by the British psychologist Havelock Ellis. By 1913, however, under increasing pressure from Japanese socialist feminists, the magazine had become a forum for discussion of wider social issues such as suffrage and more overt criticism of the political and social discrimination against Japanese women.

Hiratsuka herself opposed the idea of women working outside the home and as a result neglecting their children. This view led to a debate among Japanese feminists in the magazines *The Sun* and *Women's Consensus* on how women could reconcile their needs and duties as mothers with their desire for greater economic independence and political equality with men. In her thinking on this issue, Hiratsuka was strongly influenced by the writings of Key and had translated and published extracts from her book *Love and Marriage* in *Bluestocking* in 1911. According to Hiratsuka, children were part of society as well as members of individual families, and therefore the state must ensure their protection and, by association, the security of their mothers by providing aid and subsidies to mothers. This attitude was in marked contrast to the ideas of Hiratsuka's contemporary Ito Noe, who felt that women's only hope lay in total economic independence from husbands and from the state.

Despite its moderate tone, the magazine *Bluestocking* was frequently banned as a supposed pernicious influence on morals. In 1913, Hiratsuka published a scorching attack on women who condoned the prevailing system of male privilege in Japan and their own subjugation in marriage. She argued that they should have the right to marry for love instead of effectively prostituting themselves by submitting to the sexual demands of husbands. This opinion prompted an official warning to the magazine's editors from the government. Hiratsuka and her contributors continued to suffer constant harassment in their work and were derided as "new women" by those who had little understanding of the concept. Issues of the magazine were often banned because of the nature of their content, and Hiratsuka's home was vandalized.

In her private life, Hiratsuka lived with a man younger than herself, the artist Okumura Hiroshi, by whom she had two children. After Okumura became sick with tuberculosis, the couple ran up debts, and Hiratsuka was so discouraged by the stresses of keeping the magazine going and by the flagging support for its increasingly political position among more conservative women that she handed over the running of *Bluestocking* to Ito Noe in January 1915. Plagued by debts and government interference, the magazine was finally closed in February 1916.

Hiratsuka did not entirely abandon her social concerns: she continued to lecture and in 1918 became concerned about the conditions of women workers in the textile and other industries. She began campaigning and raising funds to set up a new organization dedicated to women's rights to suffrage and equality with men and to calls for higher standards of female education and the protection of mothers. In March 1920 the New Woman's Society was inaugurated by Hiratsuka and Ichikawa Fusae to work toward seeing women "fulfill our natural obligations and attain our natural rights" (Robins-Mowry 1983, 66). As a nationwide organization, it was also dedicated to obtaining the abolition of the notorious Article 5 of the 1887 Police Security Regulations banning women from political organizations and rallies. The society gathered petitions to the Diet in July 1920, calling for amendments to Article 5 of the law, finally achieved in 1922. It also asked for controls to be placed on men with venereal disease being able to marry and for the rights of their wives to divorce them—both of which were rejected. Despite numerous setbacks, the society continued to regularly petition for repeal of Article 5. However, personal conflicts and differences of opinion made it impossible for Hiratsuka and Ichikawa to continue working together, and in 1921 they both left the New Woman's Society.

Hiratsuka withdrew once more from activism and in 1922 the society was dissolved after the legal restrictions on women's political organizations were lifted. By this time the society had ingrained a sense of mission in other women who were to follow and campaign for reform later in the 1920s. After women were given the vote at the end of World War II, Hiratsuka took a guiding role as president of the Federation of Japanese Women's Societies and turned her energies to world peace. In 1951, together with Ichikawa Fusae, she organized Women Opposing Remilitarization of Japan; later she protested the Vietnam War.

See also Goldman, Emma; Ichikawa Fusae; Ito Noe; Key, Ellen; Schreiner, Olive.

References and Further Reading

Jayawardena, Kumari. 1986. *Feminism and Nationalism in the Third World.* London: Zed Books.
Robins-Mowry, Dorothy. 1983. *The Hidden Sun: Women of Modern Japan.* Epping, Essex: Bowker.
Sievers, Sharon. 1983. *Flowers in Salt: The Beginnings of Feminist Consciousness in Modern Japan.* Stanford: Stanford University Press.

Hobhouse, Emily
(1860–1926)
United Kingdom/South Africa

In 1900 Emily Hobhouse, the daughter of a country rector, found herself having to bear witness to the terrible conditions suffered by Afrikaner women and children in the British internment camps set up during the Boer War of 1899–1902. Her official report would establish her as a foremost humanitarian in the first years of the twentieth century.

Hobhouse's early life is a classic tale of the sublimation of the hopes and aspirations of a young Victorian woman to filial duty. She was born at a country rectory near Liskeard, Cornwall, and was educated at home. Her family was well connected and had a reputation for philanthropy. As the youngest, unmarried daughter of the family, however, Hobhouse suffered the fate of many of her contemporaries. She was saddled with the responsibility, from age nineteen, of caring for her clergyman father in his widowhood, until his death in 1895 finally freed her at the age of thirty-five. Throughout this time, she was allowed to indulge in only the least controversial acts of local charity among the poor. But by then, her lonely early life had left its mark on a nature that would remain deeply melancholic.

At last free to embrace the social concerns that had for so long preoccupied her, Hobhouse traveled to the United States and studied the social work carried out by Jane Addams at Hull House before undertaking welfare among Cornish emigrant miners at the town of Virginia, Minnesota. In this remote mining town near the Canadian border, she organized Sunday schools, visited the sick, and campaigned for temperance and against prostitution. For a while she was engaged to an American businessman and prepared herself for a life ranching with him in Mexico City. After she waited for him to join her in Mexico City, he eventually jilted her, and Hobhouse returned to England in 1899. She lived in Chelsea, became involved in housing projects with the social reformer Octavia Hill, and worked for the Women's Industrial Council, where she met and became friends with the pacifist Kathleen Courtney. At the outbreak of the Boer War in 1899, Hobhouse became a member of the pacifist group the South African Conciliation Committee and was appointed secretary of its women's group, helping to organize antiwar rallies.

In 1900 Hobhouse founded the Relief Fund for South African Women and Children after reports filtered back to her about the sufferings of Afrikaner women and children uprooted by General Horatio Kitchener's policy of land clearance and held in detention camps. The fund was supported mainly by Quakers and other humanitarians at a time when the majority of the British population were fiercely jingoistic and anti-Boer. Through it, Hobhouse raised money to buy supplies of food, which were sent to Capetown in December 1900. During the early part of 1901, Hobhouse visited the concentration camps in and around Bloemfontein in the Orange River Colony. As she distributed supplies of food, clothing, and medicine, she observed the lack of sanitation and primitive conditions in which the inmates were housed under canvas structures; there was also terrible malnutrition and endemic disease.

Back in London in January 1901, she denounced the "methods of barbarism" employed by British troops in their displacement of Afrikaner families in South Africa, met with the secretary of war to encourage the government to take steps to improve the situation, but still found herself up against a wall of apathy from the British government. She turned for support to Sir Henry Campbell-Bannerman and other radical Liberal opposition members of Parliament. The impact of Hobhouse's horrifying account was unprecedented and provoked considerable outrage. Her subsequent canvassing, speech making, and raising of public awareness resulted in an official British Commission being

sent out to South Africa in August and September under Millicent Garrett Fawcett to inspect the camps and improve their administration. Hobhouse was not invited to join the commission, and when she tried to return to South Africa later in 1901, Kitchener had her deported. But Fawcett's subsequent report validated Hobhouse's findings.

In 1902 Hobhouse published *The Brunt of War and Where It Fell,* a collection of women's narratives of the Boer War that she edited. Another collection, *War without Glamour: Or, Women's War Experiences Written by Themselves, 1899–1902,* was published in 1924. She also annotated and wrote the introduction for an Afrikaner woman's diary, *Tant Alie of the Transvaal: Her Diary, 1880–1902,* a firsthand account of the destruction wreaked upon the homes of settlers.

Hobhouse eventually returned to South Africa in 1903 to raise money for the dispossessed families in the Transvaal and Orange River Colony in the aftermath of the war. In 1905 she set up the first of several schools to teach spinning, lace making, and weaving to Afrikaner girls and promoted home industries, although continuing to criticize the shortcomings of British reconstruction in the region.

Hobhouse remained an outspoken pacifist during World War I and decried South African support for the British war effort, supporting the international congress held by women pacifists in The Hague in 1915. During the war she worked for the International Committee of Women for Permanent Peace that had been set up at the congress and visited German prisoner-of-war camps and German-occupied Belgium. She was closely monitored by both British and German intelligence, but it was only her failing health that eventually prevented her from continuing with relief work, as a founder of the Swiss Relief Fund, among the displaced peoples of central Europe in the aftermath of the war. In 1921 her Afrikaner friends and supporters in South Africa, who had dubbed her the "Angel of Love," raised £2,300 to buy the ailing Hobhouse a home at St. Ives in Cornwall. When she died, as a mark of the deep esteem in which she was held by Afrikaners, Hobhouse's ashes were buried at the National Women's Monument at Bloemfontein, which commemorates the 26,251 women and children who died in one of the most futile wars of the Victorian era.

See also Addams, Jane; Courtney, Kathleen D'Olier; Fawcett, Millicent Garrett; Hill, Octavia.

References and Further Reading

Balme, Jenifer Hobhouse. 1994. *To Love One's Enemies: The Work and Life of Emily Hobhouse.* Cobbe Hill, BC: Hobhouse Trust.

Fisher, John. 1971. *That Miss Hobhouse.* London: Secker and Warburg.

Fry, Ruth. 1929. *Emily Hobhouse: A Memoir.* London: Jonathan Cape.

Hobhouse, Emily. 1901. *Report of a Visit to the Camps of Women and Children in the Cape and Orange River Colonies.* London: Friars Printing Association.

Liddington, Jill. 1989. *The Long Road to Greenham: Feminism and Anti-Militarism in Britain since 1820.* London: Virago.

Oldfield, Sybil. 2001. *Women Humanitarians: A Biographical Dictionary of British Women Active between 1900 and 1950.* London: Continuum.

Reenen, Rykie van. 1984. *Emily Hobhouse: Boer War Letters.* Cape Town: Human and Rousseau.

Holtby, Winifred
(1898–1935)
United Kingdom

The feminist journalist, pacifist, and close friend of Vera Brittain was continually torn between a career as a writer and her sensitivity to the guilt suffered by many women forced to choose between the independent working life and the family. Her preoccupation with humanitarian concerns and social justice led her to dislike the emphasis being placed by women reformers on purely feminist issues: she was first and foremost a believer in equal rights and racial harmony, which in the last nine years of her life prompted her to come to the defense of black workers in South Africa after visiting the country in 1926. Holtby's untimely death has created problems for her biographers, however, with her saintly reputation set in aspic in Brittain's *Testament of Friendship* and a previous lack of emphasis on her social concerns by historians only now being addressed.

Holtby grew up at Rudston in the East Riding of Yorkshire, in a well-off farming family. Her mother, who also came from a farming background, was a local county councilor. Holtby studied at home with governesses and then at Queen Margaret's School in Scarborough; when she showed literary talent in her teens, her mother had her poetry privately printed. Holtby won a scholarship to study history at Somerville College, Oxford, in 1917, where she met her life-long friend Vera Brittain, with whom she shared the same political and feminist beliefs and dedication to social justice. Soon after, Holtby decided to put her studies on hold to serve in France with the Women's Auxiliary Army Corps (1918–1919). Returning to Oxford to complete her degree in 1919, she graduated in 1921.

Throughout her life, Holtby battled with her own ambivalent feelings toward life as an independent woman; having opted for a life as a writer, she sublimated many of her emotional and sexual needs into her work. She moved to London in 1921, sharing a flat in Bloomsbury with Brittain, and became a skilled and prolific journalist, writing for the *Manchester Guardian,* the *Yorkshire Post, Good Housekeeping,* the *Daily Express,* and the *News Chronicle* as well as the specialist teacher's journal, the *Schoolmistress.* In 1923 she published her first novel, *Anderby Wold,* set in the farming milieu in Yorkshire where she had grown up.

During the 1920s, Holtby, as a pacifist, supported the work of the League of Nations and undertook lecture tours in Europe, speaking on politics and feminist and social issues. She supported the Labour Party by canvassing for its candidates in the 1932 election. When the voting age for women was lowered to twenty-one in 1928, she published a pamphlet, "A New Voter's Guide to Party Programs," encouraging women to make full use of the franchise. With Vera Brittain, she was also active in Lady Margaret Rhondda's Six Point Group, which advocated equal pay and work opportunities for women in the public sphere, such as teaching and the civil service: these centered around the introduction of widows' pensions and family allowances, equal custody rights, nursery care, and access to birth control. The group also lobbied against the exclusion of married women from certain professions.

In 1926 Holtby was invited to South Africa, where she conducted a lecture tour to "Rotary clubs, student unions, Jewish guilds, University women, boys' and girls' high schools, training colleges, synods of clergy and Sons of England" (Brittain 1940, 199) under the auspices of the League of Nations Union. She was distressed by the racial oppression she encountered there, particularly of black workers at the Kimberley diamond mines and in the slums of Johannesburg, in which latter city she met with Zulu trade union leaders and British liberals campaigning for racial justice. She noted the continuing manifestations of British imperialism, the indifference of white administrators, and the increasing racial tension at a time when the Colour Bar Bill was in the process of segregating the black and white communities. Holtby returned to the United Kingdom, convinced that the white minority there were living off the backs of the deprived black majority. Her advocacy of racial justice in South Africa would cause her to retain close links with and give financial support to the work among blacks in South Africa of the Scottish trade unionist William Ballinger and the Industrial and Commercial Workers' Union for Black South Africans. Through an informal "Africa Group" that Holtby set up in the UK on her return (from 1934 known as the Friends of Africa) she met black intellectuals and civil rights advocates, such as the Jamaican Una Marson, with whom she developed a close friendship shortly before her death.

On her return to England in 1926, Holtby accepted the job as director and editor of Lady Rhondda's radical journal, *Time and Tide,* which she used as a forum for her advocacy of egalitarianism and world peace. She shared a home with Brittain, whose husband spent the academic year in the United States, and the two women's relationship, for long rumored to be a lesbian one, was undoubtedly one of profound mutual respect and emotional dependency.

Holtby produced several other novels, many of them featuring independently minded women: *The Crowded Street* (1924); *The Land of Green Ginger* (1927), which she herself described as embracing "passion, tuberculosis, suicidal mania, neurasthenia, lack of sanitary accommodation and stifled creative desire" (Brittain 1940 221); and *Poor Caroline* (1931). Her 1933 novel *Mandoa, Mandoa!* was a satirical depiction of African colonialism drawn from her experiences there. She also published a notable study of Virginia Woolf in 1932.

Undoubtedly, the work that has now attracted critical attention from feminists is Holtby's *Women in a Changing Civilisation* (1927). In its assessment of the contribution of women to social progress since the eighteenth century, Holtby reflected with growing apprehension that there was still a long way to go in the overturning of traditional male prejudices on women's role. She also spoke out in it against the chauvinistic male backlash against women's emancipation. Women had gained rapid ground with their postwar enfranchisement and greater employment opportunities, but Holtby noted the ominous official antifeminism now rearing its head in totalitarian states. The social revolution of the 1920s, which witnessed women shortening their skirts and cutting off their long hair, had prompted diehards such as fascist leader Sir Oswald Mosley to call for women to act once more like "real" women, in response to which Holtby had commented: "He can find them at their quintessence in the slave markets of Abyssinia, or in the winding alleys of a Chinese city" (Holtby 1934, 193). She felt that evolutionary change in the role of women had brought about changes to the female psyche and women's view of the world, a belief that she discussed in her 1935 article, "A Generation of Women's Progress." In it, she optimistically hoped that women's equality could be achieved by constructive methods emphasizing the common humanity of the sexes rather than by means that polarized them even further.

In 1931 Holtby's health had begun failing, and she was eventually diagnosed with a fatal kidney complaint, Bright's disease. She underwent painful therapy in order to buy some time, during which she set about writing her last and most famous novel, *South Riding,* which she completed a month before she died in 1935. Published posthumously in 1936, the novel is set in the Yorkshire farming community and reflects Holtby's great love of her home country. In its depiction of a feisty heroine, the school headmistress Sarah Burton, Holtby created a vivid account of one woman's struggle to raise educational standards against the obduracy of local officialdom. The book is also a powerful study in the vagaries of local government (for which reason her mother sought to prevent it being published). It won the James Tait Black Memorial Prize, and was made into a feature film in 1938 and a successful British television series in 1974.

Winifred Holtby died shortly after her thirty-seventh birthday. A generous and warmhearted woman, she seemed to go out of her way to accommodate the needs of others to the detriment of her own personal and emotional needs (she had an on-off relationship for years with Harry Pearson but never married). Holtby once declared that her life seemed to her "like a clear stream which has simply reflected other people's stories and problems" (Shaw 1999). It is hoped that continuing scholarship will bring the woman so long remembered primarily as the friend of the better-known Vera Brittain out from the shadows of unjustified neglect. See the website detailing the Winifred Holtby Collection at Hull at http://www.hullcc.gov.uk/holtby.

See also Brittain, Vera; Marson, Una.
References and Further Reading
Berry, Paul, and Alan Bishop, eds. 1985. *Testament of a Generation: The Journalism of Vera Brittain and Winifred Holtby.* London: Virago.
Brittain, Vera. 1940. *Testament of Friendship: The Story of Winifred Holtby.* London: Macmillan.
Brittain, Vera, and G. Handley-Taylor, eds. 1960. *Selected Letters of Winifred Holtby and Vera Brittain 1920–1935.* London: A. Brown.
Bush, Barbara. 1998. "Britain's Conscience on Africa: White Women, Race, and Imperial Politics in Inter-War Britain." In Clare Midgeley, ed., *Gender and Imperialism.* Manchester: Manchester University Press.
Daley, Caroline, and Melanie Nolan. 1994. *Suffrage and Beyond: International Feminist Perspectives.* New York: New York University Press.
Holtby, Winifred. 1934. *Women in a Changing Civilization.* London: John Lane.
Kennard, Jean E. 1989. *Vera Brittain and Winifred Holtby: A Working Partnership.* Hanover: University Press of New England.
Shaw, Marion. 1999. *The Clear Stream: A Life of Winifred Holtby.* London: Virago.
Spender, Dale. 1982. *Women of Ideas, and What Men Have Done to Them.* London: Routledge and Kegan Paul.
Waley, M. 1976. *Winifred Holtby: A Short Life.* Privately printed.

Hopkins, (Alice) Ellice
(1836–1904)
United Kingdom

The activities in Britain of social purity campaigner and rescuer of fallen women Ellice Hopkins were, in their day, greatly admired. Her endless stream of evangelical tracts and pamphlets on the subject sold in the thousands and were influential in promoting similar movements across the British Commonwealth and in the United States. With time, however, her very Victorian brand of pious self-denial and reformist zeal became unfashionable, and historically, Hopkins was supplanted in later years by more identifiably feminist and socialist figures. She also rapidly lost ground to the charismatic Josephine Butler, with whom for many years she collaborated in rescue work among prostitutes and campaigns for an end to the sexual double standard.

Hopkins, christened Alice but known throughout her career by her sexually neutral second name, Ellice, was the daughter of William Hopkins, a Cambridge mathematician. Brought up as a high-church Anglican and provided with a good education by her father at home, she began teaching Sunday school and soon astonished the church authorities at Barnwell, where she lived, with her preaching skills. She was allowed to exercise these in the evenings, holding evangelical meetings for working men at which she effected moral and spiritual conversions among her audiences. Inspired by the work of reformer Annie McPherson in the East End of London, she initiated the construction of a local Working Men's Institute and Club in Barnwell, which offered recreation and literacy lessons and where audiences of as many as 600–800 men would gather to hear her speak, many pledging themselves to reformed sexual behavior and temperance.

After her father's death in 1866, Hopkins's health broke down, and she turned to writing poetry and a book for convalescents, *Sick-Bed Vows and How to Keep Them* (1869). She and her mother moved to Brighton that year, where between 1866 and 1870 she wrote her first pamphlets publicizing local work among prostitutes by a Mrs. Vicars, notably "Work among the Lost" and "Work in Brighton," the latter with a preface by Florence Nightingale. Pamphlets such as these were endlessly reprinted, and it was not uncommon for 20,000–30,000 copies to end up in circulation. In Brighton, Hopkins also took up an interest in the social purity campaigns among soldiers being run by Sarah Robinson at her Soldier's Friend Institute, once again throwing herself into lectures, meetings, endless letter writing, and running night schools. The two women also made a concerted attack on moral standards in Portsmouth, considered at that time by social purity reformers to be the "very stronghold of Satan" (Barrett 1907, 55) because of its large naval and military population. Hopkins was active in the establishment there in 1874 of a Soldiers' Institute, of which she became trustee. In 1875 Hopkins described her activities in the tract "An English Woman's Work among Workingmen."

It was her meeting in 1872 with the surgeon and philosophical writer James Hinton that had the most profound and galvanizing effect on Hopkins's life. Hinton had been deeply impressed by Hopkins's sense of reformist mission and encouraged her to join him in the rescue of young women who had fallen into prostitution (not without having first of all been obliged to explain a few of the medical facts of life to his ingenuous pupil, who had led the most modest and sheltered of lives). By the time Hinton died in 1875, he had inculcated in Hopkins a sense of sacred duty in saving young women from the clutches of prostitution. Inspired by his teaching, Hopkins established the first of a network of Ladies' Associations for the Care of Friendless Girls in Brighton in 1876. She applied herself in earnest to the rescue of fallen women, patrolling the streets and public houses in search of vulnerable young women who might be preyed upon by men. It was also a policy of the association to visit brothels on a weekly basis, where Hopkins, having struggled to overcome her own sense of delicacy and revulsion to cross the threshold, would persuade prostitutes to kneel down with her and pray for forgiveness.

Branches of this association soon sprang up in many large towns, and local committees raised funds to rent houses that would serve as refuges for eight to ten girls under the supervision of a matron. The girls would be offered a modicum of vocational training, generally for domestic service, and after three months, they were given a uniform (the cost of which they repaid through clothing clubs) and placed in work. If they subsequently lost their jobs, they had to once more return to the homes to await new employment. The associations also gave classes in child care to unmarried mothers and helped them board out their babies with foster families so that they could enter rehabilitation programs at the homes. In 1881 Hopkins described this work in her pamphlet "Preventive Work, or the Care of Our Girls"; in 1895 the National Union of Women Workers grew out of this rescue work.

During an intense ten-year campaign from 1878 to 1888, Hopkins traveled Britain, proselytizing on moral reform and rescue work and in particular lobbying for the raising of the age of consent under a new Criminal Law Amendment Act (1885). She constantly had to fight against recurring bouts of ill health, a characteristic of many Victorian women reformers, who despite their frailty took on the most exhausting itineraries in their reform work. In Hopkins's case, one of her many admirers, the bishop of Durham, averred that she had "done the work of ten men in ten years" and was "the ablest woman I have ever met" (Barrett 1907, 102). Hopkins visited the major cities of the north of England, Scotland, and Wales, attracting huge audiences and everywhere she went selling thousands of copies of her many pamphlets.

Hopkins's assault on public morals and prostitution was at all times a clearly defined one, engaged on three levels. Aside from establishing homes where young girls at risk of being lured into prostitution could be safely housed, she also rescued children from the brothels in which they lived with their prostitute mothers. Hopkins saw this as a pressing social problem, claiming in 1880 that there were as many as 10,000 children in this situation. These children would be sent for rehabilitation to special industrial schools established under the 1880 amendment to the Industrial Schools Act (popularly known as the Ellice Hopkins Act), which made it a criminal offense for children under sixteen to live in brothels. Hopkins took advice from the pioneer of children's homes, Dr. Thomas Barnardo, and proceeded to set up a network of industrial schools along the lines of a prototype she had opened in Plymouth in 1879. Some would see the act as an infringement of civil liberties, in that it denied mothers who were prostitutes the right of custody over their children and granted police the authority to forcibly remove children from brothels. Hopkins herself was dissatisfied with the provisions of the act, but for different reasons: she would have liked the legislation to go further and to be extended to women up to the age of twenty-one.

Concerned with the overcrowding in city slums, the second strand of Hopkins's three-pointed attack on public morals was aimed at control of unnatural sexual relations within the family. She lectured to working-class mothers on how they could preserve levels of decency and chastity in their homes by teaching their children about sexual matters and personal hygiene, in hopes of reducing the incidence of incest and adolescent sex brought about by families comprising all ages and sexes sleeping in such close proximity to each other in overcrowded tenements. But Hopkins's most innovative work came with her personal crusade to control men's sexual behavior and reform them through the establishment of male chastity leagues. With this in mind, she began touring garrison towns, proselytizing among soldiers on social purity and temperance. In 1879 Hopkins founded the Church Penitentiary Association to persuade working men to pledge to "the protection of women and children and to the propagation among their own sex of a high ideal of masculine conduct and responsibility" (Hall and Howes 1999, 24).

From the 1870s, through the National Vigilance Association, Hopkins was also a regular collaborator with Josephine Butler and William Thomas Stead in the campaign against the traffic in young virgins for prostitution, finally achieved with the passing of the Criminal Law Amendment Act of 1885. Hopkins contributed regular articles to the *Shield,* the official publication of the Ladies' National Association for the Repeal of the Contagious Diseases Acts, which had been established in 1869. But Hopkins and Butler differed in their approach to moral reform: Hopkins considered her campaigning to be essentially preventive but viewed Butler's work, which sought to repeal or change existing laws such as the Criminal Law Amendment Act and the Contagious Diseases Acts, as primarily remedial. Nevertheless, the two women were central figures in the campaigning on this issue, writing endless letters and pamphlets on the subject and encouraging women to lobby their members of Parliament, particularly in the light of Stead's newspaper exposé of the white slave trade in 1885.

In 1883, after years of lobbying and after finally winning the support of the bishop of Durham, Hopkins managed to persuade the Church of England to take an official position on moral reform. This decision had finally come when she published a tract in 1879, "A Plea for the Wider Action of the Church of England in the Prevention of the Degradation of Women," in which she had demanded that the established church rise from its apathy and do something about prostitution and the sexual double standard. It was not poverty that brought about and perpetuated vice, she felt, but the uncontrolled sexual behavior of men. With clerical backing, she founded the Church of England Purity Society and the White Cross Army (the two organizations amalgamating in 1891 to become the White Cross League) in order to launch a wide-reaching campaign for chastity. The White Cross League became a potent social force, with its exhortations to working men to join in brotherhood in the defense of women and children from prostitution and degradation. It spread very rapidly, particularly among the pit men of the Durham and Yorkshire coalfields and in major Scottish cities such as Glasgow and Edinburgh, with other branches appearing especially among the military, in army barracks and even on board ships. In 1883, with the help of the Salvation Army, Hopkins established a huge social purity camp in Plymouth characterized by an "extravagant blend of military, revolutionary and bureaucratic rhetoric" (Walkowitz 1980, 242). During the 1880s and 1890s, Hopkins turned out a vast industry of tracts and pamphlets in support of the league's work, which were also widely disseminated by the Moral Reform Union, and which influenced the work of Grace Dodge in the United States.

Recruits to the White Cross League promised not only to be respectful of women but also to modify both their language and behavior. Soon the word spread to Ireland; to British colonies such as India, Australia, New Zealand, South Africa, Jamaica, and Canada; to the United States, where a major branch was established in Chicago in 1885; and even to Japan. And again, Hopkins was tireless in the promotion of the league's activities, conducting a huge correspondence and producing pamphlets such as "True Manliness" (which sold over 300,000 copies within a year), and addressing mass meetings of working men. The White Cross League continued to work for the moral reform of men until the outbreak of World War II; Hopkins also endorsed the similar work of the Gospel Purity Association, established in 1884 for the benefit of recalcitrant men and women who promised to reform their sexual behavior.

In 1886 Hopkins published *The Present Moral Crisis: An Appeal to Women,* in which she urged women also to organize in defense of their sex. She had by that time come to the conclusion that political empowerment through the vote would help women in their fight for moral reform. Her point of view, as F. K. Prochaska argues, was based on her belief that "votes for women were simply a means by which society might be made more compassionate, by which the relations of men and women might be made equal and holy" (1980, 219). In her view, women had and would always hold the moral high ground and could be the leaders in creating a truly Christian society that would eradicate the visible signs of lack of moral will. In 1888 Hopkins's health once again collapsed, and she was forced to give up active campaigning, although she did not stop writing. After traveling to Europe and recuperating in Italy and Spain, she returned to England in 1890, living mainly in Brighton. She devoted the remainder of her life to writing, producing after six years' labor, in 1899, one of her most passionately argued works, *The Power of Womanhood, or Mothers and Sons,* in which she gave an account of her life's work and commended the collaboration of the sexes in future social and moral reform. She published *The Story of My Life,* a timid attempt at sex education based on an explanation of natural history and physiology, in 1903.

After Hopkins's death, her story died with her. Sheila Jeffreys argues that "only church historians" (1985, 18) have taken any note of her work, with most commentators assuming, wrongly, that she was a spinsterly prude. Yet in many of her written works, Ellice Hopkins was an innovator in her perception of the greater social and economic ills that lay at the root of prostitution and moral degeneration, and although her work was guided by her Christian impulses toward the rehabilitation of the sinner, she also offered cogent arguments for efficient methods of preventive work as well as legal reform and "had more influence than any other woman or man on the development of 1880s social purity" (Jeffreys 1985, 9).

See also Butler, Josephine; Dodge, Grace; Nightingale, Florence.

References and Further Reading

Barrett, Rosa M. 1907. *Ellice Hopkins.* London: Wells, Gardner Darton and Company.

Bartley, Paula. 1999. *Prostitution and Reform in England 1860–1914.* London: Routledge.

Bristow, Edward J. 1977. *Vice and Vigilance: Purity Movements in Britain since 1700.* London: Gill and Macmillan.

Hall, M. P., and I. V. Howes. 1999. *The Church in Social Work.* 1965. London: Routledge.

Hartmann, Mary, and Lois W. Banner, eds. 1975. *Clio's Consciousness Raised: New Perspectives on the History of Women.* London: Harper and Row.

Heasman, Kathleen. 1962. *Evangelicals in Action: An Appraisal of Social Work in the Victorian Era.* London: Geoffrey Bles.

Jeffreys, Sheila. 1985. *The Spinster and Her Enemies: Feminism and Sexuality, 1880–1930.* London: Pandora.

Melnyk, Julie. 1998. *Women's Theology in Nineteenth-Century Britain: Transfiguring the Faith of Their Fathers.* New York: Garland.

Morgan, Sue. 1999. *A Passion for Purity: Ellice Hopkins and the Politics of Gender in the Late Victorian Church.* Bristol: Center for Comparative Studies in Religion and Gender.

———. 2000. "Faith, Sex and Purity: The Religio-Feminist Theory of Ellice Hopkins." *Women's History Review* 9(1): 9.

Prochaska, F. K. 1980. *Women and Philanthropy in Nineteenth-Century England.* Oxford: Clarendon Press.

Walkowitz, Judith. 1980. *Prostitution and Victorian Society: Women, Class and the State.* Cambridge: Cambridge University Press.

Walton, Ronald G. 1975. *Women in Social Work.* London: Routledge and Kegan Paul.

Hossain, Begum Rokeya Sakhawat
(1880–1932)
India

The daughter of a prosperous landowner, the writer and pioneer educator Begum Hossain was born in the Bengal presidency (now Bangladesh) and went on to found a well-patronized Muslim school for girls in Calcutta in 1911. Despite her enlightened attitude toward girls' education, she was obliged to remain mindful of her family's Muslim traditions (her mother was one of four wives) and had to be pragmatic in her criticism of religious practice. While she exposed and satirized the hypocrisy and absurdities of purdah in her novels and essays, such as *The Secluded Ones,* and in her public speeches, she toed the traditional line in her school sufficiently to ensure that it would have enough pupils. Within the limitations of the morality and religious views of her time, Hossain was able at least to ensure that the girls who graduated from her school were better equipped and more enlightened for their subsequent roles as wives and mothers.

At home, as a girl, Hossain was taught Arabic

and Urdu in order to read prescribed religious and moral texts but was forbidden from studying Bengali and English, the languages of non-Muslims, in which she might read texts containing emancipatory ideas. She was taught to read English in secret by her elder brother, who was a supporter of women's education. In 1896 Hossain was married off to Sakhawat Hossain, a widower twice her age. Her liberal-minded husband, who had been educated in Europe and was the deputy magistrate of Bhagalpur, was convinced that women's education was the necessary foundation of social change, and he also gave her private instruction. With his blessing, when she was twenty-one, Hossain began to publish articles on women's issues and short stories such as "Sultana's Dream" (1905), published in the *Indian Ladies' Magazine.*

In many of her essays, such as "The Female Half," "The House," "The Veil," and "The Ideal Housewife," Hossain called for the education of women and for their liberation from hidebound convention. She also published articles on the confinement of women in purdah and the use of the veil—even within the home—arguing that education, even in a limited form, would make better wives and mothers of Indian women. Her husband died in 1909; with the aid of 10,000 rupees that he had bestowed for the purpose, Hossain set up a school for Muslim girls in Bhagalpur in the state of Bihar. But a feud over property with her late husband's family and their moral objection to her educational activities forced her to close the school down and transfer her activities to Calcutta. There she opened the Sakhawat Memorial Girls' School in March 1911 with only eight pupils. By 1915 the number had risen to eighty-four, and the school was offering a curriculum that comprised reading and writing in Urdu, gardening, making handicrafts, cooking, and physical fitness, as well as instruction in the preservation of Islamic cultural and religious values. Once the school had been inspected and officially approved by the wife of the viceroy of India, the numbers went up, and by 1930 it was well established as a leading high school patronized by upper-class families. Although Bengali and English had been added to the curriculum, the school mandated Muslim standards of modesty in dress and respected the wishes of those who chose to observe purdah. But in her essays and speeches, Hossain

continued to argue that education for Muslim girls was a positive approach to retaining traditional culture.

In Calcutta, Hossain also became involved in women's rights issues. She cofounded the Bengali Muslim Women's Association in 1916 and chaired the Bengal Women's Education Conference in Calcutta in 1926 and the Indian Women's Conference at Aligarh in 1932. Throughout her life, Hossain conducted an unobtrusive campaign against the repressive traditions of purdah but was heavily criticized for doing so. Opposition to her position was heightened when she came out in support of Katherine Mayo's controversial book *Mother India,* published in 1927, in which the American journalist attacked the practice of child marriage and exposed the terrible sufferings in childbirth of young girls denied proper medical care. At the time of her death, Hossain was preparing an essay entitled "The Rights of Women." The date of her death, 9 December, is now commemorated as Rokeya Day in Bangladesh.

References and Further Reading
Forbes, Geraldine. 1996. *Women in Modern India.* New Cambridge History of India, vol. 4. Cambridge: Cambridge University Press.
Jahan, Roshan, ed. and trans. 1981. *Inside Seclusion: The Avarodhbasini of Rokeya Sakhawat Hossain.* Dacca: BRAC Printers.

Howe, Julia Ward
(1819–1910)
United States

The abolitionist, women's rights campaigner, and advocate of prison reform Julia Ward Howe was also one of the leaders of women's peace mediation. As a woman of deep religious faith and author of "The Battle Hymn of the Republic," she also supported women's religious ordination and was an unofficial lay preacher.

The daughter of a wealthy banker, Howe was educated by governesses and at private schools until she was sixteen, studying Latin, Greek, French, German, and Italian and the social graces of singing and piano playing. Romantic and impressionable, she read the novels of George Sand, Honoré de Balzac, and the German Romantic poet Johann Wolfgang von Goethe. She reached marriageable age beautiful, wealthy,

Julia Ward Howe (Library of Congress)

and accomplished but disappointed her guardians (her mother and father were dead) by marrying a man twenty years her senior, Samuel Gridley Howe, a reformer, teacher, and director of the New England Asylum of the Blind.

Howe spent most of her life in south Boston after enjoying a honeymoon in Europe and meeting Charles Dickens, Thomas Carlyle, and William Wordsworth in London. On the voyage home, she met Florence Nightingale and was so impressed that she named her second child after her. Isolated at home with, eventually, five children, Howe began writing plays and poetry and continued with her self-study of languages and philosophy. The family home, meanwhile, had become a meeting place for local abolitionists, but her husband refused Howe any active role in the movement. In 1853 he briefly allowed her to help edit his antislavery journal, *The Commonwealth;* mindful of his reservations about her work and his dismissive attitude toward her literary gifts, she published her first volume of poetry, *Passion Flowers,* anonymously in 1854. In twenty years of marriage, Samuel Howe never acknowledged any of Julia's many accomplishments, a fact that led to their increasing alienation until his death in 1876.

During the Civil War, the Howes visited Washington, D.C., where after the Battle of Bull Run, Julia witnessed Union troops being reviewed by General George McClellan at a camp near the Potomac River in November 1861. It was here that she heard soldiers singing "John Brown's Body," the popular wartime song set to a traditional folk song. Howe's husband had been a supporter of John Brown, and Julia, as a poet, wanted to honor his memory. She did so in song, inspired by her religious feelings to write what she felt were more appropriate, respectful lyrics to fit the haunting melody she had heard the soldiers singing. The "Battle Hymn of the Republic" was written by her in her room at the Willard Hotel in Washington, and published in February 1862 in the *Atlantic Monthly.* She may have only been paid four or five dollars for it, but the song's enduring popularity in the United States ensured Howe's subsequent fame when she was in her forties.

At the end of the Civil War and after the emancipation of the slaves, Howe turned her attentions to the growing women's rights campaign. After the death of her son in 1868, she attempted to dissipate her grief by throwing herself into religious and philosophical study—of Immanuel Kant, Johann Fichte, G. W. F. Hegel, and Baruch Spinoza—and giving public lectures on social ethics, in the 1870s addressing such bodies as the Boston Radical Club and the Concord School of Philosophy. With Lucy Stone, she founded the New England Women's Club in 1868, initially a loose network of study clubs in which women could take literacy classes and which also offered community libraries, playgrounds, and child care facilities and lobbied for women's education and strengthening of their rights over their property and children. The society also donated funds to run holiday schools for children and provided bursaries for students of academic promise. Howe's work for women's clubs, as president of the society almost uninterruptedly from 1871 to 1910, would also involve her in the establishment of the Association for the Advancement of Women and the General Federation of Women's Clubs, which would eventually boast 2 million members. After the split in the women's suffrage movement in 1869, Howe, already president of the moderate New England Woman Suffrage Association (1868–1877, 1893–1910), became a founder with Stone of the American Woman Suffrage Association and for twenty years edited the *Woman's Journal.*

During 1870–1878 and 1891–1893, she was also president of the Massachusetts Woman Suffrage Association. In 1878 she attended the first international women's rights congress held in Paris, France.

As an ardent pacifist, Howe was one of the first women in the United States to elaborate on the idea of an international network of peace activists. In 1870 she published an "Appeal to Womanhood throughout the World," exhorting women to come together and hold a conference to set up international cooperation and peace mediation to avert future wars. Horrified by the carnage of the Franco-Prussian War in Europe (1870–1871), she lent further support to the idea of an international women's peace movement as president of the U.S. branch of Marie Goegg's International Association of Women from 1871. She visited England in 1872 in hopes of organizing a women's peace conference there, but when this failed to materialize, Howe had to accept the difficulty for women of coming together from many countries for such a conference. She suggested instead the founding of a Woman's Peace Party in the United States, supported by national branches and the inauguration of 2 June as a women's international peace day, but not until 1915 would a Woman's Peace Party be established in the United States and the International Committee of Women for Permanent Peace be set up in The Hague. Howe's international sympathies and interests would continue to be reflected in her 1891 foundation of the American Friends of Russian Freedom and her presidency, from 1894, of the United Friends of Armenia.

Howe was a devout Unitarian and believed in women's ability and right to be ordained as ministers. She became an unofficial lay minister, giving sermons wherever the opportunity arose, mainly in Unitarian and Universalist churches, beginning in 1870. In 1873 she initiated the first of annual private conventions of women preachers at her home, providing such women with an opportunity to be mutually self-supporting.

Howe continued writing into her old age, in 1895 producing a work of social criticism (*Is Polite Society Polite?*) in which she criticized contemporary cultural values. She promoted the work of her feminist precursor Margaret Fuller, writing a biography, *Margaret Fuller* (1883), and editing *The Love-Letters of Margaret Fuller 1845–1846* (1903). Her *Reminiscences, 1819–1899* appeared in 1900. She was awarded three honorary doctorates, and in 1908 she was the first woman elected to the American Academy of Arts and Letters. Howe was also one of the first to address women's capacity for academic study, in her *Sex and Education* (1874), in which she argued for coeducation.

By the time she died at the age of ninety-one, Howe was revered as the "Dearest Old Lady in America," and the images of her in old age, sitting demurely in her lace cap, testify to that perception of her. At her memorial service in 1910, the voices of 4,000 mourners were raised in singing "The Battle Hymn of the Republic." Although the public affection for the woman who wrote the unofficial national anthem of the United States endured, the memory of her work in support of many social issues receded into the background.

See also Fuller, (Sarah) Margaret; Goegg, Marie Pouchoulin; Nightingale, Florence; Sand, George; Stone, Lucy.

References and Further Reading

Bolton, Sandra Knowles. 1895. *Famous Leaders among Women*. New York: Crowell.

Clifford, Deborah. 1979. *Mine Eyes Have Seen the Glory: A Biography of Julia Ward Howe*. Boston: Little, Brown.

Flexner, Eleanor. 1975 [1959]. *A Century of Struggle: The Woman's Rights Movement in the United States*. Rev. ed. Cambridge, MA: Belknap Press of Harvard University Press.

Frost, Elizabeth, and Kathryn Cullen DuPont. 1992. *Women's Suffrage in America: An Eyewitness History*. New York: Facts on File.

Grant, Mary Hetherington. 1994. *Private Woman, Public Person: An Account of the Life of Julia Ward Howe from 1819–1868*. Brooklyn, NY: Carlson Publishing.

Hall, Florence Howe. 1916. *The Story of the Battle Hymn of the Republic*. New York: Harper.

Howe, Julia Ward. 1899. *Reminiscences, 1819–1899*. Boston: Houghton Mifflin.

Reynolds, Moira Davison. 1988. *Nine American Women of the Nineteenth Century: Leaders into the Twentieth*. Jefferson, NC: McFarland.

Richards, Laura E., and Maude How Elliot. 1970 [1915]. *Julia Ward Howe 1819–1910*. Reprint, Boston: Houghton Mifflin.

Williams, Gary J. 1999. *The Hungry Heart: The Literary Emergence of Julia Ward Howe*. Amherst: University of Massachusetts Press.

How-Martyn, Edith
(1875–1954)
United Kingdom

The socialist suffrage campaigner Edith How-Martyn was a defector from the militant Women's Social and Political Union (WSPU) and a cofounder of the Women's Freedom League (WFL) in 1907. After 1915, much of her life's work was devoted to the birth control movement, first in Britain. After World War I, she moved onto the international stage, where she worked closely with Margaret Sanger through the Birth Control International Information Center (BCIIC), taking its message to India and other parts of Asia.

Edith How was born in Cheltenham and educated at Frances Buss's North London Collegiate School for Ladies. She studied physics and mathematics at University College in Aberystwyth and at the London School of Economics, becoming one of the first women to win a science degree, which she obtained after marrying Herbert Martyn in 1899. Soon after, she was appointed a lecturer in mathematics at Westfield College, part of the University of London. In 1906, having already been politically active as a member of the Independent Labour Party (ILP), she joined the WSPU, becoming joint honorary secretary with Charlotte Despard in June. In October 1906 How-Martyn was one of the first suffragettes to be jailed (serving one month of a two-month sentence), after she had tried to make a speech at the House of Commons.

How-Martyn soon came to dislike the domination of the WSPU by the Pankhursts and objected to their rigid autocratic rule, favoring a less centralized organization that gave greater autonomy to regional branches. As a socialist, she was also disillusioned when the Pankhursts broke off their relationship with the Independent Labour Party; along with other members of the WSPU, How-Martyn favored continuing collaboration with the ILP as the best means of furthering the suffrage cause in Parliament.

After the WSPU conference for 1907 was cancelled and the Constitution suspended (in September) by the Pankhursts, there was a serious breach in the union, prompting a mass exodus of members. Heading this group were How-Martyn, Despard, and Teresa Billington-Greig, three of the WSPU's most experienced political campaigners

through their links with the ILP. Together they established a third women's suffrage organization to rival the WSPU and Millicent Garrett Fawcett's National Union of Women's Suffrage Societies, the Women's Freedom League.

The WFL, after having briefly operated as a splinter group within the WSPU, came into official being in November 1907. It was organized along more democratic lines than the WSPU, with Despard as president and treasurer and How-Martyn as secretary (until 1911). As a result of its emphasis on input from regional branches at regular annual conferences, its Glasgow and Edinburgh branches became particularly influential. By allowing room for debate and difference in its ranks, however, the WFL was subject to sometimes bitter debate, and in time, Charlotte Despard's controlling influence over WFL policy prompted How-Martyn to voice objections similar to those she had had about the WSPU.

One of the strategies adopted by the WFL, in what it described as its "constitutional militancy" (Fulford 1957, 147), was passive resistance to government. This policy was manifested through the nonpayment of taxes and the boycotting of the 1911 census, which How-Martyn endorsed. But her support for the WFL was fading by 1911 as she became disillusioned with the union's political failures, and she resigned. After women were enfranchised in 1918, How-Martyn was one of seventeen women who stood for election to Parliament. She campaigned for a seat as an independent member of Parliament for Herndon on a program of feminist issues, but only one woman (Constance de Markievicz) was elected (although, as a member of Sinn Féin, she never took her seat). How-Martyn turned instead to local government, in 1919 becoming the first woman member of the Middlesex County Council and serving for three years. In 1928, when women were finally granted suffrage on an equal basis with men at age twenty-one, How-Martyn was a cofounder with Lilian Lenton of the Suffragette Fellowship, which she served as chair. This organization did valuable work in collecting and preserving suffrage memoirs and descriptions of women's activism, particularly their experiences in prison, with How-Martyn sending out questionnaires to former suffragists. This material was collected in an archive that is now preserved in the Museum of London.

For the rest of her active career after about 1915, How-Martyn devoted herself to the birth control movement. In 1910 she had joined the Malthusian League, which at that time was the only organization in Britain promoting family planning. The subject was still contentious, even among suffragists and in the ILP, and would remain so for some time. But eventually How-Martyn found Malthusianism insensitive to the needs and circumstances of individual women; birth control was, she believed, "the Pivot, the Cornerstone of reconstruction and emancipation" (Soloway 1982, 180), and she joined Marie Stopes's birth control campaign. In 1921, How-Martyn helped Stopes set up one of England's first birth control clinics. In 1923, with other women in the Labour Party, she launched a concerted drive to disseminate birth control literature through welfare clinics run by local authorities in England.

In her birth control work, How-Martyn was increasingly drawn to the international movement led by the U.S. reformer Margaret Sanger, whom she had first met in 1915. In 1927, with Sanger, she organized the World Population Conference in Geneva and a year later set up a birth control center in London, briefly entertaining the idea of standing for Parliament again in 1929—this time on a birth control ticket. In 1930 How-Martyn's center was reconstituted as the Birth Control International Information Center, with Sanger as president and How-Martyn as director, and in 1931, she published *The Birth Control Movement in England*.

How-Martyn began traveling and lecturing extensively in India on behalf of birth control. After attending the All-India Women's Conference (AIWC) in Karachi in 1934, she toured India for two months, lecturing on the subject, and returned for the 1935 conference, afterward touring with Sanger and speaking at a wide range of venues. In December 1935, thanks to their influence, the AIWC passed its first resolution on contraception. In her later pamphlet, "Round the World for Birth Control," How-Martyn described how she had addressed 41 of the 105 meetings on birth control, covering 6,500 miles back and forth across India, during her tour with Sanger. She returned to India on several occasions in the following four years to supervise its growing network of birth control clinics. How-Martyn became adept at lobbying for support among the Indian medical profession and also engaged in public debate with Mahatma Gandhi over his views on celibacy as a means of birth control. Altogether, she spent a year (1935–1936) with Sanger on a world tour for birth control. Together they visited and lectured in India, Burma, Malaya, China, the Philippines, Japan, and Hawaii before traveling on to Canada and down the West Coast of the United States.

In 1938 the BCIIC merged with the National Birth Control Association of England (later the Family Planning Association and after that the International Planned Parenthood Association). With war looming in the late 1930s, How-Martyn's international work for birth control was interrupted, and in 1939 she and her husband emigrated to Australia, where she was obliged to remain because of failing health. In Australia she established a branch of the Suffragette Fellowship. She died in Sydney. The recent acquisition of Edith How-Martyn's papers on birth control by the Margaret Sanger Papers Project provides an insight into the work of this neglected pioneer. For information, contact http://www.nyu.edu/projects/sanger/howmarty.htm.

See also Billington-Greig, Teresa; Buss, Frances; Despard, Charlotte; Fawcett, Millicent Garrett; Markievicz, Constance de; Pankhurst, Christabel; Pankhurst, Emmeline; Pankhurst, (Estelle) Sylvia; Sanger, Margaret.

References and Further Reading
Banks, Olive, ed. 1985, 1990. *The Biographical Dictionary of British Feminists*, vol. 1, *1800–1930*; vol. 2, *1900–1945*. Brighton: Harvester Wheatsheaf.
Crawford, Elizabeth. 1999. *The Women's Suffrage Movement, 1866–1928: A Reference Guide*. London: University College of London Press.
Fulford, Roger. 1957. *Votes for Women: The Story of a Struggle*. London: Faber and Faber.
Johnson-Odim, Cheryl, and Margaret Strobel, eds. 1992. *Expanding the Boundaries of Women's History: Essays on Women in the Third World*. Bloomington: Indiana University Press.
Newsome, Stella. 1957. *The Women's Freedom League 1907–1957*. London: Women's Freedom League.
Purvis, June, and Sandra Stanley Holton, eds. 2000. *Votes for Women*. London and New York: Routledge.
Soloway, Richard Allen. 1982. *Birth Control and the Population Question in England, 1877–1930*. Chapel Hill: University of North Carolina Press.

Huerta, Dolores
(1930–)
United States

The neglected civil and economic rights of the mainly Hispanic migrant fieldworkers in the United States found a determined advocate in the Chicana activist Dolores Huerta, when she joined with labor leader Cesar Chavez in 1962 to found the National Farm Workers Association, the precursor of today's United Farm Workers of America (UFW). In her many years of service, Huerta has proved the effectiveness of the nonviolent boycott in obtaining improved rights for migrant workers and has been recognized as one of the most effective lobbyists on behalf of ethnic minorities in the United States.

Huerta was born in a poor mining town in New Mexico and grew up in the farmworking community of Stockton, California, the daughter of a union activist and a mother who ran a boardinghouse for migrant farmworkers. She studied at high school and Stockton College, and after obtaining a teaching diploma at the University of the Pacific's Delta Community College, she took up a teaching post. However, soon after, she resolved to take up community work for local underpaid Chicano farmworkers, many of whose hungry and poorly clothed children were among her pupils. Huerta married young and, as a devout Catholic, was soon the mother of seven children from two marriages.

In 1955 she became a member of Stockton's Community Service Organization (CSO), a Mexican American self-help body dedicated to improving living conditions in Mexican American communities of the barrios and encouraging immigrants in California to settle into the community and register to vote. But her real vocation would begin in 1958, when she took up work with rural laborers for the Agricultural Workers Association in the Stockton area. A year later, she returned to the CSO to work with its director, Chavez, assisting workers involved in legal cases, lobbying for changes to citizenship requirements that prevented migrant workers from receiving pensions and public welfare, and defending the rights of Spanish-speaking people to vote in their own language.

Frustrated by the continuing reluctance of the CSO to establish a trade union, Huerta and Chavez left in 1962 to campaign more specifically for farmworkers. They cofounded the National Farm Workers Association, known from the early 1970s as the United Farm Workers of America, with Huerta as vice president. The UFW's objective was to defend the rights of migrant workers in the San Joaquin Valley, many of whom worked on the 38,000 acres of vineyards there, and achieve for them the same kind of wages and health and safety standards enjoyed by workers in factories. Soon after, Huerta was appointed to lead and train picketers and enlisted the UFW in helping Filipino workers take a stand against grape producers in what would become the historic, five-year Delano grape strike of 1965–1970. Together with Chavez, Huerta organized a huge national consumer boycott of California table grapes and mobilized large-scale picketing of wholesalers and supermarkets. By 1970, with 17 million people across the United States joining in the boycott, the growers finally capitulated.

Huerta became adept at negotiating contracts with growers. In 1966 she broke new ground in trade union history when she led grape workers in collective bargaining with one of the biggest Californian growers, the Schenley Wine Company. During the 1970s, the UFW backed further boycotts by migrants working in iceberg lettuce and grape picking. Huerta continued to assist in the negotiation of contracts and wage agreements; initiated welfare programs, such as death benefits and unemployment insurance; and oversaw the establishment of the Juan De La Cruz Farm Worker Pension Fund and a Farm Workers Credit Union, all the while receiving only a minimal wage. The increasing muscle of the UFW would result in recognition of the rights of its members to collective bargaining on wages and working conditions under California's 1975 Agricultural Labor Relations Act, the first U.S. law to recognize such rights. Throughout the 1970s, Huerta was also involved in the long and difficult negotiations that often flared up into open and bitter conflict over the relationship between the UFW and the powerful Teamsters union. Eventually, in 1977, she achieved an agreement whereby the Teamsters would represent the interests of the canners, packers, and truck drivers in the food-growing industry, while the UFW would continue to look after the rights of fieldworkers.

During the 1980s, the UFW began running a radio station, KUFW-Radio Campesina, as part of its National Farm Workers Service Center, which now runs five Spanish-language radio stations. Huerta continued to lead campaigns to change government policy on immigrants, particularly those illegal ones who had lived in the United States for several years and paid taxes. Her work led to declaration of an amnesty in 1985 and passage of the immigration act that year, which gave such workers citizenship.

Huerta's expertise in liaising with legislators and government bureaucrats resulted in her becoming a familiar and powerful public speaker for the UFW, which since its inception has grown to a membership of 70,000 and has more recently engaged in representing the rights of fields workers in the strawberry-producing industry. Huerta has extended her defense of workers' rights to include those of other minority groups and women workers. She has testified to legislative committees on issues such as the use of pesticides and their toxic effects on farmworkers and the environment, under the auspices of the United Farm Workers Organizing Committee, lobbying to have the use of DDT (banned in 1972) and parathion in crop spraying outlawed.

For more than thirty years, Huerta worked with Chavez (from the 1960s until his death in 1993) and eventually married his brother, Richard (her third husband, with whom she had four more children). Huerta's high profile on picket lines and in demonstrations has led to her being arrested more than twenty times, including a severe beating in 1988 from which she needed two years to recuperate. She has been the recipient of honorary doctorates and numerous awards, including the Outstanding Labor Leader Award (1984), the Roger Baldwin Medal of Liberty Award of the American Civil Liberties Union, and the Eugene V. Debs Foundation Outstanding American Award. In 1998 she was voted one of *Ms.* magazine's "Women of the Year." Aside from continuing to serve as secretary-treasurer of the UFW at its headquarters in La Paz, Mexico, Huerta serves as vice president of the Coalition for Labor Union Women. For links to several sites about Huerta's life and work, contact http://www.inconnect.com/rvazquez/huerta.html/. For further information about the United Farm Workers of America, contact http://www.farmworkers.org/.

References and Further Reading

Current Biography. 1997. New York: H. W. Wilson.

De Ruiz, Dana Catharine, and Richard Larios. 1992. *La Causa: The Migrant Farmworkers' Story.* Austin, TX: Raintree Steck-Vaughn.

Felner, Julie. 1998. "Dolores Huerta." *Ms.* January-February, 46–49.

García, Richard A. 1993. "Dolores Huerta: Woman, Organizer, and Symbol." *California History* 72(1): 56–72.

Gregory Dunn, John. 1976. *Delano: The Story of the California Grape Strike.* New York: Farrar, Straus, and Giroux.

Jensen, Joan M., ed. 1981. *With These Hands: Women Working on the Land.* New York: McGraw-Hill.

Perez, Frank. 1996. *Dolores Huerta.* Austin, TX: Raintree Steck-Vaughn.

I

Ichikawa Fusae
(1893–1981)
Japan

Ichikawa Fusae was a pioneer of the Japanese women's suffrage and women's organized labor movements between the two world wars, remaining politically active until her death at the age of eighty-seven. Her inspired leadership as a member of the Japanese Diet for twenty-five years was instrumental in convincing the government to finally sign the United Nations Convention on the Elimination of All Forms of Discrimination Against Women in 1979.

Ichikawa came from a poor background in Nagoya, and the regime of frugality under which she grew up became so ingrained in her that she lived extremely modestly throughout her life. After leaving school, she became a teacher and also worked as a reporter. Finding her social passions aroused by the unequal wages paid to men and women teachers, she became involved in the labor movement through her association with Christian reformers in Japan and acted as secretary of the women's department of the trade union the Fraternal Organization in 1919. In 1920 she founded the New Woman's Society with Hiratsuka Raicho and, with it, the journal *Women's League* as the voice of the Japanese suffrage movement. She rapidly established a reputation for challenging Japanese conventions of female modesty by cutting her hair short, adopting Western clothes, and daring to smoke in public and in 1920 was arrested for her political activities.

A year later, Ichikawa traveled to the United States and spent the next three years meeting feminist leaders such as Jane Addams, Carrie Chapman Catt, and Alice Paul. She studied the U.S. women's movement, its involvement in paci-

Ichikawa Fusae (Library of Congress)

fism and social reform, and the organization of women's labor and trade unions. Ichikawa also made diligent use of her time by studying and taking extension courses at Columbia University.

On her return in 1924, Ichikawa worked for the Tokyo branch of the International Labour Organization and oversaw its coordination of relief work after the devastating Kanto earthquake of 1923. But she gave up this role to concentrate her energies on the fight for women's suffrage, collaborating with Kubishiro Ochimi later that year to set up the League for the Realization of Women's Suffrage, which a year later became the League for Women's Suffrage. In its manifesto the league, which was enlisting women for a nationwide campaign for suffrage, declared that it was time for women of all political and religious persuasions to join in challenging their unequal place in politics, asserting that "women, who form one-half of the population of the country, have been left entirely outside the field of political activity" (Fujimura-Fanselow and Atsuko Kameda 1995, 7). For the next sixteen years, until the outbreak of World War II, Ichikawa frequently took the podium on suffrage issues and canvassed politicians across all political parties for their support, rather than limiting herself, as other suffragists felt she should, to a drive for support among sympathetic socialists only.

After Kubishiro left the league, Ichikawa became general secretary and led support for a government bill in 1931 that would have allowed women to vote in local elections, but a long petition organized by Ichikawa and her colleagues was thrown out by the House of Peers. During Japan's invasion of Manchuria in the late 1930s and the ensuing world war, Japanese women were diverted away from their own cause and into support of Japanese militarism and the war effort, with appeals being made to women to help mobilize the national spirit. Although successful in getting a bill passed to provide financial support to widowed and deserted women, Ichikawa was forced to accept that suffrage would have to wait, as also would her vision of promoting ties between Japanese suffragists and feminists and the International Council of Women, based in Brussels. Support for the cause of women's suffrage waned dramatically, and after the League for Women's Suffrage disbanded in 1940, Ichikawa was forced to concede that women could best demonstrate their worthiness of the vote by supporting the national war effort; by 1942 Japanese women's organizations were all amalgamated under the umbrella of the Greater Japan Women's Association.

As a journalist, Ichikawa herself was dragooned into the Patriotic Press Association, which ran Japanese propaganda during the war. After Japan's defeat in 1945, Ichikawa's long campaign for suffrage finally bore fruit when the American occupation forces in Japan demanded the introduction of universal suffrage. Japanese feminists regrouped as the Committee to Formulate Postwar Policy Measures for Women under the leadership of Ichikawa and others, once more calling for their democratic rights. In December 1945, Japanese women finally received the vote, and a new Constitution ratified a year later initiated reforms of property and inheritance laws in women's favor, promoted their rights to obtain an education and work, and introduced protective legislation for women workers. Meanwhile, Ichikawa herself was excluded from political activities from 1947 to 1950 by the occupation forces as a punishment for having publicly promoted the Japanese war effort.

After supporting herself for several years by writing articles and growing vegetables, Ichikawa accepted the leadership of the Japanese Women's Voter's Alliance, toured the United States as a Japanese cultural envoy, and in 1953 was elected to the House of Councilors. She was returned on five more occasions between 1958 and 1980, during which time she spearheaded a campaign to clean up electoral procedures and party politics, in 1976 taking part in an investigation of the corrupt practices of Prime Minister Kakuei Tanaka. In 1974 she received the Ramon Magsaysay award; she was a leading organizer of a national coalition of women's groups, which ran the Japanese International Women's Year conference a year later.

See also Addams, Jane; Catt, Carrie Chapman; Hiratsuka Raicho; Paul, Alice.

References and Further Reading

The Annual Obituary. 1981. New York: St. Martin's Press.

Ashby, Ruth. 1995. *Herstory: Women Who Changed the World.* New York: Viking.

Fujimura-Fanselow, Kumiko, and Atsuko Kameda. 1995. *Japanese Women: New Feminist Perspectives on the Past, Present, and Future.* London: Feminist Press.

Golden, Kristen, and Barbara Findlen, eds. 1998. *Remarkable Women of the Twentieth Century: 100 Portraits of Achievement.* New York: Friedman/Fairfax Publishers.

Murray, Patricia. 1975. "Ichikawa Fusae and the Lonely Red Carpet." *Japan Interpreter* (2): 171–189.

Pharr, Susan J. 1981. *Political Women in Japan: The Search for a Place in Political Life.* Berkeley: University of California Press.

Vavich, Dee Ann. 1967. "The Japan Woman's Suffrage Movement: Ichikawa Fusae—A Pioneer in Woman's Suffrage." *Monumenta Nipponica* 22(3/4): 401–436.

Inglis, Elsie
(1864–1917)
United Kingdom

The Scottish medical pioneer Elsie Inglis was in the first generation of women to study at Sophia Jex-Blake's School of Medicine for Women in Edinburgh, later setting up her own medical college in rivalry with Jex-Blake's. Her concern at the sufferings endured by poor women during successive pregnancies and the lack of compassion demonstrated by male doctors in their treatment of women's gynecological complaints prompted Inglis to open a women's hospital in Edinburgh, where she worked for higher standards in midwifery and maternity care. During World War I, Inglis, herself terminally ill, endured appalling conditions to nurse wounded Serbian troops on the Balkan front and in Romania.

Inglis was born in northern India at a remote hill station, Naini Tal, in the foothills of the Himalayas, where her Scottish father was in the civil service. When John Inglis retired in 1875, the family spent time in Hobart, Tasmania, visiting an older son, before returning to England in 1877. They settled in Edinburgh, where Inglis's father, as an advocate of women's equal opportunities, provided the best of educations for his daughter, after which she spent a year in Paris.

Between 1886 and 1889, Inglis studied at Edinburgh School of Medicine for Women but, like Elizabeth Garrett Anderson before her, found Jex-Blake a difficult, authoritarian personality and disliked the way she managed the school. After the unfair expulsion of two women students by Jex-Blake, Inglis left the school and, with financial assistance from her father and other wealthy supporters, set up the Scottish Association for the Medical Education of Women and a rival establishment, the Medical College for Women, offering lower tuition fees than Jex-Blake's establishment. Meanwhile, she continued with her own training, first at Edinburgh Medical College and then at the Glasgow Royal Infirmary, where she studied under Sir William McEwen.

In 1892, having obtained her license at both Edinburgh and Glasgow, Inglis took up a post as resident medical officer at Anderson's New Hospital for Women in London. While in London, she was active in the suffrage movement and joined the Women's Liberal Federation. After further study of obstetrics at the Rotunda Dublin, she returned to Edinburgh in 1894, where she established a private practice with another woman doctor, Jessie Macgregor. Later that year when women students were finally admitted to medical degrees at Edinburgh University, Inglis helped establish a hall of residence for them.

In 1894 Inglis took up a lectureship in gynecology at her Medical College for Women and opened a seven-bed hospital for women and children, the George Square Nursing Home. She was determined to do something about the lack of proper maternity care for poor women in Edinburgh and in 1904 moved the home to new premises in a slum area and renamed it the Hospice. In 1910, it amalgamated with Edinburgh's Bruntsfield Hospital. Staffed by women, the Hospice was one of the first to offer poor women anesthetics in childbirth. Inglis, who was noted for her compassion and generosity with patients, often waived her fees; with her staff, however, she was a legendary martinet and a stickler for discipline.

During the 1900s, Inglis traveled abroad to investigate gynecological methods in women's clinics in Germany, Vienna, New York, Chicago, and Minnesota. As a liberal, she had supported Irish home rule and was a member of the Women's Liberal Federation but was disappointed in the continuing lack of support among Liberal members of Parliament for women's suffrage. In the years leading up to World War I, Inglis became a leading figure in the Scottish suffrage movement, as honorary secretary of the Edinburgh National Society for Women's Suffrage and in 1906 as founder of the Scottish Women's Suffragette Federation. In 1909, she became secretary of the Federation of Scottish Suffrage Societies and gave up her affiliation with the Liberal Party to promote the National Union of Women's Suffrage Societies Election Fighting Fund, which supported prosuffrage Labour Party candidates.

In 1914, on the outbreak of World War I, Inglis missed out on being included in Anderson's Women's Hospital Corps. Although she knew she was ill (and kept that illness secret), she offered her services as a doctor to the War Office but was told to "go home and keep quiet" (Strachey 1978, 338). Undaunted, she advertised in the suffrage journal the *Common Cause,* raised funds of £25,000 through the suffrage network in Scotland, and with those funds established the Scottish Women's Hospitals (SWH) to raise all-female medical units to volunteer for service on the Western Front. Ignored by the British War Office, the organization sent out fourteen of these units, first of all to bases in France—where a fine hospital with 200 beds was set up at Royaumont Abbey in 1915—and later to Serbia, Corsica, Salonika, Romania, and Russia.

In April 1915, eager to serve, Inglis went to help run an SWH unit that had been set up in a schoolhouse at Kragujevac, south of Belgrade in Serbia. Upon her arrival, she discovered that typhus, enteric fever, pneumonia, and other infectious diseases were raging among 60,000 prisoners of war who had been abandoned in the area by the Austrians. After three months, the typhus epidemic was finally under control. Forced to retreat from Kragujevac in November 1915, Inglis's unit was sent to attend prisoners in military hospitals farther south at Kruševac, remaining even when German troops invaded. After these field hospitals were closed in February 1916 by the Austrians, she was sent back to England. Her request to be sent to serve with British troops in Mesopotamia was turned down, but Inglis soon returned to the Eastern Front in August with another medical unit, funded by the London Suffrage Society, to nurse wounded Serbs in the Russian army—volunteers who had opted to fight with the Russian army rather than for the Austro-Hungarian Empire (of which Serbia was then part).

In September 1916, traveling by sea, Inglis's "London Unit" entered Russia at the northern port of Archangel and traveled down to Odessa on the Black Sea and across to the Dobrudja district of Romania to nurse Serb divisions fighting there. The conditions they encountered were horrible, with very high casualty rates and a desperate lack of medical supplies. Inglis remained in the region, running a unit at Reni near the Black Sea when the Allies withdrew from the Dobrudja, her hospital again overflowing with wounded after a German counterattack. Despite collapsing in September, Inglis kept the seriousness of her illness from her colleagues, staying with her Serbian division and ensuring its safe evacuation out of Russia via Archangel after the October Revolution in 1917. Traveling by icebreaker, she arrived in Newcastle-upon-Tyne on 25 November after sailing up the River Tyne. The next day, her mission complete, Inglis's astonishing willpower ebbed away, and she died that evening. One of the nurses on her unit later summed up Inglis's extraordinary character, describing a woman who was "as light as a leaf and as gallant as a guardsman." There was, Elsie Butler said, "a driving-power in her fragile body which would have put a Rolls-Royce to shame, a genius for getting miracles to happen, and administrative gifts hardly distinguishable from statesmanship. . . . Her words of praise were rare and greatly treasured; but her wrath was terrible" (Leneman 1994, 217).

Inglis's funeral in Edinburgh was attended by members of the British and Serbian royal families. Soon after, a hospital for Serb children suffering from tuberculosis was set up in her memory in the south of France; her own medical unit returned to Macedonia until the end of the war. When the Scottish Women's Hospitals was disbanded at the end of hostilities, its remaining funds were used toward the construction of the Elsie Inglis Memorial Maternity Hospital, which opened in Edinburgh in 1925. Inglis was the recipient in April 1916 of Serbia's highest decoration, the Serbian Order of the White Eagle; she was also awarded Russia's Gold St. George Medal.

See also Anderson, Elizabeth Garrett; Jex-Blake, Sophia.

References and Further Reading

Balfour, Lady Frances. 1918. *Dr Elsie Inglis.* London: Hodder and Stoughton.

Bell, Enid Moberley. 1953. *Storming the Citadel: The Rise of the Woman Doctor.* London: Constable.

Crawford, Elizabeth. 1999. *The Women's Suffrage Movement, 1866–1928: A Reference Guide.* London: University College of London Press.

Jus Suffragii, 1 February 1918. Obituary notice.

Lawrence, Margot. 1971. *Shadow of Swords: A Biography of Elsie Inglis.* London: Michael Joseph.

Leneman, Leah. 1994. *In the Service of Life: The Story of Elsie Inglis and the Scottish Women's Hospitals.* Edinburgh: Mercat Press.

Leneman, Lori. 1995. *"A Guid Cause": The Women's Suffrage Movement in Scotland.* Rev. ed. Edinburgh: Mercat Press.

McLaren, Eva Shaw, ed. 1919. *A History of the Scottish Women's Hospitals.* London: Hodder and Stoughton.

Mitchell, David. 1966. *Women on the Warpath: The Story of Women of the First World War.* London: Jonathan Cape.

Strachey, Ray. 1978 [1928]. *The Cause: A Brief History of the Women's Movement.* Reprint, London: Virago.

Ishimoto Shizue
(Kato Shizue)
(1897–)
Japan

With support from the American birth control pioneer Margaret Sanger, Ishimoto Shizue broke from her extremely traditional family background to lead the Japanese campaign during the interwar years. Her primary argument in support of her activities was that if women were emancipated enough to be able to control the size of their families, then the well-being of society as a whole would improve as a result.

Born into a wealthy former samurai family, Ishimoto had a Westernized upbringing and was educated at the Peeresses' School. Soon after her graduation, she married into wealth and status as the wife of Baron Ishimoto Keikichi. The baron, himself an enlightened liberal and humanist, encouraged Ishimoto to take an interest in labor unions, and in 1919–1920 she went with him to the United States, where she studied English and mixed with American socialists. Through the Young Women's Christian Association (YWCA) and U.S. journalist Agnes Smedley, she met Margaret Sanger.

Sanger subsequently visited Japan on a lecture tour in 1922, where she was forced to circumvent attempts at controlling her public campaigning by speaking in private homes. Inspired by Sanger's example, Shizue and her husband founded the Japan Birth Control Institute with other like-minded supporters, and Ishimoto, who had already published articles on birth control in popular magazines such as the *Housewife's Friend* and *Women's Salon* before Sanger's visit, set out to bring birth control ideas to the working and uneducated classes. Because she was not an averred socialist, others working for birth control criticized her campaigning as eugenics-based and guided by a desire to control the population rather than improve the lot of workers. Ishimoto always contended that control of rising birthrates was essential to the improvement of living conditions for workers and that birth control would give women relief from unwanted pregnancies that weakened their health and thus

Ishimoto Shizue (left), with Margaret Sanger (right) (Sophia Smith Collection)

release them sooner back into the workplace. In Ishimoto's view, birth control should not be a contentious issue because it enables women to be better mothers to the children they do have and reinforces happy family life. In a 1922 article in the *Housewife's Friend,* she also argued that birth control was a tool for world peace because overpopulation was at the root of unrest and war, and control of population could therefore be a stabilizing factor.

Throughout the 1920s, Ishimoto had to rely on private fund-raising to support her birth control campaign. She also ran a yarn shop alongside the knitting classes she offered, where she proselytized on birth control. In 1932, with the support of leading feminists, Ishimoto helped set up the Women's Birth Control League of Japan. By that time, she had become increasingly dependent on financial support from the United States, where she returned in 1932 to give a series of lectures. She spent time in New York during 1933–1934 gaining more knowledge of the medical and scientific background of the latest methods at Margaret Sanger's Birth Control Research Institute. By the end of her time in the United States, Ishimoto had become something of a celebrity. In 1935 she published her autobiography in English, made another lecture tour in 1936, and was able to go back to Japan with funding from a U.S. patron of birth control.

On her return, Ishimoto set up her own clinic and began offering private consultations to women, recommending the use of the Dutch cap. But her campaigning during the 1930s proved an uphill struggle when political considerations entered the birth control campaign and divided its support in the wake of growing opposition to birth control from the medical profession. In 1937, with the outbreak of war against China, Ishimoto's clinic was closed down by the authorities, and the government actively encouraged population increase by banning contraceptives and issuing official policies in support of larger families. Ishimoto was arrested and imprisoned. Such was the outrage of her Western supporters, who lobbied the government, that she was soon released, only to be forced again in January 1938 to close down her clinic at a time when the Japanese, taking a page from Joseph Stalin's book, were offering incentives to mothers who had more children.

Throughout the war years, the birth control movement in Japan was put on hold. Ishimoto was, in her own words, forced into "silent resistance" until the political climate changed with Japan's defeat in 1945. In 1944 she married for a second time, to labor organizer Kato Kanju. Her career entered a new phase at war's end, with Ishimoto becoming a leading Japanese politician of the post–World War II era. She was elected to the Japanese Diet in 1946, where she retained her seat for twenty years as an independent. In tandem with her political career, she retained her connection with the birth control movement through numerous activities. She was one of the founders of the Japanese Family Planning Association in the 1950s and president of the Family Planning Federation of Japan from 1974. After the war, and until 1984, she was vice president of the Japanese Organization for International Cooperation in Family Planning. Ishimoto was frequently dubbed "the Margaret Sanger of Japan," but her achievements during the course of a long career in public service underlined her contribution in her own right as one of Japan's great female humanitarians and social reformers.

See also Sanger, Margaret.

References and Further Reading

Ishimoto Shizue. 1935. *Facing Two Ways: The Story of My Life by Baroness Shidzué Ishimoto.* New York: Farrar and Rinehart.

———.1936. *East Way, West Way: A Modern Japanese Girlhood by Baroness Shidzué Ishimoto.* New York: Farrar and Rinehart.

Robins-Mowry, Dorothy. 1983. *The Hidden Sun: Women of Modern Japan.* Epping, Essex: Bowker.

Sanger, Margaret. 1931. *My Fight for Birth Control.* New York: Farrar and Rinehart.

Tipton, Elise K. 1997. "Ishimoto Shizue: The Margaret Sanger of Japan." *Women's History Review* 6(3): 337–356.

Ito Noe
(1895–1923)
Japan

One of the most forceful Japanese "new women" of the 1910s who took over the editorship of the feminist journal *Bluestocking,* Ito Noe had demonstrated a precocious talent for writing with her first articles, published when she was seventeen. She was an outspoken leader of the women's movement of that time, moving increasingly toward anarchism. Her life was tragically cut short when she was murdered in her prison cell at the age of twenty-eight.

She began her professional life working as a clerk in the post office, but dissatisfied with her lack of education, she went to Tokyo to study at the Ueno Women's School with financial assistance from the (male) novelist Murakami Namiroku. Despite her desire for self-improvement through education, she was obliged to accede to an arranged marriage at Kyushu but left her husband soon after to go and live with another man in Tokyo.

In the autumn of 1912, with financial assistance from Hiratsuka Raicho, the editor of *Bluestocking* who had been impressed by the passion of her commitment, Ito managed to go home to get a divorce and returned to Tokyo, where she began writing for the magazine. By 1913 she was its leading proponent of social and political reform. In her work, Ito went further than the purely literary-minded, elite Japanese women who confined their activities to debate on the pages of *Bluestocking* and other short-lived feminist publications. Inspired by the writings of the German anarchist Emma Goldman, Ito became politically active and encouraged the board of *Bluestocking* to tackle more fundamental political issues. In September 1913 she published a translation of extracts from Goldman's essay "The Tragedy of Women's Liberation" and drew criticism and a withdrawal of support from other members of the Bluestocking group who disliked her increasingly extremist views. With the departure of Hiratsuka Raicho from the editorial board in January 1915, Ito, still only twenty, was left at the helm. Until its demise in 1916, the magazine, under her influence, welcomed the wider discussion of women's issues such as abortion and prostitution.

Ito wrote many essays on male-female relationships and emphasized the hypocrisy of men who argued for greater female chastity while doing nothing to change their own sexual habits. Nor were prostitutes any worse than many married women, in her view, for women within loveless marriages were equally the sexual and economic slaves of men. Ito felt that Christian campaigns for moral reform could never be effective; the solution for her was social upheaval, and people's behavior could only change under the aegis of a new and equitable society.

After physical exhaustion brought an end to her work on *Bluestocking*, Ito went to live with her still-married lover, the political activist Osugi Sakae. Because of their anarchist sympathies, the couple were under constant police surveillance. Over the next six years (1917–1923), Ito had five children by Osugi, and they lived in penury. In April 1921 she helped found the Red Wave Society, the first socialist organization for women, which was committed to the achievement of social equality before suffrage and eager to enlist women in socialist education programs and rallies. But the leaders were arrested, and the society was forced underground in 1922. In September 1923 Ito and Osugi were taken in for questioning by the police and murdered by an officious officer, who deemed they were a danger to society and strangled them. The Red Wave Society was disbanded in 1925.

See also Goldman, Emma; Hiratsuka Raicho.

References and Further Reading

Hane, Mikiso. 1988. *Reflections on the Way to the Gallows: Rebel Women in Pre-War Japan.* Berkeley: University of California Press.

Jayawardena, K. 1986. *Feminism and Nationalism in the Third World.* London: Zed Books.

Sievers, Sharon. 1983. *Flowers in Salt: The Beginnings of Feminist Consciousness in Modern Japan.* Stanford: Stanford University Press.

J

Jackson, Helen Hunt
(1830–1885)
United States

Helen Hunt Jackson (Library of Congress)

What Harriet Beecher Stowe did for the African American in *Uncle Tom's Cabin*, Helen Hunt Jackson hoped to do for Native Americans with her 1884 novel *Ramona*. Her concern for the rights of displaced American Indian tribes was aroused after she settled in Colorado in the 1870s and prompted her to rise to their defense in the last five years of her life.

Jackson grew up in a strict Calvinist environment in Massachusetts, where her father was a professor at Amherst College and friendly with the Beecher family. After losing both parents to tuberculosis, Jackson was brought up by relatives and educated at the Female Seminaries in Falmouth and Ipswich, Massachusetts, and the Abbott School in New York. She was a childhood friend of the poet Emily Dickinson, with whom she corresponded regularly and whom she encouraged to publish her poetry.

She married army engineer Edward Bissell Hunt in 1852 and spent her life traveling with him from one posting to another. The deaths of her husband in an accident and her two young sons from illness left Jackson, by 1865, prostrate with grief. She moved to Newport, Rhode Island, and turned to writing to support herself, submitting anonymous book reviews for East Coast publications such as the *Evening Post* and the *Nation*, as well as poetry. After spending 1868–1870 traveling in Europe, Jackson published an account in *Bits of Travel* (1872); her first collection of poetry, *Verses*, was published in 1870. During Jackson's lifetime, her verse was much admired by fellow poets such as Ralph Waldo Emerson, but Jackson, who throughout her life had an am-bivalent view of women's entry into public life, shunned the literary limelight and continued to publish under various pseudonyms.

After remarrying in 1875, Jackson settled in the dry climate of Colorado Springs, hoping to improve her bronchial condition. Her second husband, William Sharpless Jackson, was a Quaker banker, and although she never became a Quaker herself, Jackson shared the Quaker movement's sentiments on the rights of Native Americans. Jackson began to publish novels, including a fictionalized biography of Dickinson, *Mercy Philbrick's Choice* (1876), and wrote several short stories that were remarked on for their vivid portrayal of local settings.

On a trip to Boston in 1879, her husband took Jackson to hear Native American leaders Standing Bear and Susette La Flesche (Bright Eyes) speak on the abuse of their rights to their traditional homelands. In 1877 the Ponca peoples had been forcibly resettled in Indian Territory (now Oklahoma) from their hunting grounds on the Dakota-Nebraska border, which had been made over to the Dakota tribe. The Ponca tribe suffered miserably in this new environment and rapidly succumbed to disease. In protest, their chief Standing Bear led thirty-four of them 600 miles back north to Nebraska, where they sought refuge but were arrested and turned back. Appalled by this story, Jackson went against her inherent distaste for becoming a "woman with a cause"—and this despite her innately public persona as a charismatic, feisty, and energetic woman—and set out to research their case and that of other Indian tribes in official documents. In 1881, after several years of fierce campaigning, letters to the press and church leaders, and confrontation with the officials responsible for the Ponca resettlement, Jackson published a 457-page critique of U.S. treatment of its native peoples and of its wars against them in the West. In *A Century of Dishonor: A Sketch of the United States Government's Dealings with Some of the Indian Tribes,* she exposed the shameful betrayal by the federal government of successive Indian treaties. At her own expense, Jackson ensured that the report was widely circulated in official quarters, including to members of Congress.

The official response to *A Century of Dishonor* came a year later, when Jackson was appointed a special commissioner to investigate the social conditions of the California Mission Indians (twenty-one groups of Native Americans Christianized by Spanish Franciscan missionaries in California from the mid-eighteenth century), who were also being systematically dispossessed. Her equally penetrating report on the subject, published in 1883 after extensive travel in and around southern California, failed to carry a bill in Congress.

Frustrated by official and public indifference, Jackson decided to follow Harriet Beecher Stowe's example and produce a fictionalized critique, which she wrote intensively over a period of three months and which appeared as the novel *Ramona* in 1884. In this depiction of the Spanish community in California, written with the same intentions as Stowe had for *Uncle Tom's Cabin,* Jackson graphically described the exploitation of local Native Americans and the erosion of both their way of life and culture and those of Hispanic peoples. Jackson stated: "If I can do one-hundredth part for the Indians as Mrs. Stowe did for the Negroes, I will be thankful" (Reynolds 1988, 112). Reform of government policies toward Native Americans followed with the passage of the 1887 Dawes Act, or General Allotment Act, under which tribal lands were allotted to individual Native Americans, who then became U.S. citizens. Ultimately, however, the novel was a success for the wrong reasons—not for its social criticism but for its sentimental and romantic elements and its nostalgic depiction of early settler life in California, which prompted numerous later film versions, including a silent one by D. W. Griffith in 1910 and a Hollywood version in 1936 starring Loretta Young and Don Ameche.

Jackson died prematurely at the age of fifty-five, after complications set in when she broke her leg in several places. Three volumes of her verse were published posthumously: *Sonnets and Lyrics* (1886), *Glimpses of Three Coasts* (1886), and *Between Whiles* (1887). To this day, the story *Ramona* is remembered in the words of the popular song of the same name (with lyrics in 1917 by Mabel Wayne), and a dramatization is still mounted as an annual stage pageant in Hemet, California. For further information on the *Ramona* pageant, contact www.ramonapageant.com.

See also La Flesche, Susette; Stowe, Harriet Beecher.

References and Further Reading
Banning, Evelyn I. 1973. *Helen Hunt Jackson.* New York: Vanguard.
Jackson, Helen Hunt. 1964 [1881]. *A Century of Dishonor; A Sketch of the United States Government's Dealings with Some of the Indian Tribes.* Reprint, Minneapolis: Ross and Haines.
———. 1994. *Westward to a High Mountain: The Colorado Writings of Helen Hunt Jackson.* Denver: Colorado Historical Society.
Mathes, Valerie Sherer. 1990. *Helen Hunt Jackson and Her Indian Reform Legacy.* Austin: University of Texas Press.
Odell, Ruth. 1939. *Helen Hunt Jackson.* New York: D. Appleton-Century.
Rader, Emily. 2000. "The Indian Reform Letters of Helen Hunt Jackson, 1879–1885." *Pacific Historical Review* 69(2): 296–297.
Reynolds, Moira Davison. 1988. *Nine American Women of the Nineteenth Century: Leaders into the Twentieth.* Jefferson, NC: McFarland.

Senier, Siobhan. 2001. *Voices of American Indian Assimilation and Resistance: Helen Hunt Jackson, Sarah Winnemucca, and Victoria Howard.* Norman: University of Oklahoma Press.

Jacobi, Mary Putnam
(1842–1906)
United States

Women's medical education in the United States found one of its first pioneers in the work of Mary Putnam Jacobi. A woman who dedicated her life to improving standards in clinical practice as well as campaigning against the traditional chauvinism of the male medical profession, she ranks alongside Elizabeth Garrett Anderson in Britain in her mission to change preconceptions of women's traditional physical "frailty." In so doing, she endorsed and extended the similar arguments of Julia Ward Howe's *Sex and Education* (1874) and Antoinette Brown Blackwell's *The Sexes throughout Nature* (1875).

Born during a family visit to London, Jacobi was from the famous Putnam publishing family of New England. She grew up in several homes in New York state and was encouraged in her love of science by her father, who allowed her to study anatomy as part of her education at home. From an early age, she set her heart on a career in medicine; despite her father's aversion for medicine as a "repulsive pursuit" for a woman, he did not stand in her way. She managed to gain admittance to the New York School of Pharmacy to study chemistry and pharmacy and, after graduating in 1863, trained for one year at the Female Medical College of Pennsylvania. But the medical training open to women in the United States at that time was extremely limited, and after working for a few months at Marie Zakrzewska's New England Hospital for Women and Children in Boston, Jacobi went to Paris to seek further clinical experience. While there, she supported herself by sending articles to magazines back home, such as *Putnam's Magazine* and *Scribner's Monthly.* She doggedly lobbied to be admitted to the prestigious Ecole de Médecine, eventually, in 1867, becoming the first woman to study there (a considerable achievement, since she knew no French when she first arrived) thanks to the personal intervention of the French minister of public education. Jacobi was in the midst of writ-

Mary Putnam Jacobi (Archive Photos)

ing her thesis in 1870 when Paris came under siege during the Franco-Prussian War (1870–1871), but she remained in the city, working as a hospital intern.

Having obtained her medical degree with high honors in France in 1871, Jacobi returned to New York, where she set up in private practice. She rapidly established her preeminence as a teacher at the Women's Medical College run by Emily Blackwell and at her sister Elizabeth Blackwell's New York Infirmary for Women and Children, serving in the capacity of professor of *materia medica* and from 1873 also lecturing on therapeutics. But in 1896 Jacobi gave up the post because of differences of opinion with Emily Blackwell over the curriculum and Jacobi's continuing dissatisfaction with her students' inability to meet her own rigorous standards.

Determined to raise the profile of women's medical training, which was still embryonic at the end of the nineteenth century, Jacobi was a prolific contributor to medical journals and tireless in her promotion of the work of women doctors, founding the Association for the Advancement of the Medical Education of Women (AAMEW) in 1872, of which she remained president until 1903. Jacobi's lobbying on behalf of the AAMEW eventually secured the admission of women to medical courses at Cornell University.

In 1873 Mary married Dr. Abraham Jacobi, who despite being an able pediatrician had lost two wives in childbirth and five children in infancy. He was also president of the Medical Society for the County of New York and an influential figure in medical reform. Together the couple collaborated on a book about the care of babies, *Infant Diet* (1874). They became leading figures in American medicine, and their home was a venue for the medical world. The Jacobis set up clinics for the poor and campaigned for social reforms that would improve the living environments of the working classes in New York's slums; they also campaigned for new health and safety standards in the workplace. In addition, Mary concerned herself with the diseases affecting children, holding lectures on the subject at the New York Post-Graduate Medical School during 1882–1885 and a year later setting up a children's ward at the New York Infirmary for Women and Children.

In 1876 Jacobi published "Question of Rest for Women during Menstruation." Written in response to a Harvard University essay competition on menstruation, it was based on answers to 1,000 questionnaires sent out by Jacobi. It would be one of the first medical challenges to the widespread emphasis on women's physical and emotional instability during menstruation and the public perception of it as being incapacitating. Jacobi contested the conventional medical belief that women should reduce their physical activities during menstruation, concluding that inactivity—both physical and sexual—only heightened women's levels of menstrual pain. The essay won the competition and the $200 Boylston Medical Prize.

Jacobi was also a vigorous activist for women's suffrage from 1894, when she joined the New York City campaign for women's right to vote at state level and published a collection of her public lectures on the subject, *"Common Sense" Applied to Woman Suffrage* (1894). She was a founder of the Working Women's Society (later the New York Consumers' League), which, among its many activities, tried to put a stop to the exploitation of mainly female workers in sweatshops.

Two of the several medical textbooks written by Jacobi are *Essays on Hysteria, Brain-Tumor, and Some Other Cases of Nervous Disease* (1888) and *Physiological Notes on Primary Education and the Study of Language* (1899). She made significant contributions to medical journals, covering a range of topics from physiology to pediatrics, neurology, and pathology, and became an authority on the gynecological and psychosomatic complaints of women, such as nervous breakdown. In the summer of 1896, Jacobi diagnosed the first signs of the meningeal brain tumor that would destroy her ability to speak and eventually kill her.

See also Anderson, Elizabeth Garrett; Blackwell, Antoinette Brown; Blackwell, Elizabeth; Howe, Julia Ward; Zakrzewska, Marie.

References and Further Reading
Blake, Catriona. 1990. *The Charge of the Parasols: Women's Entry to the Medical Profession*. London: Women's Press.

Bonner, Thomas Neville. 1992. *To the Ends of the Earth: Women's Search for Education in Medicine*. Cambridge, MA: Harvard University Press.

Dictionary of American Biography 1946–1958, and indexes to Supplements 1–10, 1981–1996. New York: Scribner's.

Levin, Beatrice. 1988. *Women and Medicine*. Lincoln: Media Publishing.

Putnam, Ruth, ed. 1925. *Life and Letters of Mary Putnam Jacobi*. London: G. P. Putnam's Sons.

Sicherman, Barbara, and Carol Hurd Green. 1980. *Notable American Women 1607–1950: A Biographical Dictionary*, vol. 4, *The Modern Period*. Cambridge, MA: Belknap Press of Harvard University.

Wells, Susan. 2001. *Out of the Dead House: Nineteenth-Century Women Physicians and the Writing of Medicine*. Madison: University of Wisconsin Press.

Women's Medical Association of New York. 1925. *Mary Putnam Jacobi, M.D. A Pathfinder in Medicine, with Selections from Her Writings and a Complete Bibliography*. New York: G. P. Putnam's Sons.

Jacobs, Aletta
(1851–1929)
Netherlands

The first woman to qualify as a doctor in the Netherlands and president of the Dutch Woman Suffrage Association (1903–1919), Aletta Jacobs was an outstanding figure in the Dutch women's movement and the first woman to develop a systematic approach to contraception and birth control. She also worked exhaustively for legal reforms, to improve the working conditions of shop girls, and in disseminating the ideals of the international pacifist movement.

Jacobs came from a family of assimilated Jews and was one of eleven children. Her father, a doctor and an enlightened liberal who encouraged her and her sisters in their academic aspirations, helped her gain admission to a boys' high school in a small nearby town by petitioning the prime minister for girls to attend secondary school without special license. But since the age of five, Jacobs had longed to be a doctor. Although she was refused admittance to university to do so, in 1870 she sat the standard matriculation exam, qualifying for entry to train as a pharmacist's assistant. She passed with distinction and decided to lobby to enter the university medical school. Her father again appealed to the prime minister, and in 1871 Jacobs was allowed to take the one-year preparatory course in philosophy and then in 1872 was given permission to proceed with medical studies at the University of Groningen. She was finally awarded her medical degree in Utrecht in April 1878.

Awarded a doctorate in 1879, Jacobs was urged to restrict her activities to midwifery because of continuing public resistance to the idea of women doctors. She traveled to England to see for herself how women doctors were pioneering work there and for a while worked at various London hospitals, including Great Ormond Street. She also gained a lasting respect for the work of Elizabeth Garrett Anderson, whom she observed at her women's hospital on the Marylebone Road. She returned to Amsterdam in September 1879, where, upon attending a conference on the advancement of medical science, she was swamped by requests for her medical skills by so many Amsterdam women that she decided to set up in practice on the Herengracht as an independent woman doctor.

Aletta Jacobs (left) (Library of Congress)

In England, Jacobs had been impressed with the work of pioneers such as Annie Besant, who had disseminated literature on birth control and been prosecuted as a result. She had also met and associated with radical groups, such as the Fabians, and with suffragists, having supported the campaign for women's franchise since her student days. At her practice in Amsterdam, Jacobs became increasingly concerned during the 1880s about the need for working-class women to receive better instruction in hygiene and child care and began running a twice-weekly free clinic for poor people attached to the Dutch General Trade Union, where for fourteen years she treated needy women until a bout of ill health forced her to stop.

In the course of this work, Jacobs became all too painfully aware of the misery and deprivation suffered by working-class people as a result of the bad conditions in which they worked and the unhealthy accommodation their large families inhabited. In 1882, at the age of thirty-three, she decided that birth control was the only means of controlling overpopulation and social misery and founded the first birth control clinic in the world that year in Amsterdam. Although many similar clinics sprang up in the Netherlands over the next few years, Jacobs would wage a thirty-year battle against ignorance and prejudice (even among doctors) regarding her pioneering work on contraception. With the Netherlands being the only country that sanctioned birth control for some time, Jacobs pioneered the adoption of the "Dutch cap," the popular name for the Messinga pessary (cervical cap), the first effective contraceptive device. Jacobs's work was central to the worldwide birth control movement that would nurture other women pioneers such as Marie Stopes and Margaret Sanger more than thirty years later.

Beginning in 1882, Jacobs also became active in the suffrage movement. Her first step in effecting political change came in 1883, when she challenged the voting qualifications as laid down in the Dutch Constitution, asking the burgomaster of Amsterdam to register her to vote because she was a taxpayer. Technically, the wording of the Dutch Constitution did not deny the vote to women, but she was still refused. In order to provoke debate on the subject, she took her case to court, and it was eventually rejected in the Court of Appeal. The Constitution was subsequently amended to specify that suffrage applied to men only. In 1893 Jacobs was invited to join the committee, which established the Woman Suffrage Association, the brainchild of a group of women from the Free Women's Movement. In 1895 she became president of the association's Amsterdam section and from 1903 to 1919 was president of the national association. During the association's twenty-five-year campaign, Jacobs lobbied for women's suffrage all over the Netherlands.

In the late 1880s, Jacobs launched a personal campaign in the Netherlands to improve the working conditions of Dutch shop girls. During their visits to her clinic, she had noticed how frequently they suffered gynecological problems as a result of standing on their feet during working days that could last from 8 A.M. until 11 P.M. When a government commission was set up in 1886 to investigate working conditions in factories and elsewhere, she urged that conditions for shop girls also be looked into and asked that shopkeepers provide some kind of seating for girls to take occasional brief rests. This suggestion was rebuffed by management on the grounds that it would appear disrespectful to customers. Faced with indifference from shop owners and officials alike, Jacobs published a newspaper appeal in 1894, drawing public attention to the detrimental affects such long hours had on the health of shop girls. The appeal received limited support from the public and shopkeepers, with a few women's committees springing up in local towns in support of the

idea and other groups demanding shorter opening times for shops and department stores. It would be 1902, however, before Jacobs's campaign would be officially acknowledged by the government, when it finally initiated a change to the laws on working hours.

Prostitution was another subject that elicited Jacobs's concern, from a medical rather than a moral standpoint, prompting her to publish an article in 1895 in the weekly newspaper, the *Amsterdammer*. In it, she argued for the dissemination of educational literature outlining the dangers of prostitution and the risk of sexually transmitted diseases, preferring this approach to joining the campaign to abolish state-regulated prostitution. She was invited to give a lecture at the Society for the Advancement of Women's Interests in November 1897, which was later published, provoking vilification of Jacobs in the press for having dared to raise such a "disgusting" subject in public. However, as a positive response, Jacobs received requests from female university students to write for their student paper on the social consequences of various kinds of sexual behavior.

In 1904 Jacobs became a member of the International Woman Suffrage Alliance (IWSA), and her major work for the IWSA from the turn of the twentieth century would make her one of the most respected international figures in the women's movement. She attended the inaugural meeting of the alliance in Berlin, on which occasion the Netherlands was one of the six founding members. In 1908 Jacobs was the major organizer of the IWSA's fourth annual congress, held for the first time in Amsterdam. It was a year that marked a turning point in the Dutch suffrage campaign, with women's suffrage at last being taken seriously in the Netherlands. The Woman Suffrage Association grew rapidly in the following years, from 2,500 to 6,000 members.

Within the IWSA, Jacobs became a close friend and correspondent of Carrie Chapman Catt and Anna Howard Shaw, accompanying them on numerous promotional trips in Europe. She responded to a request to help South African suffragists organize and in 1910 lectured on suffrage and prostitution in Cape Town, Johannesburg, and other cities, where she was appalled to see the complete disregard for safety and hygiene in preventing the spread of venereal disease. Before leaving South Africa, Jacobs published an

"Open Letter to the Women of South Africa" in which she outlined the dangers of prostitution and called for better sex education among men as well as women. And the next year, after attending the annual IWSA conference in Stockholm (1911), Jacobs and Catt embarked together on a yearlong world tour in a major drive to arouse women's interest in their civil and political rights in South Africa, the Middle East, the Philippines, and Japan.

During World War I, Jacobs was highly active in the pacifist movement, as a close associate of the U.S. pacifist Jane Addams. Back in 1899, she had attended the first peace conference to be held in the Netherlands, where she met and became an admirer of the peace campaigner Bertha von Suttner, who tried and failed to persuade her to give up medicine in favor of full-time pacifist work. In 1915 Jacobs was involved in one of numerous peace initiatives by women, when together with Addams, Rosika Schwimmer, and other radical feminists, she called on European women, independently of any established organizations, to attend an international congress for future peace, which ran from 28 April to 1 May at The Hague. Attended by 1,136 delegates representing 150 women's organizations from twelve different countries, the congress established the International Committee of Women for Permanent Peace (in 1919 changed to the Women's International League for Peace and Freedom). Jacobs, elected vice chair and secretary of the committee, was a member of a delegation of women that toured neutral European countries in an attempt to mediate for peace. During August and September 1915, she spent time in the United States with Catt, Emily Greene Balch, and Addams, discussing plans to establish a League of Neutral Countries.

After the war, Jacobs made a study tour of Germany, where she detailed the consequences of military destruction and food shortages on the starving German population and set up an action committee, the work of which was later taken over by the Red Cross. When women gained the vote in the Netherlands in 1919, she continued to work for the IWSA.

See also Addams, Jane; Anderson, Elizabeth Garrett; Balch, Emily Greene; Besant, Annie; Catt, Carrie Chapman; Sanger, Margaret; Schwimmer, Rosika; Shaw, Anna Howard; Stopes, Marie; Suttner, Bertha Félice Sophie von.

References and Further Reading

Bosch, Mineke. 1990. *Politics and Friendship: Letters from the International Woman Suffrage Alliance, 1902–42.* Columbus: Ohio State University Press.

Bussey, Gertrude, and Margaret Tims. 1980 [1960]. *Pioneers for Peace: Women's International League for Peace and Freedom 1915–1965.* Reprint, London: George Allen and Unwin.

Evans, Richard. 1977. *The Feminists: Women's Emancipation Movements in Europe, America and Australasia 1840–1920.* London: Croom Helm.

Jacobs, Aletta. 1996. *Memories: My Life as an International Leader in Health, Suffrage, and Peace.* New York: Feminist Press.

Josephson, Harold, Sandi Cooper, and Steven C. Hause et al., eds. 1985. *Biographical Dictionary of Modern Peace Leaders.* Westport, CT: Greenwood Press.

Liddington, Jill. 1989. *The Long Road to Greenham: Feminism and Anti-Militarism in Britain since 1820.* London: Virago.

Rupp, Leila J. 1997. *World of Women: The Making of an International Women's Movement.* Princeton: Princeton University Press.

Van Voris, Jacqueline. 1987. *Carrie Chapman Catt: A Public Life.* New York: Feminist Press.

Jameson, Anna Brownell
(1794–1860)
Ireland

One of five daughters of a painter of miniatures, the Irish writer, feminist, and social critic Anna Jameson was born in Dublin and found herself orphaned in her teens. Faced with the only option open to unmarried women of her time, she became a governess to a series of aristocratic families, beginning with that of the marquis of Winchester. For the next fifteen years she lived in miserable servitude, only to make an unwise marriage in 1825 to a man of whose true personality she felt uncertain, the barrister Robert Jameson.

Jameson's marriage failed, and her husband left for Dominica in 1829, by which point, as much out of necessity as desire, she had begun to discover her literary and political voice. Her first novel, *The Diary of an Ennuyée,* had been published in 1826 and was a fictionalized account of her time spent in Europe as a governess. In subsequent works such as *Celebrated Female Sovereigns* (1831) and *Characteristics of Shakespeare's Women* (1832), she began to explore women's issues. Jameson's work was particularly popular in Germany, where she lived from 1834 to 1835.

After a final attempt at reconciliation between Jameson and her husband failed during her trip to Canada in 1837–1838, Robert Jameson, by then attorney general of Canada, agreed to a settlement of £300 per year, which gave Jameson a small but significant degree of financial freedom to take up the issues that interested her. Her account of her travels in Canada, *Winter Studies and Summer Rambles in Canada* (1838), was not only an engaging travelogue, but also tackled women's and Aboriginal rights. Jameson noted the sorry plight of women settlers in remote areas, considering such an existence to be that of a "dependent drudge" and remarking that "I have not often in my life met with contented and cheerful-minded women, but I have never met with so many repining and discontented women as in Canada" (Thomas 1967, 137). As for the Aboriginals, these she admired in the tradition of the "Noble Savage" who yet had something to teach the "civilized" world. But in her opinion they were doomed to extinction if they did not adapt: "The hunter must make way before the agriculturist, and the Indian must learn to take the bit between his teeth, and set his hand to the ploughshare, or *perish*" (138).

During the 1840s, Jameson wrote a series of articles about women, including the 1846 pamphlet on a subject close to her own heart, "The Relative Position of Mothers and Governesses." She also gave her support to the reformers of the Langham Place Circle, becoming a mentor to women such as Jessie Boucherett and Bessie Rayner Parkes in their work in the Society for the Promotion of the Employment of Women and Barbara Bodichon in her 1857 petition for a Married Women's Property Act. Bodichon had a particular admiration for Jameson's dogged pursuit of her own living at a time when such single-mindedness and independence in women were frowned upon.

As a single woman who had endured years as a governess and then as an unwanted and neglected wife, Jameson devoted much space in her writings to the difficulties experienced by women in their attempt to live alone and be self-supporting. She was influenced in much of her work by French feminists such as Madame de Staël, and believed that women had a unique contribution to make to society and should be given more scope for self-improvement in order to prove their worth. She herself had discovered the economic independence that could be won by women through writing, a fact she demonstrated by supporting through her work the several elderly female relatives who were entirely dependent on her.

In 1842 Jameson was awarded a civil list pension but continued with her feminist activities, giving public and private lectures, writing on social issues, and urging that women should not be confined to being caretakers in the home. She advocated that they take up useful employment as nurses, teachers, and workhouse administrators. She supported the work of the Governesses' Benevolent Association and joined a campaign of women artists to put pressure on the elitist Royal Academy to allow female students to study in its art schools.

A friend and colleague of many pioneering social reformers and a woman who fought against the prevalent misogyny of the publishing world and literary critics, Jameson was a major impetus behind the establishment of the groundbreaking *English Woman's Journal* in 1859, which is seen by many as marking the origin of the women's movement in Britain.

See also Bodichon, Barbara; Boucherett, Jessie.

References and Further Reading
Banks, Olive, ed. 1985. *The Biographical Dictionary of British Feminists,* vol. 1, *1800–1930.* London: Harvester Wheatsheaf.
Baylen, J. O., and N. J. Gossman. 1979–1984. *Biographical Dictionary of Modern British Radicals.* 3 vols. Hassocks, Sussex: Harvester Press.
Johnston, Judith. 1997. *Anna Jameson: Victorian, Feminist, Woman of Letters.* Brookfield, VT: Ashgate.
Ó Céirin, Kit, and Cyril Ó Céirin, eds. 1996. *Women of Ireland: A Biographical Dictionary.* Kinvara, County Galway: Tír Eolas.
Shattock, Joanne, ed. 1993. *Oxford Guide to British Women Writers.* Oxford: Oxford University Press.
Thomas, Clara. 1967. *Love and Work Enough: The Life of Anna Jameson.* Toronto: University of Toronto Press.
Todd, Janet, ed. 1989. *Dictionary of British Women Writers.* London: Routledge.

Jebb, Eglantyne
(1876–1928)
United Kingdom

The work of the Save the Children Fund, the largest international voluntary agency in the United Kingdom, has gained great credence and respect since it was established in 1919. It is now a major international humanitarian organization dedicated to working with deprived children in more than 130 countries in the Third World. Its aid workers are frequently seen undertaking essential relief work in the midst of natural disasters such as floods, famines, and earthquakes. On a more mundane level, the fund also administers rural schools and play groups, provides school meals, oversees health programs, and is involved in the campaign to clear landmines. Yet the name of its original founder, Eglantyne Jebb, is rarely mentioned, nor is it generally known that it was she who drafted the League of Nations' 1924 Declaration of Geneva on children's rights that would be the basis of the 1945 United Nations Declaration of the Rights of the Child.

Jebb was born into a wealthy Shropshire family and grew up on the family estate at Ellsmere. As a young woman, she had a passionate love of rural life and the solitary pleasures of country walks. She was also sensitive to her own position of social and economic privilege and developed a dislike of class distinction that would remain at the root of her humanitarianism.

Jebb was encouraged by her maiden aunt, who had taken a hand in her education at home, to study at St. Margaret Hall at Oxford University in 1895–1898, where Jebb won first-class honors in English language and literature. She went on to teacher-training college at Stockwell in south London in 1898 and obtained her first post at a progressive primary school in Marlborough, Wiltshire, which promoted the education theories of Friedrich Froebel. Ill health forced her to give up her job in 1901, however. When she recovered, Jebb took up social work in Cambridge in 1903 for the Charity Organisation Society, in 1906 publishing her findings on poverty in the city, *Cambridge: A Brief Study in Social Questions.* In the book, she drew attention to the plight of poor children she had encountered in the streets "on whose faces the dull suffering of hopelessness has left its indelible stamp" (Oldfield 1984, 297) and first laid out her ideas on development programs among the underprivileged. She remained at Cambridge until 1908 but was still troubled by intermittent illness caused by thyroid problems. During 1910–1912 she traveled in Europe with her sick mother in search of a rest cure, during which time she wrote a novel, *The Ring Fence,* an examination of the class system.

In 1913 Jebb was encouraged by her brother-in-law Charles Buxton to join him and her sister Dorothy in humanitarian work in the Balkans on behalf of the Macedonian Relief Fund. The main object of relief work was to help Muslim Albanian refugees who were now being persecuted after having lost to the Serbs, who were Eastern Orthodox Christians, in the Balkan wars. After returning to England, Jebb set about fund-raising for relief supplies for these refugees, but World War I broke out soon after, and again Jebb was sidelined by ill health, until an operation for a goiter in 1916 brought with it a renewal of her energies. She helped her sister Dorothy run the *Cambridge Magazine,* established by Dorothy during the war to present a less jingoistic and more balanced view of the conflict and to analyze the social and economic ramifications of war.

As a committed pacifist, Jebb did not support the war effort but was anxious, as soon as hostilities were over, to return to Europe to do something for the many starving babies and children, particularly in Germany and Austria, who were now the victims of the Allied blockade that had followed the end of fighting. As a Christian, her message was simple—aid to children was essential, for they represented the future. Jebb traveled on to Macedonia to assist in the organization of relief supplies in the ruins of the Balkans. There she confronted an enormous refugee problem, with 4–5 million children abandoned and starving. Her response came on New Year's Day, 1919, when she set up the Fight the Famine Council (FFC) with Dorothy and others, including the reformer Emily Hobhouse, who was chair of the Russian Babies' Fund. Their objective was to galvanize support from David Lloyd George's government in raising relief supplies.

The FFC was renamed the Save the Children Fund at a meeting held at the Albert Hall in May 1919 to launch a major appeal. Initially, Jebb had to fight against considerable hostility to the idea of fund-raising to help children from the enemy side, but she came up with enterprising publicity campaigns to encourage fund-raising, which reached £400,000 in its first year alone; she also succeeded in enlisting the support of Pope Benedict XV in her work. A vast amount of money would be raised across forty countries over the next few years to provide food and clothing not just for the children in Germany and Austria, but also for those suffering the depredations of war elsewhere: in Greece, Bulgaria, Romania, Armenia, Poland, and Russia. The fund's first branch in Britain was opened in Fife, Scotland, in 1919, and the organization rapidly became staffed by professionals who established 300 branches throughout the United Kingdom.

The Save the Children Fund International Union was established in Geneva on 6 January 1920 in furtherance of Jebb's belief that aid should cut across all creeds and cultures as a unifying force for good. During the 1920s, she showed herself to be an excellent propagandist and publicist. To raise public awareness and money, she devised a new campaign geared to enlist people with respected public profiles—journalists, doctors, and businesspeople—in the building of hospitals, children's homes, and schools throughout the British Empire and subsequently the developing world. It was a policy that paid off; many international celebrities and public figures continue to endorse the organization's many visible campaigns around the world.

In August 1921, the fund was quick to respond to a terrible famine in the grain-growing regions of the River Volga in Bolshevik Russia, recognizing that its services would be needed in peacetime as well as in wartime. Public opinion was against sending assistance to the new communist regime there, but once again, Jebb's primary consideration was the plight of the children, and she organized essential food supplies between 1921 and 1923. After this crisis, Jebb lobbied hard at the League of Nations for adoption of a Declaration of the Rights of the Child, which she published in the fund's journal, *The World's Children,* and which was endorsed by the league at the Declaration of Geneva in 1924. This declaration emphasized the importance of children being the first to receive relief aid in times of distress. The child's material and spiritual development; its right to be fed, nursed, and sheltered; and its right to be socially reclaimed if delinquent were also of primary importance, as was its instruction in social and moral responsibilities. In 1945, the United Nations extended the declaration to include seven basic statements on children's rights. Jebb's work would be endorsed and promoted by other women reformers, including Emmeline Pethick-Lawrence, Charlotte Despard, Ray Strachey, and Nancy Astor.

Jebb never ceased to look for other ways of relieving suffering among impoverished communities, such as providing self-sustaining aid in the form of tools and seeds with which those in need could grow their own food. It was but one aspect of her general strategy on giving aid, which was founded on careful planning and research in order that the needy be shown how to make the best use of aid, which in itself, she believed, should always be given wisely. In her view, aid relied equally on the willingness of those receiving it to give something back to their own communities. An emphasis on families was always uppermost in Jebb's mind, and as a devout Christian, she was insistent that the provision of aid should not be governed by considerations of race or religion.

Jebb lived in Geneva for the last three years of her life. She died of exhaustion after a series of operations at the age of only fifty-two. Her sister Dorothy Buxton, a Quaker and pacifist who assisted her in founding the Fight the Famine Council and the Save the Children Fund, also undertook valuable work for refugees. Buxton was the author of *You and the Refugee: The Economics of the Refugee Problem* (1939). For further information on Jebb and the work of the Save the Children Fund, go to http://www.savethechildren.org.uk/. Information on Jebb can also be found at http://www.leader-values.com/leader/20values/Eglantyne%20Jebb.htm.

See also Astor, Nancy; Despard, Charlotte; Hobhouse, Emily; Pethick-Lawrence, Emmeline.

References and Further Reading

Buxton, Dorothy, and Edward Fuller. 1931. *The White Flame.* London: Longman's.

Freeman, Kathleen. 1965. *If Any Man Build: The History of the Save the Children Fund.* London: Hodder.

Fuller, Edward. 1953. *Her Fighting Line: Eglantyne Jebb and the Save the Children Fund.* Edinburgh: Edinburgh House Press.

Hacker, Carlotta. 1999. *Humanitarians.* New York: Crabtree.

Oldfield, Sybil. 1984. *Spinsters of This Parish: The Life and Times of F. M. Mayor and Mary Sheepshanks.* London: Virago.

———. 2001. *Women Humanitarians: A Biographical Dictionary of British Women Active between 1900 and 1950.* London: Continuum.

Wilson, Francesca M. 1967. *Rebel Daughter of a Country House.* London: George Allen and Unwin.

Jeffers, Audrey Lane
(1898–1968)
Trinidad and Tobago

In the history of women's social campaigning in the British-governed Caribbean islands of Trinidad and Tobago, Jeffers was one of the leading black women in the organization of self-help groups for women in the 1920s. Her establishment in 1921 of the Coterie of Social Workers in the capital, Port of Spain, provided the first non-white organization to offer an outlet for middle-class black and colored women to help underprivileged working women and their children.

Jeffers was from a comfortably well-off black family who lived in the uptown St. Clair suburb. She was educated at Tranquillity Girls Practising School and went to England at the age of fifteen, later taking a diploma in social science at Alexander College in north London. While in London, Jeffers was also involved in founding the Union of Students of African Descent, which later became known as the League of Coloured Peoples. During World War I, she worked among West African troops and set up a West African Soldiers' Fund.

Returning to Trinidad and Tobago in 1920, Jeffers ran a junior school at her own home but soon realized that the needs of the island's underprivileged children were more fundamental. She encouraged other socially concerned women to join her in founding the Coterie of Social Workers, which in 1926 opened a "Breakfast Shed" in Port of Spain to provide hot meals for poor schoolchildren. Several other similar centers were set up elsewhere throughout Trinidad and Tobago over the following years. The coterie extended its activities, setting up the St. Mary's Home for Blind Girls in 1928 and the Maud Reeves Hostel for Working Girls in 1935; in addition, Jeffers established a day nursery for working mothers.

In 1936 the coterie acted as host for a Conference of British West Indies and British Guiana Women Social Workers, held in Port of Spain from 20 April to 10 May. Jeffers gave the opening address, urging women social workers to set up a regional federation to support their work in the realms of education and welfare. On 8 May she gave another speech on "The Urgent Needs of Women in Trinidad," describing the plight of the "middle-class educated negress" denied gainful employment in the civil service. She also detailed the rise of prostitution in Port of Spain and the failure of men to support their illegitimate offspring. In hopes of counteracting these problems, she proposed raising money to establish a high school for girls and a women's police force to monitor the activities of prostitutes and protect young girls from being drawn into this work. Throughout her career, she constantly reminded government of its obligation to provide social welfare.

In 1936 Jeffers was the first woman to be elected to Port of Spain's city council, as an independent candidate for the western ward, with backing from the Trinidad Labour Party. She faced a barrage of opposition to her doing so as a woman and defended her decision by underlining the usefulness of a woman with social concerns to the council. A large turnout in support of her on polling day endorsed her stand, a major step forward for the women's movement in the Caribbean. In 1969, Jeffers was posthumously awarded the first national award instituted in Trinidad and Tobago, the Chaconia Gold Medal for Social Service.

References and Further Reading

Anthony, Michael. 1997. *Historical Dictionary of Trinidad and Tobago.* Lanham, MD: Scarecrow Press.

Comma-Maynard, Olga. 1971. *The Briarend Pattern: The Story of Audrey Jeffers O.B.E. and the Coterie of Social Workers.* Port of Spain: Busby's Printerie.

Wieringa, Saskia, ed. 1995. *Subversive Women: Women's Movements in Africa, Asia, Latin America and the Caribbean,* chap. 5. London: Zed Books.

Jellicoe, Anne
(1823–1880)
Ireland

The Quaker educator and founder of the Governesses' Association and Ireland's first higher education institution for women, Alexandra College, Anne Jellicoe began her philanthropic activities promoting sales of hand embroidery by poor Irish women. Born Anne Mullin in the factory town of Mountmellick, Jellicoe was the daughter of a Quaker schoolteacher. Her religious background gave the young Anne a strong awareness of women's right to education and training in some kind of useful employment, a fact brought home to her when the Quaker-run local weaving and spinning industries at Mountmellick went into decline from the 1830s. After moving to Clara in 1848, Mullin married mill owner John Jellicoe. Her first association with women workers began when she encouraged those who made the sacks for her husband's flour mill to diversify into embroidery. In 1850 she set up a school to teach embroidery on muslin and lace crochet work to these local women. By the time the school closed in 1856, Jellicoe had become determined to do more to educate and train poor women, particularly when, from the late 1850s, she saw how their hand-sewing skills were being superseded by factory produced work. Around this time, she established a local Quaker-run infant school for poor children at Cole Abbey and opened an institute that aimed to train and then find employment for educated women.

In 1860 Jellicoe took it upon herself to investigate working conditions and pay for women in Dublin manufacturing industries and in 1861 reported back to the National Association for the Promotion of Social Science on her findings, making particular reference to women employed in needlework, lace and shirt making, and textile manufacturing. A year later, she provided the association with a report on "A Visit to the Female Convict Prison at Mountjoy, Dublin," but by then she had become drawn to the urgent need for better education for working women. Such were the moral constraints in Irish society of that time that Jellicoe was obliged to restrict her efforts to those respectable but financially distressed middle-class women (often governesses) who needed to undertake paid employment. She founded a society in 1864, known as the Queen's Institute, for the express purpose of providing such women with technical training but unfortunately quickly discovered that to do so was impossible because the women concerned often lacked the most rudimentary education. A few such women (mainly former governesses who had some skills) were trained to copy legal documents, but although the institute had obtained employment

for 862 of its former trainees by 1870, the venture was always limited in its scope.

After being widowed in 1862, Jellicoe had a £3,000 inheritance at her disposal. She used it to provide a permanent home for the Queen's Institute, where her students could be trained for a wider range of occupations. With the support of the archbishop of Dublin, she finally opted to set up a new type of women's college, along the lines of Queen's College for Women in London. In 1866 the Alexandra College (named after the princess of Wales) opened in Dublin "for the sound and liberal education of gentlewomen," as the *Irish Times* reported. As ever, though, the emphasis was on enlisting the right kind of socially acceptable pupils, and Jellicoe's intake was restricted to the middle and upper classes. A curriculum of lessons given by professors from Dublin's Trinity College was established for women over the age of fifteen, and in 1868 Jellicoe, now formally appointed lady superintendent of the college, introduced advanced subjects such as astronomy and Greek literature for the more gifted students. But she remained preoccupied with the sorry standards of basic literacy among the majority of women and in 1869 founded the Governesses' Association of Ireland with the ambition of setting up a collegiate school, opened in 1873 as the Alexandra School, that would prepare students for Alexandra College. A fund was established by the association to provide study grants for young women wishing to train as governesses and teachers; it also set up its own employment registry to help them find suitable employment. The Alexandra School proved a success and much of its profits was ploughed back into the running of the college.

Although Jellicoe did not take a vocal role in campaigning for women's education, her quiet dedication to its principles as a morally ennobling factor in women's lives reflected her very unassuming, private personality. Little is known about her personal life; she lived quietly and died suddenly at the age of fifty-seven, but the Alexandra College remains a lasting memorial to her important contribution.

References and Further Reading

Cullen, Mary, and Maria Luddy. 1995. *Women: Power and Consciousness in Nineteenth-Century Ireland. Eight Biographical Studies.* Dublin: Attic Press.

Ó Céirin, Kit, and Cyril Ó Céirin, eds. 1996. *Women of Ireland: A Historical Dictionary.* Kinvara, County Galway: Tír Eolas.

Jex-Blake, Sophia
(1840–1912)
United Kingdom

Indomitable and *difficult* are words frequently used to describe the English medical reformer Sophia Jex-Blake. In the estimation of her fellow medical pioneer Elizabeth Garrett Anderson, Jex-Blake's intense mood swings and her abrasive and at times downright willful character made her unsuited to a medical career. Certainly, Jex-Blake's complex personality made her campaigning for women's medicine extremely turbulent, placing her in the firing line of much criticism and hostility. As a young woman, her original ambition had been to open a women's college, but after witnessing the pioneering work in women's medicine in the United States, she decided to become a doctor and applied her considerable reserves of dedication and determination to taking on the British medical and university establishment in order to do so, eventually setting up the London School of Medicine for Women and her own hospital in Edinburgh.

Born in Hastings, Sussex, Jex-Blake had a reputation for being high strung as a child. Her strict upbringing by evangelical Anglican parents was conservative and authoritarian. After being educated at private schools, where her spirit was crushed by harsh discipline, she overcame her father's resistance and studied for a year (1858) at Queen's College for Women in London. She stayed on at the school for three more years (1859–1861), teaching mathematics, although her father, who was opposed to women entering paid employment, would not allow her to accept any salary. Jex-Blake then spent some time teaching English in a girls' school at Mannheim, Germany. Rebelling against parental pressures to return home and play the dutiful daughter, in 1865 she traveled to the United States to study teaching methods at women's colleges and published her findings in *American Schools and Colleges.*

On visiting Marie Zakrzewska's New England Hospital for Women and Children in Boston, Jex-Blake met and came under the influence of its resident physician, Dr. Lucy Sewall, who gave her work in the hospital dispensary and in record keeping and encouraged her to take up medicine. Unsuccessful in her attempt to enter Harvard Medical School, Jex-Blake went to New York, where she was one of the first women to register for study at Elizabeth Blackwell's Women's Medical College at the New York Infirmary for Women and Children. After three years, her studies were cut short by her father's death, and Jex-Blake was obliged to return to England to care for her mother. Determined to continue her medical training, in 1869 Jex-Blake decided to lobby for admission to lectures at Edinburgh Medical School and was soon joined in her campaign by Edith Pechey-Phipson. She argued her case strongly in her 1869 essay, "Medicine as a Profession for Women," which was published in Josephine Butler's book, *Woman's Work and Woman's Culture,* and described how women in many European countries had been granted medical training since the Middle Ages, in contrast to the present situation in Britain. Jex-Blake also emphasized the desperate need for women practitioners to attend women patients on gynecological matters, particularly in childbirth, when many women preferred to suffer without proper medical help rather than be attended by men.

Jex-Blake succeeded in persuading the university authorities to provide private lectures for a group of five women students in the prerequisite subjects, which they not only successfully completed but at which they excelled alongside the male students. But a year later, when they moved on to anatomy classes, the continuing hostility and harassment from other male students escalated into a near riot at Surgeons Hall, when the five women were mobbed by male students as they attempted to take their anatomy examination. They struggled on, constantly restricted and having to be escorted to and from lectures; they were also charged double the fees of male students. In 1872, when they applied to take their final examinations, they were informed that the university would only grant them a "certificate of proficiency." Jex-Blake was incensed, and the women took the university to court for reneging on its commitment to allow them to study. In July 1872, with Jex-Blake having borne much of the burden of dealing with lawyers and university authorities as well as continuing her own studies, the case came to court. The court found in their favor, and the women entered the final phase of their clinical work at the Royal Infirmary. However, when they took their exams in October, Jex-Blake failed—the only one of the five women to do so. The case against them was also reversed on appeal in 1873, and they were not, after all, granted their full medical degrees. Jex-Blake's hot temper meanwhile had also got the better of her in 1871, and she had been taken to court for libeling a college doctor during a meeting of the university's board of managers. When the libel case ended, she was left with the bill for costs of £1,000, which was raised by sympathizers.

Despite the whole affair prompting considerable debate in the press and academia, and her case now being argued in the House of Commons by Russell Gurney, a sympathetic member of Parliament, Jex-Blake had to concede temporary defeat in obtaining her medical degree. She decided instead to fly in the face of opposition and establish a women's medical school. With the support of Elizabeth Garrett Anderson, in October 1874 she obtained the lease of a premises in London, where she established the London School of Medicine for Women, which later offered lectures from another medical pioneer, Elizabeth Blackwell. In August 1875, the passage of the Enabling Act allowed British medical examining boards to grant licenses to women (although it was not incumbent upon them to admit women to medical schools), the first to do so being King's and Queen's College of Physicians in Dublin. Meanwhile, Jex-Blake spent the winter of 1876–1877 in Switzerland, at the University of Bern, in order to complete her clinical training. Having obtained her medical degree there in the spring of 1877 after presenting a thesis on puerperal fever, Jex-Blake returned to Britain and also passed her licensing exams in Dublin. In May 1877 she was finally entered on the register of practitioners of the British Medical Association.

Expecting to be given a senior post at the London School of Medicine, she returned to find that in her absence a woman named Isabel Thorne had been appointed over her head as executive secretary, and, already aware of the personality clash between herself and the pacific Anderson, Jex-Blake returned to Edinburgh. She set herself up in private practice that June and also opened her own Dispensary for Women and Children, acting as its attending medical officer. In 1885 it became the Edinburgh Hospital for Women and Children, which was staffed by women. Jex-Blake was now determined to set up a medical school for women and did so in 1886, with herself as dean. When, in 1894, women students were finally admitted to study alongside male students at British universities, including the Edinburgh Medical School, she closed her own school. Jex-Blake served as honorary treasurer of the National Association for Promoting the Medical Education of Women and was a member of the Medical Society of the Irish College of Physicians. She also accepted an appointment as lecturer in midwifery at the Edinburgh Extra-Mural School. Her other medical publications were *Medical Women* (1872; revised and republished in 1886) and *The Care of Infants* (1884); she also wrote articles for the *Fortnightly Review* and the *Nineteenth Century*. Jex-Blake retired to the south of England in 1899.

During her early years in London, Jex-Blake had associated with feminists in the Langham Place Circle. In 1859 she supported their establishment of the Society for Promoting the Employment of Women, and she was a founder, with Josephine Butler, Frances Power Cobbe, and Florence Nightingale, of the Ladies' National Association for the Diffusion of Sanitary Knowledge, which in its advocacy of sanitary reform emphasized the need for rational dress (no tight corseting), fresh air, and clean water as well as improved maternity and child care. Jex-Blake was also active in the suffrage movement: she was a signatory of Barbara Bodichon's 1866 petition on women's suffrage and an active member of the Edinburgh branch of the National Society of Women's Suffrage and encouraged women in Edinburgh to take up public service by serving as Poor Law Guardians.

Jex-Blake paid the price for her difficult personality in her private life. She was happy only in the company of other women, but her abrasive personality lost her many female friends, most particularly the reformer Octavia Hill. Their close friendship faltered as a result of Jex-Blake's high-strung nature and was never restored, although Jex-Blake left all her property to Hill in her will.

See also Anderson, Elizabeth Garrett; Blackwell, Elizabeth; Bodichon, Barbara; Butler, Josephine; Cobbe, Frances Power; Hill, Octavia; Nightingale, Florence; Pechey-Phipson, Edith; Zakrzewska, Marie.

References and Further Reading

Balfour, Margaret I., and Ruth Young. 1929. *The Work of Medical Women in India.* London: Oxford University Press.

Bell, Enid Moberley. 1953. *Storming the Citadel: The Rise of the Woman Doctor.* London: Constable.

Blake, Catriona. 1990. *The Charge of the Parasols: Women's Entry to the Medical Profession.* London: Women's Press.

Bonner, Thomas Neville. 1992. *To the Ends of the Earth: Women's Search for Education in Medicine.* Cambridge, MA: Harvard University Press.

Lovejoy, Dr. Esther Pohl. 1957. *Women Doctors of the World.* New York: Macmillan.

Roberts, Shirley. 1993. *Sophia Jex-Blake: A Woman Pioneer in Medical Reform.* London: Routledge.

Strachey, Ray. 1978 [1928]. *The Cause: A Brief History of the Women's Movement.* Reprint, London: Virago.

Todd, Margaret. 1918. *The Life of Sophia Jex-Blake.* London: Macmillan.

Walsh, Mary Roth. 1977. *"Doctors Wanted: No Women Need Apply": Sexual Barriers in the Medical Profession, 1835–1975.* New Haven: Yale University Press.

Jilani, Hina, and Asma Jahangir
(1951–) and (1952–)
Pakistan

The Pakistani lawyers and human rights activists Hina Jilani and Asma Jahangir have mounted a brave and difficult campaign, in defiance of traditional patriarchal attitudes, to draw attention to the practice of honor killing in Pakistan and to offer help and advice to women seeking to free themselves from unhappy marriages. The tragic murder on 6 April 1999—in Jilani's own offices—of Samia Sarwar, a mother of two seeking a divorce from her husband after being separated for five years, brought unprecedented world attention to the abuse of women's rights in Pakistan. It initiated a campaign by Jilani and her sister Jahangir, backed by Amnesty International, against the continuing abuse and subjugation of Pakistani women. Jilani has also repeatedly called for the democratization of the political system in Pakistan and amendments to the Constitution to increase the representation of women in its legislature so that, under their influence, more attention can be drawn to women's and human rights issues. She is now a leader in the promotion of nongovernmental human rights organizations in Pakistan and a member of the United Nations Center for Human Rights and the Carter Center's International Human Rights Council.

Jilani began her legal practice in 1979, setting up the first women's law firm, known as AGHS, in Lahore in 1981 with her sister Asma Jahangir and two other female lawyers. In 1987 the firm was given the status of a nongovernmental organization (NGO) in recognition of its support for human rights. Since the setting up of their Women's Legal Aid Cell in 1986 and the women's refuge known as Dastak, Jilani and Jahangir have taken on numerous test cases in the difficult history of human rights campaigning in Pakistan. Their legal work for women has attracted calls for help from more than 1,400 women since 1991, many of them seeking divorce from brutal or abusive husbands. Dastak has offered food, shelter, and training to women in distress as well as education for their children and has often been able to effect a reconciliation between them and their families. The support of a UN General Assembly Declaration on Human Rights Defenders, which upholds the right of lawyers such as Jilani and Jahangir to engage in the peaceful protection of human rights, has prompted an international appeal to the Pakistan government to uphold these civil liberties and to clamp down on the iniquitous "custom" of honor killings.

Now recognized as leading social campaigners in Pakistan, Jilani and Jahangir have set up the Aurat Foundation, through which they have extended their legal work to cover all aspects of human rights litigation, with a particular emphasis on legal representation for women and children, minority groups, and prisoners. Jilani is a founding member of the Human Rights Commission of Pakistan and the Women's Action Forum and has since become prominent in regional and international organizations working to set up standards in international human rights.

In 1998 Jilani published *Human Rights and Democratic Development in Pakistan,* in which she made detailed recommendations on democratic reform relating to human rights in Pakistan, drawing particular attention to the violation of the rights of women, who she argued were not adequately protected against acts of violence, such as the widespread fundamentalist practice of honor killings, and against sexual abuse, particularly rape. The Pakistan Penal Code in this respect was repealed after the introduction of new Islamic penal law in 1979, notably the Hadood ordinances, which Jilani argues now make it more difficult for rapists to be brought to justice. Under the ordinances, a woman in Pakistan who now accuses a man of rape must prove her own innocence and may find herself faced with a countercharge of *zina,* the crime of adultery and unmarried sex. Jilani's work has been recognized by awards from the American Bar Association and Human Rights Watch. In August 2000 the UN secretary general appointed Jilani Special Representative on Human Rights Defenders, a three-year appointment during which she will report on their work around the world.

Asma Jahangir, who has served as vice chair of the Defence for Children International in Geneva, has now taken over the chair of the Human Rights Commission of Pakistan from her sister Jilani, who has been promoted to its secretary-general. In 1993 she published *Children of a Lesser God: Child Prisoners of Pakistan,* an exposé of the widespread abuse of children in its many forms. In describing a long catalogue of maltreatment—through neglect, incest, child marriage, infanticide, the selling of children into bonded labor by their own families, and the abuse of children under the criminal justice system, Jahangir argued that since Pakistan had signed the UN Convention on the Rights of the Child, then it was duty-bound to follow the UN Standard Minimum Rules for the Administration of Juvenile Justice. In 1995 Jahangir was awarded the Ramón Magsaysay Award for public service and in 1998 the UN appointed her as Special Rapporteur on Extrajudicial, Summary and Arbitrary Executions.

Together, in 1990 Jilani and Jahangir published a study, *The Hudood Ordinances: A Divine Sanction?,* in which they discussed the effects of this new legislation on the underprivileged and disadvantaged, pointing out that this made children as young as seven, who were formerly protected by the Pakistan Penal Code, liable for punishments such as whipping. With their long track record in human rights activism, Jilani and Jahangir encountered even more violent opposition in their work on behalf of Muslim women seeking divorce. They have been the target of death threats and *fatwas* from religious groups, as well as from individual families whose wives and daughters have turned to these lawyers for help. Blood money has been offered for their assassination, and demands have been made to parliament that the two women be punished in accordance with "tribal and Islamic law." Such is the opposition of traditional society to the perceived dishonor of divorce that both the govern-

ment and the police have turned a blind eye to threats made against the sisters, their only response being to place both women under round-the-clock surveillance. In May 1999 Jilani openly accused the Pakistan government of supporting a smear campaign against their women's refuge, Dastak. Meanwhile, the honor killings continue, with 300 cases reported in Pakistan in 1998 alone.

On International Women's Day, 8 March 2001, the sisters were awarded the Millennium Peace Prize. There is considerable information on the net on the work of Jilani and Asma, but since these websites are constantly changing, readers are recommended to search for updates under their names.

References and Further Reading
Jahangir, Asma, and Hina Jilani. 1990. *The Hudood Ordinances: A Divine Sanction. A Research Study of the Hudood Ordinances and Their Effects on the Disadvantaged Sections of Pakistani Society.* Lahore: Rhotas Books.
Jahangir, Asma, and Mark Doucet. 1993. *Children of a Lesser God: Child Prisoners of Pakistan.* Lahore: Vanguard.
Jilani, Hina. 1998. *Human Rights and Democratic Development in Pakistan.* Lahore: Human Rights Commission of Pakistan.

Jiménez y Muro, Dolores
(1848–1925)
Mexico

A leading socialist activist, teacher, and writer, Jiménez worked for many years for the Mexican Liberal Party helping to initiate teaching and housing reform before later joining the Zapatistas. She also collaborated with another pioneer reformer, Juana Gutiérrez de Mendoza, on a range of social projects.

Born in the small town of Aguas Calientes, northern Mexico, Jiménez worked as a rural schoolteacher and moved to Mexico City in 1904. During the first decade of the twentieth century, she was a member of the Precursor Movement, a democratic, reformist group that opposed the dictatorship of Porfirio Díaz. She took up writing, publishing poems and articles in journals that opposed Díaz's dictatorship. In 1905 she joined the staff of the *Mexican Woman,* the journal of the Daughters of Cuauhtémoc (named after the last Aztec emperor), which ran until 1908; she also wrote for the feminist publication the *Newspaper of the Home* (*El Diario del Hogar*). During this dissident period, she was frequently arrested and imprisoned for being involved in demonstrations, and in jail she went on hunger strikes in order to win her release. In prison in 1911, she founded Regeneration and Consensus, an organization dedicated to women's rights and those of indigenous people.

Dissatisfied with the liberals' lack of muscle, Jiménez joined the opposition group led by Francisco Madero and became involved in the Complot de Tacubaya in 1911, an armed insurrection called by Madero when Díaz refused to relinquish power after losing a phony election in 1910. The complot was supported by a detailed fifteen-point plan for wide-reaching social and economic reform that Jiménez had drafted, involving agrarian reform, maximum working hours, better wages and working conditions for peasants in the countryside as well as workers in urban areas, educational reform, and the protection of Mexico's indigenous peoples. Jiménez added a qualifier, about which she felt particularly strongly, in response to the massive influx of foreign workers that Díaz had allowed to industrialize and modernize Mexico. It stated that foreign firms operating in Mexico should ensure that at least half of their workforces were Mexican nationals. She also insisted that the wages of both women and men be increased.

The ensuing demonstrations orchestrated by Francisco Madero in the Tacubaya region demanded increases in the wages of both rural and urban workers, including women. More than 10,000 participants in the rebellion were subsequently arrested, but it achieved its object of eventually bringing down Díaz's government. Meanwhile, Jiménez had joined the revolutionary leader Emiliano Zapata when she realized that Madero was never going to implement the radical program of agrarian reform she supported, a program that included the restoration of traditional, communal landownership to the indigenous people. Now in her sixties, Jiménez collaborated with the Zapatistas and undertook missions for them until Zapata's assassination in 1919, by which time she had been promoted to the rank of colonel in the Zapatista peasant guerrilla army.

After Zapata's death, Jiménez retired from ac-tivism. She received no recognition except for a meager pension. She continued to speak out against corruption in government and at the age of sixty-five was imprisoned by another despotic military administration, that of General Victoriano Huerta, whom she had criticized in the newspaper *The Voice of Juarez*. Little is known about Jiménez's personal life; she remained unmarried.

See also Gutiérrez de Mendoza, Juana Belén.

References and Further Reading

Adams, Jerome R. 1991. *Liberators and Patriots of Latin America.* Jefferson, NC: McFarland and Co.

Cockroft, James D. 1966. *Intellectual Precursors of the Mexican Revolution.* Austin: University of Texas Press.

Macías, Anna. 1983. *Against All Odds: The Feminist Movement in Mexico to 1940.* Westport, CT: Greenwood Press.

Soto, Shirlene. 1990. *Emergence of the Modern Mexican Woman: Her Participation in Revolution and Struggle for Equality, 1910–1940.* Denver: Arden Press.

Jinnah, Fatima
(1893–1967)
Pakistan

The Pakistani campaigner for the rights and welfare of Muslim women was the sister of the first governor-general of Pakistan, Muhammad Ali Jinnah, and assumed the role of his secretary and political adviser. In her seventies she took a brave stand against the oppressive regime of Mohammad Ayub Khan during the election campaign of 1964–1965.

Jinnah was born in Karachi and grew up in Bombay under the protection of her brother, after their father died when she was eighteen. She was educated at a mission school and went on to study dentistry. She lived in England from 1929 to 1933, after accompanying her brother to a Round Table Conference in London.

She joined the rejuvenated Muslim League on her return to India, when it began pushing for reform of religious and social attitudes toward women and the provision of better health care. As a member of the league's national council, she worked for women's welfare from the mid-1930s, in particular fighting against traditional patriarchal attitudes and becoming president of the All-

India Muslim Women's Committee, which set up branches throughout the country. She encouraged the development of industrial schools and cooperatives of self-employed workers, many of them women, and was patron of the Fatima Jinnah Women's Medical College in Lahore.

All through this period, Jinnah continued to support the political career of her brother Ali Jinnah, acting as his political hostess when he became the first governor-general of Pakistan after the partition of India in 1947. She went into mourning for him on his death in 1948 and retreated for the next six years from public life. She reemerged briefly to support the Muslim League in elections in the east wing of Pakistan (now Bangladesh) during 1954, but as such she held only a figurehead role, reappearing on important political or national occasions, until the abrupt change of government brought about by a military coup in 1958 caused her to speak out on the abuses of human rights under the dictatorial regime of Muhammad Ayub Khan. The various opposition parties in Pakistan gathered around Jinnah as the keeper of the flame of her brother's form of democratic government, and she was persuaded to stand in the 1965 election as the main opposition candidate. Ayub Khan retaliated by enlisting the help of orthodox religious groups to issue a *fatwa* proclaiming that a woman could not be head of an Islamic state. Jinnah lost the election despite a huge groundswell of popular support and amid accusations that Ayub had rigged the vote. Jinnah never married and was much revered as the "Mother of the Country," a fact reflected in the great public funeral accorded her in Karachi.

References and Further Reading

Jinnah, Fatima. 1976. *Speeches, Messages and Statements of Madar-i-Millat Mohtarama Fatima Jinnah (1948–1967)*. London: Research Society of Pakistan.

Roberts, Frank C., ed. 1961–1970. *Obituaries from The Times*, vol 2. Reading: Newspaper Archive Developments.

Jones, Mary ("Mother Jones")
(1830?–1930)
United States

The determined gaze of the embattled trade union leader Mother Jones speaks volumes about the life of a woman who grew up fighting and never gave in to intimidation. From her birth in poverty in Ireland, through her early life as an emigrant, first to Canada and then in the United States, Mary Jones endured personal tragedy and financial hardship in her crusading defense of the rights of U.S. workers. Jones made light of her own personal sacrifices; her only concern was to travel to wherever the fight for justice took her, and her motto was one of exemplary pragmatism: "Pray for the dead and fight like hell for the living."

Sources disagree over the date of Jones's birth in the city of Cork, Ireland. For many years, it was generally accepted that she had reached the age of 100 at the time of her death, but her 1925 *Autobiography* remains unreliable on dates, with some biographers now suggesting that she was born as late as 1836. Her father's activities for Irish independence forced him to leave Ireland sometime around 1835 (so Jones's birth could not have been much later than that), and the family joined him in Toronto, Ontario, in 1838, where her father worked on the railroad. After attending public high school in Toronto, Jones worked as a teacher, first in New England and then in a convent in Michigan. After a year, she gave up teaching for employment as a dressmaker in Chicago but returned to teaching in 1860, settling in Memphis, Tennessee.

In 1861 she married George Jones, a member of the Iron Molder's Union, and the couple began raising a family in the coalfields of Tennessee. But in 1867, Jones lost her husband and all four of their children in an epidemic of yellow fever. She bravely stayed on in Memphis to help nurse other victims of the epidemic before moving back to Chicago, where she resumed working as a seamstress. No sooner had she established a successful dressmaking business, however, than tragedy again visited her, when in 1871 she lost all her possessions and her workshop in the devastating Chicago fire. She took refuge at the meeting hall of the Knights of Labor, a workingmen's fraternity that her husband had supported, and committed herself to encouraging workers to join the trade union movement. Jones soon attracted attention and notoriety because of her spontaneity as a speaker and her defiantly outspoken views.

Thereafter, Jones subsumed her own personal pain and loss into a life of activism for the labor movement over a span of fifty years, living without a permanent home and with few possessions and traveling to wherever the labor confrontations arose. She bedded down wherever she could on the road, in tents and shantytowns, her first campaign being the 1877 Pittsburgh railroad strike on the Baltimore-Ohio line. Thereafter, as a trade union troubleshooter in the coal, steel, copper-mining, and garment industries, she pursued the cause of improved wages and working conditions. She worked on behalf of workers in the coal-mining industry as a representative of the United Mine Workers (UMW). In 1899–1900, Jones organized miners' wives to collect food and supplies for strikers during a UMW strike in Pennsylvania. She proved adept at galvanizing workers' womenfolk into action, and in 1902, during a strike by anthracite miners of the UMW in West Virginia, she led marches by strikers' wives wielding pots, pans, brooms, and mops. She broke off her campaign for the UMW in 1903 to organize miners in Colorado but opposed the union's decision to capitulate and resigned, taking up the defense of striking machinists on the Southern Pacific Railroad and copper miners in Arizona.

In 1903, in protest at the exploitation of child textile workers in the mills of Pennsylvania, who were subjected to sixty-hour workweeks, Jones led the "March of the Mill Children," a group of juvenile workers, many under sixteen, who formed part of the industry's 75,000-strong labor force. The protesters took a week to march the 100-mile journey from Kensington, Pennsylvania, to President Theodore Roosevelt's home at Oyster Bay, Long Island. Barred from taking the marchers all the way to Roosevelt's front door, Jones dressed three of the mill boys in their Sunday best and got past security men, only to be turned away again. The ensuing publicity, however, led to legislation on child labor in Pennsylvania.

A lifelong socialist, in 1898 Jones had been a cofounder of the Social Democratic Party. After giving up her organizing for the UMW in 1904, she took to the lecture circuit on behalf of the Socialist Party of America. In 1905 she supported the founding of the Industrial Workers of the World, or Wobblies, and fought the deportation from the United States of Mexican revolutionaries.

In 1911 Jones left the Socialist Party to resume work for the United Mine Workers, taking up the

Mary "Mother" Jones (Library of Congress)

cause of miners in West Virginia in their battle to get the operators of Paint and Cabin Creeks to renew their work contracts. The dispute became ugly, and violence broke out. As a result, at the age of eighty-two, Jones was prosecuted for conspiracy to commit murder after threatening to call the miners to arms. Her sentence of twenty years by a military court specially set up by the state militia was soon commuted by the new governor. Upon her release, Jones, not in the least deterred by her experience, immediately took up labor issues in Colorado in 1913, organizing miners striking in the Rockefeller-owned Colorado Fuel and Iron Company. In 1915–1916, she was in New York negotiating during strikes by streetcar and garment workers and in 1919 traveled to Pittsburgh to support a strike by steelworkers.

Jones once again left the UMW in 1922 because of differences with its leadership. She took part in her last labor dispute in 1924, in support of dressmakers in Chicago. During her long career, she wrote for many socialist and trade union newspapers, including the *United Mine Workers Journal,* and in 1895 was a founder of the socialist weekly journal, *Appeal to Reason.* Her 1925 *Autobiography of Mother Jones* proved to be a classic, appearing in new editions in 1972 and 1990.

Like other indomitable socialist campaigners of her time, such as Elizabeth Gurley Flynn—herself an admirer of Jones as a great "agitator"—Jones attracted a large amount of often hysterical publicity for her union activism. Unlike other women trade union activists, however, she was adamantly opposed to women's involvement in a separate women's rights movement. Her overriding desire was to make the world a better place for everyone, not just women. In her unique and colorful idiom, she placed the class struggle first, believing that male support for women's work for suffrage, temperance, and moral reform was a deliberate ploy to keep them away from more militant and confrontational activism. As a woman who acted on instincts and never developed a social philosophy, Jones was a hands-on campaigner with undoubted gifts of inspirational leadership. She thrived best in the thick of things, regularly claiming not to be a humanitarian but purely and simply "a hell-raiser." Such an admission ensured that in the public eye, she would be ranked alongside Emma Goldman as yet another socialist activist who was perceived as a threat to the very fabric of American society.

True to the spirit of a lifetime's campaigning, Jones was buried alongside miners who had died during a riot in the mines at Virden in 1898, at the Mount Olive Union Miners' Cemetery in the coalfields of southern Illinois. A monument to Jones was raised there in 1936. A website at http://www/execpc.com/~shepler/mojo.htr/ offers links to several sites on the life and work of Mother Jones. Information can also be obtained from the Illinois Labor History Society at http://.www.kentlaw.edu/ilhs/majones.htm/.

See also Flynn, Elizabeth Gurley; Goldman, Emma.

References and Further Reading

Atkinson, Linda. 1978. *Mother Jones: The Most Dangerous Woman in America.* New York: Crown Publishers.

Colman, Penny. 1994. *Mother Jones and the March of Mill Children.* Brookfield, CT: Millbrook Press.

Felder, Deborah G. 1996. *The 100 Most Influential Women: A Ranking of the 100 Greatest Women Past and Present.* London: Robinson.

Fetherling, Dale. 1974. *Mother Jones, the Miner's Angel: A Portrait.* Carbondale: Southern Illinois University Press.

Foner, Philip. 1979. *Women and the American Labor Movement,* vol. 1, *From Colonial Times to the Eve of World War I.* New York: Free Press.

———, ed. *Mother Jones Speaks.* New York: Monad Press.

Gorn, Elliott J. 2000. *Mother Jones: The Most Dangerous Woman in America.* New York: Hill and Wang.

Jones, Mary Harris. 1990 [1925]. *Autobiography of Mother Jones.* Edited by Mary Field Parton. Rev. ed. Chicago: Charles H. Kerr.

Josephson, Judith Pinkerton. 1997. *Mother Jones: Fierce Fighter for Workers' Rights.* Minneapolis: Lerner Publications.

Kraft, Betsy. *Mother Jones, One Woman's Fight for Labor.* New York: Clarion Books.

Long, Priscilla. 1976. *Mother Jones, Woman Organizer, and Her Relations with Miners' Wives, Working Women, and the Suffrage Movement.* Boston: Red Sun Press.

Niess, Judith. 1977. *Seven Women: Portraits from the American Radical Tradition.* New York: Viking Press.

Steel, Edward M. 1985. *The Correspondence of Mother Jones.* Pittsburgh: University of Pittsburgh Press.

———, ed. 1988. *The Speeches and Writings of Mother Jones.* Pittsburgh: University of Pittsburgh Press.

Joseph, Helen Beatrice
(1905–1992)
South Africa

As a white social worker among the poor blacks of Cape Town during the 1950s, Helen Joseph was one of the first members of the white elite to witness at close quarters the miseries wrought by racial segregation. She committed the rest of her life to fighting for racial justice and an end to apartheid. She became famous internationally as a leading white South African dissident and endured with courage accusations of treason, house arrest, abuse, death threats, and constant surveillance. Fortunately, she lived long enough to see the end of apartheid in 1992.

Born in Midhurst, Sussex, in England, Joseph attended King's College at the University of London, graduating in 1927. She taught in India for three years before emigrating to South Africa in

1931, then married, and served as an information and welfare officer in the Women's Auxiliary Air Force during World War II.

After the war and her divorce, she worked for a while in the Garment Workers' Union under its leader Solly Sachs and then trained as a social worker and ran community centers in a mixed-race area in Cape Town. Determined to work for political change and an end to segregation, in 1955 she became a cofounder of the white wing of the African National Congress (ANC), the Congress of Democrats, and that same year helped to draw up its freedom charter calling for South Africa's transition to a multiracial society. During the 1950s, in her desire to improve the position of black women, Joseph served as secretary of the Federation of South African Women. On 9 August 1956, she and Lilian Ngoyi led a major demonstration by 20,000 women of the federation against the iniquitous pass laws, which obliged all black and colored women to carry proof of racial identity. Since then, that day has been celebrated as South African Women's Day.

The ANC was outlawed, and in 1956 Joseph, along with many other activists, was arrested and held in detention for five months. A year later, she was charged with treason and held under house arrest for six months, becoming the first white person in South Africa to suffer this form of incarceration. The trial dragged on for four years, until Joseph was acquitted in 1961. Her freedom of association was strictly controlled again between 1962 and 1971; her book about her experiences, *If This Be Treason* (1963), was banned, and she was registered as a communist by the authorities in 1965. The discovery that she had cancer in 1971 led to her being released from house arrest and hospitalized. Although banned from holding office, she was elected honorary vice president of South African Students on a regular basis from 1971 to the 1980s.

After her recovery from cancer, she resumed her political activities, raising funds for the care of the jailed Nelson Mandela's daughters. She was again arrested and banned from political activism from 1980 to 1982. By that time, a new anti-apartheid group linked to the ANC had come into being, and Joseph became one of its patrons in 1983. The United Democratic Front, with black and white representatives from 575 community groups, trade unions, and women's and youth organizations, began mounting a major campaign. It called for international trade sanctions and gained international support for the rights of political prisoners and the dismantling of apartheid from organizations such as Amnesty International.

When she was eighty years old, Joseph was no longer considered dangerous to the state and was "unbanned," although the media were still not allowed to publish her interviews and statements. Before her death she was awarded the highest honor that the ANC gave to a white person, the Seaparnakoe Medal. Helen Joseph remained all her life a devout Christian, guided by an unshakeable vision of racial justice; when she died, her coffin, draped in the ANC flag, was buried in Soweto's all-black cemetery.

See also Ngoyi, Lilian.
References and Further Reading
Joseph, Helen. 1963. *If This Be Treason*. London: Deutsch.
———. 1986. *Side by Side: The Autobiography of Helen Joseph*. London: Zed Books.
Uerwey, E. J., ed. 1995. *New Dictionary of South African Biography*. Pretoria: HSRC Publishers.
Walker, Cheryl. 1991. *Women and Resistance in South Africa*. 2d ed. Cape Town: David Philip.

Joshi, Anandibai
(1865–1887)
India

Joshi, the first Hindu woman to qualify as a doctor (and also the first high-caste Indian woman to travel to the United States, where she obtained her degree), was the cousin of the feminist educator Pandita Ramabai. Joshi was born in Poona, India, into a high-caste, landowning Brahmin family and was married in 1874, on her ninth birthday. Her husband, a government post office official, had known the family for some time and had taught Joshi Sanskrit. After the death of her only child in 1878 a few days after it was born (a child she had given birth to at the age of only thirteen), Joshi was convinced that its chances of survival might have been better had there been better medical facilities available. She became convinced of the desperate need for women to train as doctors and resolved to devote herself to the medical care of women and children.

At that time it was impossible for her to study

medicine in India, and so with her husband's assistance she began to correspond with a missionary newspaper and through it eventually found a potential sponsor in the United States, a Mrs. B. F. Carpenter of Roselle, New Jersey. Meanwhile, Joshi attended a school run by the Society for the Propagation of the Gospel in Bombay. The sometimes domineering approach used by Christian missionaries during her time there to impose their beliefs on non-Christians lingered in her memory and taught her the necessity of religious tolerance.

Finally, in 1883, Joshi left her husband behind in India and set off on her own from Calcutta via Liverpool to New York to study medicine for three years at the pioneering Women's Medical College in Philadelphia. Even there, in order to preserve her reputation and prevent the loss of caste brought on by her daring to travel abroad, she had to remain scrupulous in the preparation of her own strictly vegetarian food on a smoky anthracite coal stove in her college room. She scrupulously observed Hindu rites and wore her traditional sari at all times for she had made a vow: "I will go to America as a Hindu, and come back and live among my people as a Hindu" (Sen Gupta 1944, 18). While at college she was taken under the wing of its principal, Dr. Rachel Bodley, who lodged Joshi in her own home.

Early in 1884 Joshi was invited to give a talk in the college and chose as her subject child marriage. She confounded her audience, many of whom were hostile to the practice, by endorsing it as traditional, an opinion no doubt born out of loyalty to her own culture and her own personal situation, rather than enlightened belief.

Although suffering from poor health and overwork (the result of studying sixteen hours a day), Joshi graduated eighth out of forty-two students in 1886, an occasion proudly witnessed by her cousin Ramabai, who had arrived especially for the occasion. Joshi returned to India, full of crusading zeal to at last offer constructive service to Indian women, and found herself something of a celebrity. Indeed, many admirers, in defiance of Joshi's loss of caste for having traveled abroad, came to pay their respects to her. She was offered an appointment as the resident physician on the women's ward of the Albert Edward Hospital that had just been built in Kolhapur. But tragically, she had developed tuberculosis, probably contracted in the cold winter climate of Philadelphia to which she was unused. She died within five months of returning to India, at the age of twenty-two; after cremation her ashes were sent by her husband to the United States for burial. Joshi's death prompted many eulogistic tributes in the Indian press; those who knew her would not forget her tiny physique and her quiet dignity. Despite the shortness of her life, her legacy has been an extremely important one in the history of women's medicine in India and an inspiration to the many pioneer Indian women who followed her.

See also Ramabai, Pandita Saraswati.

References and Further Reading
Chapman, Mrs. E. F. 1891. *Sketches of Some Distinguished Indian Women.* London: W. H. Allen.
Jayawardena, Kumari. 1995. *The White Woman's Other Burden: Western Women and South Asia during British Rule.* London: Routledge.
Sen Gupta, Padmini. 1944. *Pioneer Indian Women.* Bombay: Thacker.

Juhacz, Marie
(1879–1956)
Germany

The moderate women's rights activist and reformer Marie Juhacz worked in municipal welfare projects and rejected the Marxist theories of Clara Zetkin that subordinated the cause of women's rights to the waging of class war. For Juhacz, the key to achieving socialism lay in winning the confidence of working-class women by cooperating with them at the grassroots level on practical projects and encouraging their naturally protective role as mothers in welfare activism.

Born near Brandenburg into a poor farming family, Juhacz worked in a factory and then as a seamstress. Introduced to socialist literature by her brother, she began attending socialist meetings and was drawn into the movement by her sympathy for striking women weavers in Crimmitschau. After divorcing her husband in 1903, she turned to socialist and humanitarian concerns. She moved to Berlin in 1906, where she lived with her sister Elizabeth and shared with her the burden of child care. On joining the Women's and Girls' Educational Club in Schöneberg, Juhacz was asked to organize the dissemination of socialist propaganda among working women. In 1911 she entered vocational work among women in municipal welfare projects, but the outbreak of World War I kept her sidelined to local activities until after the war and the achievement of women's suffrage.

Juhacz became head of the Workers' Welfare Bureau within the Social Democratic Party in 1919 and headed its campaigns in support of welfare legislation, as well as writing for its women's journal, *Equality.* She believed that women should back, not divide, the nation in its hour of defeat and revived the concept of women's "separate spheres." She encouraged them once more to channel their work into welfare, saying: "Women are the born protectors of humanity and, therefore social work corresponds so well with their nature" (Smith 1989, 439).

Juhacz served as a social democratic member of the Reichstag from 1923 to 1933 and lobbied for higher status to be accorded women within the party. In 1929 she prepared a report on "Women in the Economy" for the annual party conference, concluding that women's greater involvement in political life could only follow their improved economic position. Like several other leading feminist socialists, she left Germany after the rise of Adolf Hitler, but returned in 1949 to resume social and welfare work.

References and Further Reading

Quaterat, Jean H. 1979. *Reluctant Feminists in German Social Democracy 1885–1917.* Princeton: Princeton University Press.

Smith, Bonnie G. 1989. *Changing Lives: Women in European History since 1700.* Lexington, MA: D. C. Heath.

Thönnessen, Werner. 1976. *The Emancipation of Women: The Rise and Decline of the Women's Movement in German Social Democracy 1863–1933.* London: Pluto Press.

K

Kanno Suga
(1881–1911)
Japan

Inspired by the poet Yosano Akiko, the Japanese anarchist Kanno took up writing and entered into some of the most advanced discussions of the social issues of her day. She lived an unorthodox lifestyle and had several affairs (including one with her stepbrother). In her political life, she saw herself as a Japanese freedom fighter in the mold of the Russian revolutionaries Vera Figner and Sofya Perovskaya and was prepared to sacrifice her life in order to achieve radical social change. Like Perovskaya in Russia, she was the first woman executed for her involvement in a plot to assassinate the ruler.

Kanno's short and tragic life began with harsh treatment at the hands of a violent stepmother and rape at the age of fifteen. Her father, a member of the samurai class, had lost his wealth when his mining business failed. Denied a secondary school education, Kanno began reading on social issues in her teens. In 1899 at the age of seventeen, she was forced to enter into an arranged marriage to Komiya Fukutaro. When her ailing father was deserted by her stepmother, she returned to nurse him and look after her younger siblings.

In early 1902, with the help of the Osaka-based (male) novelist Udagawa Bunsui, Kanno obtained a job as a reporter for the *Osaka Morning Report* and later also wrote for the *Christian World* (1903–1904). In Osaka she became involved in the moral reform movement led by Japanese Christians and socialists. She joined the Women's Moral Reform Society led by Yajima Kajiko and others, supported its drive to abolish licensed brothels, and wrote newspaper articles condemning prostitution. In 1903 Kanno became a Christian.

In 1903 Kanno published the antiwar novel *Breaking Off,* and the next year, along with other feminists in the Osaka Women's Moral Reform Society (of which she was now an elected officer), she took a pacifist stance during the Russo-Japanese War of 1903–1904. In 1906 she moved to Tanabe to work for the socialist newspaper *Muro News.* There she met and had an affair with a fellow reporter and socialist, Arahata Kanson, and moved back to Tokyo to work on the *Mainichi Telegraph.*

Despite the fact that she was suffering from tuberculosis, Kanno continued to write on women's need for self-fulfillment and the traditional mindset that viewed their role as "having nothing to do but be obedient" (as one male official had expressed it in the nineteenth century). She found herself having to fight double standards of female chastity and male promiscuity in her own relationships with men, for her newest lover, the activist Kotoku Shusui, visited brothels despite espousing the equal rights of women.

In 1908 Kanno was involved in the "Red Flag" incident, a socialist-anarchist rally that turned into a demonstration at which many of her fellow activists were arrested. She spent three months in jail, where she fell ill. Convinced that peaceful campaigning would never bring political change, Kanno became more militant. Together with Kotoku, she started the journal *Free Thought* and discussed the need for more violent means to effect political change, becoming herself drawn into the manufacture of explosives for an attack on the emperor. When the plot to assassinate the emperor was discovered in May 1910, Kanno was put on trial in December for her involvement in it. Proudly defending herself in court as one of the twenty-four ringleaders, Kanno, along with eleven men, was sentenced to death. She went to her execution a willing martyr to the cause in which her belief was unshakeable. Although her deep sense of patriotism might now seem misguided, her posthumous reputation in Japan was frequently unjustly maligned by an overemphasis on her attitudes toward free love and her liberated sense of her own sexuality.

See also Yajima Kajiko; Yosano Akiko.
References and Further Reading
Hane, Mikiso, ed. 1988. *Reflections on the Way to the Gallows: Rebel Women in Prewar Japan.* Berkeley: University of California Press and Pantheon Books.
Sievers, Sharon. 1983. *Flowers in Salt: The Beginnings of Feminist Consciousness in Modern Japan.* Stanford: Stanford University Press.

Kar, Mehrangiz
(1944–)
Iran

The radical Islamist and secular lawyer Mehrangiz Kar, a veteran campaigner for women's legal rights in Iran was one of seventeen leading Iranian intellectuals arrested in 2000 for taking part in an academic conference in Berlin. She is one of a growing number of intellectual women of her generation who have paid a high price for calling for social reform in Iran by being persecuted or silenced.

Born in the city of Ahwaz in southern Iran, since the Islamic Revolution of 1979, Kar has been a supporter of greater access for women to political representation, as well as better education, pay, and employment opportunities. She has frequently invoked the terms of the 1979 United Nations Convention on the Elimination of All Forms of Discrimination Against Women, to which the Iranian government has yet to be a signatory, and which upholds the right of all women to be granted equal human and civil rights on a par with men. She has also campaigned vigorously for better rights for women in divorce cases and in the custody and guardianship of their children, daring to suggest that the shah's 1974 Family Protection Law—now rescinded by the fundamentalist government—was at least an attempt at limiting the absolute rights of fathers under Islamic law. Since the 1979 Revolution, the law, in her view, has failed to address women's legal rights, with the patriarchal power of men over their wives and children once more becoming entrenched.

Kar wrote a series of extremely critical articles on these and other aspects of the disenfranchisement of Iranian women for the pioneering feminist journal *Women* (*Zanan*) during 1995–1996. Along with other advocates of reform she argued that women were in fact equal with men under Islamic law and that misogynist clerics had misinterpreted it down the ages in order to keep women subservient. She called for women's right to divorce violent husbands and for courts to clearly define what exactly constitutes "violence." Kar has also argued that the law should be amended so that women no longer have to produce witnesses to acts of domestic and other violence against them, a difficult thing now that people no longer live in large, extended families. In 1999 she published her defense of women's rights in Iran—*Elimination of Discrimination Against Women*—offering detailed proposals on the enhancement of their legal position.

In April 2000, Kar was invited, along with other Iranian reformists and dissidents, to attend a conference at the Heinrich Boel Cultural Institute in Berlin, organized to discuss the future of Iran in light of the landslide victory of new reformist president Muhammad Khatami in the general election of 1997. Hopes of political change had been running high, particularly among the groundswell of young and middle-class Iranian women who gave their support to Khatami, but the conservative backlash in Iran quickly defused them. On her return to Iran after the conference, Kar and the other delegates were accused of spreading propaganda against the Islamic Republic and of offending Islam and its clerical leaders in Iran. Kar herself was charged with "acting against national security" and was imprisoned pending trial along with two other activists, Shahla Lahiji and Akbar Ganji. During her two months in custody, before her release on bail she had become seriously ill with breast cancer, leading to a mastectomy and chemotherapy soon after. She was subsequently tried by a civil court on charges of violating the observance of *hijab,* denying its necessity under Islamic law and propagating against the Islamic Republic. Sentenced to four years in prison, she immediately appealed.

In 2000 Kar was nominated one of three World Women of the Year by the Italian Women Journalists Association, although she was not allowed to leave Iran to receive her award. During her detention international pressure was mounted by journalists and lawyers on the violation of Kar's human rights under the International Convention on Civil and Political Rights—of which Iran is a signatory—but her supporters are fearful for her chances of survival should she be sent to prison. For recent updates on Kar's situation readers are advised to search the web.

References and Further Reading
Afshar, Haleh, ed. 1996. *Women and Politics in the Third World.* London: Routledge.
Kandiyoti, Deniz. 1991. *Women, Islam and the State.* Macmillan: Basingstoke.

Kartini, Raden Adjeng
(1879–1904)
Indonesia

In the course of her short life, Raden Adjeng Kartini was the first Indonesian woman to openly express a profound desire not just to be better educated but also to be socially useful. In her famous correspondence with Dutch humanitarians, she vividly described the strictly secluded lives of women in Indonesia of her day, which denied them opportunities for education, fulfillment, and freedom of choice in marriage. Her intellectual grasp enabled her to enter into a wide-reaching discussion, by letter, of many of the social problems facing her country in the period leading to independence and on the brink of a new and modernizing age.

Kartini was born in Mayong, the daughter of a civil service official, Raden Adipatai Sosroningrat, and one of his four wives (who had been married to him at age fourteen). In 1880 Sosroningrat was promoted to regent of Japara (leading to the later misnomer that Kartini was a Javanese "princess"). Her father's social position in the colonial administration brought Kartini into contact with Dutch humanitarians working in Java and with it—against prevailing social conventions—an education. Kartini attended a European school for the children of plantation owners in Japara, where she learned Dutch, until the age of twelve. Her brief and liberating period of enlightenment was followed by several years (1891–1895) of strict seclusion, during which Kartini, as she herself described it, was expected to conform to the socially accepted, upper-class norm: "the ideal Javanese girl . . . quiet, as immobile as a wooden doll, speaking only when it's absolutely necessary in a tiny, whispering voice which can't be heard by ants" (Taylor 1976, 649). She was trained in the necessary domestic skills of cooking, observing the religious festivals, and making traditional handicrafts such as batik, but increasingly came to dislike the strict adherence to the complicated rules of precedence and subservience between classes. As much as possible, Kartini used the time for study, reading, for example, about the work of the Indian social reformer Pandita Ramabai.

When the feminist Marie Ovink-Soer arrived in Japara as wife of a senior Dutch official, Kartini's intellectual horizons once more opened, and she and her sisters became frequent visitors, which in itself was a break from convention (single women were usually not allowed to venture outside the home). From 1896 Kartini and her sisters were allowed by their father to make other chaperoned excursions to Samarang and Batavia. Little by little, the articulate Kartini gathered around her a group of admiring Dutch expatriates, who supported her calls for women's education, based on a view that mothers began the task of instilling the appropriate moral qualities in children and that the task should be carried on through formal education.

In 1900 Kartini began corresponding with Dutch socialist Stella Seehandelaar and discussed feminist issues with her. Such was Kartini's command of Dutch that she was able to exchange views on a wide range of subjects, particularly marriage, polygamy, and the need for women to learn skills so that they would be more economically independent. She spoke out also against the inhibiting social conventions that denied personal autonomy and that demanded that highborn girls be kept apart from society until the time came for them to submit to arranged marriages: "Everything for the man, and nothing for the woman, is our law and custom. . . . I would do the humblest work, thankfully and joyfully, if by it I could be independent" (Kartini 1964, 41–42). Her advocacy of better educational opportunities for women in Indonesia was greatly disappointed when colonial official J. H.

Abendanon failed to gain support for his proposal to establish a boarding school in Batavia for upper-class Javanese girls. Kartini resolved that she could only achieve her ideal by studying abroad. In 1902 she applied to travel to the Netherlands to train as a teacher, as well as obtain skills in first aid and hygiene (she was also a keen supporter of women's medical training). The Dutch government awarded her a scholarship, but family opposition again prevailed. Instead, Kartini and her sister Roekmini set up their own school for girls in 1903, with just ten pupils, teaching them cooking and other domestic skills, hygiene, first aid, and traditional handicrafts such as batik and woodcarving. That same year, Kartini also completed a report for the Dutch colonial government on rural poverty and social reform entitled "Educate the Javanese."

Barely a month after Kartini's school had opened and she had begun her "wonderful work," she had to submit to family pressure and get married. By this time, the well-meaning support of her Dutch benefactors had brought only more criticism upon her head in Java for challenging the traditional patriarchy, and Kartini had become demoralized. She realized that the only way forward was to use the position of privilege that her higher caste gave her to continue to fight for what she believed. To have been able to resist getting married until the age of twenty-four was, in itself, something of an achievement on her part, and Kartini agreed to marry only on the condition that her husband, a widower much older than herself, allow her to continue with her school. At her new home in Rembang, Kartini opened another school and also continued through her ensuing pregnancy to write on social problems in Java. Four days after giving birth to a son, Kartini suddenly died. Her sisters continued her work in education, and by 1930, with support from a Dutch foundation, several "Kartini schools" were in existence. A younger sister, Kardinah, fulfilled another of Kartini's visions and eventually ran a hospital that trained Javanese women as midwives.

In her expressive and often touchingly idealistic letters, written in Dutch, Kartini tackled many social and even political issues of her times, as well as conducting a discourse on her own personal conflict between duty to parents and to her own intellectual aspirations. The letters resonate with her commitment to social progress and to reforms in public health, education, and welfare. They also are a testament to her yearning to see Javanese women liberated from the seclusion of their lives, from early arranged marriages made for considerations of class and status and not for love. Although her letters were later put to good use by Dutch colonial reformers in the cause of women's education in Java, they were not mere propaganda but a profoundly loyal expression by Kartini of the positive aspects of her own culture and of her deep love for the Indonesian archipelago as a whole.

See also Ramabai, Pandita Saraswati.

References and Further Reading

Jayawardena, Kumari. 1986. *Feminism and Nationalism in the Third World*. London: Zed Books.

Kartini, Raden Adjeng. 1964. *Letters of a Javanese Princess*. Translated and edited by Agnes Louise Symmers, and introduced by Hildred Geertz. New York: W. W. Norton.

———. 1992. *Letters from Kartini: An Indonesian Feminist 1900–1904*. Translated by Joost Coté. Clayton, Victoria: Monash Asia Institute.

Taylor, Jean Stewart. 1976. "Raden Ajeng Kartinin." *Signs* 1(3): 639–661.

Kaur, Rajkumari Amrit
(1889–1964)
India

The founder of the Indian Red Cross and its president from 1950, Kaur was once described in the London *Times* as "one of the three great women thrown up by the nationalist movement," along with Sarojini Naidu and Vijay Pandit (Brittain 1979, 158). She was also a leading feminist and founding member of the All-India Women's Conference in 1926.

Kaur was born at Lucknow, a daughter of the Kapurthala royal family, which had converted to Christianity. She received a liberal education at Sherbourne School for Girls in Dorset and also studied in London and Oxford. Returning to her home in the Punjab in 1909, she declined to get married, preferring instead to take up projects with the young. As a believer in physical exercise for children she introduced sports for schoolchildren and would later be a founder of the National Sports Club of India. She also took up women's issues, such as child marriage, the pur-

Rajkumari Amrit Kaur (Indian Red Cross)

dah system, and the plight of India's underprivileged, low-caste Hindu social class, the untouchables (Harijans). Believing that women should organize themselves in order to exercise their political muscle, she was a founding member of the All-India Women's Conference in 1926, which she served as secretary and then as president, 1937–1938.

For sixteen years Kaur worked as Mahatma Gandhi's secretary, having first met him in 1919. During the 1930s, she became a leading campaigner for the women's franchise and testified in support of it to government committees, such as in 1933, when she led a delegation of female members of the Indian legislature that gave evidence to a British Joint Parliamentary Committee on Indian Constitutional Reform. As a close supporter of Gandhi, she became involved in the salt campaign of 1930 that strove to break the British monopoly on the salt industry, for which she was arrested, and the Quit India movement in 1942, for which, after leading processions and rallies, she was again arrested and imprisoned.

When India became independent, Kaur was appointed minister of health in its first govern-

ment, holding the post from 1947 to 1957 and during her time in office encouraging women's participation in sports. Her interest in medical care and hygiene motivated her to found the All-India Institute of Medical Sciences, for which she lobbied for financial support in many countries. Kar initiated important medical projects through her setting up of the Tuberculosis Association of India and the Central Leprosy Teaching and Research Institute opened in Madras. She served as vice chair of the board of governors of the League of Red Cross Societies and chair of the executive committee of the St. John's Ambulance Association; a new college of nursing was also named after her.

Kaur's work for the Red Cross brought her many awards and honorary degrees from several countries: the Count Bernadotte Gold Medal (League of Red Cross Societies) and the Gold Medal (National Red Cross societies of fourteen countries). She was the first Asian woman elected president of the World Health Assembly (1950). In 1961 Kaur was awarded the René Sand Memorial Award at the International Conference of Social Work in Rome.

See also Naidu, Sarojini; Pandit, Vijaya Lakshmi.
References and Further Reading
Brittain, Vera. 1979 *Envoy Extraordinary.* London: Allen and Unwin.

Kehew, Mary Morton
(1859–1918)
United States

A founder of the Union for Industrial Progress, the self-effacing Mary Morton Kehew was never a public personality but worked with quiet dedication for social reform in Boston and for protective legislation for women workers during and until the end of World War I. The daughter of a Boston banker and wife of a Boston merchant, Kehew exploited her position of privilege and her own private wealth in improving the quality of working women's lives. In 1886, with the support of her reformist-minded husband, she joined the Women's Education and Industrial Union (WEIU) in Boston, which through its women's clubs offered help and recreation facilities to female workers coming to Boston in search of jobs. Under Kehew's directorship

(1890–1892) and presidency (1892–1913, 1914–1918), the WEIU rapidly extended its original, modest philanthropic work to become a focus for much humanitarian work in and around Boston. It began by offering educational classes, legal advice, counseling, and vocational training to working women. Kehew helped women exploit their natural skills so that they could earn a decent wage by setting up trade schools to assist them: a dressmaking school in 1895, one in housekeeping in 1897, and another in salesmanship in 1905 were so successful that in 1910 the union also established an Appointment Bureau to assist college graduates in exploiting their skills professionally. Kehew became a trustee of Simmons College for Women, established in 1902, which eventually took over the WEIU's courses in housekeeping and sales.

In 1892 Kehew founded the Union for Industrial Progress with the assistance of the Chicago bookbinder and labor organizer Mary Kenney to defend the interests of bookbinders, laundry workers, and workers in tobacco and garment industries and organized unions for them between 1896 and 1901.

In 1903 Kehew's outstanding work for women's trade unions was recognized with her appointment as the first president of the Women's Trade Union League. The work of the WEIU, meanwhile, became increasingly influential. In 1905 a research department was established, which initiated detailed statistical studies of the working lives of women in Boston and provided a research basis for changes in legislation relating to moneylending, sanitation, pensions, and the minimum wage. The work of the research department would lead eventually to the creation of the Massachusetts Department of Labor and Industry. Kehew herself, who served on many state commissions on industrial education and child labor, would also be a guiding figure in the Massachusetts branch of the Association for Labor Legislation.

Kehew was also active in the settlement movement in Boston and in the organization of day nurseries and well-baby clinics. Much of her work for women was directed to helping those who were blind, through organizations such as the Massachusetts Association for Promoting the Interest of the Adult Blind (founded in 1903), the Loan and Aid Society for the Blind, and a settlement for blind women, Woolskin House.

References and Further Reading

Boone, Gladys. 1942. *The Women's Trade Union Leagues in Great Britain and the United States of America.* New York: Columbia University Press.

Dictionary of American Biography 1946–1958, and indexes to Supplements 1–10, 1981–1996. New York: Scribner's.

Sicherman, Barbara, and Carol Hurd Green, eds. 1980. *Notable American Women 1607–1950: A Biographical Dictionary,* vol. 4, *The Modern Period.* Cambridge, MA: Belknap Press of Harvard University.

Whitman, Alden, ed. 1988. *American Reformers: An H. W. Wilson Biographical Dictionary.* New York: H. W. Wilson.

Keller, Helen
(1880–1968)
United States

The story of the battle of the deaf, dumb, and blind Helen Keller to break out of her solitary world of darkness and silence is an extraordinary one that has been told many times. Even more extraordinary is the manner in which she surmounted enormous obstacles to obtain a university degree and enter a vigorous public career as a socialist, pacifist, and defender of the rights of the handicapped. Refusing to countenance any concessions to her disabilities, Keller was a prolific author, traveled the world, and made many appearances on the lecture circuit to become a twentieth-century icon.

Born in Tuscumbia, Alabama, the daughter of a newspaper editor, Keller was left deaf and blind after an attack of what seems likely to have been either meningitis or scarlet fever at the age of nineteen months. The impossibility of communicating her feelings and frustrations manifested itself in the growing child through uncontrollable bouts of rage and physical violence that her parents found impossible to deal with. They resisted calls by friends and relatives to resort to the conventional solution of having Keller locked away in an institution and, having the financial means, consulted every kind of medical expert. They despaired of their daughter ever making any progress, however, until in 1886 they met Alexander Graham Bell—the inventor of the telephone and himself a pioneer in the teaching of the deaf—who told them of the work of the Perkins Institution in Boston in teaching the blind. The institution responded by sending a

Helen Keller (Library of Congress)

young teacher, Anne Sullivan (who also had impaired vision), to live with the family in 1887 and teach Keller a means of communication. Sullivan would remain Keller's devoted amanuensis until she died forty-nine years later, in 1936.

Sullivan's method in breaking through the barriers that isolated Keller from the world of sound and vision was to exploit her heightened sense of touch and teach her a manual alphabet, tapped out in the palm of her hand, through which she slowly learned to associate words with objects. Once Keller had grasped the principle of the method, famously depicted in the later stage play and film, when Sullivan held one hand under running water while signing its letters in the other, she rapidly acquired her first 300 words. From there, and with further therapy at the Horace Mann School for the Deaf in Boston and lipreading (by putting her fingers on the person's mouth) at the Wright-Humason Oral School in

New York, Keller, a quick learner, grasped Braille and was eventually able to write proficiently, with a ruler guiding her hand. By 1890 Sullivan had also taught her to "listen," and later even to speak, through a painstaking process of learning to associate the different vibrations of the larynx with different sounds, although Keller's speech remained incomprehensible to all but her close caregivers.

During 1896 to 1900, Keller attended Cambridge School for Young Ladies, with Sullivan alongside to guide her through her lessons in preparation for entry to university studies. She won a place at Radcliffe College in 1900 and proved an outstanding scholar, thanks to the utter dedication of Sullivan, who accompanied her to lectures and translated them by touch into Keller's hand. Textbooks were provided for Keller in Braille, and she mastered the use of a special typewriter for her essays and examination papers. She studied French, German, Italian, Latin, and Greek and even learned to ride and swim. In 1904 she graduated with honors, having already published her autobiography, *The Story of My Life,* in 1902, an enduring and inspirational text that has since been translated into fifty languages. In 1905 Sullivan married John Macy, a tutor at Harvard who had assisted Keller in the writing of her book, but his wife's unshakable devotion to Keller would eventually lead to the breakdown of the marriage.

Because so much attention has been paid to the moving story of Keller's fight to overcome her physical handicaps, her other and considerable activities and social concerns are often overlooked. A convinced socialist, from the 1910s to the 1920s Keller was an active member first of the Socialist Party of America, which she joined in 1909, and later the more radical Industrial Workers of the World (Wobblies) led by Eugene Debs, to which she defected in 1914 after becoming impatient with the party's lack of political progress. Many of Keller's socialist articles were published in the radical press and collected as *Out of the Dark* in 1913. Inevitably, Keller's activities were monitored by the Federal Bureau of Investigation under instructions from Herbert Hoover.

In the course of her long public career, Keller never limited herself to campaigning solely within her own sphere of disability, averring that her sympathies lay with all people who struggled for justice and for racial and sexual equality. Part of this attitude no doubt stemmed from her own religious conversion in 1896 to the Swedenborgians, who emphasized the value of the individual spirit and the rights to equality of achievement of all people. In 1927 Keller would publish an account of her faith in *My Religion.*

With her passionate instinct for women's equality, Keller was a supporter of the birth control movement and votes for women and eschewed the moderate mainstream of the U.S. suffrage movement in preference for the radicalism of the Pankhursts' Women's Social and Political Union. A convinced pacifist, Keller saw all wars as destroyers of the family of human beings, and militarism as perpetuating the most exploitative aspects of capitalism. When World War I broke out in 1914, Keller opposed U.S. entry into the war and in the *New York Call* of 20 December 1915 published an essay entitled "Menace of the Militarist Program." She undertook an antiwar preparedness lecture tour around the Midwest and in 1917 called for pacifists to work toward a conciliatory "people's peace." In 1932, like many other pacifists disturbed by the rise of fascism in Germany, she joined War Resisters International, and remained vehemently antifascist, going so far as to refuse to allow her books to be translated into German. In 1938, with the threat of war escalating, Keller supported boycotts of goods from Germany, Japan, and Italy.

During World War II, Keller compromised her pacifist sympathies to support what she felt was a necessary war against fascism and supported the U.S. war effort by visiting the wounded in military and naval hospitals, in particular commiserating with those who had been blinded or had lost limbs. In the postwar years, she offered her support to blind war veterans. After she visited the devastated Japanese cities of Hiroshima and Nagasaki, she vowed to commit herself to the fight against the development of nuclear weapons.

The major part of Keller's life from the early 1920s, however, was taken up with working for the blind. After 1913, her own difficult financial situation had been eased by Andrew Carnegie's award of a lifetime pension of $5,000 per year, which enabled her and Sullivan to embark on lecture tours. Appearing in public lecture halls as well as on the vaudeville circuit (1920–1924), they demonstrated their lipreading and signing skills in order to raise public awareness of the problems of the deaf and blind. Keller also was one of the first to speak openly of the occurrence of blindness in newborn babies, passed on to them in the womb by mothers infected with venereal disease. In 1924 she and Sullivan began fund-raising for the American Foundation for the Blind; for the rest of her life, Keller would be its leading international campaigner, with Sullivan's help reaching a fund-raising target of £2 million through their lectures on their unique partnership. Keller's lobbying during the 1930s on behalf of the blind also secured the passage of the Pratt Bill, which provided for reading services for the blind, and the 1935 Social Security Act, which made blind people eligible for federal welfare assistance.

By the late 1920s Sullivan's own eyesight, which she had partially recovered after several operations, was rapidly deteriorating, and she too went blind. Her death in 1936 was a devastating blow to Keller, and in 1938 she published an account of her difficulties in adjusting to the loss of Sullivan in *Helen Keller's Journal, 1936–1937*. After Sullivan's death, Keller was assisted in her work by her secretary-housekeeper, Polly Thompson, who had joined her and Sullivan in 1914.

Keller undertook a succession of seven world tours between 1946 and 1957, promoting the welfare of the blind worldwide under the auspices of the American Foundation for Overseas Blind; her own Helen Keller Endowment Fund was used to channel donations from her many wealthy patrons into helping people suffering in the Third World. She outlived Polly Thompson, too (who died in 1960), and by the time of her death at the age of eighty-eight had received honorary degrees from Harvard and Temple Universities, the 1964 Presidential Medal of Freedom, and France's Legion of Honor. Her many autobiographical writings include *The World I Live In* (1909), *Optimism: My Key of Life* (1926), *My Religion* (1927), and *Midstream: My Later Life* (1929). A further testament to the devotion of Sullivan, *Teacher*, appeared in 1955.

Keller's story was immortalized by a 1959 Pulitzer Prize–winning Broadway play, *The Miracle Worker*, by William Gibson. Based on Keller's book, *The Story of My Life*, it became an Academy Award–winning film of the same title in 1962. There is a considerable amount of material about Keller's life and work on the World Wide Web via the site http://www.about.com. The work for the deaf and the blind inspired by Helen Keller continues through organizations such as the Royal National Institute for the Blind (www.rnib.org.uk/), American Foundation for the Blind (www.afb.org, which also has much of her writing online), Helen Keller National Center for Deaf-Blind Youth and Adults (www.helenkeller.org), and Helen Keller International (www.hki.org).

See also Pankhurst, Christabel; Pankhurst, Emmeline; Pankhurst, (Estelle) Sylvia.
References and Further Reading
Current Biography. 1942. New York: H. W. Wilson.
Felder, Deborah G. 1996. *The 100 Most Influential Women: A Ranking of the 100 Greatest Women Past and Present*. London: Robinson.
Foner, Philip. 1967. *Helen Keller: Her Socialist Years: Writings and Speeches*. New York: International Publishers.
Hermann, Dorothy. 1998. *Helen Keller: A Life*. New York: Alfred A. Knopf.
Keller, Helen. 1996 [1902]. *The Story of My Life*. Reprint, Mineola, NY: Dover Publications.
———. 2000 [1927]. *Light in My Darkness*. 2d ed. Reprint of *My Religion* edited by Ray Silverman. Westchester, PA: Chrysalis Books.
Lasch, Joseph. 1980. *Helen and Teacher: The Story of Helen Keller and Anne Sullivan*. New York: Delacorte/Seymour Lawrence.
Oldfield, Sybil. 1989. *Women against the Iron Fist: Alternatives to Militarism 1900–1989*. Oxford: Basil Blackwell.
Waite, Helen, and Elmira Waite. 1961. *Valiant Companions: Helen Keller and Annie Sullivan Macy*. London: Hodder and Stoughton.
Wymer, Norman. 1965. *Helen Keller*. London: Macdonald.

Kelley, Florence
(1859–1932)
United States

Described as an "impatient crusader" by her biographer Josephine Goldmark, Florence Kelley played a key role in defending the working rights of women and children in the sweatshops of Chicago. She was a pioneer of legislative change in this respect through the work of the National Consumers' League, serving as its general secretary from 1899 to 1932.

Born in Philadelphia into a Quaker background on her mother's side, Kelley was educated mainly at home. She was encouraged in her studies by her father, a radical Republican member of Congress, and in 1876 went to study at Cornell University. She eventually received her B.A. in literature in 1882, after ill health had forced her to withdraw temporarily. Barred, as a woman, from taking up graduate studies in law, she went on a European tour, during which she discovered that Zurich University was admitting women to its courses. Securing a place there, Kelley studied law and economics and mixed in the melting pot of socialist radicals from Russia and eastern Europe. She read the writings of Karl Marx and became a socialist, in 1887 publishing her English translation of Friedrich Engels's 1845 book, *The Condition of the Working Class in England in 1844*, in New York.

In Zurich Kelley met and married a Polish-Jewish medical student, Lazare Wischnewetsky,

Florence Kelley (Library of Congress)

veys in the United States, *Hull House Maps and Papers* (1895). Legislative changes quickly followed her reports, with the Sweatshop Act of 1893 limiting the working day for women to eight hours and prohibiting child labor in Illinois. Kelley was appointed chief factory inspector for the state in order to monitor the implementation of the act, eventually producing four more reports on child labor in Chicago. She acquired increased legal muscle in prosecuting evasion of the legislation by finally obtaining a law degree in 1894 at Northwestern University and being admitted to the bar.

In 1899 Kelley moved back to New York, where she lived and worked at the Henry Street Settlement run by Lillian Wald until 1924. She also found a new role for herself as general secretary of the National Consumers' League, eventually setting up sixty branches in twenty U.S. states and advocating the concept of the league's "white label" on goods, an indicator that their manufacture had not involved the exploitation of workers. Kelley's campaign, undertaken in consort with the Women's Trade Union League, proved highly influential.

Kelley discussed protective legislation and a minimum wage for women and child workers in her 1905 book, *Some Ethical Gains through Legislation*, also emphasizing the moral responsibility of middle-class consumers in defending workers against exploitation by boycotting goods made by unscrupulous manufacturers. She traveled extensively, arguing the case for such legislation in clubs, trade unions, and colleges, her high-profile campaigning between 1910 and 1930 resulting in major changes to labor legislation and the establishment of a minimum wage in nine states by 1913.

Kelley also crusaded against the exploitation of children in industry in her work as a member of the board of the New York Child Labor Committee (from 1902) and an organizer, with Wald, of its national body from 1904. In later years, she lobbied for passage of the Keating-Owen Child Labor Act of 1916 but was greatly discouraged when it was declared unconstitutional in 1918 and immediately began petitioning for an amendment on child labor to be included in the U.S. Constitution.

In 1909 Kelley was one of the founders of the National Association for the Advancement of Colored People. She was also a regular partici-

in 1884. After settling in New York in 1886, they joined the Socialist Labor Party but were expelled soon after because the party was unable to countenance Kelley's outspoken criticism of Marxist doctrine. Her marriage also failed, and by 1891 Kelley was left to take care of her three children. She moved to Chicago, reverted to her maiden name after obtaining a divorce, and in 1891 joined Jane Addams's Hull House, where she remained until 1899.

In 1889 Kelley had published a pamphlet, "Our Toiling Children," in which she raised the issue of child labor, and it was her main sphere of activity ever after. In 1892 she secured an appointment from the Illinois Bureau of Labor Statistics to study Chicago's sweatshops. During the course of her research, she also investigated slum housing, noting the prevalence of epidemics of smallpox and other diseases among immigrant workers. She was moved by the plight of those home workers in the sweatshop system who earned a pittance for piecework while working in filthy surroundings in unheated, unsanitary, and badly lit outbuildings, basements, and even stables. Along with the work of her colleagues, Kelley's findings were published in one of the pioneering social sur-

pant in the work of the National Conference of Charities and Corrections and in 1913 joined Eugene Debs's Socialist Party of America. As vice president of the National American Woman Suffrage Association, she found time to campaign for women's suffrage but from 1923 opposed the Equal Rights Amendment Act as a supporter of separate protective legislation for women.

From the moment war broke out in 1914, Kelley was one of many women social workers from the settlement movement who took up a pacifist position as an extension of their social concerns. She was vice chair of the short-lived American Union Against Militarism during 1916–1917, and although she did not support U.S. entry into the war, she agreed with other social reformers on the importance of monitoring the rights of workers in war industries and channeled her activities in what seemed to her to be more constructive work, as secretary of the Board of Control of Labor Standards in overseeing production of clothing for the army. After the end of World War I, Kelley was a delegate, to the International Committee of Women for Permanent Peace in Zurich, at which she was a founding member of the Women's International League for Peace and Freedom in 1919.

Kelley contributed regularly to journals such as the *American Journal of Sociology*. Her other published works include *Modern Industry in Relation to the Family* (1913); *Modern Industry in Relation to Health, Education, and Morality* (1914); and *The Supreme Court and Minimum Wage Legislation* (1925).

Kelley's eloquence and combative spirit were remarked upon by all who saw the fervent conviction, often boiling over into impatience, with which she spoke about social injustice. In 1929, eloquently arguing for assistance programs to mothers during debates on extension of the provisions of the Sheppard-Towner Maternity and Infancy Protection Act, she remarked: "Why are seals, bears, reindeer, fish, wild game in the national parks, buffalo, migratory birds, all found suitable for federal protection; but not the children of our race and their mothers?" (Chambers 1963, 51). The woman who was described by Frances Coralie Perkins as a "smoking volcano" was finally weakened by long illness, but within a couple of years of her death, many of Kelley's recommendations on labor reform were implemented by the U.S. government.

See also Addams, Jane; Perkins, Frances Coralie; Wald, Lillian D.

References and Further Reading

Blumberg, Dorothy Rose. 1966. *Florence Kelley: The Making of a Social Pioneer.* New York: Augustus Kelley.

Chambers, Clarke A. 1963. *Seedtime of Reform: American Social Service and Social Action, 1918–1933.* Minneapolis: University of Minnesota Press.

Davis, Allen F. 1967. *Spearheads for Reform: The Social Settlements and the Progressive Movement 1890–1914.* New York: Oxford University Press.

Frankel, Noralee, and Nancy S. Dye. 1991. *Gender, Class, Race, and Reform in the Progressive Era.* Lexington: University of Kentucky Press.

Goldmark, Josephine. 1976 [1953]. *Impatient Crusader: Florence Kelley's Life Story.* Reprint, Westport, CT: Greenwood Press.

Kerber, Linda K., and Jane DeHart-Mathews. 2000. *Women's America: Refocusing the Past.* New York: Oxford University Press.

Kraditor, Aileen. 1981 [1965]. *The Ideas of the Woman Suffrage Movement 1890–1920.* Reprint, New York: W. W. Norton.

Sklar, Kathryn Kish. 1986. *The Autobiography of Florence Kelley: Notes of Sixty Years.* Chicago: Charles H. Kerr.

———. 1995. *Florence Kelley and the Nation's Work: The Rise of Women's Political Culture, 1830–1900.* New Haven: Yale University Press.

———. 1998. *Social Justice Feminists in the United States and Germany: A Dialogue in Documents 1885–1933.* Ithaca: Cornell University Press.

Trattner, Walter I. 1970. *Crusade for the Children: A History of the National Child Labor Committee and Child Labor Reform in America.* Chicago: Quadrangle Books.

Kenney, Annie
(1879–1953)
United Kingdom

The image of trade unionist and militant suffragette Annie Kenney, defiantly wearing her working woman's emblems of knitted shawl and steel-tipped clogs, became a potent symbol of grassroots participation in the British suffrage movement in the 1900s. Kenney was, however, the only working-class woman entrusted with a policymaking role in the inner sanctum of the Pankhursts' Women's Social and Political Union (WSPU). This fact led to accusations that she was used by the Pankhursts as a token working-class figure who was patronizingly promoted as "the Suffragette Mill Girl"—little more than the unwitting mascot of the middle-class WSPU elite. Kenney has often been perceived as having no mind of her own; such was the utterly whole-hearted manner with which she embraced militancy and gave her undivided devotion to her idol, Christabel Pankhurst, that she was even referred to as "Christabel's blotting paper" (Vicinus 1985, 259). But Annie Kenney was no cipher. She was a woman of honesty, grit, humor, and charisma who had a strong appeal. In the words of Sylvia Pankhurst, she spoke "with a voice that cries out for the lost childhood, blighted hopes and weary, overburdened lives of the women workers whom she knows so well" (Mackenzie 1975, 43).

Kenney was born into a poor working-class family in Springhead, a village in the Pennine Chain in Lancashire. As one of twelve children, she received only a minimal education in the village school and was sent out to work part-time at the local mill in 1889, at the age of ten. She left school for full-time work (an eleven-and-a-half-hour day) in the carding room of the Woodend Mill when she was thirteen and lost a finger in an accident winding bobbins. For fifteen years, she remained at the mill, becoming the first woman representative of workers in the card and blowing rooms in her local textile union.

Although her schooling was rudimentary, Kenney's life was far from lacking in intellectual stimulus, with Annie and her brothers and sisters sharing interests in social issues and education. Annie was an avid reader who enjoyed the writings of Walt Whitman, John Ruskin, and William Morris. In 1905 she and her sisters Jessie and Jenny (who were also involved in the suffrage movement) heard Christabel Pankhurst speak at Oldham Trades Council, and Kenney volunteered to accompany her on a speaking tour among factory girls in the Lancashire mill towns that summer. Thereafter, she committed herself to women's suffrage with all the ardency of a religious convert, becoming a regular visitor to the Pankhursts' home on Nelson Street in Manchester and a speaker for the WSPU.

Kenney set the style of her campaigning—noisy and belligerent—when she took part in the first significant demonstration of the militant suffrage movement in October 1905. At the Free Trade Hall in Manchester, she and Christabel created a disturbance during a Liberal Party meeting called to endorse the candidacy of Winston Churchill in a forthcoming election. They interrupted a speech by Sir Edward Grey, challenging him on whether the Liberal Party would make women's suffrage part of its political program if it came to power. When Grey failed to answer, she and Pankhurst unfurled a banner demanding "Votes for Women." The women were jostled out and kicked down stairs. Outside, they held an impromptu protest meeting and were arrested for obstruction. Kenney and Pankhurst refused to pay their fines and thus became the first suffragettes to be sent to prison—Kenney for three days—in so doing providing the WSPU with an unprecedented and unexpected amount of publicity at home and abroad, as a result of which donations and many new recruits poured into the WSPU.

Two months later, on 21 December, after employing similar tactics during a speech by prime minister Sir Henry Campbell-Bannerman at the Royal Albert Hall, Kenney was ejected. In June 1906, she was at the head of a deputation on women's suffrage to Chancellor of the Exchequer Herbert Asquith's home in London, where she was arrested and sentenced to six weeks in prison. By that time established as a leading agitator, Kenney undertook a lecture tour in the north of England and Scotland upon her release, but by the autumn, she was back in prison yet again. In 1907, she was made a paid organizer for the WSPU and was entrusted with organizing its activities in the west of England. She based herself in Bristol for the next four years and became a local celebrity through her regular speeches at open-air rallies, which were renowned for their vigor and wit. She came into her own between March 1912 and April 1913, when after a period of intense WSPU militancy, the movement's leaders, Emmeline Pankhurst and Emmeline Pethick-Lawrence, were jailed and Christabel fled to France to avoid being imprisoned. Kenney became covert chief organizer for the WSPU and with dogged devotion made weekly trips across the English Channel to France in order to obtain briefings from Christabel and report on events in England.

In April 1913, Kenney was arrested for inciting a riot with her inflammatory speeches and sentenced to eighteen months in prison. She went on hunger and thirst strikes in Maidstone Prison, which permanently impaired her health. Under the terms of the new Cat and Mouse Act, introduced to counter the increase in hunger strikes, she would be repeatedly released and rearrested, in between traveling the country in disguise in order to evade arrest and speak at WSPU meetings. She even attempted to win sanctuary from the bishop of London at Lambeth Palace.

In 1914, when war broke out, Kenney went on a suffrage lecture tour in the United States at Christabel's behest, and after the WSPU suspended activities to support the war effort, she was enlisted to encourage women to take up munitions work. She supported Christabel Pankhurst's electoral campaign when she stood for Parliament after women won the vote in 1918, but when this campaign ended in failure, Kenney retired from politics. She married a civil servant, James Taylor, in 1920 and had one son. The couple settled in Letchworth, and there Kenney, now a convert to Theosophy and later the Rosicrucians, lived quietly and wrote her autobiography, published in 1924 as *Memories of a Militant*. Although the WSPU promoted her factory and trade union background in galvanizing support from other working women, Kenney was never an active member of the socialist movement, although Sylvia Pankhurst later argued that she made up for her lack of intellectual sophistication with her enthusiasm and directness.

See also Pankhurst, Christabel; Pankhurst, Emmeline; Pankhurst, (Estelle) Sylvia; Pethick-Lawrence, Emmeline.

References and Further Reading
Crawford, Elizabeth. 1999. *The Women's Suffrage Movement, 1866–1928: A Reference Guide*. London: University College of London Press.
Dobbie, B. M. W. 1979. *A Nest of Suffragettes in Somerset*. The Batheaston Society.
Fulford, Roger. 1957. *Votes for Women: The Story of a Struggle*. London: Faber and Faber.
Mackenzie, Midge. 1975. *Shoulder to Shoulder*. London: Penguin.
Mitchell, David. 1966. *Women on the Warpath: The Story of Women of the First World War*. London: Jonathan Cape.
Mulvey-Roberts, Marie, and Tamae Mizuta, eds. 1994. *A Militant: Annie Kenney*. London: Routledge.
Pankhurst, Christabel. 1987 [1959]. *Unshackled: The Story of How We Won the Vote*. Reprint, London: Cresset Women's Voices.
Pethick-Lawrence, Emmeline. 1938. *My Part in a Changing World*. London: Victor Gollancz.
Rosen, Andrew. 1993 [1974]. *Rise Up, Women! Militant Campaign of the WSPU 1903–1904*. Reprint, London: Routledge.
Vicinus, Martha. 1985. *Independent Women: Work and Community for Single Women, 1850–1920*. London: Virago.

Key, Ellen
(1849–1926)
Sweden

A central figure in the movement for the reform of sexual ethics and of attitudes toward love and marriage who was condemned in her home country as a "seducer and corrupter of youth" (Anthony 1915, 94), Ellen Key was a woman who combined genius with a lack of clarity verging on mysticism in her arguments for a new social order centered on the sanctity of the mother-child relationship. Such an approach has prompted some feminists to condemn her for promoting an idealized vision of motherhood above women's civil and political rights.

The daughter of a wealthy landowner, Key was born on the family estate at Sundsholm and was educated at home. Her family moved to Stockholm when her father entered parliament in 1868. For a while, Key worked as her father's secretary cum housekeeper, until the family suffered financial losses and he lost his seat in parliament in 1883. She became a teacher at Anna Whitlock's Co-educational School in Stockholm in 1880 and held the post until 1903, during which period she also gave weekly lectures to women on Scandinavian culture at the Workers' Institute in Stockholm and lectured on social reforms and economics.

Since the late 1860s, Key had been interested in the plays of Henrik Ibsen and the issues relating to women's situation that plays such as *A Doll's House* (1879) had raised. She began publishing essays on women's issues in 1884, drawing attention to the unfairness of property laws. She claimed to be the first Swedish woman to give a public speech calling for women's suffrage (in 1893) and the first peace lecture in Stockholm (1897), in which latter activity she was influenced greatly by the pacifism of Bertha von Suttner and her novel *Lay Down Your Arms!* Key supported the concept of courts of arbitration and arms limitation but opposed unilateral disarmament, for she had a deeply held moral philosophy that envisaged society naturally evolving

Ellen Key (Hulton-Deutsch Collection/Corbis)

toward harmony and cooperation, without any need for coercion, under the guiding spiritual influence of women. The greater public and political influence women had, the sooner war would be ended, in her view, and she frequently reiterated the ideals of Fredrika Bremer's 1854 call for a women's international peace union.

In 1896 Key gave a public lecture entitled "Misused Feminine Power" (also issued later as a pamphlet), which provoked a public outcry for its atheism and its views on sexual freedom. In many respects, its argument was far from progressive and was embraced by traditionalists who opposed the women's movement because of the emphasis the lecture placed on the essential role of motherhood. Key did advocate women's suffrage but exhorted women not to reject their natural function as mothers in favor of asserting their political equality alongside men. Taking the eugenicist view, Key felt that the abnegation of their maternal responsibility by women would affect the future of the human race. In 1896 Key addressed a women's conference held in Copenhagen, criticizing the current ideology of the suffrage movement

in her speech, "The Abuse of Women's Strength," for seeking to lead women into different fields of predominantly male activity rather than consolidating their role in those fields in which they excelled, primarily that most noble and self-sacrificing of roles—motherhood. Without this, the social equilibrium would be destroyed. Thus, it was Key's objective that greater social value be placed on childbearing and child rearing, through the provision of maternity and child care benefits and a reduction in working hours for working-class mothers so that they could be released from the economic and sexual slavery that was the lot of so many married women.

For Key, mothers played a unique role, and she sought the elevation of motherhood as an important social function; women should pursue their own feminine concerns in a separate sphere from men, where they could develop their "social motherliness," rather than trying to emulate men.

Key's 1900 work, *The Century of the Child,* on women's psychology, marriage and sexual roles, and the education of children was widely translated and brought her international fame. Meanwhile Key continued to seek women's emancipation as sexual beings but refused to link it with their overall political liberation. Rather than calling for equality with men, she promoted women's difference and their unique feminine qualities, in particular their compassion, pacifism, and greater respect for life. She viewed their sexual emancipation as a separate issue, not as a facet of women's liberation.

In this and other works elaborating on her views on relationships, Key was widely misinterpreted as advocating free love, and she was much vilified in her home country, although progressive reformers elsewhere in Europe responded positively to her ideas. What she in fact argued was that although marriage provided the basis for child rearing, only genuine heterosexual love made a relationship—married or otherwise—truly moral. Thus she believed that the conception of children was legitimized not by marriage but by the love in which they were conceived. Nor did she expect the vast majority of relationships founded on love to last. Sadly, she had no children of her own, although she had a celibate "affair" with a married man for ten years.

In 1903 Key set off on a six-year lecture tour of Europe and was particularly popular in Germany, where her ideas were influential in the League for the Protection of Motherhood and Sexual Reform (founded in 1904). In 1905, on a visit to Berlin, she affirmed her commitment to women's suffrage, but by then she had already begun to alienate radicals in the movement, with some commentators observing that her notoriety as a supposed advocate of free love had impeded the progress of women's suffrage in Germany.

During World War I, Key supported patriotism that respected national culture and people but opposed unilateral disarmament. She urged childless women to divert their energies into the peace movement. She believed that their influence might be the only hope in ending the war, but as the fighting continued and many suffrage and other women's groups abandoned their activities to support their national war effort, Key became deeply disillusioned. She continued to support Swedish neutrality during the war.

During her life, Key published thirty books, including influential works on motherhood and the family that were translated into many languages: *Love and Marriage* (1911), *Love and Ethics* (1912), *The Woman Movement* (1912), and *Renaissance of Motherhood* (1914), as well as pacifist works such as *War, Peace and the Future* (1922). She had a profound influence on other women writers, with whom she conducted an extensive correspondence. Key's work also found support in Japan among feminists such as Hiratsuka Raicho, who translated sections of *Love and Marriage* in 1911. At the end of her life, Key's work was honored by the Swedish government, which gave her a stretch of coast at Strand, where in 1910 she built herself a home; it was bequeathed by her as a rest home for workers.

See also Bremer, Fredrika; Hiratsuka Raicho; Suttner, Bertha Félice Sophie von.

References and Further Reading
Anthony, Katherine S. 1915. *Feminism in Germany and Scandinavia*. New York: Henry Holt.
Josephson, Harold, Sandi Cooper, and Steven C. Hause et al., eds. 1985. *Biographical Dictionary of Modern Peace Leaders*. Westport, CT: Greenwood Press.
Key, Ellen. 1976 [1912]. *The Woman Movement*. Translated by M. and B. Borthwick. Reprint, Westport, CT: Greenwood Press.
Liddington, Jill. 1989. *The Long Road to Greenham: Feminism and Anti-Militarism in Britain since 1820*. London: Virago.
Lundell, Torberg. 1984. "Ellen Key and Swedish Feminist Views on Motherhood." *Scandinavian Studies*.
Nystrom-Hamilton, L. S. 1912. *Ellen Key: Her Life and Work*. New York: G. P. Putnam's Sons.
Offen, Karen. 2000. *European Feminisms 1700–1950: A Political History*. Stanford: Stanford University Press.

Khan, Raana Liaquat Ali (Begum Sahiba)
(1905–1990)
Pakistan

The women's rights campaigner and politician Raana Liaquat Ali Khan, who as wife of the first prime minister of Pakistan used her position to push for social and welfare reform, opposed some of the repressive policies that affected Muslim women in the 1980s. The daughter of an Indian civil servant, Khan was educated at a school in Naini Tal and Lucknow University, where she studied economics and sociology. After taking a teacher-training course, she became professor of economics at a girls' college in Delhi. In 1933 she married Liaquat Ali Khan, a member of the United Provinces Legislative Council, and together with the Pakistani politician Muhammad Ali Jinnah spent the next fourteen years working toward the creation of a separate state for India's large Muslim population. When Pakistan came into being after the partition of India in 1947, Khan was instrumental in organizing medical and food aid for the thousands of refugees that poured into the new country in the wake of fierce fighting in India. Such was her indispensable role in enlisting financial support from the rich to provide food and shelter for the dispossessed and her tireless work among the sick that her example led to the setting up of the All-Pakistan Women's Association for the relief of poverty and suffering.

In 1951 Khan's husband, who had become prime minister of Pakistan in 1947, under Jinnah as governor-general, was assassinated. Unwilling to comply with traditional convention, Khan refused to withdraw from public life into purdah but instead channeled her grief into full-time work for a myriad of social concerns and important self-help organizations. She set up Pakistan Cottage Industries to foster the work of the self-employed, the Health and Nutrition Association, various centers offering health care for women, and colleges in Karachi, Dacca, and Lahore to train them in home economics. On a broader level, she maintained an interest in women's rights through the Federation of University Women and the International Women's Club. Having been looked upon as the Florence Nightingale of the refugee camps during the partition crisis of 1947, she maintained an interest in health care as a patron of the Nurses Association and the hospital named for her, the Liaquat Memorial Hospital.

In 1949 Khan briefly headed a Women's National Guard in Pakistan, but it was suppressed by the country's religious leaders, the mullahs. Undeterred, Khan continued to speak out on women's rights throughout her public life and indeed took on a higher public profile through her work at the United Nations in 1952, as only the second Muslim woman to attend as a delegate. For the next twelve years (1954–1966), she served as the first Muslim woman appointed as an ambassador (to the Netherlands, Italy, and Tunisia). From 1973 to 1976 she served as the first woman governor of Sind province.

Khan continued to resist the political and religious repression of women under the dictatorship of General Mohammad Zia-ul-Haq from 1977 to 1988, seeing many of the laws passed by his regime as undemocratic and retrograde in their discriminatory attitude toward women. In 1979 the UN recognized her distinguished services to social causes by awarding her the Human Rights Award.

References and Further Reading

The Annual Obituary. 1989. New York: St. Martin's Press.

Liaquat, Ali Khan. 1950. *Pakistan, the Heart of Asia: Speeches in the United States and Canada,* May and June 1950, by the Prime Minister of Pakistan with an appendix by Begum Liaquat Ali Khan. Cambridge, MA: Harvard University Press.

Penguin Biographical Dictionary of Women. 1998. Harmondsworth: Penguin.

Uglow, Jennifer, ed. 1998. *Macmillan Dictionary of Women's Biography.* 3d ed. Basingstoke: Macmillan.

Kingsford, Anna
(1846–1888)
United Kingdom

The vegetarian and antivivisectionist Anna Kingsford, her reputation for long reduced to the most superficial of entries in the *Dictionary of National Biography,* is now being restored to women's history. She took up the challenge of studying medicine in a man's world as a deliberate means of furthering the antivivisection and vegetarian campaigns by using sound and well-argued medical knowledge to promote them. To make such a choice, at a time when women in Britain were barred from medical schools and when any respectable woman who chose to take up a professional career of any kind was frowned upon, was in itself an extraordinary achievement, and she proved to be one of the very few medically qualified women able to speak on both subjects. In her short life, Kingsford became a leading figure in the food reform movement as a staunch advocate of vegetarianism; her forthright campaigning against vivisection was carried on, after her death, by the indomitable Frances Power Cobbe and Louise Lind-af-Hageby.

Kingsford was born Anna Bonus in Stratford, Essex, the youngest of twelve children of a merchant in the city of London. As the youngest child, she was frequently left to her own devices and began reading mythology, indulging her vivid imagination in flights of fantasy that led to the invention of imaginary friends and regular conversations with the spirit world. She became devoted to defenseless, dumb animals, later in life admitting with utter candor: "I do not love men and women. I dislike them too much to do them any good" (Elston 1987, 120). Kingsford's first literary efforts were in poetry, and she published short stories (1868–1872) in the *Penny Post* under the pseudonym of Ninon Kingsford.

When she was nineteen, Anna's father died, leaving her with an income of £700 per year. In 1867 she married her clergyman cousin, Algernon Kingsford, and had one daughter, Eadith. In 1870 Anna converted to Roman Catholicism, and the ceremony was conducted by the eminent Catholic cleric Cardinal Henry Manning. In 1872 she took over the proprietorship of the *Lady's Own Paper;* having been peculiarly sensitive to the sufferings of animals since a young age, Kingsford used the journal as a vehicle for her own views on vivisection, which had developed since she had been encouraged by her brother to give up eating meat. She embraced vegetarianism with unshakable conviction, refusing to wear fur, feathers, or leather shoes. Soon her quest to accomplish the abolition of vivisection and promote the benefits of a vegetarian diet—for its physical, chemical, hygienic, economic, moral, and spiritual benefits (as she perceived them)—prompted her to abandon her journal to go to Paris to study medicine. She was a firm advocate of women's right to an independent life (which she had insisted upon when agreeing to marry) and to higher education. She entered medical school in Paris in 1874, returning frequently to her husband and child in England, and was often chaperoned during her studies by her friend, the writer Edward Maitland. Sharing the same mystical ideas, a passion for vegetarianism, and a rejection of the material world, Kingsford and Maitland collaborated on *Keys of the Creeds* (1875) and a collection of nine of Kingsford's spiritualist lectures, *The Perfect Way, or, the Finding of Christ* (1882).

Kingsford acquired her medical degree on 22 July 1880, with a thesis in French on the vegetarian diet. Considerably enlarged and translated into English (and also German), it was published a year later as *The Perfect Way in Diet,* in which she offered her own extremely well-presented medical arguments that human beings were not by nature carnivorous and that, if anything, they were by nature fructivores (Kingsford's arguments strongly suggest that she might have been vegan rather than vegetarian). For Kingsford a return to a natural vegetable diet was the panacea for almost all social and physical ills, and the message was forcefully transmitted in all her many writings. After she qualified as a doctor, she set herself up in what would be a highly successful medical practice, specializing in women's complaints. Many middle-class women beat a path to her door, anxious to discover the secret of her luminous complexion, only to be advised by Kingsford to throw their dubious, if not dangerous, mineral-based cosmetics in the bin and embrace the cleansing properties of a vegetarian diet. She wrote regular articles on hygiene, vegetarianism, and beauty care for the *Lady's Pictorial* in the mid-1880s and brought out a book on the subject, *Health, Beauty and the Toilet* (1886), which sold well in the United Kingdom and the United States.

As an evangelist for healthy living, Kingsford was a founding member of the Food Reform Society (FRS) in 1881 and traveled the United Kingdom, making speeches on vegetarianism on behalf of the FRS and the Vegetarian Society. She also lectured against compulsory smallpox vaccination and vivisection, emphasizing at all times that "the Vegetarian movement is the bottom and basis of all the movements toward Purity, Freedom, Justice, and Happiness" (Maitland 1913, vol. 2: 248). Together with her untiring helpmate Maitland, she attended public meetings and rallies in England and abroad, speaking in French at the French Vegetarian Society in Paris and helping establish antivivisection groups in Geneva and Lausanne (although the former soon folded). Tirelessly, Kingsford and Maitland collated statistics and prepared memoranda, articles, appeals, and petitions aimed at the abolition of vivisection. Kingsford translated many of her own articles, written for journals such as the *Vegetarian Messenger, Nature,* and the *Food Reform Magazine,* into French and German, in which countries she had a respectful following. During 1881–1882, she exchanged views on vivisection on the pages of the *Nineteenth Century* (vol. 2, 1882), a debate prompted by her own essay, "The Uselessness of Vivisection." In her many articles, Kingsford regularly berated the time spent by women preparing lavish, meat-based meals, which she felt kept them chained as housekeepers and demeaned them by involving them in the handling of dead animals.

During the 1880s, Kingsford was caught up in a crisis of faith over her Christian beliefs, which had become increasingly eroded by her interest in Eastern faiths and mysticism and which had drawn her into a study of ancient philosophies such as Platonism, Buddhism, and Gnosticism. Eventually, Kingsford embraced Theosophy, in 1883 becoming president of the London Lodge of the Theosophical Society and a close associate of Madame Helena Blavatsky. Kingsford also became a noted psychic, claiming to visit the spirit world during her sleep and later giving public lectures on the content of her prophetic dreams and visions (some argued that these were hallucinations brought on by her extreme fasting and abstention from meat). In time, however, she and Maitland sought their own independent platform for their mystical beliefs, geared to the study of the soul, mystical theology, and occult science, and cofounded the Hermetic Society in 1884.

Although she had supported women's suffrage and the campaign for married women to retain the right to their own property by publishing articles in her 1870s journal, the *Lady's Own Paper,* Kingsford was reluctant about taking on overtly feminist campaigning. She saw women's activism on animal rights as affording a far more worthwhile opportunity for practical work, believing that by encouraging more conservative-minded women into the less (sexually and politically) controversial arena of antivivisection, they could thus be provided with an important outlet for philanthropic work and a role in public life. And indeed, women's contribution to the vegetarian and antivivisection movements in Victorian Britain was crucial, with between 40 and 60 percent of the leadership and patrons of the various societies being female. Queen Victoria, who was renowned for her sentimentality about animals and never went anywhere without a Pomeranian dog in her lap, was herself a patron of the Royal Society for the Prevention of Cruelty to Animals (RSPCA) and a supporter of Cobbe's antivivisectionist Victoria Street Society. Kingsford's own feminist writings were heavily slanted toward highly allegorical interpretations of women's subjugation and male cruelty toward laboratory animals, such as the now highly regarded "City of Blood"—the subject of recent feminist analysis—published in *Dreams and Dream Stories* (1888). In it, Kingsford, like other feminist writers such as Sarah Grand, drew analogies between the hidden world of vivisection and the medical abuse and domestic oppression of women behind closed doors.

In 1887, during a visit to Paris where she had hoped to observe operating techniques at the Pasteur Institute, Kingsford caught pneumonia after being soaked by torrential rain, and her illness developed into pulmonary consumption. She died four months later, after vainly seeking a rest cure on the Riviera. A woman of great ethereal beauty, whom Maitland saw as a latter-day Mary Magdalene and whom the social purity campaigner William Thomas Stead revered as "that marvellous embodiment of a burning flame in the form of a woman, divinely tall, and not less divinely fair" (Maitland 1913, vol. 2: 378), Kingsford entered the pantheon of Victorian mystics and eccentrics who rapidly became unfashionable in the modernizing twentieth century. Her occult and mystical writings, however, hold continued appeal for fringe culture; often published in new age journals such as *Lucifer* and *Light,* they include *Astrology Theologised* (1886) and *Clothed with the Sun* (1889).

Much of Kingsford's groundbreaking work was continued by the Humanitarian League, established by Maitland and Henry Salt in 1892. In 1895 the Women's Vegetarian Society was founded, and in 1896 the Humanitarian League's petition against vivisection was signed by women activists, including Isabella Ford and Margaret McMillan. By the 1900s, many militant suffragists, seeing the clear analogies to be drawn between the subjugation of women and that of animals, signed petitions organized by the Humanitarian League against blood sports, and were active in the Vegetarian Society (which Kingsford had served as a vice president). Beatrice Webb carried on much valuable work in the National Food Reform Association (as the Food Reform Society was renamed), as did the militant suffragist Lady Constance Lytton.

Meanwhile, Maitland took jealous charge of Kingsford's posthumous reputation, publishing *The Ideal in Diet: Selections from the Writings of Anna Bonus Kingsford* in 1898 and his own and Kingsford's *Addresses and Essays on Vegetarianism* in 1913. In a celebration of its hundredth anniversary in 1946 and in recognition of Kingsford as a pioneering figure, the Vegetarian Society devoted the September issue of its journal to her life and work. For further information on Kingsford's mysticism, see http://www.personal.usyd.edu.au/~apert/kingsford.html. For further information on the Vegetarian Society of the United Kingdom, see http://www.vegsoc.org/.

See also Butler, Josephine; Cobbe, Frances Power; Despard, Charlotte; Ford, Isabella; Grand, Sarah; Lytton, Lady Constance; McMillan, Margaret; Webb, Beatrice.

References and Further Reading

Basham, Diana. 1992. *The Trial of Woman: Feminism and the Occult Sciences in Victorian Literature and Society.* London: Macmillan.

Dictionary of National Biography. First published 1888–1900 in 64 vols. Supplements published every ten years, 1901–1985. London and Oxford: Oxford University Press.

Elston, Mary Ann. 1987. "Women and Antivivisection in Victorian England, 1870–1900." In Nicolaas A.

Rupke, ed. *Vivisection in Historical Perspective.* London: Croom Helm.

Greer, Mary. 1995. *Women of the Golden Dawn: Rebels and Priestesses.* Rochester, VT: Park Street Press.

Hays, Frances. 1885. *Women of the Day: A Biographical Dictionary of Notable Contemporaries.* London: Chatto and Windus.

Hogan, Anne. 1998. *Women of Faith in Victorian Culture: Reassessing the Angel in the House.* New York: St. Martin's Press.

Kean, Hilda. 1998. *Animal Rights: Political and Social Change in Britain since 1800.* London: Reaktion Books.

Lansbury, Coral. 1985. *The Old Brown Dog: Women, Workers and Vivisection in Edwardian England.* Madison: University of Wisconsin Press.

Maitland, Edward, ed. 1913. *Anna Kingsford: Her Life, Letters, Diary and Work.* 2 vols. London: John M. Watkins.

Shirley, Ralph. 1920. *Occultists and Mystics of All Ages.* London: W. Rider and Son.

Vyvyan, John. 1969. *In Pity and in Anger: A Study of the Use of Animals in Science.* London: Michael Joseph.

Kishida Toshiko
(1861–1901)
Japan

Kishida Toshiko was a leading figure and notable public speaker in the pioneering but short-lived popular rights movement that arose during the early 1880s in Meiji Japan (1868–1911). In a groundbreaking speech in 1883, she talked of the restrictions placed upon young women by Japanese society, likening them to daughters "confined in boxes," denied the fulfillment of a life in the outside world. Such a practice, she declared, was "like growing flowers in salt" and stunted their intellectual growth (Sievers 1983, 41). Kishida went on to become one of the first Japanese feminists to enter journalism in the promotion of social ideals.

Kishida was born into a wealthy Kyoto merchant family. She was fortunate in not being subjected to many of the restrictions prevailing at that time, and by the age of eighteen, such was her reputation both for beauty and intellectual accomplishments that word reached the Meiji empress, Haruko. Kishida was appointed as a lady-in-waiting in order to teach the empress literature. For two years she endured the rigid conventions of court life and the enforced separation from the real world and observed with growing dismay the ritualistic subservience of the women around her.

Leaving her post on the excuse of illness in 1882, Kishida traveled in Japan with her mother, meeting with members of the Popular Rights Movement and inspiring women wherever she went to set up their own discussion and self-help groups and lecture societies. She was the first woman in Japan to give public lectures on women's emancipation and had already earned a considerable reputation as an eloquent speaker by the age of twenty. The limitations that women's upbringing and early marriage placed on them by failing to train them in self-sufficiency, encapsulated by Kishida in the title of her speech, "A Girl in a Box, or the Imperfection of Marriage," would prove a brave challenge to long-held social conventions and an impassioned call for women's education. She delivered the speech at a Liberal Party meeting in Otsu on 12 October 1883, not long after cofounding the Kyoto Women's Society. But doing so was deemed to be in defiance of the 1880 Public Assembly Act, which banned women from political meetings and speech making, and Kishida was fined and briefly imprisoned. In 1884 she married a Liberal Party politician, Nakajima Nobuyuki, and the couple converted to Christianity. During May–June 1884, Kishida published an important ten-part article, "I Tell You, My Fellow Sisters," in the Liberal Party newspaper the *Light of Freedom.* However, continuing harassment by the police and the dissolution of the Liberal Party in 1884 forced Kishida to give up public speaking and channel her social activism into journalism. She also taught at Ferris's School for Women in Yokohama.

Kishida began writing for the Christian journal, the *Women's Education Magazine,* from the mid-1880s, where she spoke out against the traditional overvaluing of men to the detriment of women and argued for women's equal rights with them as an essential element of the modernization of Japan. She believed that the inequalities between women and men were perpetuated not by differences in mental ability between the sexes, but by women being denied access to education and by the persisting social conventions supported by men. In particular, she condemned the sexual double standard that prevailed in Japan, which condoned concubinage for men yet emphasized women's chastity, allowing men but not women to divorce their partners for adultery. For Kishida, women's rights were closely bound up with her own deep sense of patriotism and she was convinced that reform of civil and human rights would not only improve relationships within the family but also make for a better nation. But her later journalism never had the same impact as her early three-year career (1882–1884) as a public speaker.

In 1887 Kishida and her husband were exiled from Tokyo during a roundup of intellectuals. They settled in Yokohama, returning to Tokyo in 1890 when Nakajima was elected to the lower house of the Japanese Diet and Kishida became involved in the Tokyo Women's Reform Society (founded in 1886). By this time, however, Japanese feminists had become increasingly isolated by the prevailing climate of resurgent conservatism in Japan, and in 1890 a total clampdown on women's political activities under the provisions of Article 5 of the Police Security Regulations (further reinforced in 1900), meant it would be another twenty years before the women's movement that Kishida had done so much to inspire would be revived with the "new woman" and suffrage movements of the Taisho period (1912–1926). Kishida did not live to see these positive results, however. She died prematurely of tuberculosis at the age of forty.

References and Further Reading

Miyoko Fujieda. 1995. "Japan's First Phase of Feminism." In Kumiko Fujimura-Fanselow and Atsuko Kameda, eds., *Japanese Women: New Feminist Perspectives on the Past, Present, and Future.* New York: Feminist Press.

Robin-Mowry, Dorothy. 1983. *The Hidden Sun: Women of Modern Japan.* Epping, Essex: Bowker Publishing Co.

Sievers, Sharon L. 1981. "Feminist Criticism in Japanese Politics in the 1880s: The Experience of Kishida Toshiko." *Signs* 6(4): 602–616.

———. 1983. *Flowers in Salt: The Beginnings of Feminist Consciousness in Modern Japan.* Stanford: Stanford University Press.

Kollontai, Alexandra
(1872–1952)
Soviet Union

The flamboyant, irreverent, uncompromising Alexandra Kollontai was a forceful and unconventional personality in the Bolshevik government that came to power after the October Revolution of 1917. So forceful, indeed, that she had to be got out of the way. Her controversial ideas on women's sexuality (labeled the "glass of water theory of sex" in a willful misreading of her ideas), which she used as part of her greater campaign to overturn conventional bourgeois morality, have since perhaps attracted an unwarranted amount of attention. This misinterpretation, in turn, has deflected attention from her serious work in integrating women into the new socialist society as men's equals. Within the space of five years, this beautiful, challenging, and highly articulate woman became, in the eyes of the dogmatists of the party, an eccentric and a maverick with too great a propensity to argue against the mainstream commitment to economic goals above all others. In the end her call for greater democratization of the party, through her support for the Workers' Opposition, led to her speedy removal to a diplomatic post abroad.

On the superficial level, Kollontai's reputation has for long rested on the perceived incongruity of her professed sensuality and insistence on sexual freedom with the new communist order, which deemed that there was no room for such personal preoccupations. Kollontai's primary objective was always to see women fully integrated into socialist society and not exploited as its servants. Her ultimate ideal was to elevate the new Soviet woman to the status of a queen bee, serviced by anonymous male workers with whom she procreated as part of the greater project of constructing a harmonious collective society. Viewed simply, her ideas affirmed the essential need for women to free themselves from their traditional enslavement to men. But these were radical ideas that did not go down well, either with the party or with traditional, conservative popular belief.

Born Alexandra Mikhailovna Domontovich, Kollontai was from a wealthy, liberal, and aristocratic Russo-Finnish family. Her father was a general in the Russian Imperial Army and later a social democrat legislator who supported reform. Her mother was the daughter of a Finnish timber merchant, and the family moved between their family estate in Finland and their home in St. Petersburg. Kollontai spent much of her young life growing up in the isolation of the snowy Finnish wastes. She was educated privately. By the time she began writing at age sixteen, she had already developed a fiercely independent nature. In order to escape the confines of life at home, she married Vladimir Kollontai, a factory inspector, when she was twenty and soon after had a son. But she soon felt oppressed within the domestic sphere and poured out her feelings into short stories (which remain unpublished). In 1896 increasing political differences with her husband led to a rift between them, after she had accompanied him on his inspection of a textile factory. Upon witnessing the terrible working conditions there, she was appalled at her husband's complacency. She joined a group of activists in an underground organization, the Marxist Union of Struggle for the Working Class, and began making contact with striking women workers in textile factories. In 1898 Kollontai left her husband and, putting her son in the care of her parents, went to Switzerland to study Marxism and economics, mixing with Russian radicals in exile there.

On her return to St. Petersburg in 1899, Kollontai became active in illegal propagandizing among workers and was drawn into the events of the 1905 Revolution, demonstrating alongside working women at the Winter Palace on Bloody Sunday. She began mobilizing working women for mass strikes, organized a women's club for factory workers, and wrote pamphlets demanding women's economic and sexual equality with men. But she joined none of the moderate feminist groups that began agitating for women's suffrage at this time, denouncing them as bourgeois and criticizing such women for the narrowness of their campaigning.

During 1907 Kollontai convened meetings of the Union of Textile Workers, at which she lectured to women on hygiene and child care; but the Bolsheviks saw her support for women's groups as divisive and forced her to abandon them. Kollontai remained vehement about the narrowness of the Russian feminist movement, even going so far as to noisily intervene (along with a posse of forty socialist women supporters) during the First All-Russian Women's Congress,

Alexandra Kollontai (AP/Wide World Photos)

held in St. Petersburg in 1908, when she condemned its participants as timid in their objectives and elitist and bourgeois in their thinking. She countered their feeble activism (as she saw it) in 1909 by publishing *The Social Bases of the Woman Question*. This book, influenced by the socialist writings of August Bebel and Friedrich Engels, was a discussion of Marxist arguments in support of working-class women's economic independence and their liberation from the bondage of marriage. In it, Kollontai argued for a wide range of maternity care, state support for pregnant and nursing mothers, day care facilities for their children, and the protection of women in industry. She also devoted much space to endlessly reiterating the sins of the moderate suffragists, whom she felt would never win the support of working women.

Kollontai's activities soon brought her under police surveillance. She was forced to flee to exile in Germany in order to evade arrest after writing a contentious pamphlet on Finnish independence from Russia. She spent the next nine years in Europe, moving among Menshevik exiles, finally converting to Bolshevism in 1915, and joining Lenin in Berlin. Under Kollontai's influence, the Bolsheviks enlisted Inessa Armand and Nadezhda Krupskaya to set up a communist newspaper for women in 1913. The *Woman Worker* featured discussions on women's rights and working conditions, family problems, and women's health and hygiene. The journal was closed down on the outbreak of war in 1914.

During World War I, Kollontai was active in the pacifist movement, writing a pamphlet entitled "Who Needs the War?" In 1915 she toured the United States on a mission to prevent the Americans from joining the fighting. She returned to Russia after the 1917 February Revolution, at which time she was the first woman elected to the Central Committee of the Bolshevik Party. Anxious to enlist the Bolshevik government's support for women's welfare, she called a working women's conference in Petrograd (the new name for St. Petersburg) shortly after, where she proposed new maternity laws and protective legislation for workers. After the October Revolution, Lenin appointed her commissar for public welfare, in which capacity (until March 1918, when she resigned) Kollontai initiated family reforms and maternity care for working women. She also advised on reform of the divorce laws as part of the drawing up of a new family code.

As commissar for social welfare, Kollontai set up health care centers for women that offered advice on birth control and child care and became known as "palaces for the protection of motherhood and infancy." In all her work, she continually underlined state responsibility for some of the functions of the family that had for so long kept women at home, in order that women could enjoy a greater degree of personal autonomy and be given the opportunity to take part in political work. Her wide range of proposals included sixteen weeks of free health care for mothers before and after childbirth, light work for expectant mothers, a four-hour workday for them during their first month back at work, and the prohibition of night work for expectant and nursing mothers. Kollontai also called for legislation to protect women working in dangerous industries and for work for children under the age of sixteen to be made illegal. With regard to marriage, she advocated that religious ceremonies should be replaced by civil marriages and that men and women should enjoy total equality in marriage and in their rights over their children. No distinction should be made between illegiti-

mate and legitimate children, and divorce should be made easier.

After the premature death of Inessa Armand, chair of the Zhenotdel (the Women's Department of the Central Committee of the Communist Party), which had been founded in 1919, Kollontai took over the campaign it had inaugurated to target the high levels of illiteracy among peasant women. Through the Zhenotdel, she also sought to erode the traditional structures and practices of Russian family life, which Kollontai believed would not spontaneously give way to the new socialist collective. Although she had no desire to see women withdraw from their primary social duty of having children, she wanted them to do so not within individual family units but within the broader context of the community. She optimistically anticipated that the conventional family unit would be replaced by communal living, where members made their own choices for platonic or erotic love and where domestic functions would be carried out in communal kitchens, laundries, and nurseries that would take care of each new baby as a "unit of labor."

In 1921 Kollontai became increasingly concerned with the Bolshevik leadership's tightening grip over government, made possible by means of the tentacles of its wide-reaching bureaucracy. She allied herself with the Workers' Opposition, in the process having a passionate love affair with one of its leaders, Alexander Shlyapnikov. The opposition argued for decentralized political control through independent trade unions instead of the concentration of power among the elite of the Communist Party. Kollontai had also grown wary of the New Economic Policy introduced by Lenin, which was rapidly reintroducing the old economic enslavement of women, many of whom were now doubly burdened with long hours working in factories as well as looking after their children. After the proposals of the Workers' Opposition were thrown out by the Tenth Party Congress in 1921, many of its leaders were expelled from the party. In 1922 Kollontai was moved to the Commissariat for Foreign Affairs and posted to Oslo in a trade delegation. A year later she was made Norwegian ambassador. She remained in Norway until 1925 and spent a year in Mexico (1926) before returning to Norway in 1927–1930. From 1930 until 1945, she was based in the Russian embassy in Sweden, becoming ambassador in 1943.

In Oslo Kollontai returned to the fiction writing of her teenage years, producing three short stories about the Soviet new woman, published under the title "Love of Worker Bees" in 1923 (and in the United States as "Red Love" in 1927), in which she elaborated on the problems that the contemporary Soviet woman had in balancing her personal need for love and sexual fulfillment with the commitment to socialist progress. It was a subject she had broached before, in her 1918 works *The New Morality and the Working Class* and *The Family and the Communist State,* in which she had argued that economic change was not enough; a new morality and the establishment of new sexual relations had to accompany the overhaul of the old society. "Love of Worker Bees" further promoted the mutual recognition by men and women of their individual sexual rights. A new form of love would appear in Soviet society—the "winged Eros"—to serve the "solidarity love" that would transcend self-love and the competitiveness of the old bourgeois order. But the stories were violently disapproved of as being too explicit by the notoriously puritanical Lenin, and by writing them Kollontai also provided further ammunition, after his death in 1924, with which her political opponents would shoot down the last vestiges of her political reputation.

By 1926 Kollontai had made her final political foray on behalf of women when she returned briefly from Norway to debate the proposed new Soviet marriage code and in particular the issue of alimony. Originally, Kollontai had supported the idea of state subsidies for wives and mothers, but now she revised her view to suggest the introduction of a marriage contract that laid down the economic responsibilities of both partners and their equal rights to marital property. She proposed also the abolition of alimony (which in her view reinforced women's perceived weakness and financial dependence) and the creation of a general insurance fund to which all adult members of the population would contribute. This fund in turn would pay for the establishment of daytime nurseries for the children of working mothers and refuges for mothers and children in need, and provide economic support for single mothers who were unable to work. Such a fund would defuse the hostilities over financial support that so often accompanied divorce and would be another step toward a collective society in which such responsibilities were shared. Despite Kollontai's detailed suggestions, the party failed to respond, and the Marriage Code of 1926 retained alimony while upholding the right to divorce.

Thus came to an end Kollontai's increasingly solitary feminist protest in the face of a party that had persistently pressured her to put up or shut up. She did so thereafter, well out of the political limelight in her diplomatic posts abroad. She reemerged from obscurity in 1944 to negotiate an end to the Soviet war with Finland, persuading the Finns to accept a draconian peace settlement imposed by Joseph Stalin. She was even nominated for the Nobel Peace Prize in 1946 for her diplomacy. This last public success bought her readmittance into the Soviet fold, and she returned to Moscow in 1945, where she wrote her memoirs of Lenin, published posthumously in 1959.

Kollontai was, along with Lenin's widow Nadezhda Krupskaya, one of the few Old Bolsheviks to survive Stalin's Great Terror of the 1930s, her political profile, like Krupskaya's, being too conspicuous for Stalin to have had her incarcerated or murdered. In 1930 Stalin had abolished the Zhenotdels, announcing that the "woman problem" in the Soviet Union had been solved. His relentless overturning of many socialist family policies and the marginalization of women's issues ensured an end to Kollontai's utopian dream. During the 1930s, with the reintroduction of laws consolidating the Soviet nuclear family unit, Stalin would undo much of her pioneering work in support of women's social and sexual autonomy.

See also Armand, Inessa; Krupskaya, Nadezhda.
References and Further Reading
Berkin, Carol R., and Clara M. Lovett. 1980. *Women: War and Revolution.* New York: Holmes and Meier.
Boxer, Marilyn J., and Jean H. Quaterat. 1978. *Socialist Women: European Socialist Feminism in the Nineteenth and Early Twentieth Centuries.* New York: Elsevier North-Holland.
Clements, Barbara Evans. 1979. *Bolshevik Feminist: The Life of Aleksandra Kollontai.* Bloomington: Indiana University Press.
———. 1997. *Bolshevik Women.* Cambridge: Cambridge University Press.
Holt, Alix, ed. 1977. *Selected Writings of Alexandra Kollontai.* London: Allison and Busby.

Kollontai, Alexandra. 1975. *The Autobiography of a Sexually Emancipated Communist Woman.* Edited by Irving Fetscher, translated by Salvator Altanasio. New York: Schocken Books.

———. 1977. *Love of Worker Bees.* Translated by Cathy Porter. London: Virago.

Porter, Cathy. 1980. *Alexandra Kollontai: A Biography.* London: Virago.

Slaughter, Jane, and Robert Kern. 1981. *European Women on the Left: Socialism, Feminism, and the Problems Faced by Political Women, 1880 to the Present.* Westport, CT: Greenwood Press.

Stites, Richard. 1991 [1978]. *The Women's Liberation Movement in Russia: Feminism, Nihilism, and Bolshevism, 1860–1930.* Reprint, Princeton: Princeton University Press.

Kovalevskaya, Sofya
(1850–1891)
Russia

The brilliant career of the Russian mathematician and educator Sofya Kovalevskaya was cut short by premature death from pneumonia at the age of forty-one. She has been embraced by mathematical science as one of its first women pioneers, and she also has the reputation of being one of the first nineteenth-century Russian women admitted to university (although she was forced to study outside her own country). Although not an active reformer, she was hugely significant in the history of women's higher education in Russia. Kovalevskaya's academic achievements galvanized many other young Russian women into following her example and fighting to make new inroads into the male-dominated spheres of academic study.

Like most Russian pioneers of women's education, Kovalevskaya came from the moneyed upper classes. She was born Sofya Korvin-Krukovskaya on the family estate at Palibino near Vitebsk. Her father was an artillery general, and she was educated at home. But her childhood was unhappy, and she became timid, withdrawn, and sickly. Legend has it that on finding the walls of her playroom temporarily papered with old mathematical notes of her father's, Kovalevskaya became absorbed in their perplexing formulas and developed a precocious interest in mathematics. It was encouraged from the age of six, and she received further encouragement from the family tutor, Joseph Malevich, until 1867.

In 1868 Sofya unsuccessfully petitioned to be admitted as an auditor to classes at the Naval Academy at a time when women in Russia were not allowed to study at university. She married paleontologist Vladimir Kovalevsky that year, in order to be able to go with him to Germany to study. But even in Heidelberg she found herself prohibited from attending lectures at the university, so the couple moved to Berlin in 1870, where she obtained private tuition under the eminent mathematician Karl Weierstrass for the next four years. Weierstrass finally persuaded the authorities at the University of Göttingen to allow her a doctorate in 1874 on the strength of her three theses, on partial differential equations, Saturn's rings, and Abelian integrals.

Kovalevskaya's academic credentials were exceptional, yet despite this she was unable to find work after her return to Russia in 1874. The Russian educational authorities were only prepared to let her teach in the lower classes of a girls' gymnasium (high school). Now the mother of a daughter, Kovalevskaya worked for a while on private research into the refraction of light and tried her hand at fiction and journalism. She returned to Berlin with her daughter to try to find a teaching post; but while she was away her husband lost money in bad investments and committed suicide in 1883. Weierstrass came to Kovalevskaya's rescue soon after, using his connections to obtain her a five-year extraordinary professorship in mathematics at Stockholm University from 1884. She made a great success of her career there; in 1885 she was promoted to chair of mechanics. In 1888 the French Academy of Sciences awarded her the Borodin Prize, increased from 3,000 to 5,000 francs, for what it deemed an exceptional piece of work, her account "On the Rotation of a Solid Body about a Fixed Point." In 1889 she was elected a corresponding member of Russia's Imperial Academy of Sciences.

Kovalevskaya never had time to develop her literary talents, although she cowrote a play, *Struggle for Happiness,* with her friend Anne Leffler (1885) and published an account of the Polish rebellion of 1863 in Swedish during her time in Stockholm. Of her forays into fiction, her novella *The Nihilist* (written in 1880 and translated into English in 1895 as *The Woman Nihilist*) has been of some posthumous interest. It is the story of the self-sacrifice of an ardent female revolutionary out to solve Russia's social ills who marries another revolutionary to save him from hard labor and goes into exile with him, and was very much a product of the idealistic sense of mission among Russian feminists of her time. Kovalevskaya's memoirs were first published in English in 1895 as *Recollections of Childhood.*

References and Further Reading

Engel, Barbara Alpern. 1983. *Women of the Intelligentsia in Nineteenth-Century Russia.* Cambridge: Cambridge University Press.

Kennedy, D. H. 1983. *Little Sparrow: A Portrait of Sophia Kovalevsky.* Athens: Ohio University Press.

Koblitz, Ann Hibner. 1983. *A Convergence of Lives: Sofia Kovalevskaia, Scientist, Writer, Revolutionary.* Boston: Birkhauser.

Kovalevskaia [sic], S. V. V. 1978. *A Russian Childhood.* Translated and edited by Beatrice Stillman. New York: Springer-Verlag.

Porter, Cathy. 1976. *Fathers and Daughters: Russian Women in Revolution.* London: Virago.

Krog, Gina
(1847–1916)
Norway

The initiator of the moderate, short-lived Norwegian women's movement prior to World War I, Gina Krog founded the Women's Suffrage Union in 1885 with only twelve members. She became a member of the International Council of Women and an important figure in the international movement for women's suffrage.

The women's movement in Norway was slow to gather impetus, taking its lead from writings on women's and social issues such as those by Camilla Collett. Krog's group campaigned modestly, working for municipal suffrage and improved opportunities for women in education and employment and advocating changes in the legal status of married women. Nor was its tenor stringently feminist.

In 1884 Krog had become active in the Norwegian Association for the Promotion of Women's Interests. A year later, in 1885, after Krog gave a public lecture on the subject of women's suffrage, demanding equal voting rights for both sexes, she founded the Woman Suffrage Union with links to the National Woman Suffrage Association in the United States. The twelve

founding members divided the country between them, lecturing, organizing petitions, and in 1887 founding their own periodical, *New Ground,* which Krog edited until her death. With the rise of a radical political movement in Norway in the 1880s, Krog and other suffragists were encouraged to demand full female suffrage. Women's suffrage was first debated in the Storthing in 1890; encouraged by this, Krog created another suffrage group, the National Women's Suffrage Union, in 1895. Under its auspices, she sought to broaden women's activism from its modest, purely economic, and educational national concerns toward the universal issues of suffrage and moral reform that were gathering ground throughout Europe. She did, however, limit her vision of women's suffrage as being linked to property, achieved in 1901 when women in Norway who owned property or were married to property owners were allowed to vote in municipal elections.

In 1904 Krog was instrumental in bringing Norway's National Council of Women into the International Council of Women (ICW), which had been founded in Washington, D.C., in 1888 to encourage international collaboration between women activists. Krog was one of several Norwegian delegates to the Fourth Congress of the International Council of Women, held in Berlin in 1904, at which the International Woman Suffrage Alliance (IWSA) was established, by which time she had formed strong personal friendships with U.S. feminists Elizabeth Cady Stanton and Susan B. Anthony. She also attended IWSA congresses in Amsterdam in 1908, Toronto in 1909, and Rome in 1914.

As a conservative movement, the Norwegian suffrage campaign achieved its objective ahead of many of the much more forceful national suffrage movements. While their more militant sisters in Britain and the United States were still out campaigning in 1907, 300,000 Norwegian women taxpayers were enfranchised under suffrage linked to a small property qualification; in 1911 the government approved the appointment of women to cabinet posts. Finally, in 1913 women were given the vote on the same basis as men.

An outstanding Norwegian suffrage leader alongside Krog and another familiar figure in the IWSA was Louise Quam (1833–1935). Wife of a former Norwegian prime minister, she served as vice president of the Norwegian National Council of Women from 1904 to 1913.

See also Collett, Camilla.
References and Further Reading
Blom, Ida. 1980. "The Struggle for Women's Suffrage in Norway, 1885–1913." *Scandinavian Journal of History* 5: 3–22.
Evans, Richard. 1977. *The Feminists: Women's Emancipation Movements in Europe, America and Australasia 1840–1920.* London: Croom Helm.
Rasmussen, Janet E. 1982. "Sisters across the Sea: Early Norwegian Feminists and Their American Connections." *Women's Studies International Forum* 5(6): 647–654.

Krupskaya, Nadezhda
(1869–1939)
Russia/Soviet Union

The wife of Lenin and grand old lady of the Bolsheviks Nadezhda Krupskaya found an important niche for herself after the 1917 Russian Revolution in spearheading the drive against illiteracy. She developed new education standards and revisions to the school curriculum and also devoted much energy to Soviet schemes for women and young people. As the widow of the Soviet leader Vladimir Ilyich Lenin, who died in 1924, her position became precarious as she increasingly tried to resist his successor Stalin's dominating and intimidating presence. Eventually, her inability to penetrate the darker complexities of Stalinist political intrigue marginalized her, and her brave resistance evaporated in the escalating climate of terror, leaving her, in her last days, an isolated and frightened remnant of the Bolshevik old guard.

Krupskaya came from a family of impoverished gentry; her father was an army artillery officer. Like many bright young women of her time, she grew up trapped in a rural backwater, where she began absorbing the mass of periodical literature then available on socialism and the theories of Karl Marx and Friedrich Engels. Under the influence of these writings, she went to St. Petersburg, hoping to become a teacher. In 1889 she studied in the Bestuzhev Higher Courses for Women but soon left to mix with more radical students from the Technological Institute, influenced by revolutionary literature that had been smuggled in from Russian communities in exile.

She was soon acting as a propagandist for the Russian social democrats among factory workers, as well as teaching groups of workers in evening and Sunday schools.

In 1894 she met Lenin at a Marxist study group and on his behalf undertook the gathering of information on the lives of workers in the factory districts. Lenin was arrested in 1895 and sent into exile in Siberia in 1897. A year later Krupskaya, after being arrested too, followed him out to Siberia. Upon her arrival the couple married, on Nadezhda's mother's and the authorities' insistence (the mother went everywhere with them ever after), in July 1898. It seems unlikely that their sexual relationship lasted for very long. Perhaps some of Krupskaya's very evident unselfishness was due in part to her inability to have children, for which both she and Lenin showed genuine affection. In their absence, she threw her energies into working for education after Lenin made her vice commissar of education in the Bolshevik government.

Although Alexandra Kollontai has cornered the ideological limelight on the status of women in Soviet Russia, which she first discussed in her 1908 publication, *The Social Bases of the Woman Question*, Krupskaya had in fact made her own more modest contribution. It was a pamphlet titled "The Working Woman," which she wrote in exile in 1900 (based on the information gathering she had done for Lenin). In it, as a Tolstoyan believer in the virtues of the peasant, she drew simplistic comparisons between the life of the oppressed woman factory worker and woman peasant under capitalism—poor, overworked, malnourished, and with too many children—and the socialist utopia yet to come. There women would enjoy full equality, and there would be no exploitation of the workforce; all human needs would be attended to by the state. It would, however, be the far more forceful and confrontational personality, Kollontai, who would boldly develop controversial ideas on the new Soviet woman in the years to come, only to be met with derision from most of the Bolshevik leadership. Krupskaya, with her typical modesty and self-effacing character, devoted her attentions instead to education and organizing women within the party.

For the whole of Lenin's life, Krupskaya unquestioningly served him as his loyal helpmate, secretary, and, after a serious stroke, nurse. She followed him doggedly around Europe during his long years of exile, constantly on the move from one bolt-hole to another in Munich, Vienna, Paris, Zurich, and London, incessantly reading, studying, writing, and debating. To her, Lenin's work was sacrosanct, and so devoted was she to Lenin as the leader of a great cause that she even condoned his close relationship with the beautiful Inessa Armand, for whom she was no physical match. Indeed, such had been Krupskaya's unprepossessing, matronly appearance that her Zurich landlady had even remarked: "Frau Lenin would have made a good *Hausfrau,* but she always had her mind on other work" (Wilson 1967, 467). On Lenin's death, Krupskaya even proposed that he be buried alongside Armand in the Kremlin Wall rather than being subjected to the indignity of being put on display in the Lenin Mausoleum.

After the Revolution in October 1917, Lenin made Krupskaya vice commissar of education and over the next five years she would be the chief formulator of mass adult education programs that would make considerable inroads in literacy levels. She was happy to stay out of party politics and devoted the same level of dedication to her work at the commissariat of education as she had to her work for Lenin. She targeted adult illiteracy by sending teachers out into the factories and the communes and devising new syllabuses of adult education. She launched a major drive against illiteracy; under her aegis 30,000 classes were set up across the Soviet Union for adult illiterates. She also spearheaded a campaign in 1919 to disseminate political propaganda on the Bolshevik Party and gave a series of lectures at educational conferences. In 1920 she and Inessa Armand began editing a theoretical journal for women, the *Communist Woman,* which featured articles by women in factories and in rural areas.

Over the following years, Krupskaya battled her own ill health to continue with her diligent efforts, in the belief that equality of the sexes had to be achieved first and foremost through education. She traveled the Soviet Union visiting schools, libraries, and reading circles, speaking at factory meetings and at conferences, and further developing and refining the political education program. But after Lenin was disabled and politically sidelined by several strokes in 1922–1923, she found herself having to deal increasingly with his would-be successor, Joseph Stalin. She

Nadezhda Krupskaya (Hulton-Deutsch Collection/ Corbis)

attempted to keep Lenin abreast of political events while he was recuperating outside Moscow, at a time when he had become increasingly mistrustful of Stalin's ambitions. After Lenin's death in 1924, Krupskaya remained a thorn in Stalin's side and a constant reminder of the old guard of the party that he was now seeking to eliminate. In 1926 she published her *Reminiscences of Lenin.* Although she continued her work for the Commissariat of Education, in 1928 the system she had built up over ten or more years was dissolved. Stalin also opposed her plans to establish polytechnic schools. Krupskaya refused to be intimidated and struggled to carry on with her educational propaganda.

Stalin was incensed by Krupskaya's continuing stubbornness, but because she was the widow of Lenin, he could not get rid of her. Nor could he deprive her of her role as the keeper of Lenin's flame, although in the past he had been heard by Vyacheslav Molotov to grumble that "she may use the same lavatory as Lenin, but that doesn't mean she knows anything about Leninism"

(Radzinsky 1997, 214). In 1935 the last straw came for Stalin when Krupskaya joined with other Bolsheviks of the old guard in an attempt to defend Lev Kamenev, who had come under attack by Stalin. It is then that he is said to have made his classic remark that if Krupskaya continued to meddle in political affairs, the party would nominate someone else as Lenin's widow, by deliberately fabricating an until-then-undisclosed divorce and announcing, posthumously, that Lenin had in fact "remarried" to someone more appropriate, like the leading apparatchik Elena Stasova. At this point Krupskaya's resistance to Stalin finally crumbled, and she spent her last few years in fear for her life.

In 1938, after being formally denounced at the Central Party Control Commission by Stalin's henchman, the head of the secret police Nikolay Ezhov, Krupskaya collapsed. She was by then very sick and plagued with the thyroid trouble that had caused her eyes to bulge. But she still refused to give up her work for education, in that year alone speaking at 172 meetings and writing 2,500 letters on educational matters. She died in February 1939 of "a sudden attack of appendicitis." However, some of the symptoms described on her death certificate (vomiting and cyanosis) suggest a different scenario.

See also Armand, Inessa; Kollontai, Alexandra.

References and Further Reading

Clements, Barbara Evans. 1997. *Bolshevik Women.* Cambridge: Cambridge University Press.

Elwood, R. C. 1992. *Inessa Armand: Revolutionary and Feminist.* Cambridge: Cambridge University Press.

Krupskaya, Nadezhda. 1970. *Memories of Lenin.* London: Panther.

McCauley, Martin. 1997. *Who's Who in Russia since 1900.* London: Routledge.

McNeal, Robert. 1972. *Bride of the Revolution: Krupskaya and Lenin.* Ann Arbor: University of Michigan Press.

Radzinsky, Edvard. 1997. *Stalin.* London: Sceptre.

Service, Robert. 2000. *Lenin: A Biography.* London: Macmillan.

Vasilieva, Larissa. 1994. *Kremlin Wives.* London: Weidenfeld and Nicolson.

Wilson, Edmund. 1967 [1960]. *To the Finland Station.* London: Fontana.

Kuliscioff, Anna (Anna Rozenstein) (1854–1925) *Russia/Italy*

The Italian socialist feminist and doctor Anna Kuliscioff, the first woman to practice medicine in Italy, became a radical campaigner for protective legislation for women and children. Her activities were hampered, however, by the conflict she experienced between loyalty to feminist issues and her espousal of Marxism.

Born in the Jewish district of Kherson, then part of the Russian empire, Anna Rozenstein, as she then was called, was the daughter of wealthy, assimilated Jews. Beautiful and cultivated, she grew up in Simferopol in the Crimea and graduated from high school with honors at the age of sixteen. She was supported in her studies by her liberally minded parents. Unable to enter university in Russia, she followed the path of other emancipated young Russian women of her time and went to Switzerland, where she studied engineering at Zurich University in 1871–1872.

In Zurich she became one of a tight group of Russian exiles and utopian socialists called the Zhebunists, who were admirers of the St. Simonians (followers of the radical Frenchman Jules Simon). Inspired by meetings with the Russian anarchists Peter Lavrov and Mikhail Bakunin, in 1872 Kuliscioff decided to become a revolutionary. She tore up her university papers and returned to Russia as part of a wave of student propagandists who inaugurated the "To the People Movement" of 1873, which took the ideas of socialism to the peasants. She married fellow revolutionary Peter Markelovich in the early 1870s and evaded arrest when the vast majority of these students, including her husband, were rounded up and put on trial by the tsarist authorities. Kuliscioff worked with revolutionary groups in southern Russia until their activities too were curtailed and she was forced into exile in Switzerland in 1877.

She lived in Lugano for seven years with the Italian anarchist Andrea Costa, by whom she had a child, and in 1878–1879 they lived in Florence. Ten years after graduating from Zurich University, she decided to become a doctor and returned to Bern University to study medicine in 1882–1884; on her return she set up a practice in a working-class district in Milan, where she specialized in gynecology and maintained strong links with industrial workers. By the mid-1880s, the edges had long been rubbed off Kuliscioff's youthful anarchism; she became a committed Marxist and joined the Socialist League of Milan. In 1884 she entered into a forty-year relationship with Marxist leader Filippo Turati, with whom she corresponded daily over a long period, especially during their imprisonment in 1898–1899. In 1890 they cofounded and edited the journal *Social Criticism,* which ran until 1910. In 1892 Turati and Kuliscioff founded the Italian Socialist Party and became leading figures, with Kuliscioff rapidly gaining a reputation for herself as "the most intelligent man in Italian socialism" (Berkin and Lovett 1980, 151).

In 1890 Kuliscioff organized a conference entitled "The Monopoly of Man" at the Philological Society of Milan, which discussed women's social and economic subordination. In her speech of that title, which was also published as a pamphlet, she described the humiliation of women's economic dependence, which destroyed both character and spirit and turned them into parasites. And for working women, the burden was doubled by having to labor long hours for low wages in addition to fulfilling their duties at home. What is more, she dared to suggest that working-class men oppressed their wives as much as men from other classes. In 1892 Kuliscioff visited the factories of Milan, urging women to unite to fight for their labor rights, equal pay, and protective legislation; she also lobbied the government for legislation that would restrict the working hours of women and children. In 1894 she addressed an International Congress on Injuries at Work, a subject that, as a doctor, particularly concerned her, since she believed weak and overworked women produced sickly children. In 1902 a law restricting women's and children's labor was finally passed.

Kuliscioff became an increasingly independent feminist figure from the 1890s, when her concerns were more and more diverted into socialism and the class struggle and away from separate women's issues. By 1897 she had completely detached herself from other women's groups, believing as she did that socialism and feminism were two separate issues that were not necessarily compatible. She channeled her efforts on behalf of women workers into the Socialist Party but found herself drawn into a debate over the situation of working women with the other major figure in Italian feminism, Anna Mozzoni, who challenged her as to whether socialism really would bring women sexual emancipation. Mozzoni felt that Kuliscioff's calls for specific labor legislation and welfare for working women did nothing but perpetuate the image of them as the weaker sex. For her part, Kuliscioff felt that middle-class feminist campaigning such as Mozzoni's went no further than the limited reformist work that had been undertaken by enlightened men since the French Revolution. It was only through socialism, she averred, that women would be liberated; but they needed to be patient, accepting minimal economic reforms until the proletarian revolution overturned the old capitalist system that bound them, paving the way for a radical reform of society, and with it the roles of the sexes, and the family.

Despite her avowed Marxism, Kuliscioff did not have the conventional shabby appearance espoused by Russian members of the movement. Although she had contracted tuberculosis after a period in prison in 1878–1879 that had left her an invalid by 1890, she was always elegant and well dressed, referred to wherever she went as "Signora Kuliscioff." As cofounder of the Socialist Party in Italy, she was deeply disappointed when a feminist movement failed to develop out of it and she had to fight her own battles with the leaders of the party, who opposed women's suffrage as "bourgeois." Thus in 1901 she found herself having to choose between her loyalty to her sex and her loyalty to the party, when the Socialist Party failed to make women's suffrage part of its program.

The problem here, as in other male-dominated national socialist parties, was that promotion of women's suffrage as an essential element of party policy remained a contentious issue, with many socialists—even female ones—wanting the campaign for women's suffrage to be postponed until after the winning of the class struggle (see, for example, Clara Zetkin). Kuliscioff believed that political change would only come if there was unity between the sexes in their work for socialist goals, the achievement of which in turn would emancipate both men and women. She pursued more intensely her arguments within the party for female suffrage throughout 1910–1912, having already come into conflict with her partner Turati over the issue. In 1910 she prepared a report on universal suffrage that she read at the congress of the Italian Socialist Party, held in Milan. In 1911 she became editor of the bimonthly publication *Defense of the Women Workers,* and through its pages and those of the journal *Avanti* (Forward; January–November 1912), she demanded women's suffrage as a basic civil right. For a short period in 1912, Kuliscioff led the women's auxiliary of the International Socialist Party, again working for women's unionization and suffrage. But by the end of the year, her reformist group within the party had been cold-shouldered. Kuliscioff remained active in socialist journalism until her death, which came at a low point in Italian social democracy, as Benito Mussolini rose to power.

See also Mozzoni, Anna Maria.
References and Further Reading
Berkin, Carol R., and Clara M. Lovett. 1980. *Women: War and Revolution.* New York: Holmes and Meier.
Boxer, Marilyn, and Jean H. Quaterat. 1978. *Socialist Women: European Socialist Feminism in the Nineteenth and Twentieth Centuries.* New York: Elsevier North-Holland.
La Vigna, Claire. 1991. *Anna Kuliscioff: From Russian Populism to Italian Socialism.* New York: Garland.
Slaughter, Jane, and Robert Kern. 1981. *European Women on the Left: Socialism, Feminism, and the Problems Faced by Political Women, 1880 to the Present.* Westport, CT: Greenwood Press.

Kuzwayo, Ellen
(1914–)
South Africa

As a teacher, social worker, and civil rights campaigner in the Johannesburg township of Soweto, Kuzwayo was a leading figure in the black consciousness movement that grew up there in the late 1960s. She has described the crucial contribution of black South African women to the struggle for racial justice in her autobiography, *Call Me Woman,* and has devoted her life to fighting against the second-class status accorded black women in South Africa.

Kuzwayo was an only child and grew up on her family's farm in the Orange Free State. She was educated at boarding school in Natal and Adams College in Durban. In 1937 she gained a primary higher teacher's certificate at Adams College in Amanzitoti and began teaching. In the mid-1930s she regularly attended African National Congress (ANC) conferences and in 1946 became secretary of its Youth League.

She married her second husband, Godfrey Kuzwayo, in 1950 and gave up teaching to train as a social worker at the Jan Hofmeyr School of Social Work at the University of Witwatersrand (1953–1955). She took her first job in 1956, working for the Johannesburg city council and from 1957 to 1962 worked for the Southern African Association of Youth Clubs.

In 1969, while serving as general secretary of the Young Women's Christian Association (YWCA) for the Transvaal region (1964–1976), Kuzwayo joined the black consciousness movement, working closely with its leader, Steve Biko. Her determination to fight for racial justice was reinforced in 1974, when she was dispossessed of the family farm she had inherited because the South African government designated that area as whites-only.

In 1976 Kuzwayo taught at the School of Social Work at the University of Witwatersrand before moving to the Soweto township in Johannesburg, where she set up women's self-help projects to administer funds from Britain, in cooperation with the Soweto Women's Self-Help Coordinating Council and the Black Housewives League. During the civil unrest in Soweto that year that led to riots among children and students and a mass protest movement culminating in a death toll of 575, she was a member of the Committee of Ten and was actively involved in the protest. In 1977, with the death of Steve Biko and the banning of eighteen black civil rights organizations, Kuzwayo again ran up against the authorities and spent five months in detention without charge under Section 10 of the Internal Security Act (1977–1978).

Since the 1970s Kuzwayo has continued to work for the rights of women in South Africa by promoting various self-help groups and acting since 1978 as consultant to the Zamani Soweto Sisters Council. The council now runs a Skills Training Centre (set up in 1987) to teach weaving to 500 women and girls annually. In 1979 Kuzwayo was named woman of the year by the *Johannesburg Star* and was asked to become chair of the Maggie Magaba Trust, a fund established in memory of a black nurse to give financial assistance to black women's self-help groups and individual families in financial need in Soweto.

Kuzwayo has also been awarded an honorary doctorate by the University of Natal. In 1984 she became the first president of the Black Consumer Union of South Africa, an organization that represents 50,000 members of various organizations throughout South Africa. The publication of *Call Me Woman* in 1985 modestly underplays her own role in the civil rights movement, with Kuzwayo setting out to provide a positive image of black women in South Africa by recording the heroism of numerous unsung figures in the fight for racial equality. In the new post-apartheid government of South Africa, Kuzwayo was elected an ANC member of parliament for the constituency of Dobsonville.

References and Further Reading
Kuzwayo, Ellen. 1985. *Call Me Woman.* London: Women's Press.
———. 1996. *Sit Down and Listen: Stories from South Africa.* Claremont, South Africa: D. Philip.

L

La Flesche, Susette (Susette Tibbles; Inshta Theumba, or "Bright Eyes")
(1854–1903)
United States

The Omaha Indian Susette La Flesche took part in a campaign in support of the rights of Native Americans to their historical homelands. She was born in Bellevue, Nebraska, and her French baptismal name came to her through her grandfather, a French fur trader. She was the daughter of Iron Eye, the last officially recognized chief of the Omaha tribe (1853–1888), and grew up on a reservation on the Missouri River in northeastern Nebraska, where she was educated in the English language in the local Presbyterian mission school (1862–1869). When her academic abilities became apparent, La Flesche, together with her sister Susan, was sent to Elizabeth, New Jersey, in 1869 to attend the Institute for Young Ladies. La Flesche returned to the Omaha tribe as a teacher in 1873, working in the local government school.

In 1879 La Flesche was drawn into the campaign being waged by the chief of the Ponca tribe, Standing Bear, for his people to be allowed to return to their homelands in Nebraska. They had been forcibly resettled in Indian Territory (now Oklahoma) in 1877, where they had suffered greatly and their numbers had been decimated by disease. When Standing Bear and thirty-four of his people were arrested after making the long and difficult journey north, back to Nebraska, the incident flared up into a national cause célèbre. Standing Bear was eventually acquitted under a historic ruling, when the presiding judge, Elmer Dundy, recognized his status as a person before the law.

Standing Bear set out on a lecture tour in the East, giving speeches on the injustice meted out to the Poncas in particular and Native Americans in general under government policies of arbitrary resettlement. La Flesche accompanied him as an interpreter and in 1881 married the newspaper editor, Thomas Tibbles, who had publicized the cause in the *Omaha Herald*. Their campaign was supported by other activists such as Helen Hunt Jackson, who had heard Standing Bear lecture in Boston, and the poet Henry Wadsworth Longfellow, who took a personal shine to La Flesche as the incarnation of his own Native American princess, Minnehaha (the heroine of Longfellow's narrative poem, *The Song of Hiawatha*).

Along the East Coast, La Flesche and Standing Bear appeared in major cities such as Boston, Philadelphia, and Washington, D.C. La Flesche and her husband gave evidence to several congressional committees, and such was the support for their campaign that Congress passed the Dawes Severalty Act of 1887, which gave land and citizenship rights to individual Native Americans and put an end to their forcible settlement on reservations.

In 1886 La Flesche and her husband left the United States on a ten-month lecture tour, visiting England and Scotland, where they gave a series of lectures on Native American culture and aroused much public interest. Upon her return to the United States in 1890, she continued to lecture on Native American women and culture and investigated life for Indians in South Dakota in the aftermath of the Wounded Knee massacre in 1890. For two years, La Flesche and her husband lived in Washington, D.C. (1893–1895), before returning to live on a farm in Bancroft, Nebraska. There La Flesche, by that time in poor health, spent her final years with the Omaha tribe, dying at the early age of forty-nine. During this period, she published numerous magazine stories and articles and illustrated a book about Indian life in Omaha, *Oo-mah-ha Ta-wa-tha* (1898), by Fannie Reed Giffen. In 1881 she had also illustrated and edited the anonymous work *Ploughed Under: The Story of an Indian Chief.*

Susette La Flesche's sister, Susan Picotte La Flesche (1865–1915), became one of the first Native American doctors after training at the Woman's Medical College of Pennsylvania. She too returned to her native home among the Omaha to found a hospital and serve as official doctor to the Omaha tribe and was also active in defense of the civil rights of Native Americans.

See also Jackson, Helen Hunt.
References and Further Reading
Dictionary of American Biography 1946–1958, and indexes to Supplements 1–10, 1981–1996. New York: Scribner's.

Jackson, Helen Hunt. 1994. *Westward to a High Mountain: The Colorado Writings of Helen Hunt Jackson.* Denver: Colorado Historical Society.

Odell, Ruth. 1939. *Helen Hunt Jackson.* New York: D. Appleton-Century.

Sicherman, Barbara, and Carol Hurd Green. 1980. *Notable American Women 1607–1950: A Biographical Dictionary,* vol. 4, *The Modern Period.* Cambridge, MA: Belknap Press of Harvard University.

Labarca Hubertson, Amanda
(1886–1975)
Chile

Educator, scholar, and feminist Labarca was a pioneer of the women's suffrage movement in Chile who did much to draw public attention to a wide range of women's issues and encouraged women to become socially active outside the domestic sphere. Labarca has been seen as very much a middle-class feminist whose activities were constrained by her observance of convention. Apparently, she did not feel sufficiently liberated to take an active role in the women's movement until after her husband had died, and supported the preservation of traditional male and female roles, emphasizing instead gender equality on a spiritual and moral level.

Born in Santiago, where she later studied at the Pedagogic Institute of the University of Chile,

Labarca undertook further studies at Columbia University Teachers' College in New York City. She also studied at the Sorbonne in Paris. Having married the Radical Party politician and educator Guillermo Labarca Hubertson, who later became minister of justice and education under President Arturo Alessandri Palma, Labarca was soon drawn into Radical Party activities.

In 1910 she attended the First International Congress of Women, held in Buenos Aires, Argentina, and in June 1915 she founded the Women's Reading Circle, an independent group (i.e., in this period not oriented to the Roman Catholic Church) for the study of literary and philosophical works and Chilean culture, which was patronized by university lecturers and professional women. She also collaborated in setting up a more general Women's Club. According to Elsa Chaney, the club "let a breath of fresh air into a closed, colonial Chile, with the best of thought, science and literature" (Chaney 1979, 336). Although the society, which had about 300 members by 1916, was independent in outlook and nonpartisan, it inevitably became linked to Labarca's husband's Radical Party, whose policies for secularizing Chilean society and reducing the influence of the church drew opposition to its activities from the Catholic establishment. In 1916, Labarca also became director of a girls' high school in Santiago, where she introduced new educational methods and attracted pupils from the middle and upper classes. In 1919 the Women's Reading Circle and the Women's Club combined to create the National Council of Women (NCW), with Labarca as its first president. The council would be the prime mover in the Chilean feminist movement throughout the 1920s and fostered an influential circle of feminists in Chile. In 1923 it was affiliated with the International Council of Women. The organization initiated a program calling for compulsory primary education, the establishment of a home for girl students who came to the capital to study, and the institution of laws protecting the civil and juridical rights of women. During the 1930s the NCW provided relief and health care to the unemployed and their wives and children in Chile. The NCW also collaborated with the government on prison reform and the protection of minors and initiated adult literacy programs.

From 1922, when she became the first woman to hold a university professorship, Labarca devised courses on education at the University of Chile. As a founding member that same year of the Pan-American Association for the Advancement of Women, Labarca traveled in the United States and studied education methods there. She wrote on a wide range of subjects, publishing several titles on education: *Secondary Schools in the United States* (1919), *History of Chilean Education* (1939), *Contemporary Feminism* (1940), and *Realities and Problems in Chilean Education* (1953). In 1928 she published *Feminine Activities in Chile,* in which she outlined her ideas on sex education. Labarca also contributed articles on Chilean working women in 1931 to the leading feminist journal in Chile, *We Women* (*Nosotras*), the journal of the Women's Union of Chile, and produced studies on women's education for the program of the umbrella group, the Movement for the Emancipation of the Women of Chile.

In 1933 Labarca drew attention to the anomalous situation regarding divorce, whereby the rich could buy religious annulments of marriages through subterfuge, but women who had legally separated from their husbands suffered the social stigma of public and religious disapproval, as did their children. She also brought to the fore the issues of illegitimacy and parental responsibility, arguing that men should not be allowed to ignore their financial responsibility for the children they fathered outside marriage.

Labarca led the campaign that finally achieved women's right to vote in municipal elections in 1934. That same year she also published *Whither Woman?* But she was not convinced that the political arena was the right place for women, fearing that their decency and moral sense would be corrupted if they forced themselves into such a fiercely competitive environment.

In 1937 Labarca became head of the editorial council of the journal *Women's Action,* the official organ of the Civic Women's Party that had been founded in 1922, and worked to defend the rights of indigenous people. She continued to be a regular participant in Latin American and pan-American scientific congresses. In 1944 at the first national congress of women in Chile, Labarca's years of keeping up the pressure resulted in a much broader base of support for the women's rights movement under her leadership of a newly amalgamated Federation of Women's Organizations. Her status as a preeminent woman in the campaigns for civil and social rights

was recognized in 1949, when Labarca became honorary president of Chile's National Council of Women, just after women in Chile finally won the vote in December 1938. From this date on, however, the feminist movement went into decline, with groups dwindling into discord among themselves and the percentage of women in government so diminished that by the time Salvador Allende came to power in 1970, only one woman was, briefly, a cabinet member.

References and Further Reading
Chaney, Elsa M. 1979. *Supermadre: Women in Politics in Latin America.* Austin: Institute of Latin American Studies, University of Texas Press.
Lavrin, Asunción. 1995. *Women, Feminism, and Social Change in Argentina, Chile, and Uruguay 1890–1940.* Lincoln: University of Nebraska Press.
Tenenbaum, Barbara A., ed. 1996. *Encyclopedia of Latin American History and Culture.* Vol 3. New York: Charles Scribner's Sons.

Lange, Helene
(1848–1930)
Germany

An educator and conservative feminist leader in Berlin, Helene Lange worked with Minna Cauer and Franziska Tiburtius to set up, in 1889, the first German educational institution, the Realkurse, to prepare women for university entrance. As a staunch believer that girls were intellectually capable of studying the same subjects as boys and were worthy of an education that did more than simply prepare them for marriage, she defended women's right to secondary and university education as an essential element of national, social, and moral reform. She felt that in their role as mothers, women had the most important and sacred of roles, as the educators of future generations. They should, therefore, "bring their unique talent to bear on the cultural evolution of humanity, which until now has onesidedly borne the stamp of men" (Joeres and Maynes 1986, 116–117).

Born in Oldenburg, the daughter of a merchant, Lange lost her mother at the age of six. After her father's death during her teens, she was brought up by maiden aunts and attended a private girls' school. Upon leaving school, Lange took a job as an au pair at a girls' boarding school in Alsace, teaching literature and grammar and studying French and music. She returned to Germany in 1867 as governess to the daughters of a rich industrialist in Osnabruck. In 1871, despite the reservations of her family, she was now old enough to study without their permission and moved to Berlin to fulfill her ambition of training as a teacher. After receiving her diploma, she taught privately and continued her own education, studying Latin and philosophy and attending lectures at the Victoria Lyceum, an institution founded in 1868 to give women access to higher education.

Lange arrived early at the conclusion that would lie at the heart of her later campaigning, that male teachers were not the best equipped to give moral instruction to adolescent girls and that the teaching profession should be opened up to women. In 1876, having obtained a post as director of a higher girls' school in Berlin, she began meeting with other educators, including Henriette and Franziska Tiburtius (both also women pioneers in dentistry and medicine, respectively). Eventually, Lange and her circle of supporters obtained the support of Crown Princess Victoria, Queen Victoria's eldest daughter and a keen advocate of women's education. In 1887 Lange published a pamphlet outlining her ideas, the "Yellow Brochure," which would provide the impetus for a concerted campaign to extend higher school education for German girls.

With other women, Lange petitioned the Prussian minister of education to allow women teachers to have a greater role in the education of girls in higher grades, most particularly in the teaching of German and religion, and also called for the establishment of an institute dedicated to the training of women teachers. She denigrated the traditional views that women's education was merely a preparation for marriage or that women should be deemed intellectually incapable of studying the same subjects as men and argued that male teachers taught too much factual knowledge and neglected "ethically oriented" subjects. Despite the fact that her views were met with derision, at the Victoria Lyceum Lange adapted the curriculum to offer more challenging courses. A visit to England in 1888 only reinforced Lange's view that the English system of girls' schools, which was mainly run by women, was far superior. The following year, with Franziska Tiburtius and Minna Cauer, Lange raised money to open the Realkurse in Berlin, a higher girls' school to prepare women for useful employment, which offered a two-year course in mathematics, science, economics, history, modern languages, and Latin. In 1893 another, more prestigious, classical four-year course offering Greek and Latin as well was inaugurated at the Realkurse, promoting it to a Gymnasialkurse, a type of school that took graduates from the higher girls' schools and prepared them for university entrance.

In 1890 Lange consolidated her work for women's education by founding, with Marie Stritt, the General German Women Teachers' Association, which would become one of the most important professional associations for German women. It lobbied on behalf of its 16,000 members (by the end of the nineteenth century) for wage parity between male and female teachers, the continuing expansion of the school curriculum, and the employment of more female teachers and school administrators. In 1893 Lange founded the journal *The Woman* with Gertrud Bäumer, which would become the leading organ of the women's movement in Germany.

In 1894 Lange tried to take over Minna Cauer's role in the Women's Welfare Association (established in 1888) and set up a new group in Berlin with Lily Braun. But by 1900 she was forced by ill health to give up her active leadership in the education movement, concentrating instead on compiling with Bäumer an ambitious *Handbook of the Women's Movement* (1901–1906). In 1908 the Prussian government finally allowed women who had completed their education at a recognized secondary institution to enter the universities, and Realkurse graduates were now no longer obliged to seek university education in Switzerland.

See also Bäumer, Gertrud; Braun, Lily; Cauer, Minna; Stritt, Marie; Tiburtius, Franziska.

References and Further Reading

Albisetti, James. 1982. "Could Separate Be Equal? Helene Lange and Women's Education in Imperial Germany." *History of Education Quarterly* (Fall): 301–318.

Joeres, Ruth-Ellen B., and Mary Jo Maynes, eds. 1986. *German Women in the Eighteenth and Nineteenth Centuries: A Social and Literary History.* Bloomington: Indiana University Press.

Sklar, Kathryn Kish. 1998. *Social Justice Feminists in the United States and Germany: A Dialogue in Documents 1885–1933.* Ithaca: Cornell University Press.

Lanteri-Renshaw, Julieta
(1873–1932)
Argentina

The socialist feminist founder and president of the National Feminist Union (NFU) of Argentina, who pioneered the women's suffrage movement in that country, Lanteri-Renshaw was a colorful and at times notorious figure who was in the first wave of women doctors to qualify in Argentina, along with Cecilia Grierson. Together with Grierson and María Abella de Ramírez, Lanteri-Renshaw guided the early activities of Argentine feminists, but her unrepentant individualism lost the movement support among more conservative elements.

Born in Italy, Lanteri-Renshaw went to Argentina at the age of six. She obtained a special permit—the first woman to do so—allowing her to enter the National College in La Plata, where she obtained a degree in pharmacology in 1898. She went on to earn her medical degree at the University of Buenos Aires in 1906 and took up a lectureship in mental illness and diseases affecting women and children. The all-pervading prejudice toward women in medicine at that time meant her attempt to be appointed professor of psychiatric ailments at the Medical School of the University of Buenos Aires was blocked.

In 1905 Lanteri-Renshaw became involved in the establishment of the Argentine Association of Free Thought (AAFT), a society that emphasized civil freedom above political emancipation. In 1908 she published *The Freethinking Woman,* and at a National Congress of Freethinkers that year, she spoke out in support of women's suffrage and their rights to own property as well as to have personal autonomy within marriage. Her independent position led her to found the National League of Women Freethinkers in 1909 in Buenos Aires and its associated journal, *The New Woman,* the following year.

Lanteri-Renshaw was granted Argentine citizenship in 1910 on her marriage to a fellow physician, Albert Renshaw, and was thus able to take up a post in the faculty of medicine at the university. Between 1907 and 1920, she made frequent visits to Europe to explore for herself the standards in hospitals, mental asylums, and schools. Armed with this information, she sought to implement health care reforms and in particular to improve the care of women, children, and unmarried mothers in Argentina. This she did by founding the League for the Rights of the Woman and the Child in 1911 in Buenos Aires, over which she presided and where she sought to encourage their welfare through legislation. In 1913 Lanteri-Renshaw was an organizer, along with other notable Argentine feminists—Alicia Moreau de Justo, Elvira Rawson de Dellepiane and Carolina Muzzilli—and president of the first Argentine National Congress on the Child.

By this time, disliking the right-wing philanthropy of the dominant women's group, the National Council of Women (established in 1900), Lanteri-Renshaw became involved in the more radical work of the Argentine Association of University Women and the Feminist Socialist Center. She continued to be a regular speaker at the Argentine Association for Free Thought meetings, where she took male members of her audiences to task for their continuing subordination of women. Eventually she became discontented with the line taken by the AAFT on universal suffrage; the majority of male members did not wish to fight simultaneous campaigns for male and female universal suffrage but were content to let women's suffrage wait until after universal male suffrage had been attained.

In 1918, Lanteri-Renshaw founded her own party, the National Feminist Union, and served as its president, leading a wide-reaching campaign for women's suffrage and civil and labor rights. In her frequent lectures, speeches, and publications, she urged the granting of the vote to women as essential official confirmation of their adulthood. Although she asserted the value of motherhood, Lanteri was determined that women's biological differences from men should not be the foundation for their exclusion from political life. And she made sure that she herself did not succumb to the discomforts of fashion by eschewing tight corsets and long, heavy skirts.

In 1919 Lanteri-Renshaw turned her attention to government and, in a test case, ran in local elections as a national deputy to the Argentine Congress. In March and November 1920 she stood as an unofficial candidate for government office with the support of the NFU's 3,000 members, in a mock election exercise to test women's political eligibility for the vote and gauge public support for women in politics. Under the law in Argentina at that time, all "citizens" were obliged to register for military service. Lanteri-Renshaw challenged the definition of "citizens" by calling for herself and other NFU members to be registered for military service. When this request was rejected, she argued that women could not, therefore, be technically classed as "citizens." After Lanteri-Renshaw made this challenge again in 1927, the Supreme Court refused to give an opinion on whether, in order to have the vote, women had to be classified as "citizens" (which in turn required them to undertake military service). Her actions aroused the antagonism of fellow reformer Alicia Moreau de Justo, who felt that Lanteri-Renshaw's political activities were self-seeking and that she should have more willingly subordinated herself to work with the NFU. Lanteri-Renshaw, however, did not wish to confine herself to women's issues and wanted to show that women could work with men in electoral campaigning. Much was made in the press of her electoral campaign, with papers such as the *Buenos Aires Herald* nominating her in March 1920 as "the Pankhurst of Argentina" (Carlson 1988, 159). An American suffragist, Katharine Dreier, who traveled to Buenos Aires to observe Lanteri-Renshaw's campaign remarked on her courage in dealing with abuse and hostility out on the streets and at an open-air rally for 2,000 people in March.

Lanteri-Renshaw's political program was ambitious: she called for universal suffrage and male-female equality under the civil code; for legislation in the workplace regulating working hours; for equal pay, pensions, maternity benefits, and protection of women and children workers; for professional training for women; and for specialist care for delinquent children, prison reform, and the abolition of capital punishment. As a doctor, she placed a strong emphasis on social hygiene and the introduction of efficient provisions against infectious diseases, for greater safety regulation in factories, and for bans on the manufacture and sale of alcohol.

But despite Lanteri-Renshaw's passionate commitment to a wide range of reform, she was greeted with overwhelming indifference from the population at large and had a poor showing in the election. Such a response was indicative of the general failure of women's groups in Argentina during this period to arouse a groundswell of popular support. As Narifran Carlson has pointed out, it needed a demagogue such as Juan Perón and a willing and iconic accomplice, his wife Eva, to touch a nerve with working-class people, especially women, and galvanize grassroots support for political change. Even though women such as Lanteri had been trying for years to persuade women of their own power to change things, it was ultimately Eva Perón who in the 1940s won over popular support. It is no wonder that the rise of Juan and Eva Perón filled Argentine feminists with despair and disillusion, for in the end the Argentine working classes responded to a cosmetic campaign staged by the Peróns where the committed reformers had failed. For a while Lanteri-Renshaw remained a popular figure; when she died in a car crash in May 1932, more than 1,000 people attended her funeral.

See also Abella de Ramírez, María; Grierson, Cecilia.
References and Further Reading
Carlson, Narifran. 1988. *Feminismo! The Woman's Movement in Argentina from Its Beginnings to Eva Perón.* Chicago: Academy Chicago Publications.
Lavrin, Asunción. 1995. *Women, Feminism, and Social Change in Argentina, Chile, and Uruguay 1890–1940.* Lincoln: University of Nebraska Press.

Laperrière de Coni, Gabriela
(1866–1906/1907)
Argentina

Together with her husband, Emilio, Gabriela Laperrière de Coni did innovative work in public health in the 1900s that led to legislation improving the lives of ordinary workers, particularly women and children, in Argentina. As a journalist, socialist, and public health activist, she became a founder of the Feminist Socialist Center run by the Argentine Socialist Party, and was the first woman to serve on the executive committee of the party, which had been founded in the 1890s. Laperrière's life was cut short by illness, but her influence was nevertheless considerable.

Born in Bordeaux, France, Laperrière worked as a schoolteacher and took up writing and journalism, contributing to several newspapers. Before she left France, she published a naturalistic novel about a female doctor striving to help sick children in a hospital. Her social conscience already aroused, she found a sympathetic partner in her husband, Dr. Emilio Coni, whom she married in Buenos Aires in 1899. He was a doctor and city council member thirty years her senior and a leading socialist involved in public health. Laperrière joined her husband in raising public awareness about health issues, many of them exacerbated by overcrowding and the spread of disease in the wake of industrialization and urban growth. Aware of the terrible toll of diseases such as tuberculosis and syphilis and the high levels of infant mortality, the couple took their proselytizing into the factories and tenement housing, as well as into the brothels of Buenos Aires.

As a convinced feminist, Laperrière dedicated herself to the defense of women. She felt they should be released from some of the burden of domestic duties and given better access to education in order to exercise greater control over their lives. She also defended their right to work in environments that were safe and free of disease. But as the twentieth century began, she involved herself more and more in politics. In 1900 she served as press secretary for the Argentine National Council of Women but gave up the post when she realized its objectives were not radical enough for her. In 1901 she organized a national peace conference and a year later founded a Pacifist League for factory workers.

In 1901 she also became the first factory inspector in Buenos Aires, when the mayor, possibly at her husband's suggestion (he was a member of the city's Board of Health), appointed Laperrière to undertake research on factory conditions for women and children. She was appalled by what she saw: women and children working in cramped, badly lit, and poorly ventilated rooms, often forced to adopt constricting and uncomfortable work positions that she felt would deform them physically and even cause infertility. She put forward suggestions to the National Congress on protective legislation for workers, with the emphasis on protecting women's physical potential as mothers and more generally combating the worrying incidence of tuberculosis.

Laperrière's completed survey had four parts, the first of which was published in November 1901. In it, she reported on the filthy and polluted conditions in which some workers, including children as young as age ten, worked. The eighteen specific recommendations of her study gave weight to a 1902 proposal for new legislation relating to women and child workers. Its main suggestions were that children under fourteen should not be allowed to work in factories unless they had been vaccinated against smallpox and that they should only work a six-hour day. Women and children over the age of eighteen should only work eight hours between 6 A.M. and 6 P.M. and should have Sundays off; they should not undertake work involving heavy machinery. Women who were breastfeeding children should have a space set aside for them to do so in factories. Laperrière recommended the introduction of maternity leave and also raised the moral issue of the kind of factories and workplaces to which women and children should be exposed, suggesting that they should be excluded from certain kinds of dangerous work. Some of Laperrière's recommendations were taken up in 1904 in legislation known as the "Alfredo Palacios Law" (named after the socialist deputy who had submitted Laperrière's suggestions to the Chamber of Deputies); it became law in 1907.

In addition to her work inspecting factories, Laperrière became a popular speaker on public health issues such as hygiene and nutrition. She was a prominent campaigner on the dangers of tuberculosis and its causes, which she listed as "alcoholism, unhealthy habitation, poor nourishment, excessive physical, mental or moral labor, and poor hygiene" (Guy 1989, 243). Women who worked long hours in the factories as well as performing domestic tasks in the home and enduring often unwanted pregnancies were particularly vulnerable. Laperrière founded the Argentine Anti-Tuberculosis League in 1901 and published articles in which she suggested women should be relieved of some of the cooking at home by setting up soup kitchens for workers near factories, a suggestion that eventually resulted in the establishment of some subsidized restaurants.

By 1902 Laperrière had extended her activities to mediate in labor disputes. She cofounded the Feminist Socialist Center and began organizing women workers, such as dressmakers, telephone operators, and cigarette rollers, to call for better working conditions through the Women's Labor Union established by Fenia Chertkoff de Repetto. She defended the right of 800 women workers in an espadrille factory to work an eight-hour day, but her campaigning was stymied by the unwillingness of management to negotiate with someone who was not a member of the workforce. By this time, Laperrière had come to the conclusion that women and children would do better to leave the factories altogether, in the somewhat idealistic if not naive belief that since they had no bargaining power with their employers, they should proudly withdraw their labor. She believed it was better for them to live in penury than allow themselves to be exploited.

Information on Laperrière's life becomes very sketchy after 1904. At this point, she left her husband to marry her lover, syndicalist leader Julio Arraga, which led to her ostracization by the Socialist Party and would condemn her to the footnotes of the early history of Argentine feminism. In the saddest of ironies, she herself succumbed to tuberculosis, a highly infectious disease that she had probably caught during her public health campaigning. But her work had not been for nothing: it was taken up by other health care pioneers such as Carolina Muzzilli, who would later produce public health programs to combat tuberculosis.

See also Chertkoff de Repetto, Fenia; Muzzilli, Carolina.

References and Further Reading

Carlson, Narifran. 1988. *Feminismo! The Woman's Movement in Argentina from Its Beginnings to Eva Perón*. Chicago: Academy Chicago Publications.

Guy, Donna J. 1989. "Emilio and Gabriela de Coni: Reformers, Public Health and Working Women." In William Beezley and Judith Ewell, eds., *The Human Tradition in Latin America: The Nineteenth Century*. Wilmington, DE: Scholarly Resources.

Lavrin, Asunción. 1995. *Women, Feminism, and Social Change in Argentina, Chile, and Uruguay 1890–1940*. Lincoln: University of Nebraska Press.

Tenenbaum, Barbara A., ed. 1996. *Encyclopedia of Latin American History and Culture*. Vol. 2. New York: Charles Scribner's Sons.

Lathrop, Julia
(1858–1932)
United States

In her work through the U.S. Children's Bureau and her advocacy of separate care for the mentally ill, Julia Lathrop was one of a gifted and devoted group of women who pioneered social work from the 1890s at Hull House in Chicago. She went on to devote forty years of her life to the advancement of women's role in government and to social reforms at the federal level.

Born in Rockford, Illinois, Lathrop was imbued with a sense of social justice and women's rights by her suffragist mother and her Republican lawyer father. Educated at Rockford Seminary and then at Vassar College, she graduated in 1880. She then worked for ten years as a secretary in her father's law office and, eventually, at the age of thirty-two, decided to put into practice her growing interest in social causes. In 1890 she joined Jane Addams at Hull House in Chicago, the beginning of a close association that would last for twenty years.

During the economic depression of 1892, Lathrop was already investigating the social conditions of those seeking relief in the Hull House district, when her work came to the attention of the Illinois Board of Public Charities, which appointed her its first woman inspector (1893–1901, 1905–1909). She took time out during the winter of 1893–1894 to conduct an exhausting survey of the hospitals, asylums, and almshouses in Cook County, later contributing much of this evidence to the important social document, *Hull House Maps and Papers* (1895).

Lathrop's research in Cook County alerted her to the misery suffered by the mentally ill in public institutions, and like another similar pioneer, Dorothea Lynde Dix, she advocated the care of these people within special-purpose institutions rather than their incarceration in prisons along with the sick and the elderly. In order to broaden her knowledge, she studied methods of extramural care of the insane on trips to Europe in 1898 and 1900, publishing her ideas in *Suggestions for Visitors to County Poorhouses and to Other Public Charitable Institutions* (1905). In 1909 she joined Clifford W. Beers's National Committee for Mental Hygiene, having by then twice resigned from the Illinois Board of Public Charity in protest at its mismanagement and its failure to reform its methods of staffing state institutions.

As a result of her observations of the care of the mentally ill, Lathrop became convinced of the need to improve nursing care and worked toward acceptance of women doctors and nurses in state hospitals and asylums, as well as improvements in the training of caretakers for state institutions, by becoming a founder and later trustee of the Chicago Institute of Social Science in 1903–1904, where she set up the first courses in the new discipline of social work and was a regular lecturer in the initial stages. These classes were further developed in 1908, when the institute was renamed the Chicago School of Civics and Philanthropy (which in 1920 then became the School of Social Service Administration of the University of Chicago) under the auspices of Sophonisba Breckinridge and Edith Abbott in the training of social workers; Lathrop was later president of the National Conference of Social Work. In 1908 the three women also founded the Immigrants' Protective League, in which Lathrop remained active until her death, and in 1922 she served on a commission to investigate conditions for immigrants arriving at the reception center on Ellis Island, New York.

Lathrop's firsthand observations in Cook County had also led her to lobby for the establishment of a juvenile court. The first such court was established in Chicago in 1899, across the road from Hull House. Lathrop organized a Juvenile Court Committee to raise money to pay the salaries of probation officers who would follow the rehabilitation efforts for juveniles. She later described her work in *The Child, the Clinic and the Court* (1925).

The latter part of Lathrop's career was taken up with reform of infant health care and child labor, after she was appointed head of the newly established Children's Bureau by President William Howard Taft in 1912. As a subsidiary of the Department of Commerce and Labor, the bureau pioneered studies of the rates of illegitimacy and infant and maternal mortality (which led to the introduction of birth registration), nutrition, child labor, juvenile delinquency, and pensions for mothers. The major task of the Children's Bureau was to enforce the measures protecting child workers under the 1916 Keating-Owen Child Labor Act, but the law was declared unconstitutional in 1918 by the Supreme Court, as an infringement of state laws. Lathrop turned her energies to achieving the passage in 1921 of the first building block in the United States' new social welfare program, the Sheppard-Towner Maternity and Infancy Protection Act.

Lathrop was forced to resign from the Children's Bureau in 1921 because of ill health, having by that time garnered huge public support and offers of help for the work of the agency, particularly as a result of its sterling efforts in assisting poor, pregnant, and nursing women in remote rural areas and advising them on child rearing. She was succeeded by the equally able and energetic Edith Abbott but remained a supporter of its work until her death. From 1922 to 1924, she served as president of the Illinois League of Women Voters. She was also a member of the Child Welfare Committee of the League of Nations from 1925 to 1932.

See also Abbott, Edith; Addams, Jane; Dix, Dorothea Lynde.

References and Further Reading

Addams, Jane. 1935. *My Friend, Julia Lathrop.* New York: Macmillan.

Davis, Allen F. 1967. *Spearheads for Reform: The Social Settlements and the Progressive Movement 1890–1914.* New York: Oxford University Press.

Frankel, Noralee, and Nancy S. Dye. 1991. *Gender, Class, Race, and Reform in the Progressive Era.* Lexington: University of Kentucky Press.

Lindenmeyer, Kriste. 1997. *"A Right to Childhood": The U.S. Children's Bureau and Child Welfare, 1912–1946.* Urbana: University of Illinois Press.

Marchand, C. Roland. 1972. *The American Peace Movement and Social Reform, 1898–1918.* Princeton: Princeton University Press.

Tobey, James A. 1925. *The Children's Bureau: Its History, Activities and Organization.* Baltimore: Johns Hopkins University Press.

Lawson, Louisa
(1848–1920)
Australia

The Australian feminist and suffragist Louisa Lawson, a founding mother of the movement in that country, is also remembered as a pioneer of women's journalism through her publication *The Dawn* (1888–1905), which was staffed and produced by women. As an outspoken patriot who had lived in the outback, she was unqualified in her respect for other Australian women—albeit only the white ones—who had also struggled in the face of cultural repression and political disenfranchisement and "braved the bush for strenuous years / To make Australia's name" (Lake 1999, 22).

Lawson was the daughter of a first-generation Australian immigrant and was born on a station at Guntawang in the outback of New South Wales. She attended the local national school at Mudgee. When she was fifteen, her family moved to the goldfields at Gulgong, where she worked in the family's store and boardinghouse and helped looked after her eleven siblings. In 1866, in order to escape the drudgery of home life and her father's hard drinking, she married a Norwegian gold prospector, Neils Hertzberg Larsen, who later anglicized the name to Lawson. Her married life was tough, with Lawson living and giving birth to seven children (of whom only four survived) in a series of makeshift bark huts in the goldfields of New South Wales. Eventually, they established a homestead of sorts on land at Eurunderee. But her husband was frequently away from home for long stretches, working as a carpenter. Miserable and impoverished, Lawson suffered a desperate sense of isolation, which, compounded by her husband's improvidence, aroused her feminist consciousness.

In 1883, unable to tolerate her unhappy marriage any longer, Lawson left her husband and took their children to Marrickville, in Sydney, where she supported them as a seamstress, took in washing, and ran a boardinghouse. She made new friends at the Progressive Spiritualist Lyceum, where she was first introduced to suffragists. She remained a woman of puritan values, painfully aware of the suffering of women trapped in unhappy marriages with drunken and abusive husbands. Therefore, divorce and custody rights were a major issue for her. Lawson was determined to liberate women from domestic drudgery and degradation and lives of unrewarded self-sacrifice and sought to raise their levels of independence, their powers of wage-earning, and their self-respect.

In 1887, already having dabbled with writing patriotic verse, Lawson bought a journal, the *Republican*, which she edited with her son Henry (also a notable Australian poet), calling for Australian independence from British rule. A year later, she set up Australia's first feminist journal, *The Dawn*, which she ran and edited for seventeen years, using an all-woman editorial and printing team (against which male trade unionists made strong objections). In addition to offering a range of household advice, the journal published short stories and gave the debate on suffrage center stage. It promoted dress reform and legal changes to enhance women's rights in marriage, custody of their children, and their own property. *The Dawn* attracted a wide readership and made money. By 1890 it had 2,000 subscribers, many of them overseas, and Lawson employed ten women in its production.

A women's suffrage group called the Dawn Club followed in 1889 as an offshoot of the magazine and was intended as a forum for women's mutual development and aid, advocating dress reform and temperance, social purity, protective legislation for women and children, and women's education. Lawson was a passionate advocate of women's right to work, as she herself had demonstrated, urging that girls should be better equipped through education to earn their living and be given the opportunity to enter professional work—for example, as prison warders, doctors, magistrates, and factory inspectors. In 1891 the group transferred its activities to Dora Montefiore and Rose Scott's Womanhood Suffrage League, which demanded women's equal voting rights with men; Lawson was elected to its council. That year *The Dawn* published one of the first recorded public speeches on women's suffrage, in which Lawson argued categorically that the enfranchisement of women would make for a better and nobler society. She frequently allowed the editorial offices of *The Dawn* to be used for suffrage meetings and did some of the league's printing, but after suffering from physical strain and becoming disheartened by the ousting of her friend Lady Mary Windeyer from the presidency, Lawson resigned in 1893. In 1901 she joined a rival suffrage group, the Women's Progressive Association, publicizing its activities in *The Dawn* in support of women's appointment to public office.

A tram accident in 1900 left Lawson with permanent injuries and coincided with a legal dispute over a patent and a decline in her financial fortunes. Her impaired health forced the closure of *The Dawn*, which was also in decline, in 1905. Lawson lived in poverty for the rest of her life, making a little money from publication of her poetry and short stories but dying alone and embittered in the New Hospital for the Insane in Gladesville, New South Wales, in 1920. She suffered the fate of many other feminist pioneers: until her rediscovery by the second wave of feminists, her subsequent posthumous reputation was built largely on the fact that she had been the mother of Australia's more famous poet, Henry Lawson.

See also Montefiore, Dora; Scott, Rose.
References and Further Reading
Fry, Eric, ed. 1983. *Rebels and Radicals.* Sydney: Allen and Unwin.

Lake, Marilyn. 1999. *Getting Equal: The History of Australian Feminism.* London: Allen and Unwin.

Lawson, Olive, ed. 1990. *The First Voice of Australian Feminism: Excerpts from Louisa Lawson's* The Dawn *1888–1895.* Brookvale, NSW: Simon and Schuster.

Matthews, Brian. 1987. *Louisa.* Melbourne: McPhee Gribble Publishers.

Midgely, Clare. 1998. *Gender and Imperialism.* Manchester: Manchester University Press.

Oldfield, Audrey. 1992. *Woman Suffrage in Australia: A Gift or a Struggle?* Melbourne: Cambridge University Press.

Ollif, Lorna. 1978. *Louisa Lawson: Henry Lawson's Crusading Mother.* Adelaide: Rigby.

Pearson, Sharyn. 1992. *The Shameless Scribbler: Louisa Lawson.* London: Sir Robert Menzies Centre for Australian Studies.

Lee Tai-Young
(1914–1998)
Korea

The Korean lawyer Lee Tai-Young is an outstanding role model and revered figure for Korean women. As the country's first female lawyer and later its first female judge and as the founder of Korea's first legal aid center in 1956, she almost single-handedly provided a much-overdue advice and counseling facility for thousands of distressed and needy women and lobbied tirelessly for extensive revisions to Korean family law. She achieved her legal qualification while raising four children on her own during her husband's imprisonment and suffered persecution herself under the repressive regime of the 1970s. A devout Christian, Lee Tai-Young dedicated her life to the ideals of service to women and the community, and was a lifelong defender of democracy and a reunified Korea.

Lee was a third-generation Methodist, born in Pukjin in the mountains of northwestern Korea, a gold-mining area that had attracted Chinese, Japanese, and U.S. prospectors. Her father, who worked in the Pukjin Gold Mine, was killed in a mining accident when she was a baby, leaving her hardworking mother to bring up her three children alone. Lee was educated at Kwang Dong Primary School in Pukjin and was a regular attendee of the local Sunday school. A bright and extraordinarily forthright child, at the age of only seven she took part in a speaking contest, choosing as her title "I Am a Girl" and asserting, in what was then an extremely chauvinistic society, the rights of girls to do what boys did. When she was older, she entered a similar competition, winning first prize for a speech that challenged "Why Aren't Girls Given an Education?"

After the family moved to Youngbyun, where Lee attended a Methodist school, she came under the influence of her missionary teachers. At the age of thirteen, she left home, after excelling in the entrance exams, to attend Chung-Eui High School on Pyongyang and was already nursing an ambition to become a lawyer. There, she was elected president of the student Young Women's Christian Association (YWCA) and began a lifelong affiliation with the movement. After graduating in 1931, Lee returned to Youngbyun, where her mother was already planning an arranged marriage. But Lee had set her sights on further education and in 1932 took the entrance examination for Ewha Women's College (now a university), the first establishment of its kind for Korean women. She majored in home economics, but she was determined to do something to improve the lot of women confined to the domestic sphere and began privately studying law.

In 1935 Lee took part in the first All-Korea Woman Student's Speaking Contest, where she spoke on women's liberation from domesticity, choosing as her topic "The Second Nora," inspired by Henrik Ibsen's play *A Doll's House.* In her speech she was highly critical of the submissiveness of Korean women, who in her opinion behaved as little more than domestic dolls, and advocated that they should eject the men who oppressed them rather than leave home as Nora did. After her graduation in 1936, Lee taught economics and piano at the Pyongyang Women's Bible College. Still resisting the idea of marriage, she became involved in women's issues, taking a particular interest in the social position of the *kisaeng* (the Korean equivalent of the Japanese geisha) and studying them at their training school in Pyongyang. Sympathetic to what she saw as the *kisaeng*'s loss of selfhood—many of them had been forced to take up their work to help support their families—she listened to their stories and became even more determined to help these and other oppressed women through the channels of the law.

At this time, Lee had begun helping a

Methodist minister, Chyung Yil-Hyung, who was doing social work among the poor in Pyongyang's industrial wasteland at Sinlee. She helped at his summer camp and taught Bible school, and he in turn encouraged her desire to return to her studies. They married in October 1936 but lived in very straitened circumstances, with few possessions. Chyung was closely involved with the Korean independence movement and during their years together would suffer persecution for this and his Christian beliefs. Meanwhile, the couple settled in Seoul, where Lee taught in a girls' high school. After the Japanese attack on Pearl Harbor in 1941 and the declaration of war between Japan and the United States, the political situation in Korea tightened, and in 1945 Lee's husband was detained without trial by the Japanese on a charge of subversion and was imprisoned for five years. Lee took on extra work as a seamstress in order to support her children, making and selling quilts and opening a small store.

At the end of World War II and after her husband's release, she finally entered Seoul National University at the age of thirty-two as its first woman student. She was also the first woman to graduate from that institution with a degree in jurisprudence, in 1949. Meanwhile, Korea was once again the scene of political conflict, and after the Korean War of 1950–1953, the country was divided into two separate states: South Korea and the communist-backed North Korea. Despite having four children, Lee successfully passed her judicial qualification and obtained a master's degree in 1957 at Seoul National University (in South Korea), presenting a thesis on divorce. Meanwhile, she had already set up her own independent law office, where she rapidly became aware of the huge demand for women lawyers to offer counseling and advice to Korean women seeking release from unhappy marriages. In South Korea at that time, women were greatly discriminated against under existing laws and were traditionally brought up under the Confucian principles of the "three obediences"—to father, husband, and son. Determined to fight the patriarchal customs that subordinated women and left them powerless, Lee worked to make legal counseling more widely available and in 1956 founded the Women's Legal Counseling Center.

The center was an immediate success, and Lee soon extended its work to help men as well as women, changing its name to the Korean Legal Aid Center for Family Relations. By 1966 it had relocated to bigger premises and had a staff of 20, backed up by 470 volunteers, who offered legal advice to about 80 people a day. It even offered a free wedding ceremony to those who could not afford one. Lee's 1958 booklet, "100 Questions and Answers about Legal Counseling Cases for Women," was updated and expanded, incorporating her outlines for revision of Korean family law, and was republished in 1976 as *What Can I Do?*

In 1963 Lee accepted the post of dean of the law college of Ewha University, with a view to encouraging more women to take up legal training. Over the next eight years, she instituted radical changes to the curriculum, devising a program of clinical legal education for women students and sending students out into the field to monitor legal work. In 1971 she resigned to work for her husband's political candidacy in upcoming elections but continued to fund-raise for the purchase of a bigger, permanent home for the constantly growing Korean Legal Aid Center, for which land was eventually bought on Yoi Island. Work was completed on the One Hundred Women's Building (named after its major subscribers) at the end of 1976, and the new premises offered a nursery, auditorium, and library, as well as counseling rooms.

The opening of the Korean Legal Aid Center had reinforced Lee's conviction that all the counseling in the world would not help if the Korean legal system, which upheld the sexual double standard, was not reformed. In the late 1950s, she and other women had begun to petition for changes, lobbying the Ministry of Justice and the National Assembly to revise family law to match the standards of the Constitution of the Republic of Korea (i.e., South Korea), by putting an end to sexual discrimination. Thanks to the campaigning of Lee and other Korean feminists, revisions to the family law were introduced in 1957 and finally became effective in January 1960. They abolished the obligation of married women to seek the approval of their husbands in bringing legal actions, reduced the age until which parental consent was required for marriage to twenty-seven for men and to twenty-three for women, allowed women and men equal grounds to divorce and equal rights in the adoption of children, and granted married women the right to inherit property.

In 1973 Lee was central to the founding of the Pan-Korean Women's Group to Promote the Revision of the Family Law, an umbrella organization of sixty-one women's groups dedicated to reform that launched a concerted propaganda drive on radio, on TV, and in the press. Further reforms came with another revision of the family law in January 1979, which permitted women to inherit an equal share of family wealth with males, provided a definition of joint married property and equal parental rights, reduced the age for parental consent to marriage to twenty, and allowed divorce by mutual agreement.

By the time of the twenty-fifth anniversary of the Korean Legal Aid Center in 1981, Lee had achieved many of her major objectives: the introduction of preventive educational programs, legal literacy for all, family law reform, and the drafting of a family charter. But she was a woman who never for one moment stood still. Beginning in the 1970s, she had taken a stand on human rights issues in Korea, serving as vice chair of the Human Rights Committee of the Korean National Council of Churches and taking charge of a team of human rights lawyers. With Kim Chong-Rye, she founded the Citizens' Association for the Restoration of Democracy in 1975 and spoke out against emergency measures in South Korea in 1976. She was one of a group of eminent Koreans, including her husband, who on calling for the restoration of democracy were arrested and put on trial. Although her sentence of three years in jail was suspended, she was disbarred for ten years. No longer allowed to give legal advice at her center, Lee accepted a speaking tour in the United States in 1979. After the coup d'état in South Korea that year, she suffered further political oppression under the dictatorship of General Doo Hwan Chun. She would die still longing for the reunification of Korea.

During her long career, Lee Tai-Young traveled to the United States, Europe, Africa, and the Middle East, attending functions such as the World Peace Through Law conference in Belgrade in 1971, where she won the conference award; the Moral Rearmament Conference in Geneva; the World YWCA Convention in Ghana; and the International Federation of Women Lawyers Conference in Israel. She was the recipient of many legal awards, including the International Legal Aid Association Award in 1978 and the World Methodist Peace Award in 1984, and

was made an honorary doctor of law at Drew University in Madison, New Jersey, in 1981. In 1975 she received what has been dubbed the "Asian Peace Prize"—the Ramón Magsaysay Award—"for effective service to the cause of equal juridical rights for the liberation of Korean women" (Strawn 1988, 211).

Lee was the author of fifteen books on women's issues, including *The Divorce System in Korea* (1957), *Commonsense in Law for Women* (1972), *Women of North Korea* (1979, expanded 1988), and *Born a Woman* (1987). A great admirer of the social reforms of Eleanor Roosevelt, she translated Roosevelt's 1958 book, *On My Own*, into Korean (1964). Lee also published a volume of memoirs, *Dipping the Han River out with a Gourd* (1984); its title alluded to a Korean saying that expresses in metaphor the huge wellspring of human need and the small contribution she felt that she had made. With eloquence, Lee Tai-Young summed up her mission as having been to "build a dam which can produce energy and power to lighten the darkened corners of society and reinvigorate its stalled and rusty engines" (Strawn 1988, 225). Lee Tai-Young's story has received virtually no attention outside South Korea. The generosity of Seunghee Han in sending me a copy of Sonia Reed Strawn's book from Seoul is gratefully acknowledged.

References and Further Reading
Strawn, Sonia Reid. 1988. *Where There Is No Path: Lee Tai-Young, Her Story.* Seoul: Korea Legal Aid Center for Family Relations.

Lind-af-Hageby, Louise
(1878–1963)
Sweden/United Kingdom

In 1903 and again in 1913, the Swedish-born antivivisectionist Louise Lind-af-Hageby was at the center of an extremely contentious debate between animal rights campaigners and the medical establishment in Britain. For many years after, she was an important figure in the campaign in England, dominated by women activists, to defend animals against the inhuman practices of medical experimentation, adding her voice to the debate that had been pioneered by Frances Power Cobbe and Anna Kingsford before her.

Despite the fact that she was active in the animal rights movement until the 1950s, details have yet to emerge of Lind-af-Hageby's early life and career. It is known that she came from a wealthy Swedish family in Stockholm, prominent in the nobility, and was the granddaughter of the chamberlain of Sweden. She was educated at one of England's top girls' schools—Cheltenham Ladies College—afterwards studying (c. 1900) in Paris for a while, before returning to the United Kingdom. She was provided by her family with a private income that sustained her subsequent years of activism, first in the suffrage and social purity movements as a member of the Women's Freedom League, and her increasing and vigorous support for many animal rights organizations, such as the Humanitarian League.

Lind-af-Hageby found herself first in the public eye in 1903, when she and a Swedish friend, Liese Schartau, published *The Shambles of Science: Extracts from the Diary of Two Students of Physiology,* in which they detailed their observations of painful experiments they had witnessed on an unanesthetized terrier dog over a period of two months at University College in London. They had originally enrolled in physiology classes at the London School of Medicine for Women in 1902, but upon discovering that it did not permit vivisection, obtained permission to attend lectures at University College, which was known to be a center for animal experimentation in Britain. Like Anna Kingsford before her, Lind-af-Hageby had taken up scientific study with the objective of being able to expose the practices of vivisection, which she first witnessed on the terrier dog on 2 February 1903. In their book, Lind-af-Hageby and Schartau condemned what they perceived as the relish with which the vivisection had been undertaken by Dr. William Bayliss, the professor concerned, which they felt discredited the entire medical profession. In exposing the techniques used on the dog, Lind-af-Hageby and her promoter, Stephen Coleridge of the National Anti-Vivisection Society, were sued for libel by Bayliss, who won the case and was awarded damages of £2,000.

The fact that they lost the case mattered little to Lind-af-Hageby in comparison to the huge publicity it had attracted, in both the national and the medical press, which contributed directly to the establishment in 1906 of the Second Royal Commission on Vivisection, at which Lind-af-Hageby gave evidence. Many suffragists were also dedicated vegetarians and animal

rights campaigners and had come out in strong support of Lind-af-Hageby and Schartau. After the libel case, subscriptions were raised to erect a drinking fountain with a statue—the Old Brown Dog, as it became known—at the Latchmere Recreation Ground in a working-class district of Battersea. It was unveiled in 1906, in memory not just of the terrier dog whose sufferings had been the inspiration for *The Shambles of Science* but also of 232 other dogs that protesters claimed had been vivisected in the medical school that year. The monument quickly became the symbol of the animal rights movement and a rallying point for both campaigners, nicknamed "browndoggers," and their opponents; in November 1907 a group of medical students intent upon wrecking the monument were arrested after a scuffle with police. The monument was promoted in a pamphlet titled "The Old Brown Dog and His Memorial" and in several popular songs of the time, and local trade unionists in Battersea rallied to the defense of the antivivisectionists in protecting it from attack and defacement. Over the next three years, antivivisectionists and vivisectionists (mainly medical students) frequently clashed in heated public meetings and debates over the statue's removal; by March 1910 the authorities had had enough, and the statue was removed by Battersea Council. In 1985 a fund-raising campaign was mounted by animal rights campaigners to replace it. Lind-af-Hageby retained her connections with Battersea as a member of the board of the Battersea Anti-vivisection Hospital, established for the free treatment of the poor and working classes. Her objection to medical experimentation on animals also extended to humans and in line with the hospital's policy, she opposed compulsory vaccination.

Although Lind-af-Hageby was obliged by the court decision of 1903 to withdraw the libelous edition of *The Shambles of Science* and take out the offending passages, she replaced them with an account of the trial and republished the book later that year. It was reprinted four more times in the next ten years, while uncensored copies were still surreptitiously sold. In 1906 Lind-af-Hageby was a cofounder with Nina, duchess of Hamilton and Brandon, of the Animal Defence and Anti-Vivisection Society (ADAVS). (It is notable that the movement attracted a considerable number of upper-class ladies with titles.) It was by no means the first society of its kind; similar societies had been set up in Britain as early as the mid-1870s under the impetus of Frances Power Cobbe, who, like many feminist supporters of the cause, drew clear analogies between the abuse of women by medical practitioners and that of animals. Lind-af-Hageby remained totally dedicated to her work, organizing numerous antivivisection demonstrations and rallies from 1906 to 1912 and covering reform of slaughterhouse practices in the *Anti-Vivisection Review,* of which she was editor, beginning in 1909 and continuing for many years.

In 1906 Lind-af-Hageby published the pamphlet "Is Vivisection Morally Justifiable and Necessary to Science and Humanitarianism?" and in 1906 and again in 1907 took part in public debates on vivisection, with Dr. W. D. Halliburton, professor of physiology at King's College, and with Dr. B. J. Collingwood, demonstrator of physiology at St. Mary's Hospital. The proceedings of both were published as ADAVS pamphlets. She also served as secretary of the British Section of the International Medical Anti-Vivisection Association and was the instigator and organizer of its July 1909 congress in London, which drew distinguished delegates from around the world.

In 1912 Lind-af-Hageby took British citizenship. A year later, she was involved in another expensive libel case, pleading her own case during a sixteen-day action against the *Pall Mall Gazette.* It had come about as the result of an exhibition of antivivisection propaganda set up by Lind-af-Hageby, as secretary of ADAVS, in a shop in London's Picadilly. The display of graphic photographs and diagrams of vivisection attracted crowds of horrified onlookers; it had been written up in a disparaging article in the May 1912 issue of the *Pall Mall Gazette* by Dr. Caleb Williams Saleeby, who had accused the ADAVS of mounting a "systematic campaign of falsehood" against the medical profession. Lind-af-Hageby lost her libel action against Saleeby and the proprietors of the *Pall Mall Gazette,* but even the *British Medical Journal,* in reporting the case in its 26 April 1913 issue, applauded her "marvellous power" and her ability to "stand in court day after day showing no sign of fatigue, not losing her temper and able to cross examine as well as any counsel at the bar" (917–918). The *Lancet* also commended her eloquence and dexterity with legal arguments. At the end of the trial, the

medical profession went away content that it had been vindicated; the gallant Lind-af-Hageby, left to pay the costs, was feted at a grand vegetarian dinner held in her honor.

During World War I, Lind-af-Hageby was a committed pacifist and a member of the International Committee of Women for Permanent Peace, established in The Hague in 1915. She lectured against militarism and published "Mountain Meditations, and Some Subjects of the Day and War" in 1917. She became greatly distressed by the sufferings of animals in war, particularly horses on the battlefield, and at a Conference on the Pacifist Philosophy of Life in July 1915, she urged the founding of a rescue service for animals in wartime. The ADAVS subsequently set up veterinary hospitals for sick and wounded horses, and Lind-af-Hageby went to France to promote animal welfare, as well as to undertake humanitarian aid—in 1916 opening a sanatorium for wounded French soldiers at Carqueiranne in the south of France. During the 1920s, she continued to propagandize for peace in pamphlets such as "Be Peacemakers. An Appeal to Women of the Twentieth Century to Remove the Causes of War" (1924). She protested cruel sports, such as the hunting of pregnant hares by schoolboys at Eton, as a supporter of the Our Dumb Friends' League; opposed the trade in old horses for slaughter; and during World War II again expressed her concern for the animal victims of war in an ADAVS pamphlet, "Bombed Animals—Rescued Animals—Animals Saved from Destruction: Typical Cases from the Records of the Animal Defence Society's War Work and Some Comment" (1941).

In 1950 Lind-af-Hageby attended The Hague World Congress for the Protection of Animals and is last recorded as purchasing the duchess of Hamilton's Ferne Estate in Dorset in 1954, which she turned into an animal sanctuary.

See also Cobbe, Frances Power; Kingsford, Anna.
References and Further Reading
Bekoff, Marc, ed. 1998. *The Encyclopedia of Animal Rights and Animal Welfare.* London: Fitzroy Dearborn.
Kean, Hilda. 1998. *Animal Rights: Political and Social Change in Britain since 1800.* London: Reaktion Books.
Lind-af-Hageby, Louise, and Liese K. Schartau. 1903. *The Shambles of Science: Extracts from the Diary of Two Students of Physiology.* London: Ernest Bell.

Rupke, Nicolaas A. 1987. *Vivisection in Historical Perspective*. London: Routledge.

Vyvyan, John. 1971. *The Dark Face of Science*. London: Michael Joseph.

Linton, Eliza Lynn
(1822–1898)
United Kingdom

The novelist and essayist Eliza Lynn Linton is generally acknowledged as the first woman in England to earn her living by journalism. Although she expressed feminist views in her early novels, she became one of the most dedicated and vocal of antifeminists, producing, in 1868, a much contested essay, "The Girl of the Period," on the arguments for and against women's emancipation. In her lambasting of what she saw as the self-seeking and mercenary behavior of her female contemporaries, Linton called for a return to the uncontroversial and unchallenging "womanly" virtues of sweetness, domesticity, and acquiescence.

Linton was the youngest of the twelve children of a vicar of strict conservative outlook and grew up at Keswick in the Lake District. Her mother died when she was a baby, and in her early life she felt deeply lonely and unloved. Her father paid little attention to her educational needs; she was mainly self-taught, learning to speak French, Italian, German, and Spanish. Her introspection and isolation combined with the austerity of her home life led Linton to become religious in her late teens, but religious obsession turned to loss of faith and eventual breakdown. In 1855 she resolved to leave home and go to London to pursue a writing career. Living in extremely reduced circumstances, she produced her first novel, *Azeth the Egyptian*, in 1846, a historical story based on her research in the British Museum. *Amynone*, set in ancient Greece, followed in 1848. But the novels were not successful enough to provide an income, and Linton turned to journalism in 1849, working for the *Morning Chronicle* (1849–1851) and publishing stories in Charles Dickens's journal *All the Year Round*. For a while, she moved in radical, freethinking circles, associating with Walter Savage Landor, George Henry Lewes, and Dickens before leaving for Paris in 1851, where she spent the next three years working as a foreign correspondent.

Eliza finally married in 1858; her husband, William Linton, was an engraver and a widower with seven children. After her marriage, Linton tried to set herself up in a literary salon, but her modest inheritance was run through by her husband, and the marriage failed soon after, although the couple never divorced. Linton turned once again to fiction, producing a string of novels that in various ways dealt with women's issues. *Grasp Your Nettle* (1865) discussed the difficulties of rural life for women, and *Sowing the Wind* (1867) described an unhappy marriage. *The True History of Joshua Davidson, Christian and Communist* (1872) and *The Atonement of Leam Dundas* (1877) were particularly well regarded.

By the end of the 1860s, Linton had become highly critical of the younger generation, a fact demonstrated after she joined the staff of the *Saturday Review,* a forum for antifeminist writing. Linton published the first of a series of essays on women entitled "The Girl of the Period" in the 14 March 1868 issue. In it, she condemned young women for being immodest and egocentric and lacking the traditional qualities of domesticity. In her view, they had become materialistic slaves to fashion, interested only in their own status and willing to sell themselves to the highest bidder in the marriage market to ensure a comfortable lifestyle. The essays were widely debated, by turns applauded and satirized, and were republished in *The Girl of the Period and Other Essays* (1883).

In 1889 Linton was a signatory of "An Appeal against Female Suffrage," organized by the prominent novelist Mrs. Humphry Ward and other antisuffragists, who argued that for women to agitate for political power was to betray their traditional roles as wives and mothers; nor did Linton and her kind believe that women had either the political common sense or the physical stamina to take on public roles. She refused to accept the arguments of feminists that emancipated women would create a better world, seeing them rather in their demands to enter the masculine sphere of politics as being a threat to the stability of the social fabric, the sacred institutions of the empire, and the security of the family.

Linton continued in a similar vein, between July 1891 and March 1892 producing three articles on "The Wild Women as Social Insurgents" in the *Nineteenth Century.* In their repudiation of traditional domestic roles and marriage and the loss of their feminine figures (she decried flat chests and lean hips), Linton criticized emancipated women for seeking to dominate men, in the process losing their sense of duty, patriotism, and morals. Women's demands for political equality with men were, she argued, the product of mere "sexual enmity" and an unwillingness to admit that they were the weaker sex. Political arguments were best left to men, as far as she was concerned. For women to join what she called "The Shrieking Sisterhood" (Fulford 1957, 62) of public speaking for suffrage and other feminist issues was emasculating of men and demeaning of the female sex and the womanly ideal. Women should accept the elevated status of the male intellect and should content themselves with basking in reflected glory as the wives of successful husbands. Linton also took particular exception to women's smoking in the company of men. To do so, in her estimation, reduced them to the level of miner women, who could be seen in industrial regions smoking their dirty old pipes outside their cottage back doors. A vigorous response to Linton's castigation of her sex came with Sarah Grand's famous essay on the new woman (1894—see entry) and subsequent emancipatory novels by her and other feminist novelists of the fin-de-siècle.

Further onslaughts came from Linton in 1894, when she attacked women's higher education at Girton College, Cambridge, in her novel *The One Too Many* and disapprovingly portrayed emancipated women smoking and drinking. An 1894 article, "Nearing the Rapids," criticized moves to introduce the franchise for women householders, with Linton complaining that such women lacked character and a good enough level of basic education to be accorded this right. Nothing that the modern, emancipated woman did won Linton's approval. Her antifeminism even extended to criticism of women taking up cycling, a further endorsement of their increasingly mannish behavior in her view, and a pursuit that she condemned as "a queer cross between the treadmill and the tightrope, a work of penance rather than pleasure" (McCrone 1988, 178–179).

In her own private life, Linton had a troubled sexuality: she formed close attachments to other women but condemned lesbianism in *The Rebel of the Family* (1880). However, one of her best novels, *The Autobiography of Christopher Kirkland* (1885), was based on her own life but recounted through the eyes of a man. In the light of her own failed marriage, perhaps, Linton ad-

vocated reform of the divorce laws and supported the campaign for a Married Women's Property Act, arguing for an end to women's economic enslavement and for the equality of partners within marriage in her 1870 essay, "The Modern Revolt," published in *Macmillan's Magazine*. She also supported calls for protective legislation for women workers. In two of her novels, *Joshua Davidson* and *Under Which Lord?* (1879), she was critical of the Church of England, attacking the hypocrisy of the clergy and elements of church ritual.

See also Grand, Sarah; Ward, Mary.

References and Further Reading
Anderson, Nancy Fix. 1987. *Woman against Women in Victorian England: A Life of Eliza Linton*. Bloomington: Indiana University Press.
Fulford, Roger. 1957. *Votes for Women: The Story of a Struggle*. London: Faber and Faber.
Harman, Barbara, and Susan Meyer, eds. 1996. *The New Nineteenth Century: Feminist Readings of Underread Victorian Fiction*. New York: Garland.
Harrison, Brian. 1978. *Separate Spheres: The Opposition to Women's Suffrage in Britain*. London: Croom Helm.
Holcombe, Lee. 1983. *Wives and Property: Reform of the Married Women's Property Law in Nineteenth-Century England*. Toronto: University of Toronto Press.
Linton, Eliza. 1899. *My Literary Life*. London: Hodder and Stoughton.
McCrone, Kathleen E. 1988. *Sport and the Physical Emancipation of English Women 1870–1914*. London: Routledge.
Sanders, Valerie. 1996. *Eve's Renegades: Victorian Anti-Feminist Women Novelists*. London: Macmillan.
Showalter, Elaine. 1999 [1977]. *A Literature of Their Own: British Women Novelists from Brontë to Lessing*. Reprint, London: Virago.
van Thal, Herbert. 1929. *Eliza Lynn Linton*. London: Allen and Unwin.

Liu-Wang Liming
(1897–1970)
China

A nonpartisan Chinese feminist who resisted communist ideology and political alignment while remaining a committed patriot, Liu-Wang ultimately succumbed to the drive of the Chinese Communist Party (CCP) for dominance over feminist activity in postwar China. She was eventually condemned for her nonalignment during the Cultural Revolution of the 1960s.

Having lost her father when she was nine, Liu-Wang was fortunate in being accepted into an American-run boys' missionary school when she was ten years old. She was a quick learner and soon demonstrated her independent spirit by unbinding her feet when she was twelve. After graduating from Jiujiang Ruli Academy, she stayed on as a teacher there. Having come under the influence of the Woman's Christian Temperance Union (WCTU), which had opened branches in China in the 1890s–1900s, she obtained a scholarship to study biology at Northwestern University in Illinois. While in the United States, she married in 1920.

On her return to China, Liu-Wang joined the Chinese women's movement in Shanghai and became a member of the Committee to Promote the National Assembly in 1924, which called for women's political representation. She later took a post on the Guomindang's committee on the women's movement while remaining active both in the Women's Suffrage Association during the 1930s and the WCTU, which she served as general secretary from 1926 until the 1950s. The WCTU, like the Young Women's Christian Association (YWCA), was influential in its work for underprivileged women and workers in China. The WCTU, funded in part with money from the United States, opened a vocational school to help women train for careers, and offered accommodation for single working women at the Shanghai Women's Apartment. Apart from temperance, it advocated birth control and monogamy, discouraged opium smoking, castigated men who abandoned their wives, and undertook social work among prostitutes. It also supported women's suffrage as well as peace initiatives during the Russo-Japanese War of 1903–1904. Inevitably, however, it alienated communist feminists who disliked the religious overtones of the WCTU, some of them accusing Liu-Wang of harboring the conventional Confucian ethic of "good wife, wise mother" at the root of her feminist thinking.

Supported financially by her husband, Liu-Wang was able to devote herself full-time to the WCTU and in 1933 published *The Chinese Women's Movement,* in which she not only upheld changing sexual attitudes that she felt were essential to social evolution in China, such as the right of women to marry for love and to seek divorce, but also looked forward to an end to class conflict and the introduction of democratic socialism, which would guarantee equality for women in the workplace and make them truly independent economically. She elaborated on her views in the biweekly magazine the *Women's Voice,* which she began publishing in October 1932. Liu-Wang's feminism was criticized by the Chinese Communist Party as being too "narrow," however. She defied her critics during the crisis with Japan over Manchuria in the 1930s by asserting her patriotism in an individualistic manner rather than through the machinery of the CCP, and called on Chinese women to support the National Salvation Alliance, make donations to the war effort, and boycott Japanese goods. However, in 1937, after the Japanese attacked northern China, she moved toward more overt support for the communists by joining the Shanghai National Salvation Alliance. Left a widow with three children after her husband's assassination by Japanese agents in 1938, Liu-Wang continued her activities in Chongqing. Here she set up an organization for orphans, the Zhan'en Institute for Refugee Children, and became principal of the West China Women's Vocational School. Her organization of the Chinese Women's Friendship Association also reflected her encouragement of women's participation in the war effort, which for a brief period in 1937 saw the collaboration of women in the CCP and the Guomindang under a united front.

Toward the end of World War II Liu-Wang optimistically anticipated the establishment of democracy in China, and in 1944 she was elected to the central committee of the Chinese Democratic League, only to witness China's spiral into civil war. She revived the *Women's Voice* and reestablished the activities of the WCTU in Shanghai in 1945. In 1947, however, the Chinese Democratic League was outlawed by the Guomindang, and Liu-Wang fled to Hong Kong.

After Mao Zedong gained power in 1949, Liu-Wang returned to China and in Beijing represented the Chinese Democratic League at the Chinese People's Political Consultative Conference. When the WCTU was incorporated as a member society of the newly established All-China Women's Federation in 1949, as a federation dedicated to unifying the women's movement under the CCP, Liu-Wang became a member of the executive committee. She went on to hold other offices within the federation and retained her guiding influence over the WCTU, which culminated in her election in 1956 as vice chair of the latter. The WCTU had continued its pacifist campaigning into the communist period, in later years against nuclear weapons, and in 1958 was instrumental in obtaining the passing of an antiprostitution bill. By this time, however, Liu-Wang had become a casualty of the communist antirightist campaign that engineered the purging of many leading figures from public activities. Both of Liu's societies, the WCTU and the All-China Women's Federation, lost their autonomy in the rigid political alignment of independent groups under CCP control that soon followed. In 1966 Liu Wang was arrested on charges of spying for the Central Intelligence Agency. She died in prison in Shanghai in 1970 and was reacknowledged by the Chinese government in 1980.

References and Further Reading

Wang Zheng. 1999. *Women in the Chinese Enlightenment.* Berkeley: University of California Press.

Livermore, Mary
(1820–1905)
United States

Mary Livermore (Library of Congress)

In addition to campaigning for suffrage and temperance, Mary Livermore was, with Dorothea Lynde Dix and Clara Barton, an important figure in the organization of medical and relief services during the Civil War in the United States. After long playing a prominent role in the Woman's Christian Temperance Union (WCTU), she espoused Christian socialism in her later years.

Born in Boston and brought up a Calvinist, Livermore converted to the Baptist faith when she was fourteen. She was educated at the Hancock Grammar School and at Martha Whiting's Female Seminary in Boston and stayed on at the seminary, teaching French, Latin, and Italian until 1838. In 1839 she took a post as private tutor to the children of a plantation owner in North Carolina, where she soon became repulsed by the ill treatment of slaves. After three years in the South, she returned to Massachusetts to teach at a coeducational school in Duxbury and married a Universalist minister and temperance leader, Daniel Parker Livermore, in 1845.

Although her time was primarily taken up with raising her three daughters, Livermore wrote articles to supplement the family's income and was active in the local temperance movement. In 1857 the Livermores moved to Chicago, where from 1857 to 1869, Mary and her husband edited the Universalist journal the *New Covenant;* she remained active in the abolitionist movement and worked for temperance as a member of the Washingtonians. She also gave time to charitable work for poor women and children through such bodies as the Home for Aged Women, the Hospital for Women and Children, and the Home for the Friendless.

During the Civil War, Livermore put her children in the care of her housekeeper and a governess, and after volunteering for the Chicago (later Northwestern) Sanitary Commission, spent the next four years undertaking a tour of military hospitals and assessing the supplies needed by them. Placed in charge of the Chicago branch of the Sanitary Commission in December 1862 and with the help of a woman named Jane Hoge, Livermore organized 3,000 local relief groups in the Midwest to raise medical and food supplies for General Ulysses S. Grant's Union Army. She also raised $70,000 in funds to buy essential medical supplies by staging a Sanitary Fair in October 1863 that inspired numerous similar ventures across the North. Early in 1863, Livermore responded promptly to a threatened outbreak of scurvy among Grant's troops by haranguing farmers to send mountainous supplies of canned and dried fruit and fresh vegetables south by rail to Vicksburg. Livermore went to Vicksburg and sent back her account of her experiences to the *New Covenant.* In 1887 she published *My Story of the War: A Woman's Narrative of Four Years Personal Experience,* which became a best-seller.

The experience of the Civil War heightened Livermore's growing sense of women's ability to play an important, reformist role in public life, and crucial to that role was their right to suffrage. When the war was over, she became an active supporter of the emergent women's suffrage movement in the United States, in 1868 calling a local convention of women suffragists and becoming president of the newly founded Illinois Woman Suffrage Association. A year later, she founded the association's journal, the *Agitator,* a forum for campaigning on temperance and women's suffrage, which she also edited. Responding to the call of Lucy Stone to establish an American Woman Suffrage Association (AWSA), Livermore became its vice president. In 1870 she merged the *Agitator* with the AWSA's official publication, the *Woman's Journal,* and moved back to Boston to take up its editorship. From 1875 to 1878, she was AWSA president.

In 1870 Livermore cofounded the Massachusetts Woman Suffrage Association, at a time when she was being increasingly drawn into a public career in lecturing; she was its president from 1893 to 1903. For the next twenty-five years, she toured on the lecture circuit as one of the most popular figures in the AWSA, noted for her passionate advocacy of women's education. She had been the first president, in 1873, of the Association for the Advancement of Women, and championed women's education in her much-called-for lecture, "What Shall We Do with Our Daughters?" (published in 1883). In 1872 Livermore gave up her editorship of the *Woman's Journal* because of her increased lecture commitments, which included speech making on behalf

of the WCTU after she had been instrumental in founding its Massachusetts branch in 1874 (which she served as president for ten years). Livermore covered many topics in her lectures, including moral reform, religion, suffrage, marriage and divorce, immigration, women's need for physical exercise, and dress reform. In 1878 she was a delegate to the First International Congress on Women's Rights held in Paris, France, with Julia Ward Howe of the AWSA.

By the time she retired from public speaking in 1896, Livermore had acquired a high public profile as a leading voice in the women's temperance and suffrage movements in Massachusetts. She continued her good works through the Beneficent Society of New England and the Women's Education and Industrial Union of Boston and published her autobiography, *The Story of My Life,* in 1897–1899.

See also Barton, Clara; Dix, Dorothea Lynde; Howe, Julia Ward; Stone, Lucy.

References and Further Reading

Bordin, Ruth. 1981. *Woman and Temperance: The Quest for Power and Liberty, 1873–1900.* Philadelphia: Temple University Press.

Ginzberg, Lori D. 1990. *Women and the Work of Benevolence: Morality, Politics, and Class in the Nineteenth-Century United States.* New Haven, CT: Yale University Press.

Hersch, Blanche G. 1978. *Slavery of Sex: Feminist Abolitionists in America.* Urbana: University of Illinois Press.

Livermore, Mary. 1897. *The Story of My Life.* Hartford, CT: A. D. Worthington.

———. 1995. *My Story of the War.* Reprint, New York: Da Capo Press.

Massey, Mary E. 1966. *Bonnet Brigades: American Women and the Civil War.* New York: Alfred A. Knopf.

Lockwood, Belva Ann
(1830–1917)
United States

Belva Lockwood was the first woman lawyer to appear before the U.S. Supreme Court after waging an intense struggle for the right to do so. As a bold and eloquent advocate of women's rights, she believed that no professional doors should be closed to women. In her view, if Queen Victoria could reign over large portions of the globe, then women in general should be given the roles they aspired to alongside men in education, the church, and the legal system and be paid an equal wage for equal work.

Born in Royalton, New York, Lockwood was forced to leave school at age fifteen in order to help support her family during financial difficulties. She taught for four years and married in 1848, but after her husband was killed in an accident in 1853, she returned to teaching. Determined to continue her own education, Lockwood took up her studies again at Genesee College (later Syracuse University) in New York state, graduating in 1857. She took a post as superintendent of the Lockport Union School, where she pioneered progressive education for girls, encouraging their participation in outdoor activities and physical education. During this time, she also became friendly with the women's rights activist Susan B. Anthony. Lockwood went on to open her own coeducational school in Washington, D.C., the McNall Seminary (under the name of her first husband), after moving there in 1866. In 1868 she met and married her second husband, a dentist and Baptist minister named Ezekiel Lockwood, who helped her run the school and encouraged her in her ambition to study law.

Lockwood's application to do so was turned down by Columbia, Georgetown, and Harvard Universities. Eventually, in 1871, she was allowed to study for a law degree at the new National University Law School (NULS) in Washington, a fact that aroused persistent controversy. She completed her studies in 1873 at the age of forty-three, only to be blocked in her ambitions by Ulysses S. Grant, then president of the United States and ex-officio president of the NULS, who initially refused to grant her degree. Lockwood wrote a personal letter to Grant demanding her diploma and within twenty-six days had obtained her degree. In 1873 she was admitted to the bar in the District of Columbia but, as a woman, experienced tremendous difficulty in pursuing her career. In 1875, when she was hired to represent Charlotte von Corts in a dispute over infringement of her patent, Lockwood used it as a test case to gain the right to plead before the Court of Claims. She took her campaign straight to the U.S. Supreme Court in a bid to overturn established legal custom, which prohibited female lawyers from pleading cases in the high court. Lockwood's determined campaign-

Belva Ann Lockwood (Library of Congress)

ing eventually won through, when in 1879, under new legislation, she became the first American woman permitted to enter the Court of Claims to plead a case.

Throughout her career, Lockwood regularly defended the challenges made to traditional political practice, in 1872 supporting Victoria Claflin Woodhull's bold candidacy for president in a challenge to the wording of the Fourteenth Amendment, which had failed to specify that women had equal rights with men. That year she also lobbied the U.S. Congress to introduce legislation giving women employed by the government equal pay for equal work and in her own legal work frequently represented government employees over pension claims.

Lockwood became a much-respected figure in Washington, who could be seen bicycling from her office to court. She encouraged other women to study for the bar and supported a broad base of reform of laws affecting women in the District of Columbia, including the property rights of married women and their right to equal guardianship of children. She had also been a suffragist since 1867 and was a founder of the Washington Universal Franchise Association as well as a member of the National Woman Suffrage Association. As a lawyer, she prepared amendments on women's suffrage for debate in the states of Oklahoma, New Mexico, and Arizona in 1903.

In 1884, as a member of the National Equal Rights Party, Lockwood was nominated as its candidate for the presidency. In her election campaign, she demanded equal rights in marriage and divorce for women and equality for Native Americans, blacks, and immigrants. Ultimately, Lockwood garnered enough support in the West to win 4,149 votes (male) in five states. She repeated her campaign in 1888 with little public attention. An account of her campaigning, "How I Ran for the Presidency," was published by Lockwood in the *National Magazine* in 1903.

In 1906 Lockwood was at the center of a famous case, when she defended the rights of the Eastern Cherokee against the U.S. government for nonpayment for Native American lands upon which it had encroached. Lockwood won the case and an award of $5 million plus interest for the Eastern Cherokee people.

In her later years Lockwood became increasingly interested in pacifism. During the 1880s and 1890s, she was active in the Universal Peace Union (UPU) and sat on the editorial board of its journal, the *Peacemaker*. Her skills acquired during years of high-profile lobbying for women in the legal profession were put to good use as a publicist and speechwriter for the peace movement, and she represented the UPU at European peace congresses in 1889, 1906, 1908, and 1911. As secretary of the International Peace Bureau (founded in 1891), she assisted in drawing up arbitration treaties and joined in efforts to mediate after the United States intervened in Cuba in 1898 to provoke the Spanish-American War. She also supported the 1899 and 1907 peace conferences in The Hague in their efforts to set up international courts of arbitration and justice.

From 1893 Lockwood was a member of the International Council of Women and also served on the nominating committee for the Nobel Peace Prize. She was joined by her daughter in a thriving legal practice in Washington, but it sadly collapsed after her daughter's premature death in 1894. Lockwood spent her remaining years beset by ill health.

See also Anthony, Susan B.; Woodhull, Victoria Claflin.

References and Further Reading

Berry, Dawn Bradley. 1997. *The Fifty Most Influential Women in American Law.* Los Angeles: Lowell House.

Calabre, Marian. 1996. *Great Courtroom Lawyers: Fighting the Cases That Made History.* New York: Facts on File.

Dictionary of American Biography 1946–1958, and indexes to Supplements 1–10, 1981–1996. New York: Scribner's.

Emert, Phyllis Raybin. 1996. *Top Lawyers and Their Famous Cases.* Minneapolis: Oliver Press.

Fox, Mary Virginia. 1975. *Lady for the Defense: A Biography of Belva Lockwood.* New York: Harcourt, Brace, Jovanovich.

Josephson, Harold, Sandi Cooper, and Steven C. Hause et al., eds. 1985. *Biographical Dictionary of Modern Peace Leaders.* Westport, CT: Greenwood Press.

Whitman, Alden, ed. 1988. *American Reformers: An H. W. Wilson Biographical Dictionary.* New York: H. W. Wilson.

Lowell, Josephine Shaw
(1843–1905)
United States

A reformer whose work was initially prompted by her faith in social Darwinism and enlightened philanthropy, Josephine Shaw Lowell believed in organizing voluntary work with efficiency by ensuring an ongoing commitment to the social rehabilitation of those receiving welfare. In her objective that offenders and the underprivileged be assisted in becoming useful and self-supporting members of society, she worked toward the establishment of separate prisons for women. The women from upper-class privileged backgrounds who helped in this work, Lowell believed, would in turn redeem themselves from lives of idleness.

Born in West Roxbury, Massachusetts, Lowell came from a wealthy, established Boston family of Unitarian abolitionists. Her family was friendly with reformers in and around the Boston area, notably the feminists Lydia Maria Child and Margaret Fuller. In 1847 the family moved to Staten Island, and in 1851 they embarked on a five-year European tour, during which Lowell was educated in Paris and Rome. On her return to New York in 1856, she completed her studies at Miss Gibson's School in New York City and Boston, where she too became involved in the abolitionist cause.

When the Civil War broke out, Lowell's family staunchly supported the North. Her brother volunteered for military service but was soon killed at the battle of Fort Wagner in July 1863. Lowell threw herself into war work, joining the Women's Central Association of Relief for the Army and Navy, where she had her first taste of administering charity on a large scale. In 1863 she also met and married Colonel Charles Lowell, nephew of the poet James Russell Lowell, but he died of wounds received in battle less than a year later. The couple's daughter Carlotta died soon after.

At end of the Civil War, Lowell joined the National Freedmen's Relief Association of New York and became a leading fund-raiser, trying to dissipate her grief in good works by inspecting schools set up for newly freed slaves in Virginia. Meanwhile, Lowell's home in New York was becoming a meeting place for activists and reformers. In 1872 she began work for the State Charities Aid Association, which sought to monitor standards of care in almshouses, hospitals, prisons, and orphanages. Lowell was horrified by the neglect and the lack of aftercare she witnessed, and her reports on vagrancy and the sufferings of paupers in Westchester County attracted the attention of the governor, who in 1876 appointed her the first woman commissioner on the New York Board of Charities (a post she held until 1889). Thereafter, Lowell spent much time touring and inspecting public institutions as an advocate of the new school of "scientific philanthropy," in which welfare was based on careful study of needs and reports on findings. In particular, she worked for women convicts to be held in separate institutions from males (such as the women's reformatory set up in Bedford Hills, New York) and for reform of the care of the mentally ill. Lowell was of the view that mental disabilities were linked to deprivation and crime and espoused the new eugenics-led theories that the only way to minimize social problems was to prevent the passing on of hereditary traits, such as pathological behavior and mental retardation, from one generation to the next. She advocated the establishment of an asylum for feebleminded women, and her efforts resulted in the foundation of the Newark Custodial Asylum for Feeble-Minded Women of Child-Bearing Age, the first of its kind in the United States. Lowell was also a prime mover in the establishment of the House of Refuge for Women in 1886 (later the State Training School for Girls) in Hudson, New York, which sought to rehabilitate inmates through vocational training. In 1888 she achieved another first with the introduction of matrons in police stations.

In 1882 Lowell had founded and been first director of the New York Charity Organization Society, and for the next twenty-five years, she oversaw the work of various charities, making many donations to charity from her own private income. She passed on her years of experience and the principles that she had developed for organized relief and welfare work in her book *Public Relief and Private Charity* (1884). She was the author of many articles and over forty reports, in all of them, including her notable "One Means of Preventing Pauperism," emphasizing that the palliative of the unquestioning administration of handouts did nothing to confront the underlying causes of pauperism. Real change required the encouragement of personal, moral reform in the individual and the adoption of viable future means of support for the destitute. Increasingly, Lowell came to underline links between labor problems and poor wages and living conditions and looked for new preventive measures that would be far more effective than philanthropy. In 1889, convinced that the only solution to pauperism lay in active campaigning for such improvements and for better wages and rights for workers, she resigned from the New York Board of Charities to concentrate on trade union activities. She joined Mary Elisabeth Dreier, her sister Margaret Dreier Robins, and Lillian D. Wald in liaising with the Working Woman's Association (WWA), founded in 1886 to support women in their fight for recognition of their labor rights.

In 1890 Lowell was the principal impetus behind the reformation of the WWA as the Consumers' League of New York with her friend Maud Nathan and served as its first president (1890–1896). Together, they urged consumers to take responsibility to ensure that the goods they bought did not involve the exploitation of workers and, in particular, were made by companies that supported the rights of shop girls. The findings of her trade union research were published as *Industrial Arbitration and Conciliation: Some Chapters from the Industrial History of the Past Thirty Years* (1893). During the economic depression of 1893, Lowell returned to organizing relief for New York's East Side unemployed and mediated during a tailors' strike.

During her final years, Lowell's home in New York became a venue for eager young social reformers and philanthropists who gained important insights from Lowell into the Progressive Era school of preventive social work, which was replacing traditional charitable activities. Lowell set up a lobbying group, the Woman's Municipal League (1894), to work toward political changes that would support these numerous humanitarian reform programs and also founded a women's branch of the Civil Service Reform Association of New York state in 1895. Her final activities were in the anti-imperialist movement against aggressive U.S. foreign policy, particularly during the Spanish-American War of 1898.

See also Child, Lydia Maria; Dreier, Mary Elisabeth; Fuller, (Sarah) Margaret; Robins, Margaret Dreier; Wald, Lillian D.

References and Further Reading
Dictionary of American Biography 1946–1958, and indexes to Supplements 1–10, 1981–1996. New York: Scribner's.
Ginzberg, Lori D. 1990. *Women and the Work of Benevolence: Morality, Politics, and Class in the Nineteenth-Century United States.* New Haven, CT: Yale University Press.
McGuire, William, and Leslie Wheeler, eds. 1993. *American Social Leaders: From Colonial Times to the Present.* Denver: ABC-CLIO.
Sicherman, Barbara, and Carol Hurd Green, eds. 1980. *Notable American Women 1607–1950: A Biographical Dictionary,* vol. 4, *The Modern Period.* Cambridge, MA: Belknap Press of Harvard University.
Stewart, William Rhinelander. 1911. *The Philanthropic Work of Josephine Shaw Lowell.* New York: Macmillan.
Waugh, Joan. 1997. *Unsentimental Reformer: The Life of Josephine Shaw Lowell.* Cambridge, MA: Harvard University Press.

Luisi, Paulina
(1875–1950)
Uruguay

One of the first women in Uruguay to qualify as a doctor, Luisi, a leading sex educator of her day, took part in a wide range of international conferences, held important teaching posts, and was in charge of the gynecological clinic at the University of Montevideo's Faculty of Medicine.

Paulina Luisi (Uruguay Embassy)

During a long and active career, in a country considered to be the most progressive in Latin America at that time, Luisi worked for many social issues, notably against state-regulated prostitution and for better public health care and sex education. She was also involved in the campaigns for women's suffrage, working rights, and education. In the international arena, she was a leading voice on the welfare of children.

Society in Luisi's home country had been strongly influenced by its many European colonizers at the turn of the century, who had brought with them a reformist spirit that supported women's emancipation and the legalization of divorce. Under President José Batlle y Ordóñez, Uruguay had developed the first welfare state in South America and had been the first to set up a network of social services. Nevertheless, Luisi still had to fight diehard prejudices in her long campaign for sex education.

Born into a comfortably-off German-Italian family, Luisi enjoyed the privilege of being among the first women in Uruguay to study for a *bachillerato* and to receive a university education. She subsequently became the first Uruguayan woman to earn a medical degree, graduating from the University of Montevideo in 1909. She went on to attend the prestigious Columbia Teachers' College in New York City before World War I and worked for a while as a secondary school teacher.

By 1916 she had become active in numerous organizations. That year she founded the National Council of Women, the Uruguayan branch of the International Council of Women, in Montevideo and led the Uruguayan delegation to the First American Congress of the Child, held in Buenos

Aires, where she spoke on sex education. At this time, she first became interested in the popular movement of eugenics, joining the League of Social Prophylaxis in an effort to find solutions to such rampant social problems as poor levels of health among Uruguay's poor and working classes, a situation that perpetuated itself through the birth of weak and sickly children. Luisi's approach was to tackle controllable social ills such as drug and alcohol abuse and the spread of venereal disease through health and welfare programs, moral guidance, and better sex education; she opposed the state regulation of prostitution. Like her contemporary, the Argentine campaigner Alicia Moreau de Justo, Luisi felt that such campaigning should be addressed to all strata of society.

As early as 1906, Luisi had attempted to introduce sex education when she had urged that French doctor Alfred Fournier's sex manual be distributed among schoolboys aged twelve to fourteen. Such a suggestion inevitably invited condemnation from the church and the Catholic press, as well as the conservative majority among elite philanthropists and reformers, who considered Luisi immoral. It was an accusation that would dog Luisi throughout her long battle to introduce sex education programs. She was deeply committed to her crusade to see this curriculum adopted as official government policy, and her commitment to an in-depth understanding of the subject took her to Europe in 1913 to study methods there.

During the 1920s and 1930s, Luisi's activism was ambitious. In 1921 she gave a paper on sex education at the Ninth Medical Congress in Uruguay, and in 1922 she was appointed to the Council of Public Welfare and served as Uruguayan delegate in Paris at the International Congress of Propaganda for Social Hygiene, Prophylaxis, and Moral Education. From 1925 to 1930 she organized lectures for secondary school children on social hygiene, and in 1926 she took part in a congress on syphilis in Buenos Aires. From 1922 to 1925, she was a member of the League of Nations consultative committee on the Treaty to End Traffic in Women and Children, and was also active for many years in the International Abolitionist Federation. All these activities earned her a high profile at home and abroad. It was also at this time that she developed a detailed plan for sex education embracing a basic understanding of the physiology of sex

and reproduction, an explanation of the consequences of unprotected sex (pregnancy, venereal disease), and a code of moral behavior emphasizing respect for human life.

Like many feminists, Luisi argued that sexual responsibility was not solely a women's issue and that men should be equally responsible, both morally and financially, for their sexual behavior and the illegitimate children that they fathered. In addition, men should exercise more self-discipline and cease resorting to prostitutes. Much of the pursuit of casual sexual gratification, she felt, was encouraged by advertising and the media, and Luisi was in favor of film censorship and degrees of modesty in fashion. In some of her ideas, Luisi was driven by what might be perceived now as a rather naive belief that moral codes and a sense of social responsibility had far more power to change individual behavior than they do in reality. She believed that self-discipline and voluntary chastity before marriage could go some way toward overcoming the social ills resulting from unbridled sexual behavior. But in everything her overriding concern was to protect the well-being of the mother and child. She was influenced by eugenics in her belief that parents, from whatever social class, who suffered from genetic illness or disease should not pass it on to their children. A combination of moral guidance, education, and control of transmittable diseases was, in her estimation, the key to a better generation of people.

Luisi also dedicated much of her energy to women's suffrage. In 1919 she founded the Uruguay Alliance of Women for Suffrage, which was allied to the country's National Council of Women. Again, Luisi's activities as the leading light of the Uruguayan National Council of Women between 1922 and 1932 took her into the international arena and a prominent role in the International Woman Suffrage Alliance (which from 1920 on regularly reported on women's suffrage activities in Uruguay in its journal, *International Woman Suffrage News*). She represented the Uruguayan alliance at the Pan-American Women's Conference in Baltimore in 1922, at which she was elected an honorary vice president. Over the next ten years, she attended numerous feminist congresses at which she talked of her own comprehensive social program embracing suffrage, education, housing, taxation, and public health. By 1924 she had drawn away from the National Council of Women, feeling that its objectives were too narrow. She believed that feminism and the fight for women's suffrage were but the basis for a much wider program of social reform and doubted that women's political parties could ever achieve radical social change alone. She did, however, retain her leadership of the Uruguayan alliance and in 1926 was voted president for life.

As Uruguayan delegate to the first assembly of the League of Nations in 1919–1920, Luisi supported the goals of international peace and disarmament and became a committed pacifist. Throughout her career, she collaborated closely with her friend Alicia Moreau de Justo on women's education and political rights as well as sex education (they shared similar views on the role of eugenics). Between them, the two women worked hard to initiate support for suffrage throughout Latin America and organized feminist groups in Santa Fé and Córdoba, Argentina. Luisi's comprehensive campaigning for women's rights extended to concerns over the rights of working women. She argued that they should have equal rights with male workers, enjoy freedom of choice in the employment they took, and be protected by the same industrial legislation, with the exception of enjoying maternity rights.

Luisi shared her social concerns with her two equally enlightened sisters, Luisa and Clotilde, who were also leading female activists in Uruguay: Luisa, an educator, poet, and feminist critic, became head of a girls' secondary school; Clotilde was the first woman in Uruguay to practice as a lawyer. In 1932 women's suffrage was achieved in Uruguay; in 1942, with reform of the civil code, Luisi saw the enactment of many of the civil and political rights for which she had so long campaigned.

See also Moreau de Justo, Alicia.

References and Further Reading

Carlson, Narifran. 1988. *Feminismo! The Woman's Movement in Argentina from Its Beginnings to Eva Perón.* Chicago: Academy Chicago Publications.

Lavrin, Asunción. 1995. *Women, Feminism, and Social Change in Argentina, Chile, and Uruguay 1890–1940.* Lincoln: University of Nebraska Press.

Tenenbaum, Barbara A., ed. 1996. *Encyclopedia of Latin American History and Culture.* Vol. 3. New York: Charles Scribner's Sons.

Lutz, Bertha
(1894–1976)
Brazil

One of the most prominent, internationally admired, and respected Latin American feminists of her day, Lutz became a familiar figure at many international congresses. She devoted herself to vigorously leading the fifteen-year campaign for women's suffrage in Brazil in the belief that women's access to the vote and to better education was the key to their exercising a greater reformist influence in society.

Lutz's father, an eminent authority on tropical medicine, was originally Swiss; her mother was an English nurse who had worked with lepers in Hawaii. Lutz was born in São Paolo in 1894 after her family had emigrated there, but she returned to Europe (1911) to further her education for seven years. She studied biology at the science faculty of the Sorbonne and gained a doctorate from the Pasteur Institute in Paris. While in France, she became active in women's rights campaigning and kept in close touch with English suffragists, monitoring their campaign in Britain.

Before returning to Brazil, Lutz published seminal articles in Brazilian newspapers in which she underlined women's ability to contribute to society, as women had so ably demonstrated in the war effort in Britain. Although she accepted that men needed to be educated to show greater respect for women, Lutz also felt that women had to find a role for themselves. In particular, Lutz despised women who lived idle lives, exploited their sexuality, and allowed themselves to be pampered and spoiled by men. She felt they should begin taking on responsibilities that would allow them to contribute to economic and social progress in Brazil.

These early articles did much to lay the foundation for the women's movement in Brazil, which she headed when she returned to Rio de Janeiro in 1918. On her arrival, she immediately suggested that a League of Brazilian Women be founded to undertake social welfare projects and encourage other women to take up education so that they could become worthy of political responsibility. Once women had obtained the vote and used it to further social change, Lutz felt that their value to society would be recognized, and they would then play an influential role in both the economic and the moral improvement of the country.

In 1919 Lutz began running the administrative commission of the League of Brazilian Women, but she soon became dissatisfied with the organization's limited objectives. Together with the feminist writer and teacher María Lacerda de Moura, in 1920 she founded a secular study group in Rio de Janeiro, the League for the Intellectual Advancement of Woman, which sought to differentiate itself from the Roman Catholic Church–oriented philanthropic societies that until then had been dominated by upper-class women. Lutz and Moura's new league set about publishing articles and proclamations to encourage women to educate themselves, in the belief that education was the key to women's intellectual emancipation, employment, and eventually suffrage. Lutz appealed directly to the minister for education to provide better secondary education for women so that they could enter universities and be better trained.

In 1919 Lutz herself set an objective for women when she won a high position, against competition from male candidates, to become the first woman appointed to the government post of secretary of the National Museum in Rio de Janeiro, only the second woman in Brazil to hold a senior post in the civil service. She later gained an additional degree in law at the University of Rio de Janeiro (1933) and for many years, as an accomplished scientist like her father, taught zoology at the same university.

Within a year of her return from Europe in 1918, Lutz had begun traveling again to international conferences around the world. In 1919 she represented Brazil at an International Labor Organization conference on conditions for working women. In 1922 she represented Brazil at the 2,000-delegate Pan-American Women's Conference in Baltimore, Maryland, and made her mark as an international feminist. The success of the conference, at which she was elected vice president, prompted Lutz to cooperate in the founding of the Pan-American Association for the Advancement of Women, becoming its vice president, and to refashion the League for the Intellectual Advancement of Woman into a more comprehensive national organization. Renamed the Brazilian Federation for the Advancement of Women (BFAW) in 1922, it represented twenty Brazilian states and comprised a wide range of

Bertha Lutz (Bettmann/Corbis)

professional associations, reformist groups, and charities. It ambitiously staged a women's congress in Rio de Janeiro that December, helping to develop close friendships between Brazilian feminists and those from other countries in the Americas, as well as fostering the establishment of the Brazilian Alliance for Female Suffrage, with Lutz as its general secretary. Although this new suffrage alliance would officially lead the struggle for women's suffrage in Brazil, with Lutz at its helm, the BFAW, in which she remained active, would, as the largest women's organization in Brazil, play a crucial role in the campaign, particularly after it was affiliated, in 1923, with the International Woman Suffrage Alliance. That year, Lutz traveled to Rome as a delegate to the alliance's ninth congress, and from then on worked closely with its leader, Carrie Chapman Catt, with whom she became very close friends and conducted a regular correspondence.

The major focus of Lutz's work through the BFAW during the 1920s remained not just the Brazilian suffrage campaign but also other issues affecting women's lives: their education, particularly at school; protection of the rights of mothers and children; and protective legislation for working women. It also had the general objective of broadening women's social and political awareness and in so doing encouraged them to exercise their political rights.

Lutz devoted much of her time to lobbying political leaders and raising public opinion by publishing manifestos and many articles in the press, giving interviews, making public speeches at women's conferences, and taking part in debates in the Senate. She even went up by plane over Rio de Janeiro to drop leaflets in support of women's rights.

In 1930 after Getúlio Vargas came to power as provisional president in the wake of a popular revolt, Lutz was asked to join a government commission set up to draft a new Constitution, which included electoral reform. She composed a thirteen-point document that included women's suffrage, their equality with men before the law, their right to equal pay and maternity leave, and their right to hold public office. Her plan also embraced welfare programs and legislation to institute minimum wages and statutory working hours for women workers. Lutz saw working-class women as having to shoulder the double burden of working long hours in factories as well as bringing up families and carrying out domestic chores. As early as 1922, she had joined with the Union of Commercial Employees in Rio de Janeiro to reduce the working day of shop assistants. After suffrage was achieved in 1931 and became part of the civil code the following year, Lutz worked on the draft that would guarantee women equal national and political rights with men. When passed in 1934, this law introduced the principle of equal pay for equal work and an eight-hour day. Lutz's program of reform was incorporated into the constitution of 1934.

In 1934 Lutz was elected as an alternate candidate to the federal district of Rio. After being promoted to the Chamber of Deputies upon the death of a male member in 1936, she joined the Commission on the Code for Women to deal with the particular social problems experienced by women and to initiate legislation on their status and social rights. She also proposed that the government set up a National Women's Department to handle issues relating to child protection and the rights of women workers. This idea placed particular emphasis on encouraging women to improve their own economic status rather than simply relying on limited handouts from the state; unfortunately, the inauguration of this department was preempted by a military coup in 1937.

The dictatorship of Vargas's Estado Novo from 1937 to 1945, which dismissed democratic politics, was a fallow time for feminist activity in Brazil, although Lutz took a critical stance on his government's failure to give roles in government to women or to allow them their promised rights under the 1934 Constitution. She continued with her high-profile international work, taking part in the inaugural meeting of the United Nations in San Francisco in 1945, where she managed to get the phrase "nondiscrimination on the grounds of sex" added to its list of basic principles. In 1952 Lutz became a founding member of the UN Commission on the Status of Women and helped to create its charter. In 1975 she represented Brazil at the UN Conference on Women, held in Mexico City, and a year later, at the age of eighty-one, she attended the UN-sponsored International Women's Year Conference in Mexico City.

A highly intelligent, energetic, and multilingual campaigner, Lutz retained a lifelong interest in science. Her experience in the international arena and her wide range of feminist contacts were a huge bonus to the Brazilian feminist movement, although her frequent trips abroad at times separated her from the grass roots of the Brazilian movement.

See also Catt, Carrie Chapman.
References and Further Reading
Hahner, Judith E. 1990. *Emancipating the Female Sex: The Struggle for Women's Rights in Brazil, 1850–1940.* Durham, NC: Duke University Press.
Miller, Francesca. 1992. *Latin American Women and the Search for Social Justice.* Hanover, NH: University Press of New England.
Tenenbaum, Barbara A., ed. 1996. *Encyclopedia of Latin American History and Culture.* Vol. 3. New York: Charles Scribner's Sons.

Lytton, Lady Constance
(1869–1923)
United Kingdom

Along with Emily Wilding Davison, Lady Constance Lytton is an iconic figure in the history of British suffragism, remembered for the self-sacrificing stand she took on the treatment of suffragettes in prison. After discovering that a double standard operated, one for ordinary suffragettes and another for suffragettes such as herself from the upper classes, she rejected any preferential treatment and sought to be allowed to suffer for her cause on the same level as her comrades.

Born in Vienna, Lytton was the daughter of a British diplomat who, later, as the first Earl of Lytton, was viceroy of India. Her great-grand-mother was the pioneering socialist feminist and writer Anna Doyle Wheeler; her mother, Edith, was a lady-in-waiting to Queen Victoria from 1892. Much of Lytton's childhood was spent abroad during her father's postings, including India (1873–1880) and Paris (1887–1891). Living in genteel isolation from the outside world, she was educated by governesses before the family finally returned to Knebworth, their grand country estate in Hertfordshire. Lytton's young life, however, had been circumscribed by frail health caused by a rheumatic heart, and she came increasingly under the control of her domineering mother, particularly after her father died in 1891. An unrequited love in 1892 for a man she had met on a trip to South Africa caused her to retreat even further from public view, and she surrendered to the stultifying life of imposed inactivity, refusing even the offer in 1900 to become lady-in-waiting to Princess Marie Louise of Schleswig-Holstein.

In 1906, after inheriting some money from a great-aunt, Lytton's donation of the money to a folk dance movement brought her into contact with the Esperance Guild for working girls and in turn an introduction, in 1908, to militant suffragette Emmeline Pethick-Lawrence. The suffrage cause appealed to Lytton's strong sense of egalitarianism and public service, and she began visiting suffragettes in prison, finally joining the Women's Social and Political Union (WSPU) in 1909, eager to earn her spurs as a militant and willing to go to jail. She was arrested four times from 1909 to 1911, the first time in February 1909, when she was sentenced to four weeks in Holloway Prison. There she found herself assigned to the prison's First Division (for political and higher-grade prisoners of social standing), and after doctors confirmed her heart condition, she was removed to the relative comfort of the prison hospital before insisting that she be returned to her cell. Dismayed at being segregated in this way and not wishing to have her genuine medical condition used as a mitigating factor in her treatment, Lytton took the extreme step of self-mutilation in protest and attempted to carve

the slogan "Votes for Women" across her chest. On her second arrest, she was sent to Newcastle Prison, where she went on hunger strike for fifty-six hours. The authorities, again aware of her status and her medical condition, did not force-feed her as they did other suffragette prisoners, and she was soon released.

During her short suffrage career, Lytton became an energetic lobbyist and campaigner for the WSPU, producing a pamphlet entitled "No Votes for Women: A Reply to Some Recent Anti-Suffrage Publications" in 1909 and addressing suffrage rallies. In 1910, during a suffrage demonstration in Liverpool against the treatment of suffrage prisoners, she was arrested after throwing stones and breaking windows at the home of the governor of Walton prison. But this time, Lytton had preempted being singled out as a special prisoner by adopting a disguise. She had deliberately dressed herself as a working-class woman, cut her hair short, and had even rejoined the WSPU under a false name and identity—as Jane Warton, a seamstress. Lytton's wish for martyrdom was granted; sent to Walton jail, she was incarcerated in the far less salubrious, hard-labor Third Division for two weeks. She promptly went on a hunger and thirst strike. After four days, she was declared fit enough to be force-fed, and the doctors did not bother to check first on her medical condition (as they were supposed to do for all prisoners before this procedure was undertaken). Lytton later described the brutal treatment meted out to her. During force-feeding, a metal gag was used to hold her mouth open in an unnaturally wide and painful position, after which "an inordinately wide stomach tube about four feet long was thrust down her oesophagus" (Mulvey-Roberts 2000, 167). She nearly died of asphyxiation and suffered terribly during each of the eight occasions on which she was subjected to force-feeding.

Although Lytton gained an almost perverse sense of pride from the subterfuge she had adopted in order to win her badge of courage as a suffrage martyr, her health was irrevocably damaged. In a fascinating study, Marie Mulvey-Roberts (2000, 171) argues that Lytton's sufferings in prison were for her a form of religious ecstasy akin to that of the postulant willing to be "tortured for the faith"; to others, such action seemed an incomprehensible act of deliberate and perverse self-destruction. But it drew important press coverage of the horrors of force-feeding; Lytton's brother wrote to *the Times* demanding a public inquiry into the practice, and Lytton recounted her experiences to a public meeting in January 1910. The continuing public outcry over Lytton's and other cases eventually resulted in the abandonment of force-feeding by the prison authorities, with the government resorting instead to the iniquitous Cat and Mouse Act of April 1913, whereby hunger strikers were released until they had sufficiently regained their strength and were then promptly rearrested.

In June 1910, Lytton became a full-time paid organizer for the WSPU on a salary of £2 per week; she also joined the Church League for Women's Suffrage but suffered a slight stroke at the end of the year. She recovered sufficiently to join a 1911 deputation of suffrage societies to Prime Minister Herbert Asquith in an attempt to convince him to introduce a bill for women's suffrage and, after another campaign of window smashing, was again sent to Holloway but was quickly released. In May 1912, she was finally felled by a stroke at the age of only forty-three, which left her partially paralyzed down one side. Unable to continue with her activism for suffrage, she was forced once more to give herself up to the ministrations of her overweening and devoted mother, retiring to Homewood, their house on the Knebworth estate. Lytton's willpower was undimmed, however, and she succeeded in writing her memoirs, *Prisons and Prisoners* (1914), with her left hand. This classic account would provide valuable insight into the prison system and call for improvements to prison conditions. Her generosity extended to offering financial and moral support to another damaged hunger striker, Rachel Peace, who had suffered nervous collapse after being force-fed

and had never recovered. After years of invalidism at Knebworth, in 1923 Lytton abruptly removed herself from her mother's care to undergo medical "treatment" with a dubious practitioner, Homer Lane, who based his practices on psychoanalysis and ignored Lytton's clinical case history. Within three weeks, Lady Conny, "one of the finest, most unselfish, and most loyal of loyalists" in the words of Annie Kenney (Kenney 1924, 88), was dead.

See also Davison, Emily Wilding; Pethick-Lawrence, Emmeline; Wheeler, Anna Doyle.

References and Further Reading
Balfour, B., ed. 1925. *Letters of Constance Lytton.* London: William Heinemann.

Crawford, Elizabeth. 1999. *The Women's Suffrage Movement, 1866–1928: A Reference Guide.* London: University College of London Press.

Kenney, Annie. 1924. *Memories of a Militant.* London: Edward Arnold.

Lytton, Constance. 1914. *Prisons and Prisoners, Some Personal Experiences by Constance Lytton and "Jane Warton, Spinster."* London: William Heinemann.

Mulvey-Roberts, Marie. 2000. "Militancy, Masochism, or Martyrdom? The Public and Private Prisons of Constance Lytton." In June Purvis and Sandra Stanley Holton, eds., *Votes for Women.* London and New York: Routledge.

Mulvey-Roberts, Marie, and Tamae Mizuta, eds. 1994. *The Militants: Suffragette Activism.* (Perspectives in the History of British Feminism.) London: Routledge.

Pankhurst, E. Sylvia. 1977 [1931]. *The Suffragette Movement: An Intimate Account of Persons and Ideals.* Reprint, London: Virago.

Vicinus, Martha. 1985. *Independent Women, Work and Community for Single Women, 1850–1920.* London: Virago.